Lecture Notes in Computer Science   1514

Edited by G. Goos, J. Hartmanis and J. van Leeuwen

Springer
Berlin
Heidelberg
New York
Barcelona
Budapest
Hong Kong
London
Milan
Paris
Singapore
Tokyo

Kazuo Ohta Dingyi Pei (Eds.)

Advances in Cryptology – ASIACRYPT'98

International Conference
on the Theory and Application
of Cryptology and Information Security
Beijing, China, October 18-22, 1998
Proceedings

 Springer

Series Editors

Gerhard Goos, Karlsruhe University, Germany
Juris Hartmanis, Cornell University, NY, USA
Jan van Leeuwen, Utrecht University, The Netherlands

Volume Editors

Kazuo Ohta
NTT Information and Communication System Labs. 609A
1-1 Hikarinooka, Yokosuka, Kanagawa 249, Japan
E-mail: ohta@sucaba.isl.ntt.co.jp

Dingyi Pei
SKLOIS, Graduate School of USTC
19A Yu Quan Road, Beijing 100039, P.R. China
E-mail: dypei@sun.ihep.ac.cn

Cataloging-in-Publication data applied for

Die Deutsche Bibliothek - CIP-Einheitsaufnahme

Advances in cryptology : proceedings / ASIACRYPT '98,
International Conference on the Theory and Application of
Cryptology and Information Security, Beijing, China, October 18 -
22, 1998. Kazuo Ohta ; Dingyi Pei (ed.). - Berlin ; Heidelberg ; New
York ; Barcelona ; Budapest ; Hong Kong ; London ; Milan ; Paris ;
Singapore ; Tokyo : Springer, 1998
  (Lecture notes in computer science ; Vol. 1514)

ISBN 978-3-540-65109-3   ISBN 978-3-540-49649-6 (eBook)
DOI 10.1007/978-3-540-49649-6

CR Subject Classification (1991): E.3, G.2.1, D.4.6, K.6.5, F.2.1-2, C.2, J.1

ISSN 0302-9743

Typesetting: Camera-ready by author
SPIN 10692702   06/3142 – 5 4 3 2 1 0   Printed on acid-free paper

Preface

ASIACRYPT'98, the international conference covering all aspects of theory and application of cryptology and information security, is being held at Beijing Friendship Hotel from October 18 to 22. This is the fourth of the Asiacrypt conferences. ASIACRYPT'98 is sponsored by the State Key Laboratory of Information Security (SKLOIS), University of Science and Technology of China (USTC), and the Asiacrypt Steering Committee (ASC), in cooperation with the International Association for Cryptology Research (IACR).

The 16-member Program Committee organized the scientific program and considered 118 submissions. Of these, 32 were accepted for presentation. The authors' affiliations of the 118 submissions and the 32 accepted papers range over 18 and 13 countries or regions, respectively.

The submitted version of each paper was sent to all members of the Program Committee and was extensively examined by at least three committee members and/or outside experts. The review process was rigorously blinded and the anonymity of each submission are maintained until the selection was completed. We followed the traditional policy that each member of the Program Committee could be an author of at most one accepted paper.

These proceedings contain the revised versions of the 32 contributed talks as well as a short note written by one invited speaker. Comments from the Program Committee were taken into account in the revisions. However, the authors (not the committee) bear full responsibility for the contents of their papers.

We are very grateful to the members of the Program Committee for generously spending so much of their time on the difficult task of selecting the papers. They are: Thomos A. Berson, Colin Boyd, Zongduo Dai, Marc Girault, Xuejia Lai, Tzonelih Hwang, Burt Kaliski, Kwangjo Kim, Kouichi Sakurai, Mitsuru Matsui, Andrew Odlyzko, Guozhen Xiao, Lam Kwok Yan, Yuliang Zheng. We also thank the following outside experts who assisted the Program Committee in evaluating various papers: Masayuki Abe, Kazumaro Aoki, Fabrice Boudot, Dengguo Feng, Atsushi Fujioka, Eiichiro Fujisaki, Henri Gilbert, Louis Goubin, Shaoquan Jiang, Masayuki Kanda, Shiho Moriai, Tatsuaki Okamoto, Haiwen Ou, Jacques Patarin, Philippe Toffin, Jacques Traore, Shigenori Uchiyama, Yujie Zhou, Moti Yung, We apologize for any omission in this list.

We would like to appreciate all who have submitted papers to ASIACRYPT'98 and the authors of accepted papers for their on-time preparation of camera-ready manuscripts.

We are also pleased to thank Shu Chang and Chen Lan for their help with preparation of the various tasks of the program co-chairs.

August 1998   Kazuo Ohta
                                                                Dingyi Pei

ASIACRYPT'98
Beijing, October 18-22, China

International Conference on the Theory and Application of Cryptology and Information Security

Sponsored by
The State Key Laboratory of Information Security
University of Science and Technology of China

and
The Asiacrypt Steering Committee

In cooperation with
The International Association for Cryptologic Research

Gerneral Chair
Keqin Feng (Vice President of USTC)

Program Committee
Thomos A. Berson (Anagram Labs., USA)
Colin Boyd (Queensland Univ. of Tech., Australia)
Zongduo Dai (Chinese Academy of Sciences, China)
Marc Girault (France Telecom, France)
Xuejia Lai (R3 Security Engineering, Switzerland)
Tzonelih Hwang (National Cheng Chung Univ., Taiwan)
Burt Kaliski (RSA Labs., USA)
Kwangjo Kim (Information and Communication Univ., Korea)
Kouichi Sakurai (Kyushu Univ., Japan)
Mitsuru Matsui (Mitsubishi Electric Corp., Japan)
Andrew Odlyzko (AT&T, USA)
Kazuo Ohta (Co-chair, NTT, Japan)
Dingyi Pei (Co-chair, SKLOIS, China)
Guozhen Xiao (Xidian Univ., China)
Lam Kwok Yan (National Univ. of Singapore, Singapore)
Yuliang Zheng (Monash Univ., Australia)

Organizing Committee
Qing Chang (National Nature Science Fundation, China)
Guang Hua (Graduate School of USTC, China)
Kan Zhang (Chinese Academy of Sciences, China)
Xinkao Song (Beijing Scientific and Technical Society, China)
Zhansheng Zhao (Chairman, SKLOIS, China)

ASIACRYPT'98

Beijing, October 18-22, China

**International Conference on the Theory and
Application of Cryptology and Information Security**

Sponsored by
**The State Key Laboratory of Information Security
University of Science and Technology of China**

and
The Asiacrypt Steering Committee

In cooperation with
The International Association for Cryptologic Research

Gerneral Chair
Keqin Feng (Vice President of USTC)

Program Committee
Thomos A. Berson (Anagram Labs., USA)
Colin Boyd (Queensland Univ. of Tech., Australia)
Zongduo Dai (Chinese Academy of Sciences, China)
Marc Girault (France Telecom, France)
Xuejia Lai (R3 Security Engineering, Switzerland)
Tzonelih Hwang (National Cheng Chung Univ., Taiwan)
Burt Kaliski (RSA Labs., USA)
Kwangjo Kim (Information and Communication Univ., Korea)
Kouichi Sakurai (Kyushu Univ., Japan)
Mitsuru Matsui (Mitsubishi Electric Corp., Japan)
Andrew Odlyzko (AT&T, USA)
Kazuo Ohta (Co-chair, NTT, Japan)
Dingyi Pei (Co-chair, SKLOIS, China)
Guozhen Xiao (Xidian Univ., China)
Lam Kwok Yan (National Univ. of Singapore, Singapore)
Yuliang Zheng (Monash Univ., Australia)

Organizing Committee
Qing Chang (National Nature Science Fundation, China)
Guang Hua (Graduate School of USTC, China)
Kan Zhang (Chinese Academy of Sciences, China)
Xinkao Song (Beijing Scientific and Technical Society, China)
Zhansheng Zhao (Chairman, SKLOIS, China)

Contents

Public Key Cryptosystems

Generating RSA Moduli with a Predetermined Portion 1
  Arjen K. Lenstra (Citibank, USA)

Generation of Shared RSA Keys by Two Parties.. 11
  Guillaume Poupard, Jacques Stern (ENS, France)

An Attack on RSA Given a Small Fraction of the Private Key Bits.................. 25
  Dan Boneh, Glenn Durfee (Stanford Univ., USA)
  Yair Frankel (Certco, USA)

C^*_{-+} and HM: Variations Around Two Schemes of T.Matsumoto and H.Imai.......... 35
  Jacques Patarin, Louis Goubin (BULL, France),
  Nicolas Courtois (Univ. de Toulon, France)

Invited Talk

ECC/DLP and Factoring-Based Cryptography: A Tale of Two Families.............. 50
  Burt S. Kaliski Jr. (RSA Labs., USA)

Elliptic Curve Cryptosystems

Efficient Elliptic Curve Exponentiation Using Mixed Coordinates......................... 51
  Henri Cohen (Univ. Bordeaux I, France),
  Atsuko Miyaji (MEI., Japan),
  Takatoshi Ono (MISRLNC., Japan)

Efficient Implementation of Schoof's Algorithm...................................... 66
  Tetsuya Izu, Jun Kogure, Masayuki Noro,
  Kazuhiro Yokoyama (Fujitsu Labs, LTD., Japan)

Design of Hyperelliptic Cryptosystems in Small Characteristic and a Software 80
Implementation over $F_2 n$ ....
  Yasuyuki Sakai (MEC., Japan)
  Kouichi Sakurai (Kyushu Univ., Japan)

Construction of Secure Elliptic Cryptosystems Using CM Tests and Liftings.......... 95
  Jinkui Chao, Osamu Nakamura, Kohji Sobataka,
  Shigeo Tsujii (Chuo Univ., Japan)

Elliptic Curve Discrete Logarithms and the Index Calculus.......................... 110
  Joseph H. Silverman (Brown Univ., USA)
  Joe Suzuki (Osaka Univ., Japan)

Cryptanalysis 1

Cryptanalysis of Rijmen-Preneel Trapdoor Cipher..................................... 126
  Hongjun Wu (Nat. Univ. of Singapore),
  Feng Bao, Robert H.Deng (Kent Ridge Digital Labs., Singapore),
  Qin-Zhong Ye (Nat. Univ. of Singapore)

Improved Truncated Differential Attacks on SAFER................................. 133
  Hongjun Wu (Nat. Univ. of Singapore),
  Feng Bao, Robert H.Deng (Kent Ridge Digital Labs., Singapore),
  Qin-Zhong Ye (Nat. Univ. of Singapore)

Optimal Resistance Against the Davis and Murphy Attack.......................... 148
  Thomas Pornin (ENS, France)

Signature

A Group Signature Scheme with Improved Efficiency............................... 160
  Jan Camenisch (Univ. of Aarhus, Denmark)
  Markus Michels (r3 security engineering, Switzerland)

A Study on the Proposed Korean Digital Signature Algorithm...................... 175
  Chae Hoon Lim (Future Systems Inc., Korea)
  Pil Joong Lee (POSTECH, Korea)

Cryptanalysis 2

Cryptanalysis of the Original McEliece Cryptosystem.............................. 187
  Anne Canteaut, Nicolas Sendrier (INRIA Project CODES, France)

Improving the Security of the McEliece Public-Key Cryptosystem................. 200
  Hung-Min Sun (Chaoyang Univ. of Tech., Taiwan)

Cryptanalysis in Prime Order Subgroups of Z_n^*..................................... 214
  Wenbo Mao (Hewlett-Packard Labs., UK)
  Chae Hoon Lim (Future Systems Inc., Korea)

Finite Automata

Weak Invertibility of Finite Automata and Cryptanalysis on FAPKC.............. 227
  Zongduo Dai (SKLOIS, China)
  Ding Feng Ye, Kwok Yan Lam (Nat. Univ. of Singapore, Singapore)

Authentication Codes

Bounds and Constructions for Multireceiver Authentication Codes................ 242
  Rei Safavi-Naini, Huaxiong Wang (Univ. of Wollongong, Australia)

Electronic Cash

FairOff-Line e-Cash Made Easy... 257
  Yair Frankel (CertCo, USA)
  Yiannis Tsiounis (GTE Labs., USA)
  Moti Yung (CertCo, USA)

Off-Line Fair Payment Protocols Using Convertible
Signatures..................... 271
  Colin Boyd, Ernest Foo (Queensland Univ. of Tech., Australia)
Efficient Fair Exchange with Verifiable Confirmation of Signatures.............. 286
  Liqun Chen (Hewlett-Packard Labs., UK)

Adaptively Secure Oblivious Transfer.. 300
  Donald Beaver (Transarc Corp. USA)

Steam Ciphers

ML-Sequences over Rings $Z/(2^n)$.. 315
  Wenfeng Qi (ZIEI, China)
  Junhui Yang (Academia Sinica, China)
  Jingjun Zhou (ZIEI, China)

Analysis Methods for (Alleged) RC4.. 327
  Lars R.Knudsen (Univ. of Bergen, Belgium)
  Willi Meier (HTL Brugg-Windisch, Belgium)
  Bart Preneel, Vincent Rijmen, Sven Verdoolaege (ESAT, K. U. Leuven,
  Belgium)

Reduced Complexity Correlation Attacks on Two Clock-Controlled
Generators 342
  Thomas Johansson (Lund Univ., Sweden)

Cryptographic Protocols

A New and Efficient All-Or-Nothing Disclosure of Secrets Protocol 357
  Julien P. Stern (UCL Crypto Group, Belgium)

The Béguin-Quisquater Server-Aided RSA Protocol fom Crypto'95 is Not
secure ....
  Phong Nguyen, Jacques Stern (ENS, France)   372

Key Escrow

Equitable Key Escrow with Limited Time Span (or How to Enforce Time
Expiration Cryptographically).. 380
  Mike Burmester (Univ. of London, UK)
  Yvo Desmedt (Univ. of Wisconsin-Milwaukee, USA),
  Jennifer, Seberry (Univ. of Wollongong, Australia)

New Cryptography

Audio and Optical Cryptography.. 392
  Yvo Desmedt, Shuang Hou (Univ. of Wisconsin-Milwaukee, USA),
  Jean-Jacques Quisquater (Univ. Catholique de Louvain, Belgium)

Information Theory

Strong Security Against Active Attacks in Information-Theoretic Secret-Key
Agreement... 405
  Stefan Wolf (ETH, Switzerland)

Some Bounds and a Construction for Secure Broadcast Encryption............... 420
  Kaoru Kurosawa, Takuya Yoshida (Tokyo Institute of Technology, Japan)
  Yvo Desmedt, (Univ. of Wisconsin-Milwaukee, USA)
  M.Burmester(Univ. of London, UK)

Author Index

Author Index 435

Generating RSA Moduli with a Predetermined Portion

Arjen K. Lenstra

Citibank, N.A., 4 Sylvan Way, Parsippany, NJ 07054, U.S.A.
arjen.lenstra@citicorp.com

Abstract. This paper reviews and generalizes a method to generate RSA moduli with a predetermined portion. The potential advantages of the resulting methods are discussed: both the storage and the computational requirements of the RSA cryptosystem can be considerably reduced. The constructions are as efficient as generation of regular RSA moduli, and the resulting moduli do not seem to offer less security than regular RSA moduli.

1 Introduction

In [18] Vanstone and Zuccherato presented several methods to generate RSA moduli that contain a certain predetermined portion. They describe scenarios where such moduli may be useful by reducing the storage requirements of RSA moduli without compromising security. For instance, all members of a group of users may share some fixed number of bits of their RSA moduli, or users may want to include a binary representation of their personal data in their RSA modulus. For DSA keys with a predetermined portion see [13].

For an N-bit RSA modulus Vanstone and Zuccherato are able to specify up to N/2 leading bits. Their method for doing so is, however, quite inefficient. They also present a faster method that allows specification of up to N/4 leading bits, and a compromise scheme of intermediate speed that specifies between N/4 and N/2 leading bits. All these methods are rather cumbersome and require factorization of the number given by the specified leading bits. A more serious disadvantage of the leading bits methods from [18] is that Coppersmith has shown in [12] that the resulting moduli are substantially easier to factor than a general product of two large primes.

Perhaps the most surprising aspect of the Vanstone/Zuccherato method is why they chose such a complicated method and apparently overlooked the obvious and straightforward trick that is reviewed in this paper. Not only is it elementary, it also does not seem to be affected by any known attack. This 'follow your nose' approach was known to at least some people, among them Coppersmith (cf. [3]), Quisquater (cf. [12]), and Shamir (cf. [16]), but most people, including the present author, were unaware of it. Allegedly (cf. [12]), it is used in a 1984 French banking standard. Attempts to access the reference [9] to this standard failed. Sakurai pointed out that the method is described in [19] for a different application. Apparently, the trick was independently reinvented many times, which is not so strange given how simple it is.

K. Ohta and D. Pei (Eds.): ASIACRYPT'98, LNCS 1514, pp. 1-10, 1998.
© Springer-Verlag Berlin Heidelberg 1998

The method presented in this paper allows generation of RSA moduli with any number of predetermined leading bits, with the fraction of specified bits only limited by security considerations. The basic method is as efficient as regular generation of RSA moduli. Several generalizations are described as well: a slower version that allows specification of slightly more bits, a method to specify any number of trailing bits, and combined methods where the specified bits are split among the leading and trailing bits of the modulus. In all methods 'bits' may be replaced by digits with respect to any radix. The method to specify trailing bits is a simple modification of the basic method. It was already described in [18] and is included for completeness.

Coppersmith's attack does not affect any of the methods presented here (and therefore neither the security of the Vanstone/Zuccherato trailing bits method). Neither does any other known attack seem to affect the security of the moduli as generated by the methods presented here. Obviously that does not imply a proof of security. It can be proved that for a randomly selected predetermined portion the resulting moduli cannot be distinguished from regular RSA moduli. This is about the strongest security result one may hope for in this context. Proving absolute security of the schemes themselves is an entirely different matter. Such a proof is unlikely. Some confidence in the strength of the methods may be provided by the fact that several eminent cryptanalists have been aware of the basic method for many years without being able to break it.

More or less the opposite approach to randomly selecting a predetermined portion is to select it in such a way that the resulting moduli are relatively close to a power of 2. According to [12] both Quisquater and the French banking standard focussed on this particular application, because it allows entirely division-free and thus much faster modular multiplication. Intuitively it sounds like a bad idea, but when a few straightforward precautions are taken no published factoring method can take substantial advantage of the special form of the modulus. Both in the May 1998 draft of the forthcoming ANSI X9.31 standard (cf. [1]) and in [17] it is mentioned that RSA moduli of the form $2^{64x} \pm c$ should not be used because they would be 'readily susceptible' to the special version of the number field sieve integer factoring algorithm. Neither [1] nor [17] specify how such moduli are generated, but if one of the methods presented in this paper is used, then they are not vulnerable to such an attack.

The X9.31 standard contains a number of criteria to be satisfied by primes dividing an RSA modulus. Some of these criteria make sense and can easily be satisfied, either by construction or by rejecting the (sufficiently small) fraction of moduli that violate one of the criteria. Other criteria are meant to protect against certain attacks but do, in fact, not offer any additional protection and provide only a false and misleading sense of security. Attempts to satisfy these latter criteria simply do not make sense, as argued in [15] as well. Therefore, the X9.31 criteria have not been incorporated in the methods presented in this paper. It should be kept in mind, however, that incorporation is possible and that in practical circumstances some of the criteria will have to be taken into account.

This paper is organized as follows. In Section 2 the basic method and its generalizations are presented. Section 3 comments on the security of the proposed methods, and in Section 4 RSA moduli that are relatively close to a power of 2 are discussed.

2   Generating RSA Moduli with a Predetermined Portion

Throughout this section $d \in \mathbf{Z}_{>1}$ denotes a fixed radix. A *digit* refers to a digit in the radix d representation. For a positive integer r its *length* $|r|$ refers to the length of r's radix d representation with non-zero leading digit.

The length of the RSA modulus n to be constructed is denoted by N, the length of the predetermined portion s of n is denoted by K with $K < N$, and $L = N-K$. The concatenation of two arrays of digits a_1 and a_0 is denoted $a_1 \| a_0$. In this section methods are presented to construct RSA moduli with radix d representation $s\|r$, $r\|s$, and $s_1\|r\|s_0$, where r is an array of L digits and $s = s_1\|s_0$. Throughout this section it is assumed that N, K, and L are sufficiently large.

(2.1) Fixing the leading digits of n. Let s be a number of length K. First compute the number $n' = s * d^L$ of length N. Next, pick a random prime p of length at most L, round n' up to the nearest multiple of p, and let q' be the integer such that $n' = p * q'$. Finally, find the smallest non-negative integer m such that $q = q' + m$ is prime. If the resulting $n = p * q$ is of the form $s\|r$, then return n, p, and q, and terminate; otherwise start all over again with the same s.

Remarks. Note that $[p * q'/d^L] = s$ and that $n = s\|r$, i.e., $[n/d^L] = [p * (q'+m)/d^L] = s$, holds if $p-1+m*p < d^L$ (where the 'p-1' results from the rounding up). Because of the Prime Number Theorem, m may on average be expected to be of order $\ln(N-|p|)$. It follows that if p is chosen such that $|p|$ is approximately equal to $L-\ln(K)$, then Algorithm (2.1) may be expected to find an RSA modulus in time $O(\ln(L)+\ln(K))$: $O(\ln(L))$ steps to find a random p and $O(\ln(K))$ to find q given q'. This is the same as the expected time needed for regular generation of an RSA modulus of length N consisting of the product of a length L and a length K prime.

If $|p|$ is chosen closer to L (or, equivalently, if the length of s is chosen larger while keeping $|p|$ fixed) then Algorithm (2.1) may be expected to require more iterations before it is successful. The largest $|p|$ (or, equivalently, largest $|s|$) would require q' to be prime, in which case Algorithm (2.1) may be expected to find an RSA modulus in time $O(\ln(L)*\ln(K))$. This is of course substantially slower than regular RSA modulus generation, but maximizes the length of the predetermined portion as $N-|p|$.

If $L-|p|$ is chosen larger, then q can be chosen at random from among the primes in a much wider range above q'. Obviously, for random s, this makes q much closer to a random prime than is the case in Algorithm (2.1).

The number n' may also be defined as $s * d^L + d^L - 1$, rounded down instead of up, after which the smallest non-negative m such that q'-m is prime should be determined. Or the last L digits of n' may be randomized in either version. Also, truly random digits may be appended to s, or p may be the product of several (sufficiently large) primes. Or any of numerous other minor modifications may be applied to Algorithm (2.1). Note that Algorithm (2.1) does not impose any size restrictions on p and q in addition to the standard size restrictions for factors of RSA moduli.

A similar straightforward construction can be used to fix the trailing digits of n. Instead of dividing the (shifted) pattern by a random prime and appropriately changing the trailing digits, the pattern may be divided by a random prime modulo a power of the radix, after which the leading digits are changed appropriately. The resulting method is identical to the method in Section 7 of [18]:

(2.2) Fixing the trailing digits of n. Let s be an array of K digits that corresponds to an odd number (where s may have leading digits zero). First pick a random prime p of length at most L, and a random number x of length $L-|p|$. Next, let $q' = x*d^K + ((s/p)$ mod $d^K)$ and let $n' = p*q'$. Finally, find the smallest non-negative integer m such that $q' + m*d^K$ is prime, and let q be $q' + m*d^K$. If the resulting $n = p*q$ has length N, then return n, p, and q, and terminate; otherwise start all over again with the same s.

Remarks. The inverse of p modulo d^K exists since p is prime and d may be assumed to be much smaller than p. Furthermore, $|n'| \approx K+L-|p|+|p| = N$ and n mod $d^K = p*(q'+ m*d^K)$ mod $d^K = p*(x*d^K + ((s/p)$ mod $d^K))$ mod $d^K = s$ mod $d^K = s$. The resulting n has length at most N as long as m is not too large. Combined with the fact that the Prime Number Theorem also holds in arithmetic progressions it follows that the run time analysis of Algorithm (2.2) is similar to the run time analysis of Algorithm (2.1). Also, more or less the same modifications can be applied.

Algorithms (2.1) and (2.2) can be combined into at least two different methods to predetermine leading and trailing portions of the digits of an RSA modulus. The conceptual ideas of the two methods are presented below. Let $s = s_1||s_0$ with $|s_1| = K_1$, $|s_0| = K_0$, $K = K_1+K_0$, s_0 odd if $K_0 > 0$, and assume that $N \approx 2K$. The constructions immediately generalize to any $N > 2K$. In general $N < 2K$ cannot be achieved, i.e., at most half the bits of the resulting modulus can be predetermined.

(2.3) Fixing the leading and trailing digits of n. Pick a random prime p of length K, and write $p = p_1||p_0$ with $|p_1| = K_1$ and $|p_0| = K_0$. As in Algorithm (2.1) divide s_1 by p_1 to get q_1, the leading K_1 digits of q. As in Algorithm (2.2) divide s_0 by p_0 modulo d^{K_0} to get q_0, the trailing K_0 digits of q. Let $q' = q_1||q_0$. Find the smallest non-negative integer m such that $q'+m*d^{K_0}$ is prime, and let $q = q'+m*d^{K_0}$.

(2.4) Alternative (slow) method of fixing the leading and trailing digits of n. Pick a number p_1 at random with $|p_1| = K_1$, the leading K_1 digits of p. As in Algorithm (2.1) divide s_1 by p_1 to get q_1, the leading K_1 digits of q. Pick an array q_0 of K_0 random digits, the trailing K_0 digits of q. As in Algorithm (2.2) divide s_0 by q_0 modulo d^{K_0} to get p_0, the trailing K_0 digits of p. Iterate choice of q_0 (or add 1 to q_0 and adapt p_0 accordingly) until $p = p_1||p_0$ and $q = q_1||q_0$ are prime.

Remarks. In both (2.3) and (2.4) the resulting $n = p*q$ has trailing K_0 digits equal to s_0 and leading K_1 digits close to s_1. The leading K_1 digits can be made equal to s_1 by including breathing space after the K_1-th but before the K_0-th digit, similar to the construction explained in the analysis of Algorithm (2.1). The details can be filled in easily.

Algorithm (2.3) runs in expected time $O(\ln(K))$: p is selected first after which q follows, as in Algorithms (2.1) and (2.2). In Algorithm (2.4) parts of p and q are selected at random, after which the complementary parts follow. Because the primes are constructed simultaneously Algorithm (2.4) runs in expected time $O(\ln(K)^2)$. It is unclear if the approach of spreading the randomness between the two factors as in Algorithm (2.4) has any advantages compared to the more direct approach of Algorithm (2.3). With $K_0 = 0$ Algorithm (2.3) generalizes to Algorithm (2.1) with $N \approx 2K$, and with $K_1 = 0$ Algorithm (2.3) generalizes to Algorithm (2.2) with $N \approx 2K$.

The lengths of p and q do not have to be the same, as follows from the following generalized version of Algorithm (2.3).

Pick a random prime p of length L ($L = N-K$), and write $p = p_1\|p_0$ with $|p_1| = L_1$ and $|p_0| = L_0$. As in Algorithm (2.1) divide $s_1 d^{L_1}$ by p_1 to get q_1, the leading K_1 digits of q. As in Algorithm (2.2) divide s_0 by p_0 modulo d^{K_0} to get q_0, the trailing K_0 digits of q. Let $q = q_1\|q_0$. Keep adding d^{K_0} to q until q is prime.

A similar change applies to Algorithm (2.4). In both generalizations at most half the bits of the resulting modulus can in general be predetermined.

3   Security Considerations

During regular generation of RSA moduli two primes, say p and q, are randomly and independently selected, and their product, say n, is made public. Despite the independence of p and q, however, the prime q is determined by p and a complementary portion of only $[\log_d(n)-\log_d(p)]$ leading and/or trailing radix d digits of n, for any $d > 1$. In Algorithms (2.1), (2.2), and (2.3) the prime factor q is, by construction, determined by the choice of p and the predetermined portion s of complementary length. It follows that this situation is identical to regular RSA moduli, as long as the complementary portion s of the modulus is randomly selected and as long as only $m = 0$ is allowed in Algorithms (2.1), (2.2), and (2.3). (Instead of requiring $m = 0$, a much larger range of m's may be allowed than in Algorithms (2.1), (2.2), and (2.3), to deal with the 'unfair' advantage of primes ending a long arithmetic progression of composites. Note, however, that many efficient prime generation methods used in RSA moduli generation have the same bias.) A slightly more involved argument applies if portions of p and q are randomly selected (and s is random), as in Algorithm (2.4). Thus, if the predetermined portion is randomly selected then the moduli as constructed by the proper variations of the methods from Section 2 cannot be distinguished from regular RSA moduli. A similar argument appeared in [19].

Even if the predetermined portion is not randomly selected it is in general unclear how to distinguish any particular modulus constructed as in Section 2 from a regular RSA modulus. A predetermined portion that looks random to an unsuspecting outsider may consist of some contrived encoding of useful information, such as a key merged with a block cipher encryption using that key. An insider who knows the encoding scheme for the predetermined portion has an advantage if no precautions are taken to hide the length of the factors. How this advantage may be used to factor the modulus is unclear, as long as none of the factors is chosen too small and p does not depend on the predetermined portion (as in [19]). Hiding the length of the factors may for instance be done by adding truly random bits to the predetermined portion s, as mentioned in Section 2, or by forcing m as in Section 2 to be such that s gets extended, a modification not explicitly mentioned in Section 2.

Once a predetermined portion has been recognized, for instance because it is shared by many moduli, it is hard to imagine how it would help to factor any of them, since anyone can generate such moduli. Furthermore, it is very unlikely that the security of a regular RSA modulus is affected by using one of the algorithms from Section 2 to generate a modulus having a large portion in common with it. Note that shared leading digits can easily be recognized, mostly irrespective of the d used during construction and the radix used for representation of the moduli. A common trailing portion may be harder to recognize if different radices are used during construction and representation. One very minor problem with a shared portion is that there is a larger probability that two participants end up with the same modulus, but this probability is of the same order of magnitude that someone guesses one of the factors of an RSA modulus, and may thus be neglected.

Predetermined portions that lead to special computational properties of the resulting moduli are discussed in the next section.

4   Moduli of a Special Form

Algorithm (2.1) can be used to generate RSA moduli of the form $d^N \pm t$ for positive t's that are substantially smaller than d^N. On computers where numbers are internally represented using radix d numbers, arithmetic operations modulo such RSA moduli can be carried out very efficiently because divisions can entirely be avoided. Let the radix d representation of t have N/c digits for some $c > 1$. Then reduction modulo $d^N \pm t$ of a product of approximately 2N radix d digits can be done in approximately $N/(N-N/c)$ multiplications of two numbers of $N-N/c$ and N/c radix d digits, plus some additions. In standard arithmetic this amounts to approximately N^2/c multiplications, which is c times faster than ordinary or Montgomery reduction (cf. [10]) modulo numbers of the same size. Moreover, ordinary reduction requires on the order of N low level divisions. The above division-free reduction can be expected to make modular exponentiation approximately $5c/(2c+3)$ times faster, a speed-up that can be increased by using Karatsuba multiplication during the reduction process.

Algorithms (2.3) or (2.4) or their generalizations can be used to generate RSA moduli of the form $d^N \pm t d^M \pm 1$ with $M < N/2$ and $|t| \approx N/2$. As above, reduction modulo $d^N \pm t d^M \pm 1$ of a product of approximately 2N radix d digits can be done in approximately $N^2/2$ multiplications. Algorithm (2.2) can be used to generate N-digit RSA moduli of the form $t d^M \pm 1$. It is easy to see that such moduli lead to similar speed-ups, not only when using standard arithmetic but also when Montgomery arithmetic (cf. [10]) is used.

It is suggested in [1] and [17] that such special form moduli are easier to factor than regular RSA moduli. If that is indeed the case, then using them cannot be recommended. Below some characteristics of the currently known factoring algorithms are discussed and how their speed may be affected by factoring the above N-digit special composites as opposed to regular RSA moduli having N radix d digits. Without loss of generality it is assumed that $d = 2$ and that regular 1024-bit RSA moduli may be considered to be sufficiently secure against factoring attacks. The question addressed is how small t may be chosen so that the factorization of $2^{1024} \pm t$ does not become substantially easier than the factorization of a regular 1024-bit RSA modulus.

Elliptic curve method. The elliptic curve method (cf. [8]) is good at finding small factors, with only polynomial dependence on the size of the number being factored. Given ample practical experience with this method it may safely be assumed that $2^{1024} \pm t$ cannot be factored by the elliptic curve method as long as the smallest factor is at least 2^{300}, even if the implementation takes advantage of the special arithmetic properties of the number $2^{1024} \pm t$ being factored. Because in Algorithm (2.1) the size of t corresponds to the size of one of the factors it follows that t should be at least 2^{300} and at most 2^{724}.

Other special purpose methods. With a smallest prime factor that is already at least 2^{300} it may safely be assumed that $2^{1024} \pm t$ is secure against trial division and Pollard's rho method, and may be expected to be secure against Pollard's p−1 method and variations thereof (cf. [6]). Since the size of t corresponds to the size of the factor p that is randomly selected at the beginning of Algorithm (2.1), explicit protection against the latter methods may even be included (despite [15] and the author's reservations about such protections).

Number field sieve. If $2^{1024} \pm t$ can be written as f(m) for an integer m and integral polynomial f of reasonably low degree d, say between 3 and 10, and with coefficients substantially smaller than the d-th or (d+1)-st root of n, then the number field sieve (cf. [7]) runs substantially faster than for general 1024-bit numbers. Actually, if the coefficients are bounded by constants the much faster 'special' number field sieve applies. Note that **all** coefficients need to be small to get a substantial speed-up − as long as even one of them is close to the d-th or (d+1)-st root of n hardly any speed-up will be obtained. For $2^{1024} \pm t$ with a t that may be expected to behave as a random number of at least 300 bits the probability is negligible that such a polynomial f with unusually small coefficients exists. Thus the number field sieve cannot be expected to factor numbers of the form $2^{1024} \pm t$ (as generated by Algorithm (2.1)) faster than regular 1024-bit RSA moduli, if the number $2^{1024} \pm t$ is already properly protected against the elliptic curve method.

Quadratic sieve. In the quadratic sieve factoring method (cf. [14]) one attempts to find many smooth numbers close to the square root of the number being factored, where a number is smooth when all its prime factors are smaller than some specified bound. Given the way the numbers that are inspected for smoothness are generated, their size or smoothness probability is not affected by the special form of $2^{1024} \pm t$. Thus quadratic sieve cannot be expected to factor numbers of the form $2^{1024} \pm t$ faster than regular 1024-bit RSA moduli.

Continued fraction method. The continued fraction method (cf. [11]) uses the continued fraction expansion of the squareroot of the number n being factored to generate numbers that are inspected for smoothness. In general these numbers are at most $2\sqrt{n}$. The recursion used to generate them does not produce numbers of significantly different size if n is of the form $2^{1024} \pm t$. The continued fraction method can therefore not be expected to be able to take advantage of the special form of $2^{1024} \pm t$.

Cubic sieve. If integers a, b, c, can be found such that $b^3 \neq a^2 c$ and $b^3 \equiv a^2 c$ modulo $2^{1024} \pm t$ (or if a similar identity holds), then $2^{1024} \pm t$ can be factored by means of the cubic sieve (cf. [4]) in approximately the same time it would take quadratic sieve to factor a general number of the same order of magnitude as $(\max(a,b,c))^2$. Thus, the identity $2*(2^{341})^3 \equiv \pm t$ modulo $2^{1024} \pm t$ may make it possible to factor $2^{1024} \pm t$ in the same time it would take quadratic sieve to factor a number of order $\max(2^{682}, t^2)$, assuming that t is square-free. It should be noted that this estimate is probably rather optimistic as far as the speed of the cubic sieve is concerned, because computational experience with the cubic sieve is very limited. For a conservative estimate of the security of $2^{1024} \pm t$ this optimism is justifiable.

   The number field sieve factorization of a number $\approx 10^{130}$ could have been completed in one fifth of the time of the quadratic sieve factorization of a number $\approx 10^{129}$ (cf. [5]). Combining this conservative estimate with the asymptotic run times of the number field sieve and quadratic sieve, it follows that a 780-bit number offers approximately the same amount of security against a quadratic sieve attack as a 1024-bit number offers against a number field sieve attack. Thus, for square-free t, the security of $2^{1024} \pm t$ is not affected by the cubic sieve if $\max(2^{682}, t^2) \approx 2^{780}$. It follows that t should be of the form $a^2 t'$ where t' has at least approximately 390 bits and is square-free. This condition either can be satisfied by factoring (and possibly rejecting) a 390-bit t as found by Algorithm (2.1), a rather impractical and cumbersome process, or it may safely be assumed to hold on probabilistic grounds by using a larger t of, say, 500 bits.

Zhang's method. If $2^{1024} \pm t$ can be written as $m^3 + c_2 m^2 + c_1 m + c_0$, then the method from [20] factors $2^{1024} \pm t$ in approximately the same time it would take quadratic sieve to factor a general number of the same order of magnitude as $2^{682} * \max_{0 \leq i \leq 2} c_i$. Because vulnerability to this method implies vulnerability to the number field sieve, no speed-up can be expected if the number $2^{1024} \pm t$ is already properly protected against the elliptic curve method.

Other general purpose factoring methods. There do not seem to be any special properties of any other published general purpose factoring algorithms, such as Dixon's random squares method or the various methods using class groups, that may affect the security of numbers of the form $2^{1024} \pm t$ with, say, $2^{500} < t < 2^{700}$ as constructed by Algorithm (2.1).

Conclusion. It follows from the above brief factoring survey that numbers of the form $2^{1024} \pm t$ as constructed by Algorithm (2.1) offer regular 1024-bit RSA security, as long as t is not much smaller than 2^{500}, and that square-free t's as small as 400 bits may even be used. Furthermore, t should not be much bigger than 2^{700}. Thus RSA operations could be made at least 30% faster (using the analysis presented above with c = 2), while at the same time considerably simplifying the division code and saving storage space for RSA moduli. These are a rather minor advantages compared to the enormous disadvantage of a security breach when the above conclusion happens to be incorrect.

After some straightforward modifications the same factoring analysis (and thus the same conclusion) applies to the special form moduli generated using Algorithms (2.2), (2.3), or (2.4).

Acknowledgments. Acknowledgments are due to Don Coppersmith, David Naccache, Kouichi Sakurai, Adi Shamir, and, indirectly, Moti Yung, for their help in tracking down 'prior art', and to the Asiacrypt'98 program committee for helpful remarks.

References

1. ANSI X9.31: American national standard for financial services – Digital signatures using reversible public key cryptography for the financial services industry (rDSA). Working draft (May 1998)
2. Coppersmith, D.: Finding a small root of a bivariate integer equation; factoring with high bits known. In: Maurer, U. (ed.): Advances in Cryptology – Eurocrypt'96. Lecture Notes in Computer Science, Vol. 1070. Springer-Verlag, Berlin Heidelberg New York (1996) 178-189
3. Coppersmith, D.: Personal communication (1998)
4. Coppersmith, D., Odlyzko, A.M., Schroeppel, R.: Discrete logarithms in GF(p). Algorithmica 1 (1986) 1-15
5. Cowie, J., Dodson, B., Elkenbracht-Huizing, R.M., Lenstra, A.K., Montgomery, P.L., Zayer, J.: A world wide number field sieve factoring record: on to 512 bits. In: Kim, K., Matsumoto, T. (eds.): Advances in Cryptology – Asiacrypt'96. Lecture Notes in Computer Science, Vol. 1163. Springer-Verlag, Berlin Heidelberg New York (1996) 382-394
6. Knuth, D.E.: The art of computer Programming, Vol. 2, Seminumerical algorithms, 2nd edn. Addison Wesley (1981)
7. Lenstra, A.K., Lenstra, Jr., H.W. (eds.): The development of the number field sieve. Lecture Notes in Mathematics, Vol. 1554. Springer-Verlag, Berlin Heidelberg New York (1993)
8. Lenstra, Jr., H.W.: Factoring integers using elliptic curves. Ann. of Math. 126 (1987) 649-673
9. Les Specifications et les Normes de la Carte à Memoire Bancaire, Groupement Carte à Memoire, 96 rue de la Victoire, 75009, Paris, Janvier 1984, chapitre 6: La Securité.
10. Montgomery, P.L.: Modular multiplication without trial division. Math. Comp. 44 (1985) 519-521

11. Morrison, M.A., Brillhart, J.: A method of factoring and the factorization of F_7. Math. Comp. 29 (1975) 183-205
12. Naccache, D.: Personal communication (1998)
13. Naccache, D., M'Raïhi, A., Vaudenay, S., Raphaeli, D.: Can D.S.A. be improved? – Complexity trade-offs with the digital signature standard. In: DeSantis, A. (ed.): Advances in Cryptology – Eurocrypt'94. Lecture Notes in Computer Science, Vol. 950. Springer-Verlag, Berlin Heidelberg New York (1995) 77-85
14. Pomerance, C.: Analysis and comparison of some integer factoring algorithms. In: Lenstra, Jr., H.W., Tijdeman, R. (eds.): Computational methods in number theory. Math. Centre tracts 154/155. Math. Centrum, Amsterdam (1982) 89-139
15. Rivest, R.L., Silverman, R.D.: Are 'strong' primes needed for RSA?. In: RSA'98 conference binder.
16. Shamir, A.: Personal communication (1998)
17. Silverman, R.D.: Fast generation of random, strong RSA primes. RSA Laboratories' Cryptobytes 3, number 1, (1997) 9-13
18. Vanstone, S.A., Zuccherato, R.J.: Short RSA keys and their generation. Journal of Cryptology 8 (1995) 101-114
19. Young, A. Yung, M.: The dark side of „Black-Box" cryptography, or: should we trust Capstone? In: Koblitz, N. (ed.): Advances in Cryptology – Crypto'96. Lecture Notes in Computer Science, Vol. 1109. Springer-Verlag, Berlin Heidelberg New York (1996) 89-103
20. Zhang, M.: Factorization of the numbers of the form $m^3+c_2m^2+c_1m+c_0$. In: Buhler, J.P. (ed.): Algorithmic Number Theory – ANTS-III. Lecture Notes in Computer Science, Vol. 1423. Springer-Verlag, Berlin Heidelberg New York (1998) 131-136

Generation of Shared RSA Keys
by Two Parties

Guillaume Poupard and Jacques Stern

École Normale Supérieure, Laboratoire d'informatique
45 rue d'Ulm, F-75230 Paris Cedex 05, France
email: {Guillaume.Poupard,Jacques.Stern}@ens.fr

Abstract. At Crypto'97 Boneh and Franklin proposed a protocol to efficiently generate shared RSA keys. In the case of two parties, the drawback of their scheme is the need of an independent third party. Furthermore, the security is guaranteed only if the three players follow the protocol. In this paper, we propose a protocol that enables two parties to evaluate any algebraic expression, including an RSA modulus, along the same lines as in the Boneh-Franklin protocol. Our solution does not need the help of a third party and the only assumption we make is the existence of an oblivious transfer protocol. Furthermore, it remains robust even if one of the two players deviates from the protocol.

1 Introduction

The general problem of private multi-party computation has motivated many solutions for ten years. In 1986, Yao [26] proved the existence of secure two-party protocols assuming the computational intractability of factoring large integers. Goldreich, Micali and Wigderson [16] generalized this result and showed that trapdoor functions enable to evaluate any function whose inputs are privately owned by the parties, provided a majority of them is honest. The next year, Ben-Or, Goldwasser and Wigderson [2] and independently Chaum, Crépeau and Damgård [8] solved the same problem under an information-theoretic approach. Then, many papers improved the needed assumptions [18], the theoretical bounds for subclasses of functions [9] or the simplicity and the efficiency of the methods [13].

The aim of all those papers is to solve any multi-party computation problem. Accordingly the first step is always the description of the function to be privately evaluated as a logical circuit or as a polynomial over a finite field. This enables to reduce the problem to a very small set of elementary protocols, like the computation of the logical AND of two bits, at the cost of polynomial but unpractical solutions. Consequently, even if the problem of multi-party computation is theoretically solved, the design of more specific but also more efficient protocols appears necessary.

Boneh and Franklin [5] followed this "application oriented" approach to solve the problem of generating shared RSA keys. More precisely, some parties want to

K. Ohta and D. Pei (Eds.): ASIACRYPT'98, LNCS 1514, pp. 11–24, 1998.

jointly generate an RSA modulus $N = pq$ where p and q are prime in such a way that, at the end of the computation, the parties are convinced that N is indeed a product of two large primes but none of them knows its factorization. They use the general protocol of Ben-Or, Goldwasser and Wigderson [2] to prove that the distributed computation of N by two parties can be efficiently done with the help of a third party, assuming the three players do not collude and follow the protocol. They also prove that the test $N = pq$ with p and q two prime numbers can be efficiently done by two honest parties alone, using a clever probabilistic algorithm variant of the Miller-Rabin and the Solovay-Strassen ones, under the assumption that the quadratic residuosity problem is computationally hard to solve. Finally, they show how two parties can generate shared secret keys, by themselves for small public exponents and with the help of a third party in the general case. An experimental evaluation of the performance can be found in [24]. It shows that a 1024-bit modulus N can be generated in only 10 minutes with Sparc 20 machines.

Independently Cocks [10,11] has proposed another solution for the same problem that only involves two honest players but assuming the computational intractability of a problem weaker than RSA. This protocol is analyzed and improved in [4].

More recently, Frankel, MacKenzie and Yung [15] have improved the security of the Boneh-Franklin protocol. Their generation scheme is efficient and robust even when a minority of parties are malicious. But in the case of only two parties, both of them have to be honest.

Our Results

For many applications, the protocol of Boneh and Franklin does not provide an accurate level of security for two reasons. Firstly, it needs an independent and honest third party. Secondly, the security is guaranteed only if the three players do not deviate from the protocol. In this paper, we show how two parties can efficiently generate shared RSA keys even if one of them is dishonest. From a theoretical point of view, we only assume the existence of oblivious transfer protocols.

From a practical point of view, our scheme is less efficient than the Boneh-Franklin protocol based on the Ben-Or, Goldwasser and Wigderson construction [2] which is itself based on arithmetical computation in finite fields. Anyway our protocol is much more efficient, especially when we focus on the number of rounds of communication, than those derived from general techniques.

The paper is organized as follows: we first recall the notion of an ANDOS protocol. Then we propose an efficient and general protocol for the distributed evaluation of algebraic expressions by two parties. We prove its security when the players are honest but also its robustness when one of them is malicious. Then, we use this protocol to generate shared RSA keys. Finally we compare the efficiency of our scheme with general 2-party computation protocols. We also propose in an appendix another solution, much more simple and efficient but less general, based on the higher residue cryptosystem of Naccache and Stern [19].

All-or Nothing Disclosure of Secrets Protocols

Oblivious transfer has been introduced in 1981 by Rabin [21] and a specific version, namely the oblivious transfer of one bit out of two [14], soon emerged as a very useful cryptographic primitive for many applications [18]. Brassard, Crépeau and Robert generalized this notion in various natural ways [7] and they proved the equivalence of those protocols in an information theoretic sense [6].

All-or Nothing Disclosure of Secrets (ANDOS) protocols [7] address the following problem: a *merchant* has n secret bit-strings and wishes to sell one of them to a *buyer* who has the ability to choose which one he wants. There are two privacy requirements: the merchant does not want the buyer to obtain information about any other secret and the buyer does not want the merchant to learn anything about the string he has chosen.

Oblivious transfer, and consequently ANDOS, can be based on various assumptions like the existence of trapdoor functions [16], of noisy channels [12] or of quantum channels [3]. From a practical point of view, efficient implementation can be based on the quadratic residuosity problem [7,25] or on the Diffie-Hellman assumption [1,23].

In this paper we use ANDOS as a cryptographic primitive. In order to formalize its properties, let us consider that Alice sells a secret to Bob. Using the terminology of [17], we define the *view* of Alice to be everything she sees during the execution of the protocol. Let $View_A$ be the random variable whose value is this view. It depends on the secrets $s_1, ... s_n$ sold by Alice, on the index i_B of the secret bought by Bob and on the random tape ω_A of Alice considered as a polynomial time Turing machine. We also use the three well-known notions of indistinguishability of random variables: the perfect one, the statistical one and the computational one (see [17] for complete definitions). In the paper, we just talk about indistinguishability without any other precision for simplicity reasons but all the definitions and proofs hold in the three models and the choice of one of them only depends on the properties of the underlying ANDOS.

We model the ANDOS protocol as a scheme that enables Alice to sell one secret out of n to Bob in such a way that:

(ANDOS$_1$) Alice does not learn anything about the index i_B of the secret she has sold:

$$\forall j \in [1, n] \quad View_A(\omega_A, s_1, ... s_n, i_B)$$
$$\text{is indistinguishable from } View_A(\omega_A, s_1, ... s_n, j)$$

(ANDOS$_2$) Bob does not learn anything about the other secrets:

$$\forall s'_1, ... s'_n \text{ such that } s'_{i_B} = s_{i_B} \quad View_B(\omega_B, s_1, ... s_n, i_B)$$
$$\text{is indistinguishable from } View_B(\omega_B, s'_1, ... s'_n, i_B)$$

2   Efficient Two-Party Evaluation of Algebraic Expressions

The General Problem

Let us consider two players, Alice and Bob, modelled as polynomial time Turing machines, who have private randomly chosen data $d_A \in \mathcal{E}_A$ and $d_B \in \mathcal{E}_B$. We want to design a two-party computation protocol which enables Alice and Bob to compute a public function $f(d_A, d_B)$ (whose result is encoded as an integer value) modulo a prime public modulus P.

This protocol has to meet two main properties. Informally, it must be *correct*, i.e. the result of the computation must be $f(d_A, d_B) \bmod P$. It must also be *private*, i.e. a party must not be able to learn information about the other's secret. The exact meaning of those two properties will be made precise further on. At the moment, let us stress that we do not develop a general two-party computation protocol but just an efficient scheme suitable to the generation of shared RSA keys. Consequently we need weaker notions of privacy and correctness than those described in more general papers [2,8,16,26].

The Protocol

Let us consider polynomial size sets $\mathcal{E}_A$ and $\mathcal{E}_B$ and any prime modulus P. The following protocol enables Alice and Bob to compute $f(d_A, d_B) \bmod P$ without revealing there private inputs $d_A \in \mathcal{E}_A$ and $d_B \in \mathcal{E}_B$:

(1) Alice randomly chooses $(\alpha_A, \beta_A) \in \mathbb{Z}_P^* \times \mathbb{Z}_P$ (the coefficients of a secret line).
(2) Alice and Bob perform an ANDOS protocol where Alice sells
     $\{\gamma_d\}_{d \in \mathcal{E}_B} = \{\alpha_A \times f(d_A, d) + \beta_A \bmod P\}_{d \in \mathcal{E}_B}$ and Bob buys $\gamma_{d_B} = y_B$.
(3) Bob randomly chooses $(\alpha_B, \beta_B) \in \mathbb{Z}_P^* \times \mathbb{Z}_P$.
(4) Alice and Bob perform an ANDOS protocol where Bob sells
     $\{\delta_d\}_{d \in \mathcal{E}_A} = \{\alpha_B \times f(d, d_B) + \beta_B \bmod P\}_{d \in \mathcal{E}_A}$ and Alice buys $\delta_{d_A} = y_A$.
(5) Alice and Bob broadcast (simultaneously) (α_A, β_A, y_A) and (α_B, β_B, y_B).
(6) They verify $\alpha_A \in \mathbb{Z}_P^*$, $\alpha_B \in \mathbb{Z}_P^*$ and $(y_B - \beta_A) \times \alpha_A^{-1} = (y_A - \beta_B) \times \alpha_B^{-1} \bmod P$. If this equality holds, $f(d_A, d_B) = (y_A - \beta_B) \times \alpha_B^{-1} \bmod P$; we say that the protocol ends *successfully*. Otherwise, the protocol fails and the players stop cooperation.

Security Analysis for Honest Players

We first consider that Alice and Bob behave honestly, i.e. follow the protocol.

Theorem 1 (Correctness). *If the two players follow the protocol, it always succeeds and both of them obtain the correct value $f(d_A, d_B) \bmod P$.*

Proof. The correctness of the protocol when the two players are honest is obvious according to the graphical representation of figure 1.   □

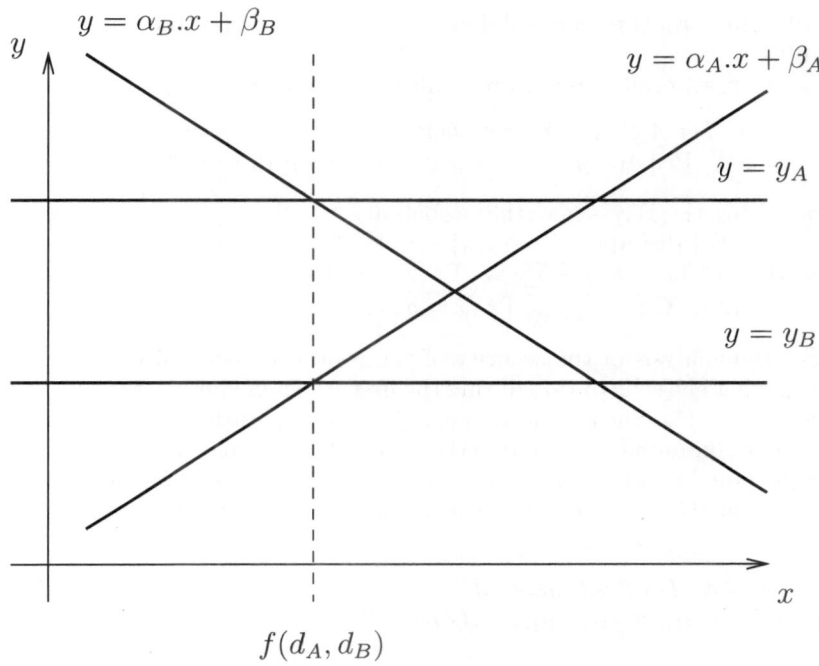

$$y = \alpha_B.x + \beta_B$$

$$y = \alpha_A.x + \beta_A$$

$$y = y_A$$

$$y = y_B$$

$$f(d_A, d_B)$$

Fig. 1. Graphical representation of the two-party computation protocol

Theorem 2 (Privacy). *Given $f(d_A, d_B)$ mod P and their own private data, Alice and Bob can each simulate the transcript of the protocol. Consequently they learn nothing more than the value $f(d_A, d_B)$ mod P.*

Proof. We show how to simulate Alice's view but the same proof holds for Bob. The simulator randomly chooses $\alpha_B \in \mathbb{Z}_P^*$, $\beta_B \in \mathbb{Z}_P$, $\delta_d \in \mathbb{Z}_P$ for all $d \in \mathcal{E}_A - \{d_A\}$. It computes $\delta_{d_A} = y_A = \alpha_B \times f(d_A, d_B) + \beta_B$ mod P and $\gamma_d = \alpha_A \times f(d_A, d) + \alpha_B$ mod P for all $d \in \mathcal{E}_B$ (including $y_B = \gamma_{d_B}$). It then randomly choose $d \in \mathcal{E}_B$ and simulates the buying of the secret γ_d by Bob. The property (ANDOS$_1$) shows that the view of Alice during the simulation is indistinguishable from what she sees when Bob really buys γ_{d_B}. It also simulates the buying of $\delta_{d_A} = y_A$ by Alice. Property (ANDOS$_2$) proves that the view of Alice is indistinguishable from her view when the secrets $\{\delta_d\}_{d \in \mathcal{E}_A - \{d_A\}}$ are really computed by Bob. Finally, the simulator reveals α_A, β_A, y_A, α_B, β_B, y_B whose distribution is the same as in a real interaction between Alice and Bob.   □

Security Analysis when one Player is Malicious

We only consider the situation where Alice is malicious and Bob honest. For the reverse case, even though the protocol is not symmetrical for the two players, the following proofs remain valid because they do not use the order of the steps (1) to (4).

Let us first recall a useful probabilistic lemma [20]:

Lemma 3. *Let $A \subset X \times Y$ such that $\Pr \{A(x,y)\} = \varepsilon$ and, for any $\alpha < \varepsilon$, let $X_0 = \{a \in X / \Pr \{A(x,y)/x = a\} > \varepsilon - \alpha\}$. Then $\Pr \{x \in X_0\} \geq \alpha$.*

Proof. Using the Bayes law, the probability $\varepsilon = \Pr_{(x,y)\in X\times Y} \{A(x,y)\}$ is equal to $\Pr \{x \in X_0\} \Pr \{A(x,y)/x \in X_0\} + \Pr \{x \notin X_0\} \Pr \{A(x,y)/x \notin X_0\}$ and this is less than $\Pr \{x \in X_0\} + \sum_{a\notin X_0} \Pr \{x = a\} \Pr \{A(x,y)/x = a\}$.
So $\varepsilon \leq \Pr \{x \in X_0\} + \sum_{a\notin X_0} \Pr \{x = a\} (\varepsilon - \alpha)$. □

For the analysis of the security of the protocol when Alice is malicious, we note $\widetilde{\gamma}_d$ what she sells to Bob during the first ANDOS and $\widetilde{y_A}$ the value she broadcasts at step (5). Such a notation enables to distinguish potentially false values from those computed according to the protocol. The tuple $(\{\widetilde{\gamma}_d\}_{d\in\mathcal{E}_B}, \alpha_A, \beta_A, \widetilde{y_A})$ is simply noted t and Δ denotes the size of $\mathcal{E}_B$. Finally, we often omit the modular reduction $\mod P$ for simplicity reasons but all the computation are performed in $\mathbb{Z}_P$.

Definition 4. *For fixed values of d_A, d_B and t, Alice is said to be* pseudo-honest *(PH) if $\widetilde{\gamma}_{d_B} = \alpha_A \times f(d_A, d_B) + \beta_A \mod P$ and $\widetilde{y_A} = y_A$.*

Definition 5. *For fixed values d_A and d_B, the predicate $success_{d_A,d_B}(t, \alpha_B, \beta_B)$ is true if the protocol ends successfully i.e. if $\alpha_A \neq 0$ and $(\widetilde{\gamma}_{d_B} - \beta_A) \times \alpha_A^{-1} = (\widetilde{y_A} - \beta_B) \times \alpha_B^{-1} \mod P$.*

Before proving the correctness of the protocol, let us state a lemma whose proof comes from elementary algebra arguments and that essentially says that the intersection of two non-parallel lines is reduced to one point in $(\mathbb{Z}_P)^2$.

Lemma 6. *For fixed values of d_A, d_B, y_A and for a given tuple t, if there exists two different pairs (α_B^1, β_B^1) and (α_B^2, β_B^2) such that $y_A = \alpha_B^1 \times f(d_A, d_B) + \beta_B^1 = \alpha_B^2 \times f(d_A, d_B) + \beta_B^2$ and $success_{d_A,d_B}(t, \alpha_B^i, \beta_B^i)$ for $i \in \{1,2\}$, then Alice is pseudo-honest.*

Lemma 7. *If Alice has a cheating strategy such that the protocol ends successfully with probability ε, she is pseudo-honest with probability greater than $\varepsilon - \frac{1}{1-P}$.*

Proof. The probability distribution of $t = (\{\widetilde{\gamma}_d\}_{d\in\mathcal{E}_B}, \alpha_A, \beta_A, \widetilde{y_A})$ a priori depends on d_A, d_B, α_B and β_B. Property ANDOS_2 applied to the second ANDOS (where Alice buys $y_A = \alpha_B \times f(d_A, d_B) + \beta_B \mod P$ to Bob) shows that for a fixed value y_A, the distribution of t does not depend of α_B and β_B such that $y_A = \alpha_B \times f(d_A, d_B) + \beta_B \mod P$. Consequently, this distribution only depends on $(d_A, d_B, y_A) = s$. Let us note $\mathcal{D}$ the distribution of the pairs (α_B, β_B) such that $y_A = \alpha_B \times f(d_A, d_B) + \beta_B \mod P$ and $\mathcal{T}$ the (non uniform) distribution of tuple t for fixed values of d_A, d_B and y_A. Let ε be the probability of success of the protocol according to the cheating strategy of Alice and ε_s be this probability for fixed values of d_A, d_B and y_A; $\varepsilon = \sum_s \Pr\{s\}\varepsilon_s$ and $\varepsilon_s = \Pr_{(\alpha_B,\beta_B)\in\mathcal{D},t\in\mathcal{T}}\{success_{d_A,d_B}(t,\alpha_B,\beta_B)\}$. Let X_s be the set of the tuples t such that $\Pr_{(\alpha_B,\beta_B)\in\mathcal{D}}\{success_{d_A,d_B}(t,\alpha_B,\beta_B)\} > \frac{1}{P-1}$. Lemma 3, with $\alpha = \varepsilon_s - \frac{1}{P-1}$, proves that $\Pr_{t\in\mathcal{T}}\{t\in X_s\} \geq \varepsilon_s - \frac{1}{P-1}$.

For fixed values of d_A, d_B and y_A, there are exactly $P-1$ pairs (α_B,β_B) such that $y_A = \alpha_B \times f(d_A,d_B) + \beta_B \mod P$ and the distribution $\mathcal{D}$ of those pairs is uniform since Bob chooses them randomly. If t belongs to X_s, the probability $\Pr_{(\alpha_B,\beta_B)\in\mathcal{D}}\{success_{d_A,d_B}(t,\alpha_B,\beta_B)\}$ is greater than $\frac{1}{P-1}$ so there exists two different pairs (α_B^1,β_B^1) and (α_B^2,β_B^2) such that $y_A = \alpha_B^i \times f(d_A,d_B) + \beta_B^i \mod P$ and $success_{d_A,d_B}(t,\alpha_B^i,\beta_B^i)$ for $i \in \{1,2\}$. According to lemma 6, this proves that Alice is pseudo-honest.

We can now evaluate the probability for Alice to be pseudo-honest:

$$\sum_s \Pr\{s\} \Pr_{t\in\mathcal{T}}\{t\in X_s\} \geq \sum_s \Pr\{s\}\left(\varepsilon_s - \frac{1}{P-1}\right) = \varepsilon - \frac{1}{P-1}$$

□

Theorem 8 (Correctness). *Assume Alice has a cheating strategy such that the protocol ends successfully with probability ε. If an execution of the protocol is successful, the probability for the result to be $f(d_A,d_B)$ is greater than $\frac{\varepsilon - \frac{1}{P-1}}{\varepsilon}$.*

Proof. The probability for Alice to be pseudo-honest conditioned by the knowledge that the protocol ends successfully is $\Pr\{success(t,\alpha_B,\beta_B)/\text{Alice PH}\} \times \Pr\{\text{Alice PH}\}/\Pr\{success(t,\alpha_B,\beta_B)\}$.

Lemma 7 proves $\Pr\{\text{Alice is pseudo-honest}\} \geq \varepsilon - \frac{1}{P-1}$, by definition the probability of success is ε and finally $\Pr\{Success/\text{Alice PH}\} = 1$ because when Alice is pseudo-honest the protocol is successful so the result of a successful execution is correct with probability $\geq 1 - \frac{1}{\varepsilon(P-1)}$. □

Dealing with multiparty computation, an important characteristic is how fair the protocol is. During the shared generation of RSA keys, neither Alice nor Bob can take advantage to stop the interaction before the normal end because such keys cannot be used alone. So our protocol is unfair but it does not matter since our aim is not to design a general multiparty computation scheme but rather to obtain a scheme with no more properties than those needed for the generation of shared RSA keys.

Lemma 9. *The knowledge of $f(d_A,d_B) \mod P$ enables Alice to simulate the transcript of successful executions of the protocol.*

Proof. We already said in lemma 7 that the probability distribution of t depends on y_A. Furthermore, for randomly chosen $(\alpha_B,\beta_B) \in \mathbb{Z}_P^* \times \mathbb{Z}_P$ and for any fixed value of $f(d_A,d_B)$, the distribution of $y_A = \alpha_B \times f(d_A,d_B) + \beta_B \mod P$ is uniform.

Most of the simulation of Alice's view is the same as in the case of honest players (theorem 2). For fixed value of $f(d_A, d_B)$, the view of Alice during the first ANDOS is simulated by the buying of $\widetilde{\gamma}_{d_0}$ for a random value d_0. Her view during the second ANDOS is simulated by the buying of $y_A = \delta_{d_A} = \alpha_B f(d_A, d_B) + \beta_B \mod P$ for randomly chosen α_B, β_B and δ_d for $d \neq d_A$. Then the simulator broadcasts α_A, β_A, $\widetilde{y_A}$, α_B, β_B, y_B, where $y_B = \widetilde{\gamma}_d$ for a randomly chosen d. Finally the simulator is reset until the verification succeeds.   □

Theorem 10 (Privacy). *Assume Alice has a cheating strategy such that the protocol ends successfully with probability ε. After a successful execution of the protocol, Alice cannot learn more than $\frac{1}{\varepsilon(P-1)} \log \Delta - \frac{\varepsilon - \frac{1}{P-1}}{\varepsilon} \log \left(\varepsilon - \frac{1}{P-1} \right)$ bits of information about d_B in addition to the result $f(d_A, d_B)$.*

Proof. Let $\nu_{d_A,t}$ be the random variable equal to the number of $\widetilde{\gamma}_d$ correctly computed by Alice according to the revealed line $y = \alpha_A.x + \beta_A \mod P$, i.e. such that $\widetilde{\gamma}_d = \alpha_A f(d_A, d) + \beta_A \mod P$. For fixed d_A and t, the probability for Alice to be pseudo-honest is exactly ν/Δ if she reveals $\widetilde{y_A} = y_A$ so the probability ε' for Alice to be pseudo-honest is less than $\sum_{d_A,t} \Pr\{d_A, t\}\nu/\Delta$. Furthermore, if the protocol is successful, she exactly learns that $\widetilde{\gamma}_{d_B}$ has been correctly computed and consequently learns that d_B belongs to a set of size ν. In order to estimate the information Alice learns in addition to the result $f(d_A, d_B)$, we evaluate the expected value of $\log \nu$ in case of success, $E(\log \nu/success) = \frac{1}{\varepsilon} \sum_{d_A,t} \Pr\{d_A, t\}\frac{\nu}{\Delta} \log \nu$. A convexity inequality applied to the function $F(x) = x \log x$ shows that

$$E(\log \nu/success) \geq \frac{1}{\varepsilon\Delta}F(\varepsilon'\Delta) \geq \frac{\varepsilon - \frac{1}{P-1}}{\varepsilon} \left(\log(\varepsilon - \frac{1}{P-1}) + \log \Delta \right)$$

□

Furthermore, it is important to notice that, if the final verification fails, Bob is convinced that Alice has tried to cheat because the protocol is always successful when the players behave honestly.

Theorem 10 does not prove strict privacy because, with non negligible probability, a malicious player can obtain a few bits about the other player's secret without being caught. But, if we consider Alice and Bob as polynomial time Turing machines and if the probability of success is non-negligible, Alice does not learn much more information than what she could have guessed. More precisely, for example in the case of the generation of an RSA modulus N, if the knowledge of about $-\log \varepsilon$ bits of information enables Alice to factorize N in polynomial time, we can use her to factorize N in polynomial time without any other information.

When P is large enough, the previous results are simpler:

Theorem 11. *Assume Alice has a cheating strategy such that the protocol ends successfully with probability ε. If $\frac{1}{P-1} = o(\varepsilon)$, the result of a successful execution is correct and Alice cannot learn more than $-\log \varepsilon$ bits of Bob's secret in addition to $f(d_A, d_B)$.*

Special Case of Algebraic Expressions

The protocol has been stated for polynomial size sets $\mathcal{E}_A$ and $\mathcal{E}_B$. When f is an algebraic expression in $\mathbb{Z}_M$ and the inputs d_A and d_B are tuples of elements of $\mathbb{Z}_M$, if M can be factored in small relatively prime factors $M = \prod_{i=1}^{k} m_i$, with k and m_i polynomial in the security parameter, the protocol can also be used, even though M is not polynomial.

Instead of performing the protocol previously described with the large modulus M, we can use it k times with each modulus m_i. Finally, if $P > m_i$, Alice and Bob obtain $f(d_A, d_B) \bmod m_i$ for all i and the result $f(d_A, d_B) \bmod M$ is computed with the Chinese remainder theorem. The more M can be factored in relatively prime factors, the more the protocol is efficient. Consequently, as much as possible, we use a modulus M equal to the product of the first k prime numbers. Notice that theorem 10 can be generalized because if Alice learns less than $-\log \varepsilon_i$ bits of information with probability ε_i at round i, she learns less than $\sum_i -\log \varepsilon_i = -\log\left(\prod_i \varepsilon_i\right) = -\log \varepsilon$ with probability $\prod_i \varepsilon_i = \varepsilon$.

3 Computation of Shared RSA Keys

The computation of shared RSA keys by two parties can be efficiently performed using the protocol of the previous section. The first step consists in computing a candidate $N = (p_A + p_B) \times (q_A + q_B)$ and then to test whether N is the product of two prime numbers. Such a test has be proposed by Boneh and Franklin. Then, the second part of the generation consists in computing a shared secret key associated with a public exponent e.

3.1 Computation of the Modulus N

Let n be the size of the modulus we want to generate and $\mathcal{E}_A = \mathcal{E}_B = [0, 2^{n/2-1}[^2$ be the range where Alice and Bob randomly choose their private input $d_A = (p_A, q_A)$ and $d_B = (p_B, q_B)$. They want to compute $f((p_A, q_A), (p_B, q_B)) = (p_A + p_B) \times (q_A + q_B) = N$. We choose M as the smallest product of the first prime numbers greater than 2^n. Consequently, the result of the computation modulo M is the same as if the computation were done with integers. The function f is an algebraic expression so that we can use the efficient protocol described in section 2. This solves the problem of the efficient computation a shared RSA modulus by only two parties, even if one of them is malicious.

3.2 Trial Division Test

Since Alice and Bob first choose their private data, compute N and, only afterwards, test that $p_A + p_B$ and $q_A + q_B$ are indeed prime numbers, the generation procedure has to be repeated about $n^2/4$ times in order to obtain an RSA modulus N. Boneh and Franklin have proposed to perform a trial division test just after the random choice of p_A and p_B to check that $p_A + p_B$ is not divisible by a small prime number. This allows a reduction of the number of trials and consequently of the complexity of the generation.

We can use our protocol again to test if a small prime number p divides $p_A + p_B$, just taking $d_A = p_A \bmod p$, $d_B = p_B \bmod p$, $\mathcal{E}_A = \mathcal{E}_B = \mathbb{Z}_p$ and $f(x, y) = 0$ if $x + y = 0 \bmod p$ and $f(x, y) = 1$ otherwise. If during one trial division test the result 1 is obtained, Alice and Bob try again with new values p_A and p_B. Consequently, if the test succeeds, Alice only learns that $p_A + p_B \neq 0 \bmod p$, and she would have learned it anyway after the test $N = pq$.

In addition to the generic cheating strategy analyzed in theorem 10, Alice can use an input value $\widetilde{p_A}$ different from $p_A \bmod p$ as input. If she does this, she learns that $\widetilde{p_A} + p_B \neq 0 \bmod p$, i.e $\log(p)/p$ bits of p_B. Since Bob cannot know if she tried to cheat, Alice can make the protocol restart until she learns as much information as possible. If we note $\mathcal{P}$ the set of tested prime numbers, the information learned by Alice if she is malicious is less than $\sum_{p \in \mathcal{P}} \log(p)/p$ bits. If $\mathcal{P}$ is the set of the first ℓ prime numbers, this leads to a maximal amount of information less than $\log(\ell \ln \ell)$. As an example, for $n = 1024$ one can test the first 200 prime numbers as it is adviced in [24]. With our protocol, Alice can learn at most 9 bits of information about p_B.

3.3   Efficiency Improvement

A more efficient and more secure way to choose secret data that have more chance to lead to an RSA modulus consists in choosing p_A and p_B (resp. q_A and q_B) such that $p_A + p_B$ is not divisible by a very small prime number. More precisely, let M' be a product of the first odd prime numbers such that $M' \approx 2^{n/2-1}$. The choice of p_A and p_B by Alice and Bob is performed as follows:

(1) Alice randomly chooses $p'_A \in \mathbb{Z}^*_{M'}$, $p_A \in \mathbb{Z}_{M'}$,
(2) Bob randomly chooses $p'_B \in \mathbb{Z}^*_{M'}$, $\rho_B \in \mathbb{Z}_{M'}$,
(3) Alice and Bob perform a protocol as described in section 2 with
    $d_A = (p'_A, p_A)$, $d_B = (p'_B, \rho_B)$ and
    $f((p'_A, p_A), (p'_B, \rho_B)) = p'_A \times p'_B - p_A - \rho_B \bmod M'$,
(4) Bob obtains the value δ and computes $p_B = \delta + \rho_B \bmod M'$.

This protocol enables Alice and Bob to privately and efficiently obtain p_A and p_B such that none of the first prime numbers divides $p_A + p_B$.

Alice could try to cheat using $p'_A \notin \mathbb{Z}^*_{M'}$ but the design of the two-party computation protocol obliges Alice and Bob to input data in $\mathbb{Z}^*_{M'} \times \mathbb{Z}_{M'}$. Furthermore, the knowledge of $p_B = p'_A \times p'_B - p_A \bmod M'$ does not help Bob to learn more than $p_A + p_B \in \mathbb{Z}^*_{M'}$ because $\forall p'_B \in \mathbb{Z}^*_{M'}$, $p'_B \times \mathbb{Z}^*_{M'} = \mathbb{Z}^*_{M'}$. After this preliminary step, Bob could use a different p_B but this would just reduce the efficiency of the protocol and cannot be used as a way to cheat. The aim of this computation is just to help Bob in choosing a reasonable p_B.

In conclusion, an efficient strategy to compute a good N consists in generating p_A and p_B with this protocol, possibly testing a few more trial divisions, doing the same with q_A and q_B, computing N and finally testing if N is actually the product of two large prime integers.

It would be interesting to generate an RSA modulus N such that the prime factors p and q are *strong* primes. We do not know how to achieve this but we can test if $(p-1)/2$ is divisible by small prime numbers or not. To do this, we just use the protocol designed for the trial division test, with the function $f(x, y) = 0$ if $(x + y - 1)/2 = 0 \bmod p$ and $f(x, y) = 1$ otherwise.

3.4 Generation of the Shared Private Keys

When N has been generated and tested, the last step is the choice of a public exponent e and of a secret one d. More precisely, we want Alice to know d_A and Bob d_B such that $e \times (d_A + d_B) = 1 \bmod \phi(N)$.

Let ϕ_A be $N - p_A - q_A + 1$ and ϕ_B be $p_B + q_B$. Let M'' be the smallest product of the first prime integers greater than $2e \times 2^n$.

(1) Alice randomly chooses $\zeta_A \in \mathbb{Z}_e$,
(2) Alice and Bob privately compute $(\phi_A + \phi_B)^{-1} - \zeta_A \bmod e$ and only Bob obtains the result ζ_B, as in the protocol of section 3.3,
(3) Alice randomly chooses $T_A \in \mathbb{Z}_{M''}$,
(4) Alice and Bob privately compute $(\phi_A + \phi_B) \times (\zeta_A + \zeta_B) + 1 - T_A \bmod M''$ and only Bob obtains the result T_B,
(5) Alice computes its secret share $d_A = \lfloor T_A/e \rfloor$,
(6) Bob computes its secret share $d_B = \lceil T_B/e \rceil$,
(7) Alice and Bob verify that $e(d_A + d_B) = 1 \bmod \phi(N)$.

In order to verify if d_A and d_B has been correctly computed, Alice chooses a random message m and sends $c = m^{e \times d_A} \bmod N$ to Bob who replies the original message m to prove that he knows d_B. Then Bob verifies in the same way that Alice owns a correct exponent d_A.

This protocol is based on the algorithm Boneh and Franklin used to compute $e^{-1} \bmod \phi(N)$. They have noticed that this computation can be done without reduction modulo $\phi(N)$ but just with reductions modulo e. Their algorithm is the following: first compute $\zeta = -\phi(N)^{-1} \bmod e$ and then take $T = \zeta\phi(N) + 1$. Since e divides T, $d = T/e$ verifies $ed = 1 \bmod \phi(N)$.

4 Comparison with General 2-Party Computation Schemes

We said in the introduction that, from a theoretical point of view, there already exist general protocols that enable to privately evaluate expressions like $N = (p_A + p_B) \times (q_A + q_B)$ in polynomial time [26,16,18,13]. All those schemes transform 2-party computations into secure evaluation of logical circuits. This enables to reduce any computation to the combination of a very small set of elementary protocols, like the computation of the logical AND of two bits, at the cost of polynomial but unpractical solutions.

If we focus on the multiplication $N = (p_A + p_B) \times (q_A + q_B)$, with p_A, p_B, q_A and q_B, four $(n/2 - 1)$-bit integers, the most practical logical circuit able to evaluate N needs $O(n^2)$ gates and is depth is $O(n)$. Using the results of [13], we obtain a protocol that enable to privately compute N with a communication complexity of $O(n^2)$ and with at least $O(n)$ rounds of communication (for a fixed value of the security parameter).

In order to compare this complexity with our scheme's, we need to choose an ANDOS protocol. The one described in [25] has a communication complexity $C(t) = 2^{\alpha(\sqrt{\log t})}$ when one secret out of t is sold and needs a constant number of rounds of communication ($\alpha \approx 1.1$). The global communication complexity of our scheme is $2\sum_{i=1}^{k} C(p_i^2)$ with $2^n \approx \prod_{i=1}^{k} p_i$ and p_i the ith prime number. Consequently, this complexity is about $2\int_2^n 2^{\alpha\sqrt{\log t}}/\log t\, dt$ (see for example [22]) and this expression is about $2n \times 2^{\alpha\sqrt{\log n}}/\log n = o(n^\beta)\ \forall \beta > 1$. So, asymptotically, our solution is about $O(n)$ times more efficient than general ones in term of communication complexity. Furthermore, the k ANDOS can be parallelized so the resulting protocol as a constant number of rounds of communication while general solutions need at least $O(n)$ rounds.

¿From a more practical point of view, using the results of [25], we estimate the communication to 2MB when $n = 768$ bits. A general solution would clearly be much less efficient since it would need at least $(n/2)^2 \approx 150.000$ Rabin oblivious transfer [21] and a few hundred rounds of communication.

In conclusion, our scheme is much more practical than those derived from general solutions while it is still based on very general security assumptions. But the secure computation of a shared RSA keys always seems to need efficient computers linked by high rate networks. We propose in appendix an alternative solution, less general since it is based on a specific number theoretical problem but that enables very efficient computations and transmissions.

References

1. M. Bellare and S. Micali. Non-Interactive Oblivious Transfer and Application. In *Crypto '89*, LNCS 435, pages 547–557. Springer-Verlag, 1990.
2. M. Ben-Or, S. Goldwasser, and A. Wigderson. Completeness Theorems for Non-Cryptographic Fault-Tolerant Distributed Computation. In *Proc. of the 20th STOC*, pages 1–10. ACM Press, 1988.
3. C.H. Bennett, G. Brassard, C. Crépeau, and M.-H. Skubiszewska. Practical Quantum Oblivious Transfer. In *Crypto '91*, LNCS 576, pages 351–366. Springer-Verlag, 1992.
4. S. Blackburn, S. Blake-Wilson, M. Burmester, and S. Galbraith. Shared Generation of Shared RSA Keys. Technical Report CORR 98-19, University of Waterloo, 1998. Available at http://www.cacr.math.uwaterloo.ca.
5. D. Boneh and M. Franklin. Efficient Generation of Shared RSA Keys. In *Crypto '97*, LNCS 1294, pages 425–439. Springer-Verlag, 1997.
6. G. Brassard, C. Crépeau, and J-M. Robert. Information Theoretic Reductions among Disclosure Problems. In *Proc. of the 27th FOCS*, pages 168–173. IEEE, 1986.
7. G. Brassard, C. Crépeau, and J-M. Robert. All-or Nothing Disclosure of Secrets. In *Crypto '86*, LNCS 263, pages 234–238. Springer-Verlag, 1987.

8. D. Chaum, C. Crépeau, and I. Damgård. Multiparty Unconditionally Secure Protocols. In *Proc. of the 20th STOC*, pages 11–19. ACM Press, 1988.
9. B. Chor and E. Kushilevitz. A Zero-One Law for Boolean Privacy. In *Proc. of the 21st STOC*, pages 62–72. ACM Press, 1989.
10. C. Cocks. Split Knowledge Generation of RSA Parameters. In *Cryptography and Coding: Proceedings of 6th IMA Conference*, LNCS 1355, pages 89–95. Springer-Verlag, 1997.
11. C. Cocks. Split Generation of RSA Parameters with Multiple Participants. Technical report, 1998. Available at http://www.cesg.gov.uk.
12. C. Crépeau and J. Kilian. Achieving Oblivious Transfer Using Weakened Security Assumptions. In *Proc. of the 29th FOCS*, pages 42–52. IEEE, 1988.
13. C. Crépeau, J. van de Graaf, and A. Tapp. Commited Oblivious Transfer and Private Multy-Party Computation. In *Crypto '95*, LNCS 963, pages 110–123. Springer-Verlag, 1995.
14. S. Even, O. Goldreich, and A. Lempel. A Randomized Protocol for Signing Contracts. *Communications of the ACM*, 28:637–647, 1985.
15. Y. Frankel, P. MacKenzie, and M. Yung. Robust Efficient Distributed RSA-Key Generation. In *Proc. of the 30th STOC*. ACM Press, 1998.
16. O. Goldreich, S. Micali, and A. Wigderson. How to Play any Mental Game. In *Proc. of the 19th STOC*, pages 218–229. ACM Press, 1987.
17. S. Goldwasser, S. Micali, and C. Rackoff. The Knowledge Complexity of Interactive Proof Systems. *SIAM journal of computing*, 18(1):186–208, february 1989.
18. J. Kilian. Founding Cryptography on Oblivious Transfer. In *Proc. of the 20th STOC*, pages 20–31. ACM Press, 1988.
19. D. Naccache and J. Stern. A New Public Key Cryptosystem Based on Higher Residues. In *Proc. of the 5th CCCS*. ACM press, 1998.
20. D. Pointcheval and J. Stern. Security Proofs for Signature Schemes. In *Eurocrypt '96*, LNCS 1070, pages 387–398. Springer-Verlag, 1996.
21. M. Rabin. How to exchange secrets by oblivious transfer. Technical Report TR-81, Harvard Aiken Computation Laboratory, 1981.
22. J.N. Rosser and L. Schoenfeld. Approximate Formulas for some Functions of Prime Numbers. *Illinois Journal of Mathematics*, 6(1):64–94, march 1962.
23. K. Sakurai and H. Shizuya. A Structural Comparison of the Computational Difficulty of Breaking Discrete Log Cryptosystems. *Journal of Cryptology*, 11(1):29–43, 1998.
24. S. Spalding and R. Wright. Experimental Performance of Shared RSA Modulus Generation. In *proc. of Algorithms and Experiments 98*, pages 34–43, 1998.
25. J.P. Stern. A New and Efficient All-Or-Nothing Disclosure of Secrets Protocol. In *Asiacrypt '98*, LNCS. Springer-Verlag, 1998.
26. A. C. Yao. How to Generate and Exchange Secrets. In *Proc. of the 27th FOCS*, pages 162–167. IEEE, 1986.

A   An Efficient Solution Based on Higher Residues Cryptosystem

Using a specific number theoretical problem, we can also propose a much more simple and efficient solution that does not need to perform many rounds of communication. It is based on a trapdoor version of the discrete logarithm problem. More precisely, Alice chooses parameters for the Naccache Stern cryptosystem [19] based on higher residues, i.e σ a squarefree odd B-smooth integer greater than 2^n, where B is a small integer, an RSA modulus N_A such that σ divides $\phi(N_A)$, g an element whose multiplicative order modulo N_A is a large multiple of σ.

The computation of $N = (p_A + p_B) \times (q_A + q_B)$ can be easily done with the following protocol that, on secret inputs x_A and x_B of Alice and Bob make them obtain y_A and y_B such that $y_A + y_B = x_A \times x_B \mod \sigma$:

- Alice chooses a random x, computes $x^\sigma g^{x_A} \mod N_A = c$ and sends it to Bob,
- Bob chooses $y_B \mod \sigma$ and x', computes $c^{x_B} x'^\sigma g^{-y_B} \mod N_A = d$ and sends d to Alice,
- Alice decrypts d and obtains $y_A = x_A \times x_B - y_B \mod \sigma$.

The security analysis of this protocol is out of the scope of this appendix. We can just notice that a commitment of p_A, p_B, q_A and q_B and a verification of the correctness of the result have to be added (as in [4]). This can be done using modular exponentiation and its homomorphic property.

An Attack on RSA Given a Small Fraction of the Private Key Bits

Dan Boneh[1], Glenn Durfee[1], and Yair Frankel[2]

[1] Computer Science Department, Stanford University, Stanford, CA 94305-9045
{dabo,gdurf}@cs.stanford.edu
[2] Certco, 55 Broad St., New York, NY 10004
yfrankel@cs.columbia.edu

Abstract. We show that for low public exponent RSA, given a quarter of the bits of the private key an adversary can recover the entire private key. Similar results (though not as strong) are obtained for larger values of e. For instance, when e is a prime in the range $[N^{1/4}, N^{1/2}]$, half the bits of the private key suffice to reconstruct the entire private key. Our results point out the danger of partial key exposure in the RSA public key system.

1 Introduction

Let $N = pq$ be an RSA modulus and let e, d be encryption/decryption exponents, i.e. $ed = 1 \mod \phi(N)$. We study the following question: how many bits of d does an adversary require in order to reconstruct all of d? Surprisingly, we show that for low public exponent RSA, given only a quarter of the least significant bits of d an adversary can efficiently recover all of d. We obtain similar results, summarized in the next subsection, for larger values of e as well. Our results show that RSA, and particularly low public exponent RSA, are vulnerable to *partial key exposure*. We refer to this class of attacks at *partial key exposure attacks*.

To motivate this problem consider a computer system which has an RSA private key stored on it. An adversary may attempt to attack the system in a variety of ways in order to obtain the private key. Some attacks (e.g. a timing attack [3]) are able to reveal some bits of the key, but may fail to reveal the entire key [5]. Our results show that attacks, such as the timing attack on RSA, need only be carried out until a quarter of the least significant bits of d are exposed. Once these bits are revealed the adversary can efficiently compute all of d. Another scenario where partial key exposure comes up is in the presence of covert channels. Such channel are often slow or have a bounded capacity. Our results show that as long as a fraction of the private exponent bits can be leaked the remaining bits can be reconstructed.

It is natural to ask the analogous question in the context of discrete log schemes. For instance, given a fraction of the bits of the private key in the ElGamal public key system [2], can one efficiently recover the entire key? There is no known method for doing so. Furthermore, the common belief is that no such

K. Ohta and D. Pei (Eds.): ASIACRYPT'98, LNCS 1514, pp. 25–34, 1998.
© Springer-Verlag Berlin Heidelberg 1998

efficient algorithm exists. This resistance to partial key exposure is an interesting distinction between RSA and discrete log schemes.

We note that Wiener [7] showed that RSA is insecure whenever the private exponent d is less than $N^{1/4}$. In other words, given that the 3/4 most significant bits of d are zero an adversary can efficiently recover the remaining quarter. This result does not apply to our problem: Wiener's continued fractions approach does not work when the most significant bits of d are given to the adversary, but they are non-zero. Instead, we derive our results using powerful tools due to Coppersmith [1].

Let $N = pq$ be an n-bit RSA modulus. Throughout the paper we view the private exponent d as an n-bit string. When referring to the t most significant bits of d we refer to the t left most bits of d when viewed as an n-bit string. For instance, it is possible that the t most significant bits of d are all zero, for some t. Similarly, a quarter of the bits of d always refers to $n/4$ bits.

1.1   Summary of Results

We summarize our results in the following two theorems. The proofs are given in the body of the paper. The first theorem applies to low public exponent RSA. The second applies to larger values of e. Throughout we assume $N = pq$ is an RSA modulus with $\sqrt{N}/2 < q < p < 2\sqrt{N}$.

Theorem 1. *Let $N = pq$ be an n-bit RSA modulus. Let $1 \leq e, d \leq \phi(N)$ satisfy $ed = 1 \bmod \phi(N)$. There is an algorithm that given the $\frac{n}{4}$ least significant bits of d computes all of d in polynomial time in n and e.*

We note that the running time of the attack algorithm in the above theorem is *linear* in e. Consequently, as long as e is not "too large" the attack can be efficiently mounted. For a very small value of e such as $e = 3$ the attack runs in a reasonable amount of time. For larger values, such as $e = 65537$, the attack is still feasible, though clearly takes much longer.

Theorem 2. *Let $N = pq$ be an n-bit RSA modulus. Let $1 \leq e, d \leq \phi(N)$ satisfy $ed = 1 \bmod \phi(N)$.*

1. *Suppose e is a prime in the range $[2^t \ldots 2^{t+1}]$ with $\frac{n}{4} \leq t \leq \frac{n}{2}$. Then given the t most significant bits of d there is a polynomial time (in n) algorithm to compute all of d.*
2. *More generally, suppose $e \in [2^t \ldots 2^{t+1}]$ is the product of at most r distinct primes with $\frac{n}{4} \leq t \leq \frac{n}{2}$. Then given the factorization of e and the t most significant bits of d there is an algorithm to compute all of d in polynomial time in n and 2^r.*
3. *When the factorization of e is unknown, we obtain a weaker result. Suppose e is in the range $[2^t \ldots 2^{t+1}]$ with $t \in 0 \ldots n/2$. Further, suppose $d > \epsilon N$ for some $\epsilon > 0$. Then there is a polynomial time (in n and $\frac{1}{\epsilon}$) algorithm that given the $n - t$ most significant bits of d, computes all of d.*

Theorem 2 applies to public exponents e in the range $2^{n/4} \leq e \leq 2^{n/2}$. Unlike the previous theorem, Theorem 2 makes use of the most significant bits of d. When e is prime, at most half the bits of d are required to mount the attack. Fewer bits are needed when e is smaller. Indeed, if e is close to $N^{1/4}$ only a quarter of the MSB bits of d are required. The same result holds when e is not prime, as long as we are given the factorization of e and e does not have too many distinct prime factors. The last part of the theorem applies to $e < N^{1/2}$ when the factorization of e is not known. To mount the attack, at least half the MSB bits of d are required. More bits are necessary, the smaller e is. The attack algorithm works for most e, but may fail if d is significantly smaller than N.

One may refine Theorem 2 in many ways. It is possible to obtain other results along these lines for public exponents $e < N^{1/2}$. For instance, consider the case when the factorization of e is unknown. If the adversary is given half the most significant bits of d and a quarter of the least significant bits then we show the adversary can recover all of d. When $e < N^{1/4}$ this is better than the results of Theorem 2 part (3). However, we view attacks that require a non-consecutive segment of d as artificial. We briefly sketch these variants in Section 4.3.

1.2   Notation

Throughout the paper we let $N = pq$ denote an n-bit RSA modulus. We assume the primes p and q are distinct and close to $\sqrt{N}$. More precisely, we assume

$$4 < \sqrt{N}/2 < q < p < 2\sqrt{N} \tag{1}$$

We denote the set of such n-bit RSA moduli by $\mathbb{Z}_{(2)}(n)$. Our results also apply to RSA moduli $N = pq$ where p is much larger than q, but we do not give the details here.

Notice that equation 1 implies $p + q < 3\sqrt{N}$. For convenience, throughout the paper we set

$$s := p + q.$$

Under the assumption $p > q$ this implies:

$$p = \frac{1}{2}(s + \sqrt{s^2 - 4N}). \tag{2}$$

Furthermore, it follows by equation 1 that

$$N/2 < N - 4\sqrt{N} < \phi(N) < N. \tag{3}$$

Let $1 \leq e, d \leq \phi(N)$ be encryption/decryption exponents. Then $ed \equiv 1 \pmod{\phi(N)}$. Throughout the paper we denote by k the unique integer such that:

$$ed - k\phi(N) = ed - k(N - s + 1) = 1. \tag{4}$$

Since $\phi(N) > d$ we know that $k < e$.

2   Finding Small Solutions to Bivariate Polynomials

Our results make heavy use of seminal results due to Coppersmith. Using the lattice basis reduction algorithm of Lenstra, Lenstra, and Lovasz [4], Coppersmith [1] shows how to find small solutions (x_0, y_0) to a bivariate polynomial $f(x, y)$, provided appropriate bounds on x_0 and y_0 are known in advance.

Theorem 3 (Coppersmith[1]). *Let $f(x, y)$ be a polynomial in two variables over $\mathbb{Z}$, of maximum degree δ in each variable separately, and assume the coefficients of f are relatively prime as a set. Let X, Y be bounds on the desired solutions x_0, y_0. Define $\tilde{f}(x, y) := f(Xx, Yy)$ and let D be the absolute value of the largest coefficient of $\tilde{f}$. If $XY < D^{2/(3\delta)}$, then in time polynomial in $(\log D, 2^\delta)$, we can find all integer pairs (x_0, y_0) with $p(x_0, y_0) = 0, |x_0| < X, |y_0| < Y$.*

We make use of an immediate consequence of this theorem, which is a slight generalization of a result in [1].

Corollary 1. *Let $N = pq$ be an n-bit RSA modulus. Let $r \geq 2^{n/4}$ be given and suppose $p_0 := p \bmod r$ is known. Then it is possible to factor N in time polynomial in n.*

Proof. From $p_0 := p \bmod r$ we may find $q_0 := q \equiv N/p_0 \bmod r$. We seek a solution (x_0, y_0) to $f(x, y) = (rx+p_0)(ry+q_0)-N$, where $0 \leq x_0 < X = 2^{n/2+1}/r$ (similarly $y_0 < Y = 2^{n/2+1}/r$). Notice, however, that the greatest common divisor of the coefficients of the polynomial $f(x, y)$ is r, so to use Theorem 3, we must divide through by r to get a new polynomial $g(x, y) = f(x, y)/r$. Now notice that the largest coefficient of $\tilde{g}(x, y) = g(Xx, Yy)$ is at least $2^{n+2}/r$. So, to use Theorem 3 we require

$$XY = r^{-2}2^{n+2} < (2^{n+2}/r)^{2/3},$$

which is satisfied whenever $r > 2^{(n+2)/4}$. By doing exhaustive search on the first two bits of x_0 and y_0 this can be reduced to $r \geq 2^{n/4}$.   □

3   Partial Key Exposure Attack on Low-exponent RSA

In this section we consider attacks on the RSA cryptosystem with a "small" exponent e. For our purposes, "small" implies that exhaustive search on all values less than e is feasible. In particular, since $k \leq e$ holds, our attack algorithm can try all possible values of k (recall that k is the unique integer satisfying $de - k\phi(N) = 1$). We can now prove Theorem 1.

Theorem 4. *With the notation as in Section 1.2, given the $\frac{n}{4}$ least significant bits of d, we can factor N in polynomial time in n and e.*

Proof. Suppose we are given the least-significant $\frac{n}{4}$-bit block of d; that is, we know $d_0 = d \bmod 2^{n/4}$. By Equation 4, we have

$$ed_0 \equiv 1 + k(N - s + 1) \pmod{2^{n/4}},$$

Recall that $s = p + q$. The attack algorithm tries all candidate values for k in the range $[0 \dots e]$. For each candidate value, the algorithm solves the above equation for $s \bmod 2^{n/4}$. Given a candidate value for $s \bmod 2^{n/4}$ the algorithm can find $p \bmod 2^{n/4}$ by solving the quadratic equation

$$p^2 - sp + N \equiv 0 \pmod{2^{n/4}}$$

Given a candidate value for $p \bmod 2^{n/4}$ we run the algorithm of Corollary 1 to try to factor N. After at most e attempts the correct value of $p \bmod 2^{n/4}$ is obtained and the factorization of N is exposed. The total running time is linear in e. $\square$

We did not employ the full generality of Corollary 1, as $\bmod r$ bits could have been used for any $r \geq 2^{n/4}$. This will be used in the next section where we consider more sophisticated key exposure attacks.

One may wonder whether a similar partial key exposure attack is possible using the most significant bits of d. The answer is no. The reason is that low public exponent RSA leaks half the most significant bits of d. In other words, the adversary may obtain *half* the most significant bits of d from e and N alone. Consequently, revealing the most significant bits of d does not help the adversary in exposing the rest of d. This is stated more precisely in the following fact.

Fact 5. *With the notation as in Section 1.2, suppose there exists an algorithm $\mathcal{A}$ that given the $n/2$ MSB bits of d discovers all of d in time $t(n)$. Then there exists an algorithm $\mathcal{B}$ that breaks RSA in time $et(n)$.*

Proof. Observe that by Equation 4, we have $d = (1 + k(N + 1 - p - q))/e$. Let $\tilde{d}$ be

$$\tilde{d} = \left\lfloor \frac{1 + k(N + 1)}{e} \right\rfloor$$

Then

$$0 \leq \tilde{d} - d \leq k(p + q)/e \leq 3k\sqrt{N}/e < 3\sqrt{N}$$

It follows that $\tilde{d}$ matches d on the $n/2$ most significant bits of d. Hence, once k is known, the half most significant bits of d are exposed. With this observation, algorithm $\mathcal{B}$ can work as follows: try all possible values of k in the range $[0 \dots e]$. For each candidate, compute the value $\tilde{d}$. Run algorithm $\mathcal{A}$ giving it half the most significant bits of $\tilde{d}$. Once the correct k is found the entire private key is exposed. $\square$

Fact 5 explains why for low exponent RSA one cannot mount a partial key recovery attack given the most significant bits of d. It is natural to ask whether one can expose all of d given a quarter of the low order bits of d that are not necessarily the least significant ones. For instance, can the attack be mounted given the $n/4$ bits in positions $n/4$ to $n/2$? At the moment this is an open question.

Fact 5 also demonstrates that computing the exponentiation for the upper order bits in an RSA computation can be performed by an untrusted server. This may be used in a server aided RSA like computation where chinese remaindering is not possible such as for threshold RSA.

4   Partial Key Exposure Attack on Medium Exponent RSA

We describe several attacks on the RSA system that can be employed when the public key e is in the range $2^{n/4}$ to $2^{n/2}$. Unlike the previous section, these attacks require the *most significant* bits of d to be given. We mount the attack by carefully studying equation (4):

$$ed - k(N - s + 1) = 1$$

Recall that $s = p + q$.

The key to mounting these attacks is in finding k. Searching for k by brute force is infeasible, since k is an arbitrary element in the range $[0, e]$. Fortunately, given sufficiently many MSB's of d, we may compute k directly, eliminating it as an unknown from equation 4. Once k is revealed, we are left with two unknowns, d and s which we recover using various methods. The main tool for discovering k is presented in the following theorem. It shows that as long as $e < \sqrt{N}$ we can find k given only $\log_2 e$ MSB bits of d. The theorem produces a small constant size interval containing k. As always, we try all possible values of k in the interval until our attack algorithm succeeds.

Theorem 6. *With the notation as in Section 1.2, let t be an integer in the range $[0 \ldots \frac{n}{2}]$. Suppose $2^t < e < 2^{t+1}$ and we know the t most significant bits of d. Then we can efficiently compute the unique k satisfying Equation 4 up to a constant additive error.*

The proof of Theorem 6 relies on the following lemma, which provides general conditions under which k can be deduced by rounding.

Lemma 1. *Suppose d_0 is given such that the following two conditions hold:*

(i) $|e(d - d_0)| < c_1 N$, *and*
(ii) $ed_0 < c_2 N^{3/2}$.

Then the unique k satisfying $ed - k\phi(N) = 1$ is an integer in the range $[\tilde{k} - \Delta, \tilde{k} + \Delta]$ where $\tilde{k} = (ed_0 - 1)/N$ and $\Delta = 2(8c_2 + 2c_1)$.

Proof. Let $\tilde{k} = (ed_0 - 1)/N$. Then

$$\left| \tilde{k} - k \right| = \left| (ed_0 - 1) \left(\frac{1}{\phi(N)} - \frac{1}{N} \right) + \frac{e(d - d_0)}{\phi(N)} \right| < c_2 N^{3/2} \left(\frac{N - \phi(N)}{\phi(N)N} \right) + c_1 \frac{N}{\phi(N)}$$

Since $N - \phi(N) < 4\sqrt{N}$ and $\phi(N) > N/2$ it follows that

$$\left| \tilde{k} - k \right| < 8c_2 + 2c_1.$$

Consequently, k is an integer in the range $[\tilde{k} - \Delta, \tilde{k} + \Delta]$ as required.   □

We are now prepared to prove Theorem 6.

Proof of Theorem 6
The t most significant bits of d enable us to construct an integer d_0 satisfying $|d - d_0| < 2^{n-t}$. We use Lemma 1 to compute k. By the restriction on e, condition **(i)** is satisfied with $c_1 = 2$. Since $d_0 < N$, condition **(ii)** holds with $c_2 = 2$. Hence k is an integer in a known interval of width 40.   □

4.1   Prime Public Key

We are now ready to prove part (1) of Theorem 2. Theorem 6 enables us to find k. Once k is found we reduce equation (4) modulo e. This removes d from the equation. We can then solve for $s \bmod e$. Given $s \bmod e$ we are able to factor the modulus.

Theorem 7. *With the notation of Section 1.2, let t be an integer in the range $\frac{n}{4} \le t \le \frac{n}{2}$. Suppose e is a prime in the range $[2^t \ldots 2^{t+1}]$. Furthermore suppose we are given the t most significant bits of d. Then we can factor N in polynomial time.*

Proof. The assumptions of the theorem satisfy the conditions of Theorem 6. Consequently, k is known to be an integer in a constant size range. We try all candidate values for k. For each one we do the following:

1. Compute $s \equiv N + 1 - k^{-1} \pmod{e}$. This is well-defined since $\gcd(e, k) = 1$.
2. Find $p \bmod e$ by finding a root x_0 of the quadratic

$$x^2 - sx + N = 0 \pmod{e}$$

   This can be done efficiently (in probabilistic polynomial time) since e is prime. Indeed, if $s = p + q \bmod e$ then $x_0 = p \bmod e$.
3. Use Corollary 1 to find p given $p \bmod e$. This is possible since $e \ge 2^{n/4}$.

Once the correct value of k is found (after a constant number of attempts) the factorization of N is exposed.   □

A surprising consequence of this theorem is that, when e is prime and is roughly $\cong 2^{n/4}$, only the first $\frac{n}{4}$ MSB's of d are needed to mount the attack. This attack is as strong as the one on low public exponent RSA. In any case, for prime $e \in 2^{n/4}..2^{n/2}$ the first $\frac{n}{2}$ most significant bits of d always suffice.

The proof shows that it is not necessary for e to be prime. As long as we can solve the quadratic in step (2) the proof can be made to work. In order to solve the quadratic we must be given the factorization of e. Unfortunately, modulo a composite, the quadratic may have many roots. We must try them all. If e has r distinct prime factors, there are 2^r solutions to consider. As a result, we must also bound the number of prime factors of e. We obtain part (2) of Theorem 2.

Corollary 2. *As in Theorem 7 suppose e is an integer in the range $[2^t \ldots 2^{t+1}]$. If e has at most r distinct prime factors, and its factorization is known, then given the t most significant bits of d we can factor N in polynomial time.*

We point out that when e is close to $2^{n/2}$ the same attack can be mounted even if the factorization of e is unknown. In other words, for all e sufficiently close to $2^{n/2}$, half the MSB's of d are sufficient to reconstruct all of d. Indeed, the range $1..2^{n/2+2}/e$ can be searched exhaustively to find s/e. Given the value of s/e we can obtain s (since $s \bmod e$ is already known.) Since s is now known in the integers we can directly find p using equation 2.

4.2   Public Key with Unknown Factorization

We now turn to proving part (3) of Theorem 2. We consider the case when e is in the range $[2^t \ldots 2^{t+1}]$ with $0 \le t \le \frac{n}{2}$. The factorization of e is unknown. The following result establishes that we can still find all of d, given some of its MSB's. Our attack works as long as k is not significantly smaller than e. At the end of the section we note that the attack heuristically works for almost all e in the range $[2^t, 2^{t+1}]$.

Theorem 8. *With the notation as in Section 1.2, let t be an integer in the range $[0 \ldots n/2]$. Suppose e is in the range $[2^t \ldots 2^{t+1}]$. Further suppose $k > \epsilon \cdot e$ for some $\epsilon > 0$. Then there is an algorithm that given the $n - t$ most significant bits of d finds all of d. The algorithm runs in time $O(n^3/\epsilon)$.*

Proof. Given the $n - t$ most significant bits of d we can construct a d_0 such that $0 \le d - d_0 < 2^t$. Since $e < 2^{n/2}$ we can use d_0 and Theorem 6 to limit k to a constant size interval. For each of the candidate k we do the following:

1. Compute $d_1 = e^{-1} \bmod k$. This is possible since e and k are relatively prime. Since $ed - k\phi(n) = 1$ we know that $d_1 = d \bmod k$.
2. By assumption $k > \epsilon 2^t$. Note that at this point we know $d \bmod k$ as well as the $n - t$ MSB's of d. We determine the rest of the bits by an exhaustive search. More precisely, write

$$d = kd_2 + d_1$$

   Then $d_2 = d_0/k + (d - d_0)/k - d_1/k$. The only unknown term in this sum is $v = (d - d_0)/k$. Since $k > \epsilon 2^t$ we know that $v = (d - d_0)/k < 1/\epsilon$. To find v we try all possible candidates in the range $[0, \frac{1}{\epsilon}]$. For each candidate we compute the candidate value of d and test it out.

3. Once the correct values of v and k are found d is exposed. Testing each candidate d takes $O(n^3)$ time and there are $O(1/\epsilon)$ candidates to try out.

$\square$

Theorem 8 works without having to know the factorization of e. Unfortunately, the results are not as strong as in the previous section. When e is close to $N^{1/4}$ Theorem 8 implies that $3/4$ of the bits of d are needed to reconstruct d. This is much worse than the corresponding bound achieved in the previous section, where only $1/4$ the bits were required. When e is close to $N^{1/2}$ the theorem produces results similar to the previous section.

Theorem 8 can only be applied when $k > \epsilon \cdot e$. Intuitively k behaves roughly as a random integer in the range $[1, e]$. As such, we should have $k > e/10$ for about 90% of the $e \in [2^t, 2^{t+1}]$. Hence, heuristically the attack works efficiently for almost all e.

4.3   More Results

What if the factorization of e is unknown and e was not randomly chosen? Although it may be computationally infeasible, it is possible for e, d to be specifically chosen as factors of $1 + k\phi(N)$ for very small k, violating the conditions of Theorem 8. We stress that this is particularly unlikely, as not only would the rather large value of $1 + k\phi(N)$ would need to be factored into ed, but a factor e in the range $[2^{n/4} \ldots 2^{n/2}]$ would need to be obtained, and one that itself cannot easily be factored (making it vulnerable to Corollary 2). However, under these circumstances, the above attacks would not apply. We conclude with the following general result which holds for for all $e < 2^{n/2}$. Unfortunately, the result requires non-consecutive bits of d.

Theorem 9. *With the notation as in Section 1.2, let t be an integer in $[1, \frac{n}{2}]$ and e in $[2^t \ldots 2^{t+1}]$. Suppose we are given the t most significant bits of d and the $\frac{n}{4}$ least significant bits of d. Then in polynomial time we can factor N.*

Proof Sketch. Using Theorem 6 we may compute a constant size interval I containing k. Observe that the proof of Theorem 4 applies for all e, as long as k and the $n/4$ least significant bits of d are known. To recover d, run the algorithm of Theorem 4 on all candidate values of k in I. $\square$

In fact, Theorem 4 can be viewed as a special case of Theorem 9 in which exhaustive search is performed on the requisite $O(\log n)$ MSB bits of d.

5   Conclusions

We study RSA's vulnerability to partial key exposure. We showed that for low exponent RSA, a quarter of the least significant bits of d are sufficient for efficiently reconstucting all of d. We obtain similar results for larger values of e as long as $e < \sqrt{N}$. For instance, when e is close to $\sqrt{N}$ half the most significant bits of d suffice. These results demonstrate the danger of leaking a fraction of the bits of d. We note that discrete log schemes (e.g. DSS, ElGamal) do not seem vulnerable to partial key exposure. A fraction of the DSS private key bits does not seem to enable the adversary to immediately break the system.

There are a number of related open problems. Our results do not apply to values of e that are substantially larger than $\sqrt{N}$. A natural question is whether bits of d enable one to break the system for all values of e.

For e in the range $N^{1/4} \ldots N^{1/2}$ our most effective results (requiring the fewest bits of d) apply only once the factorization of e is known. It seems that one should be able to obtain similar results even when the factorization is unknown.

References

1. D. Coppersmith, "Finding a small root of a univariate modular equation", Proc. of Eurocrypt '96, pp. 155–165.
2. T. ElGamal, "A public key cryptosystem and a signature scheme based on the discrete logarithm", IEEE Transactions on Information Theory, 31(4):469–472, 1985.
3. P. Kocher, "Timing attacks on implementations of Diffie-Hellman, RSA, DSS, and other systems", Proc. of Cyrpto 96, pp. 104–113.
4. A. K. Lenstra, H. W. Lenstra, L. Lovász, "Factoring Polynomials with Rational Coefficients", Mathematische Annalen, vol. 261, no. 4, 1982, pp. 515-534.
5. J.J. Quisquater, private communications.
6. R. L. Rivest, A. Shamir, and L. Adleman. "A method for obtaining digital signatures and public-key cryptosystems." Communications of the ACM 21(2):120-126, Feb. 1978.
7. M. Wiener, "Cryptanalysis of short RSA secret exponents", IEEE Transactions on Info. Th., Vol. 36, No. 3, 1990, pp. 553–558.

C^*_{-+} and *HM*: Variations Around Two Schemes of T. Matsumoto and H. Imai

Jacques Patarin[1], Louis Goubin[1], and Nicolas Courtois[2]

[1] Bull Smart Cards Terminals
68 route de Versailles - BP 45
78431 Louveciennes Cedex - France
e-mail : {J.Patarin,L.Goubin}@frlv.bull.fr
[2] Modélisation et Signal
Université de Toulon et du Var - BP 132
83957 La Garde Cedex - France
e-mail : courtois@univ-tln.fr

Abstract. In [4], H. Imai and T. Matsumoto presented new candidate trapdoor one-way permutations with a public key given as multivariate polynomials over a finite field. One of them, based on the idea of hiding a monomial field equation, was later presented in [7] under the name C^*. It was broken by J. Patarin in [8]. J. Patarin and L. Goubin then suggested ([9], [10], [11], [12]) some schemes to repair C^*, but with slightly more complex public key or secret key computations. In part I, we study some very simple variations of C^* – such as C^*_{-+} – where the attack of [8] is avoided, and where the very simple secret key computations are kept. We then design some new cryptanalysis that are efficient against some of – but not all – these variations.

[C] is another scheme of [4], very different from C^* (despite the name), and based on the idea of hiding a monomial matrix equation. In part II, we show how to attack it (no cryptanalysis had been published so far). We then study more general schemes, still using the idea of hiding matrix equations, such as *HM*.

An extended version of this paper can be obtained from the authors.

1 Introduction

What is – at the present – the asymmetric signature algorithm with the most simple smartcard implementation (in terms of speed and RAM needed), and not broken ? We think that it is one simple variation of the Matsumoto-Imai C^* algorithm that we present in part I.

C^* was presented in [4] and [7], and was broken in [8], due to unexpected algebraic properties. However, many ways are possible to avoid the cryptanalysis of [8]. In [9], J. Patarin suggested to use a "hidden polynomial" instead of a "hidden monomial". These "HFE" algorithms are still unbroken. However, the secret key computations in HFE schemes are sensibly more complex than in the original C^* scheme. In [10], [11] and [12], J. Patarin and L. Goubin also studied

K. Ohta and D. Pei (Eds.): ASIACRYPT'98, LNCS 1514, pp. 35–50, 1998.
© Springer-Verlag Berlin Heidelberg 1998

some variations, where the public equations are given in different forms (some of these schemes are also presented in [5]), but here again, in order to avoid the attacks, the secret key computations or the public key computations are generally slightly more complex than in the original C^* scheme.

In part I, we design and study very simple variations of the original C^* scheme. We keep a quadratic public key and the main secret key operation is still the computation of a monomial function $f : x \mapsto x^h$ in a finite field. (The length of the elements of this finite field is much shorter than for RSA, and this explains why the implementations are much more efficient.) We break some of the new variations. However, some others still resist our attacks. They are related to some problems of orthogonal polynomials (how to complete a set of orthogonal polynomials, how to eliminate some random polynomials linearly mixed with orthogonal polynomials, etc).

These variations of C^* can also be applied to the more general HFE scheme of [9] or to Dragon schemes of [10]. We concentrate on C^* because its secret computations are particularly efficient, and because we want to see if these simple ideas can be sufficient or not to enforce the security (in HFE, the analysis is more difficult since no efficient attacks are known at the present).

In part II, we study a very different (despite the name) algorithm of [4], called [C], based on the idea of hiding (with secret affine transformations) a monomial matrix equation. Since the multiplication of matrices is a non-commutative operation, it creates a scheme with very special features. However, as in C^* or HFE, the public key is still given as a set of multivariate polynomials on a finite field, and some of the ideas used in [8] are also useful.

We show how to break the original [C] scheme (no cryptanalysis of this scheme was published before). We then study some more general algorithms, based on the same idea of hiding matrix equations.

Since all those unbroken schemes are new and very similar to broken ones, we certainly do not recommend them for very sensible applications. However, we believe that it is nice to study them because they have very efficient implementations and provide a better understanding of the subtle links between the concept of asymmetric cryptosystem and the computations required for security.

Part I: Variations around C^*

2   A Short Description of HFE and C^*

We present a short description of the HFE and C^* schemes. See [7] (for C^*), or [9] (for HFE) for more details.

The quadratic function f: Let $K = \mathbf{F}_q$ be a finite field of cardinality q. Let $\mathbf{F}_{q^n}$ be an extension of degree n over $\mathbf{F}_q$. Let

$$f(a) = \sum_{i,j} \beta_{i,j} a^{q^{\theta_{ij}} + q^{\varphi_{ij}}} + \sum_k \alpha_k a^{q^{\xi_k}} + \mu \in \mathbf{F}_{q^n}[a]$$

be a polynomial in a over $\mathbf{F}_{q^n}$, of degree d, for integers θ_{ij}, φ_{ij} and $\xi_k \geq 0$.

Since $\mathbf{F}_{q^n}$ is isomorphic to $\mathbf{F}[x]/(g(x))$, if $g(x) \in \mathbf{F}_q[x]$ is irreducible of degree n, elements of $\mathbf{F}_{q^n}$ may be represented as n-uples over $\mathbf{F}_q$, and f may be represented by n polynomials in n variables a_1, ..., a_n over $\mathbf{F}_q$:

$$f(a_1, ..., a_n) = (f_1(a_1, ..., a_n), ..., f_n(a_1, ..., a_n)).$$

The f_i are quadratic polynomials, due to the choice of f and the fact that $a \mapsto a^q$ is a linear transformation of $\mathbf{F}_{q^n}$.

Secret affine transformation of f: Let s and t be two secret affine bijections $(\mathbf{F}_q)^n \to (\mathbf{F}_q)^n$, where $(\mathbf{F}_q)^n$ is seen as an n-dimensional vector space over $\mathbf{F}_q$.

Using the function f above and some representation of $\mathbf{F}_{q^n}$ over $\mathbf{F}_q$, the function $(\mathbf{F}_q)^n \to (\mathbf{F}_q)^n$ that assigns $t(f(s(x)))$ to $x \in (\mathbf{F}_q)^n$ can be written as

$$t(f(s(x_1, ..., x_n))) = (P_1(x_1, ..., x_n), ..., P_n(x_1, ..., x_n)),$$

where the P_i are quadratic polynomials due to the choice of s, t and f.

The "basic" HFE (cf [9]): The public key contains the polynomials P_i, for $i = 1, 2, ..., n$, as above. The secret key is the function f and the two affine bijections s and t as above.

To encrypt the n-uple $x = (x_1, ..., x_n)$, compute the ciphertext $y = (P_1(x_1, .., x_n), ..., P_n(x_1, ..., x_n))$ (x should have redundancy, or a hash of x should also be sent). To decrypt y, first find all the solutions z to the equation $f(z) = t^{-1}(y)$ by solving a **monovariate** polynomial equation of degree d. This is always feasible when d is not too large (say $d \leq 1000$ for example) or when f has a special shape (as in the case of C^* described below). Next, compute all the $s^{-1}(z)$, and use the redundancy (or the hash of x) to find M from these.

HFE can also be used in signature, as explained in [9] (essentially, the idea is that now x is the signature and y the hash of the message to be signed. If the equation $f(z) = t^{-1}(y)$ has no solution z, we compute another hash).

The C^* algorithm (cf [7]): C^* can be seen as a special case of the more general HFE scheme, where the function f is $f(a) = a^{1+q^\theta}$. Such a function f has some practical advantages: if K is of characteristic 2 and if $1 + q^\theta$ is coprime to $q^n - 1$, then f is a bijection, and the computation of $f^{-1}(b)$ is easy since $f^{-1}(b) = b^{h'}$, where h' is the inverse of $1 + q^\theta$ modulo $q^n - 1$.

However, C^* was broken in [8], essentially because – in the case of a C^* scheme – there always exist equations such as

$$\sum_{i,j} \gamma_{ij} x_i y_j + \sum_i \alpha_i x_i + \sum_j \beta_j y_j + \mu_0 = 0 \tag{1}$$

from which it is possible to break the scheme (see [8]). (Here x is the cleartext (or the signature), y is the ciphertext (or the hash of the message), and γ_{ij}, α_i, β_i and μ_0 are elements of K.) Throughout this paper, we call "equation of type (1)" any equation like (1).

In the case of HFE, no cryptanalysis has yet been found (when f is well chosen), but the secret key computations are more complex.

3 Three Simple Variations of C^* (and HFE)

3.1 Less Public Polynomials: the C^*_- Scheme

The polynomials $(P_1, \ldots, P_n)$ of the "basic" HFE algorithm give y from x. However, it is possible to keep some of these polynomials secret. Let k be the number of these polynomials P_i that we do not give in the public key, so that only P_1, P_2, ..., P_{n-k} are public.

In an encryption scheme, k must be small, because in order to recover x from y, we compute the q^k possibilities for y, compute all the corresponding possible x, and find the good x thanks to the redundancy. When q is not too large, and when k is very small, for example with $k = 1$ or 2, this is clearly feasible.

In a signature scheme, k may be much larger. However, we must still have enough polynomials P_i in order that the problem of finding a value x, whose images by P_1, ..., P_{n-k} are given values, is still intractable. A value $k = 1$, 2, or $k = \frac{n}{2}$ for example may be practical and efficient.

3.2 Introducing Some Random Polynomials: the C^*_+ Scheme

Let P_i be the public polynomials in x_1, x_2, ..., x_n, of a "basic" HFE scheme. We introduce k random extra quadratic polynomials Q_i in x_1, ..., x_n, and we mix the polynomials Q_i and P_i with a secret affine bijection in the given public key.

In a signature scheme, k must be small, because for a given x, the probability to satisfy these extra Q_i equations is $\frac{1}{q^k}$. When m and k are small, the scheme is efficient: after about q^k tries, we obtain a signature.

In an encryption scheme, k may be much larger. However, the total number $k + n$ of quadratic public equations must be such that the problem of finding x from a given y is still intractable (and thus be $< \frac{n(n+1)}{2}$, because with $\frac{n(n+1)}{2}$ equations, the values $x_i x_j$ are found by Gaussian reductions, which gives the x_i). A value $k = 1$, 2 or $k = \frac{n}{2}$ for example may be practical and efficient.

Note: We may combine the variations of sections 3.1 and 3.2. For example, it is possible to design a signature or an encryption scheme from a "basic" HFE with polynomials P_1, ..., P_n, by keeping P_n secret, introducing a random polynomial Q_n instead of P_n, and computing the public key as a secret affine transformation of P_1, ..., P_{n-1}, Q_n. In the case of a C^* scheme, we call C^*_{-+} such algorithms.

3.3 Introducing More x_i Variables

Due to the lack of space, we refer the reader to the extended version of the paper.

4 Toy Simulations of C^*_{-+} with $n = 17$

We have made some toy simulations with $K = \mathbf{F}_2$ and $n = 17$ of C^*_{-+}, with $K = \mathbf{F}_2$ and $n = 17$. (Note that, in real examples, n must be ≥ 64 if $K = \mathbf{F}_2$.)

In all these simulations, we have computed the exact number of independent equations between the 17 bits of the input x_1, ..., x_{17}, and the 17 bits of the output y_1, ..., y_{17} of type (1) (see section 2), or type (2) or (3) defined by:

$$\sum \gamma_{ijk} x_i y_j y_k + \sum \mu_{ij} x_i y_j + \sum \nu_{ij} y_i y_j + \sum \alpha_i x_i + \sum \beta_i y_i + \delta_0 = 0 \quad (2)$$

$$\sum \gamma_{ijk} x_i x_j y_k + \sum \mu_{ij} x_i y_j + \sum \nu_{ij} x_i x_j + \sum \alpha_i x_i + \sum \beta_i y_i + \delta_0 = 0 \quad (3)$$

As shown in table 1, the attacks of [8] do not work directly against C^*_{-+} if we have less public polynomials, at least if $f(x) = x^3$ is avoided and if two or more polynomials are kept secret.

Note: In this table, we have subtracted the number of independent "trivial" equations, such as $x_i^2 = x_i$, or $y_i \cdot "y_j" = "y_i" \cdot y_j$, where "$y_i$" and "$y_j$" are written with their expression in the x_k variables. The notation $[\alpha]$ means that, when the y_k variables are given explicit values, we obtain in average α independent equations in the x_k variables.

Scheme	Type	x^3	x^5	x^9	x^{17}	x^{33}	x^{65}	x^{129}
C^*	(1)	34 [16]	17 [16]	17 [16]	17 [16]	17 [16]	17 [16]	17 [16]
	(2)	612 [16]	340 [16]	323 [16]	340 [17]	323 [16]	374 [16]	323 [16]
	(3)	578 [153]	442 [153]	476 [153]	493 [153]	476 [153]	459 [153]	493 [153]
C^*_{-+1}	(1)	17 [15]	1 [1]	1 [1]	1 [1]	1 [1]	1 [1]	1 [1]
	(2)	340 [15]	52 [15]	36 [15]	36 [15]	36 [15]	87 [15]	36 [15]
	(3)	443 [153]	307 [152]	341 [153]	358 [153]	341 [152]	324 [152]	358 [153]
C^*_{-+2}	(1)	1 [1]	0 [0]	0 [0]	0 [0]	0 [0]	0 [0]	0 [0]
	(2)	54 [13]	0 [0]	0 [0]	0 [0]	0 [0]	0 [0]	0 [0]
	(3)	309 [151]	173 [135]	207 [151]	224 [152]	207 [150]	190 [152]	224 [153]
C^*_{-+3}	(1)	0 [0]	0 [0]	0 [0]	0 [0]	0 [0]	0 [0]	0 [0]
	(2)	0 [0]	0 [0]	0 [0]	0 [0]	0 [0]	0 [0]	0 [0]
	(3)	176 [153]	51 [68]	74 [91]	91 [108]	74 [91]	57 [74]	91 [108]
C^*_{-+4}	(1)	0 [0]	0 [0]	0 [0]	0 [0]	0 [0]	0 [0]	0 [0]
	(2)	0 [0]	0 [0]	0 [0]	0 [0]	0 [0]	0 [0]	0 [0]
	(3)	44 [61]	0 [17]	0 [17]	0 [17]	0 [17]	0 [17]	0 [17]

Table 1 (for $K = \mathbf{F}_2$ and $n = 17$)

5   First Cryptanalysis of C^*_-

This section in given in appendix 1.

6   The C^*_{--} Algorithm

When $q^r \geq 2^{64}$, the cryptanalysis given in section 5 is not efficient. The scheme is then called C^*_{--}. It cannot be used for encryption any more, but it is still a very efficient scheme for signatures, and its security is an open problem.

7   Cryptanalysis of C_+^*

The cryptanalysis of C_+^* is very simple: it just works exactly as the original cryptanalysis of C^*. We first generate all the equations of type (1). Since in C_+^*, we just have **added** some equations (and eliminated none), we find at least as much equations (1) as in the original C^*, from which – as explained in [8] – we can find x from y (and thus break the system). Moreover, we can eliminate the random added equations and recover an original C^*, because an equation (1) generally comes from only the y_i of C^* (and not from the added equations). Therefore, by writing (1) as $x_1(P_1(y)) + x_2(P_2(y)) + \ldots + x_n(P_n(y))$ (where P_1, ..., P_n are polynomials of degree one in y_1, ..., y_{n+k}), and by making the change of variables $y_1' = P_1(y)$, ..., $y_n' = P_n(y)$, the variables y_1', ..., y_n' are the outputs of an original C^* scheme.

Note: However, this idea of adding an equation may be much more efficient in a scheme where no equation (1) exist (as in some HFE schemes) (or when we add **and** eliminate some equations, as in C_{-+}^* below).

8   Cryptanalysis of C_{-+}^*, Second Cryptanalysis of C_-^*

Cryptanalysis of C_{-+1}^*:   We know that from the variables of the original C^* we have at least n independent equations of type (1), so that – by multiplying these equations by one x_k, $1 \leq k \leq n$ – we generate n^2 independent equations of type (3).

By Gaussian reductions, we obtain at least $n^2 - \frac{n(n+1)}{2}$ $\left(= \frac{n(n-1)}{2} \right)$ equations of type (3) with no terms in y_1 (because we have at most $\frac{n(n+1)}{2}$ terms in $y_1 x_i x_j$ or $y_1 x_i$). Giving then explicit values for y, we obtain (by Gaussian reductions on the $X_{ij} = x_i \cdot x_j$ variables) the x_i values. As a result, with the equations (3) we can break C_{-+1}^*, i.e. recover an x from a given y. This attack works because (as shown in our simulations of section 4) the number of independent equations does not decrease significantly when the y_k variables are given explicit values.

Cryptanalysis of C_{-+r}^*, for $r = 2, 3$:   As shown in table 1, we generally have more than $\frac{n(n-1)}{2}$ equations of type (3), so that the attack also works very well when $r = 2$ or $r = 3$, since we have more equations (3) than expected. Of course, when – after Gaussian reductions – we still have a few variables to guess, we can guess them by exhaustive search (if this number is very small).

Cryptanalysis of C_{-+r}^*, for $r \geq 4$:   When $r \geq 4$, the attack given above may not work, so that we may need to generalize this attack by generating more general equations such as equations of total degree $d \geq 4$ (instead of three), and of degree one in the y_i variables.

We know that from the variables of the original C^* we have at least n independent equations of type (1). So by multiplying these equations by $d - 2$ variables x_k, $1 \leq k \leq n$, we generate about $n \cdot \frac{n^{d-2}}{(d-2)!}$ independent equations of the following type:

$$\sum \gamma_{i_1 i_2 \ldots i_d} x_{i_1} x_{i_2} \ldots x_{i_{d-1}} y_d + \ldots = 0. \qquad (*)$$

By Gaussian reductions, we obtain at least $n \cdot \frac{n^{d-2}}{(d-2)!} - r \cdot \frac{n^{d-1}}{(d-1)!}$ equations $(*)$ with no terms in y_1, y_2, ..., y_r (because we have at most $\frac{n^{d-1}}{(d-1)!}$ terms in $y_\mu x_{i_1} x_{i_2} \ldots x_{i_{d-1}}$, and r values μ such that $1 \leq \mu \leq r$). Giving then explicit values for y, we obtain (by Gaussian reductions on the $X_{i_1 \ldots i_{d-1}} = x_{i_1} \ldots x_{i_{d-1}}$ variables) the x_i values if $n \cdot \frac{n^{d-2}}{(d-2)!} - r \cdot \frac{n^{d-1}}{(d-1)!} \geq \frac{n^{d-1}}{(d-1)!}$ (because as shown in our simulations the number of independent equations does not dramatically decrease when we give explicit values for y), i.e. when $r \leq d - 2$.

Complexity: The complexity of this attack is essentially the complexity of Gaussian reductions on $\mathcal{O}(n^d)$ terms, i.e. $\mathcal{O}(n^{\omega d})$, with $\omega = 3$ in the usual Gaussian reduction algorithms, or $\omega = 2.3755$ in the best known general purpose Gaussian reduction algorithm (see [1]). As a result, this complexity increases in $\mathcal{O}(n^{\omega r})$, i.e. exponentially in r.

Since our simulations show that this attack works sensibly better than described above (because we have a few more equations $(*)$), we may expect to attack C^*_{-+r} when $r \leq 10$ approximately. Therefore, we think that any $r \leq 10$ is insecure. However, the complexity of the attack increases a lot when r increases. Hence, at the present, for practical applications, it is an open problem to find efficient cryptanalysis of C^*_{-+r} when $r > 10$.

Can we recover the corresponding C^*_- from C^*_{-+} ?
 This is sometimes feasible. For example, when we have equations of type (2) (this is generally the case only when r is very small: see table 1), they generally come from y_k variables of the original C^*_-, and not from the added random quadratic equations. Therefore, by looking at the terms in factor of a monomial $x_i x_j$ in those equations (2), we find the vector space generated by the public equations of the original C^*_- equations. (C^*_{-+} can then be attacked as a C^*_- algorithm.)

Part II: Schemes with a Hidden Matrix

9   The [C] Scheme

Let us recall the description of the [C] scheme, presented by H. Imai and T. Matsumoto in [4]. Let $K = \mathbf{F}_{2^m}$ be a *public* finite field of cardinality $q = 2^m$. The basic idea is to use the transformation $A \mapsto A^2$ of the set $\mathcal{M}_2(K)$ of the 2×2 matrices over the field K.

This transformation is not one-to-one, but it can be proved (see the extended version) that its restriction Φ to the set $\mathcal{E} = \{M \in \mathcal{M}_2(K), \operatorname{tr}(M) \neq 0\}$ is a bijection whose inverse is given by:

$$\Phi^{-1}(B) = \frac{1}{\sqrt{\operatorname{tr}(B)}} \cdot \left(B + \sqrt{\det(B)} \cdot I\right),$$

where $\sqrt{}$ denotes the inverse of the bijection $\lambda \mapsto \lambda^2$ on $\mathbf{F}_{2^m}$. The function $\sqrt{}$ is easy to compute, since $\sqrt{\lambda} = \lambda^{2^{m-1}}$ for any $\lambda \in \mathbf{F}_{2^m}$.

The set $\mathcal{M}_2(K)$ can be considered as a vector space of dimension 4 over K. Therefore, we can choose $s : K^4 \to \mathcal{M}_2(K)$ and $t : \mathcal{M}_2(K) \to K^4$ two *secret* linear bijections such that s maps the hyperplane $\{x_1 = 0\}$ of K^4 onto the hyperplane $\{\operatorname{tr}(M) = 0\}$ of $\mathcal{M}_2(K)$, whereas t maps the hyperplane $\{\operatorname{tr}(M) = 0\}$ of $\mathcal{M}_2(K)$ onto the hyperplane $\{x_1 = 0\}$ of K^4.

Each message M is represented by a 4-uple $(x_1, x_2, x_3, x_4) \in K^4$ such that $x_1 \neq 0$. The message space is $\mathcal{M} = \{(x_1, x_2, x_3, x_4) \in K^4,\ x_1 \neq 0\}$.

The quadratic function f is defined on the message space by:

$$f : \begin{cases} \mathcal{M} \to \mathcal{M} \\ x \mapsto t\big(s(x)^2\big) \end{cases}.$$

The hypotheses made on s and t show that the function f is a bijection.

[C] **used in encryption mode:** The public key is the 4-uple (P_1, P_2, P_3, P_4) of 4-variate quadratic polynomials over K that represent f. They are defined by:

$$f(x_1, ..., x_4) = \big(P_1(x_1, ..., x_4), P_2(x_1, ..., x_4), P_3(x_1, ..., x_4), P_4(x_1, ..., x_4)\big).$$

The secret key is the two linear bijections s and t.

To encrypt the message M represented by $x = (x_1, x_2, x_3, x_4) \in \mathcal{M}$, compute the ciphertext $y = (y_1, y_2, y_3, y_4)$ with the following formulas:

$$(\mathcal{S}) \quad \begin{cases} y_1 = P_1(x_1, x_2, x_3, x_4) \\ y_2 = P_2(x_1, x_2, x_3, x_4) \\ y_3 = P_3(x_1, x_2, x_3, x_4) \\ y_4 = P_4(x_1, x_2, x_3, x_4) \end{cases}$$

To decrypt the ciphertext $y \in \mathcal{M}$, compute:

$$x = s^{-1}\left(\frac{1}{\sqrt{\operatorname{tr}(t^{-1}(y))}} \cdot \left(t^{-1}(y) + \sqrt{\det(t^{-1}(y))} \cdot I\right)\right).$$

10   First Cryptanalysis of [C]

This section is given in appendix 2.

11   The More General $[C_n]$ Scheme

The $[C_n]$ scheme is a generalization of $[C]$, which involves $n \times n$ matrices over K, instead of 2×2 matrices.

As in the case of $[C]$, we take a public finite field $K = \mathbf{F}_{2^m}$ of cardinality $q = 2^m$. The basic idea is still to use the transformation $A \mapsto A^2$ of the set $\mathcal{M}_n(K)$ of the $n \times n$ matrices over the field K. The set $\mathcal{M}_n(K)$ can be considered as a vector space of dimension n^2 over K, so that we can choose $s : K^{n^2} \to \mathcal{M}_n(K)$ and $t : \mathcal{M}_n(K) \to K^{n^2}$ two *secret* affine bijections.

Each message M is represented by a n^2-uple $(x_1, ..., x_{n^2}) \in K^{n^2}$. The message space is $\mathcal{M} = K^{n^2}$.

The quadratic function f is defined on the message space by:

$$f : \begin{cases} \mathcal{M} \to \mathcal{M} \\ x \mapsto t\big(s(x)^2\big) \end{cases}.$$

$[C_n]$ **used in encryption mode:**   The public key is the n^2-uple $(P_1, ..., P_{n^2})$ of n^2-variate quadratic polynomials over K that represent f. They are defined by:

$$f(x_1, ..., x_{n^2}) = \big(P_1(x_1, ..., x_{n^2}), ..., P_{n^2}(x_1, ..., x_{n^2})\big).$$

The secret key is the two affine bijections s and t.

To encrypt the message M represented by $x = (x_1, ..., x_{n^2}) \in \mathcal{M}$, compute the ciphertext $y = (y_1, ..., y_{n^2})$ with the following formulas:

$$\begin{cases} y_1 = P_1(x_1, ..., x_{n^2}) \\ \quad \vdots \\ y_{n^2} = P_{n^2}(x_1, ..., x_{n^2}) \end{cases}$$

To decrypt the ciphertext $y \in \mathcal{M}$, one has to solve the equations $A^2 = B$, where $B = t^{-1}(y)$, and then to compute the cleartext $x = s^{-1}(A)$.

# pre-images	$n = 2$	$n = 3$	$n = 4$	# pre-images	$n = 2$	$n = 3$	$n = 4$
0	6	252	34440	13-15	0	0	0
1	8	160	22272	16	0	0	672
2	0	42	5040	17-21	0	0	0
3	0	0	0	22	0	2	240
4	2	56	2240	23-315	0	0	0
5-11	0	0	0	316	0	0	2
12	0	0	630	> 316	0	0	0

Table 2: number of pre-images for $[C_n]$ over $\mathbf{F}_2$ (toy examples)

It is important to notice that $A \mapsto A^2$ is not a bijection any longer (contrary to the original $[C]$ scheme described in section 9). As a result, there may be several possible cleartexts for a given ciphertext. One solution to avoid this ambiguousness is to put some redundancy in the representation of the messages, by making use of an error correcting code or a hash function (for details, see [9] p. 34, where a similar idea is used in a different scheme).

The feasibility of choosing the right cleartext among the possible ones is due to the fact that – for an average B – the number of solutions A of the equations $A^2 = B$ remains reasonable, as shown in table 2 above.

To solve the equation $A^2 = B$ when $B \in \mathcal{M}_n(K)$, two methods can be used:

The first one is based on the Jordan reduction of matrices, and provides a polynomial time algorithm to compute the square roots of a given matrix. For details, see [3] (chapter VIII, p. 231).

The second one is based on the Cayley-Hamilton theorem. Let us denote by

$$\chi_M(\lambda) = \lambda^n + \alpha_{n-1}(M)\lambda^{n-1} + \ldots + \alpha_1(M)\lambda + \alpha_0(M)$$

the characteristic polynomial of a matrix $M \in \mathcal{M}_n(K)$. Since K is a field of characteristic 2, it is easy to prove that $\alpha_i(M^2) = \left(\alpha_i(M)\right)^2$ ($0 \le i \le n - 1$). Suppose now that A satisfies $A^2 = B$ for a given B. Then, from the Cayley-Hamilton theorem ($\chi_A(A) = 0$), we obtain the following formula:

$$A = \left(\sqrt{\alpha_0(B)} \cdot I + \sqrt{\alpha_2(B)} \cdot B + \ldots\right)\left(\sqrt{\alpha_1(B)} \cdot I + \sqrt{\alpha_3(B)} \cdot B + \ldots\right)^{-1}.$$

This method can only be used when $\alpha_1(B) \cdot I + \alpha_3(B) \cdot B + \ldots$ is invertible.

Note: The scheme can also be used in signature. To sign a message M, the basic idea is to compute x from $y = h(R\|M)$ (as if we were deciphering a message), where h is a hash function and R is a small pad. If we succeed, (x, R) is the signature of M. If not (because the function is not a bijection), we try another pad R (for variants and details, see [9], where a similar idea is used).

12   Cryptanalysis of $[C_n]$

This section is given in appendix 3.

13   A Suggestion: the *HM* Scheme

The cryptanalysis of $[C_n]$ described in section 12 uses the fact that A and B commute when $B = A^2$. In order to avoid that very special algebraic property, we suggest to replace the transformation $B = A^2$ by the equation $B = A^2 + MA$, where M is a *secret* matrix randomly chosen in $\mathcal{M}_n(K)$.

The description of the obtained scheme – called *HM* – is exactly the same as for $[C_n]$. As in section 11, the transformation is generally not one-to-one, but the scheme can be used in a practical way because – as in the case of $[C_n]$ –, the number of pre-images of a given average matrix B remains under a reasonable limit. Table 4 below illustrates this fact (for a randomly chosen matrix M).

To obtain a practical scheme, one has to be able to solve the equation $A^2 + MA = B$ for a given matrix $B \in \mathcal{M}_n(K)$. There indeed exist a polynomial time algorithm to perform this computation (see [3], chapter VIII). The basic idea of this algorithm is to use the fact that $B = A^2 + MA$ implies $g(A) = 0$, where $g(\lambda) = \det(\lambda^2 + \lambda \cdot M - B)$ is a polynomial with *scalar* coefficients (notice that this property is a generalization of the Cayley-Hamilton theorem). The equation $g(A) = 0$ can be solved by using the Jordan reduction of matrices.

# pre-images	$n = 2$	$n = 3$	$n = 4$	# pre-images	$n = 2$	$n = 3$	$n = 4$
0	6	284	39552	16	0	0	72
1	8	112	12024	17	0	0	0
2	0	42	6576	18	0	0	12
3	0	32	2256	19	0	0	24
4	2	34	1868	20	0	0	24
5	0	0	960	21	0	0	0
6	0	0	972	22	0	0	24
7	0	0	168	23-25	0	0	0
8	0	2	324	26	0	0	36
9	0	0	48	27	0	0	0
10	0	2	144	28	0	0	6
11	0	0	96	29-33	0	0	0
12	0	4	162	34	0	0	4
13	0	0	56	35-39	0	0	0
14	0	0	72	40	0	0	8
15	0	0	48	> 40	0	0	0

Table 4: **Number of pre-images for** *HM* **over** $\mathbf{F}_2$ **(toy examples)**

	$n = 2$	$n = 3$	$n = 4$
$p = 2$	10 16 39	3 11 133	3 18 49
$p = 3$	1 1 14	1 1 11	1 1 18
$p = 31$	0 0 1	0 0 1	0 0 1
$p = 127$	0 0 0	0 0 0	0 0 0

Table 5: **Number of equations of**

type 1   type 4
type 2

for *HM* **over** $K = \mathbf{F}_p$

The *HM* scheme seems less vulnerable to attacks based on affine multiple (*i.e.* on equations such that those of type (1), (2) or (4)), as shown in table 5 above (equations (4) are defined in appendix 3). However, we have made computations (see table 6 below, in which the y_i variables have been replaced by explicit values) showing that equations of type (3) (defined in section 4) still exist, and also equations of "type (5)", defined by:

$$\sum \mu_{ij} x_i y_j + \sum \nu_{ij} x_i x_j + \sum \alpha_i x_i + \sum \beta_i y_i + \delta_0 = 0 \qquad (5)$$

HM	$n = 2$	$n = 3$	$n = 4$
Equations (5)	7	17	31
Equations (3)	9	30	58

Table 6: Number of linearly independent equations

Note: It may be noticed that $B = A^2$ implies the two following identities:

$$\begin{cases} AB - BA = AMA - MA^2 & \text{(type (5))} \\ A^2B - BA^2 = BMA - MAB & \text{(type (3))} \end{cases}$$

This explains – in part – the existence of such equations of types (5) and (3).

The existence of such equations threatens the HM scheme. In fact they make the cryptanalyst able to distinguish between a random quadratic transformation of K^{n^2} and a quadratic transformation corresponding to the HM scheme. This explains that we do not recommend the HM scheme. However, at the present, the existence of equations of type (5) and type (3) does not seem sufficient to break the scheme. Therefore, the question of the security of HM remains open...

14 Conclusion

Among cryptologists that have studied the problem, two main opinions arise as concerns public key schemes built with multivariate polynomials. Some of them think that most of these schemes should be vulnerable to attacks based on general principles, still to be found. According to others, the status of those many schemes can be compared to the one of most secret key algorithms: no relative proof of security is known, but the great flexibility for the choice among the possible variants of the schemes, together with the relative easiness for building efficient schemes that avoid known attacks, may support a certain confidence in the security of the schemes, at least – a priori – for those which do not seem too close to known cryptanalytic techniques.

The present article does not settle the question once and for all. Nevertheless, it gives arguments for both opinions. On the one hand, we have shown how to break some schemes for which no cryptanalysis had been given before. On the other hand, we have studied some simple and general ideas (removing equations, adding ones, introducing new variables...) that might – a priori – sensibly enforce the security of some asymmetric schemes. Interesting mathematical questions naturally arise: better understanding and detecting orthogonal polynomials, using a non commutative ring of matrices to generate multivariate equations on a (commutative) field, etc. If we had to take a strong line as concerns the unbroken schemes, our current opinion is that the most provocative schemes (C^{*}_{--},

C^*_{-+}, HM) may be too close to known cryptanalysis to be recommended, but more complex schemes (such as HFE_{-+}) may be really secure... However, it is still too soon to have a definitive opinion, and we think that – above all – the important point is to go further into the understanding of the mysterious links between mathematics and the concepts of asymmetric cryptography and cryptanalysis.

References

1. D. Coppersmith, S. Winograd, *Matrix Multiplication via Arithmetic Progressions*, J. Symbolic Computation, 1990, vol. 9, pp. 251-280.
2. J.C. Faugere, *Rough evaluation* (personal communication).
3. F.R. Gantmacher, *The Theory of Matrices*, volume 1, Chelsae Publishing Company, New-York.
4. H. Imai, T. Matsumoto, *Algebraic Methods for Constructing Asymmetric Cryptosystems*, Algebraic Algorithms and Error Correcting Codes (AAECC-3), Grenoble, 1985, Lectures Notes in Computer Science n° 229, pp.108-119.
5. N. Koblitz, *Algebraic Aspects of Cryptography*, Algorithms and Computation in Mathematics, Volume 3, Springer, 1998.
6. R. Lidl, H. Niederreiter, *Finite Fields*, Encyclopedia of Mathematics and its applications, Volume 20, Cambridge University Press.
7. T. Matsumoto, H. Imai, *Public Quadratic Polynomial-Tuples for Efficient Signature-Verification and Message-Encryption*, Advances in Cryptology, Proceedings of EUROCRYPT'88, Springer-Verlag, pp. 419-453.
8. J. Patarin, *Cryptanalysis of the Matsumoto and Imai Public Key Scheme of Eurocrypt'88*, Advances in Cryptology, Proceedings of CRYPTO'95, Springer, pp. 248-261.
9. J. Patarin, *Hidden Fields Equations (HFE) and Isomorphisms of Polynomials (IP) : Two New Families of Asymmetric Algorithms*, Advances in Cryptology, Proceedings of EUROCRYPT'96, Springer, pp. 33-48.
10. J. Patarin, *Asymmetric Cryptography with a Hidden Monomial*, Advances in Cryptology, Proceedings of CRYPTO'96, Springer, pp. 45-60.
11. J. Patarin, L. Goubin, *Trapdoor One-way Permutations and Multivariate Polynomials*, Proceedings of ICICS'97, Springer, LNCS n°1334, pp. 356-368.
12. J. Patarin, L. Goubin, *Asymmetric Cryptography with S-Boxes*, Proceedings of ICICS'97, Springer, LNCS n°1334, pp. 369-380.

Appendix 1: First Cryptanalysis of C^*_-

Principle of the attack: Let P be the complete public form of C^*. We suppose that the first r public equations have been removed. Let $P_{(r+1)...n}$ be the remaining part of P. The aim of the attack is to recover the public equations $P_{1...r}$ and then to use the classical attack of [8]. Obviously, those equations can be found only modulo the vector space generated by all the public equations. The basic idea is to use the so-called *polar* form of P, defined by

$$Q(x,t) := P(x+t) - P(x) - P(t).$$

Description of the algorithm:
1) Choose randomly $t \neq 0$ and $x^{(0)}$.
2) Compute $z_{(r+1)...n} := Q_{(r+1)...n}(x^{(0)}, t)$.
3) Solve the equation

$$Q_{(r+1)...n}(x, t) = z_{(r+1)...n}, \qquad (**)$$

where x is the unknown. There are at least two solutions ($x^{(0)}$ and $x^{(0)} + t$) and at most 2.2^r solutions, because – for a given value $z_{1...r}$ – (among 2^r possible), the equation $Q(x, t) = z$ has 0 or 2 solutions (see the extended version for a proof).

Steps 1, 2 and 3 are repeated until we obtain the maximum number of solutions: 2.2^r (we use each time a different choice for $t \neq 0$ and $x^{(0)}$). The average number of necessary tries is estimated to be about 2^r.
4) Suppose we have found $t \neq 0$ and $x^{(0)}$ such that the $(**)$ equation has exactly 2.2^r solutions: $x^{(0)}, x^{(0)} + t, x^{(1)}, x^{(1)} + t, ..., x^{(2^r-1)}, x^{(2^r-1)} + t$. Let k be an integer such that $1 \leq k \leq r$. For half of the solutions, we have $Q_k(x, t) = 0$, and for the other half, we have $Q_k(x, t) = 1$, and this remains true if we consider only the subset $\{x^{(0)}, ..., x^{(2^r-1)}\}$ of the set of solutions. Therefore

$$\sum_{\nu=0}^{2^r-1} Q_k(x^{(\nu)}, t) = 2^{r-1},$$

which gives an equation of degree one on the $\frac{n(n-1)}{2} + 1$ coefficients of Q_k (this equation is the same for all the values k, $1 \leq k \leq r$).
5) By repeating steps 1-4 $\mathcal{O}(n^2)$ times, with different choices of $(x^{(0)}, t)$, we expect to find $\frac{n(n-1)}{2} + 1 - n$ equations on the coefficients of the Q_k ($1 \leq k \leq r$). This gives $Q_1, ..., Q_r$ modulo the vector space generated by all the public equations.
6) Once Q is completely known, we deduce $P_1, ..., P_n$ (there is a technical problem when the characteristic of K is 2, see the extended version), and the classical attack of [8] can be applied, so that C_-^* is broken for small r values. The complexity of this cryptanalysis is $\mathcal{O}(q^r)$, plus the complexity of the cryptanalysis of the original C^* scheme.

Note: This cryptanalysis uses deeply the fact that C^* is a permutation polynomial. A general theory about permutation polynomials, and the related notion of orthogonal systems of equations, can be found in [6], chapter 7.

Appendix 2: First Cryptanalysis of [C]

The security of the cryptosystem is based on the difficulty of solving the system $(\mathcal{S})$ (defined in section 9) of 4 quadratic equations in 4 variables over $K = \mathbf{F}_{2^m}$. Unfortunately, such a system can always be easily solved by using an algorithm based on Gröbner bases. At the present, the best implementations of Gröbner bases can solve any set of n quadratic equations with n variables over any reasonable field K, when $n \leq 16$ approximately (cf [2]). Therefore, the original $[C]$ is not secure.

This first cryptanalysis shows that the parameter n must not be too small if we want to avoid attacks based on algebraic methods for solving systems of multivariate polynomial equations. That is why we are going to describe a generalization of the scheme to higher dimensions (for which Gröbner bases algorithms are inefficient) in section 11.

Appendix 3: Cryptanalysis of $[C_n]$

In this section, we describe a polynomial attack against the $[C_n]$ algorithm, which proves that this scheme is insecure. The key idea is to use the fact that $B = A^2$ implies $AB = BA$ (whereas two random matrices A and B do not commute in general). We begin by computing all the equations of type (1). The relation $AB = BA$ gives a priori n equations of this type. In fact, when we give explicit values to the y_i variables, we cannot obtain n independent linear equations on the x_i variables, since $AB = BA$ is also true when $B = P(A)$, where P is any polynomial in $K[X]$. The exact number of independent linear equations coming from $AB = BA$ is given by the following result of [3]:

Theorem 141 *The number N of linearly independent matrices that commute with the matrix B is given by the formula $N = n_1 + 3n_2 + \ldots + (2t - 1)n_t$, where $n_1, n_2, \ldots, n_t$ are the degrees of the non constant invariant polynomials of B.*

See [3], chapter VI, for the definition of the invariant polynomials, and chapter VIII for a proof of the theorem. In particular, we have $n \leq N \leq n^2$, with $N \simeq n$ in most of the cases. It remains – a priori – to perform an exhaustive search on $\simeq n$ variables to end the attack. In fact, we have made some simulations (see table 3 below) that suggest that there also exist many equations of type (2) (defined in section 4), and type (4) defined by:

$$\sum \gamma_{ij} x_i y_j + \sum \mu_{ij} y_i y_j + \sum \alpha_i x_i + \sum \beta_i y_i + \delta_0 = 0 \qquad (4)$$

	$n = 2$	$n = 3$	$n = 4$
$p = 2$	10 16 39	10 18 153	17 32 292
$p = 3$	4 4 28	9 9 89	16 16 271
$p = 31$	3 3 14	8 8 79	15 15 254
$p = 127$	3 3 14	8 8 79	15 15 254

Table 3: Number of equations of type 1 type 4 / **type 2** for $[C_n]$ over $\mathbf{F}_p$

Note: For $p = 2$, on these examples, we obtain $(n + 1)$ (formally) linearly independent equations of type (1). This can be explained by the fact that – on the field $K = \mathbf{F}_2$ – the equations $B = A^2$ implies $\mathrm{tr}(B) = \mathrm{tr}(A)$.

These equations of type (1), (2) and (4) can be found by Gaussian reductions on a polynomial number of cleartext/ciphertext pairs. Therefore, the $[C_n]$ scheme is unlikely to be secure: by using all the found equations of type (1), (2) and (3), a cleartext is easily found by Gaussian reductions.

ECC/DLP and Factoring-Based Cryptography: A Tale of Two Families (Invited Lecture)

Burton S. Kaliski Jr.

RSA Laboratories, 20 Crosby Drive, Bedford, MA 01730, USA
E-mail: burt@rsa.com

Abstract. They came into prominence in the 1970's, though their roots extend back several centuries. In the 1980's, they survived substantial testing and many new members were added. The roles of their various members became better understood in the 1990's, as the families gained influence throughout the world.

These are, of course, the two families of public-key cryptography. One family consists of algorithms whose security is based on the discrete logarithm problem (DLP), including elliptic curve cryptography (ECC). The other bases its security on the difficulty of integer factorization. Today, both families have significant influence and applications. They have much in common, having emerged, survived and grown together.

Researchers have studied numerous aspects of these families, from underlying security, to algorithms and protocols, to generation of keys and parameters, to efficient implementation. Standards are being written with each family in mind, and it is clear that each family will play a part in the security infrastructure that is now being developed.

How the families came to be, how they are similar, how they differ, and how the strengths of each can be combined, are all questions of current interest in assessing what role each family is likely to have, as we move into the next century.

K. Ohta and D. Pei (Eds.): ASIACRYPT'98, LNCS 1514, p. 50–50, 1998.
© Springer-Verlag Berlin Heidelberg 1998

Efficient Elliptic Curve Exponentiation Using Mixed Coordinates

Henri Cohen[1], Atsuko Miyaji[2], and Takatoshi Ono[3]

[1] Laboratoire A2X, Université Bordeaux I
[2] Multimedia Development Center, Matsushita Electric Industrial Co., Ltd.
[3] Matsushita Information Systems Research Laboratory Nagoya Co., Ltd.

Abstract. Elliptic curve cryptosystems, proposed by Koblitz ([12]) and Miller ([16]), can be constructed over a smaller field of definition than the ElGamal cryptosystems ([6]) or the RSA cryptosystems ([20]). This is why elliptic curve cryptosystems have begun to attract notice. In this paper, we investigate efficient elliptic curve exponentiation. We propose a new coordinate system and a new mixed coordinates strategy, which significantly improves on the number of basic operations needed for elliptic curve exponentiation.

key words: elliptic curve exponentiation, coordinate system

1 Introduction

Koblitz ([12]) and Miller ([16]) proposed a method by which public key cryptosystems can be constructed on the group of points of an elliptic curve over a finite field instead of a finite field. If elliptic curve cryptosystems satisfy both MOV-conditions ([15,10]) and FR-conditions ([4]), and avoid p-divisible elliptic curves over $\mathbb{F}_{p^r}$ ([23,21,25]), then the only known attacks are the Pollard ρ−method ([19]) and the Pohlig-Hellman method ([18]). Hence with current knowledge, we can construct elliptic curve cryptosystems over a smaller definition field than the discrete-logarithm-problem (DLP)-based cryptosystems like the ElGamal cryptosystems ([6]) or the DSA ([5]) and RSA cryptosystems ([20]). Elliptic curve cryptosystems with a 160-bit key are thus believed to have the same security as both the ElGamal cryptosystems and RSA with a 1,024-bit key. This is why elliptic curve cryptosystems have been discussed in ISO/IEC CD 14883-3, ISO/IEC DIS 11770-3, ANSI ASC X.9, X.9.62, and IEEE P1363 ([10]). As standardization advances, fast implementations of elliptic curve cryptosystems has been reported ([9,22,27,8,3]).

There are two approaches for efficient elliptic curve exponentiation. One uses general methods valid for any elliptic curve. The other uses ad-hoc methods for special elliptic curves, which use the complex multiplication field ([26,13]). For security purposes, an elliptic curve should not be fixed and be changed periodically. Therefore an efficient algorithm valid for any elliptic curve and not for a fixed elliptic curve is desirable. This paper explores an efficient algorithm valid for any elliptic curve.

K. Ohta and D. Pei (Eds.): ASIACRYPT'98, LNCS 1514, pp. 51–65, 1998.
© Springer-Verlag Berlin Heidelberg 1998

Elliptic curve exponentiations involve three different factors: the field of definition, the addition-chains ([11,17,14,22]), and the coordinate systems. For the field of definition, we may choose optimal fields on which modular reduction is efficient ([3]) or on which inversion is efficient ([22]). For the addition-chains, the addition-subtraction method is usually mixed with the window method ([11,17,14,22,3]). On the other hand, the optimal coordinate systems have not been so thoroughly studied, though there have been some proposals ([1]). In this paper, we study optimal coordinates for the case of a field of definition $\mathbb{F}_p$ (with p larger than 3). We propose a new coordinate system and a new mixed coordinates strategy for elliptic curve exponentiation.

1. Coordinates of an elliptic curve
An elliptic curve can be represented using several coordinate systems. For each such system, the speed of additions and doublings is different. Therefore a good choice of coordinate system is an important factor for elliptic curve exponentiations. Affine coordinates and projective coordinates are well known ([24]). Two more coordinate systems, the Jacobian coordinates and the five element Jacobian coordinates (which we will call the Chudnovsky Jacobian coordinates) have been proposed in [1]. The efficiency of Jacobian coordinates for elliptic curve exponentiation is discussed in [3].

In the present paper, we introduce what we call modified Jacobian coordinates, which gives faster doublings than affine, projective, Jacobian and Chudnovsky Jacobian coordinates. Since doublings take the largest part of the time for an elliptic curve exponentiation, this leads to noticeable improvements.

2. Strategy of elliptic curve exponentiation
Although we have at our disposal five coordinate systems including our new one, there is no single system which gives both fast doublings and fast additions: for example, the Jacobian coordinates have faster doublings but slower additions than the Chudnovsky Jacobian coordinates. Up to now, for fast elliptic curve exponentiation, a single coordinate system has been used which minimizes the total computation time ([9,22,27,8,3]). This is not the best method since some coordinates are good at additions and others are good at doublings. In this paper, we propose a new strategy using mixed coordinate systems for efficient elliptic curve exponentiation: for doublings, we use the best possible system for doublings, and for additions, we use the best possible system for additions.

This paper is organized as follows. Section 2 discusses the four known coordinate systems. Section 3 presents our new coordinate system and investigates strategies using mixed coordinate systems. The number of basic field operations for elliptic curve exponentiation using mixed coordinates is also estimated. Section 5 presents an implementation of our strategy.

2   The Coordinate Systems

An elliptic curve can be represented by several coordinate systems. We give here the addition and doubling formulas for affine coordinates ([24]), projective coordinates ([14]), Jacobian coordinates ([1,3]), and Chudnovsky Jacobian coordinates ([1]), as well as the necessary number of field operations. From now on, we assume that $\mathbb{F}_p$ is a field with $p > 3$.

2.1   The Addition Formulas in Affine Coordinate

Let

$$E : y^2 = x^3 + ax + b \quad (a, b \in \mathbb{F}_p, 4a^3 + 27b^2 \neq 0).$$

be the equation of an elliptic curve E over $\mathbb{F}_p$.

The addition formulas for affine coordinates are the following. Let $P = (x_1, y_1)$, $Q = (x_2, y_2)$ and $P + Q = (x_3, y_3)$ be points on $E(\mathbb{F}_p)$.
• **Curve addition formulas in affine coordinates** $(P \neq \pm Q)$

$$x_3 = \lambda^2 - x_1 - x_2, \; y_3 = \lambda(x_1 - x_3) - y_1, \tag{1}$$

where $\lambda = (y_2 - y_1)/(x_2 - x_1)$;
• **Curve doubling formulas in affine coordinates** $(P = Q)$

$$x_3 = \lambda^2 - 2x_1, \; y_3 = \lambda(x_1 - x_3) - y_1, \tag{2}$$

where $\lambda = (3x_1^2 + a)/(2y_1)$.

Here we discuss the computation times for these formulas in detail. For simplicity, we neglect addition, subtraction and multiplication by a small constant in $\mathbb{F}_p$ because they are much faster than multiplication and inversion in $\mathbb{F}_p$. Let us denote the computation time of an addition (resp. a doubling) by $t(\mathcal{A} + \mathcal{A})$ (resp. $t(2\mathcal{A})$) and represent multiplication (resp. inverse, resp. squaring) in $\mathbb{F}_p$ by M (resp. I, resp. S). Then we see that $t(\mathcal{A} + \mathcal{A}) = I + 2M + S$ and $t(2\mathcal{A}) = I + 2M + 2S$.

2.2   The Addition Formulas in Projective coordinates

For projective coordinates, we set $x = X/Z$ and $y = Y/Z$, giving the equation

$$E_P : Y^2 Z = X^3 + aXZ^2 + bZ^3.$$

The addition formulas in projective coordinates are the following. Let $P = (X_1, Y_1, Z_1)$, $Q = (X_2, Y_2, Z_2)$ and $P + Q = R = (X_3, Y_3, Z_3)$.
• **Curve addition formulas in projective coordinates** $(P \neq \pm Q)$

$$X_3 = vA, \; Y_3 = u(v^2 X_1 Z_2 - A) - v^3 Y_1 Z_2, \; Z_3 = v^3 Z_1 Z_2, \tag{3}$$

where $u = Y_2 Z_1 - Y_1 Z_2, v = X_2 Z_1 - X_1 Z_2, A = u^2 Z_1 Z_2 - v^3 - 2v^2 X_1 Z_2$;
• **Curve doubling formulas in projective coordinates** $(R = 2P)$

$$X_3 = 2hs, \; Y_3 = w(4B - h) - 8Y_1^2 s^2, \; Z_3 = 8s^3, \tag{4}$$

where $w = aZ_1^2 + 3X_1^2, s = Y_1 Z_1, B = X_1 Y_1 s, h = w^2 - 8B$.

The computation times are $t(\mathcal{P} + \mathcal{P}) = 12M + 2S$ and $t(2\mathcal{P}) = 7M + 5S$, where $\mathcal{P}$ means projective coordinates.

2.3   The Addition Formulas in Jacobian and Chudnovsky Jacobian coordinates

For Jacobian coordinates, we set $x = X/Z^2$ and $y = Y/Z^3$, giving the equation

$$E_J : Y^2 = X^3 + aXZ^4 + bZ^6.$$

The addition formulas in the Jacobian coordinates are the following. Let $P = (X_1, Y_1, Z_1)$, $Q = (X_2, Y_2, Z_2)$ and $P + Q = R = (X_3, Y_3, Z_3)$.

● **Curve addition formulas in Jacobian coordinates** $(P \neq \pm Q)$

$$X_3 = -H^3 - 2U_1H^2 + r^2, \ Y_3 = -S_1H^3 + r(U_1H^2 - X_3), \ Z_3 = Z_1Z_2H, \quad (5)$$

where $U_1 = X_1Z_2^2, U_2 = X_2Z_1^2, S_1 = Y_1Z_2^3, S_2 = Y_2Z_1^3, H = U_2 - U_1, r = S_2 - S_1$;

● **Curve doubling formulas in Jacobian coordinates** $(R = 2P)$

$$X_3 = T, \ Y_3 = -8Y_1^4 + M(S - T), \ Z_3 = 2Y_1Z_1, \quad (6)$$

where $S = 4X_1Y_1^2, M = 3X_1^2 + aZ_1^4, T = -2S + M^2$.

The computation times are $t(\mathcal{J} + \mathcal{J}) = 12M + 4S$ and $t(2\mathcal{J}) = 4M + 6S$, where $\mathcal{J}$ means Jacobian coordinates.

We see that Jacobian coordinates offer a faster doubling and a slower addition than projective coordinates. In order to make an addition faster, we should represent internally a Jacobian point as the quintuple (X, Y, Z, Z^2, Z^3) ([1]). This is called the Chudnovsky Jacobian coordinate and denoted by $\mathcal{J}^c$. The addition formulas in the Chudnovsky Jacobian coordinates are the following. Let $P = (X_1, Y_1, Z_1, Z_1^2, Z_1^3)$, $Q = (X_2, Y_2, Z_2, Z_2^2, Z_2^3)$ and $P + Q = R = (X_3, Y_3, Z_3, Z_3^2, Z_3^3)$.

● **Curve addition formulas in Chudnovsky Jacobian coordinates** $(P \neq \pm Q)$

$$X_3 = -H^3 - 2U_1H^2 + r^2, Y_3 = -S_1H^3 + r(U_1H^2 - X_3), Z_3 = Z_1Z_2H, Z_3^2 = Z_3^2, Z_3^3 = Z_3^3, \quad (7)$$

where $U_1 = X_1(Z_2^2), U_2 = X_2(Z_1^2), S_1 = Y_1(Z_2^3), S_2 = Y_2(Z_1^3), H = U_2 - U_1, r = S_2 - S_1$;

● **Curve doubling formulas in Chudnovsky Jacobian coordinates** $(R = 2P)$

$$X_3 = T, \ Y_3 = -8Y_1^4 + M(S - T), \ Z_3 = 2Y_1Z_1, \ Z_3^2 = Z_3^2, \ Z_3^3 = Z_3^3, \quad (8)$$

where $S = 4X_1Y_1^2, M = 3X_1^2 + a(Z_1^2)^2, T = -2S + M^2$.

The computation times are $t(\mathcal{J}^c + \mathcal{J}^c) = 11M + 3S$ and $t(2\mathcal{J}^c) = 5M + 6S$.

3   A new Strategy for Elliptic Curve Exponentiation

In this section, we investigate a new strategy for elliptic curve exponentiation. Up to now, since only one kind of coordinate system is used, it has been necessary that it should offer both an addition and a doubling with reasonable speed (not the fastest but not too slow) ([8,9,27,26,22,3]). The Chudnovsky Jacobian coordinate system is a good example: it reduces the computation time of an addition by slightly increasing the doubling time, but this is still worthwhile since Jacobian coordinates have a rather faster doubling but slower addition times than projective coordinates.

On the contrary, here we further improve on the Jacobian coordinate system in order to offer even faster doublings, and there will be no loss in elliptic curve exponentiation since we are going to use a new strategy of mixed coordinate systems.

3.1 The Modified Jacobian Coordinates

Here we modify the Jacobian coordinates in order to obtain the fastest possible doublings. For this, we represent internally the Jacobian coordinates as a quadruple (X, Y, Z, aZ^4). We call this the modified Jacobian coordinate system, and denote it by $\mathcal{J}^m$. The addition formulas in the modified Jacobian coordinates are the following. Let $P = (X_1, Y_1, Z_1, aZ_1^4)$, $Q = (X_2, Y_2, Z_2, aZ_2^4)$ and $P + Q = R = (X_3, Y_3, Z_3, aZ_3^4)$.

• **Curve addition formulas in modified Jacobian coordinates** $(P \neq \pm Q)$

$$X_3 = -H^3 - 2U_1H^2 + r^2,\ Y_3 = -S_1H^3 + r(U_1H^2 - X_3),\ Z_3 = Z_1Z_2H,\ aZ_3^4 = aZ_3^4,\quad (9)$$

where $U_1 = X_1Z_2^2, U_2 = X_2Z_1^2, S_1 = Y_1Z_2^3, S_2 = Y_2Z_1^3, H = U_2 - U_1, r = S_2 - S_1$;

• **Curve doubling formulas in modified Jacobian coordinates** $(R = 2P)$

$$X_3 = T,\ Y_3 = M(S - T) - U,\ Z_3 = 2Y_1Z_1,\ aZ_3^4 = 2U(aZ_1^4),\qquad (10)$$

where $S = 4X_1Y_1^2, U = 8Y_1^4, M = 3X_1^2 + (aZ_1^4), T = -2S + M^2$.

The computation times are then $t(\mathcal{J}^m + \mathcal{J}^m) = 13M + 6S$ and $t(2\mathcal{J}^m) = 4M + 4S$. Obviously a modified Jacobian coordinate doubling is faster than a projective, Jacobian or Chudnovsky Jacobian coordinate doubling. Furthermore it is faster than an affine coordinate doubling unless $I < 3.6M$ (S is set to $0.8M$), which seems extremely unlikely if p is larger than 100 bits, independently of the field of definition $\mathbb{F}_p$ and of the implementation of inversion.

3.2 Using Mixed Coordinates

It is evidently possible to mix different coordinates, i.e. to add two points where one is given in some coordinate system, and the other point is in some other coordinate system. We can also choose the coordinate system of the result. Since we have five different kinds of coordinate systems (represented by the symbols $\mathcal{A}$, $\mathcal{P}$, $\mathcal{J}$, $\mathcal{J}^c$, and $\mathcal{J}^m$), this gives a large number of possibilities. Generalizing slightly the notation used above, let us denote by $t(\mathcal{C}^1 + \mathcal{C}^2 = \mathcal{C}^3)$ the time for addition of points in coordinates $\mathcal{C}^1$ and $\mathcal{C}^2$ giving a result in coordinates $\mathcal{C}^3$, and by $t(2\mathcal{C}^1 = \mathcal{C}^2)$ the time for doubling a point in coordinates $\mathcal{C}^1$ giving a result in coordinates $\mathcal{C}^2$. Table 1 gives the computation times for additions and doublings in various coordinates (not all possible combinations are given, only the most useful ones).

A small discussion is necessary if we want to compare computation times. The ratio S/M is almost independent of the field of definition and of the implementation, and can be reasonably taken equal to 0.8. On the other hand, the ratio I/M deeply depends on the field of definition and on the implementation: it can be estimated to be between $9M$ and $30M$ in the case of p larger than 100 bits. From Table 1, we see that for a doubling using a fixed coordinate system, $\mathcal{J}^m$ is the best choice. On the other hand, for an addition using a fixed coordinate system, we cannot decide what is the best coordinate system independently of the relative speed of inversion: it will usually be $\mathcal{J}^c$, unless $I/M < 10.6$, in which case it will be $\mathcal{A}$.

doubling		addition	
operation	computation time	operation	computation time
$t(2\mathcal{P})$	$7M + 5S$	$t(\mathcal{J}^m + \mathcal{J}^m)$	$13M + 6S$
$t(2\mathcal{J}^c)$	$5M + 6S$	$t(\mathcal{J}^m + \mathcal{J}^c = \mathcal{J}^m)$	$12M + 5S$
$t(2\mathcal{J})$	$4M + 6S$	$t(\mathcal{J} + \mathcal{J}^c = \mathcal{J}^m)$	$12M + 5S$
$t(2\mathcal{J}^m = \mathcal{J}^c)$	$4M + 5S$	$t(\mathcal{J} + \mathcal{J})$	$12M + 4S$
$t(2\mathcal{J}^m)$	$4M + 4S$	$t(\mathcal{P} + \mathcal{P})$	$12M + 2S$
$t(2\mathcal{A} = \mathcal{J}^c)$	$3M + 5S$	$t(\mathcal{J}^c + \mathcal{J}^c = \mathcal{J}^m)$	$11M + 4S$
$t(2\mathcal{J}^m = \mathcal{J})$	$3M + 4S$	$t(\mathcal{J}^c + \mathcal{J}^c)$	$11M + 3S$
$t(2\mathcal{A} = \mathcal{J}^m)$	$3M + 4S$	$t(\mathcal{J}^c + \mathcal{J} = \mathcal{J})$	$11M + 3S$
$t(2\mathcal{A} = \mathcal{J})$	$2M + 4S$	$t(\mathcal{J}^c + \mathcal{J}^c = \mathcal{J})$	$10M + 2S$
–	–	$t(\mathcal{J} + \mathcal{A} = \mathcal{J}^m)$	$9M + 5S$
–	–	$t(\mathcal{J}^m + \mathcal{A} = \mathcal{J}^m)$	$9M + 5S$
–	–	$t(\mathcal{J}^c + \mathcal{A} = \mathcal{J}^m)$	$8M + 4S$
–	–	$t(\mathcal{J}^c + \mathcal{A} = \mathcal{J}^c)$	$8M + 3S$
–	–	$t(\mathcal{J} + \mathcal{A} = \mathcal{J})$	$8M + 3S$
–	–	$t(\mathcal{J}^m + \mathcal{A} = \mathcal{J})$	$8M + 3S$
–	–	$t(\mathcal{A} + \mathcal{A} = \mathcal{J}^m)$	$5M + 4S$
–	–	$t(\mathcal{A} + \mathcal{A} = \mathcal{J}^c)$	$5M + 3S$
$t(2\mathcal{A})$	$2M + 2S + I$	$t(\mathcal{A} + \mathcal{A})$	$2M + S + I$

Table 1. Computation amount of addition and doubling

3.3   Use of Mixed Coordinate Systems

Elliptic curve exponentiation kP usually combines the addition-subtraction method with the window method ([8,14,26,22,3]). We will set $n = \lfloor \log_2(k) \rfloor + 1$ (i.e. n is the number of bits of k), and we denote the width of a window by w. Some representations in signed binary are reported in [11,14,3]. Since our discussion does not depend on this representation, we restrict here k to be in the following representation,

$$k = 2^{k_0}(2^{k_1}(\cdots 2^{k_{v-1}}(2^{k_v}W[v] + W[v-1])\cdots) + W[0]) \tag{11}$$

where $W[i]$ is an odd integer in the range $-2^w + 1 \leq W[i] \leq 2^w - 1$ for all i, $W[v] > 0$, $k_0 \geq 0$ and $k_i \geq w + 1$ for $i \geq 1$. This representation is easy to obtain inductively by looking at the bit pattern of k ([3]). Then kP can be computed using the following procedure: first precompute points $P_i = iP$ for odd integers i and $1 \leq i \leq 2^w - 1$, set $P_{-i} = -P_i$ for each i, and then repeat doublings and addition/subtractions with these precomputed points.

The first stage of computation, that is $2^{k_v} P_{W[v]}$, can be modified in order to reduce the computation amount as follows. In the case of $W[v] = 1$, k_v doublings are reduced to $(k_v - w)$ doublings and 1 addition by setting

$$2^{k_v} P_1 = 2^{k_v - w}(P_{2^w - 1} + P_1).$$

In the case of $W[v] = 3$, k_v doublings are reduced to $(k_v - w + 1)$ doublings and 1 addition by setting

$$2^{k_v} P_3 = 2^{k_v - w + 1}(P_{2^w - 1} + P_{2^{w-1}+1}).$$

Similar modifications can be made for all $W[v] < 2^{w-1}$, and one can show that the most significant doublings $2^{k_v} P_{W[v]}$ can be reduced by $(w^2 + 5w - 2)/(2w + 4)$ doublings minus $(w + 1)/(w + 2)$ additions on average.

Up to now, we have used a single coordinate system in all the procedure. Here we propose to mix different coordinate systems by dividing the computation into three parts: we will use the coordinate system $\mathcal{C}^1$ for repeated *main* doublings (i.e. $2^{k_i-1}P'$), the coordinate system $\mathcal{C}^2$ for the result of a final doubling (i.e. $2(2^{k_i-1}P')$) and the coordinate system $\mathcal{C}^3$ for the precomputed points, where P' is an intermediate point in the computation of kP. Summarizing, the computation of kP is done by repeating $2^{k_i}P' + P_{W[i-1]} = 2(2^{k_i-1}P') + P_{W[i-1]}$, whose computation time is equal to

$$(k_i - 1)t(2\mathcal{C}^1) + t(2\mathcal{C}^1 = \mathcal{C}^2) + t(\mathcal{C}^2 + \mathcal{C}^3 = \mathcal{C}^1).$$

Let us now discuss suitable coordinate systems for $\mathcal{C}^1, \mathcal{C}^2$, and $\mathcal{C}^3$. Since doublings in $\mathcal{C}^1$ are repeated the most frequently, we should choose $\mathcal{C}^1$ such that $t(2\mathcal{C}^1)$ is the fastest, hence we set $\mathcal{C}^1$ equal to $\mathcal{J}^m$.

We now look at the coordinates suitable for $\mathcal{C}^2$ and $\mathcal{C}^3$. In this case, we must also consider the computation time necessary for constructing the table of precomputed points, which requires addition routines. For those, Table 1 says that

$$t(\mathcal{J}^c + \mathcal{J}^c) < t(\mathcal{A} + \mathcal{A}) \iff 9M + 2S < I, \qquad (12)$$

where $t(\mathcal{J}^c + \mathcal{J}^c)$ is the fastest of all addition routines with no inversions and a fixed coordinate system. ¿From equation (12), the optimal coordinate system depends on the relative speed of inversion. Roughly speaking, when the relative speed of I to M is fast, we use affine coordinates as $\mathcal{C}^3$. When the relative speed of I to M is slow, we use Chudnovsky Jacobian coordinates as $\mathcal{C}^3$. In the next section, we first discuss each case generally, and then investigate the ratio of I to M in the case where k has 160-bits, 192-bits, and 224-bits.

3.4   Precomputed Points in Affine Coordinates

We assume here that we choose $\mathcal{C}^3$ to be $\mathcal{A}$. For $\mathcal{C}^2$, we search for the coordinate system such that $t(2\mathcal{J}^m = \mathcal{C}^2) + t(\mathcal{C}^2 + \mathcal{A} = \mathcal{J}^m)$ is as small as possible. From Table 1, we see that both $\mathcal{J}^c$ and $\mathcal{J}$ are suitable choices for $\mathcal{C}^2$. Thus, we choose the simplest system $\mathcal{J}$. To summarize, we set $(\mathcal{C}^1, \mathcal{C}^2, \mathcal{C}^3) = (\mathcal{J}^m, \mathcal{J}, \mathcal{A})$.

To compute the table of precomputed points P_i, we have two methods. We can compute it in the straightforward way, which requires a time of

$$2^{w-1}I + 2^w M + (2^{w-1} + 1)S. \tag{13}$$

Or we can use the well known Montgomery trick of simultaneous inversions: the inverses modulo p of m numbers can be computed in time $I + (3m-3)M$ (see for example [2], Algorithm 10.3.4). We compute $(2P)$, then $(3P, 4P)$, $(5P, 7P, 8P)$,... $((2^{w-2} + 1)P, ..., (2^{w-1} - 1)P, 2^{w-1}P)$, $((2^{w-1} + 1)P, ..., (2^w - 1)P)$, giving a computation time of

$$wI + (5 \cdot 2^{w-1} + 2w - 10)M + (2^{w-1} + 2w - 3)S. \tag{14}$$

This will be almost always less than the time given in Equation (13) (for example, if $w = 4$, it will be the case if $I > 6.3M$). Furthermore the memory size necessary for constructing the table in Montgomery's trick is just the same as that in the above straightforward way. Thus, we will use this method for computing the table.

To compute the first stage of doublings, that is $2^{k_v} P_{W[v]}$, we use the modification discussed in Section 3.3: for example if $W[v] = 1$ we compute

$$t(2^{k_v} P_{W[v]}) = t(\mathcal{A} + \mathcal{A} = \mathcal{J}^m) + (k_v - w - 1)t(2\mathcal{J}^m) + t(2\mathcal{J}^m = \mathcal{J})$$

On the other hand, in the final stage, that is $2^{k_0}(P' + P_{W[0]})$, we use $t(\mathcal{J} + \mathcal{A} = \mathcal{J})$ instead of $t(\mathcal{J} + \mathcal{A} = \mathcal{J}^m)$ if $k_0 = 0$, and otherwise we use $t(2\mathcal{J}^m = \mathcal{J})$ instead of $t(2\mathcal{J}^m)$ as the final doubling.

We now discuss the total computation time. From Equations (11) and (14), the total computation time $T_w^1(n)$ including the time for constructing a table of P_i (i odd, $1 \leq i \leq 2^w - 1$) is equal to

$$T_w^1(n) = wI + (5\cdot 2^{w-1} - 12 + \frac{11}{w+2} + 4u + 8v)M + (2^{w-1} - 6 + \frac{12}{w+2} + 4u + 5v)S, \tag{15}$$

where u is equal to $\sum_{i=0}^{v} k_i$. It is easily shown that the average interval between two windows is 2 bits ([3]). More precisely, one can show that we have approximately $u = n - w/2 + \theta$ and $v = (n - w/2 - \theta)/(w+2)$, where $\theta = 1/2 - 1/(w+2)$. Thus, if we set $n_1 = n - w/2$, $T_w^1(n)$ is approximately given by the following formula:

$$T_w^1(n) = wI + (5 \cdot 2^{w-1} - 7\theta - \frac{13}{2} + 4n_1 + \frac{8}{w+2}(n_1 - \theta))M$$

$$+ (2^{w-1} - 8\theta + 4n_1 + \frac{5}{w+2}(n_1 - \theta))S. \tag{16}$$

3.5   Precomputed Points in Chudnovsky Jacobian Coordinates

We assume here that we choose $\mathcal{C}^3$ to be $\mathcal{J}^c$. For $\mathcal{C}^2$, we search for the coordinate system such that $t(2\mathcal{J}^m = \mathcal{C}^2) + t(\mathcal{C}^2 + \mathcal{J}^c = \mathcal{J}^m)$ is as small as possible. ¿From Table 1, we see that both $\mathcal{J}^c$ and $\mathcal{J}$ are suitable choices for $\mathcal{C}^2$. Thus, we choose the simplest system $\mathcal{J}$. To summarize, we set $(\mathcal{C}^1, \mathcal{C}^2, \mathcal{C}^3) = (\mathcal{J}^m, \mathcal{J}, \mathcal{J}^c)$.

The computation time for constructing a table of P_i (i odd, $1 \leq i \leq 2^w - 1$) is

$$t(2\mathcal{A} = \mathcal{J}^c) + (2^{w-1} - 2)t(\mathcal{J}^c + \mathcal{J}^c) + t(\mathcal{A} + \mathcal{J}^c = \mathcal{J}^c) = (11 \cdot 2^{w-1} - 11)M + (3 \cdot 2^{w-1} + 2)S.$$

The first computation of $2P$ can be done instead using affine coordinates. In this case, the computation time for a table is

$$t(2\mathcal{A}) + (2^{w-1} - 2)t(\mathcal{A} + \mathcal{J}^c = \mathcal{J}^c) + t(\mathcal{A} + \mathcal{A} = \mathcal{J}^c) = I + (2^{w+2} - 9)M + (3 \cdot 2^{w-1} - 1)S.$$

However, this is never optimal if $224 \geq k \geq 100$ so we omit this case.

To compute the first stage of doublings, that is $2^{k_v} P_{W[v]}$, we use the modification discussed in Section 3.3: for example if $W[v] = 1$, we compute

$$t(2^{k_v} P_{W[v]}) = t(\mathcal{A} + \mathcal{J}^c = \mathcal{J}^m) + (k_v - w - 1)t(2\mathcal{J}^m) + t(2\mathcal{J}^m = \mathcal{J})$$

On the other hand, in the final stage of addition, that is $2^{k_0}(P' + P_{W[0]})$, we use $t(\mathcal{J} + \mathcal{J}^c = \mathcal{J})$ instead of $t(\mathcal{J} + \mathcal{J}^c = \mathcal{J}^m)$ if $k_0 = 0$, and otherwise we use $t(2\mathcal{J}^m = \mathcal{J})$ instead of $t(2\mathcal{J}^m)$ as the final doubling.

Here we discuss the total computation amount. We obtain a total computation time $T_w^2(n)$ including the time for constructing a table of P_i (i odd, $1 \leq i \leq 2^w - 1$), given by

$$T_w^2(n) = (11 \cdot 2^{w-1} - 2w - 7 - \frac{4}{w+2} + 4u + (11 - 3/2^{w-1})v)M$$
$$+ (3 \cdot 2^{w-1} - 2w - 1 + \frac{12}{w+2} + 4u + 5v)S. \tag{17}$$

Note that the term $3/2^{w-1}$ comes from the fact that although the P_i for $i > 1$ are in Chudnovsky Jacobian coordinates, P_1 is in affine coordinates so addition with P_1 is faster.

In the same way as in Section 3.4 with $n_1 = n - w/2$, we get approximately

$$T_w^2(n) = (11 \cdot 2^{w-1} - 2w + 8\theta - 9 + 4n_1 + \frac{11 - 3/2^{w-1}}{w+2}(n_1 - \theta))M$$
$$+ (3 \cdot 2^{w-1} - 2w - 8\theta + 5 + 4n_1 + \frac{5}{w+2}(n_1 - \theta))S. \tag{18}$$

4   Time Comparisons Depending on the Ratio I/M

4.1   The Case of $k = 160$ Bits

To fix ideas, we assume here that k has 160 bits and that $S = 0.8M$. In this case, the optimal value of w is equal to 4, u is approximately equal to 158.33, and v is approximately equal to 26.28. We obtain the following results:

1. $I < 30.5M$

   The optimal mixed coordinate system is as in Section 3.4: $(\mathcal{C}^1, \mathcal{C}^2, \mathcal{C}^3) = (\mathcal{J}^m, \mathcal{J}, \mathcal{A})$. In other words, we use affine coordinates for computing the table, modified Jacobian coordinates in the main doublings (i.e. $2^{k_i-1}P'$), and we compute the result of a final doubling (i.e. $2(2^{k_i-1}P')$) using Jacobian coordinates. The computation time is given by $T_4^1(160) = 4I + 1488.4M$ (Equation (15)).

2. $I > 30.5M$

   The optimal mixed coordinate system is as in Section 3.5: $(\mathcal{C}^1, \mathcal{C}^2, \mathcal{C}^3) = (\mathcal{J}^m, \mathcal{J}, \mathcal{J}^c)$. In other words, we use Chudnovsky Jacobian coordinates for computing the table, modified Jacobian coordinate in the main doublings (i.e. $2^{k_i-1}P'$), and we compute the result of a final doubling (i.e. $2(2^{k_i-1}P')$) using Jacobian coordinates. The computation time is given by $T_4^2(160) = 1610.2M$ (Equation (17)).

Let us compare our new method using mixed coordinate systems with the traditional method using a single coordinate system. If we use Jacobian coordinates and addition-subtraction with the window method as above, the computation time for elliptic curve exponentiation is approximately $1869.1M$, which is the best known among projective, Jacobian or Chudnovsky Jacobian coordinate systems. If we use our new modified Jacobian coordinates instead of the Jacobian coordinates, the computation time of elliptic curve exponentiation is improved to approximately $1708.2M$. On the other hand, affine coordinates would be worse. We thus see that the use of modified Jacobian coordinate $\mathcal{J}^m$, together with a clever use of mixed coordinate systems, with a computation time of at most $1610.2M$, gives a very significant improvement.

4.2   The Case of $k = 192$ Bits

We assume here that k has 192 bits and that $S = 0.8M$. In this case, the optimal value of w is equal to 4, u is approximately equal to 190.33, and v is approximately equal to 31.61. We obtain the following results:

1. $I < 33.9M$

   The optimal mixed coordinate system is as in Section 3.4: $(\mathcal{C}^1, \mathcal{C}^2, \mathcal{C}^3) = (\mathcal{J}^m, \mathcal{J}, \mathcal{A})$. The computation time is given by $T_4^1(192) = 4I + 1782.8M$ (Equation (15)).

2. $I > 33.9M$

   The optimal mixed coordinate system is as in Section 3.5: $(\mathcal{C}^1, \mathcal{C}^2, \mathcal{C}^3) = (\mathcal{J}^m, \mathcal{J}, \mathcal{J}^c)$. The computation time is given by $T_4^2(192) = 1918.5M$ (Equation (17)).

Let us compare our new method using mixed coordinate systems with the traditional method using a single coordinate system. If we use Jacobian coordinates and addition-subtraction with the window method as above, the computation time for elliptic curve exponentiation is approximately $2228.6M$. If we use our new modified Jacobian coordinates instead of the Jacobian coordinates, the computation time of elliptic curve exponentiation is improved to approximately $2030.3M$. We thus see that the use of modified Jacobian coordinate $\mathcal{J}^m$, together with a clever use of mixed coordinate systems, with a computation time of at most $1918.5M$, gives a very significant improvement.

4.3   The Case of $k = 224$ Bits

We assume here that k has 224 bits and that $S = 0.8M$. In this case, the optimal value of w is equal to 4 except for the mixed coordinate system of $(\mathcal{C}^1, \mathcal{C}^2, \mathcal{C}^3) = (\mathcal{J}^m, \mathcal{J}, \mathcal{A})$ in Section 3.4. In the case of $(\mathcal{C}^1, \mathcal{C}^2, \mathcal{C}^3) = (\mathcal{J}^m, \mathcal{J}, \mathcal{A})$, the optimal value of w is determined by the relative speed of I to M: if $I > 17.7M$, then $w = 4$, otherwise $w = 5$. Here we assume that w is equal to 4 since $I > 17.7M$ in our implementation. Then u is approximately equal to 222.33, and v is approximately equal to 36.94. We obtain the following results:

1. $I < 37.4M$
   The optimal mixed coordinate system is as in Section 3.4: $(\mathcal{C}^1, \mathcal{C}^2, \mathcal{C}^3) = (\mathcal{J}^m, \mathcal{J}, \mathcal{A})$. The computation time is given by $T_4^1(224) = 4I + 2077.2M$ (Equation (15)).
2. $I > 37.4M$
   The optimal mixed coordinate system is as in Section 3.5: $(\mathcal{C}^1, \mathcal{C}^2, \mathcal{C}^3) = (\mathcal{J}^m, \mathcal{J}, \mathcal{J}^c)$. The computation time is given by $T_4^2(224) = 2226.8M$ (Equation (17)).

Let us compare our new method using mixed coordinate systems with the traditional method using a single coordinate system. If we use Jacobian coordinates and addition-subtraction with the window method as above, the computation time for elliptic curve exponentiation is approximately $2588.1M$. If we use our new modified Jacobian coordinates instead of the Jacobian coordinates, the computation time of elliptic curve exponentiation is improved to approximately $2352.5M$. We thus see that the use of modified Jacobian coordinate $\mathcal{J}^m$, together with a clever use of mixed coordinate systems, with a computation time of at most $2226.8M$, gives a very significant improvement.

5   Implementation

5.1   Elliptic Curves

Elliptic curves $E/\mathbb{F}_p$ with order divisible by a prime of at least 160-bits are secure if the trace of E ([24]) is equal to neither 0 nor 1 ([15,23]). Here we implement two elliptic curves with 160-bit, 192-bit and 224-bit key size.
Elliptic curve E_1 (160-bit key size)

  – a field of definition $\mathbb{F}_{p_1}$: $p_1 = 2^{160} - 2933$

- an elliptic curve E_1: $y^2 = x^3 + a_1 x + b_1$, where
  $a_1 = 2603045587824984789379475768845327827216503225 28$
  $b_1 = 1735363725216656526252983845896885218144335483 52$,
  $\#E_1(\mathbb{F}_{p_1}) = 3 \cdot 5 \cdot 157 \cdot q_1$, where q_1 is a prime
  $q_1 = 620595175087432237029165529381611169224913337$
- a point P_1: $(x_1, y_1) \in E_1(\mathbb{F}_{p_1})$ with order q_1, where
  $x_1 = 1274\ 10436\ 88184\ 50369\ 80533\ 90568\ 22189\ 38631\ 36302\ 30379$
  $y_1 = 572\ 21905\ 85804\ 38390\ 03353\ 99912\ 01426\ 54787\ 42865\ 52166$

Elliptic curve E_2 (192-bit key size)

- a field of definition $\mathbb{F}_{p_2}$: $p_2 = 2^{192} - 3345$
- an elliptic curve E_2: $y^2 = x^3 + a_2 x + b_2$, where
  $a_2 = 4297310835543015216800382740563318937925360220792632159597$
  $b_2 = 2864873890362010144533588493708879291950240147195088106398$,
  $\#E_2(\mathbb{F}_{p_2}) = 5^2 \cdot q_2$, where q_2 is a prime
  $q_2 = 251084069415467230553431576922046178864919281484010333019$
- a point P_2: $(x_2, y_2) \in E_2(\mathbb{F}_{p_2})$ with order q_2, where
  $x_2 = 523\ 46903\ 86238\ 76826\ 11193\ 52046\ 88411\ 23614\ 71708\ 15234$
  $y_2 = 23\ 91039\ 55423\ 03027\ 66388\ 76206\ 81604\ 62176\ 43806\ 46680$

Elliptic curve E_3 (224-bit key size)

- a field of definition $\mathbb{F}_{p_3}$: $p_3 = 2^{224} - 1025$
- an elliptic curve E_3: $y^2 = x^3 + a_3 x + b_3$, where
  $a_3 = 12404576574124969701442337182895859753361802999610504592418729761688$
  $b_3 = 9703580062017113395483118602749180613516894281953378592456586991002$,
  $\#E_3(\mathbb{F}_{p_3}) = 69 \cdot q_3$, where q_3 is a prime
  $q_3 = 390723864741313620212565436043762777712823516673432244734573782061$
- a point P_3: $(x_3, y_3) \in E_3(\mathbb{F}_{p_3})$ with order q_3, where
  $x_3 = 24976530810051270927037584984009121071093885269663350011731968108524$
  $y_3 = 84130267739323594344612082059586609672896599366392331321934278 28113$

5.2   The Running Time

We present the running times of elliptic curve exponentiation over our 160-bit and 192-bit field of definition using our methods. We compare each strategy of Section 3.4 with the traditional method using a single coordinate. Our modulo arithmetic uses the GNU MP Library GMP ([7]), so as to make easy comparisons possible, since GMP may well be the most popular multiprecision library. The platform is an UltraSPARC (143 MHz/Solaris 2.4). Table 2 shows the running times. We see that our new strategy gives a very significant improvement.

6   Conclusion

In this paper, we have introduced modified Jacobian coordinates $\mathcal{J}^m$, which offer the fastest doubling of all known coordinate systems. The new modified Jacobian

	160 bit key	192 bit key	224 bit key
field operations (μsec)			
160/192/224 bit addition	0.59	0.64	0.71
160/192/224 bit multiplication	6.50	8.93	12.00
160/192/224 bit squaring	5.35	7.22	9.01
reduction ($320/384/448 \rightarrow 160/192/224$ bit)	2.37	2.77	2.62
160/192/224 bit inverse	166	213	261
elliptic curve operations (msec)			
addition ($t(\mathcal{A} + \mathcal{A})$)	0.203	0.257	0.314
addition ($t(\mathcal{J}^c + \mathcal{J}^c)$)	0.130	0.171	0.215
addition ($t(\mathcal{J} + \mathcal{J})$)	0.144	0.191	0.239
doubling ($t(2\mathcal{J}^m)$)	0.079	0.103	0.127
doubling ($t(2\mathcal{J})$)	0.094	0.122	0.148
elliptic curve exponentiation (msec)			
mixed coordinates (case 1)	16.17	24.93	35.73
mixed coordinates (case 2)	16.66	25.54	37.53
single coordinate (Jacobian coordinate)	18.66	28.79	41.86
single coordinate (projective coordinate)	20.33	30.17	44.79

Table 2. Times for elliptic curve operations (UltraSPARC)

coordinates improve the computation time of 160-bit elliptic curve exponentiation to approximately $1708.2M$ even with the traditional method which uses a single coordinate system: the use of modified Jacobian coordinates reduces the computation time of the best known method by 9%.

Furthermore we have proposed a new method using mixed coordinate systems, which divides elliptic curve exponentiation into three parts, and in each part we choose the optimal system. For these choices we have presented three cases according to the relative speed of inversion to multiplication over $\mathbb{F}_p$. We have seen that the use of modified Jacobian coordinates together with a clever use of mixed coordinate systems, having a computation time of at most $1610.2M$, gives a very significant improvement. Our new strategy with modified Jacobian coordinates reduces the computation time of the best known method by more than 14%.

References

1. D. V. Chudnovsky and G. V. Chudnovsky "Sequences of numbers generated by addition in formal groups and new primality and factorization tests" *Advances in Applied Math.*, **7** (1986), 385–434.
2. H. Cohen, "A course in computational algebraic number theory", Graduate Texts in Math. **138**, Springer-Verlag, 1993, Third corrected printing, 1996.
3. H. Cohen, A. Miyaji and T. Ono, "Efficient elliptic curve exponentiation", *Advances in Cryptology-Proceedings of ICICS'97*, Lecture Notes in Computer Science, **1334** (1997), Springer-Verlag, 282–290.
4. G. Frey and H. G. Rück, "A remark concerning m-divisibility and the discrete logarithm in the divisor class group of curves", *Mathematics of computation*, **62**(1994), 865-874.
5. "Proposed federal information processing standard for digital signature standard (DSS)", *Federal Register*, **56** No. 169, 30 Aug 1991, 42980–42982.
6. T. ElGamal, "A public key cryptosystem and a signature scheme based on discrete logarithms", *IEEE Trans. Inform. Theory*, **IT-31** (1985), 469–472.
7. Torbjorn Granlund, The GNU MP LIBRARY, version 2.0.2, June 1996. ftp://prep.ai.mit.edu/pub/gnu/gmp-2.0.2.tar.gz
8. Jorge Guajardo and Christof Paar "Efficient algorithms for elliptic curve cryptosystems", *Advances in Cryptology-Proceedings of Crypto'97*, Lecture Notes in Computer Science, **1294** (1997), Springer-Verlag, 342–356.
9. G. Harper, A. Menezes and S. Vanstone, "Public-key cryptosystems with very small key lengths", *Advances in Cryptology-Proceedings of Eurocrypt'92*, Lecture Notes in Computer Science, **658** (1993), Springer-Verlag, 163–173.
10. *IEEE P1363 Working Draft*, June 16, 1998.
11. D. E. Knuth, *The art of computer programming, vol. 2, Seminumerical Algorithms*, 2nd ed., Addison-Wesley, Reading, Mass. 1981.
12. N. Koblitz, "Elliptic curve cryptosystems", *Mathematics of Computation*, **48** (1987), 203–209.
13. N. Koblitz, "CM-curves with good cryptographic properties", *Advances in Cryptology-Proceedings of CRYPTO'91*, Lecture Notes in Computer Science, **576** (1992), Springer-Verlag, 279–287.
14. K. Koyama and Y. Tsuruoka, "Speeding up elliptic cryptosystems by using a signed binary window method", *Advances in Cryptology-Proceedings of Crypto'92*, Lecture Notes in Computer Science, **740** (1993), Springer-Verlag, 345–357.
15. A. Menezes, T. Okamoto and S. Vanstone, "Reducing elliptic curve logarithms to logarithms in a finite field", *Proceedings of the 22nd Annual ACM Symposium on the Theory of Computing* (1991), 80–89.
16. V. S. Miller, "Use of elliptic curves in cryptography", *Advances in Cryptology-Proceedings of Crypto'85*, Lecture Notes in Computer Science, **218** (1986), Springer-Verlag, 417–426.
17. F. Morain and J. Olivos, "Speeding up the computations on an elliptic curve using addition-subtraction chains", *Theoretical Informatics and Applications* **24** No.6 (1990), 531–544.
18. S. C. Pohlig and M. E. Hellman, "An improved algorithm for computing logarithms over $GF(p)$ and its cryptographic significance", *IEEE Trans. Inf. Theory*, **IT-24** (1978), 106–110.
19. J. Pollard, "Monte Carlo methods for index computation (mod p)", *Mathematics of Computation*, **32** (1978), 918–924.

20. R. Rivest, A. Shamir and L. Adleman, "A method for obtaining digital signatures and public-key cryptosystems", *Communications of the ACM*, **21** No. 2 (1978), 120–126.
21. T. Satoh and K. Araki "Fermat quotients and the polynomial time discrete log algorithm for anomalous elliptic curves", *Commentarii Math. Univ. St. Pauli.*, vol. **47** (1998), 81-92.
22. R. Schroeppel, H. Orman, S. O'Malley and O. Spatscheck, "Fast key exchange with elliptic curve systems", *Advances in Cryptology-Proceedings of Crypto'95*, Lecture Notes in Computer Science, **963** (1995), Springer-Verlag, 43–56.
23. I. A. Semaev "Evaluation of discrete logarithms in a group of p-torsion points of an elliptic curve in characteristic p", *Mathematics of computation*, **67** (1998), 353-356.
24. J. H. Silverman, *The Arithmetic of Elliptic Curves*, GTM **106**, Springer-Verlag, New York, 1986.
25. N. P. Smart "The discrete logarithm problem on elliptic curves of trace one", to appear in J. Cryptology.
26. Jerome A. Solinas "An improved algorithm for arithmetic on a family of elliptic curves", *Advances in Cryptology-Proceedings of Crypto'97*, Lecture Notes in Computer Science, **1294** (1997), Springer-Verlag, 357–371.
27. E. D. Win, A. Bosselaers and S. Vandenberghe "A fast software implementation for arithmetic operations in $GF(2^n)$", *Advances in Cryptology-Proceedings of Asiacrypt'95*, Lecture Notes in Computer Science, **1163** (1996), Springer-Verlag, 65–76.

Efficient Implementation of Schoof's Algorithm

Tetsuya Izu, Jun Kogure, Masayuki Noro, and Kazuhiro Yokoyama

FUJITSU LABORATORIES LTD., 4-1-1 Kamikodanaka
Nakahara-ku Kawasaki 211-8588, Japan
{izu, kogure}@flab.fujitsu.co.jp, {noro, yokoyama}@para.flab.fujitsu.co.jp

Abstract. Schoof's algorithm is used to find a secure elliptic curve for cryptosystems, as it can compute the number of rational points on a randomly selected elliptic curve defined over a finite field. By realizing efficient combination of several improvements, such as Atkin-Elkies's method, the isogeny cycles method, and trial search by match-and-sort techniques, we can count the number of rational points on an elliptic curve over $GF(p)$ in a reasonable time, where p is a prime whose size is around 240-bits.

1 Introduction

When we use the elliptic curve cryptosystem [9,17] (ECC for short), we first have to define an elliptic curve over a finite field. Then, all cryptographic operations will be performed on the group of rational points on the curve. Since all the curves are not necessarily secure, we should be very careful when we choose an elliptic curve for ECC. There are several methods to select a curve for ECC, such as Schoof's method [22], CM(Complex Multiplication) method [2,18,10,3], and so on. The security of an elliptic curve for ECC depends mainly on the "cardinality" of the curve (the number of rational points on the curve or the order of the group of rational points on the curve). For example, the cardinality should have a large prime factor to guard against Pohlig-Hellman's attack. Recent studies [16,27,21] on special curves, supersingular curves and anomalous curves, suggest that there might exist certain efficient attacks on those curves using their speciality. From this point of view, Schoof's method is believed best to obtain most secure elliptic curves for ECC, as it can compute the cardinality of a randomly selected curve. Moreover, there are heuristic but strong evidence that random search on curves can find certainly good ones with prime cardinality. (See [11].)

Schoof's algorithm was not efficient in its original form. Thanks to the contributions of many people, such as Atkin[1], Elkies[7], Morain[19], Couveignes[6], Lercier[14], and so on, the algorithm became remarkably faster. In the process of computing the cardinality of a given curve, we can combine several improvements on Schoof's algorithm, such as Atkin-Elkies' method, Lercier's method, and the isogeny cycles method. However, as far as the authors know, there were no explicit criteria that give a good combination of these improvements as subprocedures.

K. Ohta and D. Pei (Eds.): ASIACRYPT'98, LNCS 1514, pp. 66–79, 1998.

The purpose of this paper is to develop an explicit criterion by introducing several new strategies. In more detail, we introduce an "intelligent choice system" on several subprocedures based on estimate of the costs of them, and investigate its effects by practical experiments. By our implementation, one can count the cardinality of one curve for ECC corresponding to the RSA with 1024bit moduli within about one minutes in average on a PC with Pentium II 300MHz CPU. And the average time for counting the cardinality suggests that its complexity is $O(\log(p)^{5\pm\epsilon})$ for some $\epsilon \ll 1$. Thus, incorporated with the "early abort" strategy [13], Schoof's method is recommended, as a practical one, to find good secure curves.

In the following sections, we consider curves over fields of odd characteristic. The proposed strategy/methods, however, can be applied *independent* of the characteristics of the base field. In section 2, we will briefly look over the improvements of Atkin-Elkies. In section 3, we will introduce new improvements and show an explicit criterion. In section 4, we will give our experimental results to show our improvements are actually efficient.

2   Overview of Previous Works

Let p be an odd prime. We will consider an elliptic curve E defined over the finite field $GF(p)$ of order p: $E : y^2 = x^3 + Ax + B$, where $A, B \in GF(p)$ with $4A^3 + 27B^2 \neq 0 \pmod{p}$. For the mathematical background, see [15,25,26].

2.1   Schoof's Algorithm

First we will briefly recall the Schoof's algorithm [22]. We denote the subgroup of ℓ-torsion points of E by $E[\ell]$ for a prime ℓ. The *Frobenius endomorphism* $\phi : (x, y) \rightarrow (x^p, y^p)$ of E is also defined on Tate module $T_\ell(E)$ as a linear map and satisfies the equation: $\phi^2 - t\phi + p = 0$, where t is the *trace* of the Frobenius map which does not depend on ℓ. Then

$$\#E(GF(p)) = p + 1 - t . \tag{1}$$

If we find an integer t_ℓ such that

$$\phi^2(P) + pP = t_\ell \phi(P) \tag{2}$$

for any $P \in E[\ell]$, we get $t \equiv t_\ell \pmod{\ell}$. By Hasse's theorem, t must satisfy $-2\sqrt{p} \leq t \leq 2\sqrt{p}$. Therefore if we compute $t \bmod \ell$ for various small primes until their product exceeds $4\sqrt{p}$, we can uniquely determine the cardinality of the curve by means of the Chinese Remainder Theorem. By the theory of prime distribution, the largest prime ℓ necessary to find t is bounded by $O(\log(p))$.

We denote the ℓ-th *division polynomial* by f_ℓ, whose degree is $(\ell^2-1)/2$ for $\ell \geq 3$, and which vanishes precisely on the x-coordinates of the ℓ-torsion points. As we compute (2) in the ring $GF(p)[x, y]/(y^2-x^3-Ax-B, f_\ell(x))$, the dominant steps is the computation of x^p and y^p in that ring. From this, the complexity of this algorithm will be $O(\log^8(p))$.

2.2   Atkin-Elkies' Improvement (SEA)

Elkies' idea [7,23] is to make use of a degree $(\ell - 1)/2$ factor g_ℓ of f_ℓ when it is possible to compute g_ℓ in $GF(p)[x]$. (In this case, ℓ is called an *Elkies prime*. Otherwise ℓ is called an *Atkin prime*). The factor g_ℓ represents an eigenspace of the Frobenius map ϕ, which can be computed as a kernel of an isogeny map. Thus, $t \bmod \ell$ is calculated by the eigenvalue of the eigenspace. As the ratio of Elkies primes is expected $1/2$, this method will reduce the complexity to $O(\log^6(p))$. Rather than determining the unique value of $t \bmod \ell$, Atkin [1,23] obtained certain restrictions on the value. Then the real value of t is found among a lot of candidates by, for example, the match-and-sort technique [12].

The Schoof-Elkies-Atkin(SEA) method is obtained by combining the above two and so it is consisting of two stages, namely, (I) *collecting information stage* and (II) *trial search stage*:

SEA
(I) Collecting informations on $t \bmod \ell$ for various ℓ's until $\prod \ell > 4\sqrt{p}$:

   (i) Compute the modular polynomial $\Phi_\ell(x, j)$.
   (ii) Check if $\bar{\Phi}(x) = \Phi_\ell(x, j(E)) \bmod p$ has a root in $GF(p)$.
      (ii-E) If $\bar{\Phi}(x)$ has a root in $GF(p)$ (we call ℓ an Elkies prime)
         calculate $t_\ell = t \bmod \ell$ using g_ℓ.
      (ii-A) Otherwise (we call ℓ an Atkin prime)
         calculate possible values of $t \bmod \ell$. We denote the set of possible values
         of $t \bmod \ell$ by $\mathcal{T}_\ell$.

The set of Elkies primes is represented by $\mathcal{E}$, and the set of Atkin primes is represented by $\mathcal{A}$.

(II) Determining the value of t by trial search:
   Now, there are candidates T for the value of t, where

$$T \bmod \ell = t_\ell \text{ for } \ell \in \mathcal{E}, \quad \text{and} \quad T \bmod \ell \in \mathcal{T}_\ell \text{ for } \ell \in \mathcal{A}.$$

The value of t is (uniquely) determined by trial search, that is, by testing if $(p + 1 - T)P = \mathcal{O}$ for each candidate T, where P is a sample rational point of E and $\mathcal{O}$ is the point of infinity, and this test is efficiently executed by the match-and-sort technique.

2.3   Isogeny Cycles Method

According to Morain *et al.* [5,6], $t \bmod \ell^2$, $t \bmod \ell^3, \dots$ can be computed efficiently when ℓ is an Elkies prime. In the method, a factor g_{ℓ^k} of the ℓ^k-th division polynomial f_{ℓ^k} is computed, where the degree of g_{ℓ^k} is at most $\ell^{k-1}(\ell - 1)/2$. The isogeny cycles method is designed as a practical improvement to SEA, and so the following shall be modified: In (I), we replace $\prod \ell$ with $\prod \ell^k$ and in (II) $T \bmod \ell^k = t_{\ell^k}$ for each $\ell \in \mathcal{E}$, where k depends on each Elkies prime ℓ. For practical implementations and improvements, see [5,6].

From now on, we will consider methods based on SEA with the isogeny cycles method. Thus, we will gather informations of $t \bmod \ell^k$ for some $k > 0$ in the stage (I) and we call the product of all primes or prime powers whose informations will be used in the trial search stage (II) the `counter`. So, when `counter` exceeds $4\sqrt{p}$ in the stage (I), we enter the next stage (II).

3   Intelligent Choice System

In implementation of SEA with the isogeny cycles method, the following choices are very important for the total efficiency;

1. decision whether to apply the isogeny cycles method for $t \bmod \ell^k$ or not, when we find an Elkies prime ℓ,
2. decision whether to compute the candidates for the value of t or just abandon it, when we find an Atkin prime, and
3. the setting on `counter` and usage of informations with respect to Atkin primes.

To give an efficient choice in various situations, and to optimize the total computation, we have to examine how the total efficiency will be changed for each choice. From this point, the estimate (guess) of the computational cost shall be very helpful. Here, as an attempt for this optimization, we will propose new strategies, usage of the estimate of costs to make an "efficient choice" at each step and systematic treatment of Atkin primes. We call the total system with these strategies an *intelligent choice system*. Of course, we can incorporate strategies in previous works into our system, as those were proposed to improve the efficiency of *each* subprocedure (method). (See Remark 2 (1).) Here we note that to make our approach effective, estimates should correspond to the real costs precisely, which requires "efficient implementation" of each operation.

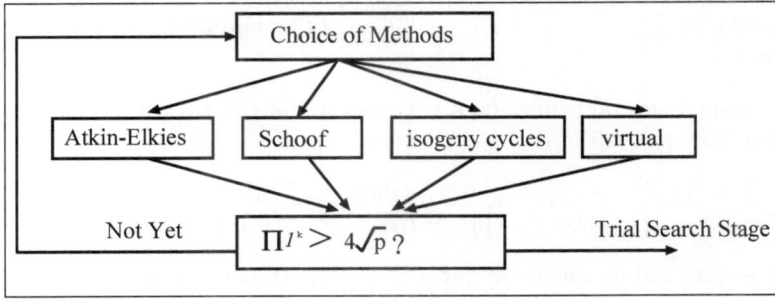

Fig. 1. The diagram of choice of methods

So far we have three methods (categories) to get the information on $t \bmod \ell^k$:

(a) *Schoof's original algorithm*, i.e. finding $t \bmod \ell$ in (2) for $P \in E[\ell]$,
(b) *Atkin-Elkies' method*, i.e. the part (I-ii) of SEA for ℓ, and
(c) *the isogeny cycles method* for ℓ^k.

Now we add *virtual methods* to take a shortcut to the trial search stage (II), which we call *virtual Atkin and virtual isogeny cycles method*.

3.1   Shortcut to the Trial Search Stage

In the stage (I), to make good use of Atkin primes ℓ, we allow candidates for $t \bmod \ell$ as information on t. Thus, in the stage (II), we search a correct value of t among all candidates constructed from informations in the stage (I). And it takes $O(\sqrt{N_C})$ additions of points on the curve, where N_C denotes the total number of candidates, by most efficient algorithm (match-and-sort/baby-step-giant-step algorithm). If N_C gets too large, the search will take much time. Therefore we set an upper limit to the total number of candidates, which we denote by CanMAX. We define CanMAX from experiments according to the size of p based on the complexity for doing match-and-sort algorithm. In "lucky" cases, we enter the stage (II) with much smaller N_C than CanMAX. In this case, by introducing *virtual methods*, we can take a shortcut to the stage (II).

From now on, $\mathcal{T}_{\ell^k}$ denotes the set of candidates for $t \bmod \ell^k$, which is obtained by Schoof's original method, Atkin-Elkies' method or the isogeny cycles method.

Virtual (Atkin/Isogeny Cycles) Method: Suppose that $\mathcal{T}_{\ell^k}$ is already computed. (For $k = 0$, we have no information on mod ℓ.) If a prime ℓ satisfies the following three conditions, we regard the candidates for $t \bmod \ell^{k+j}$ for some $j > 0$ as $\mathcal{T}_{\ell^{k+j}} = \{a + b\ell^k | a \in \mathcal{T}_{\ell^k}, 0 \le b \le \ell^j - 1\}$.

(i) For primes $\ell_1, \ldots, \ell_s$, we have already computed $\mathcal{T}_{\ell_i^{k_i}}$ and $4\sqrt{p} > \text{counter}$,

   i.e. $4\sqrt{p} > (\prod_{1 \le i \le s; \ell_i \ne \ell} \ell_i^{k_i}) \times \ell^k$.

(ii) $4\sqrt{p} < (\prod_{1 \le i \le s; \ell_i \ne \ell} \ell_i^{k_i}) \times \ell^{k+j}$. (The updated counter exceeds $4\sqrt{p}$.)

(iii) CanMAX $> (\prod_{1 \le i \le s; \ell_i \ne \ell} \#\mathcal{T}_{\ell^{k_i}}) \times \#\mathcal{T}_{\ell^{k+j}}$. (The updated N_C does not exceed CanMAX.)

We can consider several primes ℓ_m's at the same time. In this case, we can replace the inequalities (ii), (iii) with

(iia) $4\sqrt{p} < (\prod_i \ell_i^{k_i}) \times (\prod_m \ell_m^{k_m + j_m})$, where $\ell_i \ne \ell_m$.
(iiia) CanMAX $> (\prod_i \#\mathcal{T}_{\ell^{k_i}}) \times (\prod_m \#\mathcal{T}_{\ell^{k_m + j_m}})$, where $\ell_i \ne \ell_m$.

By this, we can reduce the candidates as well as the operations in the search.

3.2   Choice of Methods Based on Estimate of the Complexity

Now we have four methods to get the information on $t \bmod \ell^k$: (a) Schoof's original algorithm, (b) Atkin-Elkies' method, (c) the isogeny cycles method, and

(d) the virtual method. In each step we should be careful in choosing one of these method, as the choice will effect the total time of computations. For example, when counter is very close to $4\sqrt{p}$, it might be more efficient to compute t mod ℓ^k for a small Elkies prime ℓ, rather than to compute t mod ℓ for a large prime ℓ. Thus, as for the isogeny cycles method, it is very important to decide when we apply it and which prime we use.

Estimate of the Complexity: Here, we propose a simple strategy where we will estimate the complexity of each method and choose the most efficient one and a prime ℓ as a most efficient systematic choice. As a simple but practical example, we construct the following "complexity estimate function" by estimating the dominating computations. (We count the number of arithmetic operations over $GF(p)$.) For simplicity, we only deal with t mod ℓ^2 in the isogeny cycles case and assume that $\ell \ll \log(p)$. The function is very simple, but it works very well for actual computation. (See Section 4.2.) In the implementation we fix each *weight* $w_s, w_a, w_{i,1}, w_{i,2}, w_{i,3}$ to fit the actual computation. Here we denote by $M(n)$ the time needed to compute the product of two polynomials of degree n.

Complexity Estimate Function (Weights $w_s, w_a, w_{i,1}, w_{i,2}, w_{i,3}$ are positive numbers.)

(a) In Schoof's (original) algorithm case, we estimate its complexity at
    $w_s M((\ell^2-1)/2) \log(p)$ for a prime ℓ.
(b) In Atkin-Elkies' method case, we estimate its complexity at
    $w_a M(\ell+1) \log(p)$ for a prime ℓ.
(c) In the isogeny cycles method case, we estimate its complexity at
    $w_{i,1} M(U) \log(p) + w_{i,2} M(\ell+1) \log(p) + w_{i,3} M((\ell-1)/2) \log((\ell-1)/2) \log(p)$
    for an Elkies prime ℓ, where U is the degree of a factor g_{ℓ^2} of f_{ℓ^2} that is used in computing t mod ℓ^2.
(d) If we can apply the virtual method, i.e. three conditions for the virtual method is satisfied, we estimate its complexity at 0. Otherwise, we estimate its complexity at ∞.

We explain the above estimate briefly. In each method, its dominant step is the computation of $h_0(x)^p$ mod $h(x)$ or that of $h_0(x)^{(p-1)/2}$ mod $h(x)$ for polynomials h_0, h. In more detail, $h_0 = x, y(= x^3+ax+b)$ and $h = f_\ell$ for (a), and $h_0 = x$ and $h = \Phi_\ell(x, j(E))$ for (b). For (c), $h_0 = x$ and $h = \Phi_\ell(x, j(E/C))$, $h_0 = x$ and $h = g_{\ell^2}$, and randomly chosen h_0 and $h = \hat{g}_\ell$. (See Lemma 1 for E/C and $\hat{g}_\ell$.) By the experimental analysis in [14] and our experiment, these steps amount to more than 2/3 of the total time, which shall support the validity of the function.

In (a) we assume that we apply Schoof's original method to smaller ℓ and so the computation of $\phi(P)$ is dominant. (See Remark 2 (3).)

In (b) we count only the cost to check if $\Phi_\ell(x, j(E))$ has a root in $GF(p)$. If ℓ is an Atkin prime and we execute Atkin's method, i.e. (ii-A) in SEA, additional cost does not effect the total cost so much. But, if ℓ is an Elkies prime and we execute Elkies' method, i.e. (ii-E) in SEA, additional computations, the computation of

$\phi(P)$ and finding the eigenvalues, have certain effect on the total cost. See the paragraph Further Discussion on Practical Choice for more precise estimate.

In (c) the degree U is guessed by the following lemma used in [6], which can be shown easily by seeing the action of the Galois group.

Lemma 1 *Suppose that ℓ is an odd Elkies prime and g_ℓ corresponds to an eigenspace C of ϕ in $E[\ell]$ with eigenvalue s_0. Let d_0 be the order of s_0 in the multiplicative group $GF(\ell)^*$ and set $d = d_0/\gcd(2, d_0)$. Then, g_ℓ has a factor of degree d over $GF(p)$ and so its corresponding polynomial $\hat{g}_\ell$ with respect to the isogeny curve E/C, has also a factor of degree d over $GF(p)$. Moreover, f_{ℓ^2} has a factor g_{ℓ^2} of degree ℓd over $GF(p)$, which can be used for computing $t \bmod \ell^2$.*

In the computation of $\phi(P)$, the step $x^p \bmod g_{\ell^2}$ is dominant. (See Section 4.1.) In the computation of $\hat{g}_\ell$, the step $x^p \bmod \Phi_\ell(x, j(E/C))$ is dominant, and in the computation of a factor of $\hat{g}_\ell$, the steps $h_1^{(p-1)/2} \bmod \hat{g}_\ell$ are dominant, where h_1 are randomly chosen polynomials. See [24] for details of factoring polynomials.

Remark 2 (1) By the isogeny cycles method, we can compute $t \bmod \ell^k$ exactly, however, its cost tends large compared with Atkin-Elkies' method for the same ℓ. So its arrangement is very important. In existing works, the isogeny cycles method was considered as an option to Elkies primes, and it is applied for ℓ just after Elkies' method was executed for the same ℓ ([14]). (The power k for ℓ^k is also decided at this step.) But, for primes $\ell_1 < \ell_2$, there are many cases where the cost for $t \bmod \ell_1^2$ by the isogeny cycles method exceeds that for $t \bmod \ell_2$ by Atkin-Elkies' method. Moreover, for Elkies primes $\ell_1 < \ell_2$, the cost for $t \bmod \ell_1^2$ is not always smaller than that for $t \bmod \ell_2^2$. (See Lemma 1.)

(2) The condition for the virtual method shall depend on the cost of search in the stage (II). To guarantee the efficiency of the intelligent choice system, the current setting is derived from an assumption that the cost of search among CanMAX candidates corresponds to that of Atkin-Elkies' method just before closing the stage (I).

(3) As a common strategy for Schoof's original algorithm, we apply it only for small primes and so we set a bound on the largest prime for which Schoof's original algorithm can be applied. Then, the estimated cost for Schoof's original algorithm for large primes become ∞ in the intelligent choice system.

Examples 3 Here we demonstrate the detail of actual computation by examples. We select typical examples for which virtual methods work well. In the below, series of triples represent the trace of computation, where each triple consists of the selected method, the selected prime, and the actual cost (in seconds). For simplicity, we write **a,e,i** for Atkin's method, Elkies' method and the isogeny cycles method, respectively. (In the implementation, we computed $t \bmod 2$ by checking if E has a rational point of order 2. Thus, each series begins with $\ell = 3$.) Let $p = 2^{155} + 15$ and E defined by $y^2 = x^3 + ax + b$.

(1)

$(a, b) = (1, 5)$:
[e,3,0.1], [a,5,0.1], [i,3,0.11], [e,7,0.26], [e,11,0.51], [e,13,0.56], [i,7,0.4],
[e,17,1.05], [e,19,1.05], [i,11,0.83], [a,23,1.31], [i,13,1.66], [a,29,1.84],
[e,31,2.75], [i,17,2.4], [e,37,3.5], [e,41,4.99], [e,43,5.23]

Then, the virtual method was applied with the following setting: $2 \to 2^4$, $3 \to 3^2$, $7^2 \to 7^3$, $11^2 \to 11^3$. The trial search took 1.67 seconds.
(2) $(a, b) = (1, 64)$:

    [e,3,0.18], [e,5,0.18], [i,3,0.12], [e,7,0.25], [i,5,0.25], [a,11,0.32], [e,13,0.55], [e,17,0.92], [a,19,0.73], [a,23,1.32], [i,13,1.25], [e,29,2.55], [i,7,0.97], [a,31,2.09], [i,17,2], [e,37,3.49], [a,41,3.59], [e,43,5.32], [a,47,4.33]

Then, the virtual method was applied with the following setting: $2 \to 2^3$, $3^2 \to 3^3$, $5^2 \to 5^3$, The trial search took 1.04 seconds.

Further Discussion on Practical Choice: Here we proposed a strategy based on complexity estimate as a practical optimization. But, from precise analysis, it might be better to use the following "contribution index" instead of the complexity estimate function.

1. **Contribution Index:** On the choice of methods, the "gain" in counter must be taken into account. (Informations for large moduli shall contribute much more than those for small moduli.) As a realization of such "contribution", we may set the *contribution index* for each method by

$$\frac{\text{the estimate of the complexity}}{\text{the gain in counter}}.$$

We can give a precise argument on the gain. As for Atkin-Elkies' method with a prime ℓ, if ℓ is an Elkies prime, then the gain is exactly ℓ, however, if ℓ is an Atkin prime, the gain varies according to the number of candidates of $t \bmod \ell$ and the amount of already computed candidates. So, we might compute the "expected gain" by taking the probabilities into account. (See Section 3.3 for usage of Atkin primes.)
2. **Cost of Virtual Method:** We can give a "more reasonable" estimate to the cost of the virtual method. As the virtual method has much influence on searching the real value of t, it is better to add the estimate of the cost of search to the original estimate, and to compare it with the expected total cost for the case where we do not apply the virtual method.

By our experiment, there is little difference between the original complexity estimate function and the contribution index for 300 curves over $GF(2^{160}+7)$. So, "simple estimate of the cost" seems work well for curves over finite fields of 160-240 bits order. But, to deal with curves over larger finite fields, we have to consider a precise contribution index function to make the intelligent choice system efficient. As for the cost of the virtual method, we could not have any practical experiment due to the hardness to estimate actual costs of search by the match-and-sort technique. This shall be done in the future work.

3.3   Re-ordering Atkin Primes

When Atkin-Elkies' method is chosen, we check whether $\Phi_\ell(x, j(E))$ has a root in $GF(p)$ from $\gcd(x^p-x, \Phi_\ell(x, j(E)))$. Thus, we computed $x^p \pmod{\Phi_\ell(x, j(E))}$

for this check. If $\Phi_\ell(x, j(E))$ has not such a root, i.e. ℓ is an Atkin prime, then the candidates of $t \bmod \ell$ are computed from the distinct degree decomposition (DDD). Once we have $x^p \pmod{\Phi_\ell(x, j(E))}$, we can compute the DDD very efficiently and so the computation $x^p \pmod{\Phi_\ell(x, j(E))}$ is the dominant step in this case. But, to improve the total efficiency, there proposed a strategy that we do not execute any additional computation for Atkin primes when the total number N_C of candidates of t exceeds CanMAX.

Here, we propose a new strategy "re-ordering" that even if N_C exceeds CanMAX, we do not give up using new Atkin primes. A "good" Atkin prime is the one, which itself is fairly large and the number of whose candidates for t is small. We define "Atkin index" of an Atkin prime ℓ as:

$$\frac{\text{the number of candidates for the value } t}{\ell}.$$

In this context, Atkin primes of smaller index can be used more efficiently for the computation. When we find a new Atkin prime and N_C exceeds CanMAX, we look for "worse" Atkin primes and replace them with the new "better" one so that N_C does not exceed CanMAX. In good cases we can proceed to the trial search stage without further computations.

Examples 4 We consider the case where $p = 2^{160} + 7$, $E : y^2 = x^3 + x + 8$ and CanMAX $= 10^8$. In this case, successive 7 primes from $\ell = 59$ are Atkin primes and N_C exceeds CanMAX at $\ell = 71$. However, by "re-ordering", counter exceeds $4\sqrt{p}$ at $\ell = 79$ with $N_C = 47185920$. By the notation in Example 3, the following presents the record of computation:

[a,3,0.05], [a,5,0.09], [e,7,0.21], [a,11,0.29], [a,13,0.39], [e,17,0.99],
[a,19,0.78], [a,23,1.25], [e,29,2.86], [e,31,2.79], [e,37,3.74], [e,41,5.77],
[a,43,4.61], [a,47,5.6], [e,53,7.82], [a,59,7.14], [a,61,8.2], [a,67,12.05],
[a,71,14.49], [a,73,14.71], [a,79,13.91]

On the other hand, without "re-ordering", we have to search the next Elkies prime, which will be found at $\ell = 89$. Thus, the computation becomes 1.3 times slower.

Remark 5 The "re-ordering" strategy for Atkin primes obliges us to execute additional computation even for "bad" Atkin primes. But, this fact supports the validity of the complexity estimate function, because the difference between the cost for Elkies' method and that for Atkin's method for the same size prime becomes smaller.

4   Implementation and Experiment

We have implemented the intelligent choice system using Risa/Asir computer algebra system [20] developed by FUJITSU Labs. We examined its ability and efficiency by experiment on number of examples. We set $w_s = \infty$, $w_a = 1$, $w_{i,1} = w_{i,2} = 2$, $w_{i,3} = 0$, and $M(n) = n^2$. Although we used efficient multiplication techniques, where $M(n) = O(n^{1.6})$, the function gives reasonable choices for our examples. For the experiment, we pre-computed "canonical" modular polynomials [19] up to $\ell = 229$.

4.1   Details in Implementation

Here, we explain the following important operations.

Multiplication and Powering: The SEA algorithm spends most of the time for multiplications of polynomials over $GF(p)$ and so those in the field $GF(p)$. Thus, as recommended in [14], we used Karatsuba's algorithm in the multiplication of polynomials so that we can get the complexity $M(n) = O(n^{1.6})$ instead of $O(n^2)$. This will be effective when p is around 240-bit long. Moreover, almost all are *modular multiplications*, i.e. polynomial multiplications accompanied with polynomial division. Among them, as remarked in [14], powering polynomials dominates among other operations and it appears in the following steps;

(a) DDD computation of $\Phi_\ell(x, j(E))$,
(b) eigenvalue computation, i.e. finding t_ℓ by $\phi(P) = t_\ell P$.

Because both (a) and (b) require

(c) $x^{p^k} \bmod h(x)$ for some polynomial $h(x)$, or $h_0(x)^{(p-1)/2} \bmod h(x)$ for some polynomials $h_0(x), h(x)$, where $\deg(h) = O(\log(p))$.

For ordinary powering, we can convert one polynomial division into two polynomial multiplications with truncation, see [24]. For this truncated multiplication, we can extend Karatsuba's algorithm [8]. For p^k-th powering with $k \geq 2$, we can use multiplication tables, see also [24]. These techniques improve the total efficiency very much. We shall need, however, the FFT technique to attain drastical improvement for computation over much larger finite fields.

Eigenvalue Computation: In the isogeny cycles case, we made use of a match-and-sort algorithm in calculating an eigenvalue. As it was remarked in [23] that such a technique might work well for large ℓ, it seems to work well for isogeny cycles cases. We outline the implemented procedure briefly.

   Suppose that ℓ is an odd Elkies prime and we have already computed g_ℓ and a factor g_{ℓ^2} of f_{ℓ^2}. Let s_0 be the computed eigenvalue of the eigenspace corresponding to g_ℓ. By using g_{ℓ^2}, we will compute the eigenvalue $s_0 + \ell s_1$, where $s_0, s_1 \in \{0, 1, \ldots, \ell-1\}$ and $s_0 \neq 0$.

(i) We compute $P, \ldots, (\ell-1)P$, where the x-coordinate of P is a root of g_{ℓ^2}.
(ii) For $k = 1, \ldots, \ell-1$, we compute $k\phi(P)$ and check whether (ii-1) $vP = u\phi(P)$ or (ii-2) $-vP = u\phi(P)$, where $v = s_0 u \pmod{\ell}$.
If (ii-1) holds, then $s_0 + \ell s_1 = vu^{-1} \pmod{\ell^2}$. If (ii-2) holds, then $s_0 + \ell s_1 = -vu^{-1} \pmod{\ell^2}$.

This algorithm concerns only the x-coordinates of points and the number of additions of points is bounded by $2(\ell - 2)$. The following lemma gives the mathematical base for the correctness of the method.

Lemma 6 *For $s = s_0 + \ell s_1$, $s_0 \neq 0$, there exists an element $u_0 \in \{1, \ldots, \ell-1\}$ such that $u_0 s$ mod ℓ^2 belongs to $\{1, \ldots, \ell-1\} \cup \{\ell^2 - \ell + 1, \ldots, \ell^2 - 1\}$.*

Match-and-Sort Computation in Trial Search: In the trial search stage, we applied a certain kind of match-and-sort algorithm described in [12] for improving the efficiency. (See [12] for details.) In the implementation, we made use of projective coordinates and pre-computed multiples of a fixed point for computation of baby step and giant step. Moreover, we take much care of partitioning Atkin primes into the baby part and the giant part. To give a good partition, we apply "re-ordering" again to all Atkin primes. Also in the virtual method, we choose primes to optimize the algorithm.

4.2   Experimental Results

To examine the ability of the intelligent choice system, we choose 300 curves over $GF(p)$, where $p = 2^{160} + 7$, $A = 1$, and $1 \leq B \leq 300$, and measured the average time needed to compute the cardinality of one curve on a PC with Pentium II of 300MHz. We set the value of CanMAX=10^8. We also put the best and the worst time in the following table. In order to see the effect of our methods we tried several combinations of our strategies. We did not implement the Schoof's original algorithm.

Table 1. Using Intelligent Choice System (seconds):

No.	isogeny	virtual	re-ordering	best	average	worst
(1)	YES	YES	YES	34.7	66.5	334.7
(2)	NO	YES	YES	56.2	82.8	330.9
(3)	YES	NO	YES	43.7	76.1	339.4
(4)	YES	YES	NO	34.4	68.0	348.2

Table 2. Not Using Intelligent Choice System (seconds):

No.	isogeny	virtual	re-ordering	best	average	worst
(5)	YES	NO	NO	43.6	83.4	365.3
(6)	YES	NO	NO	43.6	86.9	374.1

(5) uses isogeny cycles if f_{ℓ^2} has a factor of degree ≤ 32.
(6) uses isogeny cycles if f_{ℓ^2} has a factor of degree ≤ 64.

From the above data, our strategies (in the intelligent choice system) will be characterized as follows:

1. The "estimate of the complexity" strategy has the main effect of speeding up the computation process overall.
2. The strategy on the isogeny cycles method and that on the virtual method have the main effect of speeding up the computation process in good cases. (Case we can proceed to the trial search stage early on.)

3. The re-ordering strategy should have the main effect of speeding up the computation process in bad cases. (Case the number of candidates for t exceeds `CanMAX`). Currently our implementation of calculation of x^{p^i} has not yet been tuned up. The authors believe that we can see a better effect after tuning up the process.

In Table 3 we show the timings (seconds) for 300 curves over other fields, which might assert that one can count the cardinality of curves used for elliptic curve cryptosystems in a reasonable time. And the average times suggest that the complexity of our implementation is $O(n^{5\pm\epsilon})$ for some $\epsilon \ll 1$. We also counted the cardinality of sample curves listed in X9.62 Working Draft and found the similar behavior on their timings as in Table 3. (It took 559 seconds for Example 1 with a 256-bit prime in H.5.3.)

Table 3. Statistics on Timings

prime	average time	best time	worst time	CanMAX
$2^{240} + 115$	454.1	242.8	1143.2	10^9
$2^{160} + 7$	66.5	34.7	334.7	10^8
$2^{155} + 15$	50.4	30.6	142.3	10^8

The authors are implementing the intelligent choice system for curves over finite fields of characteristic 2. As the basic arithmetics over finite fields of characteristic 2 can be done quite efficiently, the total computation over such fields seems faster than that over finite fields of odd characteristics.

4.3   Finding Elliptic Curves of Prime Cardinality

For secure ECC, it is strongly recommended to use a curve whose cardinality is a prime. For this purpose, we can use "early abort" strategy [13]. In this strategy, we check if the cardinality has a factor in each step of the computation of t mod ℓ. If we find that the cardinality is not a prime, we can abandon the curve and try the next one. The effect of the strategy is supported by mathematical analysis [11,13].

We incorporated this strategy to our implementation and searched curve with prime cardinality. For $p = 2^{240} + 115$, we could try 3569 curves in 52.5 hours, and found 16 curves whose cardinalities are prime. It means that we can handle each curve within 1 minute in average due to the effect of early abort strategy (almost 8 times faster than the average time in Table 3).

5   Conclusion

We have introduced an explicit criterion for efficient computation of the cardinality of an elliptic curve over a finite field. The experiment shows that we could speed up the process almost 20%. In the experiment we can find elliptic curves whose cardinalities are prime numbers in a reasonable time when the characteristics p of the base field is around 240-bit long.

Although our current implementation can not be the best, its experimental result is quite satisfactory in practice. We are going to tune up the *complexity estimate function* and `CanMAX` to get a better result. We will also implement FFT for the case when p is a larger prime and modify the intelligent choice system for parallel computation. Moreover, theoretical analysis will be our further studies.

References

1. Atkin, A.O., The number of points on an elliptic curve modulo a prime, preprint, 1988.
2. Atkin, A.O., Morain, F., Elliptic curves and primality proving, *Math. Comp.* **61** (1993) 29–68.
3. Chao, J., Tanada, K., Tsujii, S., Design of elliptic curves with controllable lower boundary of extension degree for reduction attacks, in *CRYPTO '94*, Y.Desmedt, Ed., Lecture Notes in Computer Science, **839**, pp.50–55, 1994.
4. Charlap, L.S., Coley, R., Robbins, D.P., Enumeration of rational points on elliptic curves over finite fields, preprint, 1991.
5. Couveignes, J.-M., Dewaghe, L., Morain, F., Isogeny cycles and the Schoof-Elkies-Atkin algorithm, LIX/RR/96/03, 1996.
6. Couveignes, J.-M., Morain, F., Schoof's algorithm and isogeny cycles, in *ANT-I*, L.Adleman and M.-D.Huang, Eds., Lecture Notes in Computer Science, **877**, pp.43–58, 1994.
7. Elkies, N.D., Explicit isogenies, preprint, 1991.
8. Izu, T., Noro, M., Fast remainder calculation in polynomial multiplication, in preparation.
9. Kobilitz N., Elliptic curve cryptosystems, *Math, Comp.* **48** (1987) 203-209.
10. Lay, G.-J., Zimmer, H.G., Constructing elliptic curves with given group order over large finite fields, in *ANT-I*, L.Adleman and M.-D.Huang, Eds., Lecture Notes in Computer Science, **877**, pp.250–263, 1994.
11. Lenstra Jr., H.W., Factoring integers with elliptic curves, *Annals of Mathematics* **126** (1987) 649–673.
12. Lercier, R., Algorithmique des courbes elliptiques dans les corps finis, Doctoral Thesis, L'École Polytechnique, 1997.
13. Lercier, R., Finding good random elliptic curves for cryptosystems defined over F_{2^n}, in *EURO-CRYPT '97*, W.Fumy, Ed., Lecture Notes in Computer Science, **1233**, pp.379–392, 1997.
14. Lercier, R., Morain, F., Counting the number of points on elliptic curves over finite fields: strategy and performances, in *EURO-CRYPT '95*, L.C.Guillou and J.-J.Quisquater, Eds., Lecture Notes in Computer Science, **921**, pp.79–94, 1995.
15. Menezes, A., Elliptic curve public key cryptosystems, Kluwer Academic Publishers, Boston, 1993.
16. Menezes, A., Okamoto, T., Vanstone, S.E., Reducing elliptic curves logarithms to logarithms in a finite field, in *STOC '91*, ACM Press, New York, pp.80–89, 1991.
17. Miller, V.S., Uses of elliptic curves in cryptography, in *CRYPTO '85*, Lecture Notes in Computer Science, **218**, pp.417-426, 1986.
18. Miyaji, A., Elliptic curves over F_p suitable for cryptosystems, in *AUSCRYPT '92*, J.Seberry and Y.Zhengs, Eds., Lecture Notes in Computer Science, **718**, pp.479–491, 1992.

19. Morain, F., Calcul du nombre de points sur une courbe elliptique dans un corps fini: aspects algorithmiques, *J. Théor. Nombres Bordeaux* **7** (1995) 255–282.

20. Risa/Asir, (`ftp://endeavor.fujitsu.co.jp/pub/isis/asir`).

21. Satoh, T., Araki, K., Fermat quotients and the polynomial time discrete log algorithm for anomalous elliptic curves, *Commentarii Mathematici Universitatis Sancti Pauli* **47** (1998) 81–92.

22. Schoof, R., Elliptic curves over finite fields and the computation of square roots mod p, *Math. Comp.* **44** (1985) 483–494.

23. Schoof, R., Counting points on elliptic curves over finite fields, *J. Théor. Nombres Bordeaux* **7** (1995) 219–254.

24. Shoup, V., A new polynomial factorization algorithm and its implementation, *J. Symbolic Computation.* **20** (1995) 364–397.

25. Silverman, J.H., The arithmetic of elliptic curves, Graduate Texts in Mathematics **106**, Springer-Verlag, 1986.

26. Silverman, J.H., Advanced topics in the arithmetic of elliptic curves, Graduate Texts in Mathematics **151**, Springer-Verlag, 1994.

27. Smart, N.P., The discrete logarithm problem on elliptic curves of trace one, preprint, 1997.

Design of Hyperelliptic Cryptosystems in Small Characteristic and a Software Implementation over $\mathbf{F}_{2^n}$

Yasuyuki Sakai[1] and Kouichi Sakurai[2*]

[1] Mitsubishi Electric Corporation,
5-1-1 Ofuna, Kamakura, Kanagawa 247, Japan
e-mail: ysakai@iss.isl.melco.co.jp
[2] Kyushu University,
6-10-1 Hakozaki, Higashi-ku, Fukuoka 812-81, Japan
e-mail: sakurai@csce.kyushu-u.ac.jp

Abstract. We investigate the discrete logarithm problem over jacobians of hyperelliptic curves suitable for public-key cryptosystems. We focus on the case when the definition field has small characteristic 2, 3, 5 and 7, then we present hyperelliptic cryptosystems that resist against all known attacks. We further implement our designed hyperelliptic cryptosystems over finite fields $\mathbf{F}_{2^n}$ in software on Alpha and Pentium-II computers. Our results indicate that if we choose curves carefully, hyperelliptic cryptosystems do have practical performance.

1 Introduction

1.1 Hyperelliptic Cryptosystems

Koblitz [Ko88,Ko89] investigated jacobians of hyperelliptic curves defined over finite fields as a source of finite abelian groups suitable for cryptographic discrete logarithm problems. As a motivation of the cryptographic research, Koblitz gave the following conjectural remark [Ko88, page–99]: *"Thus, as far as we know, discrete log cryptosystems using $\mathbf{J}(\mathbf{F}_{p^n})$ seem to be secure for relatively small p^n (even when $p = 2$). From the standpoint of implementation, this feature may outweigh the added time required to compute the more complicated group operation."*

Frey and Rück's generalization [FR94] of MOV-attack [MOV93] solved in subexponential time the discrete logarithm problems over some of Koblitz's designed hyperelliptic cryptosystems [Ko89]. However, Sakai, Sakurai and Ishizuka designed hyperelliptic cryptosystems [SSI98] that resist against all known attacks including the Frey and Rück's method [FR94]. Furthermore, Sakai et al. [SSI98] analyzed the computational complexity on the group operation in jacobians. Their results theoretically support the Koblitz's conjecture referred to above.

---

* Partially done while visiting in Columbia Univ. Computer Science Dept.

K. Ohta and D. Pei (Eds.): ASIACRYPT'98, LNCS 1514, pp. 80–94, 1998.
© Springer-Verlag Berlin Heidelberg 1998

In this work, we further explores hyperelliptic discrete logarithms for obtaining more efficient public key cryptosystems, and confirms experimentally the Koblitz's conjecture on the practical merit of hyperelliptic cryptosystems.

1.2   Our Investigated Topics

We consider the following topics to address as challenging problems after [Ko88] [Ko89,SSI98].

1. *Designing secure hyperelliptic cryptosystems with genus 2 curves over small characteristic fields*
   Koblitz [Ko88,Ko89] presented jacobians of curves $C : v^2 + h(u)v = f(u)$, where $deg(f(u)) = 5$ (genus 2), defined over $\mathbf{F}_2$. However, some discrete logarithms of the curves had been broken by Frey and Rück [FR94]. As a negative result, Sakai et al. [SSI98] experimentally showed that no secure curve exists with genus 2 among those defined over $\mathbf{F}_2$ and $h(u) = 1$.
   Recently developed other methods [BK98,FR97,CMT97] have generated secure hyperelliptic cryptosystems with genus 2. However, these require the size of the characteristic of curve's definition field to be large.

2. *Designing secure hyperelliptic cryptosystems over $\mathbf{F}_{2^n}$ with smaller n*
   Sakai et al. [SSI98] examined jacobians over $\mathbf{F}_{2^n}$ with genus $g = 3, 11$ curves $v^2 + v = u^{2g+1}$, which resist against all known attacks. However, their construction requires a large extension-degree n. For example, for achieving the security as RSA with 1024-bit key, the jacobian of the curve $v^2 + v = u^7$ must be defined over $\mathbf{F}_{2^{59}}$ or larger fields. They also confirmed that the jacobian of the curve $v^2 + v = u^{23}$ (genus 11) over $\mathbf{F}_{2^{47}}$ induces a secure hyperelliptic cryptosystem with the same level of security as RSA with 5000-bit key. This can be efficiently (without multi-precision library) implemented via software on 64-bit CPU (e.g. Alpha).
   However, no secure hyperelliptic cryptosystem is available from this curve with smaller n than 47. We want such a jacobian over $\mathbf{F}_{2^n}$ with hopefully $n \leq 32$ for an efficient software implementation on 32-bit CPU (e.g. Pentium).

3. *Implementing hyperelliptic cryptosystem in software*
   Indeed, the formulas for adding divisors in a jacobian are more complex compared to formulas for adding points in an elliptic curve. However, as we first remarked, Koblitz [Ko88] suggested that hyperelliptic cryptosystems defined over a small definition field may be efficient in practice.
   Sakai et al. [SSI98] evaluated encryption/decryption speed which should that hyperelliptic cryptosystems are indeed practical. However, their confirmation was only theoretical, and no performance via a practical implementation has been reported.

1.3   Our Results

On Design with Genus Two In the case of characteristic 2, we have found secure jacobians by considering a more wider class of $h(u)$ (degree of $h(u)$ has at most g). Moreover, in the case of $C : v^2 = f(u)$ over characteristic 3, 5 and 7 finite fields, where $deg(f(u)) = 5$ (genus 2), we have found many curves which resist against all known attacks.

On Design with Smaller Size of $\mathbf{F}_{2^n}$ By not choosing curves from $v^2 + v = u^{2g+1}$ but from a wider class $v^2 + v = f(u)$, we have found secure jacobians over $\mathbf{F}_{2^n}$ with "$n \leq 32$" that achieve the same (or higher) level of security as RSA with 1024-bit key.

On Implementation We have implemented operations in jacobians via software. One platform was Alpha 21164A (467MHz) with 64-bit word size, and another was Pentium-II (300MHz) with 32-bit word size. Programs were written in C-language and compiled with GCC. Our software implementation of secure jacobians, which have the same level of security as RSA with 1024-bit key, achieve good practical performance. In an exponentiation of a randomly chosen divisor, the jacobian over $\mathbf{F}_{2^{59}}$ of the genus 3 curve $C : v^2 + v = u^7$ achieved 83.3 msec. on Alpha 21164A (467MHz), and the jacobian over $\mathbf{F}_{2^{29}}$ of the genus 6 curve $C : v^2 + v = u^{13} + u^{11} + u^7 + u^3 + 1$ achieved 476 msec. on Pentium-II (300MHz). We have also implemented secure jacobians which have the same level of security as RSA with 5000-bit key. In an exponentiation of a randomly chosen divisor, the jacobian over $\mathbf{F}_{2^{47}}$ of the genus 11 curve $C : v^2 + v = u^{23}$ achieved 1.74 sec. on Alpha 21164A (467MHz). Note that those jacobians can be implemented without "a multi-precision library", because of the size of the definition fields.

1.4   Our Approach

Our Considered Security We design hyperelliptic cryptosystems that resist against the following four known attacks:

1. The Pohlig-Hellman method [PH78].
2. Frey-Rück's generalization [FR94] of the Menezes-Okamoto-Vanstone attack [MOV93].
3. Adleman-DeMarrais-Huang's *smooth-divisor-attack* [ADH94].
4. Rück's generalization [RU97] of the Semaev-Smart-Satoh-Araki attack [SEM98,SM97,SA97] on elliptic curves with Frobenius trace one.

   Our design further notes new attacks improving the parallerized Pollard-Lambda search [WZ98,GLV98].

On Choosing Curves and Counting the Order of their Jacobian In [KO88], Koblitz investigated the jacobians of the hyperelliptic curves $v^2 + v = u^{2g+1}$ over finite field for cryptographically intractable discrete logarithm. In [KO89], Koblitz also discussed the jacobians of the hyperelliptic curves of more general form $v^2 + h(u)v = f(u)$, however, the degree of the polynomial $f(u)$ is restricted to be 5 (i.e. genus 2) and the definition fields are only the case of characteristic 2. In order to obtain a broader class of jacobians suitable for secure discrete logarithms, we deal with a wider family of the hyperelliptic curves $v^2 + v = f(u)$ and $v^2 = f(u)$ over finite field of characteristic 2, 3, 5 and 7, where $\deg(f(u))=2g + 1$.

2   Preliminaries

In this section, we give a brief description of jacobians. See [KO98] for more detail.

Let $\mathbf{F}$ be a finite field and let $\bar{\mathbf{F}}$ be the algebraic closure of $\mathbf{F}$. A hyperelliptic curve C of genus g over $\mathbf{F}$ is an equation of the form $C : v^2 + h(u)v = f(u)$ in $\mathbf{F}[u, v]$, where $h(u) \in \mathbf{F}[u]$ is a polynomial of degree at most g, $f(u) \in \mathbf{F}[u]$ is a monic polynomial of degree $2g + 1$, and there are no solutions $(u, v) \in \bar{\mathbf{F}} \times \bar{\mathbf{F}}$ which simultaneously satisfy the equation $v^2 + h(u)v = f(u)$ and the partial derivative equations $2v + h(u) = 0$ and $h'(u)v - f'(u) = 0$. Thus, a hyperelliptic curve does not have singular points.

A divisor on C is a finite formal sum of $\bar{\mathbf{F}}$-points $D = \sum m_i P_i$, $m_i \in \mathbf{Z}$. We define the degree of D to be $\deg(D) = \sum m_i$. If $\mathbf{K}$ is an algebraic extension of $\mathbf{F}$, we say that D is defined over $\mathbf{K}$ if for every automorphism σ of $\bar{\mathbf{F}}$ that fixes $\mathbf{K}$ one has $\sum m_i P_i^\sigma = D$, where P^σ denotes the point obtained by applying σ to the coordinates of P (and $\infty^\sigma = \infty$). Let $\mathbf{D}$ denote the additive group of divisors defined over $\mathbf{K}$ (where $\mathbf{K}$ is fixed), and let $\mathbf{D}^0$ denote the subgroup consisting of divisors of degree 0. The principal divisors form a subgroup $\mathbf{P}$ of $\mathbf{D}^0$. $\mathbf{J}(\mathbf{K}) = \mathbf{D}^0/\mathbf{P}$ is called the "*jacobian*" of the curve C. In this paper, we denote $\mathbf{J}(C; \mathbf{K})$ also the jacobian defined over $\mathbf{K}$ of the curve C.

The discrete logarithm problem on $\mathbf{J}(C; \mathbf{K})$ is the problem, given two divisors $D_1, D_2 \in \mathbf{J}(C; \mathbf{K})$ of determining an integer m such that $D_2 = mD_1$ if such m exists.

3   Security Against Known Attacks

We will choose jacobians to satisfy the following four conditions to resist against all known attacks.

C1 : $\sharp \mathbf{J}(C; \mathbf{F}_q)$ is divisible by a large prime

C2 : $\mathbf{J}(C; \mathbf{F}_q)$ can not be imbedded into a small finite field $\mathbf{F}_{q^k}$

C3 : $2g + 1 \leq \log q$

C4 : Jacobian over a field of characteristic p has not a cyclic group structure of order p^n for small n.

Our design further notes new attacks improving the parallerized Pollard-Lambda search [WZ98,GLV98].

3.1   C1 : General Algorithms
The condition **C1** is to resist Pohlig-Hellman method [PH78]. The algorithm has a running time that is proportional to the square root of the largest prime factor of $\sharp \mathbf{J}(C; \mathbf{F}_q)$. Therefore, we need to choose curves such that $\sharp \mathbf{J}(C; \mathbf{F}_q)$ has a large prime factor.

3.2   C2 : Imbedding into a Small Finite Field
The condition **C2** is to resist Frey and Rück's generalization [FR94] of MOV-attack [MOV93] using Tate pairing. Their method reduces the logarithm problem over $\mathbf{J}(C; \mathbf{F}_q)$ to the logarithm problem over an extension field $\mathbf{F}_{q^k}$. Methods of avoiding MOV-attack have been discussed in [BS91,CTT94]. We take the similar approach by choosing curves such that the induced jacobian $\mathbf{J}(C; \mathbf{F}_q)$ cannot be imbedded via Tate pairing into $\mathbf{F}_{q^k}$ with small extension degree k. Therefore, we replace **C2** by the following sufficient condition:

C2' : The largest prime factor of $\sharp \mathbf{J}(C; \mathbf{F}_q)$ does not divide $(q)^k - 1$, $k < (\log q)^2$

3.3   C3 : Large Genus Hyperelliptic Curves

The condition **C3** is to resist Adleman-DeMarrais-Huang method [ADH94]. They found a sub-exponential algorithm for discrete logarithm over the rational subgroup of the jacobians of large genus hyperelliptic curves over finite fields. It is a heuristic algorithm under certain assumptions. Therefore, we need to choose curves such that the genus of curves is not so large.

3.4   C4 : Additive Embedding Attack

The condition **C4** is to resist Rück's generalization [RU97] of the Semaev-Smart-Satoh-Araki attack [SEM98,SM97,SA97] on elliptic cryptosystems with Frobenius trace one. The method uses an additive version of Tate pairing to solve the discrete logarithm of a jacobian over a finite field of characteristic p and has the running time $O(n^2 \log p)$ for a jacobian with cyclic group structure of order p^n.

We should remark that our design is in small characteristic $p = 2, 3, 5$ and 7. Subgroups of the jacobians that we consider have order prime to the characteristic p. Therefore, this additive embedding attack does not apply to our cryptosystems.

3.5   Improved Parallerized Pollard-Lambda Search

New attacks have been announced, which improved the parallerized Pollard-Lambda search [WZ98,GLV98]. For elliptic curves over $\mathbf{F}_{2^n}$ with coefficients in $\mathbf{F}_2$, this attacking time can be reduced by a factor of the square root of $2n$. For example, the time required to compute an elliptic curve logarithm on such a curve over $\mathbf{F}_{2^{163}}$ is reduced from the previous 2^{81} to 2^{77} elliptic curve operations.

This could be applicable to our designed hyperelliptic cryptosystems in characteristic 2, because the coefficients of our curves belong to $\mathbf{F}_2$. We should note that the power of this attack is not so strong as the four listed above. However, this attack is very important to our selection of the size of security-parameter, which effects the performance analysis of our cryptosystems. Therefore, we should consider the security against possible extension of this kind of attack in our design of hyperelliptic cryptosystems.

4   Our Order Counting Method

Beth and Schaefer [BS91] used zeta-function for their constructing elliptic cryptosystems and Koblitz [KO88,KO89,KO98] also used zeta-function of a hyperelliptic curve to construct jacobians of hyperelliptic curves defined over finite fields.

A technical difficulty in our computation on general hyperelliptic curves is that the zeta-function has a complicated form with larger degree. Therefore, it is not easy to compute its exact solutions unlike the previous cases [BS91,KO88,KO89,KO98]. However, it is known that the order of a jacobian can be computed without deciding the solution of its zeta-function [St93, Chapter V]. Therefore, we use this algorithm for our problems.

Throughout this section, F denotes an algebraic function field of genus g whose constant field is the finite field $\mathbf{F}_q$ and $\mathbf{P}$ denotes the set of places of

$F/\mathbf{K}$. The definition, the theorem and the corollary shown below are given in the article [St93].

Definition 1. *[St93] The polynomial* $L(t) := (1 - t)(1 - qt)Z(t)$ *is called the L-polynomial of function field* $F/\mathbf{F}_q$, *where* $Z(t)$ *denotes the zeta-function of* $F/\mathbf{F}_q$.

Theorem 1. *[St93]*

(a) $L(t) \in \mathbf{Z}[t]$ and $\deg L(t) = 2g$
(b) $L(t) = q^g t^{2g} L(1/qt)$
(c) $L(1) = h$, the class number of $F/\mathbf{F}_q$
(d) We write $L(t) = \sum_{i=0}^{2g} a_i t^i$. Then the following holds:
    (1) $a_0 = 1$ and $a_{2g} = q^g$.
    (2) $a_{2g-i} = q^{g-i} a_i$ for $0 \leq i \leq g$.
    (3) $a_1 = N - (q+1)$ where N is the number of places $P \in \mathbf{P}_F$ of degree one.
(e) $L(t)$ factors in $\mathbf{C}[t]$ in the form $L(t) = \prod_{i=1}^{2g}(1 - \alpha_i t)$. The complex numbers $\alpha_1, \cdots, \alpha_{2g}$ are algebraic integers, and they can be arranged in such a way that $\alpha_i \alpha_{g+i} = q$ holds for $i = 1, \cdots, g$.
(f) If $L_r(t) := (1 - t)(1 - q^r t)Z_r(t)$ denotes the L-polynomial of the constant field extension $F_r = F\mathbf{F}_{q^r}$, then $L_r(t) = \prod_{i=1}^{2g}(1 - \alpha_i t)$

Corollary 1. *[St93] Let $S_r := N_r - (q^r + 1)$. Then we have:*
$a_0 = 1$, *and* $ia_i = S_i a_0 + S_{i-1} a_1 + \cdots + S_1 a_{i-1}$, *for* $i = 1, \cdots, g$.

We can determine the order of jacobians by the Theorem and the Corollary in the following algorithm. We should note that it is easy to count $N_1, \cdots, N_g$ if $\mathbf{F}_q$ is small.

Order Counting	
Input	Hyperelliptic curve $C : v^2 + h(u)v = f(u)$ over $\mathbf{F}_q$ and extension degree n
Output	The order $\sharp \mathbf{J}(C; \mathbf{F}_{q^n})$
Step1	Determine $N_r = \sharp \mathbf{J}(C; \mathbf{F}_{q^r})$, for $r = 1, \cdots, g$ by counting the number of rational points of C over $\mathbf{F}_{q^r}$
Step2	Determine the coefficients of $L_{\mathbf{F}_q}(t) = \sum_{i=0}^{2g} a_i t^i$ in the following: $a_0 = 1$ for $1 \leq i \leq g$: $\quad a_i = (\sum_{k=1}^{i}(N_k - (q^k + 1))a_{i-k})/i$ for $g+1 \leq i \leq 2g$: $\quad a_i = q^{i-g} a_{2g-i}$
Step3	Compute $L_{\mathbf{F}_{q^n}}(1) = \prod_{k=1}^{n} L_{\mathbf{F}_q}(\zeta^k)$, where ζ runs over the n-th root of unity
Step4	Return $\sharp \mathbf{J}(C; \mathbf{F}_{q^n}) = L_{\mathbf{F}_{q^n}}(1)$

5 Jacobians over Finite Fields of Characteristic 2

Koblitz [Ko88,Ko89] considered the security of the discrete logarithm problem over jacobians of genus 2 curves when the definition fields have characteristic 2. However, Frey and Rück [FR94] generalized MOV-reduction to hyperelliptic curves. They have found that some of hyperelliptic cryptosystems presented by Koblitz [Ko89] are breakable in sub-exponential time. In this section, we discuss the security of genus 2 curves which have the form $v^2 + h(u)v = f(u)$ defined over characteristic 2 finite fields. We also discuss the security of genus 3, 4, 5 and 6 curves.

5.1 Genus 2 Curves

First, we examine the order of jacobians $\sharp J(C; \mathbf{F}_{2^n})$ in the case of $h(u) = 1$, where the degree of $f(u)$ equals to 5. We also examine their factorizations.

Extension degree n of $\mathbf{F}_{2^n}$ were examined from 59 to 89. The reason is that: $\sharp J(C; \mathbf{F}_{2^{59}})$ has the size of 119-bit. $\sharp J(C; \mathbf{F}_{2^{89}})$ has the size of 179-bit. Namely, if the jacobians are secure, their level of security are in the range from approximately RSA-512 to RSA-1024. [1] ("RSA-n" denotes RSA with n-bit key.) We have examined whether P_{max} of $\sharp J(C; \mathbf{F}_{2^n})$ divide $(2^n)^k - 1$ to confirm the security condition **C2'**. (P_{max} denotes the largest prime factor of $\sharp J(C; \mathbf{F}_q)$.) As a result, for example, in the case of $f(u) = u^5 + u^3$, $\sharp J(C; \mathbf{F}_{2^{89}})$ has the size of 179-bit and its P_{max} has the size of 134-bit. However, P_{max} divides $(2^n)^{12} - 1$. Therefore, the jacobian does not satisfy **C2'** (see also [FR94]).

In the case of $h(u) = 1$, We have failed to obtain secure jacobians, which satisfy **C1** and **C2'**. However, in [Ko98], Koblitz examined the case of $h(u) = u$ and showed examples of secure jacobians. We have examined the case of more wider classes such that $h(u)$ has degree at most g. As a result, $\sharp J(C; \mathbf{F}_{2^{89}})$ of $C : v^2 + (u^2 + u + 1)v = u^5 + u + 1$ has the size of 179-bit. Its P_{max} has the size of 178-bit. We also confirmed the jacobian satisfies **C2'**. The factorization of the jacobian is given in Appendix A.

5.2 Curves of Genus Larger than 2

Next, we examine $\sharp J(C; \mathbf{F}_{2^n})$ and their factorizations in the case of curves $C : v^2 + v = f(u)$ have genus 3, 4, 5 or 6, where degree of $f(u)$ equals to 7, 9, 11 or 13, respectively.

Table 1 shows the list of the size of $\sharp J(C; \mathbf{F}_{2^n})$ and the size of P_{max}. The factorizations are given in Appendix A. Extension degree n of $\mathbf{F}_{2^n}$ were examined by n such that $\sharp J(C; \mathbf{F}_{2^n})$ has the size of larger than 160-bit. Namely, if listed jacobians are secure, their level of security are approximately same as RSA-1024 or with a larger key. The listed equations of curves C have largest P_{max} in fixed extension degree n. In the case of genus 5, all prime factors of $\sharp J(C; \mathbf{F}_{2^{37}})$ have much smaller size than 160-bit. Therefore, $J(C; \mathbf{F}_{2^{41}})$ are listed.

We have examined whether P_{max} of $\sharp J(C; \mathbf{F}_{2^n})$ divide $(q^n)^k - 1$ to confirm the security condition **C2'**. All listed $\sharp J(C; \mathbf{F}_{2^n})$ satisfy **C2'**. Namely, P_{max} does

---

[1]   The notation *"same level of security"* is based on the following: One of the most efficient algorithm of integer factoring is the number field sieve method. The method takes $exp(c(\ln n)^{1/3}(\ln \ln n)^{2/3})$ time, where $1.5 < c < 1.9$ and n denotes the size of an integer. On the other hand, Pohlig-Hellman method, which is an efficient algorithm for discrete logarithm problem for elliptic curve, takes $\sqrt{P_{max}}$. Therefore, for example, EC-160 has approximately same level of security as RSA-1024.

genus	J	$C : v^2 + v = f(u)$	size of $\sharp J$	size of P_{max}
3	$J(C; \mathbf{F}_{2^{59}})$	$f(u) = u^7$	178-bit	165-bit
4	$J(C; \mathbf{F}_{2^{41}})$	$f(u) = u^9 + u^7 + u^3 + 1$	164-bit	161-bit
5	$J(C; \mathbf{F}_{2^{41}})$	$f(u) = u^{11} + u^5 + u + 1$	205-bit	201-bit
6	$J(C; \mathbf{F}_{2^{29}})$	$f(u) = u^{13} + u^{11} + u^7 + u^3 + 1$	174-bit	170-bit

Table 1. Jacobians over char 2 finite fields of genus 3,4,5 and 6 curves

not divide $(q^n)^k - 1$ with small k. Therefore, the curves shown in Table 1 are secure and have the same or higher level of security as RSA-1024. We implement group operations of the jacobians in software in a later section.

6   Jacobians over Finite Fields of Characteristic Larger than Two

In this section, we examine genus 2 curves over characteristic 3, 5 and 7 finite fields. Moreover, we examine genus 3 and 4 curves.

6.1   Genus 2 Curves

First, we examine the curve $C : v^2 = f(u)$, where $f(u)$ has degree 5. Tables 2, 3 and 4 show the list of the size of $\sharp J(C; \mathbf{F}_{p^n})$ and the size of P_{max} in the case of $p = 3, 5, 7$, respectively. Tabulated are in the case that the coefficients of the curves are in $\{0,1\}$. The factorizations of $\sharp J(C; \mathbf{F}_{p^n})$ are given in Appendix A.

In the case of characteristic 3, extension degree n of $\mathbf{F}_{3^n}$ were examined from 37 to 59. $\sharp J(C; \mathbf{F}_{3^{37}})$ has the size of 118-bit. $\sharp J(C; \mathbf{F}_{3^{59}})$ has the size of 188-bit. As in the last section, if listed jacobians are secure, their levels of security are in the range from approximately RSA-512 to RSA-1024. The listed equations of curves C have largest P_{max} in fixed extension degree n. As in the case of characteristic 3, extension degree n of $\mathbf{F}_{5^n}$ was examined from 23 to 43, and extension degree n of $\mathbf{F}_{7^n}$ was examined from 19 to 37.

We have examined whether P_{max} of $\sharp J(C; \mathbf{F}_{p^n})$ divide $(p^n)^k - 1$ to confirm the security condition **C2'**. All listed $\sharp J(C; \mathbf{F}_{p^n})$ in tables 2, 3 and 4 satisfy **C2'**. Namely, P_{max} does not divide $(p^n)^k - 1$ with small k.

6.2   Curves of Genus Larger than 2

Next, we examine the order of jacobians $\sharp J(C; \mathbf{F}_{p^n})$ and their factorizations of genus 3 and 4 curves $C : v^2 = f(u)$, where degree of $f(u)$ equals to 7 and 9, respectively.

Table 5 shows the list of the size of $\sharp J(C; \mathbf{F}_{p^n})$ and the size of the largest prime factor of $\sharp J(C; \mathbf{F}_{p^n})$. As in the case of genus 2, there exist secure jacobians which satisfy the condition **C2'**. The factorizations of $\sharp J(C; \mathbf{F}_{p^n})$ are given in Appendix A.

$\mathbf{J}$	C	size of $\sharp\mathbf{J}$	size of P_{max}
$\mathbf{J}(C;\mathbf{F}_{337})$	$v^2 = u^5 + u^3 + u + 1$	118-bit	97-bit
$\mathbf{J}(C;\mathbf{F}_{341})$	$v^2 = u^5 + u^2 + u + 1$	130-bit	116-bit
$\mathbf{J}(C;\mathbf{F}_{343})$	$v^2 = u^5 + u^4 + 1$	137-bit	118-bit
$\mathbf{J}(C;\mathbf{F}_{347})$	$v^2 = u^5 + u^3 + u + 1$	149-bit	135-bit
$\mathbf{J}(C;\mathbf{F}_{353})$	$v^2 = u^5 + u^4 + u + 1$	169-bit	147-bit
$\mathbf{J}(C;\mathbf{F}_{359})$	$v^2 = u^5 + u^4 + u^3 + u + 1$	188-bit	185-bit

Table 2. genus 2 curves over char 3 fields

$\mathbf{J}$	C	size of $\sharp\mathbf{J}$	size of P_{max}
$\mathbf{J}(C;\mathbf{F}_{523})$	$v^2 = u^5 + u^4 + u^3 + 1$	107-bit	103-bit
$\mathbf{J}(C;\mathbf{F}_{529})$	$v^2 = u^5 + u^4 + u^3 + u + 1$	135-bit	129-bit
$\mathbf{J}(C;\mathbf{F}_{531})$	$v^2 = u^5 + u^2 + 1$	144-bit	140-bit
$\mathbf{J}(C;\mathbf{F}_{537})$	$v^2 = u^5 + u^4 + u^3 + 1$	172-bit	149-bit
$\mathbf{J}(C;\mathbf{F}_{541})$	$v^2 = u^5 + u^4 + u^3 + 1$	191-bit	118-bit
$\mathbf{J}(C;\mathbf{F}_{543})$	$v^2 = u^5 + u^2 + 1$	200-bit	196-bit

Table 3. genus 2 curves over char 5 fields

$\mathbf{J}$	C	size of $\sharp\mathbf{J}$	size of P_{max}
$\mathbf{J}(C;\mathbf{F}_{719})$	$v^2 = u^5 + u^4 + u^3 + u^2 + 1$	107-bit	76-bit
$\mathbf{J}(C;\mathbf{F}_{723})$	$v^2 = u^5 + u^4 + u^3 + u + 1$	130-bit	118-bit
$\mathbf{J}(C;\mathbf{F}_{729})$	$v^2 = u^5 + u^4 + u^2 + 1$	164-bit	157-bit
$\mathbf{J}(C;\mathbf{F}_{731})$	$v^2 = u^5 + u^4 + u^3 + u^2 + 1$	175-bit	154-bit
$\mathbf{J}(C;\mathbf{F}_{737})$	$v^2 = u^5 + u^3 + u^2 + u + 1$	208-bit	203-bit

Table 4. genus 2 curves over char 7 fields

char	genus	$\mathbf{J}$	C	size of $\sharp\mathbf{J}$	size of P_{max}
3	3	$\mathbf{J}(C;\mathbf{F}_{337})$	$v^2 = u^7 + u^5 + u^3 + u^2 + 1$	176-bit	171-bit
	4	$\mathbf{J}(C;\mathbf{F}_{329})$	$v^2 = u^9 + u^6 + u^5 + u^3 + 1$	184-bit	178bit
5	3	$\mathbf{J}(C;\mathbf{F}_{523})$	$v^2 = u^7 + u^6 + u^2 + 1$	161-bit	154-bit
	4	$\mathbf{J}(C;\mathbf{F}_{519})$	$v^2 = u^9 + u^7 + u^6 + u^5 + u^3 + u + 1$	177-bit	168-bit
7	3	$\mathbf{J}(C;\mathbf{F}_{719})$	$v^2 = u^7 + u^6 + u^5 + u^3 + u + 1$	161-bit	152-bit
	4	$\mathbf{J}(C;\mathbf{F}_{717})$	$v^2 = u^9 + u^8 + u^6 + u^5 + u^3 + u + 1$	191-bit	181-bit

Table 5. genus 3 and 4 curves over char 3, 5 and 7 fields

7   Implementation and Timings

In this section, we show software implementation and timings of group operations in jacobians over characteristic 2 finite fields obtained in previous sections.

7.1   Computing in Jacobians

we show here an algorithm for addition and doubling of elements $D \in \mathbf{J}(C;\mathbf{F}_{2^n})$. A divisor D is regarded simply as a pair of polynomials $D = \operatorname{div}(a(u), b(u))$ such that $\deg b < \deg a$ and $\deg a \leq g$. We give here a brief description of the algorithm for the addition: $D_3 = D_1 + D_2$, where $D_3 = \mathrm{div}(a_3, b_3)$, $D_1 = \mathrm{div}(a_1, b_1)$, $D_2 = \mathrm{div}(a_2, b_2)$ (see [CA87,KO89] for more details).

Addition

Input: two divisors $D_1 = \mathrm{div}(a_1, b_1)$, $D_2 = \mathrm{div}(a_2, b_2) \in \mathbf{J}$
Output: $D_3 = \mathrm{div}(a_3, b_3) = D_1 + D_2$

Step A1 Compute d_1, s_1 and s_2 which satisfy
$$d_1 = \gcd(a_1, a_2) \text{ and } d_1 = s_1 a_1 + s_2 a_2$$
Step A2 If $d_1 = 1$ then
$$a := a_1 a_2, \ \ b := s_1 a_1 b_2 + s_2 a_2 b_1 \ (\mathrm{mod}\ a)$$
    else
     Compute d_2, s_1', s_2' and s_3 which satisfy
$$d_2 = \gcd(d_1, b_1 + b_2 + h) \text{ and } d_2 = s_1' a_1 + s_2' a_2 + s_3(b_1 + b_2 + h)$$
$$a := a_1 a_2/d_2^2, \ \ b := (s_1' a_1 b_2 + s_2' a_2 b_1 + s_3(b_1 b_2 + f))/d_2 \ (\mathrm{mod}\ a)$$
Step A3 While $\deg(a_3) > g$ do the following:
$$a_3 := (f - b - b^2)/a, \ b_3 := -h - b \ (\mathrm{mod}\ a_3), a := a_3, b := b_3$$
Step A4 Return $D_3 = \mathrm{div}(a_3, b_3)$

If a_1 and a_2 have no common factor, **Step A2** to be simpler case. Note that the case $\gcd(a_1, a_2) = 1$ is extremely likely if the definition field is large and a_1 and a_2 are the coordinates of two randomly chosen elements of the jacobian.

When $a_1 = a_2$ and $b_1 = b_2$, i.e., doubling an element of $\mathbf{J}(C; \mathbf{F}_{2^n})$, we can take $s_2 = 0$. Moreover, in the case of char $\mathbf{F} = 2$ and $h(u) = 1$, $d_1 = 1$, $s_1 = s_2 = 0$, $S_3 = 1$, and $a = a_1^2$, $b = b_1^2 + f$ (mod a). Therefore, In the case of $\mathbf{J}(C; \mathbf{F}_{2^n})$ and $C : v^2 + v = f(u)$, the doubling can be done in the algorithm as follows.

Doubling

Input: a divisor $D_1 = \mathrm{div}(a_1, b_1) \in \mathbf{J}$
Output: $D_2 = \mathrm{div}(a_2, b_2) = D_1 + D_1$

Step D1 $a := a_1^2$, $b := b_1^2 + f$ (mod a)
Step D2 While $\deg(a_2) > g$ do the following:
$$a_2 := (f - b - b^2)/a, \ b_2 := -h - b \ (\mathrm{mod}\ a_2), a := a_2, b := b_2$$
Step D3 Return $D_2 = \mathrm{div}(a_2, b_2)$

Addition and doubling take $O(g^3)$ field multiplications. The details of the estimation on the computational cost can be found in [SSI98].

7.2 Field Operations

All operations in addition and doubling of $D \in \mathbf{J}(C; \mathbf{F}_{2^n})$ are done by operations in a finite field, because our divisors D (pair of two polynomials) have coefficients in their definition field. We will use a polynomial basis in our implementations.

7.3 Representation of Field Elements in Memory

Elements in $\mathbf{F}_{2^n}$ can be represented as n-bit words in computer memory. If CPU has m-bit size of resisters, $\mathbf{F}_{2^n}$ such as $n \leq m$ are regarded as simply ordinary "unsigned integer". However, unfortunately, if $n > m$, we need to use "multi-precision" operations for computing. In general, we need such multi-precision operations for RSA and elliptic curve cryptosystems. On the other hand, the order of an abelian variety $\mathbf{A}(\mathbf{F}_q)$ of genus g lies in the range: $(q^{\frac{1}{2}} - 1)^{2g} \leq \sharp \mathbf{A}(\mathbf{F}_q) \leq (q^{\frac{1}{2}} + 1)^{2g}$ [St93]. Therefore, if we choose curves carefully, hyperelliptic cryptosystems, which have larger genus g curves compared to elliptic curve, can be implemented without multi-precision library, because an element of the definition field can be stored in computer registers. Such hyperelliptic cryptosystems may have practical performance even though the algorithm for addition of D, shown in the last sub-section, is much more expensive than the algorithm for addition of points on elliptic curves.

7.4   Generating Random Divisors

From cryptosystems point of view, we need to have a method of generating a "random" divisor $D \in \mathbf{J}(C; \mathbf{F}_{q^n})$. In [Ko89], Koblitz has given such a method in the following way. In our implementation, we have generated divisors D in the method.

We may regard C as defined over $\mathbf{F}_{q^n}$. Let C have the equation $v^2 + h(u)v = f(u)$. Choose the coordinate $u = x \in \mathbf{F}_q$ at random and attempt to solve $v^2 + h(x)v = f(x)$. In the case of q is even, $h(x) \neq 0$ and the change of variables $z = v/h(x)$ leads to the equation $z^2 + z = a$, where $a = f(x)/h(x)^2$. It is easy to see that this equation has a solution $z \in \mathbf{F}_q$ if $\mathrm{Tr}_{\mathbf{F}_q/\mathbf{F}_2} a = 0$ and does not have a solution if this trace is 1. In the latter case, we must choose another $u = x \in \mathbf{F}_q$ and start again. In the former case, we can find z as follows: If $q = 2^n$ is an odd power of 2, simply set $\sum_{j=0}^{(n-1)/2} a^{2^{2j}}$.

7.5   Timings

We have implemented group operations in jacobians over $\mathbf{F}_{2^n}$ and timed an exponentiation, an addition and a doubling of randomly generated divisors using the algorithms shown in the previous subsection. An exponentiation was done with a simple repeated-doubling method.

The platforms used were Alpha 21164A (467MHz) and Pentium-II (300MHz). Alpha has 64-bit registers and Pentium-II has 32-bit registers. Programs were written in C-language. When extension degree n of $\mathbf{F}_{2^n}$ has a larger size than the register size of the CPU, we used GNU-MP library (gmp-2.0.2) for multi-precision operations.

Table 6 shows the processing time of an exponentiation, an addition and a doubling of a randomly given divisor implemented on Alpha 21164A (467MHz) and Pentium-II (300MHz). The order of each jacobians $\sharp \mathbf{J}(C; \mathbf{F}_{2^n})$ have the largest prime factor which has a larger size than 160-bit, namely, they have the same or higher level of security as RSA-1024 and EC-160.

All jacobians of Table 6 are defined over finite fields $\mathbf{F}_{2^n}$ with $n \leq 64$. Therefore, we can implement with no multi-precision library over Alpha 21164A (467MHz). $\mathbf{J}(C; \mathbf{F}_{2^{59}})$ of genus 3 curve $C : v^2 + v = u^7$ achieved 83.3 msec. in an exponentiation. Moreover, in the case of Pentium, we should focus on the case

g	$\mathbf{J}(v^2+v=f(u);\mathbf{F}_{2^n})$		Addition(msec.)		Doubling(msec.)		Exp.(msec.)	
$\mathbf{F}_{2^n}$	$f(u)$		Alpha	Pentium	Alpha	Pentium	Alpha	Pentium
3	$\mathbf{F}_{2^{59}}$	u^7	0.54	67.6	0.26	34.1	83.3	$1.17\cdot10^4$
4	$\mathbf{F}_{2^{41}}$	$u^9+u^7+u^3+1$	0.55	67.2	0.26	33.3	96.6	$1.09\cdot10^4$
5	$\mathbf{F}_{2^{41}}$	$u^{11}+u^5+u+1$	0.88	109	0.48	58.7	183	$2.36\cdot10^4$
6	$\mathbf{F}_{2^{29}}$	$u^{13}+u^{11}+u^7+u^3+1$	0.83	2.68	0.44	1.45	159	476

Table 6. Timings of jacobians which have the same level of security as RSA-1024 on Alpha 21164A (467MHz) and Pentium-II (300MHz)

g	$\mathbf{J}$	C	size of P_{max}	Addition (msec.)	Doubling (msec.)	Exp. (msec.)
3	$\mathbf{J}(C;\mathbf{F}_{2^{89}})$	$v^2+v=u^7$	246-bit	85.3	42.8	$2.57\cdot10^4$
3	$\mathbf{J}(C;\mathbf{F}_{2^{113}})$	$v^2+v=u^7$	310-bit	118	58.9	$3.79\cdot10^4$
11	$\mathbf{J}(C;\mathbf{F}_{2^7})$	$v^2+v=u^{23}$	310-bit	5.04	3.13	$1.74\cdot10^3$

Table 7. Timings of jacobians of $C : v^2 + v = u^{2g+1}$ which have the same level of security as RSA-2048 or RSA-5000 over Alpha 21164A (467MHz)

$\mathbf{J}(C;\mathbf{F}_{2^{29}})$ of genus 6 curve $C : v^2 + v = u^{13} + u^{11} + u^7 + u^3 + 1$. An exponentiation took 476 msec. on Pentium-II (300MHz). This jacobian achieves good performance and faster than other jacobians of smaller genus curves, because of the field size.

Moreover, we have implemented genus 3 and 11 curves, which have the same level of security as RSA-2048 and RSA-5000. Table 7 shows the processing time of $C : v^2 + v = u^{2g+1}$ implemented over Alpha 21164A (467MHz). Even if the genus is 11, which has the same level of security as RSA-5000, exponentiation took 1.79 sec because of its small size of the definition field.

In the case of elliptic curve cryptosystems, many techniques for an efficient implementation has been developed, and timings were reported. For example, in [WBV96], an elliptic curve (over $\mathbf{F}_{2^{177}}$) exponentiation with 177-bit exponent achieved 72 msec. on Pentium 133 MHz. In [MOC97], an elliptic curve (over $\mathbf{F}_p, p = 2^{169} - 1825$) exponentiation with 169-bit exponent (of a random point) achieved 32.54 msec. on Sparc 110 MHz. On the other hand, in the case of hyperelliptic cryptosystems, no such a report has been published. Our hyperelliptic curves exponentiation, which have smaller definition fields, are a few times slower than the elliptic curves cases. However, our implementation suggests that hyperelliptic curve cryptosystems may have practical performance.

Acknowledgments

The second author would like to thank Iwan Duursma, who informed him of a method for computing the order of a jacobian without evaluating the exact roots of zeta. The second author also wishes to thank Zvi Galil and Moti Yung for their generous hospitality while his visiting Columbia Univ. Computer Science Dept.

References

ADH94. L.M. ADLEMAN, J. DEMARRAIS and M. HUANG, "A Subexponential Algorithm for Discrete Logarithm over the Rational Subgroup of the Jacobians of Large Genus Hyperelliptic Curves over Finite Fields", *Proc. of ANTS1, LNCS*, vol. 877, Springer-Verlag, (1994), 28–40

BK98. J. BUHLER and N. KOBLITZ, Joe Buhler and Neal Koblitz, "Lattice basis reduction, Jacobi sums and hyperelliptic cryptosystems,", Bull. Austral. Math. Soc. (1998)

BS91. T. BETH and F. SCAEFER, "Non supersingular elliptic curves for public key cryptosystems", *Advances in Cryptology - EUROCRYPT '91, Lecture Notes in Computer Science*, **547**, pp.316–327 (1991).

CA87. D.G. CANTOR, "Computing in the Jacobian of a Hyperelliptic Curve", *Math. Comp*, **48**, No.177 (1987), 95–101

CMT97. J. CHAO, N. MATSUDA, and S. TSUJII, "Efficient construction of secure hyperelliptic discrete logarithms", *Information and Communications Security*, Springer-Verlag, LNCS 1334 (1997), 292–301.

CTT94. J. CHAO, K. TANAKA, and S. TSUJII, "Design of elliptic curves with controllable lower boundary of extension degree for reduction attacks", *Advances in Cryptology - Crypto'94*, Springer-Verlag, (1994), 50–55.

FR97. G. FREY, "Aspects of DL-systems based on hyperelliptic curves", *Keynote Lecture in Waterloo-Workshop on Elliptic Curve Discrete Logarithm Problem*, 4th of Nov. (1997).

FR94. G. FREY and H.G. RÜCK, "A Remark Concerning m-Divisibility and the Discrete Logarithm in the Divisor Class Group of Curves", *Math. Comp*, **62**, No.206 (1994), 865–874

GLV98. ROBERT GALLANT, ROBERT LAMBERT and SCOTT VANSTONE, "Improving the parallelized Pollard lambda search on binary anomalous", A draft is available from http://grouper.ieee.org/groups/1363/contrib.html, (April,1998)

KO88. N. KOBLITZ, "A Family of Jacobians Suitable for Discrete Log Cryptosystems", *Advances in Cryptology - Crypto'88*, Springer-Verlag, (1990), 94–99

KO89. N. KOBLITZ, "Hyperelliptic Cryptosystems", *J.Cryptology*, **1** (1989), 139–150

KO98. N. KOBLITZ, "Algebraic Aspects of Cryptography", Springer-Verlag, (1998)

MOC97. A. MIYAJI, T. ONO and H. COHEN, "Efficient Elliptic curve Exponentiation", *Information and Communications Security*, Springer-Verlag, (1997), 282–290.

MOV93. A.J. MENEZES, T. OKAMOTO and S.A. VANSTONE, "Reducing elliptic curve logarithm to logarithm in a finite field", *IEEE Trans. on IT*, **39**, (1993), 1639–1646

PH78. S.C. POHLIG and M.E. HELLMAN, "An improved algorithm for computing logarithms over $GF(p)$ and its cryptographic significance", *IEEE Trans. on IT*, **24**, (1978), 106–110

RU97. H.G. RÜCK, "On the discrete logarithms in the divisor class group of curves", To appear in *Math. Comp.* (1997)

SA97. T. SATOH and K. ARAKI, "Fermat Quotients and the Polynomial Time Discrete Log Algorithm for Anomalous Elliptic Curves", *preprint*, (1997)

SEM98. I.A. SEMAEV, "Evaluation of discrete logarithms in a group of p-torsion points of an elliptic curve in characteristic p", *Math. Comp.*, Vol.76 (1998), 353–356.

SM97. N.P. SMART, "The Discrete Logarithm Problem on Elliptic Curves of Trace One", *preprint*, (1997)

SSI98. Y. SAKAI, K. SAKURAI AND H. ISHIZUKA, "Secure hyperelliptic cryptosystems and their performance", *Pre-Proc. PKC'98* (1998)

St93. H. STICHTENOTH, "Algebraic Function Fields and Codes", Springer-Verlag, (1993)

WBV96. E.D. WIN, A. BOSSELAERS, and S. VANDENBERGHE, "A Fase Software Implementation for Arithmetic Operations in GF(2^n)" *Advances in Cryptology - Asiacrypt'96*, Springer-Verlag, (1996), 65–76.

WZ98. MICHAEL WIENER AND ROBERT ZUCCHERATO, "Faster Attacks on Elliptic Curve Cryptosystems," A draft is available from `http://grouper.ieee.org` `/groups/1363/contrib.html`, (April,1998)

A Jacobians which have the Same Level of Security as RSA-1024

In this Appendix, we show jacobians such that the largest prime factor (P_{max}) of $\sharp \mathbf{J}(C; \mathbf{F}_{q^n})$ has the size of approximately 2^{160}.

A.1 Characteristic 2

Genus 2 curves

$\mathbf{J}(C; \mathbf{F}_{2^{89}}), C : v^2 + (u^2 + u + 1)v = u^5 + u + 1/\mathbf{F}_2$ (P_{max}:178-bit)

$\sharp \mathbf{J} = 2 \cdot 1915619426082424560734984182521086636153120315129149$69

Genus 3 curves

$\mathbf{J}(C; \mathbf{F}_{2^{59}}), C : v^2 + v = u^7/\mathbf{F}_2$ (P_{max}:165-bit)

$\sharp \mathbf{J} = 7 \cdot 827 \cdot 330906793242764047840375503433593497918507025120$53

Genus 4 curves

$\mathbf{J}(C; \mathbf{F}_{2^{41}}), C : v^2 + v = u^9 + u^7 + u^3 + 1/\mathbf{F}_2$ (P_{max}:161-bit)

$\sharp \mathbf{J} = 11 \cdot 2125818615244041340661452662120917241919480417187$

Genus 5 curves

$\mathbf{J}(C; \mathbf{F}_{2^{41}}), C : v^2 + v = u^{11} + u^5 + u + 1/\mathbf{F}_2$ (P_{max}:201-bit)

$\sharp \mathbf{J} = 29 \cdot 177317301435474789025319955016917384201809639869287331$9662133

Genus 6 curves

$\mathbf{J}(C; \mathbf{F}_{2^{29}}), C : v^2 + v = u^{13} + u^{11} + u^7 + u^3 + 1/\mathbf{F}_2$ (P_{max}:170-bit)

$\sharp \mathbf{J} = 23 \cdot 1040988300089925365337867649065425169641062000079783$

$\mathbf{J}(C; \mathbf{F}_{2^{29}}), C : v^2 + v = u^{13} + u^{11} + u^9 + u^5 + 1/\mathbf{F}_2$ (P_{max}:171-bit)

$\sharp \mathbf{J} = 13 \cdot 1841646667025959098054051155819603805847557201575621$

A.2 Characteristic 3

Genus 2 curves

$\mathbf{J}(C; \mathbf{F}_{3^{59}}), C : v^2 = u^5 + u^4 + u^3 + u + 1/\mathbf{F}_3$ (P_{max}:185-bit)

$\sharp \mathbf{J} = 5 \cdot 3993356222032046013312036841857758139633984955786870497$7

Genus 3 curves

$\mathbf{J}(C; \mathbf{F}_{3^{37}}), C : v^2 = u^7 + u^5 + u^3 + u^2 + 1/\mathbf{F}_3$ (P_{max}:171-bit)

$\sharp \mathbf{J} = 5 \cdot 7 \cdot 260850232596649810651780408888629089589940116274777$7

$\mathbf{J}(C; \mathbf{F}_{3^{37}}), C : v^2 = u^7 + u^6 + u^5 + u^4 + 1/\mathbf{F}_3$ (P_{max}:164-bit)

$\sharp \mathbf{J} = 47 \cdot 149 \cdot 130369244652044303216262821596779559280812713223$37

Genus 4 curves

$\mathbf{J}(C; \mathbf{F}_{3^{29}}), C : v^2 = u^9 + u^8 + u^7 + u^4 + u^3 + u^2 + u + 1/\mathbf{F}_3$ (P_{max}:177-bit)

$\sharp \mathbf{J} = 137 \cdot 161936596667550201850764509341446010074223174018351807$

$\mathbf{J}(C; \mathbf{F}_{3^{29}}), C : v^2 = u^9 + u^6 + u^5 + u^3 + 1/\mathbf{F}_3$ (P_{max}:178-bit)
$\sharp\mathbf{J} = 2 \cdot 43 \cdot 2579686168841150378155212270151370186946348590774566601$
$\mathbf{J}(C; \mathbf{F}_{3^{29}}), C : v^2 = u^9 + u^7 + u^5 + u^4 + u^3 + u + 1/\mathbf{F}_3$ (P_{max}:178-bit)
$\sharp\mathbf{J} = 2 \cdot 53 \cdot 2092954173072759861594173998895734536674244147143677781$
$\mathbf{J}(C; \mathbf{F}_{3^{29}}), C : v^2 = u^9 + u^7 + u^6 + u^2 + 1/\mathbf{F}_3$ (P_{max}:178-bit)
$\sharp\mathbf{J} = 3 \cdot 37 \cdot 1998676653598551445761192368350768314350891724717787133$
$\mathbf{J}(C; \mathbf{F}_{3^{29}}), C : v^2 = u^9 + u^7 + u^6 + u^5 + u^4 + u^3 + u + 1/\mathbf{F}_3$ (P_{max}:178-bit)
$\sharp\mathbf{J} = 5 \cdot 19 \cdot 2335295689665161152081487036077746477504835320261253357$

A.3   Characteristic 5
Genus 2 curves
$\mathbf{J}(C; \mathbf{F}_{5^{43}}), C : v^2 = u^5 + u^2 + 1/\mathbf{F}_5$ (P_{max}:196-bit)
$\sharp\mathbf{J} = 2 \cdot 2 \cdot 5 \cdot 6462348535570513460573407847319476321073981223998020578465\overline3$

Genus 3 curves
$\mathbf{J}(C; \mathbf{F}_{5^{23}}), C : v^2 = u^7 + u^6 + u^2 + 1/\mathbf{F}_5$ (P_{max}:154-bit)
$\sharp\mathbf{J} = 3 \cdot 43 \cdot 131322935738696075253413636183396467438153320\overline17$
Genus 4 curves
$\mathbf{J}(C; \mathbf{F}_{5^{19}}), C : v^2 = u^9 + u^6 + u^4 + u^3 + 1/\mathbf{F}_5$ (P_{max}:166-bit)
$\sharp\mathbf{J} = 2 \cdot 967 \cdot 684327546934217611797959011504633848359840651253\overline61$
$\mathbf{J}(C; \mathbf{F}_{5^{19}}), C : v^2 = u^9 + u^7 + u^6 + u^5 + u^3 + u + 1/\mathbf{F}_5$ (P_{max}:168-bit)
$\sharp\mathbf{J} = 3 \cdot 151 \cdot 292161172338621074756327634541902615881173270592929$
$\mathbf{J}(C; \mathbf{F}_{5^{19}}), C : v^2 = u^9 + u^8 + u^7 + u^4 + u + 1/\mathbf{F}_5$ (P_{max}:167-bit)
$\sharp\mathbf{J} = 17 \cdot 73 \cdot 106647119155998044412946215375749800145892212819953$

A.4   Characteristic 7
Genus 2 curves
$\mathbf{J}(C; \mathbf{F}_{7^{29}}), C : v^2 = u^5 + u^4 + u^2 + 1/\mathbf{F}_7$ (P_{max}:157-bit)
$\sharp\mathbf{J} = 79 \cdot 1312378870422428574310666502439881903134182183\overline01$
Genus 3 curves
$\mathbf{J}(C; \mathbf{F}_{7^{19}}), C : v^2 = u^7 + u^6 + u^5 + u^3 + u + 1/\mathbf{F}_7$ (P_{max}:152-bit)
$\sharp\mathbf{J} = 2^3 \cdot 41 \cdot 4515589388807654345104182483396611659561472503$
Genus 4 curves
$\mathbf{J}(C; \mathbf{F}_{7^{17}}), C : v^2 = u^9 + u^8 + u^6 + u^5 + u^3 + u + 1/\mathbf{F}_7$ (P_{max}:181-bit)
$\sharp\mathbf{J} = 2^4 \cdot 97 \cdot 188701387296773136203522548345057408767223350900238191\overline1$

B   Curves of $v^2 + v = u^{2g+1}$ over $\mathbf{F}_2$
In this Appendix, we show jacobians of $C : v^2 + v = u^{2g+1}$ in the case of $g = 3, 11$.
Genus 3 curves
$\mathbf{J}(C; \mathbf{F}_{2^{59}}), C : v^2 + v = u^7/\mathbf{F}_2$ (P_{max}:165-bit)
$\sharp\mathbf{J} = 7 \cdot 827 \cdot 33090679324276404784037550343593497918507025120\overline53$
$\mathbf{J}(C; \mathbf{F}_{2^{89}}), C : v^2 + v = u^7/\mathbf{F}_2$ (P_{max}:264-bit)
$\sharp\mathbf{J} = 7 \cdot 179 \cdot 2671 \cdot 70857183122325533127823325792054243244435303883153993362539\overline1$
    34263544967267
$\mathbf{J}(C; \mathbf{F}_{2^{113}}), C : v^2 + v = u^7/\mathbf{F}_2$ (P_{max}:310-bit)
$\sharp\mathbf{J} = 7 \cdot 1583 \cdot 75937 \cdot 13308715445912585039043505943639888842362635151754060420\overline76$
    3267396674295645712955519238138050393
Genus 11 curves
$\mathbf{J}(C; \mathbf{F}_{2^{47}}), C : v^2 + v = u^{23}/\mathbf{F}_2$ (P_{max}:310-bit)
$\sharp\mathbf{J} = 3 \cdot 23 \cdot 29 \cdot 34687 \cdot 254741 \cdot 381077 \cdot 836413 \cdot 4370719 \cdot 122803256446193 \cdot 10157840562191\overline6$
    029 \cdot 139636002374160122872280490593436140443948017710590946009612010801\overline3
    867835189294124093667687457

Construction of Secure Elliptic Cryptosystems Using CM Tests and Liftings

Jinhui Chao[1], Osamu Nakamura[2], Kohji Sobataka[1], and Shigeo Tsujii[2]

[1] Dept. of Electrical and Electronic Engineering, Chuo University, Tokyo, Japan
[2] Dept. of Information and Engineering Systems, Chuo University, Tokyo, Japan
jchao@elect.chuo-u.ac.jp, soba@chao.elect.chuo-u.ac.jp,
tsujii@ise.chuo-u.ac.jp

Abstract. Elliptic curves over number fields with CM can be used to design non-isogenous elliptic cryptosystems over finite fields efficiently. The existing algorithm to build such CM curves, so-called the CM field algorithm, is based on analytic expansion of modular functions, costing computations of $O(2^{5h/2}h^{21/4})$ where h is the class number of the endomorphism ring of the CM curve. Thus it is effective only in the small class number cases.

This paper presents polynomial time algorithms in h to build CM elliptic curves over number fields. In the first part, probabilistic probabilistic algorithms of CM tests are presented to find elliptic curves with CM without restriction on class numbers. In the second part, we show how to construct ring class fields from ray class fields. Finally, a deterministic algorithm for lifting the ring class equations from small finite fields thus construct CM curves is presented. Its complexity is shown as $O(h^7)$.

1 Introduction

Elliptic curves over finite fields have been used in recent public key cryptosystems, authentication and signature schemes. The discrete logarithm problems over the elliptic curves can resist all known subexponential attacks, which then can implement cryptographic schemes in higher speed and less key sizes while retain the same security comparing with traditional cryptographic functions [14][22][21].

Among the methods to construct explicitly secure elliptic curves over finite fields for cryptosystem applications, the point-counting algorithms, now known as the SEA algorithms can find secure curves over finite fields from randomly selected elliptic curves, but still be quite time consuming since they generally need to be repeated many times until a secure curve is found [27][28][8][24][20][10]. Another difficulty of this approach is that when one wishes to choose different curves for different users or periodically change curves over finite fields in the same cryptosystem, he has to undergo the whole process of the above calculations, or it always takes the same computations in order to obtain any new secure curves and cryptosystems.

K. Ohta and D. Pei (Eds.): ASIACRYPT'98, LNCS 1514, pp. 95–109, 1998.

According to [16], if the same curve over a finite field is repeatedly used in an elliptic cryptosystem, even each time with a random base point, one can easily transform the new discrete logarithm problem into the old one. Thus the old database can be made good use of such that one can attack this kind of cryptosystems faster, comparing with those which switch each time to a new or non-isogenous curve over a finite field. Furthermore, if one is willing to build a large database, then with certain variations of the Baby step Giant step algorithm, one can attack the cryptosystems using a fixed curve over a finite field in time of $O(q^{1/d})$, $d > 2$, rather than the standard complexity of the Baby step and Giant step algorithm: $O(\sqrt{q})$.

Another approach to build secure elliptic curves over finite fields, which is much faster and meets the requirement to change to non-isogenous curves frequently, is to use a family of elliptic curves defined over number fields, i.e. those with complex multiplication or CM elliptic curves [23] [2][3][4][19].

In fact, the CM curves may not be easy to find, but once a CM curve over a number field is built, one can use very simple and fast algorithms to design directly non-isogenous curves over finite fields with different and maybe prespecified (almost prime) orders, therefore different secure cryptosystems as many as one wishes, if he changes the characteristics and extension degrees of the finite definition fields. This can be done by efficient algorithms of reduced quadratic forms (see appendix) or the Cornacchia algorithm.

As to the security of using CM curves, it is known that all elliptic curves over finite fields are with CM (so usually they are not referred to as CM curves and we will leave the name exclusively to curves over number fields). Furthermore, each elliptic curve over a finite field is the reduction of an CM curve (known as its Deuring's lifting) over a certain number field. If there were any attack which works effective particularly for the elliptic cryptosystems designed from CM curves, we may need only to consider the lifting attacks which lift the elliptic curves over finite fields to their Deuring's liftings over number fields and solve the discrete logarithm problems over number fields. However, it is well known that these kind of attacks seem exponentially hard due to difficulty in lifting the rational points of elliptic curves from finite fields to number fields, the exponentially explosion of the heights of these rational points over number fields, and the finite rank of their Mordell-Weil groups. In fact, these are the same arguments known for security of general elliptic cryptosystems [22], i.e., on the immunity of generic elliptic curves from attacks of the index-calculus algorithm.

Existing algorithms used for construction of CM curves, somewhat vaguely called "CM field algorithms", are based on construction of class fields using analytic series expansions of the modular functions over C([1] and also [7][12])

Although theoretically these algorithms can build any elliptic curve over finite fields, they seemed tedious and always involved with problems such as approximation errors. Their complexity is known as an exponential function $O(2^{5h/2}h^{21/4})$ of the class number h, assuming the elliptic curves have their endomorphism rings as an imaginary quadratic order with the class number h. Therefore, they becomes impractical for large class numbers.

Besides, the scenario of the CM field algorithms, i.e. to start from a particular order of an elliptic curve over a given finite field, then calculate the j-invariant of the elliptic curve over the class field and finally define the model of the elliptic curve over the finite field with the assigned order, seems somewhat misleading and unnecessarily involved.

In fact, a clearer and simpler scenario consists of two stages. The first one is to build an explicit model of a CM curve over the class field. The second stage is to design the order of the curve over a finite field. The computation time of the first stage is obviously dominant. As long as one has a model of elliptic curve with CM over a number field, as mentioned before, he can use this curve to design different isogenous classes of secure curves over large finite fields.

It maybe interesting to notice the curves over finite fields with the Frobenius endomorphisms with small traces or the endomorphism rings of large class numbers can be most quickly calculated by the SEA algorithms, while the curves with the endomorphism rings of small class numbers or the Frobenius endomorphisms with large traces are most easily dealt by the algorithms using CM curves but are of most time consuming for the SEA algorithms.

Thus, the key issue in using CM curves to design elliptic cryptosystems is to find models of CM elliptic curves over number fields efficiently, in copious supply, and with endomorphism rings of large discriminants or class numbers.

In [25][26], we shown probabilistic algorithms to find random CM elliptic and higher genus curves by CM tests, which requires no calculation of j-invariants or class equations.

In this paper, we first show the CM test algorithms in a more complete form to find random CM curves. Then we show how to construct ring class fields or the definition fields of the CM curves without explicit construction of class equations, i.e. from ray class fields which can be easily derived using division polynomials. Finally, an efficient deterministic algorithm for lifting the ring class equations from small finite fields is presented to construct CM curves. The complexity of this algorithm is of polynomial time in the class number h: $O(h^7)$. All calculations in these algorithms are simple and easy to implement. Since there is only algebraic manipulations involved, no care is needed about approximation errors control during the calculations.

An interesting generalization of these algorithms is to Jacobian varieties of algebraic curves of higher genera [13] (see also [5]).

2   CM Tests for Elliptic Curves

We show in this section fast algorithms to test if an elliptic curve over a number field is with CM, which can be used to find random CM curves over number fields without calculation of j-invariants and their class equations.

Definition 1. *An elliptic curve E over a field F is with complex multiplication or a CM elliptic curve if its endomorphism ring $End_F E$ contains the rational integral ring $\mathbf{Z}$ as a proper subring.*

We refer the details of theory of complex multiplication to standard references. e.g. [17][32][18][31].

Definition 2. *An elliptic curve which passed a CM test is called a pseudo-CM elliptic curve.*

Let F be a number field. Bellow, we denote the residue field of a rational prime p in F as $\boldsymbol{F}_q$, D the discriminant of
an imaginary quadratic number field $\boldsymbol{Q}(\sqrt{\Delta}), \Delta < 0$, as CM fields of ordinary elliptic curves, i.e. $\mathrm{End}^\circ E := \mathrm{End} E \otimes_{\boldsymbol{Z}} \boldsymbol{Q} = \boldsymbol{Q}(\sqrt{\Delta})$.

Algorithm 1 (CM tests)

Procedure 1 (Ordinary reduction) [25]

Input : Random elliptic curves E/F;
Output : Pseudo-CM curves and the discriminants of their CM fields.
Step 1 Choose a small prime p_1 such that $E/\boldsymbol{F}_{q_1}$ is an ordinary reduction. Find the discriminant $d_1 = l_1^2 \Delta_1 (\Delta_1:$ square free) of the characteristic polynomial of the Frobenius endomorphism;
Step 2 Choose small primes $p_i, i = 2, \cdots, N$ such that $(\frac{\Delta_1}{p_i}) = 1$, then for $E/\boldsymbol{F}_{q_i}$ find the discriminant of the Frobenius endomorphism $d_i = l_i^2 \Delta_i$. If $\Delta_i = \Delta_1$ for all i, output E as a pseudo-CM curve with the discriminant D_1. Otherwise, output E/F as without CM.

Procedure 2 (Supersingular reduction)

Input : Random elliptic curves E/F;
Output : Pseudo-CM curves and the discriminants of their CM fields.
Step 1 Choose a small prime p_1 such that $E/\boldsymbol{F}_{q_1}$ is an ordinary reduction. Find the discriminant $d_1 = l_1^2 \Delta_1$ of the characteristic polynomial of the Frobenius endomorphism;
Step 2 Choose small primes $p_i, i = 2, \cdots, N$ such that $(\frac{\Delta_1}{p_i}) = -1$, then if $E/\boldsymbol{F}_{p_i^2}$ are supersingular or an additive bad reduction for all i , output E as a pseudo-CM curve with the discriminant D_1. Otherwise, output E/F as without CM.

Procedure 3 (bad reduction)

Input : Random elliptic curves E/F;
Output : Pseudo-CM curves and the discriminants of their CM fields.
Step 1 Choose a small prime p_1 such that $E/\boldsymbol{F}_{q_1}$ is an ordinary reduction. Find the discriminant $d_1 = l_1^2 \Delta_1$ of the characteristic polynomial of the Frobenius endomorphism;
Step 2 Choose small primes p_i such that $(\frac{\Delta_1}{p_i}) = 0$, then if $E/\boldsymbol{F}_{p_i^2}$ are supersingular or an additive bad reduction for all i, output E as a pseudo-CM curve with the discriminant D_1. Otherwise, output E/F as without CM.

Remark 1: The calculations in these tests can be obviously done by fast algorithms in polynomial time in $\log p_{amx}$.

Remark 2: With extra computations, the step 2 can be refined to identify the isomorphism types of the endomorphism rings by e.g. Kohel's algorithm [15]. In that case, one will be able to output the discriminants of the endomorphism rings.

Remark 3: Naturally one can combine these procedures to raise the computational efficiency. e.g. after the step 1, for the first N primes apply the step 2 of each procedures. Besides, the latter two ones should be applied first. Ordinary reductions over prime fields are also preferable.

If the class equation was known, one can use the following test which is based on the result of Gross-Zagier [11], which is very sharp but the calculation of discriminant becomes heavy for large class numbers.

Gross-Zagier test

Input $f(x) \in \mathbf{Z}[x]$: a polynomial; $d \in \mathbf{Z}_-$: discriminant of a CM field.
Output If $f(x)$ is the class polynomial $H_d(x)$.
Step 1 If the constant term of $f(x)$ is not d-smooth, output NO;
Step 2 If the discriminant of $f(x)$ is not $(3/4)d$-smooth, output NO;
Step 3 Output $f(x) = H_d(x)$.

3 Construction of Ring Class Fields from Ray Class Fields

Let $k = \mathbf{Q}(\sqrt{\Delta})$ ($\Delta < 0$: square free) be an imaginary quadratic number field, D the discriminant of k, $h(D)$ the class number of k, $\mathcal{O}_k$ the integral ring of k, $\mathcal{O}_c$ an order of $\mathcal{O}_k$ of conductor c with discriminant $d = c^2 D$, k_{ring}^c the ring class field modulo (c), k_{ray}^c the ray class field modulo (c), k_{abs} the abstract or Hilbert class field of k. $H_D(x)$ the Hilbert class equation and $H_d(x)$ the ring class equation of $\mathcal{O}_c$.

Let F be a number field, an elliptic curve E/F is with CM if its endomorphism ring $\mathrm{End}_F E$ is an order $\mathcal{O}_c$ of an imaginary quadratic number field $k = \mathbf{Q}(\sqrt{\Delta})$, where c is the conductor of $\mathcal{O}_c$. Furthermore, an elliptic curve with CM has a model over the ring class field modulo (c), k_{ring}^c. (Specifically, certain subfields sometimes called its moduli fields.)

In fact, to construct a ring class field, over which the CM elliptic curves are defined, is not the same thing to find the singular moduli or the j-invariants which generate the ring class field. As shown bellow, the former could be much easier than the latter.

It is known that one can obtain ring class fields from the genus fields when d are chosen as Euler's convenient numbers. Bellow, we obtain the ring class fields from the ray class fields easily. Let x_c be the x-coordinate of a c-torsion point in $E[c]$, $w_D = \frac{D+\sqrt{D}}{2}$, $h(w_D, \mathcal{O}_c)$ the Weber function.

Algorithm 2

Input : $d = c^2 D$: Discriminant of an imaginary quadratic order in $k = \boldsymbol{Q}(\sqrt{\Delta})$
   or c: its conductor;
Output : A moduli field $\boldsymbol{Q}(j(\mathcal{O}_c))$ of a ray (ring) class field modulo (c).
Step 1 Find an elliptic curve E/k_{abs} with CM such that

$$\text{End}_{k_{abs}} E = \mathcal{O}_k$$

   whose j-invariant equals $j(\mathcal{O}_k) \in k_{abs}$;
Step 2 Calculate the c-division polynomial of E, $\varphi_c(x) \in \boldsymbol{Z}[x]$;
Step 3 Find irreducible factors of $\varphi_c(x)$, $f_c(x)$;
Step 4 Find the moduli fields in k_{ray}^c:$\boldsymbol{Q}(j(\mathcal{O}_k), x_c) = \boldsymbol{Q}(j(\mathcal{O}_c), h(w_D, \mathcal{O}_c))$ which
   are generated by twice simple extensions with the $H_D(x)$ and $f_c(x)$ as the
   minimal polynomials.

Remark 1: Since the division polynomials can be easily calculated, one may
wish to chose $k = \boldsymbol{Q}(\sqrt{\Delta})$ with small class number $h(D)$.
Remark 2: If one chooses $h(D) = 1$, or one uses the thirteen elliptic curves
over $\boldsymbol{Q}$, then one finds in k_{ray}^c the moduli field $\boldsymbol{Q}(x_c) = \boldsymbol{Q}(j(\mathcal{O}_c), h)$ with the
minimal polynomial as $f_c(x)$.

In this way, one can readily produce a ring class field or its moduli field, which
can be used in the CM test algorithms in the previous section as definition fields
of CM elliptic curves.
However, since CM curves over a particular number field are of finite number
so the probability to find them could be very low. One may wish to use more
efficient and deterministic algorithm to find a CM curve by calculation of the
ring class equation $H_d(x)$, which is also a minimal polynomial of $\boldsymbol{Q}(j(\mathcal{O}_c))$. To
present such an algorithm will be the task of the following section.

4   Lifting CM Elliptic Curves fROM Finite Fields

Let $E(j)$ as a model of an elliptic curve with j as its j-invariant . For $p \neq 2, 3$,

$$E(j): \quad y^2 = x^3 - \frac{3j}{j - 1728}x - \frac{2j}{j - 1728}$$

or for any characteristics,

$$E(j): \quad y^2 + xy = x^3 - \frac{36}{j - 1728}x - \frac{1}{j - 1728}.$$

Algorithm 3:

Input : $d = c^2 D < 0$: Discriminant of an imaginary quadratic order in $\boldsymbol{Q}(\sqrt{\Delta})$;
Output : The ring class equation $H_d(x)$.

step 1 Using the Algorithm 2 to construct a moduli field F of a ring class field k_{ring}^c;

step 2 For small prime p_i , let F_{q_i} be the residue field of the rational prime p_i in $\mathcal{O}_F$.

1. If $(d/p_i) = 1$, find among all $E(j)/F_{q_i}$ for $\forall j \in F_{q_i}$ $h(d)$ isogenous but non-isomorphic elliptic curves $E_s, s = 1, \cdots, h(d)$ such that

$$4q_i = t_i^2 - c_i^2 d, \quad \text{where} \quad t_i = q_i + 1 - \#E_s(F_{q_i})$$

Then from the $h(d)$ j-invariants of E_s, $j_{is} \in F_{q_i}$, calculate the ring class equation modp_i as

$$H_d(X) \bmod p_i \equiv \prod_{s=1}^{h(d)} (x - j_{is})$$

2. If $(d/p_i) = -1$, find among all $E(j)/F_{p_i^2}$ for $\forall j \in F_{p_i^2}$, $h(d)$ isogenous but non-isomorphic elliptic curves $E_s, s = 1, \cdots, h(d)$ s.t. they are supersingular or additive bad reductions.
Then from $h(d)$ j-invariants of E_s, $j_{is} \in F_{p_i^2}$ calculate the ring class equation modp_i

$$H_d(X) \bmod p_i \equiv \prod_{s=1}^{h(d)} (x - j_{is})$$

3. If $(d/p_i) = 0$, find among all $E(j)/F_{p_i^2}, \forall j \in F_{p_i^2}$, $h(d)$ isogenous but non-isomorphic elliptic curves E_s s.t. $E_s/F_{p_i^2}$ are supersingular or additive bad reductions.
Then from $h(d)$ j-invariants of E_s, $j_{is} \in F_{p_i^2}$ calculate the ring class equation modp_i

$$H_d(X) \bmod p_i \equiv \prod_{s=1}^{h(d)} (x - j_{is})$$

step 3 By the Chinese Remainder Theorem (CRT) to lift the coefficients of

$$H_d(x) \bmod \prod_i p_i.$$

to $Z[x]$;

Step 4 If the $E(j)$ defined by the lifted ring class equation passes the CM tests in the Algorithm 1 or the Gross-Zagier test, then output $H_d(x) \bmod \prod_i p_i$ as the ring class equation $H_d(x)$, and $E(j)$ as a pseudo-CM elliptic curve; If not goto step 3 to add one more prime p_i or try other combinations.

Remark 1: Considering increase of the size of the coefficients of class equations, one may first calculate the Weber class invariants f from j-invariants over finite fields,

$$(x - 16)^3 \equiv jx \bmod p_i, \quad x \equiv f^{24} \bmod p_i$$

then lift the Weber class equations, which will allow us to lift the class equations of large class numbers. The details are referred to [7][1]etc.

Remark 2: To avoid the combinations, one can use only p s.t. there is few ambiguity in conductors. A more complete version should include the Kohel's deterministic algorithm to distinguish the isomorphism types of full endomorphism rings of the elliptic curves $E_s/\boldsymbol{F}_{q_i}$[15]. e.g. in ordinary lifting to choose E_s s.t.

$$\operatorname{End}_{\boldsymbol{F}_{q_i}} E_s = \mathcal{O}_c = \boldsymbol{Z} + c\mathcal{O}_k.$$

In supersingular lifting, check at first that if the endomorphism rings of the curves contain an optimal embedding of $\mathcal{O}_c$, the imaginary order which is chosen as the endomorphism ring of the target CM curve.

Remark 3: In fact, lifting from only prime fields is possible once a discriminant is chosen appropriately. Thus there is no need to build the ring class field a priori even in implicit form. Thus, by using only the lifting from prime fields, calculation of the division polynomials can also be omitted. In fact, the Hilbert class equations can also be lifted in the similar way.

5   Examples of CM Tests

We applied the ordinary reduction CM test of the Algorithm 1 to the elliptic curve over $\boldsymbol{Q}$:

$$y^2 = x^3 - \frac{3 \cdot j}{j - 1728} x - \frac{2 \cdot j}{j - 1728}$$

and take $p_1 = 709$, the other small primes $p_i > 300$ ($i = 2, \cdots, 10$). The nine tests ($i = 2, ..., 10$) for 64847 random curves are shown in the table, the second row shows the number of non-CM curves which are rejected at the i-th tests in Step 2. It can be observed that almost all of them are rejected by double or triple tests and none of the non-CM curves passed the first five tests.

i-th test	2	3	4	5	6	7	8	9	10
#{rejected curves}	64301	518	25	0	1	0	0	0	0

There are only two curves which passed the fifth and all tests, i.e. $D_1 = D_i$, ($i = 2, \cdots, 10$). Their j-invariants are

$$j = -15^3, \, -32^3.$$

As we know, they are truly CM curves.

In fact, the supersingular and bad reduction tests distinguish even sharperly between CM and non-CM curves (see proof of the algorithm 1 for reasons).

6   Examples of Construction of CM Curves

Take $h = 174$, $d = -153164$ with ($c = 118$, $D = -11$). The Weber class polynomial $W_d(x)$ is lifted from the following 19 ordinary reduction over prime fields.

$$p_i \in \{38327, 38867, 39191, 47507, 51287, 52691, 54167, 62627, 68567,$$
$$79907, 84947, 93047, 95891, 98807, 111191, 114467, 128291, 131927, 167891\}$$

Bellow, we show a part of it with small coefficients.

$W_{-153164}(x)$

$= 8307674973655724205648794126752152153 6$

$- 42323683992739640442809287757606649858768240 64x$

$+ 36808492460582737754412167232495487558362441682926960640 0x^2$

$- 26242757487982084712865000766384589091157781567446040224727 04x^3$

$+ 87686788061864213489595505702152711613698903214570636869160140 80x^4$

$- 16489781241655501731333261028106256316481417674894072363666938789888x^5$

$+ 14052650996984969061469817388935214478719631395032143945942480768204800x^6$

$+ 13169576985342755871469221521746969372303116412360116401406271758973009 92x^7$

$+ 18766520740113136384236471995335388274023721360064130874526022356826272563 2x^8$

$+ 992987098462162111028797607421941628603098507776909839140262474134009046630 4x^9$

$\cdots\cdots$

$\cdots\cdots$

$- 49838586711420444124697783858863436766203823639344917839348583706881163264 0x^{142}$

$+ 22297069162167652140111015244039228219361606696374190400090673018983101235 2x^{143}$

$+ 71080649261462583121962968317120128417730350894483994673224565837242826752x^{144}$

$- 95122601321218621133257525298511335715258057070859322566145377909417705472x^{145}$

$+ 45219601136166877968863776507347766787306724663008364023307302917660213248x^{146}$

$- 13346061303836276974162247560906288805918444808171101290600486055341195264x^{147}$

$+ 25337354737921119743913555955900626764971673794515791382507010448461660 16x^{148}$

$- 22920144971729281838465538130740262440855942474360106083391822133565849 6x^{149}$

$- 29127664490959341147148412087645366104070287020397722579723027980550144x^{150}$

$+ 14473860267302632756826256334560085209007765402939877697784495917760512x^{151}$

$- 22581124163779247862814621139644339448943651749300763200710342659276 8x^{152}$

$+ 21911932648642681673109307426395599556260798604340966006771581583 36x^{153}$

$+ 8383646868645701690055857919799505192324769588803081104803574978969 6x^{154}$

$- 2302542459957200841111491642324791656738959407389660060483351275110 4x^{155}$

$+ 38346824001633241348549492265171791789790892476907170098452263157 76x^{156}$

$- 45750540400104158618266884818286582019320209877538883429188853760 0x^{157}$

$+ 40674500946996572573885826017965346465580116302611164077330751488x^{158}$

$- 26996480849733659202175751374753523594968362217204708563571179 52x^{159}$

$+ 132458322755123835013929151419628962052310054314389457199693824x^{160}$

$- 48936156425506624551987956740332139506470223357651112513126 40x^{161}$

$+ 15671231872693057706331775571171963070832694775462500014336 0x^{162}$

$- 528594435540847885072660309214950311471713878690454649036 8x^{163}$

$+ 15521747694840492355619774008370320438513279027810156134 4x^{164}$

$- 3239096798144628226875867231556073257899072332049833728x^{165}$

$+ 9402148041750777656219877798027804355251052046370790 4x^{166}$

$$- \ 2296309607112522904450409137134279517655964685744464x^{167}$$
$$- \ 3429592761776584363504935760776221071566271657712x^{168}$$
$$- \ 975286194216666403852876236913037407425101353$6x^{169}$$
$$- \ 55317896647543571293087230877799868497505$6x^{170}$$
$$- \ 120396967902093838771093842812059854$64x^{171}$$
$$+ \ 1596600910185507016035597219$92x^{172}$$
$$- \ 17722643006531637142016x^{173} + x^{174}$$

The discriminant of the class polynomial and its constant term passed the Gross-Zagier test, the latter has factorization as

$$83076749736557242056487941267521536 = 2^{116}$$

7   Examples for Cryptosystem Design

Use the above CM curve ($d = -153164$), an almost prime elliptic curve E over a prime finite field $\boldsymbol{F}_p$ is obtained using the Algorithm 4 in the Appendix, where

$$p = 6411233586778658698012854170834647184757484423031$$
$$\#E(\boldsymbol{F}_p) = 6411233586778658698012849108768570758807340538364$$
$$= 2^2 * 3 * 1039 * p_{max}$$
$$p_{max} = 514215077540797136510494795377652450979093723$$

The curve has its j-invariant as

$$j - \text{inv} = 3779418350758177643266993966705704670627855414$4$$

The definition equation of this curve $y^2 = x^3 + ax + b$ has the following coefficients.

$$a = 4424050837045189024624780453466068541773776795332$$
$$b = 5086445086956345582420805025922261422768346004565$$

8   Proof of the Algorithms

Theorem 3. *In the Algorithm 1 ,*
(1) Any elliptic curve E/F rejected is without complex multiplication;
(2) The elliptic curves accepted are with high probability with complex multiplication.

Sketch of proof: Without loss of generality, we assume that $F \supset k$.(If not one can use $F := Fk$).
According to the Néron-Ogg-Shafarevitch criterion, the Grossencharacter $\psi_{E/F}$ is unramified if and only if the elliptic curve E/F has good reduction. In particular, for CM curves, if p_i splits in $\boldsymbol{Q}(\sqrt{\Delta})$, $E/\boldsymbol{F}_{q_i}$ is an ordinary reduction. While

only when the p_i is inert or ramified in $\boldsymbol{Q}(\sqrt{\Delta})$, $E/\boldsymbol{F}_{q_i}$ could have supersingular good reduction.

It is known by a result of Serre and Tate that CM curves have potential good reduction. Thus they only could have unstable or additive bad reduction.

Let $\mathfrak{P}_i$ be a prime ideal of $\mathcal{O}_F$ lying over p_i. By the Deuring's reduction theory of elliptic curves, the reduction mod $\mathfrak{P}_i$ induces an injective ring homomorphism of endomorphisms of the elliptic curve $\mathrm{End}_F E$ to $\mathrm{End}_{\boldsymbol{F}_{q_i}} E$. This map however induces a field isomorphism between the endomorphism fields if the elliptic curve is with CM and the reduction is ordinary.

Thus, if a curve E is non-CM and $E/\boldsymbol{F}_{q_i}$ is an ordinary reduction, then $\mathrm{End}^\circ_{\boldsymbol{F}_{q_i}} E$ will be imaginary quadratic fields with random discriminants. On the other hand, if a curve is CM, one will have the same $\mathrm{End}^\circ_{\boldsymbol{F}_q} E$ for any ordinary reduction at p.

Thus, the ordinary test will always reject non-CM curves and after N repetance of the ordinary reduction, the survived curves will be with CM in probability larger than $1 - 1/2^N$.

As to the supersingular reduction, it is known by Serre that for generic curves, the set of primes $S(x) = \{p_i < x | E/\boldsymbol{F}_{q_i} \text{ is supersingular }\}$ has density of zero and is conjectured that $\#S(x)/\pi(x) = O(1/\sqrt{x})$. The bad reduction at the chosen primes is even much rare for non-CM curves. Therefore, the later two tests can abandon non-CM curves even more efficiently or with higher probability. QED

Theorem 4. *The Algorithm 2 outputs the moduli field $\boldsymbol{Q}(j(\mathcal{O}_c))$ of the ring class field k^c_{ring} modulo (c).*

Sketch of proof: By the second main theorem of complex multiplication[17][32] [31],

$$k^c_{ray} = k_{abs}(x_c) = k(j(\mathcal{O}_k), x_c).$$

where x_c is the x-coordinate of a c-torsion point in $E[c]$, k^c_{ray} and k^c_{ring} are the ray class field and the ring class field modulo (c), $k_{abs} = k(j(\mathcal{O}_k))$ and $k^c_{ring} = k(j(\mathcal{O}_c))$.

On the other hand, one knows that

$$k^c_{ray} = k^c_{ring}(h(w_D, \mathcal{O}_c)) = k(j(\mathcal{O}_c), h(w_D, \mathcal{O}_c))$$

where $w_D = \frac{D+\sqrt{D}}{2}$, $h(w_D, \mathcal{O}_c)$ is the Weber function.

Thus, the ring class field k^c_{ring}, as an extension of k_{abs} also, can be constructed as a subfield of the ray class field k^c_{ray}. Its moduli field can be found also as a subfield. QED

Theorem 5. *The Algorithm 3 outputs the ring class equation $H_d(x)$, thus all the CM curves E with the End $E = \mathcal{O}_c \subset \mathcal{O}_k$, where $k = \boldsymbol{Q}(\sqrt{\Delta})$.*

Sketch of proof: Here we assume that the imaginary quadratic field k is not contained in the moduli field $F = \boldsymbol{Q}(j_c)$ of k^c_{ring}. Then $K = k^c_{ring} = Fk$. A rational prime $p \in \boldsymbol{Z}$ decomposes into $(p)\mathcal{O}_k = \mathfrak{p}\mathfrak{p}'$ where $\mathfrak{p}$, $\mathfrak{p}'$ are prime ideals in $\mathcal{O}_k$. Similarly, a prime ideal $\mathfrak{P}$ in $\mathcal{O}_F$ decomposes into $\mathfrak{P}\mathcal{O}_K = \mathfrak{Q}\mathfrak{Q}'$.

By the criterion of Néron-Ogg-Shararevitch, one can prove that E has every-where potentially good reduction which means that j is integral at all primes $\mathfrak{Q}$ in $\mathcal{O}_K$. Thus for CM curves, the minimal polynomials of j $H_d(x) \in \mathbf{Z}[x]$, one can find the ring class equation $H_d(x) \bmod p_i$ from $E_{s_i} \bmod \mathfrak{Q}_i$ where $\mathfrak{Q}_i$ lying over p_i then use the CRT to recover the $H_d(x)$.

The next task is to look for reduction of $h(d)$ j-invariants of CM elliptic curves which are Galois conjugates each other. This can be done using again ramificia-tion properties of the Grossencharacter $\psi_{E/K}$.

e.g. the $E \bmod \mathfrak{P}$ is a good reduction if and only if $\psi_{E/K}$ is unramified. Parti-cularly $E \bmod \mathfrak{P}$ is ordinary reduction if and only if $\mathfrak{P}$ splits in $\mathcal{O}_K$ or $\mathfrak{p} \neq \mathfrak{p}'$ or $(d/p) = 1$. $E \bmod \mathfrak{P}$ is a supersingular reduction or additive bad reduction if $\mathfrak{P}$ remains inert or ramifies in $\mathcal{O}_K$, i.e., p remains inert or ramifies in $\mathcal{O}_k$ or $(d/p) = 0, -1$.

These features can be distinguished from the endomorphism rings or calculation with the Frobenius endomorphism.

Besides, it is easy to prove that the degrees of p_i's which induce supersingular and bad reductions in the moduli field $\mathbf{Q}(j(\mathcal{O}_c))$ are less than two. Thus, it is enough to look for the candidates of CM j-invariants over $\mathbf{F}_{p_i^2}$.   QED

9 Complexity Analysis

It is known that for the CM field algorithm by Atkin and Morain, the precision needed to calculate a class equation with the class number h is by [1]

$$\mathrm{Prec}(d) = \binom{h}{\frac{h}{2}} \frac{\pi\sqrt{d}}{\log 10} \sum \frac{1}{a} + v_0$$

The number of terms required in series expansion of j-invariants is

$$\sqrt{Sa/k} \quad \text{where} \quad S = \frac{2(\log 6 + \mathrm{Prec}(d)\log 10)}{3\pi\sqrt{d}}$$

Using Sterling's formula: $n! = (n/e)^n\sqrt{2\pi n}$, and $h = O(\sqrt{d})$, $\mathrm{Prec}(d) = O(2^h h^{3/2})$ and the number of terms required in series expansion is $O(2^{h/2} h^{1/4})$. Thus its complexity is of an exponential function of h.

Now we analyze the complexity of the Algorithm 3. Since $j = O(e^{\pi\sqrt{d}})$, the largest coefficient in the class equations is in order of $j^h = O(e^{\pi h\sqrt{d}}) = O(e^{\pi h^2})$. To lift it by the CRT, it needs to repeat the lifting procedures over $O(h^2)$ finite fields $\mathbf{F}_{q_i}$, of which the sizes are also $O(h^2)$. Checks through all elements of each $\mathbf{F}_{q_i}$ as candidates of j-invariants of CM curves in step 2 cost $O(h^2)$. If e.g. in ordinary lifting the Kohel's deterministic algorithm is used to identify the isomorphism types of full endomorphism rings of the elliptic curve $E_s/\mathbf{F}_q$, which runs in time $O(q^{1/3+\epsilon})$ for any $\epsilon > 0$[15], then step 2 will cost $O(q_i^{4/3+\epsilon})$ for each $\mathbf{F}_{q_i}$, in all $O(q_i^{7/3+\epsilon}) = O(h^{14/3+2\epsilon})$. On the other hand, the calculations in step 3 to calculate the coefficients of $H_d(x)$ by the CRT will be dominant, which costs $O(h^7)$. In conclusion, the whole calculations will be in complexity of $O(h^7)$.

Acknowledgment: The authors wish to thank Prof. Yasutaka Ihara for kind suggestion of [11], Prof. Fumiyuki Momose for helpful discussions, and Mr. Kazuto Matsuo for assistance in preparation of this paper.

Appendix: Design of Secure Elliptic Cryptosystems with CM Curves

Once we have a CM elliptic curve over a number field, we can use it to design elliptic curve over finite fields using the fast algorithms of reduced quadratic forms(see appendix) or Cornnachia's algorithm[4][25][23]. Bellow, we show an algorithm using reduced quadratic forms.

Algorithm 4

Input E/F: A CM elliptic curve; d: the discriminant of its endomorphism ring.
Output q such that $E/\boldsymbol{F}_q$ is an almost prime curve.
Step 1 Choose $q = p^n$ (If $p = 2$ assume $d \equiv 1 \pmod 8$);
Step 2 Find an m_0 such that $m_0^2 \equiv d \pmod{4q}$;
Step 3 Let $n' = 4q, m' = 2m_0, l' = (m_0^2 - d)/4q$. If the reduced binary form of
$g(x', y') = n'x^2 + m'x'y' + l'y'^2$ is not $f(x, y) = x^2 - 4dy^2$, go to step 2;
Step 4 Calculate the modular transform A from $g(x', y')$ to $f(x, y)$ such that

$$\begin{bmatrix} x \\ y \end{bmatrix} = A \begin{bmatrix} x' \\ y' \end{bmatrix}, \qquad A = \begin{bmatrix} a_{11} & a_{12} \\ a_{21} & a_{22} \end{bmatrix}$$

Step 5 Let $t = a_{11}$, check if $\#E(\boldsymbol{F}_q) = q + 1 - t$ contains a large prime factor, or almost prime. If not, go to step 2 to find a new m_0 or go to step 1.

References

1. A.O.L.Atkin, F. Morain : "Elliptic Curves and Primality Proving" , Research Report 1256, INRIA, Juin (1990).
2. J. Chao, K. Tanada, S. Tsujii : "On secure elliptic curves against reduction attack and their design strategy", IEICE, Symposium on Cryptography and Information Security, SCIS'94, 10A, 1994-1. IEICE, Tech. rep. ISEC-93-100, p29-37, Mar. (1994)
3. J. Chao, K. Tanada, S. Tsujii : "Design of Elliptic Curves with Controllable Lower boundary of Extension Degree for Reduction Attacks", Yvo G. Desmedt (Ed.) Advances in Cryptology-CRYPTO'94, Lecture Notes in Computer Science, 839, Springer-Verlag, pp.50-55, (1994)
4. J. Chao, K. Harada, N. Matsuda, S. Tsujii : "Design of secure elliptic curves over extension fields with CM fields methods", IEICE, Symposium on Cryptography and Information Security, SCIS'94, A5.5, 1995-1. IEICE, Tech. rep. ISEC-95-52, p.1-12, 1995-3. Proc. of Pragocrypto'96, p.93-108, (1996)
5. J. Chao, N. Matsuda, S. Tsujii "Efficient construction of secure hyperelliptic discrete logarithm problems" Springer-Verlag Lecture Notes on Computer Science, Vol.1334, pp.292-301, "Information and Communication Security" Y. Han, T. Okamoto, S. Qing (Eds.) Proceedings of First International Conference ICICS'97, Beijing, China, Nov., (1997)

6. H. Cohen : "A course in computational algebraic number theory", Springer, GTM-138, (1995)
7. H. Cohn : "*Construction of class fields*", Cambridge Univ. Press, 1978.
8. J.-M. Couveignes, F. Morain, "Schoof's algorithm and isogeny cycles", Proceedings of ANTS'I, May, 1994. Lecture Notes in Computer Science, Springer-Verlag, pp.43-58. (1994)
9. D. Cox : "*Primes of the forms $x^2 + ny^2$*", John Wiley and Sons. (1989)
10. N. D. Elkies "Elliptic and modular curves over finite fields and related computational issues" "Computational perspectives on number theory", Proceedings of a Conference in Honor of A.O.L. Atkin, AMS, D.A.Buell, and J.T. Teitelbaum ed. pp.21-76, Sept. (1995)
11. B. Gross, D. Zagier : "On singular moduli", J. reine angew. Math. 355, pp.191-220. (1985)
12. E. Kaltofen and N. Yui, "Explicit construction of the Hilbert class fields fo imaginary quadratic fields by integer lattice reduction", New York Number Theory Seminar, 1989-1990, Springer-Verlag, pp. 150-202, (1991)
13. H. Kawasiro, O. Nakamura, J. Chao, S.Tsujii : "Construction of CM hyperelliptic curves using RM families", SCIS'98, 4-1-A, Jan. 1998. IEICE Tech. Rep. ISEC97-72, p. 43-50, March, (1998)
14. N.Koblitz : "Elliptic Curve Cryptosystems",Math. Comp.,vol.48, p.203-209, (1987)
15. D. Kohel "Endomorphism rings of ellitpic curves over finite fields" PhD thesis, UCB, (1996)
16. K. Kurotani, K. Matsuo, J. Chao, S. Tsujii : "Consideration of security of hyperelliptic cryptosystems", IEICE, Symposium on Cryptography and Information Security, SCIS'98, 4.1-D, Jan. (1998)
17. S. Lang : "*Elliptic Functions*", 2nd ed., Springer-Verlag, (1987)
18. S.Lang : "Complex multiplication" Springer-Verlag, (1983)
19. G-J. Lay and H.G. Zimmer : "Constructing Elliptic Curves with Given Group Order over Large Finite Fields", Proceeding of ANTS95, May, (1994)
20. R. Lercier and F. Morain : "Counting the number of points on elliptic curves over finite fields: strategies and performances",Proceeding of EUROCRYPTO'95, (1995)
21. A.Menezes : "Elliptic Curve Public Key Cryptosystems", Kluwer Academic, (1993)
22. V.S.Miller : "Use of Elliptic Curves in Cryptography", Advances in Cryptology Proceedings of Crypto'85 , Lecture Notes in Computer Science , 218 , Springer-Verlag , p.417-426, (1986)
23. F. Morain, : "Building cyclic elliptic curves modulo large primes", Advances in Cryptology -EUROCRYPT'91, Lecture Notes in Computer Science. **547** p.328-336, (1991)
24. F. Morain, "Calcul du nombre de points sur une courbe elliptique dans un corps fini: aspects algorithmique" Actes des Journees Arithmetiques, (1995)
25. O. Nakamura, N. Matsuda, J. Chao, S. Tsujii : "On cryptosystems based on abelian varieties with CM", IEICE, Symposium on Cryptography and Information Security, SCIS'97, 12-E, 1997-1, IEICE, Tech. Rep. ISEC-96-81, Mar. (1997)
26. O. Nakamura, N. Matsuda, J. Chao, S. Tsujii : "On cryptosystems based on abelian varieties with CM", IEICE, The first symposium on algebraic curves and their applications, Sept. (1997)
27. R. Schoof : "Elliptic curves over finite fields and the computation of square roots mod p", Math. Comp., vol.44, p.483–494, (1985)
28. R. Schoof : "Counting points on elliptic curves over finite fields", Journal de The'orie des Nombres de Bordeaux 7, pp.219-254, (1995)

29. J.P.Serre , J.Tate : "Good reduction of abelian varieties", Ann. of Math. (2), 88 , p.492-517, (1968)
30. J. H. Silverman : "The Arithmetic of Elliptic Curves", Springer-Verlag , (1988).
31. J. H. Silverman : "Advanced Topics in the Arithmetic of Elliptic Curves", GTM-151, Springer-Verlag, (1994)
32. G. Shimura : "Arithmetic theory of automorphic function", Iwanami-Shoten and Princeton, (1971).
33. K. Sobataka, O. Namamura, J. Chao, S.Tsujii : "Construction of secure elliptic cryptosystems using CM tests and Lifting ", SCIS'98, 4-1-B, Jan. (1998). IEICE Tech. Rep. ISEC97-71, p. 35-42, March, (1998).
34. J.Tate : "Endomorphisms of Abelian varieties over finite fields", Invent. Math. 2, p.134-144, (1966)

Elliptic Curve Discrete Logarithms
and the Index Calculus

Joseph H. Silverman[1] and Joe Suzuki[2]

[1] Mathematics Department, Box 1917, Brown University,
Providence, RI 02912 USA ⟨jhs@math.brown.edu⟩
[2] Department of Mathematics, Osaka University, Toyonaka,
Osaka 560 Japan ⟨suzuki@math.sci.osaka-u.ac.jp⟩

Abstract. The discrete logarithm problem forms the basis of numerous cryptographic systems. The most effective attack on the discrete logarithm problem in the multiplicative group of a finite field is via the index calculus, but no such method is known for elliptic curve discrete logarithms. Indeed, Miller [23] has given a brief heuristic argument as to why no such method can exist. IN this note we give a detailed analysis of the index calculus for elliptic curve discrete logarithms, amplifying and extending miller's remarks. Our conclusions fully support his contention that the natural generalization of the index calculus to the elliptic curve discrete logarithm problem yields an algorithm with is less efficient than a brute-force search algorithm.

0. Introduction

The discrete logarithm problem for the multiplicative group $\mathbb{F}_q^*$ of a finite field can be solved in subexponential time using the *Index Calculus* method, which appears to have been first discovered by Kraitchik [14, 15] in the 1920's and subsequently rediscovered and extended by many mathematicians. (See, for example, [1] and [43], and for a nice summary of the current state-of-the-art, see [29].) For this reason, it was proposed independently by Miller [23] and Koblitz [12] that for cryptographic purposes, one should replace $\mathbb{F}_q^*$ by the group of rational points $E(\mathbb{F}_q)$ on an elliptic curve, thus leading to the *Elliptic Curve Discrete Logarithm Problem*, which we abbreviate as the ECDL problem. Indeed, Victor Miller gives in his article [23, page 423] two reasons why "it is extremely unlikely that an 'index calculus' attack on elliptic curves will ever be able to work." Miller's reasons may be briefly summarized as follows:

(1) It is difficult to find elliptic curves $\mathcal{E}/\mathbb{Q}$ with a large number of small rational points. This observation may be split into two pieces.
   (a) It is difficult to find elliptic curves $\mathcal{E}/\mathbb{Q}$ with high rank.
   (b) It is difficult to find elliptic curves $\mathcal{E}/\mathbb{Q}$ generated by points of small height.

K. Ohta and D. Pei (Eds.): ASIACRYPT'98, LNCS 1514, pp. 110-125, 1998.

(2) Given an elliptic curve $\mathcal{E}/\mathbb{Q}$, a large prime p, and a point $S \in \mathcal{E}(\mathbb{F}_p)$ in the image of the reduction map $\mathcal{E}(\mathbb{Q}) \to \mathcal{E}(\mathbb{F}_p)$, it is difficult to lift S to a point of $\mathcal{E}(\mathbb{Q})$.

Miller [23] devotes three paragraphs giving some rough heuristic reasons to justify these assertions. This lack of an index calculus for the ECDL problem is often cited as a reason for the high security of modern cryptosystems based on ECDL's, as for example in the following excerpt [6].

> Most significantly, no index-calculus-type algorithms are known for the ECDL problem as for the DLP (discrete logarithm problem). For this reason, the ECDL problem is believed to be much harder than either the IFP (integer factorization problem) or the DLP in that no subexponential-time general-purpose algorithm is known.

In view of the importance of the ECDL problem in modern cryptography, it seems worthwhile making a more detailed and in-depth analysis of the possibility of an index calculus for the ECDL problem. That is the purpose of this paper. We will explain how, using a method of Mestre, it is possible to lift an elliptic curve E modulo p to an elliptic curve $\mathcal{E}$ over $\mathbb{Q}$ of moderately high rank possessing generators of moderately low height. We will further give both numerical and theoretical evidence which suggests that if p is large, then it will never be possible to use the index calculus on such a curve $\mathcal{E}$ to solve the discrete logarithm problem in $E(\mathbb{F}_p)$. The fundamental reason, already alluded to in Miller's paper, but which we will make much more precise, is that the generators $P_1, \ldots, P_r$ on a lifted curve $\mathcal{E}/\mathbb{Q}$ of rank r will necessarily have (logarithmic) height at least

$$\hat{h}(P_i) \geq A + B \log(p) + Cr \log(r)$$

for certain positive constants A, B, C. By way of contrast, the generators (factor basis) for the multiplicative group consists of the first r primes $p_1, p_2, \ldots, p_r$ whose (logarithmic) heights

$$h(p_n) = \log(p_n) \leq \log(p_r) \leq C \log(r)$$

are exponentially smaller (as a function of r) than in the elliptic curve situation.

In summary, our theoretical and numerical work fully supports Miller's conclusion that the natural generalization of the index calculus to the elliptic curve discrete logarithm problem yields an algorithm which is less efficient than a brute-force search algorithm.

The detailed contents of this paper are as follows:

Section 1. A brief description of the discrete logarithm problem and the index calculus for the multiplicative group.

Section 2. A discussion of the discrete logarithm problem for elliptic curves and a more detailed description of Miller's obstructions.

Section 3. A theoretical discussion of elliptic curves of high rank, the size of their generators, and the number of points of bounded height.

Section 4. Mestre's method for constructing curves of moderately high rank with generating points of moderately low height, in theory and in practice.

Section 5. The problem of lifing curves and points modulo p to points in $\mathcal{E}(\mathbb{Q})$.

1. The Index Calculus for the Multiplicative Group

In this section we briefly review the index calculus method for solving the discrete logarithm problem in the multiplicative group $\mathbb{F}_p^*$ of a finite field $\mathbb{F}_p$, where p is a fixed large prime. The discrete logarithm problem (DLP) asks:

$$\boxed{\begin{array}{l} \text{Given two elements } \alpha, \beta \in \mathbb{F}_p^*, \\ \text{find } k \text{ such that } \alpha^k = \beta. \end{array}} \qquad \text{(DLP)}$$

Assuming it exists, the value of k satisfying $\alpha^k = \beta$ is denoted by

$$k = \log_\alpha(\beta).$$

The first step in the index calculus is to choose what is known as a *factor basis* consisting of the first r primes,

$$\mathcal{F}_r = \{2, 3, 5, 7, 11, \dots, p_r\},$$

where we will choose r later. We write $\langle \mathcal{F}_r \rangle$ for the semi-group generated by $\mathcal{F}_r$; that is, $\langle \mathcal{F}_r \rangle$ consists of all integers whose prime divisors are all less than or equal to p_r. Numbers in $\langle \mathcal{F}_r \rangle$ are usually called p_r-*smooth*, and it is vitally important to have an accurate count of how many smooth numbers there are, so we let

$$N(\mathcal{F}_r, B) = \#\{a \in \langle \mathcal{F}_r \rangle : 1 \le a \le B\}.$$

(This slightly non-classical notation will be useful for comparison with the elliptic curve situation. In the more usual notation, $N(\mathcal{F}_r, B)$ equals $\Psi(B, p_r)$.)

If B is large in comparison to r, then it is quite easy to estimate the size of $N(\mathcal{F}_r, B)$ as the volume of an r-dimensional simplex. Thus

$$N(\mathcal{F}_r, B) = \#\left\{ (e_1, \dots, e_r) : \begin{array}{c} e_1, \dots, e_r \ge 0 \\ e_1 \log p_1 + \cdots e_r \log p_r \le \log B \end{array} \right\} \sim \frac{1}{r!} \frac{(\log B)^r}{\prod_i \log p_i}.$$

Then using Stirlings' formula and the prime number theorem (in the form $p_i \sim i \log i$) yields

$$N(\mathcal{F}_r, B) \sim \frac{1}{\sqrt{2\pi r}} \left(\frac{e \log B}{r \log r} \right)^r \qquad \text{for } B \gg r. \qquad (1)$$

We have derived this formula for $N(\mathcal{F}_r, B)$ not because it is useful for the index calculus, it isn't, but for later comparison with the elliptic case.

The index calculus begins by computing the powers $\alpha, \alpha^2, \alpha^3, \dots$ and lifting each of these values from $\mathbb{F}_p$ to $\mathbb{Z}$, say

$$\alpha^j \equiv a_j \pmod{p} \qquad \text{with } 1 \le a_j < p.$$

Each a_j is then checked against $\langle \mathcal{F}_r \rangle$, and if it is in this semi-group, we record the value

$$a_j = \prod_{i=1}^{r} p_i^{e_i(j)}. \tag{2}$$

Notice that since $a_j = \alpha^j$ in $\mathbb{F}_p^*$, and since $\mathbb{F}_p^*$ has order $p-1$, each relation (2) gives a linear equation

$$j \equiv \sum_{i=1}^{r} e_i(j) \log_\alpha(p_i) \pmod{p-1}. \tag{3}$$

We continue computing the powers of α until we obtain r independent linear relations (3), at which point the equations can be solved for the r unknowns $\log_\alpha(p_1), \dots, \log_\alpha(p_r)$. [Remark. We will neglect the fact that, in practice, the value of r will generally be sufficiently large so as to make it extremely difficult to solve the resulting system of r linear equations, even though they tend to be extremely sparse.]

The final step is to lift the quantities $\beta, \alpha\beta, \alpha^2\beta, \dots$ to $\mathbb{Z}$, say

$$\alpha^j \beta \equiv b_j \pmod{p} \qquad \text{with } 1 \le b_j < p,$$

until we find a single value of j for which b_j lies in $\langle \mathcal{F}_r \rangle$, say

$$b_j = \prod_{i=1}^{r} p_i^{f_i}.$$

Since $b_j = \alpha^j \beta$ in $\mathbb{F}_p^*$, this yields

$$j + \log_\alpha(\beta) \equiv \sum_{i=1}^{r} f_i \log_\alpha(p_i) \pmod{p-1},$$

and since we already know the values of the $\log_\alpha(p_i)$'s, we recover the desired value of $\log_\alpha(\beta)$.

The key question in implementing the index calculus method is the choice of the number r of primes in the factor base. If r is too small, then it is very unlikely that the a_j's will lie in $\langle \mathcal{F}_r \rangle$; while if r is too large, it will be computationally difficult to determine if a given a_j lies in $\langle \mathcal{F}_r \rangle$. Notice that the latter problem is that of finding the complete factorization of a number $a < p$ by primes at most p_r, which shows how the factorization problem is closely tied into the index calculus.

The probability that a given $1 \le a < p$ lies in $\langle \mathcal{F}_r \rangle$ is approximately equal to $N(\mathcal{F}_r, p)/(p-1)$. Using the approximation (1) and taking $B \gg\!\!\ll p$, we find that this quantity is maximized for $r \gg\!\!\ll \log p / \log\log p$, which unfortunately leads to a probability which is $\ll p^{-1} \cdot p^{C/\log\log p}$, far too small to be useful. However, it turns out that (1) is not a good approximation in our situation, because for moderately large values of r, most of the numbers in $N(\mathcal{F}_r, p)$ are of the form $p_1^{e_1} p_2^{e_2} \cdots p_r^{e_r}$ with many of the e_i's equal to 0, and the rest quite small. In geometric terms, most of the numbers in $N(\mathcal{F}_r, p)$ represent points which lie on the boundary of the simplex whose volume is being approximated in the formula (1).

We will not give a detailed analysis here, since the final counting result, although by no means easy, is well-known and amply described in many sources. For example, it is proven in [5] that

$$\Psi(x, L(x)^a) \approx x L(x)^{-1/2a}, \qquad \text{where} \quad L(x) = \exp(\sqrt{\log x \log \log x}).$$

(Here, as usual, $\Psi(x, y)$ is the number of positive integers less than x whose prime factors are all at most y.) Using a weak form of this result, which suffices for comparison with the elliptic curve case, we see that

$$\text{If } r \approx e^{\sqrt{\log p}}, \text{ then } N(\mathcal{F}_r, p) > p \cdot e^{-\frac{1}{2}\sqrt{\log p}}.$$

Thus a sub-exponential value for r (i.e., r is smaller than any power of p) suffices to give a sub-exponential probability of hitting an element in $\langle \mathcal{F}_r \rangle$. The reason that $N(\mathcal{F}_r, p)$ becomes this large is because the primes $p_1, p_2, \ldots, p_r$ in the rank r factor base are small, satisfying

$$\log p_i \approx \log i \le \log r. \tag{4}$$

We want to emphasize this point because it is <u>fundamentally different</u> from what occurs for elliptic curves, where the elements of a rank r factor base have size on the order of $r \log r$.

Remark.. There are various improvements that are typically used to supplement the index calculus, including storing large factors of the a_j's not factorable in the factor base so as to take advantage of overlaps (birthday phenomenon) and using fancier factorization methods (e.g., based on the number field sieve). At present, we don't see analogous methods for elliptic curves, but even if they exist, they are unlikely to affect our overall analysis, since even saving a square root does not substantially change an exponential running time.

2. The Discrete Logarithm Problem for Elliptic Curves

The discrete logrithm problem for an elliptic curve E over a finite field $\mathbb{F}_p$ is virtually identical to the analogous problem for the multiplicative group. We change notation slightly from the multiplicative case to reflect the fact that the addition law on an elliptic curve is always written additively. We thus assume that our elliptic curve E is given by a Weierstrass equation

$$E : y^2 + a_1 xy + a_3 x = x^3 + a_2 x^2 + a_4 x + a_6$$

whose coefficients lie in the finite field $\mathbb{F}_p$. The discrete logarithm problem for elliptic curves (ECDLP) asks:

$$\boxed{\begin{array}{l} \text{Given two points } S, T \in E(\mathbb{F}_p), \\ \text{find } m \text{ such that } S = mT. \end{array}} \qquad \text{(ECDLP)}$$

Note that group operation is addition in $E(\mathbb{F}_p)$, and we are being asked to compute the integer $m = \log_T(S)$. We also let

$$N = N_p = \#E(\mathbb{F}_p)$$

denote the order of the finite group $E(\mathbb{F}_p)$. There is a polynomial-time algorithm for computing N due to Schoof [30], with improvements by Elkies [8] and Atkins [3], which makes it quite practical to compute N for moderate values of p, say for $p \leq 2^{200}$, and certainly possible for even larger values.

There are various special cases for which the ECDL problem can be solved, including the following:

(1) If $N = p+1$, the so-called "supersingular" case, then the ECDL problem can be reduced to the discrete logarithm problem on the multiplicative group. More generally, if N divides $p^k - 1$, then the ECDL problem can be reduced to the discrete logarithm problem on the multiplicative group of the finite field with p^k elements. Of course, this is only practical if k is not too large. For details, see [20] and [9].

(2) If $N = p$, the so-called "anomalous" case, then the ECDL problem can be reduced to simple addition in $\mathbb{F}_p$, essentially by lifting the curve modulo p^2. See [31], [39], and [28].

(3) If N is divisible by only small primes, then one can use the method of Pohlig and Hellman [25] and Pollard [26] which solves the discrete logarithm problem in time $O(\sqrt{p'})$, where p' is the largest prime divisor of N.

(4) Although not directly relevant, we also mention that the discrete logarithm problem can be solved on the Jacobian J of a curve of genus g provided that $g \gg p$ [2]. The reason is that in this situation, the group $J(\mathbb{F}_p)$ is highly non-cyclic. For cryptographic applications of the elliptic case, one normally chooses E so that $E(\mathbb{F}_p)$ is cyclic of prime order.

Assuming that none of these methods is applicable, it is tempting to try to adapt the index calculus method described in Section 1 directly to the elliptic curve case. Here's a brief summary of how such an index calculus would work.

(1) Choose an elliptic curve $\mathcal{E}/\mathbb{Q}$ which reduces to $E/\mathbb{F}_p$ and which has a reasonably large number of independent rational points, say $P_1, P_2, \ldots, P_r$.

(2) Compute the multiples $S, 2S, 3S, \ldots$ in $E(\mathbb{F}_p)$, and for each j, try to lift jS to a rational point $S_j \in \mathcal{E}(\mathbb{Q})$. That is, $S_j \equiv jS \pmod{p}$. If this is successful, then write S_j as a linear combination

$$S_j = \sum_{i=1}^{r} n_j P_j \quad \text{in } \mathcal{E}(\mathbb{Q}).$$

(3) After r of the jS's have been lifted, we have r linear equations

$$j = \sum_{i=1}^{r} n_j \log_S(P_j)$$

which can be solved for the individual $\log_S(P_j)$'s.

(4) Next try to lift $T, T + S, T + 2S, T + 3S, \ldots$ to $\mathcal{E}(\mathbb{Q})$, say that $T + jS$ lifts to T_j. Write

$$T_j = \sum_{i=1}^{r} m_j P_j \qquad \text{in } \mathcal{E}(\mathbb{Q}).$$

Then

$$\log_S(T) + j = \sum_{i=1}^{r} m_j \log_S(P_j),$$

and since we know the values of the $\log_S(P_j)$'s, we recover the desired value of $\log_S(T)$.

There are a number of possible difficulties with putting the above outline into practice. Victor Miller [23, page 423] has given two reasons why "it is extremely unlikely that an 'index calculus' attack on elliptic curves will ever be able to work." His reasons can be briefly summarized as follows (where all quotes are from [23]):

Rank/Height Obstruction. "Unless the rank of the curve can be made very large, and the regulator made fairly small, the probability of a point of $E(\mathbb{F}_p)$ lifting to a point on $\hat{E}(\mathbb{Q})$ whose height is bounded by something reasonable (say a polynomial in $\log p$) is vanishingly small."

Lifting Obstruction. "Even if one could somehow get around the barrier mentioned above, there is still the problem of actually lifting a point." One can try to lift first to a point $(x_1, y_1) \in \hat{E}(\mathbb{Z}/p^k\mathbb{Z})$, but "there are many possible choices for (x_1, y_1). ... Thus, unless there is a new idea, it would seem that this is another barrier, difficult to surmount."

In the remainder of this paper, we are going to analyze in more detail the elliptic index calculus and the obstructions noted by Miller. We begin in the next section with a discussion of the heights of points on elliptic curves.

3. Counting Points on Elliptic Curves Over $\mathbb{Q}$

For this section we briefly forget about elliptic curves over finite fields and discuss the distribution (theoretical, practical, and conjectural) of the rational points on elliptic curves defined over $\mathbb{Q}$. For basic facts about elliptic curves, see for example [18, 33, 34].

Let $\mathcal{E}/\mathbb{Q}$ be an elliptic curve given by a minimal Weierstrass equation

$$\mathcal{E} : y^2 + a_1 xy + a_3 x = x^3 + a_2 x^2 + a_4 x + a_6$$

and discriminant $\Delta(\mathcal{E})$. Recall that the height of a rational number $r/s \in \mathbb{Q}$ is defined to be

$$H(r/s) = \max\{|r|, |s|\}.$$

The canonical height of a point $P \in \mathcal{E}(\mathbb{Q})$ is then defined to be

$$\hat{h}(P) = \frac{1}{2} \lim_{n \to \infty} \frac{1}{n^2} \log H(x(nP)),$$

and the associated inner product for $P, Q \in \mathcal{E}(\mathbb{Q})$ is

$$\langle P, Q \rangle = \frac{1}{2}\left(\hat{h}(P+Q) - \hat{h}(P) - \hat{h}(Q)\right).$$

This inner product is positive definite on $\mathcal{E}(\mathbb{Q}) \otimes \mathbb{R}$, and the elliptic regulator of a set of points $P_1, \dots, P_r \in \mathcal{E}(\mathbb{Q})$ is defined to be

$$\mathrm{Reg}(\mathcal{E}) = \det\left(\langle P_i, P_j \rangle\right)_{1 \le i, j \le r}.$$

(Generally, $P_1, \dots, P_r$ will be set of generators for $\mathcal{E}(\mathbb{Q})/(\mathrm{tors})$, or in numerical examples, an explicitly given set of points. If the set of points is not clear from the context, we will write $\mathrm{Reg}(\mathcal{E}, P_1, \dots, P_r)$.)

We are interested in counting the number of points in $\mathcal{E}(\mathbb{Q})$ of bounded height, so we set

$$N(\mathcal{E}, B) = \#\{P \in \mathcal{E}(\mathbb{Q}) : H(x(P)) \le B\}.$$
$$T(\mathcal{E}) = \#\mathcal{E}(\mathbb{Q})_{\mathrm{tors}}.$$
$$r = r(\mathcal{E}) = \mathrm{rank}\,\mathcal{E}(\mathbb{Q}).$$
$$\alpha_r = \pi^{r/2}/((r/2)\Gamma(r/2)) = \text{Volume of unit ball in } \mathbb{R}^r.$$

Using Sterlings' formula, we have the useful approximation

$$\alpha_r \approx \frac{1}{\sqrt{\pi r}} \left(\frac{2\pi e}{r}\right)^{r/2}. \tag{5}$$

The ordinary and canonical heights are related by

$$\hat{h}(P) = \frac{1}{2} \log H(x(P)) + O_{\mathcal{E}}(1). \tag{6}$$

We will say more later about the dependence of the big-O constant on $\mathcal{E}$, but for now we will ignore its effect (which is negligble in the numerical examples presented below). Then we can estimate $N(\mathcal{E}, B)$ by simply counting lattice points in $\mathbb{R}^r$ relative to the canonical height inner product. Thus

$$N(\mathcal{E}, B) = \#\{P \in \mathcal{E}(\mathbb{Q}) : H(x(P)) \le B\}$$
$$\approx T(\mathcal{E})\#\{P \in \mathcal{E}(\mathbb{Q}) : \hat{h}(P) \le \tfrac{1}{2} \log B\} \quad \text{from (6)},$$
$$\approx T(\mathcal{E}) \frac{\alpha_r}{\sqrt{\mathrm{Reg}(\mathcal{E})}} \left(\tfrac{1}{2} \log B\right)^{r/2}$$
$$\approx T(\mathcal{E}) \frac{1}{\sqrt{\pi r}} \left(\frac{\pi e \log B}{r \cdot \mathrm{Reg}(\mathcal{E})^{1/r}}\right)^{r/2} \quad \text{from (5)}.$$

We mention that $T(\mathcal{E}) \leq 16$ by Mazur's Theorem [33, VIII.7.5], so the effect from torsion is negligible. In practice, our curves will have trivial torsion, because it has been observed experimentally that the presence of rational torsion makes it more difficult to obtain high rank.

The above formula says that we shouldn't expect to get very many points until $\log B$ and $\mathrm{Reg}(\mathcal{E})^{1/r}$ are of a comparable size, so we need to study the magnitude of the regulator.

A basic result from the geometry of numbers says that (see [17, chapter 5, corollary 7.8])

$$\mathrm{Reg}(\mathcal{E})^{1/r} \geq \left(\frac{\sqrt{3}}{2} \right)^{r-1} \min_{\substack{P \in \mathcal{E}(\mathbb{Q}) \\ \hat{h}(P) \neq 0}} \hat{h}(P). \tag{7}$$

Further, there is a conjecture of Lang [18, page 92] which says that for non-torsion points $P \in \mathcal{E}(\mathbb{Q})$,

$$\hat{h}(P) \geq c \log |\Delta(\mathcal{E})|,$$

where the constant c is independent of $\mathcal{E}$. This conjecture has been largely proven [11, 35], albeit with extremely small constants c. Thus, as Miller already observes in [23], it is not possible to get $N(\mathcal{E}, B)$ large unless one chooses

$$\log B \gg r \log |\Delta|.$$

But if $\mathcal{E}$ is the lift of an elliptic curve over $\mathbb{F}_p$, then we'll certainly have $\log |\Delta| \gg \log p$. Then there's the further difficulty that Mestre proves (subject to various "standard" conjectures)

$$\log |\Delta| \gg r \log r,$$

so if we make r large, then the value of Δ (and hence B) will be enormous.

The next step is to see how this theoretical analysis, which is essentially given by Miller [23], compares to actual practice.

4. High Rank Curves With Small Height Points

It is difficult to find elliptic curves over $\mathbb{Q}$ with high rank, as witnessed by the fact that no curves of rank 12 were known before 1982 [22], and even today the highest rank known is 23 [19].

Currently the most successful method for finding curves of high rank is to start on a one or two-parameter family such that every member of the family already contains many independent points, and then specialize to find certain members which possess even higher rank. However, this method is not suitable for our purposes, because we are starting with a curve over $\mathbb{F}_p$ that we want to lift, so we need more freedom than is provided by such a family. Thus we are going to consider an earlier method of Mestre which can be applied in great generality. Mestre's idea is simple to state, although the justification for why it should yield high rank curves depends on much deep mathematics and several unproven conjectures:

Mestre's Construction

In order to produce a curve $\mathcal{E}/\mathbb{Q}$ of high rank, use congruence conditions to choose the coefficients of $\mathcal{E}$ so that $\#\mathcal{E}(\mathbb{F}_\ell)$ is maximized for all (small) primes $\ell = 2, 3, 5, \ldots, \ell_0$, and then so that the discriminant $|\Delta(\mathcal{E})|$ is more-or-less minimized subject to the congruence conditions. Then search for integer points lying close to the rightmost real two-torsion point $(e_1, 0)$, say searching for points (x, y) with $e_1 < x < e_1 + 5000$. We will call a curve chosen according to these criteria a *Mestre curve*. The precise algorithm for constructing Mestre curves is described in [22], and some justification for the algorithm is given in [21].

In his original paper [22], Mestre lists the smallest curves of ranks 4 to 12 which he found using the above method. Two of the listings appear to have typographical errors, and for the remaining curves we gather some information in Table 1, where $P_1, \ldots, P_r$ denotes a basis for $E(\mathbb{Q})$.

Table 1. Data for Mestre's moderate rank curves

r	$\dfrac{(\mathrm{Reg}\,\mathcal{E})^{1/r}}{\frac{1}{12}\log|\Delta|}$	$\min_i \dfrac{\hat{h}(P_i)}{\frac{1}{12}\log|\Delta|}$	$\max_i \dfrac{\hat{h}(P_i)}{\frac{1}{12}\log|\Delta|}$	$\dfrac{\log|\Delta|}{r\log r}$
4	0.612	0.772	0.844	2.382
5	0.627	0.840	0.941	2.362
6	0.600	0.937	0.994	2.295
7	0.696	1.032	1.063	2.116
8	0.776	1.103	1.128	2.111
9	0.543	1.051	1.073	2.311
10	0.756	1.091	1.106	2.271
12	0.674	0.916	0.923	2.273
14	0.585	1.018	1.025	2.341

A first observation (from Mestre's paper) is that the curves constructed by his method generally have square-free, or almost square-free, discriminant. This is very reasonable, because Mestre's bound for the rank alluded to above actually has the form

$$r \log r \ll \log(\mathrm{Cond}\,\mathcal{E}),$$

where the conductor $\mathrm{Cond}\,\mathcal{E}$ is (essentially) the square-free part of Δ. Thus having a large square dividing the discriminant will make it more difficult for the curve to have large rank.

A second observation, this time from Table 1, is that the independent points constructed by Mestre's method seem to satisfy

$$\hat{h}(P_i) \approx \frac{1}{12}\log|\Delta|.$$

We can justify this observation as follows. Mestre's method yields points $P = (x, y) \in \mathcal{E}(\mathbb{Q})$ which have integer coordinates $x, y \in \mathbb{Z}$ and which are fairly close to the 2-torsion point $T = (e_1, 0)$. The local decomposition of the canonical height says that

$$\hat{h}(P) = \hat{\lambda}_\infty(P) + \sum_p \hat{\lambda}_p(P).$$

(See [34, chapter VI] for the definition and basic properties of the local height functions $\hat{\lambda}_p$.) Assuming that the discriminant Δ is (mostly) square-free and that the coordinates of P are integers, the p-adic local heights add up to give (approximately) $\frac{1}{12} \log |\Delta|$, see [34, VI.4.1]. Further, the fact that P is close to T means that $\hat{\lambda}_\infty(P) \approx \hat{\lambda}_\infty(T)$, which yields

$$\hat{h}(P) \approx \hat{\lambda}_\infty(T) + \frac{1}{12} \log |\Delta|.$$

Finally, the explicit formula [34, VI.3.4] for $\hat{\lambda}_\infty$ shows that

$$\hat{\lambda}_\infty(T) = \log^+ |j(\mathcal{E})| + O(1),$$

which will tend to be fairly small. (For explicit estimates, see [36, 37].)

An additional point to make is that the value $\frac{1}{12} \log |\Delta|$ is essentially the smallest possible value for $\hat{h}(P)$ on a Mestre curve, since the fact that the discriminant is square-free means that all of the $\hat{\lambda}_p(P)$'s satisfy

$$\hat{\lambda}_p(P) \geq \frac{1}{12} \operatorname{ord}_p(\Delta) \log p,$$

and if the coordinates of P have denominators and/or P moves further away from e_1, then the value of $\hat{h}(P)$ will tend to increase. It is thus not surprising that the points constructed by Mestre's method tend to be independent, since they represent vectors of approximately the same length L in a lattice whose smallest non-zero vector also has length L. To see why this is true, consider s vectors $\mathbf{v}_1, \mathbf{v}_2, \ldots, \mathbf{v}_s \in \mathbb{R}^r$ satisfying $|\mathbf{v}_i - \mathbf{v}_j| \geq L$ and $|\mathbf{v}_i| = L$ for all $i \neq j$. Then the balls of radius L around each $|\mathbf{v}_i|$ are disjoint, and they are contained in a ball of radius $2L$, so a simple volume counting argument shows that $r \geq \log_2(s)$.

The data in Table 1 indicates that

$$\min \hat{h}(P) \approx \frac{1}{12} \log |\Delta(\mathcal{E})| \quad \text{and} \quad \frac{1}{24} \log |\Delta(\mathcal{E})| \leq \operatorname{Reg}(\mathcal{E})^{1/r} \leq \frac{1}{15} \log |\Delta(\mathcal{E})|. \tag{8}$$

A reasonable assumption, based on this data, would be that it is possible to find Mestre curves of various ranks with

$$\operatorname{Reg}(\mathcal{E})^{1/r} \approx \frac{1}{20} \log |\Delta(\mathcal{E})|. \tag{9}$$

Using this and the other material described above, we obtain the following (heuristic) result:

Heuristic Bound. *Based on the numerical data contained in* [21] *and the above theoretical analysis, it appears to be possible to use Mestre's method to produce elliptic curves* $\mathcal{E}/\mathbb{Q}$ *so that the number of rational points*

$$N(\mathcal{E}, B) = \#\{P \in \mathcal{E}(\mathbb{Q}) : H(x(P)) \le B\}$$

in $\mathcal{E}(\mathbb{Q})$ *grows like*

$$N(\mathcal{E}, B) \approx \frac{1}{\sqrt{\pi r}} \left(\frac{20\pi e \log B}{r \cdot \log |\Delta(\mathcal{E})|} \right)^{r/2}. \tag{10}$$

Further, it is probably not possible to find elliptic curves such that $N(\mathcal{E}, B)$ *grows significantly faster than this rate.*

Remark.. We also observe from Table 1 that the discriminant tends to satisfy

$$2r \log r \le \log |\Delta(\mathcal{E})| \le 3r \log r,$$

but since for the ECDL problem we will need to impose an extra congruence condition modulo a "large" prime p, we will not use this condition directly. However, it is important to point out that this estimate implies that the generating points on a Mestre curve generally satisfy

$$\hat{h}(P) \approx \frac{1}{12} \log |\Delta(\mathcal{E})| \ge \frac{r \log r}{6}.$$

Comparing this to the analogous estimate (4) for the multiplicative group, we see that the size of the generating elements for a rank r group is exponentially worse in the elliptic curve case!

5. Lifting Mod p Curves to High Rank Curves

It's now time to put into practice the theoretical material contained in the previous sections. Table 2 lists the results of some experiments we performed using Mestre's method to lift a curve over $\mathbb{F}_p$ to a curve of moderate rank. We chose to use $p = 173$ and more-or-less randomly took the curve

$$E : y^2 = x^3 + 42x + 86.$$

(We did choose E so that $\#E(\mathbb{F}_{173}) = 158$ is small, which has the effect of making Mestre's method a little less efficient.) Although not strictly necessary, the algorithm described in [22] uses curves of a slightly different form, so we changed coordinates to the isomorphic curve

$$E : y^2 + y = x^3 + 42x + 129$$

over the field $\mathbb{F}_{173}$. We then used Mestre's method to look for lifts of this curve which have the maximum number of points modulo all primes ≤ 23, and among these curves looked for independent integral points on the ones having small discriminant. The result was that of 269280 curves tested, there were three examples of rank 6 and three examples of rank 7. The relevant data for these six curves is listed in Table 2.

Table 2. Lifting From Mod 173 To Moderate Rank

r	$\dfrac{(\mathrm{Reg}\,\mathcal{E})^{1/r}}{\frac{1}{12}\log|\Delta|}$	$\min\limits_{i}\dfrac{\hat{h}(P_i)}{\frac{1}{12}\log|\Delta|}$	$\max\limits_{i}\dfrac{\hat{h}(P_i)}{\frac{1}{12}\log|\Delta|}$	$\dfrac{\log|\Delta|}{r\log r}$
6	0.702	0.849	0.948	5.823
6	0.722	0.890	0.965	5.859
6	0.673	0.854	0.942	6.252
7	0.670	0.908	0.937	4.651
7	0.686	0.891	0.952	4.712
7	0.672	0.861	0.971	4.956

Comparing Table 2 to Table 1, we see that the relationship between the regulator, the discriminant, and the minimal and maximal heights of the generators are more-or-less the same in both tables. Not surprisingly, what has changed is that for a given rank, the discriminant is much larger in Table 2 than it is in Table 1. This is very reasonable, since Table 1 imposes no prior restrictions on the coefficients of $\mathcal{E}$, while in Table 2 we are forcing the coefficients of $\mathcal{E}$ to have specific values modulo 173. This means that the discriminant of $\mathcal{E}$ should be forced upwards by some power of p.

A reasonable assumption is that $\log|\Delta|$ will grow linearly in both $\log p$ and in $r\log r$ (the latter from Mestre's results and Table 1), say

$$\log|\Delta| \approx c_1 \log p + c_2 r \log r.$$

Fitting the data in Table 2 to this formula (note $p = 173$), we find the best fit is

$$\log|\Delta| \approx 11.93 \log p + 0.26 r \log r. \tag{11}$$

(Note that for our subsequent analysis, it would make little difference if c_1 were to be reduced to, say, 5.)

Now suppose we want to solve the ECDL problem for a given prime p by using Mestre's method to lift $E/\mathbb{F}_p$ to a curve $\mathcal{E}/\mathbb{Q}$ of moderately large rank. Looking at the Heuristic Bound (10), in order to have a reasonable chance of lifting a point of $E(\mathbb{F}_p)$ to a point of $\mathcal{E}(\mathbb{Q})$ of height at most B, we need $N(\mathcal{E}, B)$ fairly close to p, say $N(\mathcal{E}, B) \geq p/2^{10}$. Then (10) and (11) give us the lower bound

$$\log B \geq \frac{r\log(p^{11.93}r^{0.26r})}{20\pi e}\left(\frac{p\sqrt{\pi r}}{2^{10}}\right)^{2/r}. \tag{12}$$

The following table gives, for various values of p, the value of r which minimizes this lower bound and the corresponding lower bound for B.

Table 3. Best Lower Bound for B in (12)

p	r	$B \geq$	$B \geq$
2^{20}	15	$2^{72.63}$	$p^{3.63}$
2^{40}	40	$2^{398.08}$	$p^{9.95}$
2^{80}	87	$2^{1823.54}$	$p^{22.79}$
2^{120}	134	$2^{4297.13}$	$p^{35.81}$
2^{160}	180	$2^{7830.74}$	$p^{48.94}$

We thus see that for any reasonable size prime p (for cryptographic purposes, one would certainly never use a prime smaller than 2^{80}), the smallest allowable B is a substantial power of p. For the sake of argument, we will make the optimistic assumption that we can take $B = p^{20}$, but as the table makes clear, the true value of B is likely to be much larger. We will also suppose, again being optimistic, that it is possible to find a suitable lift $\mathcal{E}/\mathbb{Q}$ whose rank is on the order of 100 to 200, despite the fact that no curves of rank ≥ 24 are currently known.

However, even for $B = p^{20}$ and a curve $\mathcal{E}/\mathbb{Q}$ with known generators $P_1, \ldots, P_r$, we are confronted with the second enormous challenge posed in Miller's paper. Namely, how do we lift a given point on $E(\mathbb{F}_p)$ to a point on $\mathcal{E}(\mathbb{Q})$, even if we know that there is such a lift with height less than p^{20}? Certainly we don't want to check all suitable linear combinations $\sum n_i P_i$, since this is no better than a brute-force search through a set with $N(\mathcal{E}, B)$ elements, and we've chosen B so that $N(\mathcal{E}, B) \gg\ll p$. On the other hand, we could try to lift the given point p-adically, that is, first lift mod p^2, then mod p^3, etc. If we could do this correctly, then when we lift modulo p^{20}, we will have found the desired point in $\mathcal{E}(\mathbb{Q})$, since we know that the x-coordinate of the desired point has height less than p^{20}. Unfortunately, as Miller points out, at each step in this p-adic lifting process, we are faced with p possible lifts for each lift in the previous step. Since there is no (known) method for deciding a priori which of the lifts will lead to an actual point in $\mathcal{E}(\mathbb{Q})$, this method leads to a tree with p^{20} nodes to check, clearly not a feasible task.

Of course, if the lifting problem could be efficiently solved for (say) $p \approx 2^{160}$ and $B = p^{100} \approx 2^{16000}$, either by p-adic or other methods, then it might be feasible to solve "real-world" ECDL problems using the index calculus. However, the numbers involved are so staggeringly large that it seems very unlikely that this lifting problem has a practical solution.

The key point here is that it is necessary to choose B to be a substantial power of p in order to have enough points of height $\leq B$ to cover most of $E(\mathbb{F}_p)$, and for such a large B, there is no method other than a brute force search to find the desired lift of a given point in $E(\mathbb{F}_p)$. If it had been possible to cover $E(\mathbb{F}_p)$ with points of $\mathcal{E}(\mathbb{Q})$ having height at most (say) $\sqrt{p}$, which is essentially what happens for the discrete logarithm problem in the multiplicative group, or even height at most p, then quite possibly there is a good (i.e., efficient) way of lifting points. But the fact that the generators for $\mathcal{E}(\mathbb{Q})$ have height $\gg\!\!\ll r\log r$, as compared with height $\gg\!\!\ll \log r$ in the multiplicative case, means that we cannot hope to cover $E(\mathbb{F}_p)$ with points of $\mathcal{E}(\mathbb{Q})$ having such small height. This, then, explains why it is very unlikely that there is an index calculus for elliptic curve discrete logarithms which is directly analogous to the classical index calculus for the multiplicative group.

References

1. Adleman, L., *A subexponential algorithm for the discrete logarithm problem with applications to cryptography*, Proc. 20th IEEE Found. Comp. Sci. Symp., 1979, pp. 55–60.
2. L. Adleman, J. DeMarrais and M. Huang,, *A subexponential algorithm for discrete logarithms over the rational subgroup of the jacobians of large genus hyperelliptic curves over finite fields*, Algorithmic Number Theory, Lecture Notes in Computer Science, volume 877, Springer-Verlag, 1994, pp. 28–40.
3. A.O. Atkins, *The number of points on an elliptic curve modulo a prime*, preprint, 1988.
4. R. Balasubramanian and N. Koblitz,, *The improbability that an elliptic curve has subexponential discrete log problem under the Menezes-Okamoto-Vanstone algorithm*, Journal of Cryptology (to appear).
5. Canfield, E.R., Erdös, P., Pomerance, C., *On a problem of Oppenheim concerning 'Factorisation Numerorum'*, Journal Number Theory **17** (1983), 1–28.
6. Certicom White Paper, *Remarks on the security of the elliptic curve cryptosystem*, www.certicom.com/ecc/wecc3.htm
7. T. ElGamal, *A public-key cryptosystem and a signature scheme based on discrete logarithms*, IEEE Transactions on Information Theory **31** (1985), 469–472.
8. N. Elkies, *Explicit isogenies*, preprint, 1991.
9. G. Frey and H. Rück, *A remark concerning m-divisibility and the discrete logarithm in the divisor class group of curves*, Mathematics of Computation **62** (1994), 865–874.
10. D. Gordon, *Discrete logarithms in GF(p) using the number field sieve*, SIAM Journal on Discrete Mathematics **6** (1993), 124–138.
11. N. Hindry and J. Silverman, *The canonical height and integral points on elliptic curves*, Invent. Math. **93** (1988), 419–450.
12. N. Koblitz, *Elliptic curve cryptosystems*, Mathematics of Computation **48** (1987), 203–209.
13. ———, *CM-curves with good cryptographic properties*, Advances in Cryptology - CRYPTO '91, Lecture Notes in Computer Science, volume 576, Springler-Verlag, 1992, pp. 279–287.
14. Kraitchik, M., *Théorie des Nombres*, volume 1, Gauthier-Villars, 1922.
15. ———, *Reserches sur la théorie des nombres*, Gauthier-Villars, 1924.
16. B.A. LaMacchia and A.M. Odlyzko, *Computation of discrete logarithms in prime fields*, Designs, Codes and Cryptography **1** (1991), 47–62.
17. S. Lang, *Fundamentals of Diophantine Geometry*, Springer-Verlag, New York, 1983.
18. ———, *Elliptic Curves: Diophantine Analysis*, Springer-Verlag, New York, 1978.
19. R. Martin and W. McMillen, *An elliptic curve over $\mathbb{Q}$ with rank at least 23*, announcement, June 1997.
20. A. Menezes, T. Okamoto and S. Vanstone, *Reducing elliptic curve logarithms to logarithms in a finite field*, IEEE Transactions on Information Theory **39** (1993), 1639–1646.
21. J.F. Mestre, *Formules explicites et minoration de conducteurs de variétés algébriques*, Compositio Math. **58** (1986), 209–232.
22. ———, *Constructiuon d'une courbe elliptique de rang ≥ 12*, C.R. Acad. Sc. Paris t. **295** (1982), 643–644.

23. V.S. Miller, *Use of elliptic curves in cryptography*, Advances in Cryptology CRYPTO '85 (Lecture Notes in Computer Science, vol. 218), Springer-Verlag, 1986, pp. 417–426.

24. A. Miyaji, *On ordinary elliptic curve cryptosystems*, Advances in Cryptology - ASI-ACRYPT '91, Lecture Notes in Computer Science, volume 218, Springer-Verlag, 1993, pp. 460–469.

25. S. Pohlig and M. Hellman, *An improved algorithm for computing logarithms over GF(p) and its cryptographic significance*, IEEE Transactions on Information Theory **24** (1978), 106–110.

26. J. Pollard, *Monte Carlo methods for index computation mod p*, Mathematics of Computation **32** (1978), 918–924.

27. H. H. Rück, *On the discrete logarithms on some elliptic curves*, preprint, 1997.

28. T. Satoh and K. Araki, *Fermat quotients and the polynomial time discrete log algorithm for anomalous elliptic curves*, preprint.

29. O. Schirokauer, D. Weber, and Th. Denny, *Discrete logarithms: The effectiveness of the index calculus method*, Algorithmic Number Theory, (ANTS-II, Talence, France, 1996), Lect. Notes in Computer Sci., vol. 1122, Springer-Verlag, 1996, pp. 337–362.

30. R. Schoof, *Elliptic curves over finite fields and the computation of square roots modulo p*, Math. Comp. **44** (1985), 483–494.

31. I. Semaev, *Evaluation of discrete logarithms in a group of p-torsion points of an elliptic curve in characteristic p*, Mathematics of Computation **67** (1998), 353–356.

32. V. Shoup, *Lower bounds for discrete logarithms and related problems*, Advances in Cryptology - EUROCRYPT '97, Lecture Notes in Computer Science, volume 1233, Springer-Verlag, 1997, pp. 256–266.

33. J.H. Silverman, *The Arithmetic of Elliptic Curves*, Graduate Texts in Math., vol. 106, Springer-Verlag, Berlin and New York, 1986.

34. _____, *Advanced Topics in the Arithmetic of Elliptic Curves*, Graduate Texts in Math., vol. 151, Springer-Verlag, Berlin and New York, 1994.

35. _____, *Lower bound for the canonical height on elliptic curves*, Duke Math. J. **48** (1981), 633–648.

36. _____, *The difference between the Weil height and the canonical height on elliptic curves*, Math. Comp. **192** (1990), 723–743.

37. _____, *Computing heights on elliptic curves*, Math. Comp. **51** (1988), 339–358.

38. _____, *Computing canonical heights with little (or no) factorization*, Math. Comp. **66** (1997), 787–805.

39. N. Smart, *Announcement of an attack on the ECDLP for anomalous elliptic curves*, preprint, 1997.

40. J. Solinas, *An improved algorithm for arithmetic on a family of elliptic curves*, Advances in Cryptology - CRYPTO '97, Lecture Notes in Computer Science, volume 1294, Springer-Verlag, 1997, pp. 357–371.

41. J. Voloch, *The discrete logarithm problem on elliptic curves and descents*, preprint, 1997.

42. Weber, D., *Computing discrete logarithms with the general number field sieve*, Algorithmic Number Theory, (ANTS-II, Talence, France, 1996), Lect. Notes in Computer Sci., vol. 1122, Springer-Verlag, 1996, pp. 391–403.

43. A.E. Western and J.C.P. Miller, *Tables of Indices and Primitive Roots*, Royal Society Mathematical Tables, vol. 9, Cambridge Univ. Press, 1968.

Cryptanalysis of Rijmen-Preneel Trapdoor Ciphers

Hongjun Wu[1], Feng Bao[2], Robert H. Deng[2], and Qin-Zhong Ye[1]

[1] Department of Electrical Engineering
National University of Singapore
Singapore 119260
[2] Information Security Group
Kent Ridge Digital Labs
Singapore 119613

Abstract. Rijmen and Preneel recently proposed for the first time a family of trapdoor
block ciphers [8]. In this family of ciphers, a trapdoor
is hidden in S-boxes and is claimed to be undetectable in [8] for properly
chosen parameters. Given the trapdoor,
the secret key (used for encryption and decryption) can be recovered
easily by applying Matsui's linear cryptanalysis [6].
In this paper, we break this family of trapdoor block ciphers by developing an attack on the S-boxes. We show how to find the trapdoor in the
S-boxes and demonstrate that it is impossible to adjust the parameters
of the S-boxes such that detecting the trapdoor is difficult meanwhile
finding the secret key by trapdoor information is easy.

1   Introduction

In cryptography, design of secure trapdoor one-way functions has long been a
challenging problem. Many previous proposals have been broken and the existing "secure" ones are mostly based on the few conjectures of hard problems in
number theory.

Recently, Rijmen and Preneel proposed a family of trapdoor block ciphers
[8] which we will call RP trapdoor ciphers. In such ciphers, a trapdoor is built
into S-boxes. Knowledge of the trapdoor allows one to determine the correlation
between output bits of the cipher's round function. This correlation is in turn
used to find the secret key by performing Matsui's linear cryptanalysis on a
small amount of known plaintexts [6]. In [8], it was claimed that the trapdoor
with properly chosen parameters is undetectable and RP trapdoor ciphers may
be used for public key encryption.

In this paper, we break RP trapdoor block ciphers by developing an attack
on the trapdoor S-boxes. We first demonstrate that the trapdoor can be found
from the S-boxes. We then show that RP trapdoor block ciphers can not be
made secure by adjusting system parameters, since it is not possible for such
ciphers to meet the following two contradicting requirements simultaneously: 1)

K. Ohta and D. Pei (Eds.): ASIACRYPT'98, LNCS 1514, pp. 126–132, 1998.
© Springer-Verlag Berlin Heidelberg 1998

be resistance to our attack and, 2) be computationally efficient in finding the secret key using linear cryptanalysis once the trapdoor is known.

This paper is organized as follows. The trapdoor S-boxes and RP trapdoor ciphers are briefly reviewed in Section 2. In Section 3, we present our attack to RP trapdoor ciphers (more precisely, to the trapdoor S-boxes). In Section 4, we show that it is not possible to construct secure RP trapdoor ciphers by adjusting system parameters. We conclude the paper in Section 5.

2   RP Trapdoor Ciphers

RP trapdoor ciphers make use of the "type II" linear relations as defined in [7]: correlations that exist between output bits of a cipher's round function/S-boxes. Knowledge of the trapdoor reveals the correlations and allows linear cryptanalysis being carried out to determine the secret key from some known plaintexts.

2.1   Trapdoor $m \times n$ S-Boxes

The trapdoor in RP trapdoor ciphers is built into S-boxes. An $m \times n$ S-box has m-dimensional and n-dimensional Boolean vectors as its inputs and outputs, respectively. It can be represented by 2^m n-dimensional Boolean vectors, i.e., $S = \{v_0, v_1, \cdots, v_{2^m-1}\}$. For input $x \in \{0, 1, \cdots, 2^m - 1\}$, the output of the S-box is defined as $S(x) = v_x$ where x can be treated as an m-dimensional vector. In the following, we denote the jth bit of v_i as $v_i[j]$. That is, $v_i = < v_i[1], v_i[2], \cdots, v_i[n] >$.

In a RP trapdoor cipher, the trapdoor $m \times n$ S-box is constructed as follows. First, choose a non-zero n-dimensional Boolean vector $\beta = < \beta[1], \beta[2], \ldots, \beta[n] >$ and let $\beta[q] = 1$. Then randomly choose the values of $v_i[j]$ for $i = 0, 1, ..., 2^m - 1$ and $j = 1, ..., q-1, q+1, ..., n$. Finally, set the values of $v_i[q]$, $i = 0, 1, ..., 2^m - 1$, such that

$$\beta[1]v_i[1] \oplus \cdots \oplus \beta[q]v_i[q] \oplus \cdots \oplus \beta[n]v_i[n] = v_i \cdot \beta = 0 \qquad (1)$$

holds with probability p_T (which has a value very close to 1). Equation (1) is equivalent to a correlation

$$c_T = 2p_T - 1$$

between the constant zero function and $\beta \cdot S(x)$. The trapdoor is the Boolean vector β. It was claimed in [8] that finding β from published S-boxes is difficult for suitable parameters, say, $m = 10, n = 80$ and $p_T = 1 - 2^{-5}$. RP trapdoor ciphers are designed on this supposition.

2.2   Trapdoor Ciphers

RP trapdoor ciphers are based on the Feistel structure [4]. In a Feistel block cipher with $2n$-bit block size and r rounds, plaintext and ciphertext consist of two n-bit halves denoted as L_0, R_0 and L_r, R_r respectively. Each round operates as follows:

$$R_i = L_{i-1} \oplus F(K_i \oplus R_{i-1})$$
$$L_i = R_{i-1}$$
for $i = 1, 2, ..., r$

where K_i is the ith round subkey and F is the round function. Note that after the last round, the swapping of the halves is undone to make encryption and decryption similar.

In [8], variants on both CAST [5] and LOKI91 [3] were studied. In this paper, we only consider trapdoor CAST ciphers since all the discussions here can be extended to trapdoor LOKI91 ciphers directly.

The CAST family of ciphers are 64-bit Feistel ciphers. Its round function F is based on four 8×32 S-boxes (i.e., for $m = 8, n = 32$), which have components that are either randomly chosen or are bent functions [1]. Mathematically, the round function is given by

$$F(x) = S_1(x_1) \oplus S_2(x_2) \oplus S_3(x_3) \oplus S_4(x_4)$$

where x, the 32-bit input, is the concatenation of 4 bytes $x = x_1||x_2||x_3||x_4$ and where $S_1, ..., S_4$ are four 8×32 S-boxes.

In a trapdoor CAST cipher, the four S-boxes use the same trapdoor β but possibly with different values of p_T, denoted as $p_T^{(1)}, ..., p_T^{(4)}$. The following relation holds

$$\beta \cdot F(x) = \beta \cdot S_1(x_1) \oplus \beta \cdot S_2(x_2) \oplus \beta \cdot S_3(x_3) \oplus \beta \cdot S_4(x_4)$$

Hence the round function correlates with the constant zero function with a correlation equal to

$$c_F = \prod_{i=1}^{4} c_T^{(i)}$$

It was stated in [8] that CAST should be extended in a natural way to a 128-bit block cipher by using 8×64 S-boxes. This, it claimed, will make the trapdoor undetectable. Unfortunately, this claim is false as we will show in the next section.

3   Attack on RP Trapdoor Ciphers

In this section, we show that the trapdoor in a RP trapdoor cipher can be found easily and directly from the S-boxes.

RP trapdoor ciphers as described in the last section has $l = \frac{n}{m}$ S-boxes, each consisting of 2^m n-dimensional Boolean vectors. By way of their construction as presented in Section 2.1, we know that vectors in S-boxes are randomly chosen; therefore, the total number of distinguishing vectors in the l S-boxes, denoted by N, should be very close to $l2^m$. We also know each S-box is associated with a probability $p_T^{(i)}$. Let

$$p_T = \frac{\sum_{i=1}^{l} p_T^{(i)}}{l}$$

denote the average of these probabilities.

Let all the N distinguishing vectors in the l S-boxes be denoted as $\{v_1, v_2, \cdots, v_N\}$. From Section 2.1 we know that the trapdoor β satisfies

$$v_i \cdot \beta = 0$$

for $i = 1, 2, ..., N$ with probability p_T. Hence, the problem of finding the trapdoor is to find a β such that

$$\begin{pmatrix} v_1[1] & v_1[2] & \cdots & v_1[n] \\ v_2[1] & v_2[2] & \cdots & v_2[n] \\ \vdots & \vdots & \ddots & \vdots \\ v_N[1] & v_N[2] & \cdots & v_N[n] \end{pmatrix} \begin{pmatrix} \beta[1] \\ \beta[2] \\ \vdots \\ \beta[n] \end{pmatrix} = \begin{pmatrix} \alpha[1] \\ \alpha[2] \\ \vdots \\ \alpha[N] \end{pmatrix} \quad (2)$$

for any Boolean vector $\alpha = <\alpha[1], \alpha[2], \cdots, \alpha[N]>$
of Hamming weight approximately equal to $N(1 - p_T)$

The following algorithm is used to determine the trapdoor β directly from the l S-boxes.

Algorithm 1.

Step 1. Choose n vectors, denoted as $v_{i_1}, v_{i_2}, \cdots, v_{i_n}$, randomly from $v_1, v_2, \cdots, v_N$.

Step 2. Solve the n equations for x_β:

$$v_{i_k} \cdot x_\beta = 0$$

for $k = 1, 2, ..., n$

Step 3. If non-zero solutions do not exist, go to Step 1. If solutions, say $\beta_1, \beta_2, ..., \beta_t$, are found, check whether they satisfy (2). If some β_j does satisfy (2), then it is the trapdoor β we are looking for; otherwise, go to Step 1.

Observations

1. If we happen to choose $v_{i_1}, v_{i_2}, \cdots, v_{i_n}$ in Step 1 such that $v_{i_k} \cdot \beta = 0$ has non-zero solutions for $k = 1, 2, ..., n$, then β must be among these solutions. By checking them one by one against (2), we can find this β.
2. If we can find another $\beta'(\neq \beta)$ also satisfying (2), this β' can also be used as trapdoor information in linear attack for finding the secret key.
3. Since $v_i \cdot \beta = 0$ with probability p_T, such "lucky choice" happens with probability about $(p_T)^n$. Hence, it is guaranteed to find a trapdoor with this probability. (The probability in fact should be $C_{Np_T}^n / C_N^n$. This number is very close to $(p_T)^n$ when N is much larger than n and p_T is close to 1. Here C_N^n denotes the number of ways of choosing n objects from N objects.)

4. The number of solutions t won't be very large. This is because the vectors of the S-boxes are randomly chosen except for one bit(at bit position q), therefore, the rank of the matrix in (2) is close to n with large probability.

Now let's look at a trapdoor CAST cipher with 128-bit block size ($n = 64$) and $p_T = 1 - 2^{-5}$ (this value of p_T was given in [8] as an example to illustrate the strength of the RP trapdoor cipher). The value of $(p_T)^n$ is about 0.1311. By repeating Steps 1 and 2 of the algorithm 32 times, we expect to get the value of β with probability 98.89%. This example shows clearly that RP trapdoor block ciphers are very vulnerable under our attack.

4   The Impossibility of Designing Secure RP Trapdoor Ciphers

In Section 3, we developed an attack to RP trapdoor ciphers. We demonstrated that the trapdoor can be determined easily from S-boxes. In this section, we show that it is impossible to design secure practical RP trapdoor ciphers.

We observe that there is a tradeoff between resisting our attack (i.e., Algorithm 1) and the effort required to find the secret key from trapdoor using linear cryptanalysis. This tradeoff can be adjusted by selecting system parameters r (number of rounds), m, n, and p_T. The smaller $(p_T - 0.5)$ is, the more difficult it is to succeed in Algorithm 1, but at the same time, the more difficult it is to find the secret key from the given trapdoor using linear cryptanalysis. Also, large values of m and n increases the computational complexity of Algorithm 1 , as well as that of S-boxes. To simplify our notations and without loss of generability, in the following we assume that $p_T^{(1)} = p_T^{(2)} = \cdots = p_T^{(l)}$.

Two basic requirements must be met in the design of a practical secure block cipher:

Requirement 1. The block cipher should be secure in the sense that it resists all the known attacks.

Requirement 2. The block cipher should be practical in the sense that the program size should not be too large.

To design a practical secure trapdoor cipher, two more requirements must be met:

Requirement 3. The trapdoor should is secure in the sense that it is hard to find the trapdoor even if its general form is known.

Requirement 4. The trapdoor should be practical in the sense that the secret key can be found easily once the trapdoor is given.

We now show that it is not possible to design a RP trapdoor cipher to satisfy the above four requirements simultaneously. We do this by showing that if a RP trapdoor cipher meets the first three requirements, then it can not meet the fourth requirement.

To satisfy the first requirement, the round number can not be too small. Thus, we expect that

$$r \geq 8 \tag{3}$$

To satisfy the second requirement, the total size of S-boxes is expected to be less than 128 Megabytes (i.e., 2^{30} bits). It is the same as to say that

$$\frac{n}{m}(n2^m) \leq 2^{30} \tag{4}$$

To satisfy the third requirement, we expect the following relation holds:

$$(p_T)^n \leq 2^{-64} \tag{5}$$

For a RP trapdoor cipher that **satisfies conditions** (4), (5) **and** (6) **simultaneously**, we evaluate the amount of known plaintexts required to carry out a successful linear cryptanalysis according to Matsui's algorithm 2 in [6]. The minimum numbers of plaintexts with respect to different value of m are listed in Table 1.

m	Number of plaintexts required	m	Number of plaintexts required
6	2^{175}	15	2^{74}
7	2^{150}	16	2^{70}
8	2^{132}	17	2^{67}
9	2^{118}	18	2^{65}
10	2^{107}	19	2^{64}
11	2^{97}	20	2^{65}
12	2^{90}	21	2^{78}
13	2^{84}	22	2^{126}
14	2^{78}	23	not exist since $p_T < 0.5$

Table 1. The number of known plaintexts required to carry out the linear cryptanalysis for a RP trapdoor cipher satisfying the first three requirements.

From table 1, we see that too many plaintexts are required to carried out the linear cryptanalysis based on knowledge of the trapdoor in order to discover the secret key. Although there may be some other methods to reduce the amount of known plaintexts (e.g., reducing the round number or increasing the size of S-boxes to a certain value), we believe that the number of known plaintexts required to carry out a successful linear cryptanalysis is still very large. Thus, we are forced to conclude that it is impossible to design practical secure RP trapdoor block ciphers.

132   H. Wu et al.

5 Conclusions

Security of RP trapdoor block ciphers lies on the undetectability of a trapdoor built into S-boxes. It was claimed in [8] that it is hard to obtain the trapdoor from S-boxes and therefore RP trapdoor ciphers can be used for public key encryption. In this paper, we showed how to break such ciphers by finding the trapdoor directly from S-boxes. We demonstrated our attack to RP trapdoor ciphers based on "type II" linear relations.

In addition to trapdoors based on "type II" linear relations, trapdoors that make use of "type I" linear relations were also proposed in [8]. "Type I" linear relations are defined in [7] as the correlations between input and output bits of the round function. Unfortunately, this latter type of trapdoors is also vulnerable to our attack.

Other than hiding linear relations, another method proposed in [8] is to hide differentials into block ciphers in order to make them vulnerable to differential cryptanalysis [2]. However, construction of this kind of trapdoors was not given in [8] and it seems that hiding differentials is more difficult than hiding linear relations. So far, trapdoors based on hiding differentials remains an open problem.

References

1. C.M. Adams, S.E. Tavares, "Designing S-boxes for ciphers resistant to differential cryptanalysis", Proceedings of the 3rd Symposium on State and Progress of Research in Cryptography, W. Wolgowicz, Ed., Fondazione Ugo Bordoni, 1993, pp. 181-190.
2. E. Biham, A. Shamir, Differential Cryptanalysis of the Data Encryption Standard, Springer-Verlag, 1993.
3. L. Brown, M. Kwan, J. Pieprzyk, J. Sebberry, "Improving resistance against differential cryptanalysis and the redesign of LOKI", Advances in Cryptology, Proceedings Asiacrypt'91, LNCS 739, H. Imai, R. L. Rivest, and T. Matsumoto, Eds., Springer-Verlag, 1993, pp. 36-50.
4. H. Feistel, W.A. Notz, J.L. Smith, "Some cryptographic techniques for machine-to-machine data communications", Proceedings IEEE, Vol. 63, No. 11, November 1975, pp. 1545-1554.
5. H.M. Heys, S.E Tavares, "On the security of the CAST encryption algorithm", Canadian Conference on Electrical and Computer Engineering, pp. 332-335, Sept. 1994, Halifax, Canada.
6. M. Matsui, "Linear cryptanalysis method for DES cipher", Advances in Cryptology, Proceedings Eurocrypt'93, LNCS 765, T. Helleseth, Ed., Springer-Verlag, 1994, pp. 386-397.
7. M. Matsui, "On correlation between the order of S-boxes and the strength of DES", Advances in Cryptology, Proceedings Eurocrypt'94, LNCS 950, A. De Santis, Ed., Springer-Verlag, 1995, pp. 366-375.
8. V. Rijmen, B. Preneel, "A family of trapdoor ciphers", Fast Software Encryption, LNCS 1267, E. Biham ed., Springer-Verlag, 1997, pp. 139-148.

Improved Truncated Differential Attacks on SAFER

Hongjun Wu[*]   Feng Bao[**]   Robert H. Deng[**]   Qin-Zhong Ye[*]

[*]Department of Electrical Engineering
National University of Singapore
Singapore 1 19260

[**]Information Security Group
Kent Ridge Digital Labs
Singapore 119613

Abstract. Knudsen and Berson have applied truncated differential attack on 5 round SAFER K-64 successfully. However, their attack is not efficient when applied on 5 round SAFER SK-64 (with the modified key schedule) and can not be applied on 6 round SAFER.

In this paper, we improve the truncated differential attack on SAFER by using better truncated differential and additional filtering method. Our attack on 5 round SAFER (both SAFER K-64 and SAFER SK-64) can find the secret key much faster than by exhaustive search. Also, the number of chosen plaintexts required are less than those needed in Knudsen and Berson's attack. Our attack on 6 round SAFER (both SAFER K-64 and SAFER SK-64) can find the secret key faster than by exhaustive search.

1 Introduction

In [6], Massey proposed an encryption algorithm, SAFER K-64. It is an iterated block cipher with 64-bit block size. The suggested number of rounds is minimum 6 and maximum 10 [6,7]. Knudsen discovered a weakness in the key schedule of SAFER and suggested a modified version [3]. Later, this new key schedule was adopted by Massey which resulted in SAFER SK-64 [8]. Also, Massey suggested 8 rounds to be used for SAFER with 64-bit key. The other variants of SAFER with 128-bit key are SAFER K-128 and SAFER SK-128 corresponding to SAFER K-64 and SAFER SK-64, respectively.

Evidence was given in [7] that SAFER is secure against differential cryptanalysis [1] after 5 rounds. In [2], SAFER is shown to be secure against linear cryptanalysis [9] after 2 rounds. In [5], Knudsen and Berson applied truncated differential cryptanalysis [6] on 5 round SAFER K-64 successfully. Their result showed that the secret key of 5 round SAFER K-64 can be found much faster than by exhaustive search. However, their attack is not efficient when applied on 5 round SAFER SK-64. Also, their attack cannot be extended to attack 6 round SAFER since too many wrong pairs are not filtered out.

In this paper, we improve the truncated differential cryptanalysis and apply it on 5 round and 6 round SAFER. We propose better truncated differential and additional filtering method in our attacks. For 5 round SAFER (both SAFER K-64 and SAFER SK-64), our truncated differential is with probability of about 2^{-69} in average and about 2^{38} chosen plaintexts (a large reduction in the amount of chosen plaintexts) are needed to find the secret key. This attack runs in time similar to 2^{46} encryptions of 5-round SAFER. For 6 round SAFER, our truncated differential has a probability of about 2^{-84}

K. Ohta and D. Pei (Eds.): ASIACRYPT'98, LNCS 1514, pp. 133-147, 1998.
© Springer-Verlag Berlin Heidelberg 1998

and about 2^{53} chosen plaintexts are needed. This attack runs in time similar to 2^{61} encryptions of 6-round SAFER.

The paper is organised as follows. Section 2 briefly reviews the SAFER algorithms. Section 3 introduces Knudsen and Berson's truncated differential attack on 5 round SAFER K-64. In Section 4, we present our attack on 5 round SAFER. Our attacks on 6 round SAFER are given in Section 5. Section 6 discusses the strength of 7 round SAFER and Section 7 concludes the paper.

2 Description of SAFER

SAFER K-64 is an iterated block cipher with both block and key sizes of 64 bits and with all the operations done on bytes. The key is expanded to $2r + 1$ round keys each of 8 bytes, where the round number r was suggested to be 6 [6] and then 8 [8], respectively. Each round takes 8 bytes of text input and two round keys each of 8 bytes. Each round consists of 4 layers as shown in Fig. 1.

The first layer consists of xor'ing or adding modulo 256 with the first round key. In the second layer, the 8 bytes pass through two permutations or S-boxes: $X(a) = (45^a \bmod 257) \bmod 256$, and the inverse of X, $L(a) = \log_{45}(a) \bmod 257$ for $a \neq 0$ and $L(0) = 128$. The third layer consists of adding modulo 256 or xor'ing with the second round key. The final layer is the *Pseudo-Hadamard Transformation (PHT)*. It is defined by three layers of the 2-*PHT*:

$$2\text{-}PHT(x, y) = (2x + y, x + y)$$

where each coordinate is taken modulo 256. After the last round, an output transformation is applied, which consists of xor'ing or adding modulo 256 with the last round key and is the same as the first layer of the round operation. We call this the last half round in the rest of the paper.

The PHT-transformation is simply described by a matrix M [6]. Let the input be a vector $v = [v_1, v_2, \ldots v_8]$, then the output is obtained by $v \cdot M$. M and its inverse M^{-1} are given, respectively, by

$$M = \begin{bmatrix} 8 & 4 & 4 & 2 & 4 & 2 & 2 & 1 \\ 4 & 2 & 4 & 2 & 2 & 1 & 2 & 1 \\ 4 & 2 & 2 & 1 & 4 & 2 & 2 & 1 \\ 2 & 1 & 2 & 1 & 2 & 1 & 2 & 1 \\ 4 & 4 & 2 & 2 & 2 & 2 & 1 & 1 \\ 2 & 2 & 2 & 2 & 1 & 1 & 1 & 1 \\ 2 & 2 & 1 & 1 & 2 & 2 & 1 & 1 \\ 1 & 1 & 1 & 1 & 1 & 1 & 1 & 1 \end{bmatrix} \quad M^{-1} = \begin{bmatrix} +1 & -1 & -1 & +1 & -1 & +1 & +1 & -1 \\ -1 & +1 & +1 & -1 & +2 & -2 & -2 & +2 \\ -1 & +2 & +1 & -2 & +1 & -2 & -1 & +2 \\ +1 & -2 & -1 & +2 & -2 & +4 & +2 & -4 \\ -1 & +1 & +2 & -2 & +1 & -1 & -2 & +2 \\ +1 & -1 & -2 & +2 & -2 & +2 & +4 & -4 \\ +1 & -2 & -2 & +4 & -1 & +2 & +2 & -4 \\ -1 & +2 & +2 & -4 & +2 & -4 & -4 & +8 \end{bmatrix} \quad (1)$$

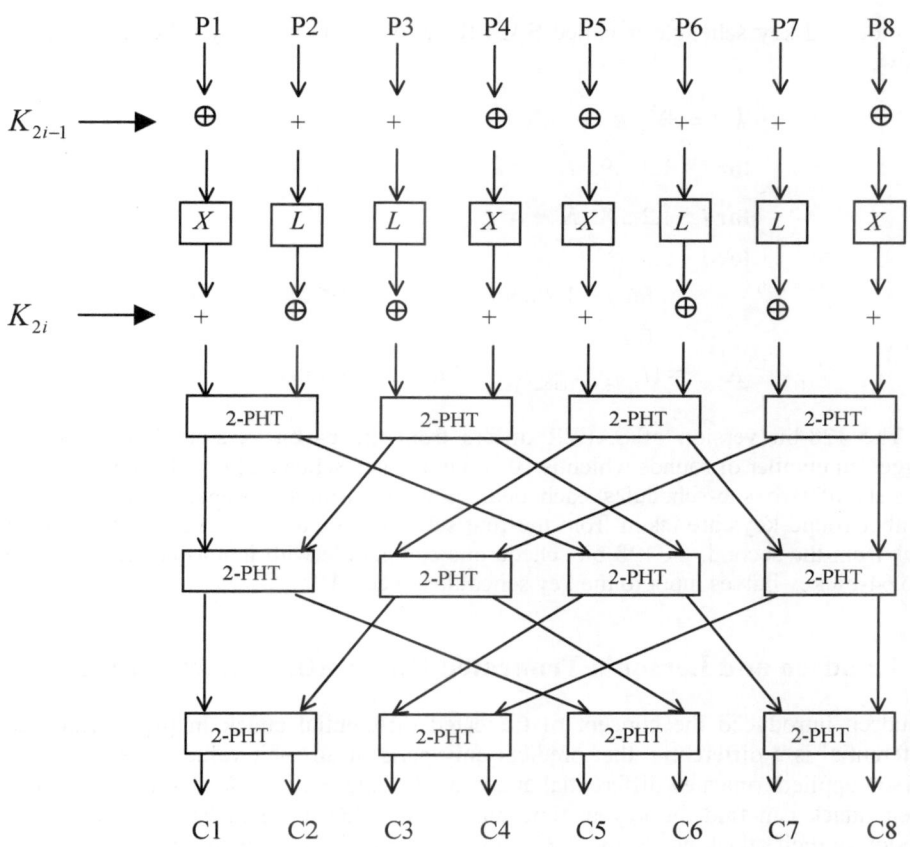

Fig. 1. One round of SAFER

The 8-byte key is expanded to $2r + 1$ round keys each of 8 bytes. The original key schedule works as follows. Let $K = (k_1, ..., k_8)$ be an 8-byte key. The round key byte j in round i is denoted as $K_{i,j}$. The round key bytes are derived as follows:

for $j = 1, 2, ... 8$: $\quad K_{1,j} = t_{1,j} = k_j$
for $i = 2, ..., 2r + 1$,
$\qquad$ **for** $j = 1, 2, ... 8$: $\quad t_{i,j} = t_{i-1,j} << 3$
$\qquad$ **for** $j = 1, 2, ... 8$: $\quad K_{i,j} = (t_{i,j} + bias[i,j]) \bmod 256$

where '<<3' is a bitwise rotation 3 positions to the left and $bias[i, j] = X[X[9i + j]]$, where X is the exponentiation permutation.

Knudsen suggested a modified key schedule for SAFER to eliminate the key schedule weakness found by him [3]. Later, this key schedule was adopted for SAFER by Massey in [8]. The original SAFER is now called SAFER K-64 and the one with the modified key schedule is called SAFER SK-64. The new key schedule is given below.

$$k_9 = \oplus_{i=1}^{8} k_i$$

for $j = 1,2,...9$: $t_{1,j} = k_j$

for $j = 1,2,...8$: $K_{1,j} = t_{1,j}$

for $i = 2,..., 2r + 1$:

    for $j = 1,2,...9$: $t_{i,j} = t_{i-1,j} << 3$

    for j $=$ $1,2,...8$:

$$K_{i,j} = (t_{i,(i+j-2 \bmod 9)+1} + bias[i,j]) \bmod 256$$

The 128-bit version of SAFER differs from the 64-bit version SAFER in the suggested number of rounds which is 10 and in the key schedule [7]. The key schedule consists of two sub-schedules each dealing with 64-bit key separately. The odd number round keys are taken from the first sub-schedule and the even number round keys from the second. A 128-bit schedule is compatible with its 64-bit version if the two 64-bit key halves input to the key schedule are equal.

3   Knudsen and Berson's Truncated Differential Attack on SAFER

Knudsen introduced the concept of truncated differential attack in [4]. Truncated differential is a differential that predicts only parts of an n-bit value. Knudsen and Berson applied truncated differential attack on 5 round SAFER K-64 successfully [5]. Their attack can find the key in time much faster than by exhaustive search. One version of their attack needs about 2^{45} chosen plaintexts and runs in time similar to 2^{46} encryptions of 5-round SAFER. Another version of their attack needs about 2^{46} chosen plaintexts and runs in time similar to 2^{35} encryptions of 5-round SAFER. We introduce their truncated differential attack on SAFER below.

3.1   Truncated Differential of SAFER

The notation of "expanded view" from [7] is used to denote a one round differential by three tuples of each 8 entries. The first tuple indicates the difference in the 8 bytes of the inputs to the round, the second tuple indicates the difference of the bytes before the PHT-transformation and the third tuple indicates the difference of the bytes after the PHT-transformation, i.e. the difference of the outputs of the round (it is also the difference of the inputs of the next round). A difference of two bytes (a,b) is defined as

$$(a - b) \bmod 256.$$

The one round truncated differential is obtained from the properties of the PHT-transformation and S boxes $(X$ and $L)$. The properties of the PHT-transformation is obtained from the matrix M. These properties are also listed in the six tables (table 4 to table 10) of [7]. The properties of the S boxes $(X$ and $L)$ used in obtaining the round differential are listed in table 3 of [6]. Knudsen and Berson listed the one round truncated differentials (together with the probability) for SAFER with inputs different in less than or equal to four bytes in table 2 and table 3 of [5]. For example, the following one round truncated differential is with probability 2^{-24}:

$$[0, 0, a, b, 0, 0, c, d], [0, 0, e, -e, 0, 0, -e, e], [e, 0, 0, 0, e, 0, 0, 0]$$

It is denoted simply as

$$3478 \rightarrow 15, \quad p = 2^{-24}$$

where 3478 denotes that the inputs are different at the bytes 3, 4, 7 and 8 and where 15 denotes that the outputs are different at the bytes 1 and 5.

One round truncated differentials can be concatenated to get   truncated differentials of more than one round. For examples, the following one round truncated differentials

$$3478 \rightarrow 15, \quad p = 2^{-24} \qquad \text{and} \qquad 15 \rightarrow 1357, \qquad p = 2^{-8}$$

are concatenated to get a two round truncated differential

$$3478 \rightarrow 15 \rightarrow 1357, \quad p = 2^{-32}$$

However, when the one round truncated differentials are concatenated, its feasibility need be considered. This problem has been mentioned in [7]. Specifically, we note that the input difference of 128 to the S boxes cannot result in output difference of 128. Thus some one round truncated differential like 24→24 cannot be concatenated with itself. It is also noted that the input difference of 128 to the exponential permutation X results in odd output difference. Thus some one round differentials like 5→78 and 78→3478 cannot be concatenated.

3.2   Knudsen and Berson's Truncated Differential Attack on 5 Round SAFER K-64

Before introducing Knudsen and Berson's truncated differential attack on 5 round SAFER, the proposition 4 in [7] is given below:

Proposition 1. *For byte differences $\Delta V = V \oplus V^*$ and $\widetilde{\Delta V} = V - V^*$,*

  a) $\widetilde{\Delta V} = 0$ if and only if $\Delta V = 0$;

  b) $\widetilde{\Delta V} = 128$ if and only if $\Delta V = 128$;

  c) $\widetilde{\Delta V}$ is odd if and only if ΔV is odd.

Knudsen and Berson's attack on 5 round SAFER K-64 uses the following 4-round truncated differential with input difference

$$[a, 0, 0, b, c, 0, 0, d]$$

and output difference $[0, 0, 0, 128, 0, 0, 0, 0]$. There are four differentials in this truncated differential which are listed below. The first two differentials are with probability of $2^{-71.68}$. The last two differentials are each of probability $2^{-72.19}$, not $2^{-71.7}$ as stated in [5]. However, this small error does not affect Knudsen and Berson's attack too much.

$$1458 \rightarrow 1357 \rightarrow 1357 \rightarrow 13 \rightarrow 4 \qquad (2)$$
$$1458 \rightarrow 2468 \rightarrow 1357 \rightarrow 13 \rightarrow 4 \qquad (3)$$
$$1458 \rightarrow 1357 \rightarrow 2468 \rightarrow 13 \rightarrow 4 \qquad (4)$$
$$1458 \rightarrow 2468 \rightarrow 2468 \rightarrow 13 \rightarrow 4 \qquad (5)$$

The probabilities in the first two rounds are each of 2^{-16} and the probability in the third round is 2^{-24}. Now we look at the differential in the fourth round. For the first two differentials, the differential in the fourth round is

$$[2v, 0, v, 0, 0, 0, 0, 0], \quad [128, 0, 128, 0, 0, 0, 0, 0], \quad [0, 0, 0, 128, 0, 0, 0, 0]$$

This round has probability $2^{-15.68}$, which can be found by direct calculation. However, for the last two differentials, the differential in the forth round is

$$[v, 0, v, 0, 0, 0, 0, 0], \quad [128, 0, 128, 0, 0, 0, 0, 0], \quad [0, 0, 0, 128, 0, 0, 0, 0]$$

This round has a probability of $2^{-16.19}$, which is also found by direct calculation. So the probabilities are each of $2^{-71.68}$ for the first two differentials and $2^{-72.19}$ for the last two differentials. The probability for the 4-round differential is thus $2^{-69.9}$, not $2^{-69.7}$ as stated in [5]. This 4-round differential is concatenated with the fifth round differential

$$[0, 0, 0, 128, 0, 0, 0, 0], \quad [0, 0, 0, x, 0, 0, 0, 0], \quad [2x, x, 2x, x, 2x, x, 2x, x]$$

where the value of x is odd. This differential has probability 1 since the input difference 128 to the exponential permutation table always yields an odd output difference.

After the final output transformation consisting of byte wise xor'ing and add'ing with the last round key, the output difference is:

$$[z_1, x, 2x, z_2, z_3, x, 2x, z_4] \qquad (6)$$

where x is odd, z_1 and z_3 are even number while z_2 and z_4 are odd number according to c) of proposition 1.

The probability for this truncated differential is $2^{-69.9}$. About 2^{70} pairs are needed to get one right pair. Every structure consisting of 2^{32} chosen plaintexts yields about $(2^{32} \times (2^{32} - 1))/2 \approx 2^{63}$ pairs with the desired input difference. 128 such structures are required to get one right pair, a total of 2^{39} plaintexts. This analysis can be performed on each structure and thus the memory requirements are 2^{32} 64-bits quantities.

The filtering processes are carried out at the last half round and the first round. The filtering at the last half round is carried out firstly. Note that the difference at the second byte of the ciphertexts (denoted as x) should be odd. The differences in bytes 3, 6 and 7 have values 2x, x and 2x, respectively. The differences at the first and fifth bytes are even and the difference at the forth and eighth bytes are odd.   After considering these, all but one out of 2^{29} pairs are discarded. 2^{41} pairs are left and each of the pair suggests 16 values of the bytes 1, 4, 5 and 8 of the last round key.   Next, the filtering process is carried out at the first round. After checking whether the suggested key yields the desired difference at the output of the first round, every pair suggests about $16 \times 2^{-15} = 2^{-11}$ values of 4 key bytes 1, 4, 5 and 8. Totally, 2^{41} pairs suggest 2^{30} values of the four bytes of the key. An exhaustive key search at this point can be done in time about $1/2 \times 2^{30} \times 2^{32} = 2^{61}$. By repeating the attack 64 times (using 2^{45} chosen plaintexts), the complexity is reduced to 2^{46}. The complexity is reduced further to 2^{35} if the attack is repeated 128 times by using 2^{46} chosen plaintexts.

In the filtering process at the last half round, sorting n items requires about $n \log n$ simple operations. A method is given in [5] to reduce the time requirements for the first filtering process.   Let a ciphertext be denoted $(c_1, ..., c_8)$ which is hashed to $(c_3 - 2c_2, \ c_6 - c_2, \ c_7 - 2c_2)$. The ciphertexts with the same hash value are candidates for a right pair after the first filtering process. Thus, the complexity is reduced to n simple operations.

4   Improved Attack on 5 Round SAFER

Knudsen and Berson's attack is able to find out the secret key of 5 round SAFER K-64 much faster than by exhaustive search. However, when it is used to attack 5 round SAFER SK-64, the suggested key by each pair is 56 bits and it is infeasible to keep a counter for each 56-bit key and repeat the attack. Knudsen and Berson left their attack on 5 round SAFER SK-64 as an open problem [5]. In the following, we improve Knudsen and Berson's attack on 5 round SAFER SK-64 by using better truncated differential and additional filtering process.   Our truncated differential attack on 5 round SAFER SK-64 needs about 2^{38} chosen plaintexts and runs in time similar to 2^{46} encryptions of 5-round SAFER. A similar attack can be applied to 5 round SAFER K-64 and the same result can be obtained. Compared with one version of Knudsen and Berson's attack on 5 round SAFER K-64 that requires about 2^{45} chosen plaintexts and runs in time similar to 2^{46} encryptions of 5 round SAFER, our attack uses much less chosen plaintexts (reduced by a factor of about 2^7) and runs in about the same time (if the filtering time is not considered).

4.1   Attack on 5 Round SAFER SK-64

Our attack on 5 round SAFER SK-64 uses the following 4-round truncated differential with input difference

$$[0, 0, 0, 0, a, b, c, d]$$

and output difference [0, 0, 0, 0, 0, 0, 128, 0]. There are 8 differentials (see (7)-(14)) in this 5-round truncated differential. The probabilities are about $2^{-71.7}$ for half of the differentials, and are about 2^{-72} for another half of the differentials.

$$5678 \rightarrow 12 \rightarrow 1256 \rightarrow 15 \rightarrow 7 \qquad (7)$$
$$5678 \rightarrow 12 \rightarrow 3478 \rightarrow 15 \rightarrow 7 \qquad (8)$$
$$5678 \rightarrow 34 \rightarrow 1256 \rightarrow 15 \rightarrow 7 \qquad (9)$$
$$5678 \rightarrow 34 \rightarrow 3478 \rightarrow 15 \rightarrow 7 \qquad (10)$$
$$5678 \rightarrow 56 \rightarrow 1256 \rightarrow 15 \rightarrow 7 \qquad (11)$$
$$5678 \rightarrow 56 \rightarrow 3478 \rightarrow 15 \rightarrow 7 \qquad (12)$$
$$5678 \rightarrow 78 \rightarrow 1256 \rightarrow 15 \rightarrow 7 \qquad (13)$$
$$5678 \rightarrow 78 \rightarrow 3478 \rightarrow 15 \rightarrow 7 \qquad (14)$$

The probabilities in the first round and the third round are each of 2^{-24} and the probability in the second round is 2^{-8}. Now we look at the differential in the fourth round. For those differentials with $1256 \rightarrow 15$ at the third round, the differential in the fourth round is

$$[2v, 0, 0, 0, v, 0, 0, 0], \quad [128, 0, 0, 0, 128, 0, 0, 0], \quad [0, 0, 0, 0, 0, 0, 0, 128, 0]$$

The probability for this round differential varies slightly with values of key and is about 2^{-16} on average. For those differentials with $3478 \rightarrow 15$ at the third round, the differential in the forth round is

$$[v, 0, 0, 0, v, 0, 0, 0], \quad [128, 0, 0, 0, 128, 0, 0, 0], \quad [0, 0, 0, 0, 0, 0, 128, 0]$$

The probability for this round differential also varies with values of the key and is larger than $2^{-15.7}$ on average. So the probabilities are each of 2^{-72} for half of the differentials and $2^{-71.7}$ for another half of the differentials. The probability for the 4-round differential is thus larger than $2^{-68.9}$ on average. This 4-round differential is concatenated with the fifth round differential

$$[0, 0, 0, 0, 0, 0, 128, 0], \quad [0, 0, 0, 0, 0, 0, 0, x, 0], \quad [2x, 2x, x, x, 2x, 2x, x, x]$$

This differential has probability 1.

After the final output transformation consisting of byte wise xor'ing and add'ing with the last round key, the output difference is:

$$[z_1, 2x, x, z_2, z_3, 2x, x, z_4] \qquad (15)$$

where z_1 and z_3 are even numbers while the least significant bits of z_2 and z_4 are the same as that of x according to c) of Proposition 1.

The probability for this differential is about $2^{-68.9}$. About 2^{69} pairs are needed to get one right pair. Every structure consisting of 2^{32} chosen plaintexts yields about 2^{63} pairs with the desired input difference. 64 such structures are required to get one right pair, a total of 2^{38} plaintexts. The analysis can be performed on each structure and thus the memory requirements are 2^{32} 64-bit quantities.

The filtering processes are carried out at the last half round, the first round and the fifth round. The filtering process at the last half round is very similar to that in Knudsen and Berson's attack except that the value of x may be odd and even. After this filtering process, 2^{41} pairs are left. Each pair suggests 16 values for the bytes 1,4,5 and 8 of the last round key ($K_{11,1}$ $K_{11,4}$ $K_{11,5}$ $K_{11,8}$). It is the same as to say that 16 values are suggested for k_2, k_5, k_6 and k_9 according to the key schedule of SAFER SK-64. Next we carry out the filtering process at the first round. For each of these 16 values, the check in the first round of differentials will give us about 2^{-6} values of the key bytes k_5, k_6, k_7 and k_8. Thus, each remaining pair suggests $16 \times 2^{-6} = 2^{-2}$ values for the key bytes k_2, k_5, k_6, k_7, k_8 and k_9. The remaining 2^{41} pairs suggest 2^{39} values for these 6 key bytes. We denote each remaining pair with one of its suggested 48-bit key as a unit. We are left with 2^{39} units after the filtering processes at the last half round and at the first round. An exhaustive key search at this point can be done in time about $\frac{1}{2} \times 2^{39} \times 2^{16} = 2^{54}$. However, an additional filtering process at the fifth round will reduce the complexity of the key search by a factor of 2^8. This additional filtering process is the major improvement of our filtering processes compared with that of Knudsen and Berson. Before introducing this filtering process at the fifth round, we first present the following theorem.

Theorem 1. Consider the following two equations (X denotes the exponential permuation)

$$X[V \oplus K] - X[V' \oplus K] = 128$$
$$\Delta V = V - V'$$

Then each pair (ΔV, K) suggests one value of V on average.

Proof: The result is obtained by direct calculation.

In applying Theorem 1, all the solutions ($\Delta V, K, V$) are precomputed, so that table lookup can be used to find out the value of V quickly once the values of ΔV and K are given.

For the fifth round, the value at the seventh byte of the input to the *PHT*-transformation is expressed as

$$V = (c_1 \oplus K_{11,1}) - 2(c_2 - K_{11,2}) - (c_3 - K_{11,3}) + 2(c_4 \oplus K_{11,4})$$
$$- 2(c_5 \oplus K_{11,5}) + 4(c_6 - K_{11,6}) + 2(c_7 - K_{11,7}) - 4(c_8 \oplus K_{11,8}) \quad (16)$$

This expression is obtained by using the expression of M^{-1}, see (1). If the value of V is known, (16) reveals 8-bit information of the key. Since the key bytes k_2, k_5, k_6, k_7, k_8 and k_9 are suggested already, the values of ($K_{11,1}$ $K_{11,4}$ $K_{11,5}$ $K_{11,6}$ $K_{11,7}$ $K_{11,8}$) are suggested. So (16) can be written as

$$2K_{11,2} + K_{11,3} = T \quad (17)$$

where T is calculated from

$$T = V - ((c_1 \oplus K_{11,1}) - 2c_2 - c_3 + 2(c_4 \oplus K_{11,4}) - 2(c_5 \oplus K_{11,5})$$
$$+ 4(c_6 - K_{11,6}) + 2(c_7 - K_{11,7}) - 4(c_8 \oplus K_{11,8})) \tag{18}$$

Next we carry out the filtering process at the fifth round. We are left with 2^{39} units after the filtering processes at the last half round and at the first round. For each unit, we know the values of x (the output difference at the third byte) and $K_{10,7}$ (which is derived from k_7 according to the key schedule of SAFER SK-64), they are the ΔV and K in Theorem 1, respectively (the S box L in the encryption becomes S box X in the decryption). So each unit suggests one value of V on average according to Theorem 1. The value of V is used to calculate the value of T in (18). From (17), we can predict 8-bit value for the key $K_{11,2}$ $K_{11,3}$. Thus, each unit suggests 2^8 values for the 64-bit key and 2^{39} units suggest $2^{39} \times 2^8 = 2^{47}$ values for the 64 bit key. The rest of the key can be found out by exhaustive key search in time about $\frac{1}{2} \times 2^{47} = 2^{46}$ encryptions of 5-round SAFER.

Compared with Knudsen and Berson's attack on 5 round SAFER K-64, the truncated differential used in our attack is better. Consider one of the truncated differentials in Knudsen and Beron's attack

$$1458 \rightarrow 1357 \rightarrow 1357 \rightarrow 13 \rightarrow 4$$

The probabilities of the truncated differential for the first round and second round are each of 2^{-16}. So the probability of the truncated differential for the first two rounds is 2^{-32}. The filtering process at the first round has the filtering power of about 2^{16} (which means that it is able to discard all but one out of 2^{16} suggested keys). Let's consider one of the truncated differentials used in our attack

$$5678 \rightarrow 12 \rightarrow 1256 \rightarrow 15 \rightarrow 7.$$

The probabilities for the first round and second round are 2^{-24} and 2^{-8} respectively. So the probability of the truncated differential for the first two rounds is 2^{-32}. This probability is the same as that of Knudsen and Berosn. But the filtering process at the first round has the filtering power of about 2^{24}, about 2^8 times larger than that in Knudsen and Berson's attack. So we see that the differential in our attack increases the filtering power at the first round by a factor of about 2^8 while keeping the probabilities almost the same as that in Knudsen and Berson's attack (when we consider only one of the differentials).

An additional filtering process at the fifth round is also used in our attack. A similar filtering process can be applied in Knudsen and Berson's attack and can increase the filtering power by a factor of about 2^7.

4.2   5 Round SAFER K-64, SAFER K-128 and SAFER SK-128

Our attack on 5 round SAFER K-64 is very similar to that on 5 round SAFER SK-64. The same differential is used and the same result is obtained. Our attack is much better than the attack on 5 round SAFER K-64 in [5] as mentioned at the beginning of this section.

For 5 round SAFER K-128, the attack in [5] is better than of ours. Applying our attack to 5 round SAFER K-128 directly, 2^{38} chosen plaintexts suggest 2^{63} values for 80 bits of the key. The filtering process is much tedious and it is infeasible to repeat the attack since the memory requirement is too large.

For 5 round SAFER SK-128, our attack seems better than the attack in [5] since here our truncated differential and the filtering process can predict 17 bits information of the 128-bit key while Knudsen and Berson's attack can determine only two bits of the key. However, both our attack and the attack in [5] cannot be carried out in reasonable time.

5   Attack on 6 Round SAFER

Knudsen and Berson's attack is not successful to 6 round SAFER [5]. We improve their attack by using similar methods as we used in attacking 5 round SAFER. Our differential attack on 6 round SAFER (SAFER K-64 and SAFER SK-64) needs about 2^{53} chosen plaintexts and runs in time similar to 2^{61} encryptions of 6-round SAFER.

5.1   Attack on 6 Round SAFER-K64

Consider the following 5-round truncated differential with input difference

$$[0, 0, a, b, 0, 0, c, d]$$

and output difference $[0, 0, 0, 128, 0, 0, 0, 0]$. There are 16 differentials in this truncated differential. The probabilities are $2^{-87.68}$ for half of the differentials, and are $2^{-88.19}$ for another half of the differentials. These probabilities are determined in a very similar way as in Section 3.2. These differentials are

$$3478 \to 15 \to 1357 \to 1357 \to 13 \to 4 \qquad (19)$$
$$3478 \to 15 \to 1357 \to 2468 \to 13 \to 4 \qquad (20)$$
$$3478 \to 15 \to 2468 \to 1357 \to 13 \to 4 \qquad (21)$$
$$3478 \to 15 \to 2468 \to 2468 \to 13 \to 4 \qquad (22)$$
$$3478 \to 48 \to 1357 \to 1357 \to 13 \to 4 \qquad (23)$$
$$3478 \to 48 \to 1357 \to 2468 \to 13 \to 4 \qquad (24)$$
$$3478 \to 48 \to 2468 \to 1357 \to 13 \to 4 \qquad (25)$$
$$3478 \to 48 \to 2468 \to 2468 \to 13 \to 4 \qquad (26)$$
$$3478 \to 26 \to 1357 \to 1357 \to 13 \to 4 \qquad (27)$$
$$3478 \to 26 \to 1357 \to 2468 \to 13 \to 4 \qquad (28)$$
$$3478 \to 26 \to 2468 \to 1357 \to 13 \to 4 \qquad (29)$$
$$3478 \to 26 \to 2468 \to 2468 \to 13 \to 4 \qquad (30)$$
$$3478 \to 37 \to 1357 \to 1357 \to 13 \to 4 \qquad (31)$$
$$3478 \to 37 \to 1357 \to 2468 \to 13 \to 4 \qquad (32)$$

$$3478 \to 37 \to 2468 \to 1357 \to 13 \to 4 \qquad (33)$$
$$3478 \to 37 \to 2468 \to 2468 \to 13 \to 4 \qquad (34)$$

The 6 round differential is

$$[0, 0, 0, 128, 0, 0, 0, 0], [0, 0, 0, x, 0, 0, 0, 0], [2x, x, 2x, x, 2x, x, 2x, x],$$

where the value of x is odd. This differential has probability 1 since an input difference 128 to the exponentiation permutation always yields an odd output difference. Therefore we obtain a 6 round truncated differential with input difference [0, 0, a, b, 0, 0, c, d] and output difference [2x, x, 2x, x, 2x, x, 2x, x] for odd x and with a probability $16 \times 2^{-87.9} = 2^{-83.9}$.

We need about 2^{84} pairs to get one right pair. We can use structures of each 2^{32} plaintexts yielding 2^{63} pairs with the desired difference in the inputs. Therefore about 2^{21} structures are needed, a total of 2^{53} plaintexts. We can perform our analysis on each structure and thus the memory requirements are 2^{32} 64-bit quantities.

After the final transformation in SAFER, the output difference is

$$[z_1, x, 2x, z_2, z_3, x, 2x, z_4] \qquad (35)$$

where x is odd and z_1 and z_3 are even numbers while z_2 and z_4 are odd numbers.

The filtering processes are carried out at the last half round, the first round and the sixth round. Firstly, we carry out the filtering process at the last half round. This is the same as that in Knudsen and Berson's attack on 5 round SAFER K-64. 2^{55} pairs are left and each pair suggests 16 values for the bytes 1, 4, 5 and 8 of the last round key. Next we carry out the filtering process at the first round. For each of these 16 values, the check in the first round of differentials will give us about 2^{-6} values of the key bytes k_3, k_4, k_7 and k_8. Thus, each remaining pair suggests $16 \times 2^{-6} = 2^{-2}$ values for the key bytes k_1, k_3, k_4, k_5, k_7 and k_8. Hence, 2^{55} pairs suggest 2^{53} values for these 6 key bytes. We denote each pair with one of its suggested 48 bit key as a unit. We are left with 2^{53} units. Then we carry out the filtering process at the sixth round. It will increase the filtering power by a factor of 2^7. Before the discussion of this filtering process, we introduce the following theorem.

Theorem 2. Consider the following two equations where L denotes the logarithmic permutation:
$$L[V] - L[V'] = 128$$
$$\Delta V = V - V'$$
Then each odd value of ΔV suggests two values of V.

Proof: The result can be obtained by direct calculation.

To use this theorem efficiently, all the solutions $(\Delta V, V)$ are listed in a table so that table lookup can be used to find V quickly when ΔV is given.

For the fifth round, the fourth byte of the output of the S box is expressed as

$$V = ((c_1 \oplus K_{13,1}) - (c_2 - K_{13,2}) - 2(c_3 - K_{13,3}) + 2(c_4 \oplus K_{13,4}) -$$
$$2(c_5 \oplus K_{13,5}) + 2(c_6 - K_{13,6}) + 4(c_7 - K_{13,7}) - 4(c_8 \oplus K_{13,8})) - K_{12,4} \quad (36)$$

If the value of V is known, (36) indicates 8 bits information of the key. Since the key bytes k_1, k_3, k_4, k_5, k_7 and k_8 are suggested already, the values of ($K_{13,1}$ $K_{13,3}$ $K_{13,4}$ $K_{13,5}$ $K_{13,7}$ $K_{13,8}$) are suggested. So (36) can be written as

$$K_{13,2} - 2K_{13,6} = T \quad (37)$$

where T is calculated as

$$T = V + K_{12,4} - ((c_1 \oplus K_{13,1}) - 2c_2 - 2(c_3 - K_{13,3}) + 2(c_4 \oplus K_{13,4})$$
$$- 2(c_5 \oplus K_{13,5}) + 2c_6 + 4(c_7 - K_{13,7}) - 4(c_8 \oplus K_{13,8})) \quad (38)$$

Now, we carry out the filtering process at the sixth round. We are left with 2^{53} units after the filtering process at the last half round and the filtering process at the first round. For each unit, we know the values of x (the output difference at the third byte), it is ΔV in Theorem 2 (we note that the S box X in encryption is the S box L in decryption). So each unit suggests two values of V. The value of V is used to calculate the value of T in (38). Each value of W suggests 2^8 values for the key $K_{13,2}$ and $K_{13,6}$. Thus, each unit suggests 2^9 values for the 64-bit key and 2^{53} units suggests $2^{53} \times 2^9 = 2^{62}$ values for the 64 bit key. The rest of the key can be found by exhaustive search in time about $\frac{1}{2} \times 2^{62} = 2^{61}$ encryptions of 6-round SAFER.

5.2 Attack on 6 round SAFER SK-64

To attack 6 round SAFER SK-64, we use the same truncated differential and similar filtering process as that in the attack of 6 round SAFER K-64. This attack needs about 2^{53} chosen plaintexts and runs in time similar to 2^{61} encryptions of 6-round SAFER. The result is the same as that obtained in the attack on 6 round SAFER K-64.

The filtering processes carried out at the last half round is the same as that in the attack of 6 round SAFER K-64. After this filtering process, about 2^{55} pairs are left, each pair suggests 16 values for the bytes 1, 4, 5 and 8 of the last round key. It is the same as to say that 16 values of k_2 k_4, k_7 and k_8 are suggested by each remaining pair. The filtering processes at the first round and the sixth round are different from those in Section 5.1 due to the difference in key schedules. Next, we carry out the filtering process at the first round. For each of these 16 values, the check in the first round of differentials will give us about 2^{-14} values of the key bytes k_3, k_4, k_7 and k_8. Thus, each remaining pair suggests $16 \times 2^{-14} = 2^{-10}$ values for the key bytes k_2, k_3, k_4, k_7, k_8. The remaining 2^{55} pairs suggest 2^{45} values for these 5 key bytes. We denote each pair with one of its suggested 40-bit key as a unit. We are left with 2^{45} units. Then we carry out the filtering process at the sixth round.

Since the key bytes k_2, k_3, k_4, k_7 and k_8 are suggested already, the values of ($K_{13,1}$ $K_{13,4}$ $K_{13,5}$ $K_{13,8}$) are suggested. So (36) can be written as

$$K_{13,2} + 2K_{13,3} - 2K_{13,6} - 4K_{13,7} - K_{12,4} = T \tag{39}$$

where T is calculated as

$$\begin{aligned} T = V - ((c_1 \oplus K_{13,1}) - c_2 - 2c_3 + 2(c_4 \oplus K_{13,4}) \\ - 2(c_5 \oplus K_{13,5}) + 2c_6 + 4c_7 - 4(c_8 \oplus K_{13,8})) \end{aligned} \tag{40}$$

Also, we note that

$$k_9 = k_1 \oplus k_2 \oplus k_3 \oplus k_4 \oplus .... \oplus k_8 \tag{41}$$

Now, we continue with the filtering process. We are left with 2^{45} units. For each unit, we know the value of x (the output difference at the second byte), it is the ΔV in Theorem 2. So each unit suggests two values of V. The value of V is used to calculate the value of T in (40). For each value of T, we can solve for 2^{16} values of k_1, k_5 and k_6 (It can be done simply through table lookup as explained later). Thus, each unit suggests 2^{17} values for the 64-bit key and 2^{45} units suggests $2^{45} \times 2^{17} = 2^{62}$ values for the 64-bit key. The rest of the key can be found out by exhaustive search in time about $\frac{1}{2} \times 2^{62} = 2^{61}$ encryptions of 6-round SAFER. This result is the same as that obtained in the attack on 6 round SAFER K-64.

In the filtering process at the sixth round, we need to find the value of k_1, k_5 and k_6 when the value of T is given. It can be done in short time through table lookup. From (39), (41) and the information that ($K_{12,4}$ $K_{13,2}$ $K_{13,3}$ $K_{13,6}$ $K_{13,7}$) are derived from (k_6 k_5 k_6 k_9 k_1) respectively, we can precompute the values of k_1, k_5 and k_6 for all the values of T and list the results in a table. In the filtering process, once the value of T is known, we can obtain the related 2^{16} values through table lookup. Thus, this filtering process can be implemented in relatively short time.

6   7 Round SAFER

For 7 round SAFER, we apply the similar truncated differential as that in the attack on 6 round SAFER. It has input difference [0, 0, a, b, 0, 0, c, d] and output difference [2x, x, 2x, x, 2x, x, 2x, x] with a probability of about 2^{-99}. To get a right pair, 2^{68} chosen plaintexts are required. Thus, it is impossible to carry out our attack.

7   Conclusion

In this paper, we improved the truncated differential attack on 5 round SAFER SK-64. We also carried out attacks on 6 round SAFER K-64 and SAFER SK-64. Our attack on 5 round SAFER SK-64 can find out the secret key in time much faster than by exhaustive search.   Also, our attack uses less chosen plaintexts compared with Knudsen and Berson's attack. Our attack on 6 round SAFER runs in time faster than by exhaustive search. However, our attack is not efficient when applied to 7 round SAFER. We strongly believe that 8 round SAFER is invulnerable to our attacks.

References

1   E. Biham and A. Shamir.   Differential Cryptanalysis of the Data Encryption Standard, Springer-Verlag, 1993.
2   C. Harpes, G.G. Kramer, and J.L. Massey. A generalization of linear cryptanalysis and the applicability of Matsui's piling-up lemma.   In L. Guillou and J.J. Quisquater, editors, *Advancess in Cryptology – Eurocrypt'95, LNCS 921*, pages 24-38. Springer Verlag, 1995.
3   L.R. Knudsen. A key-schedule weakness in SAFER K-64. In C. Copersmith, editor, *Advances in cryptology – CRYPTO'95, LNCS 963*, pages 274-286. Springer Verlag, 1995.
4   L.R. Knudsen. Truncated and higher order differentials. In B. Preneel, editor, *Fast Software Encryption, LNCS 1008*, pages 196-211, Springer Verlag, 1995.
5   L.R. Knudsen, T.A. Berson. Truncated Differentials of SAFER. In D. Gollmann, editor, *Fast Software Encryption – Third International Workshop, LNCS 1039*, pages 15-25, Springer Verlag, 1996.
6   J.L. Massey.   Safer K-64: A byte-oriented block-ciphering algorithm. In R. Anderson, editor, *Fast Software Encryption – Proc. Cambridge Security Workshop, Cambridge, U.K., LNCS 809*, pages 1-17. Springer Verlag, 1994.
7   J.L. Massey. SAFER K-64: One year later. In B. Preneel, editor, *Fast Software Encryption – Proc. Second International Workshop, LNCS 1008*, pages 212-241, Springer Verlag, 1995.
8   J.L. Massey. Strengthened Key Schedule for the Cipher SAFER, posted to the USNET newsgroup sci.crypt, September, 1995.
9   M. Matsui, Linear Cryptanalysis Method for DES Cipher. In T. Helleseth, editor, *Advances in Cryptology – Proc. of Eurocrypt '93, LNCS 765*, pages 386-397, Springer-Verlag, 1994.

Appendix

For the attack of 5 round SAFER SK-64, we illustrate one of the differentials to show the detail of the truncated differential. This example differential is

$$5678 \rightarrow 12 \rightarrow 1256 \rightarrow 15 \rightarrow 7$$

1st round: [0, 0, 0, 0, a, b, c, d], [0, 0, 0, 0, e, -e, -e, e], [e, e, 0, 0, 0, 0, 0, 0], $p = 2^{-24}$
2nd round: [e, e, 0, 0, 0, 0, 0, 0], [f, -f, 0, 0, 0, 0, 0, 0], [4f, 2f, 0, 0, 2f, f, 0, 0], $p = 2^{-8}$
3rd round: [4f, 2f, 0, 0, 2f, f, 0, 0], [g, -g, 0, 0, -g, g, 0, 0], [2g, 0, 0, 0, g, 0, 0, 0], $p = 2^{-24}$
4th round: [2g, 0, 0, 0, g, 0, 0, 0], [128, 0, 0, 0, 128, 0, 0, 0], [0, 0, 0, 0, 0, 0, 0, 128],

The probability for this round varies with the key and is larger than $2^{-15.7}$ in average.

Optimal Resistance Against the Davies and Murphy Attack

Thomas Pornin

École Normale Supérieure, 45 rue d'Ulm, 75005 Paris, France,
thomas.pornin@ens.fr

Abstract. In recent years, three main types of attacks have been developed against Feistel-based ciphers, such as DES[1]; these attacks are linear cryptanalysis[2], differential cryptanalysis[3], and the Davies and Murphy attack[4]. Using the discrete Fourier transform, we present here a quantitative criterion of security against the Davies and Murphy attack. Similar work has been done on linear and differential cryptanalysis[5,11].

1 Introduction

The Feistel scheme is a simple design which allows, when suitably iterated, the construction of efficient block cipher, whose deciphering algorithm is implemented in a similar way. The most famous block cipher using a Feistel scheme is DES, where the scheme is iterated 16 times, with 16 subkeys extracted from a unique masterkey. The deciphering algorithm is just the same; the only difference is that the subkeys are taken in reverse order.

The masterkey of DES is only 56 bits long; this is vulnerable to exhaustive search. Indeed, specialized DES chips, able to calculate half a million DES ciphers per second, have been considered since 1987[6] and their cost evaluated; it is estimated that a five millions dollars machine using a few thousands of such chips could break a DES with a single plaintext/ciphertext pair in two or three hours[7]; other more recent estimates give lower prices, thanks to continuous technological progress. More recently, following a challenge proposed by RSA Inc., a 56 bits DES key was retrieved from a plaintext/ciphertext pair using only the idle time of a few thousands generic purpose workstations around the world[8].

Although exhaustive search is quite feasible, other attacks have been developped. These may be applicable to other schemes than DES. The first one was differential cryptanalysis[3]; it was based upon the existence of pairs of plaintext, so that the corresponding ciphertexts differ in some predictable way related to the difference of the plaintexts, with a small but not negligible probability. DES appeared to be extremely well protected against this cryptanalysis, and, indeed, it is now established that the NSA, which created DES as an improvement over the Lucifer scheme from IBM, knew about this attack and strengthened its algorithm against it. The attack requires 2^{47} chosen plaintexts and their corresponding ciphertexts

K. Ohta and D. Pei (Eds.): ASIACRYPT'98, LNCS 1514, pp. 148–159, 2000.

In 1993, following his earlier work, Matsui[2] discovered linear cryptanalysis, which exploited some linear properties of DES; more specifically, Matsui was able to build a linear equation of some of the bits of the plaintext, the ciphertext and the key, which stand with a probability slightly different from 0.5. Matsui described and implemented a method to use this equation in order to recover a DES key from 2^{43} plaintext/ciphertext pairs. The linear and differential cryptanalysis have been unified in a common formalism by Chabaud and Vaudenay[5].

In 1993, Davies and Murphy[4] presented another attack, which uses the fact that the output of the confusion function used in the Feistel scheme is not truly random, and that this bias depends upon several key bits. Using a large quantity of plaintext/ciphertext pairs, it is thus possible to guess these key bits with a reasonnable probability of success. This attack has not proven very efficient in the case of DES, but the same attack may work on other Feistel-based ciphers. The resistance of a Feistel-based cipher against linear and differential cryptanalysis has already been formally quantified[5]; we present here a similar quantification for the Davies and Murphy attack.

2 Notations

We here present a description of the Feistel scheme that is used in DES. More complete explanations may be found in [1].

We consider a message space $\mathcal{M}$ which consists of binary messages of a fixed length; we assume that this length is an even number, so that the messages may be divided in two parts of same length (the left one, with the most significant bits, and the right one, with the least significant bits). We note $\mathcal{N}$ the space of half-messages.

We also consider a confusion function f which takes two aruguments, one from $\mathcal{N}$ and the other, K, from a subkey space denoted $\mathcal{K}$; f returns a value in $\mathcal{N}$.

If we consider a message (L, R) where L and R are in $\mathcal{N}$, the Feistel scheme calculates the message (L', R'), so that:

$$L' = R$$
$$R' = L \oplus f(R, K)$$

where $\oplus$ is the bitwise "exclusive or" operation.

Such a scheme can be iterated several times, with different subkeys. Each iteration will be called a round. If we have r rounds, we can note (L_i, R_i) the input of the i-th round (i is between 1 and r) and (L_{i+1}, R_{i+1}) its output. The subkey used for round i is named K_i. We then have the following equations:

$$L_{i+1} = R_i$$
$$R_{i+1} = L_i \oplus f(R_i, K_i).$$

When used in a cryptographic scheme, L_{r+1} and R_{r+1} are often exchanged. Thus we have:

$$(L, R) = (L_1, R_1)$$
$$(L', R') = (R_{r+1}, L_{r+1}).$$

With this last operation, the deciphering operation is implemented exactly the same way the enciphering is; only the subkeys K_i are taken in reverse order.

A four-rounds Feistel cipher is schematically represented in the figure 1.

In DES, there are 16 rounds ($r = 16$) and the elements of $\mathcal{N}$ are 32 bits long. The subkeys are 48 bits long, extracted from a 56 bits masterkey with a fixed and public algorithm. A known permutation is applied to the message before entering the 16 consecutive Feistel rounds, and the reverse of this permutation is applied afterwards. These permutations are fixed by the standard and can be easily inverted, so we forget them here.

We may note an interesting property of such ciphers; this property was discovered and used by Davies and Murphy in their attack[4]. For each round i, we have:

$$f(R_i, K_i) = L_i \oplus R_{i+1}$$

and, if i is not r:

$$R_{i+1} = L_{i+2}.$$

Therefore, if i is not r, we have:

$$f(R_i, K_i) = L_i \oplus L_{i+2}.$$

This remark is true for each round except the last one (where $i+2$ has no sense). If we take the exclusive or of these equations for i even, we obtain the following:

$$R \oplus L' = \bigoplus_{j=1}^{r/2} f(R_{2j}, L_{2j}).$$

We can make the same operation with the odd rounds, and get the following equation:

$$L \oplus R' = \bigoplus_{i=1}^{r/2} f(R_{2i-1}, L_{2i-1}).$$

Each plaintext/ciphertext pair thus gives access to the XORed value of the outputs of the f functions of the even rounds, and also the XORed value of the outputs of the f function of the odd rounds. That is why a non-uniform distribution of the output of the f function may be revealed by observing a large quantity of plaintext/ciphertext pairs.

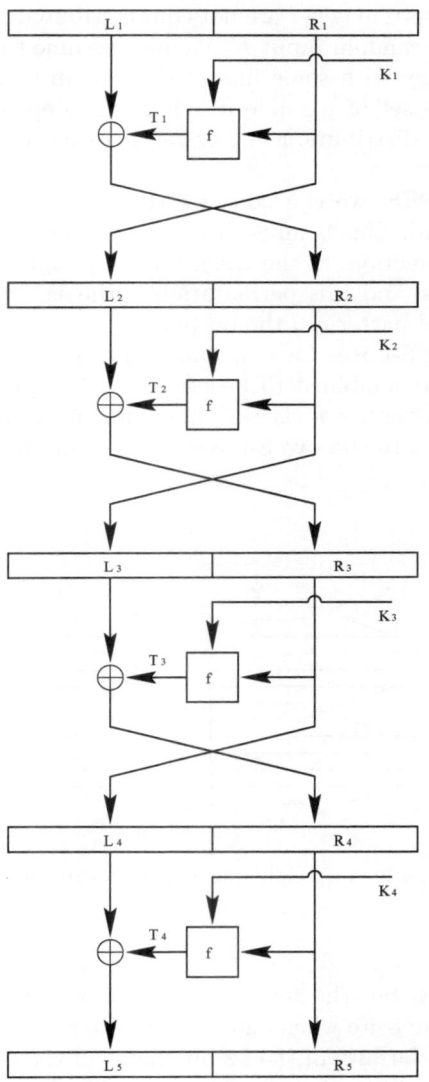

Figure 1: a four rounds Feistel cipher

3   Davies and Murphy Attack

This attack was presented in [4] and improved by Biham and Biryukov[10].

We assume that there exists a pattern of n bits, in the output of f, so that the 2^n values this pattern may get are not equidistributed, for a given key K and uniformly distributed random input R. We also assume that the distribution of the 2^n values may vary with some bits of the key, in a theorically predictable way. Thus, we have a set of possible distributions, depending on the key, and identifying the actual distribution in this set gives us some information on the key.

In the standard DES, we can consider the output of two neighbouring S-boxes in the i-th round. This is an 8-bit output; these 8 bits can be observed in the output of the f function: in the DES, a fixed permutation is applied to the output of the S-boxes, and this permutation is the same for the 16 rounds; so the 8 bits form a fixed pattern in the output of f.

Two neighbouring S-boxes have an input size of 12 bits; 12 bits of K_i but only 10 bits of R_i are combined to be used as this input. Two bits of R_i are duplicated; the two instances of each of these bits are XORed with two different key bits, and then go into the two S-boxes. This is shown in the figure 2.

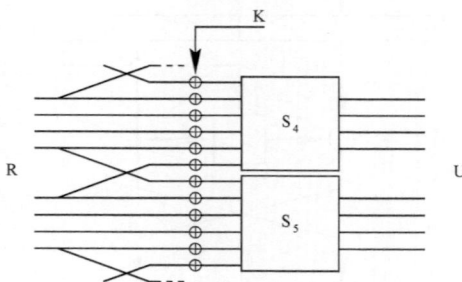

Figure 2: two neighbouring S-boxes in the DES

For each duplicated bit, the key bits condition whether the two instances of this bit are equal or opposite when entering the two S-boxes. For random R, this only implies a non-uniformity of the 12 bits input of the two S-boxes. There are two duplicated bits, and therefore four possible sets of 12 bits inputs, depending upon four key bits. Theses sets and the according output distribution of the two S-boxes can be easily enumerated.

As noted in section 2, for each plaintext/ciphertext pair, we have access to the XORed value of the outputs of the f functions of odd rounds, and thus access to the XORed value of the corresponding 8-bits paterns. If each f function of each round may have four output distributions, then the XORed value of 8 such outputs may take 165 possible distributions: the XOR is commutative, so that the order of the rounds does not matter; what only matters is the number of distributions of each of the four types described above. This leads to $\binom{11}{3} = 165$ possibilities.

Strangely enough, in DES, we end up with only two possible distributions; this is due to the specific definition of S-boxes (for a S-box, the output is a permutation of the 16 values taken by the four middle bits, and the two extreme bits determine which permutation to apply among four), which leads to some simplifications in the enumeration of the distributions. The details of this calculation may be found in [4]. The actual distribution depends upon the XORed value of several key bits (that is, an indirect key bit, that help us reduce the complexity of the exhaustive search of the key).

Therefore, identifying the actual distribution among the two possible reveals one indirect key bit. As this can be done for odd rounds as well as for even rounds, with the same plaintext/ciphertext pairs, the attack may give us two key bits.

The most efficient statistical test known is the maximum likelihood method: for each of the possible distributions, one calculates the probability of the event actually measured; the distribution which gives the highest probability is then supposed to be the right one. In the case of DES neighbouring S-boxes, we then have two distributions, which may be represented as two vectors u and v in $\mathbf{R}^{256}$; u_i with i between 0 and 255 is the probability of obtaining the 8-bits value i. Obviously, for each i, u_i is a real number between 0 and 1, and we have:

$$\sum_{i=0}^{255} u_i = 1.$$

We can also define u' (and similarly v') where

$$u_i = \frac{1}{256} + u_i'.$$

Thus we have:

$$\sum_{i=0}^{255} u_i' = 0.$$

As a consequence of the peculiar definition of S-boxes, we have:

$$u' + v' = 0.$$

More detailed explanations about this fact may be found in [4]; this is not a general property of Feistel schemes, but an artefact of the structure of the S-boxes.

Let us assume that we have access to M plaintext/ciphertext pairs; among these M pairs, each 8-bits value i appeared m_i times. If the theorical distribution is u, the probability of such an event is:

$$p_1 = \prod_{i=0}^{255} u_i^{m_i}.$$

p_2 is also defined, in the v case. Comparing p_1 and p_2 is equivalent to comparing their logarithms. We have:

$$\log p_1 = \sum_{i=0}^{255} m_i \log u_i.$$

So we have:

$$\log p_1 = \sum_{i=0}^{255} m_i \log(\frac{1}{256} + u_i').$$

As the sum of all m_i's is M, we have the following:

$$\log p_1 = \sum_{i=0}^{255} m_i \log(1 + 256u_i') - M \log 256$$

As $256u_i'$ is relatively small, compared to 1 (for a perfect cipher, u' should be 0; DES is well-designed, and a simple experiment on a few millions random plaintexts confirms that the deviation u' we deal with is really small, and thus many pairs plaintext/ciphertext are required), we can approximate the logarithms on the right hand side, which gives:

$$\log p_1 + M \log 256 \approx 256 \sum_{i=0}^{255} m_i u_i'.$$

Similarly, we have:

$$\log p_2 + M \log 256 \approx 256 \sum_{i=0}^{255} m_i v_i'.$$

Thus we compare the scalar product of m with u' and the scalar product of m with v'. We can bound these products using euclidian norms over $\mathbf{R}^{256}$. If we note $N(x)$ the euclidian norm of x, our two scalar products are:

$$s_1 = m \cdot u' \leq N(m)N(u')$$
$$s_2 = m \cdot v' \leq N(m)N(v').$$

m is what we obtain by analyzing the plaintext/ciphertext pairs; it follows a precise distribution, but may vary around this one. m_i is a random variable which counts the number of times the pattern value i was obtained among the M pairs. The probability of obtaining i for each pair is close to $1/256$, therefore the mean value of m_i is close to $M/256$, and its variance is near $(M/256)(255/256)$, which we approximate by $M/256$.

So the difference between m and its theorical value (namely M times its distribution vector) is a vector whose coordinates have an average absolute value of $(\sqrt{M})/16$; so the norm of this vector is close to $\sqrt{M}$ (where $N(m)$ is close to

$M/16$). To conclude anything from the pairs plaintext/ciphertext, the expected deviation (the difference between s_1 and s_2) must not be smaller than the standard deviation (which is the average deviation of a measure from its distribution — when dealing with uni-dimensional random variables, the standard deviation is the square root of the variance). Therefore, M must be sufficiently big so that:

$$N(m)(N(u') + N(v')) \geq \sqrt{M}.$$

This can be rewritten:

$$M \geq \frac{256}{(N(u') + N(v'))^2}.$$

In the actual DES, this leads to an attack with at least 2^{52} pairs, which may reveal two key bits. This is achieved with the two S-boxes 7 and 8. With 2^{55} pairs, the probability of success of the attack (that is, guessing correctly the two indirect key bits) is above 50%. The other pairs of S-boxes are much worse, as far as we deal with attacks.

4   The General Feistel Scheme Case

We now consider the general case of the Davies and Murphy attack; thus we ignore all simplifications induced by the specific definition of DES. We have a Feistel-based cipher, with r rounds (r is even), with a confusion function f, so that n particular bits of the output of the f function form a pattern whose 2^n possible values are not equidistributed. We also assume that the distribution of these values may vary, depending on some of the key bits of the considered round. We suppose we have q possible distributions, represented by q vectors of $\mathbf{R}^{2^n}$, denoted as u^1, u^2,... u^q.

For each plaintext/ciphertext pair, we have acces to the XORed value of $r/2$ patterns of n bits. This value follows a distribution which depends upon some key bits; we can theorically calculate these distributions, and we want to be able to determine, using several plaintext/ciphertext pairs, which distribution among the possible ones is the one actually in use; this would give us the corresponding information about the key bits involved.

The XOR operation is commutative; in each round, the pattern may have one distribution among q; what only matters in the distribution of the XORed value of the $r/2$ patterns is the number of each distribution we have among the $r/2$ rounds. The number of possible combinations is then:

$$\binom{r/2 + q - 1}{q - 1}.$$

Some of these distributions may in fact be alike, just as is the case with DES, where there are only two distributions.

We now introduce another representation for distributions of n-bits patterns, that we considered for the moment as vectors in $\mathbf{R}^{2^n}$. Such a vector can be viewed as a function from $\mathbf{Z}_2^n$ to $\mathbf{R}$, which associates to an n-bit binary vector the coordinate associated with the integer number the binary vector represents. Such a function may be decomposed using Fourier transform[9].

We consider the Fourier basis of function v_y for each vector y in $\mathbf{Z}_2^n$, so that for each vector x, we have:

$$v_y(x) = (-1)^{y \cdot x}$$

where $y \cdot x$ denotes the scalar product of y and x (namely the number of bits set to 1 in $y \& x$, where $\&$ is the bitwise AND operation).

If a is a function from $\mathbf{Z}_2^n$ to $\mathbf{R}$, we can compute its Fourier coefficients $\hat{a}(y)$ (for each vector y) as follows:

$$\hat{a}(y) = \sum_x a(x) v_y(x).$$

Using these coefficients, we can find the a function with the inverse Fourier transform:

$$a(x) = 2^{-n} \sum_y \hat{a}(y) v_y(x) = 2^{-n} \hat{\hat{a}}(x)$$

for each vector x.

The XOR operation between the output of two rounds of the cipher is, in the Fourier formalism, a convolution of the two distributions of outputs. Indeed, if a is the function representing the distribution of the output of the first round, and b is the output of the second round, then the distribution of the bitwise XOR of these two rounds will be c, where, for each x:

$$c(x) = \sum_{y \oplus z = x} a(y) b(z).$$

But, the addition in $\mathbf{Z}_2^n$ is nothing else that the XOR operation, and, for each x, we have $x \oplus x = 0$. Therefore, the equation may be rewritten this way:

$$c(x) = \sum_y a(x - y) b(y).$$

A convolution is simply calculated by multiplying term by term the Fourier coefficients. This means that, using the preceding notations, we have, for each x:

$$\hat{c}(x) = \hat{a}(x) \hat{b}(x).$$

We shall prove a similar property for the deviations to equiprobability: if we consider a', b' and c' such that $a(x) = 2^{-n} + a'(x)$ for all x, then, if c is the convolution product of a and b, then c' is the convolution product of a' and b'. Indeed, if we note d the constant function equal to 2^{-n}, its Fourier coefficients $\hat{d}(x)$ are 1 if $x = 0$, 0 otherwise. Therefore, we have the following:

$$\hat{a} = \hat{a}' + \hat{d}$$
$$\hat{b} = \hat{b}' + \hat{d}$$
$$\hat{c} = \hat{c}' + \hat{d}$$
$$\hat{c} = \hat{a}\hat{b}$$

So we have, by replacing a, b and c in the last equation by their expression in a', b' and c':

$$\hat{c}' + \hat{d} = \hat{a}'\hat{b}' + \hat{d}^2 + \hat{d}(\hat{a}' + \hat{b}')$$

We have clearly $\hat{d}^2 = \hat{d}$ (as $\hat{d}(x) = 0$ or 1 for each x), and $\hat{a}'(0) = \hat{b}'(0) = 0$ (for a function u, the first Fourier coefficient $\hat{u}(0)$ is the sum of all its values over $\mathbf{Z}_2^n$, so it is 0 in the case of a' and b', as these are the deviation of a distribution to the uniform distribution, which is the constant function equal to 2^{-n}).

In order to set a minimal bound for the complexity of the Davies and Murphy attack, we want to get a maximal bound for the size of the deviation of the pattern of the output of the f function to the uniform distribution. If we consider the m/M vector, this will follow the distribution a, which deviates from the uniform distribution by a'. The m vector comes from an actual "measure" (the plaintext/ciphertext pairs), so it will deviate from its distribution by an average distance of $\sqrt{M}$ (this is the same calculus as at the end of the section 3). We use the maximum likelihood method, so we compare the scalar products of m with the possibles deviations to equidistributions.

So we find that, if Y is a maximal bound for the euclidian norm of the deviation (in $\mathbf{R}^{2^n}$), the scalar products we consider are the number M of plaintext/ciphertext pairs needed for a succesful attack must be such that:

$$2\frac{M}{2^{n/2}}Y \geq \sqrt{M}$$

($2Y$ is a maximum for the distance between two possible distributions) which can be rewritten this way:

$$M \geq \frac{2^n}{4Y^2}$$

We note that this result stands with the approximations used in the section 3, in particular n is big enough to neglect 2^{-n} with respect to 1.

All we need is the value of Y. If the function of the distribution of the XORed value of the output of the $r/2$ rounds is a, then we may obtain Y from its Fourier coefficients $\hat{a}$. Indeed, the euclidian norm over $\mathbf{R}^{2^n}$ corresponds to the L^2 norm in the function space, and the scalar product becomes the following:

$$a \cdot b = \sum_x a(x)b(x)$$

The Fourier transform simply computes the coordinates of a function a' over the orthogonal basis (v_y). All v_y have $2^{n/2}$ as L^2 norm. We can therefore calculate the L^2 norm of a function a using the Fourier coefficients $\hat{a}$:

$$N(a') = 2^{-n/2}N(\hat{a}')$$

Therefore we have:

$$N(a) \leq 2^{n/2} \max_x |\hat{a}(x)|$$

where $N(a)$ is the L^2 norm of a. Thus, we have the proposed value Y:

$$Y = \max_x |\hat{a}(x)|$$

We have seen that the Fourier coefficients of a are obtained by multiplying those of the functions associated to each round. We then have the following security criterion:

- Calculate the Fourier coefficients of the functions representing the possible bias towards equiprobability of the distribution of the chosen pattern in the output of the confusion function of one round. This is done in the DES by expliciting the distribution of the pattern, by exhaustive enumeration of the possible inputs of two neighbouring S-boxes.
- Take the largest of these coefficients in absolute value, noted μ.
- Raise it to the r power.
- This peculiar pattern is secure against Davies and Murphy attacks up to:

$$\frac{1}{4\mu^r}$$

The global security of the scheme is therefore a question of enumeration of possible biased patterns. The criterion uses some approximations, so the actual security may in fact be higher. In the DES case, with the same pattern as the one used by Davies and Murphy to find the attack in 2^{52} (but Davies and Murphy consider the attack as useful only if it gives two correct key bits with a probability better than 0.5, and therefore calculate a complexity of 2^{55} in this case) we find a security of at least 2^{52}.

5   The Approximations Used

It must be noted that we made, in the calculation, several approximations. The main one is that we want to bound the euclidian distance between possible distributions, and we do it by bounding the deviation of these distributions to equiprobability; this is just what is necessary in the DES case, as the two possible deviations to equiprobability are just symmetric. That is why we obtain the exact result in this case.

The other calculations are also subject to some approximations. We considered that the 2^n coordinates of the m vector are gaussian independant random variables; they are not, in fact, independant, as their sum is M. If 2^n is sufficiently big, this will not be a problem. In the DES case, $n = 8$, so we neglect this effect. The m_i values follow binomial distributions, which can be approximated by a gaussian distribution if M is big enough, using the central limit theorem. Considering the precision needed, any M above 1000 will do it (and indeed M is largely above 1000). We also assume that the final distribution is close to the equiprobable one, which is desirable anyway in any symetric cipher scheme.

6   Conclusion and Open Problems

We described a method to calculate a minimal bound for the Davies and Murphy attack against a Feistel scheme. In order to apply it efficiently to a given scheme, one must first identify the patterns of bits in the output of the confusion function, whose possible values are not equidistributed. Once identified, their output distribution must then be calculated precisely, which may not be easy, depending on the scheme.

References

1. National Bureau of Standards, *Data Encryption Standard*, U.S. Department of Commerce, FIPS pub. 46, January 1977.
2. M. Matsui, *Linear Cryptanalysis Method for DES Cipher*, Lecture Notes in Computer Science, Advances in Cryptology, proceedings of EUROCRYPT'93, pp. 386–397, 1993.
3. E. Biham, A. Shamir, *Differential Cryptanalysis of the Data Encryption Standard*, Springer-Verlag, 1993.
4. D. Davies, S. Murphy, *Pairs and Triplets of DES S-Boxes*, Journal of Cryptology, Vol. 10, No. 3, pp. 195–206, 1997.
5. F. Chabaud, S. Vaudenay, *Links between Differential and Linear Cryptanalysis*, LIENS, Ecole Normale Supérieure, March 1994.
6. F. Hoornaert, J. Goubert, Y. Desmedt, *Efficient Hardware Implementation of the DES*, Lecture Notes in Computer Science, Advances in Cryptology, proceedings of CRYPTO'84, p. 147, 1984.
7. M.E. Hellman, Comments at 1993 RSA Data Security conference, 14-15 January 1993.
8. The results of the DES challenge teams were published only on the World Wide Web; see http://www.frii.com/~rcv/deschall.htm for further information.
9. W. Rudin, *Fourier Analysis on Groups*, Interscience Publishers Inc., New York, 1962.
10. E. Biham, A. Biryukov, *An Improvement of Davies' Attack on DES*, Lecture Notes in Computer Science, Advances in Cryptology, proceedings of EUROCRYPT'94, pp. 461–467, 1994.
11. K. Nyberg, *Perfect Nonlinear S-boxes*, Lecture Notes in Computer Science, Advances in Cryptology, proceedings of EUROCRYPT'91, pp. 378–385, 1991.

A Group Signature Scheme with Improved Efficiency
(Extended Abstract)

Jan Camenisch*

BRICS**
Department of Computer Science
University of Aarhus
Ny Munkegade
DK – 8000 Århus C, Denmark
camenisch@daimi.aau.dk

Markus Michels * * *

r3 security engineering ag /
Entrust Technology
P. O. Box
CH – 8301 Glattzentrum/Zurich,
Switzerland
Markus.Michels@entrust.com

Abstract. The concept of group signatures allows a group member to sign messages anonymously on behalf of the group. However, in the case of a dispute, the identity of a signature's originator can be revealed by a designated entity. In this paper we propose a new group signature scheme that is well suited for large groups, i.e., the length of the group's public key and of signatures do not depend on the size of the group. Our solution based on a variation of the RSA problem is more efficient than previous ones satisfying these requirements.

Keywords. Group signature scheme for large groups, digital signature schemes, revocable anonymity.

1 Introduction

In 1991 Chaum and van Heyst put forth the concept of a group signature scheme [16]. Participants are group members, a membership manager, and a revocation manager[1]. A group signature scheme allows a group member to sign messages anonymously on behalf of the group. More precisely, signatures can be verified with respect to a single public key of the group and do not reveal the identity of the signer. The membership manager is responsible for the system setup and for adding group members while the revocation manager has the ability to revoke the anonymity of signatures.

A group signature scheme could for instance be used by an employee of a large company to sign documents on behalf of the company. In this scenario, it is sufficient for a verifier to know that some representative of the company has signed. Moreover, in contrast to when an ordinary signature scheme would be used, the verifier does not need to check whether a particular employee is allowed to sign contracts on behalf of the company, i.e., he needs only to know

---

* Part of this work was done while this author was with ETH Zurich.
** Basic Research in Computer Science, Center of the Danish National Research Foundation.
* * * Work was done while this author was with Ubilab, UBS, Switzerland.
[1] In the original proposal, the membership manager and the revocation manager were a single entity called group manager.

K. Ohta and D. Pei (Eds.): ASIACRYPT'98, LNCS 1514, pp. 160–174, 2000.

a single company's public key. A further application of group signature schemes is electronic cash as was pointed out in [32]. In this scenario, several banks issue coins, but it is impossible for shops to find out which bank issued a coin that is obtained from a customer. Hence, the central bank plays the role of the membership and the revocation manager and all other banks issuing coins are group members. The identification as a group member is another application, e.g., in order to get access to a restricted area [28].

Various group signature schemes have been proposed so far. However, in the schemes presented in [7,16,17,36] the length of signatures and/or the size of the group's public key depend on the size of the group and thus these schemes are not suitable for large groups. Only in the two families of efficient schemes presented in [9,10] (and the blind versions thereof [32]) are the length of signatures and the size of the group's public key independent of the number of group members[2]. The schemes presented in [28] satisfy the length requirement as well, but these are inefficient.

In this paper we propose a new group signature scheme for which the length of signatures and the size of the group's public key do not depend on the size of the group. The security of our scheme relies on a variant of the so-called *strong RSA-assumption* proposed in [1,25]. Compared to the solutions in [9,10], our scheme is based on a different number-theoretic assumption and is also more efficient.

2   Model and an Approach for Realization

2.1   Model

A group signature scheme consists of the following algorithms:

setup: An interactive setup protocol between the membership manager, the group members, and the revocation manager. The public output is the group's public key Y. The private outputs are the individual secret keys x_G for each group member, the secret key x_M for the membership manager, and the secret key x_R for the revocation manager.

sign: A signature generation algorithm that on input a message m, an individual group member's secret key x_G, and the group's public key Y outputs a signature σ.

verify: A verification algorithm that on input a message m, a signature σ, and the group's public key Y returns 1 if and only if σ was generated by any group member using sign on input x_G, m, and Y.

tracing: A tracing algorithm that on input a signature σ, a message m, the revocation manager's secret key x_R, and the group's public key Y returns the identity ID of the group member who issued the signature σ together with an argument arg of this fact.

vertracing: A tracing-verification algorithm that on input a signature σ, a message m, the group's public key Y, the identity ID of a group member, and an argument arg outputs 1 if and only if arg was generated by tracing with respect to m, σ, Y, x_R.

---

[2] The other schemes [29,35] with the same properties were shown to be flawed [31,33].

The following informally stated security requirements must hold:

Unforgeability of signatures: Only group members are able to sign messages.

Anonymity of signatures: It is not feasible to find out the group member who signed a message without knowing the revocation manager's secret key.

Unlinkability of signatures: It is infeasible to decide whether two signatures have been issued by the same group member or not.

No framing: Even if the membership manager, the revocation manager, and some of the group members collude, they cannot sign on behalf of non-involved group members.

Unforgeability of tracing: The revocation manager can not accuse a signer falsely of having originated a given signature, e.g., by issuing an argument *arg* such that `vertracing` outputs 1.

The efficiency of a group signature scheme can be measured by the size of the public key Y, the length of signatures, and by the efficiency of the algorithms `sign`, `verify`, `setup`, `tracing`, and `vertracing`.

2.2   Approach of Camenisch and Stadler

The core idea of the schemes proposed in [9,10] is the following. A group's public key consists of a membership manager's public key of an ordinary digital signature scheme and a revocation manager's public key of a probabilistic encryption scheme. A user, say Alice, who wants to join the group chooses a random *secret key* x_G and computes her *membership key* $z := f(x_G)$, where f is a suitable one-way function. Alice commits to z (for instance by signing it) and sends z and her commitment to the membership manager M who returns her a *membership certificate* $u := \mathrm{sig}_M(z)$.

To sign a message m on behalf of the group, Alice encrypts z using the public key of the revocation manager (let c denote this ciphertext) and issues a *Signature of Knowledge*[3] [9] that she knows some values $\tilde{x}$ and $\tilde{u}$ such that $\tilde{u} = \mathrm{sig}_M(f(\tilde{x}))$ holds and that $f(\tilde{x})$ is encrypted in c. The verification of such a group-signature is done by checking this signature of knowledge. The revocation manager can easily revoke the anonymity of a group signature by decrypting c and forwarding this value to the membership manager.

To realize a concrete scheme along these lines, one has to find a suitable one-way function f and a suitable signature scheme that yield an efficient signature of knowledge for the values $\tilde{x}$ and $\tilde{u}$. In [9,10], two proposals based on different number theoretic assumption were put forth. The first assumption is that, given e, g, and an RSA-modulus n, finding integers u, x such that $u^e \equiv g^x + 1 \pmod{n}$ holds is hard, where g is an element of large order. The second one is that it is hard to find u and x with $|x| < |n|/2$ such that $u^3 \equiv x^5 + v \pmod{n}$ given v and n, where v is a suitably chosen integer and n is an RSA-modulus.

In the next section we will introduce an alternative assumption that allows the construction of a new group signature scheme.

---

[3] These are message dependent non-interactive arguments derived from 3-move honest-verifier zero-knowledge proofs of knowledge using the Fiat-Shamir heuristic [23,24].

3 Number Theoretic Assumptions

Recently, Barić and Pfitzmann [1] as well as Fujisaki and Okamoto [25] independently proposed a variation of the well-known RSA [39] assumption, the so-called *strong RSA assumption*. We will modify this assumption slightly. Let $k, \ell_g, \ell_1, \ell_2 < \ell_g$, and $\epsilon > 1$ be security parameters and, for simplicity, let denote $\tilde{\ell} := \epsilon(\ell_2 + k) + 1$. Furthermore, let $\mathcal{G}(\ell_g)$ denote the set of groups whose order has length ℓ_g and has two prime factors of length $(\ell_g - 2)/2$. Finally, let be $\mathcal{M}(G, z) = \{(u, e) \mid z = u^e, u \in G, e \in \{2^{\ell_1}, \dots, 2^{\ell_1} + 2^{\ell_2}\}, e \in \mathsf{primes}\}$, where $G \in \mathcal{G}(\ell_g)$ and $z \in G$.

Assumption 1 (Modified strong RSA assumption). *For all probabilistic polynomial-time algorithms $\tilde{A}$, all polynomials $p(\cdot)$, all sufficiently large ℓ_g, and suitably chosen ℓ_1, ℓ_2, k, and ϵ*

$$Pr[z = u^e \ \wedge \ e \in \{2^{\ell_1} - 2^{\tilde{\ell}}, \dots, 2^{\ell_1} + 2^{\tilde{\ell}}\} \ \wedge \ e \notin M \ : \ G \in_R \mathcal{G}(\ell_g),$$

$$z \in_R G, (U \times M) \subset_R \mathcal{M}(G, z), |M| = \mathcal{O}(\ell_g), (u, e) := \tilde{A}(G, z)] < \frac{1}{p(\ell_g)} \ .$$

Possible choices for G are discussed in Section 5. Let us remark that, given u, e, $\tilde{u}$, and $\tilde{e}$ with $z = u^e = \tilde{u}^{\tilde{e}}$, it is easy to find an element $\bar{u}$ satisfying $z = \bar{u}^{e\tilde{e}}$ using the extended Euclidean algorithm. However, as $e\tilde{e} \notin \{2^{\ell_1} - 2^{\tilde{\ell}}, \dots, 2^{\ell_1} + 2^{\tilde{\ell}}\}$ for suitable chosen parameter ℓ_g, ℓ_1, ℓ_2, ϵ, and k the integer $e\tilde{e}$ does not satisfy the range constraint. According to a result in [22,41], and as all e's in M are prime, it is infeasible to compute (u, e') satisfying $u^{e'} = z$ for an e' that does not divide the product of all e's in M as long as the standard RSA assumption holds. Hence there is no further attack except the one mentioned above.

Our group signature scheme further relies on the so-called Decision Diffie-Hellman (DDH) assumption. Let $G \in \mathcal{G}(\ell_g)$, n' be the divisor of G's order of length $\ell_g - 2$, and define the two sets

$$\mathcal{DH} := \{(g_1, y_1, g_2, y_2) \in G^4 \mid \mathrm{ord}(g_1) = \mathrm{ord}(g_2) = n' \ , \ \log_{g_1} y_1 = \log_{g_2} y_2\}$$

$$\mathcal{Q} := \{(g_1, y_1, g_2, y_2) \in G^4 \mid \mathrm{ord}(g_1) = \mathrm{ord}(g_2) = n'\}$$

of Diffie-Hellman and random 4-tuples, respectively.

Assumption 2 (Decision Diffie-Hellman assumption). *For all probabilistic polynomial-time algorithms $A : G^4 \to \{0, 1\}$, the two probability distributions*

$$Pr[a = 1 : T \in_R \mathcal{DH}, a := A(T)] \quad and \quad Pr[a = 1 : T \in_R \mathcal{Q}, a := A(T)]$$

are computationally indistinguishable.

We remark that in the case $G = \mathbb{Z}_n^*$, where n is an RSA-modulus, the DDH assumption does not hold. The Jacobi-symbol, which can be computed efficiently without knowing the factorization of n, leaks information about $\log_{g_1} y_1$ and $\log_{g_2} y_2$. For instance, if $(g_1|n) = (g_2|n) = (y_2|n) = -1$ and $(y_1|n) = 1$, then $\log_{g_1} y_1 \neq \log_{g_2} y_2$. If $G = \langle g \rangle$ is defined a subgroup of $\mathbb{Z}_n^*$ such that $(g|n) = 1$ this problem is overcome.

4   Building Blocks

In this section we introduce the building blocks for our scheme borrowing notation from [9]. These building blocks are signature schemes derived from statistical (honest-verifier) zero-knowledge proofs of knowledge using the Fiat-Shamir heuristic [23,24] and are therefore called "Signature based on a proof of knowledge", SPK for short. Usually, the security of such building blocks is argued by showing that the underlying interactive protocols is secure and then by assuming that "nothing bad happens" when the verifier is replaced with a collision resistant hash-function. This approach has been formalized as the random oracle model (e.g., see [2,37])[4]. For the signer/prover security means that the protocol should be zero-knowledge and for the verifier it means that the protocol should be a proof of knowledge. An example of this method is the Schnorr signature scheme [40] that is derived from an honest-verifier proof of knowledge of the discrete logarithm of the signer's public key.

In the following we describe four building blocks. The first one shows the knowledge of a discrete logarithm, the second the equality of two discrete logarithms, the third the knowledge of one out of two discrete logarithm, and the fourth the knowledge of a discrete logarithm that lies in a certain interval. Of course, these building blocks can be combined in the usual way (e.g., see [10]). The building blocks have in common that the prover does not know the order of G, i.e., the verifier chooses a group $G = \langle g \rangle$ of large order such that only he can know the order. However, the order of magnitude 2^{ℓ_g} of the group's order shall be known to both. Furthermore, the verifier chooses a second generator h and proves that g and h have order $p'q'$, where p' and q' are two primes of length $(\ell_g - 2)/2$ and that he does not know $\log_g h$. How this can be done is discussed in the next section. Since the group order is not publicly known, we define the discrete logarithm of an $y \in G$ to the base g to be any integer x such that $y = g^x$ holds. Finally, we assume a collision resistant hash function $\mathcal{H} : \{0,1\}^* \to \{0,1\}^k$ (e.g., $k \approx 160$).

Before we define the building blocks let us explain the notation with the following example [9]: a signature based on a proof of knowledge, denoted

$$SKP\{(\alpha, \beta) : y = g^\alpha \ \wedge \ z = g^\beta h^\alpha\} (m),$$

is used for 'proving' the knowledge of the discrete logarithm of y to the base g and of a representation of z to the bases g and h, and in addition, that the h-part of this representation equals the discrete logarithm of y to the base g. This is equivalent to the knowledge of a pair (α, β) satisfying the equations on the right side of the colon. In the sequel, we use the convention that Greek letters denote the elements whose knowledge is proven and all other letters denote elements that are known to the verifier.

---

[4] Recently, it has be shown that this approach does not work for general protocols [11], i.e., there exist protocols (although specially designed ones) which are secure in the random oracle model but that yield an insecure signature scheme. However, it is believed that the approach is still valid for the kind of protocols considered here.

4.1 Showing the Knowledge of a Discrete Logarithm

This protocol is an adaption of the protocols for proving the knowledge of a discrete logarithm [14,40] to the setting with a group of unknown order due to Girault [26,27]. A consequence of this setting is that the usual knowledge extractor for showing that a protocol is a proof of knowledge does not work; since the knowledge extractor does not know the group's order either and hence cannot compute inverses modulo this group order and therefore not extract the witness. Poupard and Stern [38] give a security proof for this adaption in a weaker security model, i.e., they show that if an attacker was able to carry out the protocol for almost all public keys, then he could also compute the discrete logarithm of the prover's public key. Since the latter is assumed to be impossible the protocol is concluded to be secure.

In the following we propose an alternative security proof using the model of Fujisaki and Okamoto [25]. In this model, the key setup is made a part of the protocol, i.e., the verifier chooses the group G and all other parameters and sends these as a first step to the prover. As a consequence, the knowledge extractor is allowed to choose the group and hence knows the group order. When turning this protocol into a signature scheme, the first steps, i.e., the key setup, are carried out interactively, and only the last three half-rounds are made non-interactive using the Fiat-Shamir heuristic.

Definition 1. *Let $\epsilon > 1$ be a security parameter. A pair $(c, s) \in \{0,1\}^k \times \{-2^{\ell_g+k}, \ldots, 2^{\epsilon(\ell_g+k)}\}$ satisfying $c = \mathcal{H}(g\|y\|g^s y^c\|m)$ is a signature of a message $m \in \{0,1\}^*$ with respect to y and is denoted $SPK\{(\alpha) : y = g^\alpha\}(m)$.*

An entity knowing the secret key $x = \log_g y$ of its public key y can compute such a signature $(s, c) = SPK\{(\alpha) : y = g^\alpha\}(m)$ of a message $m \in \{0,1\}^*$ by

- choosing $r \in_R \{0,1\}^{\epsilon(\ell_g+k)}$ and computing $t := g^r$,
- $c := \mathcal{H}(g\|y\|t\|m)$, and
- $s := r - cx$ (in $\mathbb{Z}$).

Showing that the interactive protocol corresponding to this signature scheme and the key setup is a proof of knowledge of the integer $x := \log_g y$ is straight forward. The proof that it is honest-verifier statistical zero-knowledge for any $\epsilon > 1$ is immediate from the proofs found in [38,42] for similar protocols. In [10] it is analyzed how much information (t, c, s) gives about x depending on the choice of ϵ.

4.2 Showing the Equality of two Discrete Logarithms

The next SPK is an adoption of a protocol for showing the equality of two discrete logarithms given in [15] to the setting in which the order is unknown.

Definition 2. *Let $\epsilon > 1$ be a security parameter. A pair $(c, s) \in \{0,1\}^k \times \{-2^{\ell_g+k}, \ldots, 2^{\epsilon(\ell_g+k)}\}$ satisfying $c = \mathcal{H}(g\|h\|y_1\|y_2\|y_1^c g^s\|y_2^c h^s\|m)$ is a signature of a message $m \in \{0,1\}^*$ with respect to y_1 and y_2 and is denoted*

$$SPK\{(\alpha) : y_1 = g^\alpha \ \wedge \ y_2 = h^\alpha\}(m).$$

Let $x \in \{0,1\}^{\ell_g}$ be the secret key of the signer such that $y_1 = g^x$ and $y_2 = h^x$ holds. Then a signature $SPK\{(\alpha) : y_1 = g^\alpha \wedge y_2 = h^\alpha\}(m)$ of a message $m \in \{0,1\}^*$ can be computed as follows.

- Choose $r \in_R \{0,1\}^{\epsilon(\ell_g+k)}$ and compute $t_1 := g^r$, $t_2 := h^r$,
- $c := \mathcal{H}(g\|h\|y_1\|y_2\|t_1\|t_2\|m)$, and
- $s := r - cx$ (in $\mathbb{Z}$).

The security proofs of this building block follow from the ones of the previous building block.

4.3   Showing the Knowledge of One out of Two Discrete Logarithms

The realization of the following SPK of one out of two discrete logarithms is an adoption of a protocol given in [20] to the setting with unknown order.

Definition 3. *Let $\epsilon > 1$ be a security parameter. A tuple $(c_1, c_2, s_1, s_2) \in \{0,1\}^k \times \{0,1\}^k \times \{-2^{\ell_g+k}, \ldots, 2^{\epsilon(\ell_g+k)}\} \times \{-2^{\ell_g+k}, \ldots, 2^{\epsilon(\ell_g+k)}\}$ satisfying $c_1 \oplus c_2 = \mathcal{H}(g\|h\|y_1\|y_2\|y_1^{c_1} g^{s_1}\|y_2^{c_2} h^{s_2}\|m)$ is a signature of a message $m \in \{0,1\}^*$ with respect to y_1 and y_2 and is denoted*

$$SPK\{(\alpha, \beta) : y_1 = g^\alpha \vee y_2 = h^\beta\}(m).$$

Assume that the signer knows $x \in_R \{0,1\}^{\ell_g}$ such that $y_1 = g^x$ holds. Then a signature $SPK\{(\alpha, \beta) : y_1 = g^\alpha \vee y_2 = h^\beta\}(m)$ of a message $m \in \{0,1\}^*$ can be computed as follows.

- Choose $r_1 \in_R \{0,1\}^{\epsilon(\ell_g+k)}$, $r_2 \in_R \{0,1\}^{\epsilon(\ell_g+k)}$, $c_2 \in_R \{0,1\}^k$ and compute $t_1 := g^{r_1}$, $t_2 := h^{r_2} y_2^{c_2}$,
- $c_1 := c_2 \oplus \mathcal{H}(g\|h\|y_1\|y_2\|t_1\|t_2\|m)$,
- $s_1 := r_1 - c_1 x$ (in $\mathbb{Z}$), and $s_2 := r_2$.

The security proofs of this building block follow from the ones of the previous building blocks and from [20].

4.4   Showing that a Discrete Logarithm Lies in an Interval

The last building block is based on a proof that the secret the prover knows lies in a given interval. It is related to a protocol presented by Chan et al. [13].

Definition 4. *Let $\epsilon > 1$ be a security parameter and let $\ell_1 < \ell_g$ and ℓ_2 denote lengths. A pair $(c, s) \in \{0,1\}^k \times \{-2^{\ell_2+k}, \ldots, 2^{\epsilon(\ell_2+k)}\}$ satisfying $c = \mathcal{H}(g\|y\|g^{s-c2^{\ell_1}} y^c\|m)$ is a signature of a message $m \in \{0,1\}^*$ with respect to y and is denoted*

$$SPK\{(\alpha) : y = g^\alpha \wedge (2^{\ell_1} - 2^{\epsilon(\ell_2+k)+1} < \alpha < 2^{\ell_1} + 2^{\epsilon(\ell_2+k)+1})\}(m).$$

Such a signature of a message $m \in \{0,1\}^*$ with respect to a public key $y \in G$ can be computed as follows if an $x \in \{2^{\ell_1}, \ldots, 2^{\ell_1} + 2^{\ell_2} - 1\}$ is known such that $y = g^x$ holds:

- choose $r \in_R \{0,1\}^{\epsilon(\ell_2+k)}$ and compute $t := g^r$,
- $c := \mathcal{H}(g\|y\|t\|m)$, and
- $s := r - c(x - 2^{\ell_1})$ (in $\mathbb{Z}$).

Theorem 1. *The interactive protocol corresponding to the signature scheme of Definition 4 and the key setup is a statistical honest-verifier zero-knowledge proof of knowledge of an $x \in \{2^{\ell_1} - 2^{\epsilon(\ell_2+k)+1}, \ldots, 2^{\ell_1} + 2^{\epsilon(\ell_2+k)+1}\}$ such that $y = g^x$ holds.*

Proof (Sketch). The proof that the protocol is statistical honest-verifier zero-knowledge is as before.

Let us consider the proof-of-knowledge part. Extracting the x such that $g^x = y$ is as usual. It remains to show that the extracted x lies indeed in the required interval. Let (t, c_i, s_i) be the accepting triples that the knowledge extractor got and used to compute x. Then we have $y^{c_1} g^{s_1 - c_1 2^{\ell_1}} = y^{c_2} g^{s_2 - c_2 2^{\ell_1}}$, where $c_1 \neq c_2$. Without loss of generality, we can assume that $c_2 > c_1$. Let denote $\Delta s := s_1 - s_2$ and $\Delta c := c_2 - c_1$. Then $(x - 2^{\ell_1})\Delta c \equiv \Delta s \pmod{\operatorname{ord}(g)}$ holds. As $\Delta c \in \{1, \ldots, 2^k - 1\}$ and $\Delta s \in \{-2^{\epsilon(\ell_2+k)+1}, \ldots, 2^{\epsilon(\ell_2+k)+1}\}$, we have $(x - 2^{\ell_1})\Delta c \in \{-2^{\epsilon(\ell_2+k)+1}, \ldots, 2^{\epsilon(\ell_2+k)+1}\} + j \cdot \operatorname{ord}(g)$ and thus also $(x - 2^{\ell_1}) \in \{-2^{\epsilon(\ell_2+k)+1}, \ldots, 2^{\epsilon(\ell_2+k)+1}\} + j \cdot \operatorname{ord}(g)$ for some integer j. From this it follows that $x \pmod{\operatorname{ord}(g)} \in \{2^{\ell_1} - 2^{\epsilon(\ell_2+k)+1}, \ldots, 2^{\ell_1} + 2^{\epsilon(\ell_2+k)+1}\}$. Since it is assumed to be infeasible for the prover to compute the order of g, the integer x must in fact lie in $\{2^{\ell_1} - 2^{\epsilon(\ell_2+k)+1}, \ldots, 2^{\ell_1} + 2^{\epsilon(\ell_2+k)+1}\}$ (cf. [25]). $\square$

Note that $\epsilon(\ell_2 + k) + 2 < \log(\operatorname{ord}(g)) \approx \ell_g$ should hold in order to indeed restrict the size of $\log_g y$.

5   Proposed Scheme

In this section we propose a realization of a group signature scheme the security of which is based on Assumptions 1 and 2. The basic idea of the scheme is the following. The membership manager chooses a group $G = \langle g \rangle$ and a group element z such that both assumptions hold. Furthermore, he chooses a second generators h such that $\log_g h$ is unknown. Computing discrete logs in G to the bases g, h, or z must be infeasible. Finally, computing roots in G must be feasible only to the membership manager, i.e., he is the only one who should know the order of G. The revocation manager chooses his secret key x and publishes $y = g^x$.

Each group member chooses a prime e randomly in a certain range together with the membership manager. Only the group member learns e and stores it as a secret key. A membership certificate issued by the membership manager is an element $u \in G$ such that $u^e = z$ holds. Here we slightly deviate from the approach of Camenisch and Stadler, i.e., the membership certificate and the membership key are the same value. As a consequence, the issuing of certificates must be realized in a way that the membership manager is not able to learn the group member's secret key e.

A signature of a message m by a group member consists of a triple $(a, b, d) \in G^3$ and an SPK of integers u and e such that

- u is encrypted in (a, b) of under the revocation manager's public key (which is part of the group public key)
- d commits to e,
- e lies in a given range, and
- $u^e = z$ holds.

The membership manager can reveal the identity of a signer by asking the revocation manager to decrypt (a, b).

The following paragraphs describe the new scheme in detail and provide security and efficiency analyses.

5.1   Setup of the Scheme

The setup procedure of our scheme consists of two phases. In the first phase the membership manager and the revocation manager construct the group's public key and choose their secret keys. This is described in this subsection. In the second phase of the setup, the group members choose their membership secret keys and get their membership certificates. This phase is described in the next subsection.

The membership manager chooses a group $G = \langle g \rangle$ and two random elements $z, h \in G$ with the same large order ($\approx 2^{\ell_g}$) such that Assumptions 1 and 2 hold. He publishes z, g, h, G, ℓ_g, and a proof that z, g, and h have the same, large order of the order of magnitude 2^{ℓ_g}. Also, he proves that the order of g, h, and z is not prime and not smooth. The latter would enable the membership manager to compute discrete logarithms in G. The membership manager must also proof that z and h where chosen at random. The revocation manager chooses his secret key x randomly in $\{0, \dots, 2^{\ell_g} - 1\}$ and publishes $y = g^x$ as his public key. Finally, a hash function $\mathcal{H} : \{0, 1\}^* \longrightarrow \{0, 1\}^k$ and security parameters $\hat{\ell}$, ℓ_1, ℓ_2, and ϵ are set. An example for choosing the parameters ϵ, $\hat{\ell}$, ℓ_g, ℓ_1, and ℓ_2 is given in Section 5.6.

A possible choice of $G = \langle g \rangle$ is a subgroup of $\mathbb{Z}_n^*$ such that $(g|n) = 1$. In this case the membership manager chooses two large random primes p and q ($\approx 2^{\ell_g/2}$) of form $p = 2p' + 1$ and $q = 2q' + 1$, where p' and q' are primes as well, such that $p, q \not\equiv 1 \pmod 8$ and $p \not\equiv q \pmod 8$ holds. He keeps p and q secret and publishes $n := pq$. For proving that n is of the right form, there is no efficient proof system to the best of our knowledge. Thus one has to use general zero-knowledge proof techniques (e.g., [5,6,19]) and a circuit that takes as input integers p, q, p', and q' and outputs 1 if and only if the inputs are primes and if $n = pq$, $p = 2p' + 1$, and $p = 2p' + 1$ holds. The size of p and q can be checked by the number of input bits for them (they should have at most $\lceil 0.5 \log n \rceil$ bits). This is not very efficient but must be done only once. To verify that an element a has the (large) order $p'q'$ in $\mathbb{Z}_n^*$ and Jacobi symbol 1, one needs only to test whether $a \not\equiv 1 \pmod n$ and $\gcd(a - 1, n) = 1$ holds and provide a proof should that a is a quadratic residue modulo n. An alternative choice of G is a suitable elliptic curve (e.g., see [30]).

5.2 Registration

To become a group member Alice chooses a random prime $\hat{e} \in_R \{2^{\hat{\ell}-1}, \dots, 2^{\hat{\ell}}-1\}$ such that $\hat{e} \not\equiv 1 \pmod 8$ and a random number $e_1 \in_R \{1, \dots, 2^{\ell_2} - 1\}$. She computes $\tilde{z} := z^{\hat{e}} \pmod n$ and the commitment $\hat{c} = \tilde{z}^{e_1} h^{r_{e_1}}$ with $r_{e_1} \in_R \{0,1\}^{\ell_g}$. Then she sends $\tilde{z}$ and $\hat{c}$ to the membership manager. The membership manager chooses a random number $e_2 \in_R \{1, \dots, 2^{\ell_2} - 1\}$ and sends it to Alice. Alice computes $e_3 := e_1 + e_2 \pmod{2^{\ell_2}}$ and $e := e_3 + 2^{\ell_1}$. If e is not a prime satisfying $e \not\equiv 1 \pmod 8$ and $e \not\equiv \hat{e} \pmod 8$ Alice reveals e and $\hat{e}$ to enable the membership manager checking that she hasn't cheated and they repeat the whole process. The success probability per round is roughly $1/(\ell_1 2 \ln 2)$.

If e is a prime, Alice computes $\tilde{e} := e\hat{e}$, commits to $\tilde{e}$ and $\tilde{z}$ (for instance by signing them), sends $\tilde{e}$, $\tilde{z}$, and their commitments to the membership manager, and carries out the interactive protocols corresponding to

$$W := SPK\Big\{(\alpha, \beta, \gamma, \delta, \zeta) : \hat{c} = \tilde{z}^\alpha h^\beta \,\wedge\, (-2^{\epsilon(\ell_2+k)+1} < \alpha < 2^{\epsilon(\ell_2+k)+1}) \,\wedge$$

$$\tilde{z} = z^\gamma \,\wedge\, \Big((\hat{c}\tilde{z}^{e_2-2^{\ell_2}+2^{\ell_1}})/z^{\tilde{e}} = h^\delta \,\vee\, (\hat{c}\tilde{z}^{e_2+2^{\ell_1}})/z^{\tilde{e}} = h^\zeta\Big)\Big\}(\tilde{z}) \,,$$

with the membership manager (cf. previous section). Furthermore, Alice proves that $\tilde{e}$ is the product of two primes (e.g., using the methods described in [4,43]). Using the same arguments as for the building blocks in the previous section, it can be seen that the protocol corresponding to W convinces the membership manager that Alice has formed $\tilde{e}$ and $\tilde{z}$ correctly and that $\tilde{e}/\log_z \tilde{z} - 2^{\ell_1}$ equals the sum of e_2 and the e_1 committed to in $\hat{c}$ modulo 2^{ℓ_2}.

The membership manager computes $u := \tilde{z}^{1/\tilde{e}}$ and sends u to Alice, who checks that $\tilde{z} = u^{\tilde{e}}$ holds (which is equivalent to $z = u^e$). The membership manager stores $(u, \tilde{e}, \tilde{z})$ together with Alice's identity and her commitment to $\tilde{e}$ and $\tilde{z}$ in a group-member list. Finally, Alice stores the pair (u, e) as her membership key.

Of course, $\hat{\ell}$, ℓ_1, and ℓ_2 must be chosen such that $\tilde{e}$ cannot be factored (cf. Section 5.6). In particular $\ell_2 \gg \ell_1 - (\hat{\ell} + \ell_1)/4$ must hold [18].

5.3 Signature Generation

Let us first define a group signature and then show how a group member can compute such a signature.

Definition 5. *Let ϵ, ℓ_1, and ℓ_2 be security parameters such that $\epsilon > 1$, $\ell_2 < \ell_1 < \ell_g$, and $\ell_2 < \frac{\ell_g - 2}{\epsilon} - k$ holds. A group-signature $\mathsf{sign}(x_G, (g, h, y, z), m)$ of a message $m \in \{0,1\}^*$ is a tuple $(c, s_1, s_2, s_3, a, b, d) \in \{0,1\}^k \times \{-2^{\ell_2+k}, \dots, 2^{\epsilon(\ell_2+k)}\} \times \{-2^{\ell_g+\ell_1+k}, \dots, 2^{\epsilon(\ell_g+\ell_1+k)}\} \times \{-2^{\ell_g+k}, \dots, 2^{\epsilon(\ell_g+k)}\} \times G^3$ satisfying*

$$c = \mathcal{H}(g\|h\|y\|z\|a\|b\|d\|z^c b^{s_1 - c2^{\ell_1}} / y^{s_2} \|a^{s_1 - c2^{\ell_1}} / g^{s_2} \|a^c g^{s_3} \|d^c g^{s_1 - c2^{\ell_1}} h^{s_3} \|m).$$

Remark. Such a group-signature would be denoted

$$SPK\{(\eta, \vartheta, \xi) : z = b^\eta/y^\vartheta \,\wedge\, 1 = a^\eta/g^\vartheta \,\wedge\, a = g^\xi \,\wedge\, d = g^\eta h^\xi \,\wedge$$
$$(2^{\ell_1} - 2^{\epsilon(\ell_2+k)+1} < \eta < 2^{\ell_1} + 2^{\epsilon(\ell_2+k)+1})\}(m).$$

To sign a message $m \in \{0,1\}^*$ on the group's behalf, a group member Alice

- chooses $w \in_R \{0,1\}^{\ell_g}$, computes $a := g^w$, $b := uy^w$, and $d := g^e h^w$,
- chooses $r_1 \in_R \{0,1\}^{\epsilon(\ell_2+k)}$, $r_2 \in_R \{0,1\}^{\epsilon(\ell_g+\ell_1+k)}$, and $r_3 \in_R \{0,1\}^{\epsilon(\ell_g+k)}$, and computes
- $t_1 := b^{r_1}(1/y)^{r_2}$, $t_2 := a^{r_1}(1/g)^{r_2}$, $t_3 := g^{r_3}$, $t_4 := g^{r_1}h^{r_3}$,
- $c := \mathcal{H}(g\|h\|y\|z\|a\|b\|d\|t_1\|t_2\|t_3\|t_4\|m)$,
- $s_1 := r_1 - c(e - 2^{\ell_1})$ (in $\mathbb{Z}$), $s_2 := r_2 - cew$ (in $\mathbb{Z}$), and $s_3 := r_3 - cw$ (in $\mathbb{Z}$).

The resulting signature of m is $(c, s_1, s_2, s_3, a, b, d)$. It can easily be verified that it satisfies the verification condition given in Definition 5.

5.4 Verifying Signatures, Tracing, and Verifying Tracing

A signature $(c, s_1, s_2, s_3, a, b, d)$ of a message m can be verified by checking the equation stated in Definition 5.

To reveal the originator of a given signature $\sigma := (c, s_1, s_2, s_3, a, b, d)$ of a message m, the revocation manager first checks its correctness. He aborts if the signature is not correct. Otherwise he computes $u' := b/a^x$, issues $P := SPK\{(\alpha) : y = g^\alpha \wedge b/u' = a^\alpha\}(\sigma\|m)$ (see Section 4.2), and reveals $arg := u'\|P$. He then looks up u' in the group-member list and will find the corresponding u, the group member's identity and his/her commitment to $\tilde{e}$ and $\tilde{z}$.

Checking whether the revocation manager correctly revealed the originator of a signature $\sigma = (c, s_1, s_2, s_3, a, b, d)$ of a message m can simply be done by verifying σ and arg.

5.5 Security Analysis

Before discussing the security requirements described in Section 2.1 let us have a closer look at the interactive protocol corresponding to the generation of a group signature and the parameter setup.

Theorem 2. *The interactive protocol sequentially composed of the parameter setup and the protocol corresponding to the generation of a group signature is a zero-knowledge proof of knowledge of a membership key and certificate. Furthermore, the pair (a, b) encrypts the certificate under the revocation manager's public key y.*

Proof (Sketch). Using the standard techniques (cf. Section 4), this protocol can be shown to be a statistical zero-knowledge proof of knowledge of values x_1, x_2, and x_3 such that

$$x_1 \in \{2^{\ell_1} - 2^{\epsilon(\ell_2+k)+1}, \dots, 2^{\ell_1} + 2^{\epsilon(\ell_2+k)+1}\}$$

$$z = \frac{b^{x_1}}{y^{x_2}}, \quad a^{x_1} = g^{x_2}, \quad a = g^{x_3}, \quad \text{and} \quad d = g^{x_1}h^{x_3}$$

holds. From the second and third equations we can conclude that $g^{x_2} = g^{x_3 x_1}$ and thus also $y^{x_2} = y^{x_3 x_1}$ holds. Therefore, we have

$$z = \frac{b^{x_1}}{y^{x_2}} = \frac{b^{x_1}}{(y^{x_3})^{x_1}} = \left(\frac{b}{y^{x_3}}\right)^{x_1}$$

and hence $(x_1, \frac{b}{y^{x_3}})$ is a valid membership key-pair. The triple (a, b, d) is an unconditionally binding commitment to these two values and hence the group member/prover must have known[5] them when she computed a, b, and d. Since it is assumed that the group member cannot compute roots nor discrete logarithms (as otherwise Assumption 1 would not hold), she must have had other means to get such a pair, i.e., by having run the registration protocol with the membership manager.

Finally, the commitments can be opened by the entities knowing $\log_h y$ and $\log_g h$, respectively, i.e., the values are encrypted for these entities. We recall, that the first discrete log was chosen be the revocation manager, while the second is assumed to be unknown. □

Let us now informally discuss the security properties of the proposed group signature scheme.

Unforgeability of Signatures: This is due to Theorem 2.

Anonymity of Signatures: It can be shown that the values c, s_1, s_2, and s_3 do not reveal any useful knowledge. Hence, deciding whether a signature $(c, s_1, s_2, s_3, a, b, d)$ originates from a group member with public key u' requires to decide whether $\log_g a = log_y \frac{b}{u'}$. If one was able to decide this efficiently, this would violate Assumption 2.

Unlinkability of Signatures: Linking two signatures, i.e., deciding whether two signatures $(c, s_1, s_2, s_3, a, b, d)$ and $(c', s_1', s_2', s_3', a', b', d')$ originate from the same group member requires to decide whether $\log_g \frac{a}{a'} = log_y \frac{b}{b'} = log_h \frac{d}{d'}$, as c, s_1, s_2, s_3 and c', s_1', s_2', s_3' do not reveal useful knowledge. Under Assumption 2 this is infeasible and hence signatures are unlinkable.

No Framing: Given Theorem 2, signing in the name of a group member with certificate u and requires the computation of $\log_u z$ or to factor the value $\tilde{e}$ that the membership manager received from the group member during registration. Both is assumed to be infeasible.

Unforgeability of Tracing: The pair (a, b) that is part of a signature is an El-Gamal encryption [21] of the signer's membership key under the revocation manager's public key y. Theorem 2 shows that $b/(y^{\log_g a}) = b/a^x$ is a valid membership public key. Due to Assumption 1 this must be the membership certificate of the group member who signed. Therefore, by decrypting (a, b) the revocation manager can reveal the originator of a signature at hand. In the tracing algorithm the revocation manager issues an SPK denoted *arg* which shows that he decrypted the membership public key correctly. Forging this SPK is infeasible under Assumption 1.

5.6 Efficiency Analysis

With $\epsilon = 9/8, \ell_g = \hat{\ell} = 1200, \ell_1 = 860, \ell_2 = 600$, and $k = 160$, the signature generation and verification need little less than 13'000 modular multiplications modulo a 1200-bit modulus in average, and the signature is about 1 KBytes long. Compared to the most efficient scheme given in [9], our scheme is about three

---

[5] This is important, since the knowledge-extractor knows the order, he can always find a random e and u such that $z = u^e$.

times more efficient and signatures are about three times shorter when choosing
the same modulus for both schemes. Signatures could made shorter without compromising the security of the scheme if the parameter w in the signing procedure
is chosen from a smaller domain, e.g., $\{0,1\}^{\ell_2}$ instead of $\{0,1\}^{\ell_g}$.

6   Conclusion

It is worthwhile noting that it is possible to realize blind group signatures using
the techniques given in [8,34], which are much more efficient than the blind
versions of [9,10] given in [32]. Splitting the membership and/or the revocation
manager can be done by applying the techniques of [3,12], respectively (see also
[10]). As the signature generation algorithm was derived from an interactive protocol, a group identification scheme (also called identity escrow [28]) is obtained
by using this protocol for identification.

Acknowledgments

The second author was supported by the Swiss National Foundation (SNF/SPP
project no. 5003-045293). We gratefully acknowledge the discussions with Ivan
Damgård, Markus Stadler, and Bartosz Przydatek.

References

1. N. Barić and B. Pfitzmann. Collision-free accumulators and fail-stop signature
   schemes without trees. In W. Fumy, editor, *Advances in Cryptology — EU-
   ROCRYPT '97*, volume 1233 of *LNCS*, pages 480–494. Springer Verlag, 1997.
2. M. Bellare and P. Rogaway. Random oracles are practical: A paradigm for designing
   efficient protocols. In *First ACM Conference on Computer and Communication
   Security*, pages 62–73. Association for Computing Machinery, 1993.
3. D. Boneh and M. Franklin. Efficient generation of shared RSA keys. In B. Kaliski,
   editor, *Advances in Cryptology — CRYPTO '97*, volume 1296 of *LNCS*, pages
   425–439. Springer Verlag, 1997.
4. J. Boyar, K. Friedl, and C. Lund. Practical zero-knowledge proofs: Giving hints
   and using deficiencies. *Journal of Cryptology*, 4(3):185–206, 1991.
5. J. Boyar and R. Peralta. Short discreet proofs. In U. Maurer, editor, *Advances in
   Cryptology — EUROCRYPT '96*, volume 1070 of *LNCS*, pages 131–142. Springer
   Verlag, 1996.
6. G. Brassard, D. Chaum, and C. Crépeau. Minimum disclosure proofs of knowledge.
   Journal of Computer and System Sciences, 37(2):156–189, Oct. 1988.
7. J. Camenisch. Efficient and generalized group signatures. In W. Fumy, editor,
   Advances in Cryptology — EUROCRYPT '97, volume 1233 of *LNCS*, pages 465–
   479. Springer Verlag, 1997.
8. J. Camenisch, U. Maurer, and M. Stadler. Digital payment systems with passive
   anonymity-revoking trustees. In *Computer Security — ESORICS 96*, volume 1146
   of *LNCS*, pages 33–43. Springer Verlag, 1996.
9. J. Camenisch and M. Stadler. Efficient group signature schemes for large groups.
   In B. Kaliski, editor, *Advances in Cryptology — CRYPTO '97*, volume 1296 of
   LNCS, pages 410–424. Springer Verlag, 1997.

10. J. L. Camenisch. *Group Signature Schemes and Payment Systems Based on the Discrete Logarithm Problem*. PhD thesis, ETH Zürich, 1998. Diss. ETH No. 12520, ISBN 3-89649-286-1, Hartung Gorre Verlag, Konstanz.
11. R. Canetti, O. Goldreich, and S. Halevi. The random oracle methodology, revisited. In *Proc. 30th Annual ACM Symposium on Theory of Computing (STOC)*, 1998.
12. D. Catalano and R. Gennaro. New efficient and secure protocols for verifiable signature sharing and other applications. In *Advances in Cryptology — CRYPTO '98, LNCS*. Springer Verlag, 1998.
13. A. Chan, Y. Frankel, and Y. Tsiounis. Easy come – easy go divisible cash. In *Advances in Cryptology — EUROCRYPT '98*, volume 1403 of *LNCS*.
14. D. Chaum, J.-H. Evertse, and J. van de Graaf. An improved protocol for demonstrating possession of discrete logarithms and some generalizations. In *Advances in Cryptology — EUROCRYPT '87*, pages 127–141.
15. D. Chaum and T. P. Pedersen. Transferred cash grows in size. In R. A. Rueppel, editor, *Advances in Cryptology — EUROCRYPT '92*, volume 658 of *LNCS*, pages 390–407. Springer-Verlag, 1993.
16. D. Chaum and E. van Heyst. Group signatures. In D. W. Davies, editor, *Advances in Cryptology — EUROCRYPT '91*, volume 547 of *LNCS*, pages 257–265.
17. L. Chen and T. P. Pedersen. New group signature schemes. In *Advances in Cryptology — EUROCRYPT '94*, volume 950 of *LNCS*, pages 171–181.
18. D. Coppersmith. Finding a Small Root of a Bivariatre Interger Equation; Factoring with High Bits Known In U. Maurer, editor, *Advances in Cryptology — EUROCRYPT '96*, volume 1070 of *LNCS*, pages 178–189. Springer Verlag, 1996.
19. R. Cramer and I. Damgård. Linear zero-knowledge: A note on efficient zero-knowledge proofs and arguments. In *Proc. 29th Annual ACM Symposium on Theory of Computing (STOC)*, pages 436–445. ACM press, 1997.
20. R. Cramer, I. Damgård, and B. Schoenmakers. Proofs of partial knowledge and simplified design of witness hiding protocols. In Y. G. Desmedt, editor, *Advances in Cryptology — CRYPTO '94*, volume 839 of *LNCS*, pages 174–187.
21. T. ElGamal. A public key cryptosystem and a signature scheme based on discrete logarithms. In G. R. Blakley and D. Chaum, editors, *Advances in Cryptology — CRYPTO '84*, volume 196 of *LNCS*, pages 10–18. Springer Verlag, 1985.
22. J.-H. Evertse and E. van Heyst. Which new RSA signatures can be computed from certain given RSA signatures? *Journal of Cryptology*, 5:41–52, 1992.
23. U. Feige, A. Fiat, and A. Shamir. Zero-knowledge proofs of identity. *Journal of Cryptology*, 1:77–94, 1988.
24. A. Fiat and A. Shamir. How to prove yourself: Practical solution to identification and signature problems. In A. M. Odlyzko, editor, *Advances in Cryptology — CRYPTO '86*, volume 263 of *LNCS*, pages 186–194. Springer Verlag, 1987.
25. E. Fujisaki and T. Okamoto. Statistical zero knowledge protocols to prove modular polynomial relations. In B. S. Kaliski, editor, *Advances in Cryptology — CRYPTO '97*, volume 1294 of *LNCS*, pages 16–30. Springer Verlag, 1997.
26. M. Girault. An identity-based identification scheme based on discrete logarihtms modulo a composite number. In I. B. Damgård, editor, *Advances in Cryptology — EUROCRYPT '90*, volume 473 of *LNCS*, pages 481–486. Springer-Verlag, 1991.
27. M. Girault. Self-certified public keys. In *Advances in Cryptology — EUROCRYPT '91*, volume 547 of *LNCS*, pages 490–497. Springer-Verlag, 1992.
28. J. Kilian and E. Petrank. Identity escrow. In *Advances in Cryptology — CRYPTO '98, LNCS*. Springer Verlag, 1998.
29. S. J. Kim, S. J. Park, and D. H. Won. Convertible group signatures. In *Advances in Cryptology — ASIACRYPT '96*, volume 1163 of *LNCS*, pages 311–321.

30. K. Koyama, U. Maurer, T. Okamoto, and S. Vanstone New Public-key Schemes Based on Elliptic Curves over the Ring Z_n. In *Advances in Cryptology — CRYPTO '91*, volume 576 of *LNCS*,pages 252–266.

31. C. H. Lim and P. J. Lee. On the security of convertible group signatures. *Electronics Letters*, 1996.

32. A. Lysyanskaya and Z. Ramzan. Group blind digital signatures: A scalable solution to electronic cash. In *Proc. Second Int. Conf. on Financial Cryptography*, 1998.

33. M. Michels. Comments on some group signature schemes. TR-96-3-D, Departement of Computer Science, University of Technology, Chemnitz-Zwickau, Nov. 1996.

34. T. Okamoto. Provable secure and practical identification schemes and corresponding signature schemes. In E. F. Brickell, editor, *Advances in Cryptology — CRYPTO '92*, volume 740 of *LNCS*, pages 31–53. Springer-Verlag, 1993.

35. S. J. Park, I. S. Lee, and D. H. Won. A practical group signature. In *Proc. of the 1995 Japan-Korea Workshop on Information Security and Cryptography*.

36. H. Petersen. How to convert any digital signature scheme into a group signature scheme. In *Security Protocols Workshop*, Paris, 1997.

37. D. Pointcheval and J. Stern. Security proofs for signature schemes. In U. Maurer, editor, *Advances in Cryptology — EUROCRYPT '96*, volume 1070 of *LNCS*, pages 387–398. Springer Verlag, 1996.

38. G. Poupard and J. Stern. Security analysis of a practical "on the fly" authentication and signature generation. In K. Nyberg, editor, *Advances in Cryptology — EUROCRYPT '98*, volume 1403 of *LNCS*, pages 422–436. Springer Verlag, 1998.

39. R. Rivest, A. Shamir, and L. Adleman. A method for obtaining digital signatures and public-key cryptosystems. *Comm. of the ACM*, 21(2):120–126, Feb. 1978.

40. C. P. Schnorr. Efficient signature generation for smart cards. *Journal of Cryptology*, 4(3):239–252, 1991.

41. A. Shamir. On the generation of cryptographically strong pseudorandom sequences. In *ACM Trans. on Computer Systems*, volume 1, pages 38–44, 1983.

42. M. Stadler. *Cryptographic Protocols for Revocable Privacy*. PhD thesis, ETH Zürich, 1996. Diss. ETH No. 11651.

43. J. van de Graaf and R. Peralta. A simple and secure way to show the validity of your public key. In C. Pomerance, editor, *Advances in Cryptology — CRYPTO '87*, volume 293 of *LNCS*, pages 128–134. Springer-Verlag, 1988.

A Study on the Proposed Korean Digital Signature Algorithm*

Chae Hoon Lim[1] and Pil Joong Lee[2]

[1] Future Systems, Inc., Seoul, Korea
email: chlim@future.co.kr
[2] Dept. Electronic and Electrical Eng., POSTECH, Pohang, Korea
email: pjl@postech.ac.kr

Abstract. A digital signature scheme is one of essential cryptographic primitives for secure transactions over open networks. Korean cryptographic community, in association with government-supported agencies, has made a continuous effort over past three years to develop our own signature standard. The outcome of this long effort is the signature algorithm called KCDSA, which is now at the final stage of standardization process and will be published as one of KICS (Korean Information and Communication Standards). This paper describes the proposed signature algorithm and discusses its security and efficiency aspects.

1 Introduction

The digital signature technique, a technique for signing and verifying digital documents in an unforgeable way, is essential for secure transactions over open networks. Digital signatures can be used in a variety of applications to ensure the integrity of data exchanged or stored and to prove to the recipient the originator's identity.

A group of Korean cryptographers, in association with government-supported agencies, has been developing a candidate algorithm for Korean digital signature standard, which is named KCDSA temporarily (standing for Korean Certificate-based Digital Signature Algorithm). As a result of such effort over three years, a final algorithm has been established and is now being standardized by the Korean Government. This signature algorithm, once standardized, is hopefully to be widely supported in commercial security products by Korean industries and possibly by the Government. In addition, a standard hash algorithm, developed for use with KCDSA, is also under standardization process.

* KCDSA was developed by a task force team consisting of Sang Jae Moon (Kyung Pook Univ.), Dong Ho Won (Sung Gyun Kwan Univ.), Sung Jun Park (KISA), Chung Ryong Jang (Kyung Dong Univ.), Shin Gak Kang (ETRI), Eun Jeong Lee (POSTECH), Sang Bae Park (IDIS), Chul Kim (Kwang Woon Univ.), Kyung Seok Lee (KIET), Jae Hyun Baek (ADD), Jong Tae Shin (KISA), etc., and the present authors, under the financial support of ETRI (Electronics and Telecommunications Research Institute) and KISA (Korea Information Security Agency).

K. Ohta and D. Pei (Eds.): ASIACRYPT'98, LNCS 1514, pp. 175–186, 2000.
© Springer-Verlag Berlin Heidelberg 2000

The security of most signature schemes widely used in practice is based on two difficult problems: the problem of factoring integers (e.g., RSA [16]) and the problem of finding discrete logarithms over finite fields (e.g., Elgamal [5]). The RSA scheme is used in many applications as a de facto standard. On the other hand, two variants of the Elgamal scheme have been standardized in U.S.A as digital signature standard (DSS) [19] and in Russia as GOST 34.10 (see [10]). KCDSA is also a Elgamal-type signature scheme. There have been a lot of discussions on whether our national standard should be either of RSA type or of Elgamal type. There also has been some controversy on establishing a new standard other than the widely used schemes such as RSA and DSA. Putting aside the behind story, we concluded to design our own signature scheme and KCDSA is the outcome. KCDSA is designed by incorporating several features from the recent cryptographic research and thus is believed to be secure and robust.

In this paper we describe the proposed standard for KCDSA and discuss security and efficiency aspects considered during the design process. Throughout this paper we will use the following symbols and notation:

- $a \oplus b$: exclusive-or of two bit strings a and b.
- $a \parallel b$: concatenation of two bit strings a and b.
- $\mathbf{Z}_n = \{0, 1, \cdots, n-1\}$ and $\mathbf{Z}_n^* = \{x | 1 \le x \le n-1 \ \& \ \gcd(x, n) = 1\}$.
- $|A|$ denotes the bit-length of A for integer A and the cardinality of A for set A.
- $k \in_r S$ denote that k is chosen at random over the set S.

This paper is organized as follows. We describe KCDSA parameters in Section 2 and the detailed signature algorithm in Section 3. The security and efficiency aspects of KCDSA are discussed in Sections 4 and 5, respectively. In Section 6 we briefly describe an elliptic curve variant of KCDSA and finally we conclude in Section 7.

2   KCDSA Parameters

KCDSA parameters can be divided into domain parameters and user parameters. By domain we mean a group of users who shares the same public parameters (domain parameters). Domain may consist of a single user if the user uses its own public parameters. User parameters denote parameters which are specific to each user and cannot be shared with others. These parameters must be established before normal use of digital signatures by some trusted authorities and/or by users. KCDSA makes use of the following domain and user parameters (see Appendix for a procedure that can be used to generate domain parameters):

Domain Parameters: p, q, g such that

- p : a large prime such that $L_p = |p| = 512 + 256i$ for $i = 0, 1, \cdots, 6$. That is, the bit-length of p can vary from 512 bits to 2048 bits with increment by a multiple of 256 bits.

- q : a prime factor of $p-1$ such that $L_q = |q| = 128 + 32j$ for $j = 0, 1, \cdots, 4$. That is, the bit-length of q can vary from 128 bits to 256 bits with increment by a multiple of 32 bits. Further, it is required that $(p-1)/2q$ should be a prime or at least all its prime factors should be greater than q.[1]
- g : a base element of order q mod p, i.e., $g \neq 1$ and $g^q = 1$ mod p.

User Parameters: x, y, z such that

- x : signer's private signature key such that $x \in_r \mathbf{Z}_q$.
- y : signer's public verification key computed by $y = g^{x^{-1}}$ mod p, where x^{-1} denotes the multiplicative inverse of x mod q.[2]
- z : a hash-value of *Cert_Data*, i.e., $z = h(Cert\_Data)$. Here *Cert_Data* denotes the signer's certification data, which should contain at least Signer's distinguished identifier, public key Y and the domain parameters $\{p, q, g\}$.

KCDSA is a signature algorithm in which the public key is validated by means of a certificate issued by some trusted authority. The X.509-based certificate may be used for this purpose. In this case, the *Cert_Data* can be simply the formatted certification data defined by X.509.

KCDSA also requires a collision-resistant hash function which produces L_q-bit outputs. Since q can vary in size from 128 bits to 256 bits with increment by a multiple of 32 bits, we need a family of hash functions or a hash function which can produce variable length outputs up to 256 bits. Currently standardization is being processed for a hash algorithm with 160-bit outputs called *HAS-160*. Hash functions for the other sizes of q are left as a future work.

3   The Signature Algorithm

3.1   Signature Generation

The signer can generate a signature $\{r\|s\}$ for a message m as follows:

1. randomly picks an integer k in $\mathbf{Z}_q^*$ and computes $w = g^k$ mod p,
2. computes the first part r of the signature as $r = h(w)$,
3. computes $e = r \oplus h(z\|m)$ mod q, and
4. computes the second part s of the signature as $s = x(k - e)$ mod q.

---

[1] This restriction on the size of prime factors of $(p-1)/2q$ is to take precautions against possible attacks using small order subgroups of $\mathbf{Z}_p^*$ in various applications of KCDSA (see [8] for details).

[2] Notice that there is essentially no difference in the signature algorithm if the secret-public key pair is represented by $\{x^{-1}$ mod $q, y = g^x$ mod $p\}$. We simply adopted the above notation to clarify (to the public unaware of cryptography) that we only need x for a signing purpose. This kind of key pair may be undesirable if the same key is to be used for other purposes as well (e.g., key exchange or entity authentication). However, it is a common practice in cryptographic protocol designs that the same key should not be used for different purposes.

The computation of w is the most time-consuming operation in the signing process. However, since the first two steps can be performed independent of a specific message to be signed, we may precompute and securely store the pair $\{r, k\}$ for fast on-line signature generation. The above signing process can be described in brief by the following two equations:

$$r = h(g^k \bmod p) \text{ with } k \in_r \mathbf{Z}_q^*,$$
$$s = x(k - r \oplus h(z\|m)) \bmod q.$$

3.2   Signature Verification

On receiving $\{m\|r\|s\}$, the verifier can check the validity of the signature as follows:

1. first checks the validity of the signer's certificate, extracts the signer's certification data $Cert\_Data$ from the certificate and computes the hash value $z = h(Cert\_Data)$.[3]
2. checks the size of r and $s : 0 < r < 2^{|q|}$, $0 < s < q$,
3. computes $e = r \oplus h(z\|m) \bmod q$,
4. computes $w' = y^s g^e \bmod p$ and
5. finally checks that $r = h(w')$.

The pair $\{r\|s\}$ is a valid signature for m only if all the checks succeed. The above verifying process can be described in brief by the following equations:

$$e = r \oplus h(z\|m),$$
$$r = h(y^s g^e \bmod p) \text{ ?}$$

For comparison, we summarized three signature standards, DSA, GOST and KCDSA, in Table 1.

4   Security Considerations

4.1   Security Proof under Random Oracle Model

Recently two variants of ElGamal-like signature schemes have been proven secure against adaptive attacks for existential forgery under the random oracle model [3], where the hash function is replaced with an oracle producing a random value for each new query. In the first variant, $h(m)$ is replaced with $h(m\|r)$ as in the Schnorr signature scheme. This variant was proven secure by Pointcheval and Stern [13] at Eurocrypt'96. The other variant is due to Brickell [4] at Crypto'96,

---

[3] Note that a certificate corresponds to a trusted authority's signature for the formatted data containing all information required to bind the public key and related parameters/attributes to the key owner's identity. Therefore, the computation of z can be in fact part of the certificate validation process by taking $Cert\_Data$ as the formatted data to be signed.

Schemes	$|p|$	$|q|$
DSA	$512 + 64i \ (i = 0, 1, \cdots, 8)$	160
GOST	512 or 1024	256
KCDSA	$512 + 256i \ (i = 0, 1, \cdots, 6)$	$128 + 32i \ (i = 0, 1, \cdots, 4)$

Schemes	Signature Generation	Signature Verification
	private Key : $x \in_r \mathbf{Z}_q$	public key : $y = g^x \bmod p$
DSA [19]	$k \in_r \mathbf{Z}_q^*$ $r = (g^k \bmod p) \bmod q$ $s = k^{-1}(rx + h(m)) \bmod q$	$(y^{s^{-1}r} g^{s^{-1}h(m)} \bmod p) \bmod q = r$?
GOST [10]	$k \in_r \mathbf{Z}_q$ $r = (g^k \bmod p) \bmod q$ $s = rx + kh(m) \bmod q$	$(y^{-rh(m)^{-1}} g^{sh(m)^{-1}} \bmod p) \bmod q = r$?
	private Key : $x \in_r \mathbf{Z}_q$	public key : $y = g^{x^{-1}} \bmod p$
KCDSA	$k \in_r \mathbf{Z}_q^*$ $r = h(g^k \bmod p)$ $s = x(k - r \oplus h(z\|m)) \bmod q$	$h(y^s g^{r \oplus h(z\|m)} \bmod p) = r$?

Table 1. Comparison of DSA, GOST and KCDSA

where he claimed that the variant of DSA with $r = (g^k \bmod p) \bmod q$ replaced by $r = h(g^k \bmod p)$ is also secure in the random oracle model (see [14] for its proof by Pointcheval and Vaudenay). We followed the latter approach to ensure the security of the overall design of KCDSA. From the proof under the random oracle model we can be assured that KCDSA will be secure provided that the hash function used has no weakness.

4.2 Security against Parameter Manipulation

There have been published a lot of weaknesses in the design of discrete log-based schemes due to the use of unsafe parameters (later shown insecure) (e.g., see [12,2,1,18,8]). Note that generating public parameters at random so that they do not have any specific structure is very important for security, even with a provably secure scheme (compare the results from [2] and [13]. see also [17]). KCDSA is designed to be secure against all these potential weaknesses. The (proposed) standard recommend to use the strongest form of primes [8], i.e., primes p, q such that $(p-1)/2q$ is also a prime or at least its prime factors are all greater than q. It also specifies a procedure that can be used for generation of such primes (see Appendix A). The certificate produced by this procedure can be used to verify proper generation of the parameters. Considering current algorithms and technology for finding discrete logarithms (see [11]), we recommend to use a modulus p of size 1024 bits and an auxiliary prime q of 160 bits for moderate security in most applications.

The use of the parameter $z = h(Cert\_Data)$ as a prefix message for hashing provides several advantages without much increase of computational/operational overheads.[4]

It effectively prevents possible manipulations during parameter generation, such as hidden collisions in DSS [18], since $Cert\_Data$ contains p, q, g and y. In addition, the use of z restricts the collision search in the hash function to a specific signer, since each signer uses his/her own prefix z to produce a hash code for his/her message. To see its usefulness, suppose that in the case of using the usual hash code $h(m)$ a collision is found for a specific pair of messages. Also suppose that one message out of the pair is a comfortable message that anyone can sign without reluctance. Then the collision can be used to any user to claim that the signature is for the harmful message. Realization of this scenario may be catastrophic, for example, if there exists some powerful organization willing to invest a huge amount of money to find collisions (the organization might find some unpublished weakness in the hash function which can substantially reduce the time for exhaustive search). Our new hash mode with a user-specific prefix can effectively thwart such a trial of total forgery unless a serious weakness is found for the hash function.

5   Efficiency Considerations

KCDSA is designed to avoid the evaluation of multiplicative inverses in normal use. It is only needed at the time of key pair generation. For comparison, in DSA a multiplicative inverse mod q needs to be evaluated each time a signature is generated or verified and in GOST each time a signature is verified (see Table 1). Evaluating an inverse mod q would take very little portion in the overall workload of signing/verifying on most general purpose computers. However, it may be quite expensive in a limited computing environment such as smart cards (see [15] for various comments on DSS including debates on the use of inverse). On the other hand, KCDSA needs one more call for a hash function to digest a message of length $|p|$ during both the signature generation and the verification process. This will not cost much in any environment.

We have implemented various signature schemes in the C language with inline assembly [9] and measured their timings on 90 MHz Pentium and 200 MHz Pentium Pro. The result is shown in Table 2[5] As can be expected, KCDSA and DSA show almost the same performance figures, but GOST runs about 63 % ($\approx \frac{160}{256}$) slower than KCDSA/DSA since it uses a 256-bit prime q. For comparison, we also measured the speed of RSA for the same size of modulus.

---

[4] In the present standard the hashed cert. data z is used as part of message (i.e., $z\|m$ is treated as a message to be signed). However, it may be more desirable to separate z from the message to be signed. For example, we may use z itself as a user-specific IV or complete z into one block by zero-padding and use $h(z\|pad)$ as a user-specific IV. These variants will be further discussed in the next revision.

[5] We used SHA-1 for hashing with a very short message in all the signature schemes. Multiplicative inverses were computed using an extended Euclidean algorithm.

Note that signature generation can be substantially speeded up in both RSA and ElGamal-type schemes: We can use the Chinese Remainder Theorem to speed up RSA signature generation and the precomputation technique [7] to speed up signature generation in ElGamal-type schemes. These performance figures are also shown after '/' in Sign columns. The table shows that KCDSA/DSA can sign about 6 to 10 times faster than RSA, while RSA can verify about 12 to 13 times faster than KCDSA/DSA (RSA verification key: $e = 2^{16} + 1$).

Algorithm	Lang.	Pentium/90		Pentium Pro/200	
		Sign	Verify	Sign	Verify
DSA	C	289 / 57.8°	359	95.0 / 18.9	117
($\|q\| = 160$)	D	148 /29.8	182	47.3 /9.7	58.0
	A	64.0 /13.7	79.1	17.5 /3.9	21.7
GOST	C	457 / 87.8	559	147 / 28.0	181
($\|q\| = 256$)	D	236 /44.3	287	73.4 /14.0	92.3
	A	105 /19.1	125	27.2 /5.2	35.3
KCDSA	C	287 / 56.2	359	93.3 / 18.0	116
($\|q\| = 160$)	D	145 /28.0	185	46.4 /9.0	57.4
	A	62.8 /12.4	77.7	17.0 /3.3	20.9
RSA	C	1730 / 502*	25.8	568 / 163	8.6
($e = 2^{16} + 1$)	D	878 / 254	15.8	279 / 83.5	5.3
	A	378 / 114	6.0	103 / 33.1	1.7

Notes :
   C = C only,
   D = C with double digit option (__int64) provided by MSVC,
   A = C with partial inline assembly.
   * used CRT for signature generation.
   ° used a precomputation table of 32 KBytes (6×4 config., see [7]).

Table 2. Speed of various signature schemes for 1024-bit moduli (in msec)

6   Elliptic Curve KCDSA

Much attention has been paid to elliptic curve cryptosystems in recent years, due to their stronger security and higher speed with smaller key size. An elliptic curve variant of KCDSA (EC-KCDSA for short) was not considered during the standardization process. However, we have recently worked on an alternative implementation of KCDSA over elliptic curves and completed a high-level specification of EC-KCDSA. The following brief description on EC-KCDSA is expected to be included in the next revision or as an addendum.

Let E be an elliptic curve over a finite field and $\#(E)$ be the order of E (the total number of points on E). The curve E should be chosen so that $\#(E)$ is divided by a prime q of size L_q bits. Domain parameters consist of the description of the elliptic curve E, the prime q and a point $G = (g_x, g_y)$ over E generating a cyclic group of prime order q.[6] As user parameters, each signer picks at random a private signature key x over $\mathbf{Z}_q^*$ and computes the corresponding public key Y as $Y = \overline{x}G$ over E, where $\overline{x} = x^{-1} \bmod q$. The hashed certification data z and the hash function h are the same as before. Finally, for simplicity we write $h(W)$ for an elliptic curve point $W = (w_x, w_y)$ to denote $h(w_x \| w_y)$. Note here that the two coordinates w_x, w_y are treated as bit strings and thus they are simply concatenated (without conversion from elliptic curve point to integer) and hashed.

The signing and verifying processes of EC-KCDSA are almost the same as those of KCDSA, except for the change of group operations. That is, the underlying group is changed from the multiplicative group of a prime field into the additive group of elliptic curve points. The signature for message m consists of two integers r, s of size $|q|$ generated by

$$r = h(kG) \text{ with } k \in_r \mathbf{Z}_q^*,$$
$$s = x(k - r \oplus h(z\|m)) \bmod q,$$

where the computation of r consists of computing $W = kG$ over E and then hashing the point W.

To verify the signature $\{m\|r\|s\}$, a verifier first performs the required checks on the certificate and the size of signature components as in KCDSA (see steps 1 and 2 in Sect.3.2). The verifier then recovers the point W using the received signature and checks the equality $r = h(W) = h(w_x\|w_y)$. That is, the verifying process can be described in brief by

$$e = r \oplus h(z\|m) \bmod q,$$
$$r = h(sY + eG) \ ?$$

In general, the security of EC-KCDSA will be stronger than KCDSA if both use the same size of q. However, more detailed security and efficiency analyses should be carried out after complete specification on various parameters.

7 Conclusion

We described the proposed digital signature standard for Korean community and discussed its security and efficiency. The presented algorithm is now close to publication as one of Korean Information and Communication Standards and hopefully to be widely used in security products by Korean industries and Government. We hope this publication to stimulate further investigation on its security and development of various useful applications based on it.

---

[6] According to [8], the effective key length can be reduced from $|q|$ to $2|q| - |\#(E)|$ bits in some applications of signature schemes. Therefore, considering wide applications of signature schemes, we strongly recommend that an elliptic curve should be chosen so that $\#(E)$ has as small prime factors as possible. Ideally, $|q| = |\#(E)|$.

Acknowledgments

We are very grateful to Hyo Sun Hwang (Future Systems, Inc.) for his time and effort in implementing various signature schemes for speed comparison.

References

1. R.Anderson and S.Vaudenay, Minding your p's and q's, In *Advances in Cryptology - ASIACRYPT'96*, LNCS 1163, Springer-Verlag, 1996, pp.15-25.
2. D.Bleichenbacher, Generating ElGamal signatures without knowing the secret, In *Advances in Cryptology - EUROCRYPT'96*, LNCS 1070, Springer-Verlag, 1996, pp.10-18.
3. M.Bellare and P.Rogaway, Random oracles are practical: a paradigm for designing efficient protocols, In *Proc. of 1st ACM Conference on Computer and Communications Security*, 1993, pp.62-73.
4. E.F.Brickell, Invited lecture given at Crypto'96, unpublished.
5. T.Elgamal, A public key cryptosystem and a signature scheme based on discrete logarithms, *IEEE Trans. Inform. Theory*, IT-31, 1985, pp.469-472.
6. Knuth, *The Art of Computer Programming*, Vol. 2, Addison-Wesley, 1981.
7. C.H.Lim and P.J.Lee, More flexible exponentiation with precomputation, In *Advances in Cryptology - CRYPTO'94*, LNCS 839, Springer-Verlag, pp.95-107.
8. C.H.Lim and P.J.Lee, A key recovery attack on discrete log based schemes using a prime order subgroup, In *Advances in Cryptology - CRYPTO'97*, LNCS 1294, Springer-Verlag, pp.249-263.
9. C.H.Lim, H.S.Hwang and P.J.Lee, Fast modular reduction with precomputation, *Proc. of 1997 Korea-Japan Joint Workshop on Information Security and Cryptology (JW-ISC'97)*, Oct. 26-28, 1997, pp.65-79.
10. M.Michels, D.Naccache and H.Petersen, GOST 34.10 - A brief overview of Russia's DSA, *Computers and Security*, 15(8), 1996, pp.725-732.
11. A.M.Odlyzko, The future of integer factorization, *CryptoBytes*, 1(2), 1995, pp.5-12.
12. P.C.van Oorschot and M.J.Wiener, On Diffie-Hellman key agreement with short exponents, In *Advances in Cryptology - EUROCRYPT'96*, LNCS 1070, Springer-Verlag, 1996, pp.332-343.
13. D.Pointcheval and J.Stern, Security proofs for signature schemes, In *Advances in Cryptology - EUROCRYPT'96*, LNCS 1070, Springer-Verlag, 1996, pp.387-398.
14. D.Pointcheval and S.Vaudenay, On provable security for digital signature algorithms, a manuscript, 1996, available from $http://www.dmi.ens.fr/~pointche/$.
15. R.L.Rivest / M.E.Hellman / J.C.Anderson, Responses to NIST's proposal, *Comm. ACM*, 35(7), 1992, pp.41-52.
16. R.L.Rivest, A.Shamir and L.Adleman, A method for obtaining digital signatures and public key cryptosystems, *Commun. ACM*, 21(2), 1978, pp.120-126.
17. J.Stern, The validation of cryptographic algorithms, In *Advances in Cryptology - ASIACRYPT'96*, LNCS 1163, Springer-Verlag, 1996, pp.301-310.
18. S.Vaudenay, Hidden collisions on DSS, In *Advances in Cryptology - CRYPTO'96*, LNCS 1109, Springer-Verlag, 1996, pp.83-88.
19. NIST, Digital signature standard, *FIPS PUB 186*, 1994.

A   Domain Parameter Generation for KCDSA

During the KCDSA initialization stage, a trusted authority in each domain have to generate and publish p, q, g such that

- p is a prime of specified length such that a prime q of specified length divides $p - 1$ and that all prime factors of $(p - 1)/2q$ are greater than q.
- g is a generator of a subgroup of $\mathbf{Z}_p^*$ of order q, i.e., g is an element of $\mathbf{Z}_p$ such that $g^q = 1 \bmod p$ and $g \neq 1$. Such a g can be generated by testing $g^{(p-1)/q} = 1 \bmod q$ with random $1 < g < p$.

As an example, we describe a method for generating primes p, q such that $(p-1)/2q$ is also prime. Let $PRG(s, n)$ denote a pseudorandom number generator on input s generating an n-bit random number, defined by:

$$v_i = h(s + i \bmod q) \text{ for } i = 0, 1, \cdots, k - 1,$$
$$v_k = h(s + k \bmod q) \bmod 2^r,$$
$$PRG(s, n) = v_k \parallel v_{k-1} \parallel \cdots v_1 \parallel v_0,$$

where $k = \frac{n}{L_q}$ and $r = n \bmod L_q$. The procedure for generating p, q (of size L_p, L_q, respectively) and g is as follows (see also Figure 1):

1. choose an arbitrary integer s of at least L_q bits.
2. initialize five counters: $tCount = rCount = 1$, $pCount = qCount = gCount = 0$.
3. form $Seed$ for PRG as:

$$w_2 = 0x00 \parallel i \parallel j \parallel tCount,$$
$$w_1 = rCount \parallel pCount,$$
$$w_0 = qCount \parallel gCount \parallel 0x00,$$
$$Seed = s \parallel w_2 \parallel w_1 \parallel w_0,$$

where i and j are 8 bit numbers such that $L_p = 512 + 256i$ and $L_q = 128 + 32j$, $tCount$ and $gCount$ are 8 bits long, and $pCount$, $qCount$ and $rCount$ are 16 bits long. It is assumed that $Seed$ is automatically updated whenever any counter is changed.
4. generate a random number r of length $L_p - L_q - 1$ bits as follows:

$$u = PRG(Seed, \ L_p - L_q - 1),$$
$$r = 2^{L_p - L_q - 2} \vee u \vee 1,$$

where $\vee$ denotes bitwise-or.
5. test r for primality (e.g., using the Miller-Rabin probabilistic primality test [6, page 379]). If r is prime, go to step 8.
6. increment $rCount$ by 1.
7. If $rCount < 2048$, go to step 4. Otherwise, go to step 1.

8. set $pCount = 1$ and $qCount = 1$.
9. generate a random number q of length L_q bits using the updated *Seed* as follows:

$$u = PRG(Seed, L_q),$$
$$q = 2^{L_q-1} \vee u \vee 1.$$

10. compute $p = 2qr + 1$. If $|p| < L_p$, go to step 12.
11. test q for primality. If q is prime, go to step 14.
12. increment $qCount$ by 1.
13. If $qCount < 1024$, go to step 9. Otherwise, go to step 15.
14. test p for primality. If p is prime, go to step 19.
15. increment $pCount$ by 1 and set $qCount = 1$.
16. If $pCount < 4096$, go to step 9.
17. increment $tCount$ by 1.
18. If $tCount < 256$, go to step 3. Otherwise, go to step 1.
19. set $gCount = 1$.
20. generate a random number u of length L_p bits using the updated *Seed* as follows:

$$u = PRG(Seed, L_p).$$

21. compute $g = u^{(p-1)/q} \bmod p$. If $g \neq 1$, go to step 24.
22. increment $gCount$ by 1.
23. If $gCount < 256$, go to step 20. Otherwise, go to step 17.[7]
24. terminate with output p, q, g and *Seed*.

The *Seed* output can serve as a certificate for proper generation of the parameters p, q and g. Anyone can check that p, q and g are generated as specified, since *Seed* contains all necessary information to verify their proper generation. For example, the following parameters ($|p| = 1024, |q| = 160$) were generated using the described algorithm, where we the initial user input s was taken as the first 160 bits of the fractional part of $\pi = 3.14159\cdots$. ¿From the seed, we can see that $r = (p-1)/2q$ was found by testing 991 random numbers ($rCount = 0x3df = 991$) and p was found by testing 1192 primes of q ($pCount = 0x77c = 1192$) and so on. It is easy to verify that these parameters are generated according to the above procedure.

```
Seed = 243f6a88 85a308D3 13198a2e 03707344 a4093822
       00020101 03df077c 00d10100
   p = a2951279 6e6cf682 fd9e3348 24859dfd 93299a22 7d9d6c97 226B9595
       1725c3B5 3098ceaa 3e6a0241 d0c30586 61769311 9db2e9bc 2f9cad43
       9f17fe3B 8a54f711 820421a0 394218e8 3186641d 00373299 08ab8D2f
       97ffb1c7 5afaaba3 5e356ae8 7f83d2f8 d79d031c d814318f e7865810
       16a3c871 a159056c 70722a62 cb89694f
```

---

[7] The probability of $gCount$ exceeding 255 is negligible ($gCount = 1$ for almost all cases). For completeness, we simply make the control to go back to step 3 in such an exceptional case (through steps 17, 18, 3).

```
q = ada5ff8f 174cab84 0c846634 dede6e81 5ac8f6ef

g = 1b2f2d3b a6551ffd a74ca533 011f1a92 8277d572 67297496 78a42bda
    5ba6c181 9cf283ee 14a3fb44 dacbe42b b9720d2d 7137c81e 69cfc7cf
    20a41bb1 e117fa7d 9b8d0cb0 73a91e51 15c08db8 60be3633 67a08ac2
    b59137c2 0ccf54b9 0dbc2c8c 90958555 d76c0020 2798282a 23cafc54
    7c7e7820 cf979902 2d3cde88 52d13753
```

Conditions:
$|p| = 512 + 256i$ (i=0, 1, ..., 6)
$|q| = 128 + 32j$ (j=0, 1, ..., 4)
$r = (p-1)/2q$: prime

Seed = s (user input) || 0x00 || i || j || tCount || rCount || pCount || qCount || gCount || 0x00
    (tCount, gCount : 8 bits,   pCount, qCount, rCount : 16 bits)

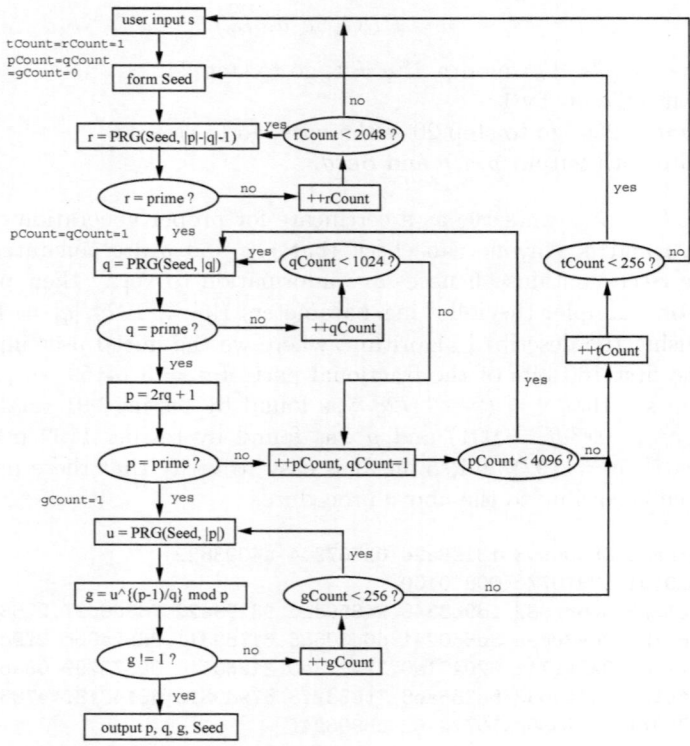

Fig. 1. Flow chart for generation of p, q, g

Cryptanalysis of the Original McEliece Cryptosystem

Anne Canteaut and Nicolas Sendrier

INRIA - projet CODES
BP 105
78153 Le Chesnay, France

Abstract. The class of public-key cryptosystems based on error-correcting codes is one of the few alternatives to the common algorithms based on number theory. We here present an attack against these systems which actually consists of a new probabilistic algorithm for finding minimum-weight words in any large linear code. This new attack notably points out that McEliece cipher with its original parameters does not provide a sufficient security level.

1 Introduction

Since the concept of public-key cryptography appeared in 1977, searching for secure public-key cryptosystems and identification schemes has been one of the most active areas in the field of cryptology. Many public-key ciphers emerged just after the invention of RSA and their underlying problems were as varied as computing a discrete logarithm, solving a knapsack problem, inverting some polynomial equations over a finite field.... But the development of some cryptanalysis methods have finally made most of them insecure. Twenty years after the fundamental paper of Diffie and Hellman, public-key cryptography has therefore become dangerously dependent on only two problems: integer factoring and discrete logarithm. However the class of public-key ciphers and identification schemes based on error-correcting codes still resists cryptanalysis. It relies on the hardness of decoding or equivalently of finding a minimum-weight codeword in a large linear code with no visible structure. The most famous of these systems are McEliece and Niederreiter ciphers [McE78,Nie86] — which are equivalent from the security point of view — and the identification schemes proposed by Stern [Ste89] and Véron [Vér95]. They are at the moment one of the few alternatives to the common public-key algorithms based on number theory. Studying their security seems therefore essential in order to anticipate a possible important progress in factoring methods for example. Moreover these public-key ciphers are particularly interesting since they run much faster than any algorithm relying on number theory.

In this paper we present an attack on these cryptosystems which consists of a new probabilistic algorithm for finding minimum-weight codewords in any linear code. We first briefly present in Section 2 some public-key cryptosystems based

K. Ohta and D. Pei (Eds.): ASIACRYPT'98, LNCS 1514, pp. 187–199, 2000.
© Springer-Verlag Berlin Heidelberg 2000

on error-correcting codes. Section 3 then describes a new algorithm for finding minimum-weight words in any linear code. Using Markov chain theory we show in Section 4 how to compute the number of elementary operations it requires. In Section 5 we finally use these results to evaluate the security of these public-key cryptosystems. We notably prove that the parameters which were originally proposed by McEliece for his cryptosystem make it insecure.

2   Some Cryptosystems Based on Error-Correcting Codes

The class of public-key cryptosystems based on the hardness of decoding or of finding a minimum-weight word in a large code contains both McEliece and Niederreiter ciphers and some zero-knowledge identification schemes like the one proposed by Stern.

2.1   McEliece and Niederreiter Public-Key Ciphers

McEliece cryptosystem uses as a secret key a linear binary code chosen in a family Γ of $[n, k]$-linear codes with error-correcting capability t for which an efficient decoding algorithm is known. In his original paper [McE78], McEliece proposed to choose this secret code amongst the irreducible binary Goppa codes of length 1024, dimension 524 and minimum distance 101.

- **private key:** it is composed of an $[n, k]$-linear binary code $\mathcal{C}$ chosen in the family Γ, a random $k \times k$ binary invertible matrix S and a random $n \times n$ permutation matrix P.
- **public key:** it consists of the $k \times n$ matrix G' defined by $G' = SGP$ where G is a generator matrix of the secret code $\mathcal{C}$.
- **encryption:** the ciphertext corresponding to the k-bit message m is $x = mG' + e$, where e is a random n-bit error-vector of weight t.
- **decryption:** the decryption procedure consists in computing $xP^{-1} = mSG + eP^{-1}$ and using a fast decoding algorithm for $\mathcal{C}$ to recover mS. The message is then given by $m = (mS)S^{-1}$.

By definition the public key is therefore a generator matrix for an other linear code $\mathcal{C}'$ which is equivalent to $\mathcal{C}$. A ciphertext in McEliece cryptosystem then corresponds to a word of the public code $\mathcal{C}'$ with t corrupted positions.

Niederreiter proposed a dual version of this system [Nie86] where the public-key is a parity-check matrix H' of a code $\mathcal{C}'$ equivalent to the secret code. A plaintext m is here an n-bit vector of weight t and the associated ciphertext x corresponds to the syndrome of m relatively to the public code, $x = mH'^t$.

McEliece and Niederreiter cryptosystems are actually equivalent from the security point of view when set up for corresponding choices of parameters [LDW94]. But for given parameters Niederreiter cipher presents many advantages. First of all it allows a public key in systematic form at no cost for security whereas this would reveal a part of the plaintext in McEliece system. The public key in Niederreiter system is then $(n - k)/n$ times smaller than in McEliece version. The systematic form of the public matrix H' and the low-weight of vector m significantly reduce the computational cost involved in the encryption in Niederreiter system. For [1024,524,101]-binary codes its transmission rate, *i.e.* the number of information symbols divided by the number of transmitted symbols, is smaller that in McEliece system. Another disadvantage of McEliece system is that it is easy to recover the plaintext if it has been encrypted twice with the same public-key. On the contrary Niederreiter cipher is deterministic since encrypting a given plaintext always leads to the same ciphertext.

Table 1 sums up the characteristics of these systems when they both use [1024,524,101]-binary codes. It then shows that it is preferable to use the version proposed by Niederreiter.

	McEliece [1024,524,101] binary code	Niederreiter [1024,524,101] binary code	RSA 1024-bit modulus public exponent = 17
public-key size	67,072 bytes	32,750 bytes	256 bytes
number of information bits transmitted per encryption	512	276	1024
transmission rate	51.17 %	56.81 %	100 %
number of binary operations performed by the encryption per information bit	514	50	2,402
number of binary operations performed by the decryption per information bit	5,140	7,863	738,112

Table 1. Performance of McEliece, Niederreiter and RSA public-key ciphers

We give for information the values corresponding to the RSA system with a 1024-bit modulus $n = pq$ when the public exponent is 17 — we here suppose that RSA encryption and decryption uses Karatsuba's method for large integer multiplication. These results point out that these public-key systems run much faster than RSA (about 50 times faster for encryption and 100 times faster for decryption). Their main disadvantages are the size of the public key and the lack of related signature scheme.

Cryptanalysis Methods There are mainly two guidelines to cryptanalyze McEliece cryptosystem :

- recover the original structure of the secret code from a generator (or parity-check) matrix of an equivalent code.
- decode the public code which has no visible structure.

The first class of attacks imposes some conditions on the family of secret codes Γ. For given length, dimension and minimal distance the family Γ must be large enough to avoid any enumeration. This aims at protecting the system from the attack which consists in enumerating all the elements of Γ until a code equivalent to the public code is found. This can be performed with an algorithm due to Sendrier [Sen96] which is able to determine from two generator matrices whether they correspond to equivalent codes and then to recover the permutation. A second condition is that a generator or parity-check matrix of a permutation equivalent code gives no information about the structure of the secret code, that means that the fast decoding algorithm requires some parameters of the secret code besides a generator matrix G'. This dismisses many families of codes like generalized Reed-Solomon codes [SS92] or concatenated codes [Sen94,Sen95].

But the family of irreducible Goppa codes is well-suited to such systems insofar as at present there exists no algorithm which is able to compute the characteristic parameters of a Goppa code from one of its permuted generator matrix. This class can even be extended to all [1024,524,101]-binary Goppa codes defined by a monic square-free polynomial of degree 50 in $GF(1024)[X]$ which has no root in $GF(1024)$. The cardinality of Γ is then $2^{498.5}$. In the case where the used family of codes satisfies the above properties, the equivalent code $\mathcal{C}'$ defined by the public key presents no visible structure; recovering a plaintext from the corresponding ciphertext then comes down to decoding any linear code.

2.2 Stern's Public-Key Identification Scheme

Stern presented at Crypto'93 [Ste93] a public-key identification scheme which relies on the hardness of finding a low-weight codeword of given syndrome. This scheme uses an $[n, k]$-random linear code over $GF(2)$. All users share a fixed parity-check matrix H for this code and an integer w slightly below the expected value for the minimal distance of a random linear code. Each user receives a secret key s which is an n-bit vector of weight w. His public key is then the syndrome sH^t. Any user can identify himself to another one by proving he knows s without revealing it thanks to an interactive zero-knowledge protocol. The minimal parameters proposed by Stern are $n = 512$, $k = 256$ and $w = 56$. Véron [Vér95] also proposed a dual version of this scheme similar to McEliece's original approach: it uses a generator matrix of the code instead of a parity-check matrix. He then suggested a new choice for the parameters in order to reduce the number of transmitted bits: $n = 512$, $k = 120$ and $w = 114$.

3   A new Algorithm for Finding Low-weight Codewords

Let $\mathcal{C}$ be a linear binary code of length n, dimension k and minimum distance d about which nothing is known but a generator matrix. We now develop an algorithm for finding a word of weight w in $\mathcal{C}$ where w is closed to d. This algorithm can also be used for decoding up to the correction capability $t = \lfloor \frac{d-1}{2} \rfloor$. If a message x is composed of a codeword corrupted by an error-vector e of weight

$w \leq t$, e can be recovered with this algorithm since it is the only minimum-weight word in the linear code $\mathcal{C} \oplus x$. Decoding an $[n, k]$-linear code then comes down to finding the minimum-weight codeword in an $[n, k+1]$-code.

Let $N = \{1, \cdots, n\}$ be the set of all coordinates. For any subset I of N, $G = (V, W)_I$ denotes the decomposition of matrix G onto I, that means $V = (G_i)_{i \in I}$ and $W = (G_j)_{j \in N \setminus I}$, where G_i is the ith column of matrix G. The restriction of an n-bit vector x to the coordinate subset I is denoted by $x_{|I} = (x_i)_{i \in I}$. As usual wt(x) is the Hamming weight of the binary word x.

Definition 1. *Let I be a k-element subset of N. I is an information set for the code $\mathcal{C}$ if and only if $G = (Id_k, Z)_I$ is a systematic generator matrix for $\mathcal{C}$.*

Our algorithm uses a probabilistic heuristic proposed by Stern [Ste89] which generalizes the well-known information set decoding method. But instead of exploring a set of randomly selected systematic generator matrices by performing at each iteration a Gaussian elimination on an $(n \times k)$-matrix as most algorithms do [LB88,Leo88], we choose at each step the new information set by modifying only one element of the previous one. This procedure is similar to the one used in the simplex method and it was first introduced in [Omu72]. If I is an information set and $G = (Id_k, Z)_I$ the corresponding systematic generator matrix, $I' = (I \setminus \{\lambda\}) \cup \{\mu\}$ is still an information set for the code if and only if the coefficient $Z_{\lambda, \mu}$ equals 1. In this case, the systematic generator matrix associated with I' is obtained from the previous one by a simple pivoting procedure which only requires $k(n - k)/2$ binary operations. Using this iterative method then leads to the following algorithm:

Initialization:
Randomly choose an information set I and apply a Gaussian elimination in order to obtain a systematic generator matrix $(Id_k, Z)_I$.

Until a codeword of weight w will be found:

1. Randomly split I in two subsets I_1 and I_2 where $|I_1| = \lfloor k/2 \rfloor$ and $|I_2| = \lceil k/2 \rceil$. The rows of Z are then split in two parts Z_1 and Z_2. Randomly select a σ-element subset L of the redundant set $J = N \setminus I$.

2. For each linear combination Λ_1 (resp. Λ_2) of p rows of matrix Z_1 (resp. Z_2), compute $\Lambda_{1|L}$ (resp. $\Lambda_{2|L}$) and store all these values in a hash table with 2^σ entries.

3. Using the hash table consider all pairs of linear combinations (Λ_1, Λ_2) such that $\Lambda_{1|L} = \Lambda_{2|L}$ and check whether wt$((\Lambda_1 + \Lambda_2)_{|J \setminus L}) = w - 2p$.

4. Randomly choose $\lambda \in I$ and $\mu \in J$ such that $Z_{\lambda, \mu} = 1$. Replace I with $(I \setminus \{\lambda\}) \cup \{\mu\}$ by updating matrix Z by a pivoting operation.

A codeword c of weight w is then exhibited when the selections I, I_1 and L satisfy

$$\text{wt}(c_{|I_1}) = \text{wt}(c_{|I_2}) = p \text{ and } \text{wt}(c_{|L}) = 0 \tag{1}$$

Parameters p and σ have to be chosen in order to minimize the running-time of the algorithm.

4   Theoretical Running-Time

We give here an explicit and computable expression for the work factor of this algorithm, *i.e.* the average number of elementary operations it requires. This analysis is essential in particular for finding the values of parameters p and σ which minimize the running-time of the algorithm.

4.1   Modelization of the Algorithm by a Markov Chain

The average number of iterations performed by the algorithm is not the same as the one performed by the initial Stern's algorithm since the successive informa-tion sets are not independent anymore. Hence the algorithm must be modelized by a discrete-time stochastic process.

Let c be the codeword of weight w to recover and $\text{supp}(c)$ its support. Let I be the information set and I_1, I_2 and L the other selections corresponding to the i-th iteration. The i-th iteration can then be represented by a random variable X_i which corresponds to the number of non-zero bits of c in I. This random variable then takes its values in the set $\{1, \ldots, w\}$. But if this number equals $2p$ we have to distinguish two cases depending of whether condition (1) is satisfied or not. The state space of the stochastic process $\{X_i\}_{i \in \mathbf{N}}$ is therefore $\mathcal{E} = \{1, \ldots, 2p-1\} \cup \{(2p)_S, (2p)_F\} \cup \{2p+1, \ldots, w\}$ where

$$X_i = u \quad \text{iff } |I \cap \text{supp}(c)| = u, \; \forall u \in \{1, \ldots, 2p-1\} \cup \{2p+1, \ldots, w\}$$
$$X_i = (2p)_F \text{ iff } |I \cap \text{supp}(c)| = 2p \text{ and } (|I_1 \cap \text{supp}(c)| \neq p \text{ or } |L \cap \text{supp}(c)| \neq 0)$$
$$X_i = (2p)_S \text{ iff } |I_1 \cap \text{supp}(c)| = |I_2 \cap \text{supp}(c)| = p \text{ and } |L \cap \text{supp}(c)| = 0$$

The success space is then $\mathcal{S} = \{(2p)_S\}$ and the failure space is $\mathcal{F} = \mathcal{E} \setminus \{(2p)_S\}$.

Definition 2. *A stochastic process $\{X_i\}_{i \in \mathbf{N}}$ is a Markov chain if the probabi-lity that it enters a certain state only depends on the last state it occupied. A Markov chain $\{X_i\}_{i \in \mathbf{N}}$ is homogeneous if for all states u and v, the conditional probability $Pr[X_i = v/X_{i-1} = u]$ does not depend on i.*

Proposition 1. *The stochastic process $\{X_i\}_{i \in \mathbf{N}}$ associated with the algorithm is an homogeneous Markov chain.*

Proof. The selections I, I_1, I_2 and L corresponding to the i-th iteration only depend on the previous information window since I_1, I_2 and L are randomly chosen. We then have for all i and for all $(u_0, u_1, \cdots, u_i) \in \mathcal{E}$,

$$Pr[X_i = u_i/X_{i-1} = u_{i-1}, X_{i-2} = u_{i-2}, \cdots X_0 = u_0] = Pr[X_i = u_i/X_{i-1} = u_{i-1}]$$

Furthermore this probability does not depend on the iteration. Hence there exists a matrix P such that :

$$\forall i \in \mathbf{N}, \ \forall (u,v) \in \mathcal{E}^2, \ \ Pr[X_i = v/X_{i-1} = u] = P_{u,v}$$

The Markov chain $\{X_i\}_{i \in \mathbf{N}}$ is therefore completely determined by its initial probability vector $\pi_0 = (Pr[X_0 = u])_{u \in \mathcal{E}}$ and its transition matrix P. Both of these quantities can be easily determined as two successive information sets differ from only one element.

Proposition 2. *The transition matrix P of the homogeneous Markov chain associated with the algorithm is given by:*

$$P_{u,u} = \frac{k-u}{k} \times \frac{n-k-(w-u)}{n-k} + \frac{u}{k} \times \frac{w-u}{n-k} \ \ \text{for all } u \notin \{(2p)_S, (2p)_F\}$$

$$P_{u,u-1} = \frac{u}{k} \times \frac{n-k-(w-u)}{n-k} \ \ \text{for all } u \neq 2p+1$$

$$P_{u,u+1} = \frac{k-u}{k} \times \frac{w-u}{n-k} \ \ \text{for all } u \neq 2p-1$$

$$P_{u,v} = 0 \ \text{for all } v \notin \{u-1, u, u+1\}$$

$$P_{(2p)_F,(2p)_F} = (1-\beta)\left[\frac{k-2p}{k} \times \frac{n-k-(w-2p)}{n-k} + \frac{2p}{k} \times \frac{w-2p}{n-k}\right]$$

$$P_{2p+1,(2p)_F} = (1-\beta)\left[\frac{2p+1}{k} \times \frac{n-k-(w-(2p+1))}{n-k}\right]$$

$$P_{2p-1,(2p)_F} = (1-\beta)\left[\frac{k-(2p-1)}{k} \times \frac{w-(2p-1)}{n-k}\right]$$

$$P_{2p+1,(2p)_S} = \beta\left[\frac{2p+1}{k} \times \frac{n-k-(w-(2p+1))}{n-k}\right]$$

$$P_{2p-1,(2p)_S} = \beta\left[\frac{k-(2p-1)}{k} \times \frac{w-(2p-1)}{n-k}\right]$$

$$P_{(2p)_F,(2p)_S} = \beta\left[\frac{k-2p}{k} \times \frac{n-k-(w-2p)}{n-k} + \frac{2p}{k} \times \frac{w-2p}{n-k}\right]$$

$$P_{(2p)_S,(2p)_S} = 1 \ \ \text{and} \ \ P_{(2p)_S,u} = 0 \ \text{for all } u \neq (2p)_S$$

$$\text{where } \beta = Pr[X_i = (2p)_S \, / \, |I \cap supp(e)| = 2p] = \frac{\binom{2p}{p}\binom{k-2p}{k/2-p}}{\binom{k}{k/2}} \frac{\binom{n-k-w+2p}{\sigma}}{\binom{n-k}{\sigma}}$$

The initial probability vector π_0 is

$$\pi_0(u) = \frac{\binom{w}{u}\binom{n-w}{k-u}}{\binom{n}{k}} \ \text{if } u \notin \{(2p)_F, (2p)_S\}$$

$$\pi_0((2p)_F) = \frac{(1-\beta)\binom{w}{2p}\binom{n-w}{k-2p}}{\binom{n}{k}}$$

$$\pi_0((2p)_S) = \frac{\beta\binom{w}{2p}\binom{n-w}{k-2p}}{\binom{n}{k}}$$

The only persistent space of this Markov chain, *i.e.* a maximal state subset which cannot be left once it is entered, exactly corresponds to the success space $\mathcal{S}$. Since this subset contains only one state which is an absorbing state, *i.e.* a state which once entered is never left, this chain is by definition an absorbing chain. A basic property of absorbing Markov chains with a finite state space is that, no matter where the process starts, the probability that the process is in an absorbing state after n steps tends to 1 as n tends to infinity. We then deduce that our algorithm converges.

Expected Number of Iterations The absorbing chain property also enables us to compute the average number of iterations performed by the algorithm.

Proposition 3. [KS60] *If $\{X_i\}_{i\in\mathbf{N}}$ is a finite absorbing Markov chain with transition matrix P, and Q is the sub-stochastic matrix corresponding to transitions among the transient states — the non-persistent states —, i.e. $Q = (P_{u,v})_{u,v\in\mathcal{F}}$ then $(Id - Q)$ has an inverse R called the fundamental matrix of the chain and*

$$R = \sum_{m=0}^{\infty} Q^m = (Id - Q)^{-1}.$$

The average number of iterations performed by the algorithm can then be deduced from this fundamental matrix.

Theorem 1. *The expectation of the number of iterations N required until $\{X_i\}_{i\in\mathbf{N}}$ reaches the success state $(2p)_S$ is given by:*

$$E(N) = \sum_{u\in\mathcal{F}} \pi_0(u) \sum_{v\in\mathcal{F}} R_{u,v}$$

where R is the corresponding fundamental matrix.

Proof.

$$E(N) = \sum_{n=0}^{\infty} n Pr[X_n \in \mathcal{S} \text{ and } X_{n-1} \in \mathcal{F}]$$

$$= \sum_{n=0}^{\infty} \sum_{m=0}^{n-1} Pr[X_n \in \mathcal{S} \text{ and } X_{n-1} \in \mathcal{F}]$$

Applying Fubini's theorem, we get

$$E(N) = \sum_{m=0}^{\infty} \sum_{n=m+1}^{\infty} Pr[X_n \in \mathcal{S} \text{ and } X_{n-1} \in \mathcal{F}]$$

$$= \sum_{m=0}^{\infty} Pr[X_m \in \mathcal{F}]$$

$$= \sum_{m=0}^{\infty} \sum_{u \in \mathcal{F}} \sum_{v \in \mathcal{F}} Pr[X_m = v \ / \ X_0 = u]$$

$$= \sum_{u \in \mathcal{F}} \pi_0(u) \sum_{v \in \mathcal{F}} \sum_{m=0}^{\infty} (Q^m)_{u,v} = \sum_{u \in \mathcal{F}} \pi_0(u) \sum_{v \in \mathcal{F}} R_{u,v}$$

Variance of the Number of Iterations The fundamental matrix also gives the variance of the number of iterations, which estimates the deviation from the average work factor of the effective computational time required by the algorithm.

Theorem 2. *The variance of the number of iterations N required until $\{X_i\}_{i \in \mathbf{N}}$ reaches the success state is given by:*

$$V(N) = \sum_{u \in \mathcal{F}} \pi_0(u) \sum_{v \in \mathcal{F}} (2R_{u,v} - \delta_{u,v}) E_v(N) \ - \left(\sum_{u \in \mathcal{F}} \pi_0(u) E_u(N) \right)^2$$

where $\delta_{i,j}$ is the Kronecker symbol and $E_u(N)$ is the average number of iterations performed by the process when it starts in state u, i.e.

$$E_u(N) = \sum_{v \in \mathcal{F}} R_{u,v}$$

Distribution of the Number of Iterations Besides the average number of iterations we often want to estimate the probability that the algorithm will succeed after a fixed number of iterations. But the approximation given by Tchebychev's inequality is usually very rough. A much more precise evaluation is obtained by raising the transition matrix of the Markov chain to the corresponding power. We actually have:

Proposition 4. *Let P be the transition matrix of the Markov chain associated with the algorithm. If $P = L^{-1} \Lambda L$ where Λ is a diagonal matrix, then the probability that the algorithm will succeed after N iterations is given by*

$$\sum_{u \in \mathcal{E}} \pi_0(u) \ \left(L^{-1} \Lambda^N L \right)_{u,(2p)_S}$$

4.2 Average Number of Operations by Iteration

We now give an explicit expression of the average number of operations performed at each iteration.

1. There are exactly $\binom{k/2}{p}$ linear combinations of p rows of matrix Z_1 (resp. Z_2); computing each of them on a σ-bit selection and putting it in the hash table requires $p\sigma$ binary additions.

2. The average number of pairs (Λ_1, Λ_2) such that $(\Lambda_1 + \Lambda_2)_{|L} = 0$ is equal to $\frac{\binom{k/2}{p}^2}{2^\sigma}$. For each of them we perform $2p - 1$ additions of $(n - k - \sigma)$-bit words for computing $(\Lambda_1 + \Lambda_2)_{|J \setminus L}$ and a weight-checking.
3. We need $K(p\binom{k/2}{p} + 2^\sigma)$ more operations to perform the dynamic memory allocation where K is the size of a computer word (K=32 or 64).
4. The average work factor involved in the pivoting procedure for updating matrix Z is $\frac{1}{2}k(n - k)$.

Hence the average number of elementary operations performed at each iteration is:

$$\Omega_{p,\sigma} = 2p\sigma\binom{k/2}{p} + 2p(n - k - \sigma)\frac{\binom{k/2}{p}^2}{2^\sigma} + K\left(p\binom{k/2}{p} + 2^\sigma\right) + \frac{k(n - k)}{2} \quad (2)$$

Proposition 5. *Suppose that the number of codewords of weight w is $\mathcal{A}_w$. The overall work factor required by the algorithm is:*

$$W_{p,\sigma} = \frac{\Omega_{p,\sigma}E(N)}{\mathcal{A}_w} \quad (3)$$

where $E(N)$ is given by Theorem 1 and $\Omega_{p,\sigma}$ by Equation (2).

Since each term in the previous expression can be explicitly computed, we are now able to determine the parameters p and σ which minimize the work factor required by the algorithm when the size of the code and the weight w of the searched codeword are given. Such a theoretical expression of the work factor is commonly used to assess the efficiency of an algorithm and to decide whether a given problem is computationally feasible. It is also applied to the automatic optimization of the parameters. But the sharpest optimization can only be performed by replacing in Equation (3) the theoretical value of $\Omega_{p,\sigma}$ by the effective average CPU time of an iteration.

5   Cryptanalysis of McEliece Cryptosystem

5.1   Work Factor Versus Probability of Success

Table 2 gives the optimal parameters and the number of binary operations involved in an attack of the previous cryptosystems.

Cryptanalyzing McEliece cipher with its original parameters then requires $2^{64.2}$ binary operations [CC98]. This new attack is certainly still infeasible but it runs 128 times faster than Lee-Brickell's attack [LB88]. As a comparison the cryptanalysis of Stern's identification scheme using van Tilburg's algorithm has an average number of iterations of $2^{57.0}$, and an estimated work factor of $2^{72.9}$ [vT94]. An obvious method for speeding up the cryptanalysis consists in distributing the algorithm: using a network of 1000 computers we only need $2^{54.2}$ operations for breaking McEliece cipher.

cryptosystem	McEliece	Stern	Véron
code	[1024,524]	[512,256]	[512,120]
w	50	56	114
optimal parameters	$p = 2, \sigma = 18$	$p = 2, \sigma = 15$	$p = 2, \sigma = 13$
average number of iterations	$9.85\ 10^{11}$	$2.16\ 10^{14}$	$1.74\ 10^{12}$
standard deviation of the number of iterations	$9.85\ 10^{11}$	$2.16\ 10^{14}$	$1.74\ 10^{12}$
work factor	$2^{64.2}$	$2^{69.9}$	$2^{61.2}$

Table 2. Work factor required for cryptanalyzing some public-key systems based on error-correcting codes

But the standard deviation of the number of iterations involved in cryptanalyzing all these systems roughly equals its average. This spread implies that an infeasible average work factor is not sufficient to guarantee that these cryptosystems are secure: it is necessary to estimate the probability that our algorithm will be successful after a feasible number of iterations. This can be done by raising the transition matrix of the associated Markov chain to the corresponding power as described in Proposition 4. We then obtain that the work factor required for decoding a [1024,524,101]-binary code up to its error-correcting capability with probability 0.5 only represents 69 % of the average work factor. And if the work factor is limited to 2^{51}, *i.e.* to 10^8 iterations, the probability that a message in McEliece cipher will be decrypt is 10^{-4}. Since 1000 iterations of the optimized algorithm are performed in 10 minutes on a workstation DEC alpha at 433 MHz, decrypting one message out of 10,000 requires 2 months and 14 days with 10 such computers (see Figure 1). The relatively high proportion of decrypted messages in a reasonable time implies that McEliece system with its original parameters is not secure as long as the enemy has a few ten fast workstations. A similar study shows that the parameters proposed in Stern's identification scheme make it much more secure. An eleven-month computation time on 10 DEC alpha enables us to recover the secret key of a user in only one case out of 100,000. This only implies that the lifetime of the keys must be less than one year. The parameters proposed by Véron significantly reduce the number of transmitted bits in each identification procedure but they impose a much shorter lifetime of the keys since 56 days on 10 of our workstations are sufficient to find the secret key of a user with a probability greater than 1/3500.

5.2   Partial Attacks on McEliece and Niederreiter Cryptosystems

McEliece and Niederreiter cryptosystems otherwise present some weaknesses since the knowledge of a small number of bits of the plaintext is sufficient to recover it in its entirety. The knowledge of some plaintext bits in McEliece cipher allows to accordingly reduce the dimension of the code we consider in the

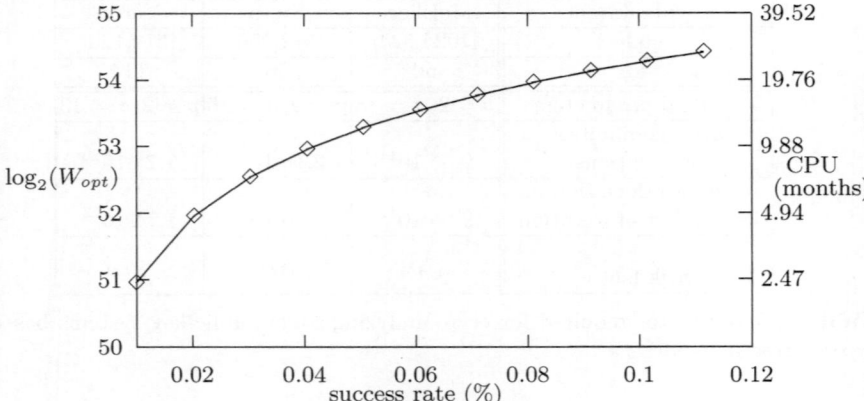

Fig. 1. Computational effort required for cryptanalyzing McEliece cryptosystem as a function of the proportion of messages successfully decrypted: the CPU time is given for 10 workstations DEC alpha at 433 MHz in parallel.

attack. If we assume that 2^{50} binary operations is a feasible work factor, it is then possible to decode up to distance 50 a [1024,404]-binary code with our algorithm. This means that the knowledge of 120 plaintext bits (*i.e.* 23 % of the plaintext) is sufficient to recover the whole plaintext in a reasonable time.

A similar attack on Niederreiter cryptosystem consists in assuming that some error positions are known by the enemy. The problem is then to determine the distance up to which a [1024,524]-binary code can be decoded. If the work factor is limited to 2^{50} binary operations, we obtain that the knowledge of 15 error positions out of the 50 introduced in McEliece and Niederreiter systems enables us to recover the plaintext. This small proportion notably implies that generating the error-vector with a noisy channel is insecure if this provides some errors whose weight is too small.

6   Conclusion

We have then proved that the security of McEliece cipher is insufficient when its original parameters are used. But this public-key system is still a valid alternative to RSA once its parameters are modified. For example if the secret key is chosen amongst the Goppa codes of length 2048, dimension 1608 and minimum distance 81, the average work factor of our attack is roughly 2^{100}. Even with these parameters the performance of McEliece cipher remains much better than the one of RSA: the costs of encryption and decryption per information bit with Niederreiter's version are respectively 45 times and 70 times lower than with RSA-1024. But the huge size of the public-key (more than 88000 bytes in this case) may often dissuade from using this cipher.

References

CC98.   A. Canteaut and F. Chabaud. A new algorithm for finding minimum-weight words in a linear code: application to McEliece's cryptosystem and to narrow-sense BCH codes of length 511. *IEEE Transactions on Information Theory*, IT-44(1):367–378, 1998.

KS60.   J.G. Kemeny and J.L. Snell. *Finite Markov chains*. Springer-Verlag, 1960.

LB88.   P.J. Lee and E.F. Brickell. An observation on the security of McEliece's public-key cryptosystem. In C.G. Günter, editor, *Advances in Cryptology - EUROCRYPT'88*, number 330 in Lecture Notes in Computer Science, pages 275–280. Springer-Verlag, 1988.

LDW94.   Y.X. Li, R.H. Deng, and X.M. Wang. On the equivalence of McEliece's and Niederreiter's public-key cryptosystems. *IEEE Transactions on Information Theory*, IT-40(1):271–273, 1994.

Leo88.   J.S. Leon. A probabilistic algorithm for computing minimum weights of large error-correcting codes. *IEEE Transactions on Information Theory*, 34(5):1354–1359, 1988.

McE78.   R.J. McEliece. A public-key cryptosystem based on algebraic coding theory. *JPL DSN Progress Report*, pages 114–116, 1978.

Nie86.   H. Niederreiter. Knapsack-type cryptosystems and algebraic coding theory. *Problems of Control and Information Theory*, 15(2):159–166, 1986.

Omu72.   J.K. Omura. Iterative decoding of linear codes by a modulo-2 linear programm. *Discrete Math*, (3):193–208, 1972.

Sen94.   N. Sendrier. On the structure of a randomly permuted concatenated code. In P. Charpin, editor, *EUROCODE 94 - Livre des résumés*, pages 169–173. INRIA, 1994.

Sen95.   N. Sendrier. On the structure of a randomly permuted concatenated code. Technical Report RR-2460, INRIA, January 1995.

Sen96.   N. Sendrier. An algorithm for finding the permutation between two equivalent binary codes. Technical Report RR-2853, INRIA, April 1996.

SS92.   V.M. Sidelnikov and S.O. Shestakov. On cryptosystems based on generalized Reed-Solomon codes. *Diskretnaya Math*, 4:57–63, 1992.

Ste89.   J. Stern. A method for finding codewords of small weight. In G. Cohen and J. Wolfmann, editors, *Coding Theory and Applications*, number 388 in Lecture Notes in Computer Science, pages 106–113. Springer-Verlag, 1989.

Ste93.   J. Stern. A new identification scheme based on syndrome decoding. In D.R. Stinson, editor, *Advances in Cryptology - CRYPTO'93*, number 773 in Lecture Notes in Computer Science, pages 13–21. Springer-Verlag, 1993.

Vér95.   P. Véron. *Problème SD, Opérateur Trace, schémas d'identification et codes de Goppa*. PhD thesis, Université de Toulon et du Var, 1995.

vT94.   J. van Tilburg. *Security-analysis of a class of cryptosystems based on linear error-correcting codes*. PhD thesis, Technische Universiteit Eindhoven, 1994.

Improving the Security of the McEliece Public-Key Cryptosystem[1]

Hung-Min Sun

Department of Information Management
Chaoyang University of Technology
Wufeng, Taichung County, Taiwan 413
Email: hmsun@mail.cyut.edu.tw

Abstract.   At Crypt'97, Berson showed that the McEliece public-key cryptosystem suffers from two weaknesses: (1) failure to protect any message which is encrypted more than once, (2) failure to protect any messages which have a known linear relation to one another. In this paper, we propose some variants of the McEliece scheme which can prevent from these attacks. These variants will not reduce the information rate in the original scheme. In addition, to improve the information rate, we also propose some variants of the McEliece scheme which can prevent from Berson-like attacks.

1   Introduction

In 1978, McEliece [16] proposed a public-key cryptosystem (*the McEliece scheme*) based on algebraic coding theory. The idea of this cryptosystem is based on the fact that the decoding problem of an arbitrary linear code is an NP-hard problem [4]. Compared with other public-key cryptosystems [8,21] which involve modular exponentiation, the McEliece scheme has the advantage of high-speed encryption and decryption. In addition, the McEliece scheme is a probabilistic encryption [6,9] that is better than other deterministic encryptions [19,21] in preventing from elimination of any information leaked with public-key cryptography. Up to now, the McEliece scheme is still not widely used. This is because the information rate of this scheme is low (close to 0.5) and it requires large binary matrices as secret key and public key. Some methods [15,18,23] were proposed to improve the information rate of the McEliece scheme. These methods use the added error vector to carry additional information. Some information bits are mapped into an error vector to be added to a codeword. Once the error vector can be identified, the additional information can be recovered. By using these methods, the information rate can be up to around 0.8 or more. For the large key problem, Sun and Hwang [24] proposed the use of a short sequence of bits (called seed-key) to specify secret key. Thus each user only needs to keep a short key, e.g., 64-bit sequence. However, the problem of large public key is still unsolved.

[1] This work was supported in part by the National Science Council, Taiwan, under contract NSC-87-2213-E-324-003.

K. Ohta and D. Pei (Eds.): ASIACRYPT'98, LNCS 1514, pp 200-213, 1998

In the past, many researchers [1,2,7,13,14,25] attempted to break the McEliece scheme. None of these were successful in the general case. Among them, Korzhik and Turkin [13] claimed that they had broken the McEliece scheme. However, most cryptographers don't believe their result to be effective because of lack of obvious evidence to confirm the time bound they claimed. At Crypt'97, Berson [5] showed that the McEliece scheme suffers from two weaknesses: (1) failure to protect any message which is encrypted more than once, (2) failure to protect any messages which have a known linear relation to one another. Although these weaknesses don't lead the McEliece scheme to be broken immediately (i.e., the private key doesn't be recovered), it is possible for an attacker to act on some behavior such that these weaknesses happen. For example, an attacker introduces some errors into the ciphertext, which is sent from the sender to the receiver, such that the receiver cannot decrypt the ciphertext correctly. If the receiver thinks this cause comes from faults in encryption phase, he will request the sender to resume again (encrypt the message and send the ciphertext again). Thus the weakness (1) will occur.

To overcome these weaknesses, Berson [5] suggested spreading randomness through the plaintext in some complicated fashion. Bellare and Rogaway's OAEP [3] *et seq.* which are commonly used to enhance the security of RSA are instructive. Thus the linear relation between the messages will be unable be found by some action of a cryptanalyst. However, these improvements will also reduce the information rate of this scheme.

In this paper we propose some variants of the McEliece public-key cryptosystem which can prevent from the attacks proposed by Berson. These variants will not reduce the information rate in the original scheme. In addition, to improve the information rate, we also propose some variants of the McEliece scheme which can prevent from Berson-like attacks. This paper is organized as follows. In section 2, we provide some background information. In section 3, we present some variants of the McEliece public-key cryptosystem which can prevent from the attacks proposed by Berson. In section 4, we propose more variants of the McEliece public-key cryptosystem which can prevent from Berson-like attacks and improve the information rate. Finally, we conclude this paper in section 5.

2   Preliminaries

2.1   The McEliece Public-Key Cryptosystem

Secret key: S is a random ($k \times k$) nonsingular matrix over GF(2), called the scrambling matrix,

G is a ($k \times n$) generator matrix of a binary Goppa code G with the capability of correcting an n-bit random error vector of weight less than or equal to t, and

P is a random ($n \times n$) permutation matrix.

Public key: $G' = S G P$

Encryption: $c = mG' + e$, where m is a k-bit message, c is an n-bit ciphertext, and e is an n-bit random error vector of weight t.

Decryption: The receiver first calculates $c' = c P^{-1} = mSG + e P^{-1}$, where P^{-1} is the inverse of P. Because the weight of $e P^{-1}$ is the same as the weight of e, the receiver uses the decoding algorithm of the original code G to obtain $m' = mS$. At last, the receiver recovers m by computing $m = m' S^{-1}$, where S^{-1} is the inverse of G.

In the original version of the McEliece scheme, the parameters k, n, and t were suggested to be 524, 1024, and 50 respectively. Many works [1,2,11,12] were to study the optimal value of these parameters such that a cryptanalyst must take the highest cost to break this system. Optimizations were suggested that if n=1024, k ranges from 524 to 654, and t ranges from 37 to 50. In this paper we use the parameter sizes of the original version without loss of generality.

An obvious attack on the McEliece scheme is to guess 524 positions of c that are not distorted by e, and then find m from $c^* = mG^*$ if G^* is invertible, where c^* and G^* are restrictions onto these positions of c and G'. Because there exist 50 errors embedded in 1024 positions, we need $C_{524}^{1024} / C_{524}^{974} \approx 1.37 \times 10^{16}$ guesses to succeed.

2.2   Berson's Attacks on the McEliece Scheme

Berson [5] proposed two attacks on the McEliece scheme, called message-resend attack and related-message attack. We restate these two attacks in the following.

Message-Resend Attack:

We assume a message m is encrypted twice because of some accident or the special action of a cryptanalyst. Then the cryptanalyst knows: $c_1 = mG' + e_1$, and $c_2 = mG' + e_2$, where $e_1 \neq e_2$ (this is called the message-resend condition). Therefore, $c_1 + c_2 = e_1 + e_2$. It is remarked that the weight of $e_1 + e_2$ is even and at most 100 because the weight of each error vector added in the McEliece scheme is 50. According to Berson's analysis, the expected Hamming weight of $e_1 + e_2$ is about 95.1 if a message-resend condition occurs. If the underlying messages are different, the excepted Hamming weight of $c_1 + c_2$ is 512. Therefore, it is easy to detect the occurrence of a message-resend condition and the weight of $e_1 + e_2$ by observing the Hamming weight of $c_1 + c_2$. If the weight of $e_1 + e_2$ is 94, we need to guess 524 positions of c_1 (c_2) that are not distorted by e_1 (e_2) from 930 possible positions with 3 wrong positions. The probability that we get a correct guess is $C_{524}^{927} / C_{524}^{930} \approx 0.0828$. This means that the cryptanalyst needs only about 12 guesses to succeed.

Similarly, if the weight of $e_1 + e_2$ is 96, only about 5 guesses are required for the cryptanalyst to succeed.

Note that the main cause that Berson's attack succeeds is that by observing the value $c_1 + c_2$ we can obtain more *information* about the positions in which the errors probably occur. In the following, we show how much information for each bit in the error vector goes through observing $c_1 + c_2$. Let $e_1(i)$, $e_2(i)$, $c_1(i)$, and $c_2(i)$ denote the i-th bit in e_1, e_2, c_1, and c_2 respectively. Here we assume the value of each bit in the ciphertext is a random variable with probability $p(c_1(i)=0)=p(c_1(i)=1)=0.5$. The entropy function [10] $H(e_1(i)|c_1(i))$

$= p(c_1(i)=0) \cdot H(e_1(i)|c_1(i)=0)+p(c_1(i)=1) \cdot H(e_1(i)|c_1(i)=1)$

$= 0.5 \cdot (\dfrac{974}{1024} \log \dfrac{1024}{974} + \dfrac{50}{1024} \log \dfrac{1024}{50})+0.5 \cdot (\dfrac{974}{1024} \log \dfrac{1024}{974} + \dfrac{50}{1024} \log \dfrac{1024}{50})$

$= 0.2814$

It is clear that $H(e_1(i)) = H(e_1(i)|c_1(i))$ and $H(e_2(i))=H(e_2(i)|c_2(i))$. This means that one cannot obtain more information on $e_1(i)$ (or $e_2(i)$) through observing $c_1(i)$ (or $c_2(i)$). However, if the message-resend condition occurs and the weight of $e_1 + e_2$ is 94, then

$H(e_1(i)|c_1(i)+c_2(i))$

$= p(c_1(i)+c_2(i)=0)H(e_1(i)|c_1(i)+c_2(i)=0)+$

$\quad p(c_1(i)+c_2(i)=1)H(e_1(i)|c_1(i)+c_2(i)=1)$

$= \dfrac{930}{1024} \cdot (\dfrac{927}{930} \log \dfrac{930}{927} + \dfrac{3}{930} \log \dfrac{930}{3})+\dfrac{94}{1024} \cdot (\dfrac{1}{2} \log 2 + \dfrac{1}{2} \log 2)$

$= 0.1203$

If the message-resend condition occurs and the weight of $e_1 + e_2$ is 96, then $H(e_1(i)|c_1(i)+c_2(i))$

$= p(c_1(i)+c_2(i)=0)H(e_1(i)|c_1(i)+c_2(i)=0)+$

$\quad p(c_1(i)+c_2(i)=1)H(e_1(i)|c_1(i)+c_2(i)=1)$

$= \dfrac{928}{1024} \cdot (\dfrac{926}{928} \log \dfrac{928}{926} + \dfrac{2}{928} \log \dfrac{928}{2})+\dfrac{96}{1024} \cdot (\dfrac{1}{2} \log 2 + \dfrac{1}{2} \log 2)$

$= 0.1139$

Related-Message Attack:

We assume two messages m_1 and m_2 are encrypted and a cryptanalyst knows a linear relation, e.g., the value $m_1 + m_2$, between these two messages. Then the cryptanalyst knows: $c_1 = m_1 G' + e_1$, and $c_2 = m_2 G' + e_2$, where $m_1 \neq m_2$, and $e_1 \neq e_2$. Therefore, $c_1 + c_2 = m_1 G' + e_1 + m_2 G' + e_2 = (m_1 + m_2)G' + (e_1 + e_2)$. Because the value $m_1 + m_2$ is known previously, $(m_1 + m_2)G'$ can be computed. Hence $c_1 + c_2 +$

$(m_1 + m_2)G' = e_1 + e_2$. As the analysis in the message-resend attack, the number of guesses required to succeed is small.

Basically, the message-resend attack is the special case of the related-message attack where the linear relation between the messages is $m_1 + m_2 = 0$. To overcome these weaknesses, Berson [5] suggested spreading randomness through the plaintext in some complicated fashion. Bellare and Rogaway's OAEP [3] *et seq.* which are commonly used to enhance the security of RSA are instructive. Thus the linear relation between the messages will be unable be found by some action of a cryptanalyst. However, these improvements will also reduce the information rate of this scheme. In the following sections, we propose some variants of the McEliece scheme, which can prevent from the attacks proposed by Berson. Some of them have the same information rate as the original McEliece scheme, and some of them have higher information rate than the original scheme.

3   Some Variants of the McEliece Scheme

In this section, we propose some variants of the McEliece scheme. These variants can prevent the McEliece scheme from the message-resend attack and the related-message attack. In addition, these variants will not reduce the information rate. The public key and the secret key in these variants are the same as those in the original McEliece scheme.

Variant I:

Encryption: $c = (m+h(e))G' + e$, where e is an n-bit random error vector of weight t, and h is a one-way hash function with an input e and an output of a k-bit vector. It is necessary to consider how to apply a well-known one-way hash function, e.g., MD5 [20], to be the function h. We omit the details here.

Decryption: First $m+h(e)$ can be obtained by using the decryption algorithm in the original scheme (the error vector can also be found in the decoding process). Secondly the receiver computes $m =(m+h(e)) +h(e)$.

Security: Let m_1 and m_2 be two messages. If $m_1 = m_2$, then $c_1 + c_2 =(h(e_1)+h(e_2))G'+e_1+e_2$. The value $(h(e_1)+h(e_2))G'$ is unknown because of lacking the knowledge of $h(e_1)$ and $h(e_2)$. We cannot obtain more information about the positions in which the error occurs. Thus the message-resend attack fails. If the value $m_1 + m_2$ is known, then $c_1 + c_2 = (m_1 + m_2 +h(e_1)+h(e_2))G' +e_1+e_2$. Although the value $m_1 + m_2$ is known, $(m_1 + m_2 +h(e_1)+h(e_2))G'$ will not be known because of lacking the knowledge of $h(e_1)$ and $h(e_2)$. We are not able to obtain any information about the positions in which the error occurs. Thus the related-message attack cannot work.

Variant II:

Encryption: $c = f(m, e)G' + e$, where e is an n-bit random error vector of weight t, and f is a trapdoor one-way function [21] with two inputs (m and e) and an output of a k-bit vector. Here f must have the property that given $f(m, e)$ it is computationally infeasible to find m and e, but it is easy to compute m given $f(m, e)$ and e. For example, DES [17], which has two inputs (message and key) and an output (ciphertext), can be one of candidates. If DES is applied, it is necessary to consider how to implement it to be the function f because DES has a 56-bit key, a 64-bit message, and a 64-bit ciphertext, while f needs an n-bit e, a k-bit m, and a k-bit output. We omit the details here.

Decryption: First $f(m, e)$ can be recovered by using the decryption algorithm in the original scheme (the receiver keeps the error vector in the decoding process). Secondly the receiver computes m by inverting the function f.

Security: If $m_1 = m_2$, then $c_1 + c_2 = (f(m_1, e_1) + f(m_2, e_2))G' + e_1 + e_2$. The value $(f(m_1, e_1) + f(m_2, e_2))G'$ is unknown because of lacking the knowledge of $f(m_1, e_1)$ and $f(m_2, e_2)$. We cannot obtain any information about the positions in which the error occurs. Thus the message-resend attack fails. If the value $m_1 + m_2$ is known, we cannot still erase the item $(f(m_1, e_1) + f(m_2, e_2))G'$. Therefore, this scheme is also secure against the related-message attack.

4   More Variants on Improving the Information Rate

In the past, some researchers [15,18,23] studied how to improve the information rate of the McEliece scheme. They use the added error vector to carry additional information. Thus the information rate of the McEliece scheme can be increased. In this section, we first formally describe their ideas as Variant III. We show that the variant is not secure against Berson-like attacks. And then, we propose some variants which can prevent from Berson-like attacks and improve the information rate.

Variant III:

Encryption: Let $m = (m_a, m_b)$ be the message. $c = m_a G' + e$, where $e = g(m_b)$, g is an invertible function which maps m_b into an n-bit error vector of weight t. Some good candidates of the function g can be found in [15,18,23].

Decryption: First m_a can be recovered by using the decryption algorithm of the code G. In the meantime, the value $g(m_b)$ can also be obtained. Then the receiver computes $m_b = g^{-1}(g(m_b))$, where g^{-1} is the inverse of g.

Information rate: By using this method, the information rate can be improved from 0.51 to 0.79 if $k=524$, $n=1024$, and $t=50$ (additional 284-bit information is carried), and from 0.63 to 0.87 if k=654, n=1024, and t=37 (additional 225-bit information is carried).

Security: Basically, the idea of this variant is the same as that of the original McEliece scheme. The main difference between both is the randomness of the error vector. The error vector of the former is not truly random, but dependent on the probability distribution of m_b. To provide better security, it is suggested that data compression technique is applied before encryption. Note that this variant is a deterministic encryption.

Let $m_1 = (m_{1a}, m_{1b})$ and $m_2 = (m_{2a}, m_{2b})$ be two messages encrypted. Because each message in this variant contains two parts, we extend the linear relation between two messages to many cases. In Table 1, we show the possible weaknesses of these cases. We give some explanations for these cases in the following.

Case III.A: If m_{1a} is known previously, then $g(m_{1b}) = c_1 + m_{1a} G'$. Thus $m_{1b} = g^{-1}(g(m_b))$.

Case III.B: If m_{1b} is known previously, then we know $m_{1a} G' = c_1 + g(m_{1b})$. It is easy to compute m_{1a} by finding $m_{1a} G^* = (c_1 + g(m_{1b}))^*$, where $(c_1 + g(m_{1b}))^*$ and G^* are restrictions onto some positions of $c_1 + g(m_{1b})$ and G' such that G^* is invertible.

Case III.C: If $m_{1a} = m_{2a}$ and $m_{1b} = m_{2b}$ are known previously, then $c_1 = c_2$. That is, $c_1 + c_2 = 0$. We cannot obtain any information about the positions in which the error occurs.

Case III.D: If $m_{1a} = m_{2a}$ and $m_{1b} \neq m_{2b}$ are known previously, then $e_1 \neq e_2$. Thus $c_1 + c_2 = (m_{1a} + m_{2a})G' + e_1 + e_2 = e_1 + e_2$. Therefore, we can obtain any information about the positions in which the errors occur. Thus m_{1a}, m_{1b}, m_{2a}, and m_{2b} can be known.

Case III.E: If $m_{1a} \neq m_{2a}$ and $m_{1b} = m_{2b}$ are known previously, then $(m_{1a} + m_{2a})G' = c_1 + c_2$. Similar to Case III.B, it is easy to compute $m_{1a} + m_{2a}$.

Case III.F: Similar to Case III.E except that $m_{1a} + m_{2a}$ has been known previously.

Case III.G: If the value $m_{1a} + m_{2a}$ and $m_{1b} \neq m_{2b}$ are known previously, then $c_1 + c_2 = (m_{1a} + m_{2a})G' + e_1 + e_2$. Because the value $m_{1a} + m_{2a}$ is known, $(m_{1a} + m_{2a})G'$ can be computed. Hence $c_1 + c_2 + (m_{1a} + m_{2a})G' = e_1 + e_2$. Therefore, we can obtain any information about the positions in which the errors occur. Thus m_{1a}, m_{1b}, m_{2a}, and m_{2b} can be known.

Table 1. The possible weaknesses in Variant III

	Information Known Previously	Information Leaked
Case III.A	m_{1a} (or m_{2a})	m_{1b} (or m_{2b})
Case III.B	m_{1b} (or m_{2b})	m_{1a} (or m_{2a})
Case III.C	$m_{1a} = m_{2a}$, $m_{1b} = m_{2b}$	None
Case III.D	$m_{1a} = m_{2a}$, $m_{1b} \neq m_{2b}$	m_{1a}, m_{1b}, m_{2a}, m_{2b}
Case III.E	$m_{1a} \neq m_{2a}$, $m_{1b} = m_{2b}$	$m_{1a} + m_{2a}$
Case III.F	$m_{1a} + m_{2a}$, $m_{1b} = m_{2b}$	None
Case III.G	$m_{1a} + m_{2a}$, $m_{1b} \neq m_{2b}$	m_{1a}, m_{1b}, m_{2a}, m_{2b}

From Table 1, it is clear that there are still many weaknesses in Variant III. To overcome these weaknesses and improve the information rate of the McEliece scheme, we propose two variants of the McEliece scheme in the following.

Variant VI:

Encryption: Let $m = (m_a, m_b)$ be the message. $c = (m_a + h(e)) G' + e$, where $e = g(r\| m_b)$, r is a q-bit random vector, g is an invertible function which maps m_b into an n-bit error vector of weight t, h is a one-way hash function with an input e and an output of a k-bit vector. Here we need the function g to have the following property. Let E be the set of 2^n possible strings of n binary digits, E_{m_b} be the set of all possible outputs of $g(r\| m_b)$ given m_b, x_i be the i-th item in E_{m_b} and $d_i = \min_{j, j \neq i}\{dist.(x_i, x_j)\}$. If we regard E as an n-dimensional Hamming space, we require that the E_{m_b} is uniformly distributed (located) in E. That is, we expect that the E_{m_b} has an approximately maximal value of $\dfrac{\sum d_i}{2^q}$. Those proposals in [15,18,23] may be the candidates of the function g.

Decryption: First $m_a' = m_a + h(e)$ and e can be found by using the decryption algorithm of the code G. Secondly the receiver computes $r\| m_b = g^{-1}(e)$, where $g^{-1}(e)$ is the inverse of g, and then discards the part r. Thus m_b is obtained. Finally, m_a can be computed by $m_a = m_a' + h(e)$.

Information rate: By using this method, the information rate can be improved from 0.51 to 0.79 if k=524, n=1024, t=50, and q=0; from 0.51 to 0.73 if k=524, n=1024, t=50, and q=64; from 0.63 to 0.87 if k=654, n=1024, t=37, and q=0; and from 0.63 to 0.8 if k=654, n=1024, t=37, and q=64.

Security: We discuss the security of this variant with parameter $q=0$ and $q=64$ respectively.

Parameter $q=0$:
In Table 2, we show the possible weaknesses in Variant IV with parameter $q=0$. Some explanations for these cases are given in the following.

Case IV.A: Assume m_{1a} is known previously. $(m_{1a}+h(g(m_{1b})))G'$ cannot be removed from c_1 because $h(g(m_{1b}))$ is unknown.

Case IV.B: If m_{1b} is known previously, then we know $(m_{1a}+h(g(m_{1b})))G' = c_1 + g(m_{1b})$. Similar to Case III.B, it is easy to compute $m_{1a}+h(g(m_{1b}))$ and hence m_{1a}.

Case IV.C: Similar to Case III.C.

Case IV.D: If $m_{1a}=m_{2a}$ and $m_{1b}\neq m_{2b}$ are known previously, then $c_1+c_2 = (h(g(m_{1b})+h(g(m_{2b})))G'+e_1+e_2$. We cannot remove $(h(g(m_{1b})+h(g(m_{2b})))G'$ from c_1+c_2. Therefore, we cannot obtain any information about the positions in which the errors occur.

Case IV.E: Similar to Case III.E.

Case IV.F: Similar to Case III.F.

Case IV.G: If the value $m_{1a}+m_{2a}$ and $m_{1b}\neq m_{2b}$ are known previously, then $c_1+c_2 = (m_{1a}+m_{2a}+h(g(m_{1b})+h(g(m_{2b})))G' +e_1+e_2$. Because the value $m_{1a}+m_{2a}$ is known, $(m_{1a}+m_{2a})G'$ can be computed. Hence $c_1+c_2+(m_{1a}+m_{2a})G'= h(g(m_{1b})+ h(g(m_{2b})))G'+e_1+e_2$. However, we cannot remove $(h(g(m_{1b})+h(g(m_{2b})))G'$ from $c_1+c_2+(m_{1a}+m_{2a})G'$.

Table 2. The possible weaknesses in Variant IV with parameter $q=0$

	Information Known Previously	Information Leaked
Case IV.A	m_{1a} (or m_{2a})	None
Case IV.B	m_{1b} (or m_{2b})	m_{1a} (or m_{2a})
Case IV.C	$m_{1a}=m_{2a}$, $m_{1b}=m_{2b}$	None
Case IV.D	$m_{1a}=m_{2a}$, $m_{1b}\neq m_{2b}$	None
Case IV.E	$m_{1a}\neq m_{2a}$, $m_{1b}=m_{2b}$	$m_{1a}+m_{1b}$
Case IV.F	$m_{1a}+m_{2a}$, $m_{1b}=m_{2b}$	None
Case IV.G	$m_{1a}+m_{2a}$, $m_{1b}\neq m_{2b}$	None

Parameter $q=64$:
In Table 3, we show the possible weaknesses in Variant IV with parameter $q=64$. Some explanations for these cases are given in the following.

Case IV.R.A: Similar to Case IV.A.

Case IV.R.B: Assume m_{1b} is known previously. Because r_1 is an unknown 64-bit random vector, the probability that we get a correct guess of the value $g(r_1 \| m_{1b})$ is only $\dfrac{1}{2^{64}}$. Therefore, we cannot remove $g(r_1 \| m_{1b})$ from c_1. Another possible attack is to guess k positions of c that are not distorted by e. Because $E_{m_{1b}}$ is uniformly distributed in E, a cryptanalyst cannot identify which positions have better chances.

Case IV.R.C: If $m_{1a} = m_{2a}$ and $m_{1b} = m_{2b}$ are known previously, then $c_1 + c_2 = (h(g(r_1 \| m_{1b}) + h(g(r_2 \| m_{2b}))G' + g(r_1 \| m_{1b}) + g(r_2 \| m_{2b})$. We cannot remove $(h(g(r_1 \| m_{1b}) + h(g(r_2 \| m_{2b}))G'$ from $c_1 + c_2$ because m_{1a}, m_{2a}, m_{1b}, and m_{2b} are unknown.

Case IV.R.D: Similar to Case IV.D.

Case IV.R.E: If $m_{1a} \neq m_{2a}$ and $m_{1b} = m_{2b}$ are known previously, then $c_1 + c_2 = (m_{1a} + m_{2a} + h(g(r_1 \| m_{1b}) + h(g(r_2 \| m_{2b}))G' + g(r_1 \| m_{1b}) + g(r_2 \| m_{2b})$. Because r_1 is a 64-bit random vector, the probability that $r_1 = r_2$ (hence $g(r_1 \| m_{1b}) = g(r_2 \| m_{2b})$) is equal to $1/2^{64}$ which is significantly small. Therefore, neither $(m_{1a} + m_{2a} + h(g(r_1 \| m_{1b}) + h(g(r_2 \| m_{2b}))G'$ nor $g(r_1 \| m_{1b}) + g(r_2 \| m_{2b})$ can be removed from $c_1 + c_2$.

Case IV.R.F: If the value $m_{1a} + m_{1b}$ and $m_{2a} = m_{2b}$ are known previously, then $c_1 + c_2 + (m_{1a} + m_{2a})G' = (h(g(r_1 \| m_{1b}) + h(g(r_2 \| m_{2b}))G' + g(r_1 \| m_{1b}) + g(r_2 \| m_{2b})$. Neither $(h(g(r_1 \| m_{1b}) + h(g(r_2 \| m_{2b}))G'$ nor $g(r_1 \| m_{1b}) + g(r_2 \| m_{2b})$ can be removed from $c_1 + c_2 + (m_{1a} + m_{2a})G'$.

Case IV.R.G: Similar to Case IV.G.

Table 3. The possible weaknesses in Variant IV with parameter q=64

	Information Known Previously	Information Leaked
Case IV.R.A	m_{1a} (or m_{2a})	None
Case IV.R.B	m_{1b} (or m_{2b})	None
Case IV.R.C	$m_{1a} = m_{2a}$, $m_{1b} = m_{2b}$	None
Case IV.R.D	$m_{1a} = m_{2a}$, $m_{1b} \neq m_{2b}$	None
Case IV.R.E	$m_{1a} \neq m_{2a}$, $m_{1b} = m_{2b}$	None
Case IV.R.F	$m_{1a} + m_{2a}$, $m_{1b} = m_{2b}$	None
Case IV.R.G	$m_{1a} + m_{2a}$, $m_{1b} \neq m_{2b}$	None

Variant V:

Encryption: Let $m = (m_a, m_b)$ be the message. $c = f(m_a, e) G' + e$, where $e = g(r \| m_b)$, g is an invertible function which maps $r \| m_b$ into an n-bit error vector of weight t, and f is a trapdoor one-way function with two inputs (m_a and e) and an output of a k-bit vector. Here the function f and the function g should have the same property as that in Variant II and that in Variant IV respectively.

Decryption: First $m_a' = f(m_a, e)$ and e can be obtained by using the decryption algorithm of the code G. Secondly the receiver computes $m_b = g^{-1}(e)$, where g^{-1} is the inverse of g. Finally, m_a can be computed by $m_a = f^{-1}(m_a', e)$, where f^{-1} is the inverse of f.

Information rate: the same as Variant IV.

Security: We discuss the security of this variant with parameter $q=0$ and $q=64$ respectively.

Parameter $q=0$:
In Table 4, we show the possible weaknesses in Variant V with parameter $q=0$. Some explanations for these cases are given in the following.

Case V.A: Similar to Case IV.A.

Case IV.B: If m_{1b} is known previously, we know $f(m_{1a}, g(m_{1b}))G' = c_1 + g(m_{1b})$. Similar to Case III.B, it is easy to compute $f(m_{1a}, g(m_{1b}))$ and hence $m_{1a} = f^{-1}(f(m_{1a}, g(m_{1b})), g(m_{1b}))$.

Case IV.C: Similar to Case III.C.

Case IV.D: If $m_{1a} = m_{2a}$ and $m_{1b} \neq m_{2b}$ are known previously, then $c_1 + c_2 = (f(m_{1a}, g(m_{1b})) + f(m_{2a}, g(m_{2b})))G' + e_1 + e_2$. We cannot erase $(f(m_{1a}, g(m_{1b})) + f(m_{2a}, g(m_{2b})))G'$ from $c_1 + c_2$.

Case IV.E: If $m_{1a} \neq m_{1b}$ and $m_{2a} = m_{2b}$ are known previously, then $c_1 + c_2 = (f(m_{1a}, g(m_{1b})) + f(m_{2a}, g(m_{2b})))G'$. We can only obtain the value $f(m_{1a}, g(m_{1b})) + f(m_{2a}, g(m_{2b}))$.

Case IV.F: Similar to Case IV.E.

Case IV.G: Similar to Case IV.D.

Table 4. The possible weaknesses in Variant V with parameter $q=0$

	Information Known Previously	Information Leaked
Case V.A	m_{1a} (or m_{2a})	None
Case V.B	m_{1b} (or m_{2b})	m_{1a} (or m_{2a})
Case V.C	$m_{1a} = m_{2a}$, $m_{1b} = m_{2b}$	None
Case V.D	$m_{1a} = m_{2a}$, $m_{1b} \neq m_{2b}$	None
Case V.E	$m_{1a} \neq m_{2a}$, $m_{1b} = m_{2b}$	None
Case V.F	$m_{1a} + m_{2a}$, $m_{1b} = m_{2b}$	None
Case V.G	$m_{1a} + m_{2a}$, $m_{1b} \neq m_{2b}$	None

Parameter q=64:
In Table 5, we show the possible weaknesses in Variant V with parameter q=64. Some explanations for these cases are given in the following.

Case V.R.A: Similar to Case IV.R.A.
Case V.R.B: Similar to Case IV.R.B.
Case V.R.C: If $m_{1a}=m_{2a}$ and $m_{1b}=m_{2b}$ are known previously, then
$$c_1+c_2 =(f(m_{1a}, \quad g(r_1\| m_{1b}))+f(m_{2a}, \quad g(r_2\| m_{2b})))G'+ \quad g(r_1\| m_{1b})$$
$$+g(r_2\| m_{2b}). \text{ We cannot remove neither } (f(m_{1a}, \quad g(r_1\| m_{1b}))+f(m_{2a},$$
$$g(r_2\| m_{2b})))G' \text{ nor } g(r_1\| m_{1b})+g(r_2\| m_{2b}) \text{ from } c_1+c_2.$$
Case V.R.D: Similar to Case V.D.
Case V.R.E: Similar to Case IV.R.E.
Case V.R.F: Similar to Case V.R.C.
Case V.R.G: Similar to Case V.G.

Table 5. The possible weaknesses in Variant V with parameter q=64

	Information Known Previously	Information Leaked
Case V.R.A	m_{1a} (or m_{2a})	None
Case V.R.B	m_{1b} (or m_{2b})	None
Case V.R.C	$m_{1a}=m_{2a}$, $m_{1b}=m_{2b}$	None
Case V.R.D	$m_{1a}=m_{2a}$, $m_{1b}\neq m_{2b}$	None
Case V.R.E	$m_{1a}\neq m_{2a}$, $m_{1b}=m_{2b}$	None
Case V.R.F	$m_{1a}+m_{2a}$, $m_{1b}=m_{2b}$	None
Case V.R.G	$m_{1a}+m_{2a}$, $m_{1b}\neq m_{2b}$	None

5   Conclusions

In this paper, we first propose two variants, Variant I and Variant II, of the McEliece scheme, which can prevent from both the message-resend attack and the related-message attack. These two variants are probabilistic encryptions, and have the same information rate as that of the original McEliece scheme. To improve the information rate and to prevent from Berson-like attacks, we also propose two variants, Variant IV and Variant V, of the McEliece scheme. In these two variants, if the parameter q is equal to 0, then they are deterministic encryptions and can improve the information rate from 0.51 to 0.79 if k=524, n=1024, t=50, or from 0.63 to 0.87 if k=654, n=1024, t=37. If the parameter q is equal to 64, then they are probabilistic encryptions and can improve the information rate from 0.51 to 0.73 if k=524, n=1024, t=50, or from 0.63 to 0.8 if k=654, n=1024, t=37.

References

1. Adams, C., and Meijer, H., „Security-Related Comments Regarding McEliece's Public-Key Cryptosystem," *Advances in Cryptology-CRYPTO'87*, Lecture notes in computer science (Springer-Verlag), pp. 224-228, 1988.
2. Adams, C., and Meijer, H., „Security-Related Comments Regarding McEliece's Public-Key Cryptosystem," *IEEE Transactions on Information Theory,* Vol. 35, pp. 454-455, 1989.
3. Bellare, M., and Rogaway, P., „Optimal asymmetric encryption," *Advances in Cryptology-EUROCRYPT'94*, Lecture notes in computer science 950 (Springer-Verlag), pp. 232-249, 1994.
4. Berlekamp, E.R., McEliece, R.J., and van Tilborg, H.C.A., „On the Inherent Intractability of Certain Coding Problems," *IEEE Transactions on Information Theory,* Vol. 24, pp. 384-386, 1978.
5. Berson, T.A., "Failure of the McEliece Public-Key Cryptosystem under Message-resend and Related-message Attack‚„, *Advances in Cryptology-CRYPTO'97*, Lecture notes in computer science (Springer-Verlag), pp. 213-220, 1997.
6. Blum, M., and Goldwasser, S., „An Efficient Probabilistic Public-Key Encryption Scheme Which Hides All Partial Information," *Advances in Cryptology-CRYPTO'84*, Lecture notes in computer science (Springer-Verlag), pp. 289-299, 1985..
7. Brickell, E.F., and Odlyzko, A., „Cryptanalysis: A Survey of Recent Results," *Proc. IEEE*, 76, (5), pp. 153-165, 1988.
8. ElGamal, T., „A Public-Key Cryptosystem and a Signature Scheme Based on Discrete Logarithms," *IEEE Trans.*, IT-31, (4), pp. 469-472, 1985.
9. Goldwasser, S., and Micali, S., „Probabilistic Encryption and How to Play Mental Poker Keeping Secret All Partial Information," *Proceedings of the 14th ACM Symposium on the Theory of Computing*, pp. 270-299, 1982.
10. Hamming, R.W., *Coding and Information Theory*, Prentice-Hall, 1986.
11. Hin, P.J.M., „Channel-Error-Correcting Privacy Cryptosystems," M.Sc. Thesis, Delft University of Technology, Delft, 1986.
12. Jorissen, F., „A Security Evaluation of the Public-Key Cipher System Proposed by McEliece, used as a combined scheme," Technical Report, Katholieke University Leuven, Dept. Elektrotechniek, Jan 1986.
13. Korzhik, V.I., and Turkin, A.I., „Cryptanalysis of McEliece's Public-Key Cryptosystem", *Advances in Cryptology-EUROCRYPT'91*, Lecture notes in computer science (Springer-Verlag), pp. 68-70, 1991.
14. Lee, P.J., and Brickell, E.F., „An observation on the security of McEliece's Public-Key Cryptosystem," *Advances in Cryptology-EUROCRYPT'88*, Lecture notes in computer science (Springer-Verlag), pp. 275-280, 1988.
15. Lin, M.C., and Fu, H.L., „Information Rate of McEliece's Public-Key Cryptosystem," *Electronics Letters*, Vol. 26, No. 1, pp. 16-18, 1990.
16. McEliece, R.J., „A Public-Key Cryptosystem Based on Algebraic Coding Theory," *DSN Progress Report*, 42-44, pp. 114-116, 1978.
17. National Bureau of Standards, NBS FIPS PUB 46, „Data Encryption Standard," *National Bureau of Standards*, U.S. Department of Commerce, Jan 1977.
18. Park, C.S., „Improving Code Rate of McEliece's public-Key Cryptosystem," *Electronics Letters*, Vol. 25, No. 21, pp. 1466-1467, 1989.
19. Rabin, M.O., „Digital Signatures and Public-Key Functions as Intractable as Factorization," MIT Lab. For Computer Science, Technical Report, MIT/LCS/TR-212, Jan 1979.
20. Rivest, R.L., „The MD5 Message Digest Algorithm," RFC 1321, Apr 1992.

21. Rivest, R.L., Shamir, A., and Adleman, L.M., „A Method for Obtaining Digital Signatures and Public-Key Cryptosystems," *Communications of the ACM*, 21, (2), pp. 120-126, 1978.
22. Schneier, B., *Applied Cryptography*, John Wiley & Sons, 1996.
23. Sendrier, N., „Efficient Generation of Binary Words of Given Weight," *Cryptography and Coding: 5th IMA Conference*, (Springer-Verlag), pp. 184-187, 1995.
24. Sun, H.M., and Hwang, T., „Key Generation of Algebraic-Code Cryptosystems", *Computers and Mathematics with Applications*, 27, (2), pp. 99-106, 1994.
25. van Tilburg, J., „On the McEliece Public-Key Cryptosystem," *Advances in Cryptology-CRYPTO'88*, Lecture notes in computer science (Springer-Verlag), pp. 119-131, 1990.

Cryptanalysis in Prime Order Subgroups of Z_n^*

Wenbo Mao[1] and Chae Hoon Lim[2]

[1] Hewlett-Packard Laboratories,
Filton Road, Stoke Gifford, Bristol BS12 6QZ, United Kingdom
wm@hplb.hpl.hp.com
[2] Future Systems Inc.,
372-2, Yang Jae-Dong, Seo Cho-Gu, Seoul, 137-130, Korea
chlim@future.co.kr

Abstract. Many cryptographic protocols and cryptosystems have been proposed to make use of prime order subgroups of Z_n^* where n is the product of two large distinct primes. In this paper we analyze a number of such schemes. While these schemes were proposed to utilize the difficulty of factoring large integers or that of finding related hidden information (e.g., the order of the group Z_n^*), our analyzes reveal much easier problems as their real security bases. We itemize three classes of security failures and formulate a simple algorithm for factoring n with a disclosed non-trivial factor of $\phi(n)$ where the disclosure is for making use of a prime order subgroup in Z_n^*. The time complexity of our algorithm is $O(n^{1/4}/f)$ where f is a disclosed subgroup order. To factor such n of length up to 800 bits with the subgroup having a secure size against computing discrete logarithm, the new algorithm will have a feasible running time on use of a trivial size of storage.

1 Introduction

Let $n = pq$ where p and q are large primes. The multiplicative group of integers modulo n, which we denote Z_n^*, has a secret order (the number of elements in the group) $(p-1)(q-1)$. It is assumed to be difficult to discover this quantity from n, and the difficulty has been used as the security basis for many cryptosystems and protocols including RSA [16], Fiat-Shamir [7], Rabin [15], Guillou-Quisquater [10], and many many more.

In the literature we also often see cryptosystems and cryptographic protocols (crypto schemes) that make use of prime order subgroups of Z_n^* (e.g., [1,2,8,9,11,13]). In the sequel, whenever we say subgroup, we refer to a prime order subgroup of Z_n^*. The order of such a subgroup is a prime number. The schemes referred above involve various ways of using such subgroups. In some use (a cryptosystem [2]), subgroup elements are disclosed while their order is hidden, and the security basis is an assumed difficulty to find the order of a given element. In another use ([1,8,9,11,13]), a subgroup is made public by disclosing both the order and the elements. This use allows zero-knowledge proof of some properties (such as possession or equality) of the discrete logarithms of the group elements.

K. Ohta and D. Pei (Eds.): ASIACRYPT'98, LNCS 1514, pp. 214–226, 1998.

We will analyze each of the crypto schemes referred in the above paragraph and itemize three classes of security failures from our analysis. Class 1: given elements of a prime order subgroup, the group order, even as a secret, cannot be used as an RSA-like hidden trapdoor. Class 2: A disclosed prime order subgroup allows to solve problems which should be difficult in Z_n^* had the subgroup not been disclosed. Class 3: the size of a disclosed subgroup versus that of Z_n^* leads to a significant reduction on the complexity for factoring n. We will formulate a simple algorithm for factoring n with a special structure designed for making use of prime order subgroups in Z_n^*. To factor such n of length up to 800 bits, our algorithm will have a feasible running time on use of a trivial size of storage.

Throughout the paper we stipulate $n = pq$ for p and q being distinct large primes. For an element $a \in Z_n^*$, we will use $ord_n(a)$ to denote the order of a modulo n, which is the least positive integer b satisfying

$$a^b \equiv 1 \,(\mathrm{mod}\,n).$$

We also confine ourselves to study subgroups of odd prime orders; namely, we exclude the case of order 2. Such subgroups merely contain elements which can be used to factor n (if they are not trivial numbers $n - 1$ or 1).

2   Class 1: Absence of RSA-like Hidden Trapdoor in any Prime Order Subgroup

Let $g \neq 1$ be a non secret element in a prime order subgroup. Since $g \bmod p$ ($g \bmod q$) is an element in Z_p^* (Z_q^*), we have the following

$$ord_p(g) \mid p - 1, \quad ord_q(g) \mid q - 1.$$

So

$$p = ord_p(g)k + 1, \quad q = ord_q(g)\ell + 1, \tag{1}$$

for some (even) numbers k and ℓ. A basic fact in number theory states the following: for every $x \in Z_n^*$,

$$m \mid n \;\text{ implies }\; ord_m(x) \mid ord_n(x). \tag{2}$$

Since $ord_n(g)$ is prime, from (2) we know either $ord_p(g) = ord_n(g)$, or $ord_p(g) = 1$. Same true for $ord_q(g)$. Obviously we do not consider the case $ord_n(g) = 1$. Thus (1) consists of one of the following three cases:

$$p = ord_n(g)k + 1, \quad q = ord_n(g)\ell + 1, \tag{3}$$

or

$$p = ord_n(g)k + 1, \quad q = \ell + 1, \quad \text{with } ord_n(g) \nmid \ell, \tag{4}$$

or

$$p = k + 1, \quad q = ord_n(g)\ell + 1, \quad \text{with } ord_n(g) \nmid k. \tag{5}$$

Note that the case (4) implies $g \equiv 1 \,(\mathrm{mod}\, q)$, or $q \mid g - 1$. Noting further $0 < g - 1 < n$, we will have (let $\gcd(x, y)$ denote the greatest common divisor of x and y)

$$\gcd(g - 1, n) = q.$$

Similarly for the case (5), we will have

$$\gcd(g - 1, n) = p.$$

We conclude to this end the following statement.

Proposition 1. *Let* $g \in Z_n^*$ *be a non secret element and* $ord_n(g)$ *be an odd prime. Then* $n = pq$ *must only use* p *and* q *with the structures shown in (3), or else the factorization of* n *will be disclosed.* $\square$

A previous cryptosystem [2] contained the above failure for using moduli with the construction (4). The failure was later discovered by Henk Meijer [3], with a suggestion for fixing by using moduli with the construction (3). Below we will examine that construction as per the system of [2], and in Section 4 we will further examine the same construction for a different danger.

2.1   The Case $n = pq = (ord_n(g)k + 1)(ord_n(g)\ell + 1)$

Further examining (3) we can see

$$n = pq = ord_n(g)(ord_n(g)k\ell + k + \ell) + 1.$$

So $n - 1$ is a multiple of $ord_n(g)$. The number $n - 1$ is publicly available even $ord_n(g)$ is kept as a secret. This fact tells us that the subgroup generated from g does not have an RSA-like trapdoor. By an RSA-like trapdoor of a group, we mean a secret number which is the inverse of a public exponent modulo the group order. The trapdoor is hidden because the group order is.

Now in the case $n - 1$ being a multiple of the group order, for any public exponent e, one can compute d to satisfy

$$ed = 1 \,(\mathrm{mod}\, n - 1). \tag{6}$$

The existence of d is not a problem. If $gcd(e, n-1) > 1$, we can replace $n-1$ in (6) with $\frac{n-1}{gcd(e, n-1)}$ which should still be a multiple of $ord_n(g)$ unless $gcd(e, n - 1) = ord_n(g)$ which is the case mostly welcome because we have discovered the hidden order.

Since $ord_n(g) \mid n - 1$, (6) implies $ed = 1 \,(\mathrm{mod}\, ord_n(g))$. Thus, in any subgroup of order $ord_n(g)$, RSA-like encryption or signature algorithms will no longer be secure. Any variations relying on the secrecy of $ord_n(g)$ will fail too. Below we review a cryptosystem that fails in this way.

2.2   Scheme Failure

The scheme [2,3] consists of a public-key encryption algorithm and digital signature algorithm. Both work in a prime order subgroup of Z_n^*. The order of the
subgroup is $r = ord_n(g)$, a prime of size 160 bits which is kept secret by the
owner of n.

In the encryption algorithm, the public key is (g, n), and the private key is
a number z computed as follows

$$z = -\frac{1}{2} \bmod r.$$

To encrypt a message $0 < m < n$, the sender picks a random number t of
size less than 160 bits, and compute the ciphertext pair (u, v) as follows

$$u := g^{2t} \bmod n,$$

$$v := mg^t \bmod n.$$

The recipient decrypts the pair (u, v) by the following calculation.

$$m := u^z v \bmod n.$$

The number $n - 1$ will suffice for a non-recipient to compute u^z and thereby
decrypt (u, v). Let

$$s := \frac{n - 1}{2^t},$$

for some t such that s is odd. A non-recipient can compute

$$z' = -\frac{1}{2} \bmod s.$$

Noting that s is a multiple of r and the latter is the order of u, it is easy to see

$$u^{z'} = u^z \bmod n.$$

This means decryption can be performed by anybody.

A similar failure in the digital signature algorithm of this cryptosystem can
be demonstrated analogously, using $n - 1$ as the trapdoor needed. The failure
allows anybody to issue signatures for the owner of the public key (g, n).

3   Class 2: Difficult Problem Made Easy Due to Disclosure of a Subgroup

Given elements in a group, zero-knowledge proofs showing some properties regarding their discrete logarithms require to make the group order public (at least
to the parties involved in the zero-knowledge protocols). But when the group in
question is Z_n^*, the order $(p-1)(q-1)$ cannot be disclosed or else no use of the

integer factorization problem can be made. A clever idea to solve this contradiction is to define zero-knowledge protocols working in a prime order subgroup of Z_n^*, with the order disclosed without leading to discovery of $(p-1)(q-1)$. A widely adopted method [1,8,9,11,13]) to achieve this is to construct p and q with the structures given in (3), and make g and $ord_n(g)$ public. Here g is chosen such that $ord_n(g) = ord_p(g) = ord_q(g)$.

A scheme failure demonstrated here is a result of transforming a problem which is known to be difficult in Z_n^*, into an easy one in a prime order subgroup.

This is a group signature scheme [13]. (In order to avoid confusion between a mathematical group and a **group** of people, in the sequel we use the bold font to refer to the latter.) A **group** signature scheme allows an individual member in a **group** (e.g., a corporation environment) to issue a signature on behalf of the **group** with the signer's identity hidden from the signature verifier (who verifies a signature using the public key of the **group**). Such signature algorithms are probabilistic ones in that, it should be computationally infeasible to decide if two signatures have been issued by the same **group** member. To prevent anonymity misuse, a **group** manager, upon inputting an administration secret and a signature, can deterministically identify the signer who has issued the signature. This is usually achieved by encrypting the signer's identity under the public key of the **group** manager in the time of signature issuance; the manager need not stay on line.

In this scheme the **group** manager's public-key cryptosystem is the ElGamal cryptosystem [6] working in a prime order subgroup of Z_n^*. Using the notation of [13], the subgroup is setup as follows. Let $n = p_1 p_2$ where p_1, p_2 are distinct large primes. Let further q be another prime of size about 160 bits, and $q \mid p_1 - 1$, $q \mid p_2 - 1$. Fixing an element $g \in Z_n^*$ of order q (modulo both p_1 and p_2), the manager's public key is y computed as follows

$$y := g^x \bmod n,$$

where $x < q$ is the private key of the manager (the above-mentioned administration secret). It is assumed that n and g are generated by a trusted center, and nobody else, even not the **group** manager or members, will know the factorization of n. The center also generates an RSA public exponent e, again with nobody else knowing the inverse of e modulo $(p-1)(q-1)$.

Let the **group** have k members. Each member i $(1 \le i \le k)$ chooses a secret $s_i \in Z_n^*$ and generates an identity by encrypting the secret s_i in RSA encryption

$$id_i := s_i^e \bmod n.$$

From the assumption in key generation, we know that even the manager cannot learn s_i, the secrets of the members. So (s)he cannot frame any member (provided each member (i) make sure not to choose s_i of order q, and this is easy to check against by checking $s_i^q \neq 1 \bmod n$). These k identities id_j $(1 \le j \le k)$ are announced to the public, together with g, e, n. So the public key of the **group** is the following tuple

$$(id_1, id_2, \cdots, id_k, g, e, n).$$

Omitting details, when the member i issuing a signature, (s)he shall use the identities of all members in the **group** and create k pairs of ElGamal-like ciphertext blocks

$$(A_j, B_j) = (g^{w_j} \bmod n, \ (\frac{id_i}{id_j})^{d_j} y^{w_j e} \bmod n), \ 1 \le j \le k,$$

where d_j are part of the signature value, and w_j are random numbers chosen by the signer i (for $j = 1, 2, \cdots, k$). The scheme also requires the signer to prove, in zero-knowledge, possession of the eth root of one of the k identities. It is thus obvious that only a **group** member is able to have generated the above ciphertext pairs, and hence to have issued a signature.

At first glance, a verifier, apart from knowing the fact that each pair (A_j, B_j) is generated via using the identity id_j (for $1 \le j \le k$), cannot identify the signer i from these pairs. On the other hand, the **group** manager can identify the signer because each pair (A_j^e, B_j) $(1 \le j \le k)$ provides ElGamal encryption of $(\frac{id_i}{id_j})^{d_j}$ under the manager's public key y, and the member i is identified because decrypting (A_i^e, B_i) will return 1.

However we notice that 1 is an element in any subgroup of Z_n^*, in particular in all subgroups of order q. Thus,

$$ord_n(B_i) = ord_n(y^{w_j e}) = q,$$

while

$$ord_n(B_j) = ord_n((\frac{id_i}{id_j})^{d_j} y^{w_j e}) \ne q, \ \text{ for } \ j \ne i.$$

These facts can easily be learned by anybody via checking whether $B_j^q \bmod n$ is 1, for $1 \le j \le k$. There is no need for an outsider to find the e-th root in Z_n^* which is well known to be a difficult problem.

A similar failure occurred in a protocol for fair-exchange of signed documents [1] (discovered by Colin Boyd [4]) which allows decryption by any non-recipient using the order of a subgroup disclosed.

The moral of this failure is that when a prime order subgroup of Z_n^* is made public, great care must be taken in protocol design not to transform a problem in Z_n^*, which is thought to be difficult, into an easy job in the subgroup.

4 Class 3: Significant Complexity Reduction for Integer Factorization

Let us now examine the structure of a composite integer $n = pq$ in which a factor of $\phi(n) = (p-1)(q-1)$ is made public. The widely adopted method for disclosing a subgroup of Z_n^* [1,8,9,11,13]) is in such a structure. Let

$$n = pq, \ p = 2p'f + 1, \ q = 2q'f + 1, \tag{7}$$

where p, q, f are distinct primes and p', q' are relatively prime integers. Here we see that the quantity

$$r = 4f^2 \tag{8}$$

is a factor of $\phi(n)$, and in the schemes referred above, the factor r is made public. (In [11], an additional factor, which is a factor of p', is also made public. We will examine that case in a moment.)

We first note

$$n + 1 = \phi(n) + p + q. \tag{9}$$

So when $r|\phi(n)$ is disclosed, we have

$$p + q \equiv n + 1 (\mathrm{mod}\ r). \tag{10}$$

For $r < p+q$ (otherwise the above congruence is an equation and $p+q$ is disclosed directly), we can rewrite the congruence (10) as

$$p + q = kr + (n + 1 \ \mathrm{mod}\ r), \tag{11}$$

where k is a unknown quantity to be determined. From (11) it is easy to see $|k| \approx |p+q| - |r|$, where $|a|$ denotes the bit length of the integer a in the binary representation. Notice that if $p + q$ becomes known, factoring n follows a simple calculation. For known r, finding $p + q$ using (11) is equivalent to finding the unknown k, and hence the difficulty of factoring n is equivalent to that of finding k. Clearly, an exhaustive search for $p+q$ based on the equation (11) will require

$$O(2^{|p+q|-|r|}) = O(2^{|(p'+q')/2f|}) \tag{12}$$

steps. This seems to be the basis for the choice of security parameters in most schemes using a prime order subgroup of Z_n^* [8,9,11,13]. However, there exists a much more efficient attack only requiring the square root of the above complexity.

Combining (9) and (11), we have

$$n + 1 - (n + 1 \ \mathrm{mod}\ r) = \phi(n) + kr. \tag{13}$$

Since $u^{\phi(n)} = 1 \,(\mathrm{mod}\ n)$ for an arbitrary u in Z_n^*, raising u to the both sides of (13) yields

$$u^{n+1-(n+1 \ \mathrm{mod}\ r)} = w^k \,(\mathrm{mod}\ n), \tag{14}$$

where $w = u^r \bmod n$ is known. Here we may assume u to have the maximum order $\lambda(n) = 2fp'q'$ since most elements in Z_n^* will have this order. Note by symmetry for $p > q$ (hence $p' > q'$) and $q' > 3$, we have

$$ord_n(u) = 2fp'q' > 2fp'3 = 3(p-1) > 2p > p+q > kr.$$

So the order of u (greatly) exceeds kr and this means in the transformation from (9), (11) to (14), the quantity k will not be reduced in modulo $ord_n(u)$.

A straightforward way to solve the equation (14) is to use Shanks' "baby-step giant-step" method (e.g., see [18,5]). It requires

$$O(2^{|k|/2}) = O(2^{(|p+q|-|r|)/2}) \tag{15}$$

steps of group computation (multiplication modulo n) and the same order of memory. This is a much lowered time complexity than that in (12) as it is the positive square root of (12).[1] However, since space is usually more expensive than time, the large space needed makes this method likely to be infeasible for k with critical sizes. Fortunately there are two memoryless variants of Shanks' method due to Pollard: the *rho* method and the *lambda* method [14] (see also [18]). Both methods have the same square-root running time, but the space requirement is negligible. Pollard's rho method requires explicit knowledge of the order of the underlying group (i.e., the order of w in (14)), so it can't be used for our purpose. However, the lambda method works even if the group order is not known; The method may produce an exponent with a small multiple of the group order added (modulo addition/subtraction). This is usually not a problem. In particular, for k with sizes of our interest, the order of w $(ord_n(w) = p'q')$ should be much larger than k. So we can extract the exact value of k from the lambda method.

In the above we have proven the following statement:

Proposition 2. *Let $n = pq$ for p, q being two distinct primes and suppose that $|p| \approx |q|$. When r is a known factor of $(p-1)(q-1)$, then n can be factored in time $O(2^{(|n|-2|r|)/4})$ using Pollard's lambda method.* □

Most schemes using the key setting in (7) base their security on both the difficulty of factoring n and the difficulty of finding discrete logarithms mod f for the known order f. Let us consider minimal requirements for choosing key parameters for such applications. For this, suppose that the current (perhaps not long-term) accepted comfortable margin for computational infeasibility is about 2^{70}. First of all, the disclosed order f should be at least 140 bits long to thwart Pollard's rho method for finding discrete logarithms mod f. Next, Proposition 2 requires that $|n| - 2|r|$ should be at least 280. Therefore, the modulus n should be at least 844 bits long (i.e., $|p| = |q| = 422$), since $|r| = 2|f| + 2 = 282$. More generally, to guarantee the security level of $2^{|f|/2}$ steps for both the above two attacks, we should have at least

$$|p| = |q| \geq 3|f|.$$

Note however that though Proposition 2 is the best result currently known (at least to the authors) on exploitation of computing small discrete logarithms, we can't exclude the possibility of existing a more efficient specialized factoring attack for such a key setting.

---

[1] A similar (less general) method for the square-root reduction was first given in [12].

$|f|$	$|k|$	complexity	actual timing
160	31	2^{15}	12 seconds
156	39	2^{20}	197 seconds
152	47	2^{24}	54 minutes
148	55	2^{28}	18 hrs 22 min

Table 1. Implementation results of Pollard's lambda method for $|n| = 704$

From the above analysis we know that 840 should be the least length setting for a modulus n in the construction (7) of which a subgroup of order f is disclosed. Any such moduli with length less than 800 bits are likely to be dangerous. For instance, for an 800-bit $n = pq$ with p, q of similar lengths and for f being a 160-bit prime, n can be factored in roughly 2^{40} steps of multiplication, well within the grasp of a determined attacker. In the case of key setting in [8,9] ($|f| = 140$, $|p| = |q| = 350$), the cost for factoring is about 2^{35} steps. The key setting in Sect.5 of [11] consists of $|f| = 160$, $|p| = |q| = 395$, and thus n can be factored in about 2^{38} steps.

A prime order subgroup used in Sect.4 of [11] uses the following construction for modulus n

$$n = pq, \ p = 2p'\gamma^d f + 1, \ q = 2q'f + 1,$$

where $gcd(\gamma, x) = 1$ for $x = p', q', f$. The numbers f, γ, and d are disclosed. Further, [11] stipulates that γ should be in the following order of magnitude

$$O(poly_1(k))^{O(poly_2(k))},$$

where $poly_1(k)$, $poly_2(k)$ are polynomials in $k = |p'| = |q'|$ (this definition of k is specified in Section 2 of [19]). In [11], no information is given on the sizes of p and q with respect to the size of γ^d. However, from the specified order of magnitude, the size of γ^d is comparable to $|p'|, |q'|$ and it may easily reach a few hundred bits. Note that in such a setting, $4f^2\gamma^d$ is a known factor of $(p-1)(q-1)$. So using this factor in the complexity bound in Proposition 2, the time for factoring n can further be lowered by $2^{|\gamma^d|/2}$ times from the case where only f is disclosed. The only way to avoid factorization is to increase the size of the modulus (and must at the same time limit the degree of $poly_2(k)$ in comparison to that of $poly_1(k)$). Such moduli are likely to exceed a practical size.

We have implemented Pollard's lambda method for solving the equation (14) to verify that our attack actually works. A number of moduli with the structure of (7) have been tested and successfully factored. As nontrivial examples (listed in A), each modulus n has 704 bits and $\phi(n)$ has a factor $r = 4f^2$ with f being prime. We computed the exponent k in (14) using our implementation of the lambda method and knowledge of n and f only. Table 1 lists the result of factoring four 704-bit moduli n with $|f| = 160, 156, 152$ and 148, corresponding to $|k| = 31, 39, 47$ and 55, respectively, on a Pentium II PC (Windows 95, 266

MHz).[2] We used the crypto-library with partial assembly coding (developed in Future Systems, Inc.), but the lambda algorithm itself was not much optimized.

Note that Pollard's lambda method can be parallelized with a perfect linear speedup (m-fold speedup with m processors) analogously to the rho method [17]. Exploiting the parallelizability, a 2^{40} level time complexity (exceeding the problems in [8,9,11]) can be handled by amateur attackers. For example, using 128 processors, each at the level of 266 MHz Pentium II, we can deduce from our experiment that a 704-bit modulus with $|f| = 140$ (resulting time complexity: 2^{35}) can be factored within one day.

5   Conclusion

We have analyzed a number of failures in cryptosystems and protocols that use prime order subgroups of Z_n^*, and shown that great care must be taken for such uses. The results of the open trapdoor revealed in Section 2, and the much lowered complexity for factoring n shown in Section 4, may not be new in mathematics; nevertheless to our belief, should be aware to the community of cryptosystem and protocol design.

Acknowledgments

We are grateful to Colin Boyd of Queensland University of Technology, Brisbane, Liqun Chen, Kenneth Paterson and Nigel Smart of HP Labs., Bristol for their constructive and critical comments. The implementation of lambda algorithm was done by Hyo Sun Hwang of Future Systems, Inc., Seoul. We would like to express special thanks for his time and effort.

References

1. Bao, F., R. Deng and W. Mao. Efficient and practical fair exchange protocols with off-line TTP. 1998 IEEE Symposium on Security and Privacy. Oakland, May 1998. pages 77–85. IEEE Compute Society.
2. Boyd, C. Digital signature and public key cryptosystem in a prime order subgroup of Z_n^*. *First International Conference on Information and Communications Security, ICICS'97 (LNCS 1334)*, pages 346–355. Springer, 1997.
3. Boyd, C. Presentation in *First International Conference on Information and Communications Security, ICICS'97* for fixing a flaw in the paper "Digital signature and public key cryptosystem in a prime order subgroup of Z_n^*". Beijing, November 1997.
4. Boyd, C. Personal communications.
5. H. Cohen. *A Course in Computational Algebraic Number Theory*. Springer-Verlag Graduate Texts in Mathematics 138. 1993.

---

[2] Actual timings may vary from instance to instance, but the presented timings were obtained from a single run for each instance.

6. ElGamal, T. A public-key cryptosystem and a signature scheme based on discrete logarithms. *IEEE Transactions on Information Theory*, IT-31(4):469–472, July 1985.

7. Fiat, A. and A. Shamir. How to prove yourself: Practical solution to identification and signature problems. *Advances in Cryptology — Proceedings of CRYPTO'86 (LNCS 263)*, pages 186–194. Springer-Verlag, 1987.

8. Girault, M. An identity-based identification scheme based on discrete logarithms modulo a composite number. In *Advances in Cryptology — Proceedings of EUROCRYPT'90 (LNCS 473)*, pages 481–486. Springer-Verlag, 1991.

9. Girault, M. and J.C. Paillès. An identity-based scheme providing zero-knowledge authentication and authenticated key-exchange. First European Symposium on Research in Computer Security–ESORICS'90, pages 173–184. 1990.

10. Guillou, L.C. and J.-J. Quisquater. A practical zero-knowledge protocol fitted to security microprocessor minimizing both transmission and memory. In *Advances in Cryptology — Proceedings of EUROCRYPT'88 (LNCS 330)*, pages 123–128. Springer-Verlag, 1988.

11. Kim, S. J., S. J. Park and D. H. Won. Convertible group signatures. *Advances in Cryptology — Proceedings of ASIACRYPT'96 (LNCS 1163)*, pages 310–321. Springer, 1996.

12. Lim, C.H. and P.J. Lee. Sparse RSA secret keys and their generation. *Proc. 3rd Workshop on Selected Areas of Cryptography*, Aug.15-16, 1996, pp.117-131, Queen's University, Ontario.

13. Park, S., S. Kim and D. Won. ID-based group signature. *Electronics Letters*. Vol.33, No.19, pages 1616–1617. September 1997.

14. Pollard, J.M. Monte Carlo method for index computation (mod p), *Mth. Comp.*, Vol.32, No.143 (1978), pages 918-924.

15. Rabin, M.O. Digital signatures and public-key functions as intractable as factorization. MIT Laboratory for Computer Science, Technical Report, MIT/LCS/TR-212. 1979.

16. Rivest, R.L., A. Shamir and L.M. Adleman. A method for obtaining digital signatures and public-key cryptosystems. *Communications of the ACM* v.21, n.2, pages 120–126. 1978.

17. Van Oorschot, P.C. and M.J. Wiener, Parallel collision search with application to hash functions and discrete logarithms, *Proc. 2nd ACM Conference on Computer and Communications Security*, Nov.2-4 1994, Fairfax, Verginia, pp.210-218. (a revised version to appear in *Journal of Cryptology*).

18. Van Oorschot, P.C. and M.J. Wiener, On Diffie-Hellman key agreement with short exponents, *Advances in Cryptology-EUROCRYPT'96* (LNCS 1070), pages 332–343, Springer-Verlag, 1996.

19. Zheng, Y., T. Matsumoto and H. Imai. Residuosity problem and its applications to cryptography. *Trans. IEICE,* Vol.E71, No.8, pages 759–767. 1988.

A   Factorization Examples

Listed here are four examples of factoring composite numbers $n_i = p_i q_i$ with $|n_i| = 704$ ($i = 1, 2, 3, 4$). Each of them is in the structure of (7) with a disclosed prime number f_i satisfying $4f_i^2|\phi(n_i)$, respectively. (Each disclosed number is the prime order of a subgroup in $Z_{n_i}^*$.) The factorization procedure, which uses knowledge of n_i and f_i only, consists of the following steps. Let $r_i = 4f_i^2$; find k_i by solving (14) using Pollard's lambda method and an arbitrary $u \in Z_{n_i}^*$; finally compute the sum of the two factors $p_i + q_i$ from (11).

$n_1 =$
4403878983927236608971167875854901858578130637648121930967501603157159110337100473118835059630202675486525459776285546455730190806180736806852837917309023035925379055536141453157681843189089797893962528442
9109969

$f_1 = 1279307573885884659565630730667563032209304623881$ ($|f_1| = 160$)

$k_1 = 2027611962$ ($|k_1| = 31$)

$p_1 + q_1 =$
13273784976299044547490668423368063756808688033061030560778659385613470153995077873141935147799796097271326

$p_1 =$
6734627128800575803512180246648669827034193598235048446630801737104548023040804821535454700449823437654803

$q_1 =$
6539157847498468743978488176719393929774494434825982114147857648508922130954273051606480447349972659616523

$n_2 =$
64554109864989573045209981572033362472631867814455170482343370081941753746147198365197379034347649276672413487013119530111186371188425802082282261069333765602676405706934984632393167881107061767091344388233210497

$f_2 = 86377634978865770214549290023394612171958862633$ ($|f_2| = 156$)

$k_2 = 538747074867$ ($|k_2| = 39$)

$p_2 + q_2 =$
16078574203113175306560234663909305050475184101648412171345388343619358401841450007235060358847689467446062

$p_2 =$
7763556732782041821097239654335578210297440729784444100583828196219292538274120851161987346342157066235939

$q_2 =$
8315017470331133485462995009573726840177743371863968070761560147400065863567329156073073012505532401210123

$n_3 =$
49717795134695045326475112627330486057331272421904875018507553084533

28535166549501577613963887317483273134902374557567913651145723535990
21740913276114932911412468599093017719864542252814715746579589808031
33009497

$f_3 = 5199318848515295611566769410707286918384452513$ ($|f_3| = 152$)

$k_3 = 130766945849270$ ($|k_3| = 47$)

$p_3 + q_3 =$
1414004770641194033062584493951204837456556488066290058212225984441
079384020823262406209041853117141243942

$p_3 =$
65528757600968992834709152083734731421153187063781982357964242382851
02130907506525723131350775223761127159

$q_3 =$
75871719463150410471549297311385752324502461816880918224158017461559
77253113316736683077691077893380116783

$n_4 =$
48674186760539467681018145523056045973888236415345231292673943613500
03686092964604087243177579323851165956239195451395380585901768379305
01449596943339226807057417747240009896818786895758692021292580430607
40210629

$f_4 = 330123952043083490387386128078634198300183001$ ($|f_4| = 148$)

$k_4 = 32139335064789130$ ($|k_4| = 55$)

$p_4 + q_4 =$
14010413393076943015390974069221998326136511372422548051245305917863
342832550005586489706641326886563369946

$p_4 =$
76366606542329158917195431596702997461688808846138079970516645219141
51997938395920083821905816573720062483

$q_4 =$
63737527388440271236714309095516985799676304878087400541936413959491
90834611609666405884735510312843307463

Weak Invertibility of Finite Automata and Cryptanalysis on FAPKC*

ZongDuo Dai[1], Ding Feng Ye[2] and Kwok Yan Lam[2]

[1]Dept. of Math., State Key Lab. of Information Security
Graduate School, Academia Sinica, 100039-08, Beijing, China,
yangdai@mimi.cnc.ac.cn

[2]Dept. of ISCS, National University of Singapore,
Lower Kent Ridge Road, Singapore 119260
yedf@iscs.nus.sg   lamky@iscs.nus.sg

Abstract

FAPKC [17, 18, 19, 20, 22] is a public key cryptosystem based weakly invertible finite automata. Weak invertibility of FAs is the key to understand and analyze this scheme. In this paper a set of algebraic terminologies describing FAs is developed, and the theory of weak invertibility of FAs is studied. Based on this, a cryptanalysis on FAPKC is made. It is shown that the keys proposed in [17, 18, 19, 20, 21] for FAPKCs are insecure both in encrypting and in signing.

Keywords: finite automaton, public key cryptosystem, cryptanalysis

1   Introduction

Finite automaton (FA) is a widely used concept in computer science and has several definitions slightly different to each other according to applications. In this context, it refers to a finite sequential state machine, which was studied widely, say for example in [1-16]. The action of such a machine is controlled by a clock which ticks with inputs, i.e., on receiving an input symbol, it produces an output symbol and its state transfers to a new one according to certain rules, and thus with an initial state and an input sequence of finite length it produces an output sequence of the same length. Hence a finite automaton is an analogue to a usual function when viewed as a transformation from input sequences to output sequences. A *weakly invertible finite automaton* (WIFA) with *delay* τ, or simply τ-*weakly invertible finite automaton*, is such a FA that any input is uniquely determined by the corresponding state and output together with the subsequent τ outputs. That is, the input information can be recovered from the outputs after waiting τ steps, or in other words, with τ delays. WIFAs are similar to the usual injective functions in the respect that one can retrieve the input

---

*This work was supported by Chinese Natural Science Foundation.

K. Ohta and D. Pei (Eds.): ASIACRYPT'98, LNCS 1514, pp. 227-241, 1998.
© Springer-Verlag Berlin Heidelberg 1998

information from the outputs. However the delay τ and the state dependence make it much more complicated for one to recover the input information than the usual injective functions. The first objective of this paper is to set up a systematic theory in dealing with the the problems such as how to construct weak invertible FAs and their weak inverses, and how to routinely retrieve input information from outputs and the initial state.

FAPKC, which is a public key cryptosystem and can do both encrypting and signing, is based on weakly invertible finite automata (WIFAs). FAPKC was first introduced in 1985 [17], named as FAPKC0. Some versions were published in 1986 [18], named as FAPKC1 and FAPKC2. Then a new version was introduced in 1995 [20], named as FAPKC3. Roughly speaking, in all these systems, the private key consists of two FAs whose weak inverses can be easy constructed, and the public key is the composition of them. It is believed in [18-21] that it is hard to decompose the public key to get the private two FAs and that it is hard to get a weak inverse of the composed FA without knowing this decomposition, hence any user can encrypt messages or verify signatures using the public key, but can neither decrypt the cipher-texts nor forge the signatures without knowing its two private components. To hide the components from the composed FA, it is proposed to use boolean functions to express the composition. Then how to maintain a moderate public key size becomes a big problem, as composition would generally yield boolean expression exploding when the outer component is nonlinear. The proposed method is to restrict the input set X equal or smaller than F^8, where F is the binary field $GF(2)$, and to restrict the nonlinear degree of the components to be small. The early versions were analysed in some papers, say in [23, 24, 25, 26].

The main contribution of this paper consists of two parts. In the first part (Section 3-5), we develop a set of algebraic terminologies to describe FAs and give a systematic treatment to the weak invertibility theory on the seperable memory FAs. In the second part (Section 6-7), based on the developed theory, we make a simple introduction to FAPKC and then a cryptanalysis on it. Our results show that all the keys proposed for FAPKC in [17, 18, 19, 20, 21] are insecure both in encrypting and in signing. Before coming to the main topic, we recall some basic definitions in the next section.

Due to lack of space, the proofs of all the lemmas and theorems in this paper are ommited.

2   Basic Definitions

For convenience, in this section we restate some basic concepts, which can be found in [8] except some concepts like the natural pairs and the right τ-weak inverses.

A *finite automaton* (FA) is a pentad $M = (X, Y, S, \delta, \lambda)$ where X, Y are input and output symbol sets respectively, S is the state set, X, Y and S are all finite, $\delta : S \times X \to S$ is the next state function, and $\lambda : S \times X \to Y$ is the output function. In the sequel, let $X^i = \{x_0 x_1 \cdots x_{i-1} | x_j \in X, 0 \le j < i\}$ be the set of all input sequence of length i, similarly for Y^i. For any $s \in S$, we use $M(s)$ and $\delta(s)$ denote the function from $\bigcup_{i \geq 1} X^i$ to $\bigcup_{i \geq 1} Y^i$ and the function from $\bigcup_{i \geq 1} X^i$ to S defined as

$$M(s)x_0 x_1 \cdots x_{i-1} = y_0 y_1 \cdots y_{i-1}$$
$$\delta(s)x_0 x_1 \cdots x_{i-1} = s_i$$

, where $s_0 = s, s_{j+1} = \delta(s_j, x_j)$, $y_j = \lambda(s_j, x_j)$, $x_j \in X$, $0 \leq j < i$. For any two FAs M, M' which have the same input space X and the same output space Y, we say a state s in M is *equivalent* to a state s' in M' if $M(s) = M'(s')$, denoted by $s \sim s'$; we say M is a *sub-automaton* of M', denoted by $M \leq M'$, if for any state s in M there exists a state s' such that $s \sim s'$; we say M and M' are *equivalent* if $M \leq M' \leq M$. We do not distinguish equivalent FAs in the rest of this paper.

A FA M is called τ-*weakly invertible*, if for any $s \in S$, $x_i, x_i' \in X$, the following condition

$$M(s)x_0' x_1' \cdots x_\tau' = M(s)x_0 x_1 \cdots x_\tau$$

implies $x_0' = x_0$. The least such τ, denoted by $\tau(M)$, is called *information delay* of M.

Let $M_1 = (X, Y, S_1, \delta_1, \lambda_1)$ and $M_2 = (Y, Z, S_2, \delta_2, \lambda_2)$ be two FAs, define the *composition* of M_2 and M_1 to be the FA $M_2 \times M_1 = (X, X, S_2 \times S_1, \delta_2 \times \delta_1, \lambda_2 \times \lambda_1)$ where

$$(\lambda_2 \times \lambda_1)((s_2, s_1), x) = \lambda_2(s_2, \lambda_1(s_1, x))$$
$$(\delta_2 \times \delta_1)((s_2, s_1), x) = (\delta_2(s_2, \lambda_1(s_1, x)), \delta_1(s_1, x))$$

$\forall (s_2, s_1) \in S_2 \times S_1, x \in X$; we usually call M_1 the *inner component*, M_2 the *outer component*. It is true that $(M_2 \times M_1)(s_2, s_1) = M_2(s_2)M_1(s_1)$.

Let $M = (X, Y, S, \delta, \lambda)$ and $M^* = (Y, X, S^*, \delta^*, \lambda^*)$ be two FAs. For $s \in S, s^* \in S^*$, we say (s^*, s) is a τ-*pair* in $M^* \times M$, or s^* is a *left* τ-*match* of s, or s is a *right* τ-*match* of s^*, if

$$(M^* \times M)(s^*, s)x_0 x_1 \cdots x_{n+\tau-1} = w_0 w_1 \cdots w_{\tau-1} x_0 x_1 \cdots x_{n-1}$$

for all $x_0 x_1 \cdots x_{n+\tau-1} \in X^{n+\tau}$, where $w_0 w_1 \cdots w_{\tau-1} \in X^\tau$ may dependent on $x_0 x_1 \cdots x_{\tau-1}$. If further $w_0 w_1 \cdots w_{\tau-1}$ is independent on $x_0 x_1 \cdots x_{\tau-1}$, we say that (s^*, s) is a *natural* τ-*pair*.

Let M and M^* be as above, M^* is called a τ-*weak inverse of* M and τ is called the *recovery delay* of M^* (with respect to M), if for any $s \in S$, there exists a $s^* \in S^*$, such that (s^*, s) is a τ-pair in $M^* \times M$. It is clear that a τ-weak inverse of M can recover the input sequence except the last τ inputs.

In studying the commutability of a FA M and its a weak inverse, we introduce the so-called right weak inverse of M. A FA M^* is called a *right* τ-*weak inverse* of M, if for any state s in M, there exists a state s^* in M^*, such that (s, s^*) is a τ-pair in $M \times M^*$.

3 Input Memory FAs and Quasi-Ring $\mathcal{F}$

From now on, we assume $X = Y = F^l$ (elements being written as column vectors), where $F = GF(2)$ is the binary field, though all the results in this paper hold true when F is any finite field. We will concentrate on the so called *input memory* FAs whose states are determined by some number of the past inputs (see below for the exact definition). Instead of investigating these FAs individually, we study them as a whole set (the quasi-ring $\mathcal{F}$) endowed with some algebraic structure. That is essential to our understanding of FAs. We begin with some definitions.

Let $\beta = \beta(t_{-h}, \cdots, t_0, u_{-k}, \cdots, u_{-1})$ be a function: $X^{1+h} \times Y^k \to Y$. Define the *memory order* of β to be the minimal integer pair (h', k') such that β is irrelevant to all the variables $\{t_{-i}, u_{-j} | i > h' \geq -1, j > k' \geq -1\}$, and denote it by $m(\beta) = (h', k')$.

This function β together with any integer pair (h, k), $h \geq h', k \geq k'$, determines a *memory FA* $M(\beta)^{(h,k)} = (X, X, S_\beta = X^h \times Y^k, \delta_\beta, \lambda_\beta)$ of type (h, k), where for any state $s_0 = (x_{-h} \cdots x_{-1}, y_{-k} \cdots y_{-1}) \in X^h \times X^k$, which is made of the past h inputs and the past k outputs, and any input $x_0 \in X$,

$$\lambda_\beta(s_0, x_0) = \beta(x_{-h}, \cdots, x_{-1}, x_0, y_{-k}, \cdots, y_{-1})$$
$$\delta_\beta(s_0, x_0) = (x_{-h+1} \cdots x_0, y_{-k+1} \cdots y_{-1} \lambda_\beta(s_0, x_0))$$

Notice that all the FAs $M(\beta)^{(h,k)}, h \geq h', k \geq k'$, are equivalent to each other, so we do not care the type (h, k), and write them by the same notation $M(\beta)$, or simply by β when there is no ambiguity.

If the function β is of the form

$$\beta = f(t_{-h}, \cdots, t_0) + g(u_{-k}, \cdots, u_{-1}) \tag{1}$$

we say $M(\beta)$ is a *separable memory FA*, written also as $M_{f,g}$. If $g = 0$, $M_{f,g}$ will be called a *input memory FA* and will be written simply as M_f; in this case, the memory order of $f = \beta$ is simply an integer h, will be denoted by $m(f) = h$.

It is clear that $M_{f,g}$ is τ-weakly invertible if and only if M_f is so, and all the problems on the weak invertibility of the separable memory FAs can be reduced to those of the input memory FAs. In order to understand the separable memory FAs, it is enough to understand the input memory FAs, so, in this paper we will mainly care about input memory FAs.

Let $\mathcal{F}$ be the set of all possible input memory FAs with $X = Y = F^l$:

$$\mathcal{F} = \{f | f = f(t_{-h}, \cdots, t_{-1}, t_0) : X^{1+h} \to X, h \geq 0, \}$$

Here $t_{-i} = (t_{-i,1}, t_{-i,2}, \cdots, t_{-i,l})^t$, where t means the transpose, and $t_{-i,j}$ is a variable taking the values from F.

Let $f = f(t_{-h}, \cdots, t_{-1}, t_0)$, $g = g(t_{-h'}, \cdots, t_{-1}, t_0) \in \mathcal{F}$. Define the *product* of f and g as

$$fg = f(g(t_{-h-h'}, \cdots, t_{-h}), \cdots, g(t_{-h'}, \cdots, t_0)) \tag{2}$$

The FA M_{fg} is denoted by the notation $C'(M_g, M_f)$ in [13]. For any state $s = (a_{-h-h'} \cdots a_{-2} a_{-1}) \in X^{h+h'} = S_{fg}$, it is known [13] that

$$s \sim (t, s_0) \in S_f \times S_g, \tag{3}$$

where

$$
\begin{aligned}
s_0 &= (a_{-h'} \cdots a_{-2} a_{-1}) \in X^{h'} = S_g \\
t &= M_g(a_{-h-h'} \cdots a_{-h-2} a_{-h-1}) a_{-h} \cdots a_{-1} \in X^h = S_f
\end{aligned}
$$

hence M_{fg} is a sub-automaton of $M_f \times M_g$.

With the above multiplication and the usual addition, $\mathcal{F}$ forms a *quasi-ring*, that is, these operations satisfy the laws of a ring except the right-distribution law.

Let $M_{m,l}(F)$ denote the set of all $m \times l$ matrices over F, similarly for $M_{m,l}(F[z])$ ... etc. Under the mapping

$$A = \sum_{0 \le i \le r} A_i z^i \mapsto \sum_{0 \le i \le r} A_i t_{-i}, \ \forall A \in M_{l,l}(F[z]), \text{ where } A_i \in M_{l,l}(F),$$

the matrix ring $M_{l,l}(F[z])$ is embedded in $\mathcal{F}$ and becomes a subring of $\mathcal{F}$, it is exactly the set of all linear FAs in $\mathcal{F}$. t_0 is the identity of $\mathcal{F}$ and will be identified with the identity matrix I and written as 1 sometimes. Similarly, t_{-i} can be identified with the matrix $z^i I$ and written as z^i sometimes.

More generally, let $\mathcal{F}_{m,l}$ be the set of input memory FAs whose output and input space have dimension m and l respectively, the set of linear FAs in $\mathcal{F}_{m,l}$ can be identified with $M_{m,l}(F[z])$. We can similarly define products of elements of $\mathcal{F}_{n,m}$ and elements of $\mathcal{F}_{m,l}$ for any n, m, l. In particular, elements in $\mathcal{F}_{m,l}$ can be multiplied by elements in $M_{n,m}(F[z])$ for any n, m, l. So the boolean expression of an element $f = f(t_{-h}, \cdots, t_0) \in \mathcal{F}$ can be written as:

$$f = CT, \ \ C \in M_{l,n}(F[z]), \ \ T = (T_1, T_2, \cdots, T_n)^t \in \mathcal{F}_{n,l} \tag{4}$$

where $T_i, 1 \le i \le n$, are distinct standard monomials, here by a standard monomial we mean a monomial of the form:

$$\prod_{0 \le i \le h} \prod_{1 \le j \le l} t_{-i,j}^{a_{i,j}}, \ \ a_{i,j} \in \{0, 1\}$$

such that there exists a j such that $a_{0,j} \ne 0$, where $t_{-i,j}^0 = 1, t_{-i,j}^1 = t_{-i,j}$.

4   Right Weak Inverses and M_f-Equations

In this section we study the problem of the existence of the right weak inverses and the problem of solving the equation determined by the operator $M_f(s)$. The following Lemma 1 is critical in our studies. From Lemma 1 one may draw an analogy between a WIFA and a usual map, as it is well known that a map between two finite sets of the same size is injective if and only if it is surjective. To start with, we need to introduce a notion which generalizes the surjectiveness of the usual functions. For a state s of M, we say $M(s)$ is τ-surjective if

$$M(s)X^{\tau+1} = (M(s)X^{\tau}) \times X$$

where $M(s)X^k = \{M(s)\underline{x} | \underline{x} \in X^k\}, \forall k \geq 1$.

Lemma 1 Let $f \in \mathcal{F}$, then f is τ-weakly invertible if and only if $M_f(s)$ is τ-surjective for all $s \in S_f$.   □

Theorem 1 Let $f \in \mathcal{F}, M^* = (X, X, S^*, \delta^*, \lambda^*)$ be a τ-weak inverse of M_f. Then M^* is also a right τ-weak inverse of f. Moreover, if (s^*, s) is a τ-pair in $M^* \times M_f$, let $s^{**} = \delta^*(s^*)M_f(s)\underline{x}^\tau$ for an arbitrary $\underline{x}^\tau \in X^\tau$, then (s, s^{**}) is a natural τ-pair in $M_f \times M^*$.   □

Remark 1 Based on the above Theorem, we may concentrate only on the weak inverses.

Theorem 2 Let $f \in \mathcal{F}$ be weakly invertible with $\tau(f) = \tau$, and let $M^* = (X, X, S^*, \delta^*, \lambda^*)$ be a $\tau'-$weak inverse of M_f, and let (s^*, s) be a τ'-pair in $M^* \times M_f$. Then

1. The M_f−equation

$$M_f(s)\underline{x} = \underline{a},\ \underline{a} = a_0 a_1 \cdots a_{n-1+\tau} \in X^{n+\tau},\ \underline{x} = x_0 x_1 \cdots x_{n-1+\tau}, n \geq 0, \tag{5}$$

   has a solution $\underline{x} \in X^{\tau+n}$ if and only if $a_0 a_1 \cdots a_{\tau-1} \in M_f(s)X^\tau$, and if it has a solution, then the first n inputs $x_0 x_1 \cdots x_{n-1}$ are uniquely determined.

2. If the equation (5) has a solution, then $\underline{x}$ is a solution if and only if it can be read out by applying $M^*(s^*)$ on $\underline{a} \underline{*}^{\tau'}$ for some $\underline{*}^{\tau'} \in X^{\tau'}$ as follows:

$$\underline{*}_1^{\tau'} \underline{x} = M^*(s^*)\underline{a} \underline{*}^{\tau'}$$

   where $\underline{*}_1^{\tau'} \in X^{\tau'}$ is irrelevant data.   □

In the sequel, a separable memory FA is denoted by the notation $M_{f,zg}$ naturally, where $f \in \mathcal{F}$ and $g \in \mathcal{F}$.

Theorem 3   1. For any $f \in \mathcal{F}$ and $g \in \mathcal{F}$, the equation $M_{f,zg}(s, r)\underline{x} = \underline{a}$ is equivalent to the equation $M_f(s)\underline{x} = \underline{a}',\ \underline{a}' = M_{1-zg}(r)\underline{a}$.

2. Let $f \in \mathcal{F}$, $\tau \geq \tau(f)$, $S_f = X^h$, $s^- \in X^{h-\tau}$, $\underline{a} \in X^n$, then the equation $M_f(s^- \underline{x}^\tau)\underline{x} = \underline{a}$ always has a solution $\underline{x}^\tau \underline{x} \in X^{\tau+n}$. Moreover, the data $\underline{x}^\tau \underline{x} \in X^{n+\tau}$ is a solution if and only if $\underline{x}^\tau \underline{x}$ satisfies:

$$M_f(\underline{b}^\tau s^-)\underline{x}^\tau \underline{x} = \underline{c}^\tau \underline{a}$$

for some $\underline{b} \in X^\tau$, $\underline{c}^\tau \in M_f(\underline{b}^\tau s^-)X^\tau$.

3. *Assume $f = f_2 f_1$ and s is equivalent to the state $(s_2, s_1) \in S_{f_2} \times S_{f_1}$ (see (3)). Assume M_2^* is a τ_2-weak inverse of M_{f_2}, and (s_2^*, s_2) is a τ_2-pair in $M_2^* \times M_{f_2}$. Then $\underline{x}$ is a solution of the equation (5) if and only if it satisfies :*

$$\underline{a}' = M_{f_1}(s_1)\underline{x}$$

where $\underline{a}'$ is obtained as follows:

$$\underline{*}_1^{\tau_2} \underline{a}' = M_2^*(s_2^*) \underline{a} \, \underline{*}^{\tau_2}, \quad \underline{*}^{\tau_2} \in X^{\tau_2}.$$ $\qquad\square$

5   Constructing WIFAs

Denote the set consisting of all possible weakly invertible elements in $\mathcal{F}$ by $\mathcal{F}^*$, and denote the set consisting of all possible τ-weakly invertible elements in $\mathcal{F}$ by $\mathcal{F}_\tau^*$. In this section, we study how to construct the elements in $\mathcal{F}^*$ and how to construct their weak inverses and the related state pairs. The last problem will be considered in Theorem 4. As will be shown, there are two types of primitive weakly invertible elements, namely weakly invertible linear FAs and 0-weakly invertible FAs, they and their weak inverses can be constructed systematically (Theorem 5 and 6). More elements in $\mathcal{F}^*$ can be generated with these two type of primitive elements by making (finite number of) the multiplicative and some proper additive operations (Theorem 7 and 8). Note that 0-WIFAs have no contribution to the information delay in such constructions, it would be interesting if one can construct systematically nonlinear WIFAs with positive delays without using any linear FAs as ingredients, but it seems a hard task.

In the sequel we denote the group consisting of all invertible $l \times l$ matrices over $F[z]$ by $GL_l(F[z])$, similarly for $GL_l(F) \ldots$ etc.

Theorem 4 *Let $M^* = (X, X, S^*, \delta^*, \lambda^*)$ be a τ-weak inverse of $f \in \mathcal{F}^*$, given a single τ-pair (b^*, b) in $M^* \times M_f$, for any state $s \in F^h = S_f$ in M_f, let $s^* = \delta^*(b^*) M_f(b) \underline{*}^d s$, then (s^*, s) is a natural τ-pair in $M^* \times M_f$, where $\underline{*}^d \in X^d$, and $d = 0$ if $h \geq \tau$ and $d = \tau - h$ if $\tau > h$.* $\qquad\square$

Remark 2 *For any given IMFA M_f and its a τ-weak inverse M_*, in order to be able to construct a τ-match for each of the states in M_f, it is enough to be able to construct only a single τ-pair in $M^* \times M_f$ according to the above Theorem.*

In order to describe all the linear elements in $\mathcal{F}^*$, we need the following kind of decompositions of matrices in $M_{l,l}(F[z])$. For any $0 \neq B \in M_{l,l}(F[z])$, by using the well-known algorithm [27] for transforming a matrix over $F[z]$ into diagonal form, one can get a decomposition of B of the form as below,

$$B = PDQ(1 - zb) \qquad (6)$$

where $P \in GL_l(F[z])$, $Q \in GL_l(F)$, $b \in M_{l,l}(F[z])$ and D is a $l \times l$ diagonal matrix determined by a tuple $\underline{n} = (n_0, n_1, \cdots, n_\tau)$ of integers

$$D = diag(I_{n_0}, zI_{n_1}, z^2 I_{n_2}, \cdots, z^\tau I_{n_\tau}, 0_n),$$
$$n = l - \sum_{0 \le i \le \tau} n_i, \ \tau \ge 0, \ n_\tau > 0, \ n_i \ge 0 \ (i < \tau),$$

where I_n is the $n \times n$ identity matrix, 0_n is the $n \times n$ zero matrix. The tuple $\underline{n}$ is uniquely determined by B and will be called the *structure parameter* of B.

Theorem 5 [15, 16, 26] *Let* $B \in M_{l,l}(F[z])$ *is of the form as in* (6), *then*

1. *B is weakly invertible if and only if* $\det(B) \ne 0$, *which is equivalent to* $l = \sum_{0 \le i \le \tau} n_i$.
2. *If B is weakly invertible, then* $\tau(B) = \tau$.
3. *If $\tau(B) = \tau$, then $M_{A,zb}$ is a τ-weak inverse of B, where $A = Q^{-1}CP^{-1}$, $C = z^\tau D^{-1}$; and $((\underline{0}, \underline{0}), \underline{0})$ is a τ-pair in $M_{A,zb} \times M_B$.* $\square$

Theorem 6 *Let* $f = f(t_{-h}, \cdots, t_{-1}, t_0) \in \mathcal{F}$, *then f is 0-weakly invertible if and only if $f(a_{-h}, \cdots, a_{-1}, t_0)$ is a permutation on X for each state $s = (a_{-h}, \cdots, a_{-1})$ in M_f, and in this case, f can be expressed as the following form:*

$$f = \sum_{1 \le i \le n} c_i(t_{-h}, \cdots, t_{-1}) P_i(t_0)$$

where $n \ge 1, P_i$ is a permutation on X, the coefficient $c_i(t_{-h}, \cdots, t_{-1})$ is a function taking the values in $\{0, 1\}$ on the understanding that $0P_i(t_0) = 0$, $1P_i(t_0) = P_i(t_0)$, and $\sum_{1 \le i \le n} c_i(t_{-h}, \cdots, t_{-1}) = 1$(as integer sum), moreover, put

$$\beta = \sum_{1 \le i \le n} c_i(u_{-h}, \cdots, u_{-1}) P_i(t_0)^{-1}$$

then the memory FA $M(\beta)$ is a 0-weak inverse of M_f, it has the same state set as M_f, and (s, s) is a 0-pair in $M(\beta) \times M_f$ for any state s in M_f. In particular, the following three types of elements are all 0-weakly invertible: 1. permutations on X; 2. $1 + zk, k \in \mathcal{F}$; 3. $1 + UkV$, where $UV = VU = 0$, $U \in M_{l,l}(F[z])$, $V \in M_{l,l}(F[z])$, and $k \in \mathcal{F}$. $\square$

It is known that $\mathcal{F}^*$ is closed under the multiplicative operation, *i.e.*, if $f_i \in \mathcal{F}^*(i = 1, 2)$, then $f_2 f_1 \in \mathcal{F}^*$. Moreover, we have

Theorem 7 *Let $f_i \in \mathcal{F}$, $i = 1, 2$, then $f_2 f_1 \in \mathcal{F}^*$ if and only if $f_i \in \mathcal{F}^*$ for $i = 1$ and 2. And in this case $\tau(f_i) \le \tau(f_2 f_1) \le \tau(f_1) + \tau(f_2)$.* $\square$

To describe the inverse of the composed FA $M_{f_2 f_1}$, the following construction is useful. Given $M = (X, X, S, \delta, \lambda)$, let

$$M^{(\tau)} = (X, X, S \times \{0, 1, \cdots, \tau\}, \delta^{(\tau)}, \lambda^{(\tau)})$$

where

$$\delta^{(\tau)}(s,i)x = \begin{cases} (s, i+1), & 0 \le i < \tau \\ (\delta(s,x), \tau), & i = \tau \end{cases}$$

and

$$\lambda^{(\tau)}(s,i)x = \begin{cases} \underline{0} \in X, & 0 \le i < \tau \\ \lambda(s,x), & i = \tau \end{cases}$$

The following theorem is well-known:

Theorem 8 *Let* $f_i \in \mathcal{F}$, $i = 1, 2$, *and* M_i^* *be a* τ_i-*weak inverse of* M_{f_i}, *then* $M_1^{*(\tau_2)} \times M_2^*$ *is a* $(\tau_1 + \tau_2)$-*weak inverse of* $M_{f_2 f_1}$. *Moreover, for any state* s *in* $M_{f_1 f_2}$, *let* (s_2, s_1) *be the state in* $M_{f_2} \times M_{f_1}$ *and equivalent to* s *(see (3)), and let* (s_i^*, s_i) *be a* τ_i-*pair in* $M_i^* \times M_{f_i}$, *then* $((s_1^*, 0), s_2^*), (s_2, s_1))$ *is a* $(\tau_1 + \tau_2)$-*pair* *in* $(M_1^{*(\tau_2)} \times M_2^*) \times M_{f_2 f_1}$. □

The next result shows that $\mathcal{F}_\tau^*$ is closed under the operation adding the elements of the form $z^{\tau+1} g$, $g \in \mathcal{F}$. To see how the inverses of $f + z^{\tau+1} g$ is related to that of f, we define the *circle product* of $M = (X, Y, S, \delta, \lambda)$ and M_β to be the FA $M \circ M_\beta = (X, Y, S \times S_\beta, \delta^\circ, \lambda^\circ)$ where $\beta = \beta(t_{-h}, \cdots, t_{-1}, t_0; u_{-k}, \cdots, u_{-1})$ is a function from $X^{h+1} \times Y^k$ to Y, $S_\beta = X^h \times Y^k$, and for any state $(s_0, r_0 = (x_{-h}, \cdots, x_{-1}, y_{-k}, \cdots, y_{-1})) \in S \times S_\beta$, and any input x_0, the functions δ° and λ° are defined as

$$\lambda^\circ((s_0, r_0), x_0) = \lambda(s_0, \lambda_\beta(r_0, x_0)),$$
$$\delta^\circ((s_0, r_0), x_0) = (\delta(s_0, \lambda_\beta(r_0, x_0)), \lambda_\beta(r_0, \lambda^\circ((s_0, r_0), x_0))).$$

Theorem 9 *Let* $f \in \mathcal{F}_\tau^*$, *and* $M^* = (X, X, S^*, \delta^*, \lambda^*)$ *be a* τ-*weak inverse of* M_f, *then*

1. $f - z^{1+\tau} g \in \mathcal{F}_\tau^*$ *for any* $g \in \mathcal{F}$, *moreover* $\tau(f - z^{1+\tau} g) = \tau(f)$.
2. $M^* \circ M_{t_0, z^{\tau+1} g}$ *is a* τ-*weak inverse of* $f - z^{1+\tau} g$. *For any state* s *in* $f - z^{1+\tau} g$, *if* (s^*, s) *is a* τ-*pair in* $M^* \times M_f$, *then* $((s^*, s), s)$ *is a* τ-*pair in* $(M^* \circ M_{t_0, z^{1+\tau} g}) \times M_{f - z^{1+\tau} g}$, *where* s *is considered naturally also as both a state of* $M_{t_0, z^{1+\tau} g}$ *and a state of* M_f. □

6   Brief Introduction of FAPKC

In this section we describe the scheme FAPKC [17, 18, 19, 20, 21] in terminologies developed above.

Choose two elements f_0 and f_1 in $\mathcal{F}^*$ whose weak inverses can be constructed easy, and let M_i^* be the constructed τ_i-weak inverse of $M_{f_i}, i = 0, 1$. Choose $g \in \mathcal{F}$. Write $f = f_0 f_1$, $\tau = \tau_1 + \tau_2$, $M^* = M_1^{*(\tau_0)} \times M_0^*$ (which is a τ-weak inverse of M_f, see Theorem 8). Write $h = h_1 + h_2$, where $h_i = m(f_i)$, $k = m(zg)$. Choose $(s, r) \in X^h \times X^k$ and $(s', r') \in X^h \times X^k$, let $(s^*, s))$ be a τ-pair in $M^* \times M_f$ (see Theorem 8), and (s', s^{**}) be a τ-pair in $M_f \times M^*$ (see Theorem 1). Write $s' = \underline{b}s^-$, where $\underline{b} \in X^\tau$, $s^- \in X^{h-\tau}$. Let $f = CT$ be the boolean expression of f (see (4)).

The keys and the algorithm in FAPKC are as below:

Public key: $C, T, g, s, r, s^-, r', \tau$.

Private key: M^*, s^*, s^{**}.

Encrypting: Suppose $\underline{p} \in X^n$ is the plaintext sequence, select $\underline{x}^\tau \in X^\tau$ randomly, then the ciphertext is $\underline{c} = M_{CT,g}(s,r)\underline{px}^\tau \in X^{n+\tau}$.

Decrypting :   The plaintext $\underline{p}$ can be read out from the equation $\underline{*}^\tau \underline{p} = M^*(s^*)M_{1-zg}(r)\underline{c}$, where $\underline{*}^\tau \in X^\tau$ is irrelevant data.

Signing :   Suppose $\underline{m} \in X^n$ is the message to be signed, select $\underline{*}^\tau \in X^\tau$ randomly, then $\underline{d}^\tau \underline{d} = M^*(s^{**})M_{1-zg}(r')\underline{mx}^\tau$ is the digital signature for $\underline{m}$.

Verifying signature: The receiver verifies whether $M_{CT,zg}(s^-\underline{d}^\tau, r')\underline{d} = \underline{m}$. The receiver accepts $\underline{d}^\tau \underline{d}$ as the legal signature if the equality holds, and rejects it otherwise.

Remark 3 *In the proposed schemes [17, 18, 19, 20], there are some restrictions on choosing the partial state s^-. These restrictions are not necessary in order to make the algorithm work, so all these restrictions have been deleted in the above description.*

Now we list the keys which are proposed in [17, 18, 19, 20, 21] as follows.

Form 1 [17, 18]: f_0 is linear, $\tau(f_1) = 0$.

Form 2 [19]: f_0 is linear, $\tau(f_1) > 0$, M_{f_1} has a weak inverse of the form $M_{A,zk}$ with $A \in M_{l,l}(F[z])$, $l = 8$ and

$$T = (t_{0,1}, t_{0,2}, \cdots, t_{0,8}, t_{0,1}t_{-1,1}, t_{0,2}t_{-1,2}, \cdots, t_{0,8}t_{-1,8})^t. \tag{7}$$

Form 3 [20]: f_0 is linear, $l = m = 8$, $m(T) = 2$ (the memory order of T), $\tau_0 = 7, \tau_1 = 8$, $h_0 + h_1 \le 20$, but no examples for f_1 are given in [20].

Form 4 [21]: $f_0 = B_0 P_0 Q_0, f_1 = B_1 P_1 Q_1$ or $f_1 = B_1$, where $B_i \in M_{l,l}(F[z])$, $Q_i \in M_{l,l}(F)$, each P_i is a permutation on X and is determined by a exponential function of the form $x^{2^a+2^b}$ which is defined over $GF(2^l)$, where $GF(2^l)$ is identified with $X = F^l$ in a natural way.

As the outer component f_0 is nonlinear, the composition $f_0 f_1$ causes an exploding boolean expression, though the nonlinear degree of f_0 is just 2. In order to keep the public key size tolerable, the parameters have to be very small. The following table is copied from [21] to illustrate the suggested parameters and the corresponding public key sizes, where $\tau_0 \le h_0 = m(f_0), \tau_1 \le h_1 = m(f_1)$, $N_1(N_2)$ is the corresponding public key size when f_1 is linear (nonlinear).

l	7	7	5	5	3	3	3
(h_0, h_1)	(1,14)	(7,8)	(1,19)	(10,10)	(1,34)	(10,25)	(17,18)
N_1(Bits)	8281	32948	4075	20950	1593	8883	13041
N_2(Bits)	105840	414512	29850	181725	5400	34560	51192

Remark 4 *In describing the basic algorithm of FAPKC3, it is stated in the section 3 of [20] that the outer component automaton of the public key is a memory finite automaton, which is not neccessarily restricted to be of the above form 3. In this paper, we consider only the latter (i.e., form 3) which is stated in the Section 4 of [20] in describing an implementation of FAPKC3, because in [20] there is neither an example nor suggested parameters for the former except the form 3. We guess it is hard to give such an example with a tolerable public key size.*

It was shown that the encrypting is insecure when the key is of the form 1 in [23] and of the form 2 in [25]. It was shown in [26] that both the encrypting and signing are insecure when the key is of the form 2 without the restriction (7).

7   Cryptanalysis on FAPKC

In this sectin we keep the notations in the last section, and consider the following

Problem 1 *How to decode the ciphertexts and how to forge the signatures without knowing the private key of FAPKC?*

We will show Problem 1 can be solved for any one of the keys of the form 1–4 listed in the last section, and also for the keys of the form 2 without the restriction shown in (7).

To decode the ciphertext is exactly to solve the equation $M_{f,zg}(s,r)\underline{p}\,\underline{x}^\tau = \underline{c} \in X^{n+\tau}$ (where $\underline{p}\,\underline{x}^\tau$ are unknowns), which is reduced to the equation $M_f^-(s)\underline{p}\underline{x}^\tau = \underline{c}'$, where $\underline{c}' = M_{t_0-zg}(r)\underline{c}$ according to Theorem 3.

To forge a signature is exactly to solve the equation $M_{f,zg}(s^-\underline{d}^\tau,r')\underline{d} = \underline{m}$ (where $\underline{d}^\tau\underline{d}$ are unknowns), which is reduced to the equation $M_f(s^-\underline{d}^\tau)\underline{d} = \underline{m}'$, $\underline{m}' = M_{1-zg}(r')\underline{m}$ according to Theorem 3 1., and further to $M_f(\underline{b}^\tau s^-)\underline{d}^\tau \underline{d} = \underline{c}^\tau \underline{m}'$ according Theorem 3 2.. Therefore Problem 1 is reduced to

Problem 2 *How to solve the M_f-equation of the form (5) for $f = f_0 f_1$?*

The following theorem shows that f, as an arbitrary element in $\mathcal{F}^*$, has a routine decomposition which will be used to reduce Problem 2. We'll say two elements f and g in $\mathcal{F}$ are similar if there exists $G \in GL_l(F[z])$ such that $f = Gg$, written as $f \simeq g$.

Theorem 10 *Assume $f = CT \in \mathcal{F}^*, C \in M_{l,n}(F[z])$, then*

1. *Using the well-known method [27] to transform a matrix over $F[z]$ to a diagonal form, we may get*

$$C = B(I,0)Q, B \in M_{l,l}(F[z]), \det(B) \neq 0, Q \in GL_n(F[z]), \qquad (8)$$

where $(I, 0)$ is a matrix of size $l \times n$, I is the identity matrix of $l \times l$ and 0 is the zero matrix of size $l \times (n - l)$, let $f^N = (I, 0)QT$, then $f = Bf^N$, where f^N is uniquely determined up to the similarity.

We'll call f^N the T-nonlinear factor of f, and call B the T-linear factor of f.

2. *For any weakly invertible linear $A \in \mathcal{F}$, denote the T-nonlinear factor of Af by $(Af)^N$, then $(Af)^N \simeq f^N$ and $\tau((Af)^N) = \tau(f^N) \leq \tau(f)$.*   □

From Theorem 10 and Theorem 7 we get

Corollary 1 *Let f^N be the T-nonlinear factor of f defined as in Theorem 10, then $\tau(f^N) \leq \tau_1$ for any one of the keys of the forms 1-4 listed in the last section, and also for the keys of the form 2 without the restriction shown in (7).* □

Notice that the weak inverses of the linear factor of f is easy constructed (see theorem 5), so basing on Theorem 10 and Theorem 3 3., Problem 2 is reduced to

Problem 3 *How to solve the equation of the form $M_{f^N}(s)\underline{x} = \underline{a}$, $\underline{a} \in X^{n+\tau}$, $n \geq 1$ (where f^N is the T-nonlinear factor of f defined as in Theorem 10) ?*

One may try to solve Problem 3 case by case by means of the divide-and-conquer searching method, or according to Theorem 2 try to solve it systematically by solving the following

Problem 4 *How to construct a τ'-weak inverse of M_f or M_{f^N} (where τ' can be chosen arbitrarily)?*

Problem 4 can be solved if we can decompose f or f^N into a product of several FAs each of which can be inverted. It is the case when the key is of the form 2 without the restriction (7), as shown in the following theorem, which characterizes the so-called quasi-linear elements defined as below.

Definition 1 *The element f in $\mathcal{F}$ is called quasi-linear if M_f has a weak inverse of the form $M_{A,zk}$ with $A \in M_{l,l}(F[z])$, $k \in \mathcal{F}$.*

Theorem 11 *Let $f \in \mathcal{F}^*$, then*

1. *f is quasi-linear if and only if f has a decomposition:*

$$f = B(1 - zg), B \in M_{l,l}(F[z]), \det(B) \neq 0, g \in \mathcal{F} \qquad (9)$$

As a consequence, if f is quasi-linear, so is Af for any $A \in M_{l,l}(F[z])$, $\det(A) \neq 0$.

2. If f is quasi-linear, then its a decomposition $f = B(1 - zg)$ of the form (9) and its a weak inverse can be obtained easy from its boolean expression $f = CT$ as follows. Assume $T = \begin{pmatrix} t_0 \\ T' \end{pmatrix}$, $C \in M_{l,n}(F[z])$, correspondingly write $C = (C_0, C'), C_0 \in M_{l,l}(F[z]), C' \in M_{l,n-l}(F[z])$. Let $C_0 = PDQ(I - zb)$ be a decomposition of C_0 of the form (6), and let $A = z^\tau Q^{-1} D^{-1} P^{-1}$, then $A \in M_{l,l}(F[z])$ and $AC' = z^{\tau+1}H$ for some $H \in M_{l,n-l}(F[z])$. Let $g = b - HT'$, $B = PDQ$. Then $f = B(1 - zg)$, and $M_{A,zg}$ is a τ-weak inverse of M_f. □

We claim that Problem 3 can be solved case by case practically by means of the divide-and-conquer searching method when the key is any one of the form 1–4 listed in the last section. To see this, we consider how large $l\tau(f)$ should be in order to resist the devide-and-conquer searching attacks on the equation of the form $M_f(s)\underline{x}^{n+\tau} = \underline{a}, \underline{a} \in X^{n+\tau}$. Let's see at first how to estimate the actual complexity of such an attack. For plain exhaustive searching, an obvious upper bound is $2^{l(1+\tau(f))}$, but the exact bound may be much smaller. When f is linear, the logarithm of the bound to base 2 can be expressed by its structure parameters defined in section 5, and the mean value for this expression is $\frac{l(1+\tau(f))}{2}$. There are no strong reasons why exhaustive searching with a nonlinear FA should be much harder than with a linear one. So, that we use $2^{l(1+\tau(f))/2}$ to estimate the complexity of the devide-and-conquer searching type attacks is not too pessimistic. Thus to resist such attacks to Problem 3, we should require, say, $\frac{l(1+\tau(f^N))}{2} > 60$. Basing on Corollary 1, the parameter $\frac{l(1+\tau(f^N))}{2}$ for any one of the keys of the forms 1–3, and for any one of the suggested keys of the form 4 is estimated as below, and one can see that non of them meets the bound 60.

1. When the key is of the form 1 and the form 2, $\frac{l(1+\tau(f^N))}{2} = 4$.

2. When the key is of the form 3, $\frac{l(1+\tau(f^N))}{2} = 36$

3. When the key is of the form 4, the parameter $\frac{l(1+\tau(f^N))}{2}$ is shown in the following table for the suggested parameters.

l	7	7	5	5	3	3	3
(h_0, h_1)	(1,14)	(7,8)	(1,19)	(10,10)	(1,34)	(10,25)	(17,18)
$\frac{l(1+\tau(f^N))}{2}$	52.5	31.5	50	27.5	52.5	39	28.5

From the above cryptanalysis of this section, we see all the keys proposed in [17, 18, 19, 20, 21] for FAPKC are insecure both in encrypting and signing.

References

[1] Huffman D.A., Canonical Forms for Information Lossless Finite State Logical Machines, IRE Transaction on Circuit Theory, IRE Trans. Cir. Theory, special supplement, 1959, pp.41-59.

[2] Massey J.L. and Sain M.K., Inverses of Linear Sequential Circuits, IEEE Trans. Comput., 1968, **17**: pp.330-337.

[3] Massey J.L. and Sain M.K., A modified Inverse for Linear Dynamical Systems, Proc. IEEE 8th Adaptive Processes Symp., 1969, pp. 5a1-5a3.

[4] Massey J.L. and Sain M.K., IEEE Trans. AC-14, No.2, 1969, pp.141-149.

[5] Forney G.D., Convolution Codes I: Algebraic Structures, IEEE Trans. I.T., 1970, **16**: pp.720-738.

[6] Tao R.J., Invertible Linear Finite Automata, Scientia Sinica, 1973, **16**: pp.565-581.

[7] Kyimit A.A., Information Lossless Automata of Finite Order, New York: Wiley, 1974.

[8] Tao R.J., Invertibility of Finite Automata (in Chinese), Beijing, Science Press, 1979: pp.39-42,68.

[9] Tao R.J., Invertibility of Linear Finite Automata over a Ring, Automata, Languages and Programming (Edited by Timo Lepisto, Arto Salomaa), Lecture Notes in Computer Sciences, Springer Verlag, 1988, **317**:pp.489-501.

[10] Lai X. and Massey J.L., Some Connections between Scramblers and Invertible Automata, Proc. 1988 Beijing Int. Workshop on Info.Th., 1988, pp. DI5.1-DI5.5.

[11] Juhani Heino, Finite Automata: a layman approach, text posted in sci,cript newsgroup, October 1994, Juhanihe@waltari.helsinki.fi, University of Helsinki, Finland, 1994.

[12] Tao R.J., Generating a kind of nonlinear finite automata with invertibility by transformation method, Laboratory for Computer Science, Institute of Software, Chinese Academy of Sciences, Beijing 100080, China, ISCAS–LCS–95–05.

[13] Tao R.J., On invertibility of some compound finite automata, Laboratory for Computer Science, Institute of Software, Chinese Academy of Sciences, Beijing 100080, China, ISCAS–LCS–95–06.

[14] Dai.Z.D., Invariants and Inversibility of Linear Finite Automata, Advances in Cryptology–ChinaCrypt'94 (In Chinease), Science Press, pp.127-134.

[15] Dai Z.D., Ye D.F., Weak Invertibility of Linear Finite Automata over Commutative Rings –Classification and Enumeration (in Chinese), KEXUE TONGBAO(Bulletin of Science), Vol.4, No.15, 8,1995, pp.1357-1360.

[16] Dai Z.D., Ye D.F., Weak Invertibility of Linear Finite Automata I, Classification and Enumeration of Transfer Functions, SCIENCE IN CHINA (Series A), Vol. 39, No. 6, June 1996, pp.613-623.

[17] Tao R.C. and Chen S.H., A Finite Automaton Public Key Cryptosystem and Digital Signatures, Chinese J. of Computer, 1985(8), pp.401-409 (in Chinese).

[18] Tao R.J. and Chen S.H., Two Varieties of Finite Automaton Public Key Cryptosystem and Digital Signatures, J. of Compt. Sci. and Tech., 1986(1), No.1, pp.9-18.

[19] Tao R.J., Conference report, ChinaCrypt'92, Xian, 1992.

[20] Tao R.J. and Chen S.H. and Chen X.M., FAPKC3: a new finite automaton public key cryptosystem, Laboratory for Computer Science, Institute of Software, Chinese Academy of Sciences, Beijing 100080, China, June, 1995. ISCAS–LCS–95–07.

[21] Chen X.M., The Invertibility Theory and Application of Quadratic Finite Automata, Laboratory for Computer Science, Institute of Software, Chinese Academy of Sciences, Beijing 100080, China, November,1996, Doctoral thesis.

[22] Schneier B., Applied Cryptography, second addition, 1994.

[23] Dai D.W., Wu K. and Zhang H.G., Cryptanalysis on a Finite Automaton Public Key Cryptosystem, Science in China, 1994 (in Chinese).

[24] Bao, F., Igarashi,Y., Break Finite Automata Public Key Cryptosystem, Automata, Languages and Programming, Lecture Notes in Computer Sciences, 944(1995), Springer,147-158.

[25] Qin Z.P., Zhang H.G., Cryptanalysis of Finite Automaton Public Key Cryptosystems (in Chinese), –Chinacrypt'96, Science Press, pp.75-86.

[26] Dai Z.D., A Class of Seperable Memory Finite Automata-Cryptoanalysis on FAPKC –Chinacrypt'96, Science Press, pp.75-86.

[27] Jacobson N., Basic Algebra I, W.H.Freeman and Company, San Francisco, pp.175-179.

[28] Wan Z.X., Algebra and Coding Theory (in Chinese), Beijing, Science Press, 1979, p.510.

Bounds and Constructions for Multireceiver Authentication Codes

R. Safavi-Naini and H. Wang

School of IT and CS
University of Wollongong, Northfields Ave
Wollongong 2522, Australia
Email: [rei, hw13]@uow.edu.au

Abstract. Multireceiver authentication codes allow one sender to construct an authenticated message for a group of receivers such that each receiver can verify authenticity of the received message. In this paper, we give a formal definition of multireceiver authentication codes, derive information theoretic and combinatorial lower bounds on their performance and give new efficient constructions for such codes, our constructions are based on the linear error-correcting codes.

Multireceiver authentication codes (MRA-codes) [4] extend Simmons' model of unconditionally secure authentication [16]. In an MRA-code [4], a sender wants to authenticate a message for a group of receivers such that each receiver can verify authenticity of the received message. Receivers are not trusted and may try to construct fraudulent messages on behalf of the transmitter. If the fraudulent message is acceptable by even one receiver the attackers have succeeded. This is a useful extension of traditional authentication code and has numerous applications. For example a director wanting to give instructions to employees in an organisation such that each employee is able to verify authenticity of the message. Providing such service using digital signature implies that security relies on unproven assumptions and the attackers have finite amount of computational resources. In unconditionally secure model, there is no computational assumptions or limitations on the attackers' resources.

A multireceiver A-code can be trivially constructed using traditional A-codes: the sender shares a common key with each receiver; to send an authenticated message it constructs n codewords, one for each receiver, concatenates them and broadcasts the result. Now each receiver can verify its own codeword and so authenticate the message. In this construction collaboration of even $n - 1$ receivers does not help them in constructing a message that is acceptable by the nth receiver simply because the n codewords are independently constructed. If we assume that the size of the malicious groups cannot be too large, for example the biggest number of collaborators is $w - 1$ (where $w < n$), then we can expect to save on the size of the key and the length of the codeword because codewords can have dependencies. This is the basis of attempting to construct codes that are more efficient than the trivial one. The first two constructions of

K. Ohta and D. Pei (Eds.): ASIACRYPT'98, LNCS 1514, pp. 242–256, 1998.
© Springer-Verlag Berlin Heidelberg 1998

(w, n) MRA-codes, given in [4], are based on polynomials over finite fields and finite geometries. DFY description of MRA-codes is basically a definition of its functionality: that is the way the code works. Kurosawa and Obana (KO) [10] studied (w, n) MRA-code, derived combinatorial lower bounds on the probability of success in impersonation and substitution attacks, and characterised Cartesian MRA-codes that satisfy the bound with equality.

In this paper we start by giving a more general definition of MRA-codes which is a natural generalisation of KO's definition. Next we derive the first information theoretic bounds on the probability of success in impersonation and substitution attacks. The bounds are used to obtain combinatorial bounds on the the number of keys of the transmitter and receivers and also the size of the tag. These latter bounds are generalisations of KO bounds to MRA-systems that are not perfect. Finally, we present two new constructions for MRA-codes using linear error-correcting codes (E-codes). The constructions are particularly important because they give MRA-codes from arbitrary E-codes and can be seen as extension of Johansson et al [9] work relating E-codes and A-codes. This established link allows us to apply bounds and constructions from the well-developed discipline of E-codes to the construction of new MRA-systems. Using maximum distance separable codes in the first construction, and special values for parameters in the second, results in new optimal MRA-codes that satisfy lower bounds on the size of keys and the tag. Besides DFY's original polynomial construction, these are the only other known optimal constructions for MRA-codes.

The paper is organised as follows. Section 1 provides basic definitions and reviews known results. In section 2 we define MRA-codes and derive information theoretic and combinatorial bounds. In section 3 we first recall DFY polynomial construction and then propose two efficient constructions from linear error-correcting codes. Finally in Section 4 we summarise our results.

1   Preliminaries

In Simmons' model of unconditionally secure authentication there are three participants: a *transmitter (sender)*, a *receiver*, and an *opponent*. The transmitter and the receiver share a *secret key* and are both assumed honest. The message is sent over a public channel which is subject to active attack. Transmitter and receiver use an *authentication code* which is a set of authentication functions f, indexed by a *key* belonging to a set E. To authenticate a message called a *source state* and denoted by $s \in S$, using a key e, transmitter forms a codeword $f(e, s)$ and sends it to the receiver who can verify its authenticity using his knowledge of the key.

Definition 1. *An authentication code C is a 4-tuple (S, M, E, f), where f is a mapping from $S \times E$ to M,*

$$f : S \times E \longrightarrow M$$

such that $f(s, e) = m$ and $f(s', e) = m$ imply $s = s'$.

In a *systematic Cartesian A-code* the codeword corresponding to a source state s using $e \in E$ is the concatenation of s and an authentication tag $t \in \mathcal{T}$, that is $m = (s,t)$. The receiver will detect a fraudulent codeword (s,t) if the tag that it calculates for s using its secret key e is different from the received tag t.

The opponent can perform an *impersonation*, or a *substitution*, attack by constructing a fraudulent codeword and succeeds if the codeword is acceptable by the receiver. In impersonation the attacker has not seen any previous communication while in substitution he has seen one transmitted codeword. A code provides *perfect protection* against impersonation if enemy's best strategy is randomly guessing a codeword. In the case of Cartesian A-codes, enemy's probability of success is $P_I = \frac{1}{|\mathcal{T}|}$. Perfect protection for substitution is defined in a similar way, it requires the enemy's best strategy to be randomly selecting one of the remainder codewords. For Cartesian A-codes the probability of success of the intruder must be $P_S = \frac{1}{|\mathcal{T}|}$.

An extension of this model, proposed by Desmedt, Frankel and Yung (DFY) [4], is when there are multiple receivers. The system works as follows. First the key distribution centre(KDC) distributes secret keys to the transmitter and each receiver. Next the transmitter broadcasts a message to all the receivers who can individually verify authenticity of the message using their secret key information. There are malicious groups of receivers who use their secret keys and all the previous communications in the system to construct fraudulent messages. They succeed in their attack even if a single receiver accepts the message as being authentic.

KO formalisation of (w,n) MRA-codes is as follows. Let $E_1, E_2.., E_n$ denote the set of decoding rules of receivers $R_1, \cdots R_n$, and S and M denote the set of source states and senders codewords, respectively.

Definition 2. *([10]) We say that $(S, M, E_1, \cdots E_n)$ is a (w,n) multireceiver A-code if for $\forall (E_{i_1}, \cdots E_{i_w})$ and $\forall (e_1, \cdots e_w)$,*

$$P(E_{i_w} = e_w | E_{i_1} = e_1, \cdots E_{i_{w-1}} = e_{w-1}) = P(E_{i_w} = e_w).$$

The probabilities of impersonation and substitution attacks, P_I and P_S, for (w,n) MRA-code are then defined as the best chance of success in impersonation and substitution attacks, respectively, against a single (arbitrary) receiver. With these definitions, they derived the following bounds. Assume $q = |M|/|S|$.

Theorem 3. *(Theorem 9 [10]) In a (w,n) MRA-code, $P_I \geq 1/\sqrt[w]{q}$. The equality holds if and only if $P(R_{i_1}, \ldots, R_{i_w} \ accept\ m) = 1/q$ and $P(R_j \ accepts\ m) = 1/\sqrt[w]{q}$ for any m and any R_j.*

Theorem 4. *(Theorem 10 [10]) In a (w,n) MRA-code without secrecy, if $P_I = 1/\sqrt[w]{q}$, then $P_S \geq 1/\sqrt[w]{q}$. The equality holds if and only if*

$$P(R_{i_1}, \ldots, R_{i_k} \ accepts\ m' | R_{i_1}, \ldots, R_{i_k} \ accepts\ m) = 1/q$$

$$P(R_j \ accepts\ m' | R_j \ accepts\ m) = 1/\sqrt[w]{q}$$

for $\forall R_j, \forall m$ and $\forall m'$ such that the source state of m is different from that of m'.

Theorem 5. *(Theorem 11 [10]) In a (w, n) MRA-code without secrecy, if $P_I = P_S = 1/\sqrt[w]{q}$, then $|E_j| \geq (\sqrt[w]{q})^2$ for $\forall j$. If the equality holds, then each rule of E_j is used with equal probability.*

KO characterised Cartesian MRA-codes that satisfy $P_I = P_S = 1/\sqrt[w]{q}$ and observed that DFY polynomial construction is in fact an optimal construction and has the least number of keys for the transmitter and the receivers and requires the smallest tag size for the authenticator.

Definition 2 only requires that the set of keys for any set of w receivers be independent. This property ensures that the probability of success in impersonation attack by any $w - 1$ receivers against a single other receiver is the same as that by an (outside) opponent. However, it does not imply a similar property for substitution, as will be shown in Example 1. (Contrary to KO's claim in page 207 [10].) We give a more general definition for MRA-codes that has KO's definition as a special case, and derive information theoretic combinatorial lower bounds on P_I and P_S for such codes. These are the first information theoretic bounds for MRA-codes.

2   Model and Bounds

An MRA-System has three phases:

1. **Key distribution:** The KDC (key distribution centre) privately transmits the key information to the sender and each receiver(the sender can also be the KDC).
2. **Broadcast:** For a source state, the sender generates the authenticated message using his/her key and broadcasts the authenticated message.
3. **Verification:** Each user can verify the authenticity of the broadcast message.

Denote by $X_1 \times \cdots \times X_n$ the direct product of sets $X_1, \ldots X_n$, and by p_i the projection mapping of $X_1 \times \cdots \times X_n$ on X_i (i.e., $p_i : X_1 \times \cdots \times X_n \longrightarrow X_i$ defined by $p_i(x_1, x_2, \ldots, x_n) = x_i$). Let $g_1 : X_1 \longrightarrow Y_1$ and $g_2 : X_2 \longrightarrow Y_2$ be two mappings; we denote the direct product of g_1 and g_2 by $g_1 \times g_2$ (i.e., $g_1 \times g_2 : X_1 \times X_2 \longrightarrow Y_1 \times Y_2$ defined by $g_1 \times g_2(x_1, x_2) = (g_1(x_1), g_2(x_2))$). The identity mapping on a set X is denoted by 1_X.

Definition 6. *Let $C = (S, M, E, f)$ and $C_i = (S, M_i, E_i, f_i)$, $i = 1, 2, \ldots, n$ be authentication codes. We call $(C; C_1, C_2, \ldots, C_n)$ a multireceiver authentication code (MRA-code) if there exist two mappings $\tau : E \longrightarrow E_1 \times \cdots \times E_n$ and $\pi : M \longrightarrow M_1 \times \cdots \times M_n$ such that for any $(s, e) \in S \times E$ and any $1 \leq i \leq n$, the following identity holds*

$$p_i(\pi f(s, e)) = f_i((1_S \times p_i \tau)(s, e)).$$

Let $\tau_i = p_i \tau$ and $\pi_i = p_i \pi$. Then we have for each $(s, e) \in S \times E$

$$\pi_i f(s, e) = f_i(1_S \times \tau_i)(s, e).$$

We assume that for each i the mappings $\tau_i : E \longrightarrow E_i$ and $\pi_i : M \longrightarrow M_i$ are surjective. We also assume that for each code C_i the probability distribution on the source states is the same with that in the A-code C, and the probability distribution on E_i is derived from that of E and the mapping τ_i.

Let T denote the sender and $R_1, \ldots, R_n$ denote the receivers. In order to authenticate a message, the sender and the receivers follow the following protocol.

1. The KDC (or the sender) randomly chooses a key $e \in E$ and privately transmits e to T and $e_i = \pi_i(e)$ to the receiver R_i for all $1 \le i \le n$.

2. If T wants to send a source state $s \in S$ to all the receivers, T computes $m = f(s, e) \in M$ and broadcasts it to all receivers.

3. Receiver R_i checks whether a source state s such that $f_i(s, e_i) = \pi_i(m)$ exists. If such an s exists, the message m is accepted as authentic. Otherwise m is rejected.

We adopt the Kerckhoff principle that everything in the system except the actual keys of the sender and receivers is public. This includes the probability distribution of the source states and the sender's keys. From Definition 6 we know that the probability distribution of the sender's key induces a probability distribution on each receiver's key.

Attackers could be *outsiders* who do not have access to any key information, or *insiders* who have some key information. We only need to consider the latter group as it is at least as powerful as the former. We consider the systems that protect against the coalition of groups of up to a maximum size of receivers, and study impersonation and substitution attacks.

Assume there are n receivers $R_1, \ldots, R_n$. Let $L = \{i_1, \ldots i_\ell\} \subseteq \{1, \ldots, n\}$, $E_L = E_{i_1} \times \cdots \times E_{i_\ell}$ and $R_L = \{R_{i_1}, \cdots, R_{i_\ell}\}$. We consider the attack from R_L on a receiver R_i, where $i \notin L$.

Impersonation attack: R_L, after receiving their secret keys, send a message m to R_i. R_L is successful if m is accepted by R_i as authentic. We denote by $P_I[i, L]$ the success probability of R_L in performing an impersonation attack on R_i. This can be expressed as

$$P_I[i, L] = \max_{m \in M} P(m \text{ is accepted by } R_i \mid e_L)$$

where $e_L \in E_L$.

Substitution attack: R_L, after observing a message m that is transmitted by the sender, replace m with another message m'. R_L is successful if m' is accepted by R_i as authentic. We denote by $P_S[i, L]$, the success probability of R_L in performing a substitution attack on R_i. We have,

$$P_S[i, L] = \max_{e_L \in E_L} \max_{m \in M} \max_{m' \ne m \in M} P(R_i \text{ accepts } m' \mid m, e_L)$$

The following two bounds are generalisation of Simmons' [16] bound and Brickell's bound [2], when attack is from a group of insiders who have access to part of the key information.

Theorem 7. *Let $P_I[i, L]$ and $P_S[i, L]$ be defined as above.*

1. $P_I[i, L] \geq 2^{-I(M;E_i|E_L)}$.
2. $P_S[i, L] \geq 2^{-I(M';E_i|M,E_L)}$.

Proof is omitted due to the lack of space, and it can be found in [15].

Corollary 8.

$$P_S[i, L] \geq 2^{-H(E_i|M,E_L)}.$$

Proof. The corollary follows from Theorem 7 by noting that $I(M'; E_i|M, E_L) = H(E_i|M, E_L) - H(E_i|M', M, E_L)$.

A (w, n) *MRA-code* is an MRA-code in which there are n receivers such that no set of $w - 1$ receivers can construct a fraudulent codeword acceptable by another receiver. We note that in this definition, the only requirement is that the chance of success of the attackers is less than one but it is possible that some coalition of attackers can have a better chance of success than an outsider. A (w, n) *MRA-code is perfect against impersonation* if the chance of success of any group of up to $w - 1$ receivers in an impersonation attack is the same as an outsider. Similarly a (w, n) MRA-code is *perfect against substitution* if the chance of success for any group of up to $w - 1$ receivers in a substitution attack is the same as an outsider.

Let $(C; C_i, \ldots, C_n)$ be an MRA-code. Define P_I and P_S as follows.

$$P_I = \max_{L \cup \{i\}} \{P_I[i, L]\}$$

$$P_S = \max_{L \cup \{i\}} \{P_S[i, L]\}$$

where the maximum is taken over all possible w-subsets $L \cup \{i\}$ ($i \notin L$) of $\{1, 2, \ldots, n\}$. In other words, P_I and P_S are the best chance of a group of $w - 1$ receivers to succeed in impersonation or substitution attacks against a single receiver, respectively.

Let $P_I[i]$ and $P_S[i]$ denote the success probabilities for an outsider in impersonation and substitution attacks, respectively. Then

$$P_I[i] = \max_{m \in M} P(R_i \text{ accepts } m) = \max_{m \in M} P(\pi_i(m) \text{ is valid in } C_i)$$

$$P_S[i] = \max_{m' \neq m \in M} P(R_i \text{ accepts } m' \mid m \text{ is valid in } C)$$
$$= \max_{m' \neq m \in M} P(\pi_i(m') \text{ is valid in } C_i \mid m \text{ is valid in } C)$$

Thus a (w, n) MRA-code is perfect against impersonation if and only if Condition (a): $P_I[i, L] = P_I[i]$ holds; and it is perfect against substitution if and only if Condition (b): $P_S[i, L] = P_S[i]$ holds.

Lemma 9. *A sufficient condition for a (w, n) MRA-code to be perfect against impersonation is that $P(e_i|e_L) = P(e_i)$ for all w-subsets $L \cup \{i\}$ ($i \notin L$) of $\{1, \ldots, n\}$.*

Proof is given in the Appendix I.

It should also be noted that an (w, n) MRA-code which is perfect for impersonation is not necessarily perfect for substitution, as the following example shows.

Example 1. Similar to the DFY polynomial scheme, the sender randomly chooses two polynomials $f(x), g(x)$ of degree at most $w - 1$ and secretly transmits $f(i), g(i)$ to receiver R_i ($i \neq 0$). For a source state $s \in GF(q)$ the sender calculates $h(x) = f(x) + sg(x)$ and broadcasts $(s, g(0), h(x))$. Each receiver R_i can verify the authenticity of the broadcasted message by checking if $h(i) = f(i) + sg(i)$. Now for any group of $w - 1$ receivers $L = \{P_{i_1}, \ldots, P_{i_{w-1}}\}$ and $i \notin L$, $P_I[i, L] = 1/q$, since L has not information about the key $(f(i), g(i))$ of R_i. But, $P_S[i, L] = 1$, since, after seeing the broadcasted message, L can calculate $f(0) = h(0) - sg(0)$, so L knows $(f(i_1), g(i_1)), \ldots, (f(i_{w-1}), g(i_{w-1}))$ and $(f(0), g(0))$. Thus L can calculate $f(x)$ and $g(x)$, and so $P_S[i, L] = 1$.

We define the *deception probability* of a (w, n) MRA-system as $P_D = \max\{P_I, P_S\}$.

Theorem 10. *Let $(C; C_1, \ldots, C_n)$ be a (w, n) MRA-code. Assume that $P_D \leq 1/q$ and suppose there is a uniform probability distribution on the source states S. Then*

(i) $|E_i| \geq q^2$, for each $i \in \{1, \ldots, n\}$.
(ii) $|E| \geq q^{2w}$.
(iii) $|M| \geq q^w|S|$.

The bounds are tight and there exists a system that satisfies the bounds with equality.

Proof is given in the Appendix I

Comparison of the bounds with KO's bounds: Theorem 10 gives combinatorial bounds for general (w, n) MRA-codes on the size of the transmitter and receivers' key when probability of deception is known. It also lower bounds the required redundancy in terms of the deception probabilities. KO's bounds only apply to (w, n) MRA-codes that are perfect against impersonation and can be seen as special cases of the combinatorial bounds derived above. Appendix II we give a more detailed comparison of the two sets of bounds.

3   Constructions

DFY [4] gave two constructions for MRA-codes: one based on polynomials and the other based on finite geometries. KO showed that the polynomial construction is optimal and has the minimum number of keys for transmitter and receivers (Theorem 9 and 11 in [10] and produces the shortest length tag for the codewords. No other optimal construction is known so far. In this section we use error correcting codes (E-codes) to construct MRA-codes. First, we present two constructions which can be used to derive an MRA-code from an *arbitrary* E-code and then show that the constructions result in new optimal MRA-codes. An linear $[n, k]$ *code* C over $GF(q)$ is a linear subspace of $GF(q)^n$ with dimension k. The *minimum distance* d_C of C is defined by $d_C = \min_{0 \neq \mathbf{u} \in C} w(\mathbf{u})$, where $w(\mathbf{u})$ is the number of nonzero coordinates of $\mathbf{u}$. A $k \times n$ matrix G over $GF(q)$ is called a *generator matrix* of C if its row vectors generate the linear subspace C. For a linear code C its dual code, denoted by $C^{\perp}$, is defined by

$$C^{\perp} = \{\mathbf{u} \in GF(q)^n; \ \mathbf{u}\mathbf{v}^T = 0 \ \text{ for all } \mathbf{v} \in C\}.$$

We briefly recall DFY's polynomial construction as it makes it easier to describe Construction I.

DFY polynomial construction: Assume there is a sender T, and n receivers $R_1, \ldots, R_n$. The key for T consists of two random polynomials $P_0(x)$ and $P_1(x)$, of degree at most $w - 1$, with coefficients in $GF(q)$. The key for R_i consists of $P_0(i)$ and $P_1(i)$. For a source state $s \in GF(q)$, T broadcasts $(s, A(x))$ where $A(x) = P_0(x) + sP_1(x)$. R_i accepts $(s, A(x))$ as authentic if $A(i) = P_0(i) + sP_1(i)$. It is proved in [4] that no group of $w-1$ receivers can perform an impersonation or substitution attacks against a single receiver, with a probability greater than $1/q$, the construction provides the following parameters $P_I = P_S = 1/q$, $|E_i| = q^2$, for all $1 \leq i \leq n$, $|E| = q^{2w}$ and $|M| = q^w|S|$.

3.1   Construction I

Let C be a linear $[n, k]$ code over $GF(q)$ with a generator matrix $G \in GF(q)^{k \times n}$. We construct an MRA-code with n receivers from C in the following way. Assume that $S = GF(q)$ is the set of source states and G is publicly known.

1. *Key distribution* T randomly chooses $(\alpha, \beta) \in GF(q)^k \times GF(q)^k$, where $\alpha, \beta \in GF(q)$. T then calculates the codewords $\alpha G = \mathbf{u} = (u_1, \ldots, u_n)$ and $\beta G = \mathbf{v} = (v_1, \ldots, v_n)$, and privately transmits (u_i, v_i) to the receiver R_i for each $1 \leq i \leq n$, which consists of the secret key of R_i.
2. *Broadcast* To authenticate a message $s \in S$, the sender T computes $\gamma = \alpha + s\beta$ and broadcasts (s, γ) to all the receivers.
3. *Verification* For each i, R_i accepts (s, γ) as authentic if $y_i = u_i + sv_i$, where $\mathbf{y} = (y_1, \ldots, y_n) = \gamma G$.

Lemma 11. *In the above construction, let the probability distribution on the source and sender's key space be uniform. Let $L = \{i_1, \ldots, i_\ell\} \subseteq \{1, \ldots, n\}$ and $i \notin L$. Then $P_I[i, L] = P_S[i, L] = \frac{1}{q}$ if and only if there exists a codeword $\mathbf{c} = (c_1, \ldots, c_n) \in C$ such that $c_{i_1} = \cdots = c_{i_\ell} = 0$ and $c_i = 1$.*

Proof. (Sketch)
Sufficiency: Assume that there exists a codeword $\mathbf{c} \in C$ satisfying the required property of the theorem. Let $\mathbf{u} = \alpha G, \mathbf{v} = \beta G$, where (α, β) is the key chosen

by the sender T. Because of the linearity of the E-code, we know that for any $t, t' \in GF(q)$ we have $\mathbf{u} + t\mathbf{c}, \mathbf{v} + t'\mathbf{c} \in C$. Since R_L have the key information $((u_{i_1}, \ldots, u_{i_\ell}), (v_{i_1}, \ldots, v_{i_\ell}))$, then for all $t, t' \in GF(q)$ $(u_{i_1}, \ldots, u_{i_\ell}, u_i + t)$, and $(v_{i_1}, \ldots, v_{i_\ell}, v_i + t')$ produce all possible keys of $R_{L \cup \{i\}}$. It follows that R_L have no information about $R_i's$ key, and hence $P_I[i, L] = P_S[i, L] = \frac{1}{q}$.

Necessity: Assume that there is no codeword $\mathbf{c}$ in C satisfying the required property of the theorem. We prove that $(u_{i_1}, \ldots, u_{i_\ell})$ and $(v_{i_1}, \ldots, v_{i_\ell})$ uniquely determine u_i and v_i. Clearly, there exist u_i and v_i such that $(u_{i_1}, \ldots, u_{i_\ell}, u_i)$ and $(v_{i_1}, \ldots, v_{i_\ell}, v_i)$ are subcodewords of C. We only need to show that such u_i and v_i are unique. Indeed, if there exist two subcodewords $(u_{i_1}, \ldots, u_{i_\ell}, u_i)$, $(u_{i_1}, \ldots, u_{i_\ell}, u'_i)$ in C, it follows that $(u_{i_1}, \ldots, u_{i_\ell}, u_i) - (u_{i_1}, \ldots, u_{i_\ell}, u'_i) = (0, \ldots, 0, u_i - u'_i)$ is also a subcodeword in C, and so is $(0, \ldots, 0, 1)$, which is a contradiction. In this case we have $P_I[i, L] = P_S[i, L] = 1$, proving the necessity.

Theorem 12. *Let C be a linear $[n, k]$ code over $GF(q)$ and let d' be the minimum distance of $C^\perp$, the dual code of C. Then Construction I results in a (w, n) MRA-code with $P_I = P_S = 1/q$, $w = d' - 1 \leq k$, and the following parameters:*

$$|S| = q, \ |M| = q^k |S|, \ |E| = q^{2k} \ and \ |E_i| = q^2.$$

Proof. We show that the resulting MRA-code is a $(d' - 1, n)$ MRA-code, but not a (d', n) MRA-code. Let G be a generator matrix of C, and let d' be the minimum distance of $C^\perp$. Recall [11] that $C^\perp$ has the minimum distance d' if and only if every $d' - 1$ columns of G are linearly independent and some d' columns of G are linearly dependent. For each $d' - 1$ columns, indexed by $\{i_1, \ldots, i_{d'-2}, i\}$, the restriction of G to these $d' - 1$ columns results in a $k \times (d' - 1)$ matrix $G_{\{i_1, \ldots, i_{d'-2}, i\}}$. It follows that $e_i \in GF(q)^{d'-1}$ can be expressed as a linear combination of the k rows of $G_{\{i_1, \ldots, i_{d'-2}, i\}}$, where $e_i \in GF(q)^{d'-1}$ is the vector with the ith entry being 1 and other entries being 0. This implies that there exits a codeword $\mathbf{c} = (c_1, \ldots, c_n) \in C$ such that $c_{i_1} = \ldots = c_{i_{d'-2}} = 0$ and $c_i = 1$. Thus, by Lemma 11 we have $P_I[i, L] = P_S[i, L] = 1/q$ for any $d' - 1$ subset $\{i\} \cup L$ of $\{1, \ldots, n\}$ with $i \notin L$, and so the resulted MRA-code is a $(d' - 1, n)$ MRA-code with $P_I = P_S = 1/q$. In a similar manner, we can prove that there exists a d'-subset $L \cup \{i\}$ of $\{1, \ldots, n\}$ such that $P_I[i, L] = P_S[i, L] = 1$, so it is not a (d', n) MRA-code.

In general the MRA-code derived from an E-code is not optimal and does not satisfy bounds in Theorem 10. In the following we will show that for a well-known class of E-codes the construction results in optimal MRA-codes.

A *maximum distance separable (MDS)* E-code has maximum possible minimum distance and its parameters satisfy $d_C = n - k + 1$. We are only interested in linear MDS codes. An important property of MDS codes is given in the following theorem.

Theorem 13. *(Theorem 2 page 318 in [11]) If C is MDS so is the dual $C^\perp$.*

This means that for an MDS code $d' = n - (n - k) + 1 = k$, or $k = d' - 1$. That is the resulting (w, n) MRA-code can protect against the largest size set of cheaters. Using this result and theorem 12 it is straightforward to prove the following.

Corollary 14. *If the linear code C in Construction I is an $[n, k]$ MDS code over $GF(q)$, then Construction I results in an optimal (k, n) MRA-code with $P_I = P_S = 1/q$. It has the following parameters*

$$|S| = q, \ |M| = q^k |S|, \ |E| = q^{2k} \ and \ |E_i| = q^2.$$

A special class of MDS codes are *Reed-Solomon code* with the following generator matrix,

$$G = \begin{bmatrix} 1 & 1 & \cdots & 1 \\ x_1 & x_2 & \cdots & x_n \\ \vdots & \vdots & \vdots & \vdots \\ x_1^{w-1} & x_2^{w-1} & \cdots & x_n^{w-1} \end{bmatrix},$$

where the x_i are n distinct elements in $GF(q)$.

Corollary 15. *If the linear code C in Construction I is an $[n, k]$ Reed-Solomon code, then Construction I coincides with DFY's construction.*

3.2   Construction II

Construction I can be seen as a generalisation of DFY's construction. Construction II is based on the properties of the dual code and can be used for large size sources which makes it of practical interest. We first describe the construction and then discuss its properties.

The basic idea is to use vectors of dual code for verification process. The sender's secret key is an $\ell \times w$ matrix U which defines the generator matrix $G = [I_\ell \,|\, U]$ of a linear code. To authenticate a source state $\mathbf{s} \in \mathcal{S}$ the sender generates the codeword $c = sG$ and broadcasts it to the receivers. Each receiver R_i has a codeword d_i of the dual code. To verify authenticity of a broadcasted vector x, receiver R_i calculates $x \cdot d_i$ ('$\cdot$' denotes vector inner product) and if it is zero, it accepts the codeword as authentic.

Let $S \subseteq GF(q)^\ell$ denote the set of source states obtained by defining an equivalence relation $\sim$ over $GF(q)^\ell \backslash \{0\}$ as follows: $\mathbf{s} \sim \mathbf{s}' \iff \mathbf{s} = r\mathbf{s}'$ for some $0 \neq r \in GF(q)$. It is easy to verify that this relation is in fact an equivalence relation. We define $\mathcal{S}$ as the set of equivalence classes obtained from $\sim$. It follows that $|S| = \frac{q^\ell - 1}{q - 1} = q^{\ell - 1} = \cdots + q + 1$.

The three phases of Construction II are as follows.

1. *Key distribution* The sender T randomly chooses an $\ell \times w$ matrix $G \in GF(q)^{\ell \times w}$)(and so $[I_\ell \,|\, U]$ is the generator matrix of a linear $[\ell + w, \ell]$ code

in its systematic form). Assume that $q \geq n$ (this assumption is not necessary[1]). T chooses n distinct elements $x_1, \ldots, x_n \in GF(q)$(these elements are public and are used as the identities of the receivers), and then calculates and secretly transmits $U(1, x_i, \ldots, x_i^{w-1})^T = \alpha_i \in GF(q)^{\ell \times 1}$ to R_i, which consists of the secret key of $R_i, i = 1, \ldots, n$.

2. *Broadcast* To authenticate a source state $\mathbf{s} = (s_1, \ldots, s_\ell) \in \mathcal{S}$, T computes $\mathbf{s}U = \mathbf{t} = (t_1, \ldots, t_w) \in GF(q)^w$ and broadcasts $(\mathbf{s}, \mathbf{t})$.

3. *Verification* For each i, R_i accepts $(\mathbf{s}, \mathbf{t})$ as authentic if $\mathbf{s}\alpha_i = \mathbf{t}(1, x_i, \ldots x_i^{w-1})^T$.

Theorem 16. *Construction II results in a (w, n) multireceiver A-code with $P_I = P_S = 1/q$. It has the following parameters*

$$|S| = \frac{q^\ell - 1}{q - 1}, \quad |M| = q^w |S|, \quad |E| = q^{\ell w} \quad and \quad |E_i| = q^\ell.$$

Proof. First, we prove that $P_I = P_S = 1/q$. It is sufficient to show that for each $L \subseteq \{1, \ldots, n\}$ with $|L| = w - 1$ and $i \notin L$, $P_I[i, L] = P_S[i, L] = 1/q$. Without loss of generality, assume that $L = \{1, \ldots, w-1\}$ and $i = w$, and that after the key distribution R_L hold their keys

$$U(1, x_1, \ldots, x_1^{w-1})^T = \alpha_1, \quad \ldots, \quad U(1, x_{w-1}, \ldots, x_{w-1}^{w-1})^T = \alpha_{w-1}.$$

Let
$\mathcal{F} = \{U \in GF(q)^{\ell \times w}; U(1, x_1, \ldots, x_1^{w-1})^T = \alpha_1, \ldots, U(1, x_{w-1}, \ldots, x_{w-1}^{w-1})^T = \alpha_{w-1}\}$. That is, $\mathcal{F}$ is the set of possibles authentication keys of the sender T in accordance with the keys of R_L. We define a mapping $\phi : \mathcal{F} \longrightarrow GF(q)^{\ell \times 1}$ by

$$\phi(U) = U(1, x_w, \ldots, x_w^{w-1})^T, \quad \forall U \in \mathcal{F}.$$

It is straightforward to verify that ϕ is one-to-one from $\mathcal{F}$ onto $GF(q)^{\ell \times 1}$. This also implies that $R_w s$ key $U(1, x_w, \ldots, x_w^{w-1})^T = \phi(U)$ is independent of the keys of R_L.

In the impersonation attack, R_L, generates a codeword $(\mathbf{s}, \mathbf{t}), \mathbf{s} \in \mathcal{S}$ and $\mathbf{t} \in \mathcal{T} = GF(q)^w$, and hope that it will be accepted by R_w as authentic. It follows

$$P_I[w, L] = \max_{(\mathbf{s}, \mathbf{t}) \in \mathcal{S} \times \mathcal{T}} \frac{|\{U; U \in \mathcal{F} \text{ and } \mathbf{s}U(1, x_w, \ldots, x_w^{w-1})^T = \mathbf{t}(1, x_w, \ldots, x_w^{w-1})^T\}|}{|\mathcal{F}|}$$

$$= \frac{q^{\ell-1}}{q^\ell}$$

$$= \frac{1}{q}.$$

In the substitution attack, R_L, after seeing a broadcast authenticated codeword $(\mathbf{s}, \mathbf{t})$, generates a new codeword $(\mathbf{s}', \mathbf{t}'), \mathbf{s}' \neq \mathbf{s}$, and hope that $(\mathbf{s}', \mathbf{t}')$ will be accepted by R_w as authentic. It follows that

$$P_S[w, L]$$
$$= \max_{\mathbf{s} \neq \mathbf{s}'} \frac{|\{U; U \in \mathcal{F}, \mathbf{s}U(1, \ldots, x_w^{w-1})^T = \mathbf{t}(1, \ldots, x_w^{w-1})^T, \mathbf{s}'U(1, \ldots, x_w^{w-1})^T = \mathbf{t}'(1, \ldots, x_w^{w-1})^T\}|}{|\{U; U \in \mathcal{F}, \mathbf{s}U(1, x_w, \ldots, x_w^{w-1})^T = \mathbf{t}(1, x_w, \ldots, x_w^{w-1})^T\}|}$$

$$= \frac{q^{\ell-2}}{q^{\ell-1}}$$

$$= \frac{1}{q}.$$

---

[1] Instead, the sender may choose a $w \times n$ matrix $M = (M_1, \ldots, M_n)$ over $GF(q)$ such that any w columns of M are linearly independent and the secret key of R_i is $\binom{-U}{I} M_i$

Similarly, we have $P_I[i, L] = P_S[i, L] = 1/q$ for any w subset $\{i\} \cup L$ of $\{1, \ldots, n\}$ with $i \notin L$. Thus we have proved that $P_I = P_S = 1/q$. The proof of the cardinality parameters are obvious.

Corollary 17. *Let $q \geq n$ be a prime power. There exists a (w, n) multireceiver A-code with the following parameters*

$$|\mathcal{S}| = q + 1, \quad |M| = q^w |\mathcal{S}|, \quad |E| = q^{2w}, \quad and \quad |E_i| = q^2,$$

and the probability of success in each attack is $P_I = \frac{1}{q}$ and $P_S = \frac{1}{q}$.

The corollary follows from the theorem when $\ell = 2$. the resulting MRA-code meets the bounds of Theorem 10 and hence is optimal.

It is interesting to note that for $w = n = 1$, the above construction results in a conventional (one-sender to one-receiver) A-code with the following parameters

$$|\mathcal{S}| = \frac{q^\ell - 1}{q - 1}, \quad |M| = q|\mathcal{S}|, \quad |E| = |E_1| = q^\ell,$$

and the probability of success in impersonation and substitution is given by is $P_I = \frac{1}{q}$ and $P_S = \frac{1}{q}$, respectively. Conventional A-code with these parameters has been constructed from finite geometries [1]. In particular, for $\ell = 2$, The A-code has the same parameters as the A-code due to Gilbert, MacWilliams and Sloane [7].

We note that Construction II is more suitable for MRA-codes with large source space. In the DFY construction and Construction I, the order of the field $GF(q)$ determines the lower bound on the success probabilities in impersonation and substitution, and at the same time bounds the size of the source that can be used in the system ($|\mathcal{S}| \leq q$). This can result in inefficient constructions for larger sources. For example a source of size 2^{100} results in probability of deception lower bounded by 2^{-100} which is unnecessarily low. The price paid for this low probability is bigger key sizes which for practical applications is not acceptable. This restriction is removed in Construction II, and by choosing appropriate ℓ the size of source can be increased to the required level.

4   Conclusions

MRA-codes are an important cryptographic primitive in secure group communication. In this paper, we gave a formal definition of MRA-codes and derived the first information theoretic bounds on their performance. The bounds result in combinatorial lower bounds which are generalisations of the previously known combinatorial bounds. We established a link between E-codes and MRA-codes by giving two constructions that can be used to derive MRA-codes from E-codes. The constructions are used to give new optimal MRA-codes.

References

1. A. Beutelspacher, Perfect and essentially perfect authentication systems, *Lecture Notes in Computer Science* **304**(1988), 167-170. (Advances in Cryptology–Eurocrypt '87).
2. E. F. Brickell, A few results in message authentication, *Congressus Numerantium*, Vol.43(1984), 141-154.
3. T. Cover and J. Thomas, Elements of Information Theory, *New York; Wiley*, 1991.
4. Y. Desmedt, Y. Frankel and M. Yung, Multi-receiver/Multi-sender network security: efficient authenticated multicast/feedback, *IEEE Infocom'92*, (1992) 2045-2054.
5. A. Fiat and M. Naor, Broadcast Encryption. In "Advances in Cryptology – Crypto '93", *Lecture Notes in Computer Science* **773** (1994), 480-491.
6. H. Fujii, W. Kachen and K. Kurosawa, Combinatorial bounds and design of broadcast authentication, *IEICE Trans.*, VolE**79**-A, No. 4(1996)502-506.
7. E. N. Gilbert, F. J. MacWilliams and N. J. A. Sloane, Codes which detect deception, *The Bell System Technical Journal*, Vol.33, No.3, 405-424(1974).
8. T. Johansson, Lower Bounds on the Probability of Deception in Authentication with Arbitration, *IEEE Trans. on Information Theory*, Vol.40, No.5, (1994) 1573-1585.
9. T. Johansson, G. Kabatianskii and B. Smeets, On the relation between A-codes and codes correcting independent errors. In "Advances in Cryptology – Eurocrypt '93", *Lecture Notes in Computer Science* **765** (1993), 1-11.
10. K. Kurosawa and S. Obana, Characterisation of (k, n) multi-receiver authentication, *Information Security and Privacy, ACISP'97*, Lecture Notes in Cpmput. Sci. **1270**,(1997) 204-215.
11. F. J. MacWilliams and N. Sloane, *The Theory of Error-Correcting Codes*, New-York; NorthHolland, 1977.
12. J. L. Massey, Cryptography - a selective survey, *Digital Communications*, North Holland(pub) (1986)3-21.
13. D. Pei, Information-Theoretic Bounds for Authentication Codes and Block Designs, *J. of Cryptology*, 8(1995)177-188.
14. R. Safavi-Naini and H. Wang, New results on multi-receiver authentication codes, *Advances in Cryptology – Eurocrypt '98*, Lecture Notes in Comp. Sci., 1403(1998), 527-541.
15. R. Safavi-Naini and H. Wang, Multireceiver Authentication Codes: Model, Bounds, Constructions and Extensions, *Information and Computation*, to appear.
16. G. J. Simmons, Authentication theory/coding theory, Lecture Notes in Comput. Sci., **196** 411-431. (Crypto '84).
17. G. J. Simmons, A survey of information authentication, in *Contemporary Cryptology, The Science of Information Integrity*, G.J. Simmons, ed., IEEE Press, (1992), 379-419.
18. B. Smeets, Bounds on the Probability of Deception in Multiple Authentication, *IEEE Trans. of Information Theory* ,Vol.40, No.5, (1994)1586-1591.
19. D. R. Stinson, The combinatorics of authentication and secrecy codes, *J. Cryptology* **2**, (1990), 23-390.
20. D. R. Stinson, Universal Hashing and authentication codes, *Designs, Codes and Cryptography* **4** (1994), 369-280.
21. D. R. Stinson, On some methods for unconditionally secure key distribution and broadcast encryption. *Designs, Codes and Cryptography*, **12**(1997), 215-243.
22. M. N. Wegman and J. L. Carter, New hash functions and their use in authentication and set equality, *J. of Computer and System Science* **22**(1981), 265-279.

APPENDIX I

Proof of Lemma 9: Consider the A-code $C_i = (S, M_i, E_i)$, we define an authenticate function $\chi(m_i, e_i)$ on $M_i \times S_i$ as

$$\chi_S(m_i, e_i) = \begin{cases} 1 \text{ if } m_i \text{ is authentic for the key } e_i \\ 0 \text{ otherwise.} \end{cases}$$

We have $P(\pi_i(m)$ is valid in $C_i) = \sum_{e_i \in E_i} \chi(\pi_i(m), e_i) P(e_i)$. We define an impersonation characteristic function χ_I on $M \times E_i \times E_L$ by

$$\chi_I(m, e_i, e_L) = \begin{cases} 1 \text{ if } m \text{ is a valid for } e \in E \text{ in } C \\ \quad \text{such that } \tau_i(e) = e_i \text{ and } \tau_L(e) = e_L \\ 0 \text{ otherwise} \end{cases}$$

From the definition of the impersonation attack we can express $P_I[i, I]$ as

$$P_I[i, L] = \max_{m \in M} P(\pi_i(m) \text{ is valid in } C_i | e_L \in E_L)$$
$$= \max_{m \in M} \sum_{e_i \in E_i} \chi_I(m, e_i, e_L) P(e_i | e_L)).$$

It follows that for any given e_L in accordance with $\tau_L(e) = e_L$ and $\tau_i = e_i$, we know $\chi(\pi_i(m), e_i) = \chi_I(m, e_i, e_L)$. Thus we have

$$P_I[i, L] = \max_{m \in M} P(m \text{ is accepted by } R_i | e_L)$$
$$= \max_{m \in M} \sum_{e_i \in E_i} \chi_I(m, e_i, e_L) P(e_i | e_L)$$
$$= \max_{m \in M} \sum_{e_i \in E_i} \chi(\pi_i(m), e_i) P(e_i | e_L)$$
$$= \max_{m \in M} \sum_{e_i \in E_i} \chi(\pi_i(m), e_i) P(e_i)$$
$$= P_I[i]$$

Proof of Theorem 10: (i) For each $(w - 1)$-subset L of $\{1, \ldots, n\}$ and any $i \in \{1, \ldots, n\}$ where $i \notin L$, by Theorem 7 and Corollary 8 we have

$$(\frac{1}{q})^2 \geq P_D^2 \geq P_I[i, L] P_S[i, L] \geq 2^{-(I(M;E_i|E_L) + H(E_i|E_L, M))} = 2^{-H(E_i|E_L)}$$

$$\geq 2^{-H(E_i)} \geq 2^{-\log|E_i|} = \frac{1}{|E_i|}.$$

It follows that $|E_i| \geq q^2$.
(ii) Assume that $L_i = \{1, \ldots, i - 1, i + 1, \ldots, w\}, i = 1, \ldots, w$. We have,

$$(\frac{1}{q})^{2w} \geq \prod_{i=1}^{w} P_I[i, L_i] P_S[i, L_i] \geq 2^{\sum_{i=1}^{w} H(E_i | E_{L_i})}$$

$$\geq 2^{-\sum_{i=1}^{w} H(E_i | E_1, \ldots, E_{i-1})} = 2^{-H(E_1, \ldots, E_w)}$$
$$\geq 2^{-H(E)} \geq 2^{-\log|E|} = \frac{1}{|E|}.$$

Therefore, $|E| \geq q^{2w}$.

(iii) Since $\tau : E \longrightarrow E_1 \times \cdots \times E_n$ induces a mapping from E to $E_1 \times \cdots \times E_w$, we have $I(M; E) \geq I(M; E_1, \ldots, E_w)$. It follows that

$$2^{-I(M;E)} \leq 2^{-I(M;E_1,\ldots,E_w)} = 2^{-\sum_{i=1}^{w} I(M;E_i|E_1,\ldots,E_w)}$$

$$= 2^{-\sum_{i=1}^{w} I(M;E_i|E_1,\ldots,E_{i-1})}$$

$$= \prod_{i=1}^{w} 2^{-I(M;E_i|E_1,\ldots,E_{i-1})} \leq \prod_{i=1}^{w} P_I[i, Q_i],$$

where $Q_i = \{1, \ldots, i-1\}$. Since for each $1 \leq i \leq w$, we have $P_I[i, Q_i] \leq P_I[i, L_i] \leq \frac{1}{q}$, it follows that,

$$2^{-I(M;E)} = 2^{-(H(M)-H(M|E))} = 2^{-H(M)} 2^{H(M|E)} \leq (\frac{1}{q})^w.$$

Since S is assumed to be uniformly distributed, we know that $H(M|E) = H(S) = \log |S|$. Hence $|M| = 2^{\log |M|} \geq 2^{H(M)} \geq q^w |S|$, which proves (iii). The bounds are tight as in the next sections we will give constructions that meet them with equality.

APPENDIX II

In the following we give we comparison between bounds obtained in Theorem 10 and the bounds derived by Kurosawa and Obana in [10]. Let $\ell = \frac{|M|}{|S|}$.

1. In [10] the first part of Theorem 9 proves that $P_I \geq 1/\sqrt[w]{\ell}$. We show that our Theorem 10 (iii) implies that $P_D = \max\{P_I, P_S\} \geq 1/\sqrt[w]{\ell}$. This is because assuming $P_D = \max\{P_I, P_S\} = 1/q$ and using Theorem 10 (iii), we have $|M| \geq q^w |S| \Longrightarrow P_D = 1/q \geq \sqrt[w]{|S|/|M|} = 1/\sqrt[w]{\ell}$.
   This is similar to KO result but uses different assumption: KO result only applies to MRA-codes that are perfect for impersonation while our result is for general MRA-codes.

2. Theorem 10 and 11 in [10] in fact prove the following result(see also the introduction in [10]).

   Theorem 18. *(KO [10]) For (w, n) MRA-code without secrecy, if $P_I = P_S = \frac{1}{\sqrt[w]{\ell}}$, then $|E| \geq \ell^2$ and $|E_i| \geq (\sqrt[w]{\ell})^2$ for all $1 \leq i \leq n$.*

   This result can be also obtained from Theorem 10. Indeed, since $P_I = P_S = \frac{1}{\sqrt[w]{\ell}}$, we have $P_D = \frac{1}{\sqrt[w]{\ell}} = \frac{1}{q}$, where $q = \sqrt[w]{\ell}$ By our Theorem 10 (i) and (ii) it follows that $|E_i \geq q^2 = (\sqrt[w]{\ell})^2$. and $|E| \geq q^{2w} = (\sqrt[w]{\ell})^{2w} = (\ell)^2$ proving the desired result.
   This result applies to *all* (w, n) MRA-codes and does not require the code to be perfect for impersonation, or the assumption that the code is without secrecy.

3. The second parts of Theorem 9, 10 and 11 in [10] do not have any counterpart in this paper.

Fair Off-Line e-Cash Made Easy

Yair Frankel* Yiannis Tsiounis** Moti Yung***

Abstract. Anonymous off-line electronic cash (e-cash) systems provide transactions that retain the anonymity of the payer, similar to physical cash exchanges, without requiring the issuing bank to be on-line at payment. Fair off-line e-cash extend this capability to allow a qualified third party (a "trustee") to revoke this anonymity under a warrant or other specified "suspicious" activity. Extensions for achieving fair off-line e-cash based on off-line e-cash require modularity to be applicable in general settings. Simplicity (for ease of understanding and implementation) and efficiency (for cost effectiveness) are of high importance, otherwise these generic extensions will be hard and costly to apply. Of course, security must also be guaranteed and understood, yet, to date, there have been no efficient systems that offer provable security.

A system which is (1) provably secure based on well understood assumptions, (2) efficient and (3) conceptually easy, is typically "elegant." In this work we make a step towards elegant fair off-line e-cash system by proposing a system which is provably anonymous (i.e., secure for legitimate users) while its design is simple and its efficiency is similar to the most efficient systems to date. Security for the bank and shops is unchanged from the security of *non*-traceable e-cash. We also present ways to adapt the functionality of "fairness" into existing e-cash systems in a modular way, thus easing advancement and maintaining version compatibility; these extensions are also provably anonymous.

Keywords: Electronic cash, anonymity revocation, decision Diffie-Hellman.

1 Introduction

Simplicity is the crux of system design; when it comes to secure systems it is even more important for two reasons: first, it limits the possibility of errors during design and implementation and eases the proof of security; second, it potentially allows the algorithms to run on reduced computational resources.

In this work we simplify the method of achieving fair off-line e-cash based on any (single-term) off-line e-cash system (we demonstrate functionality under [Bra93b]). We do so without affecting the security of the basic system, while we prove the security (i.e., anonymity of legitimate users) of the "fairness" extension using a better understood assumption, that of the decision Diffie-Hellman. Our goal is to move a step closer to "elegant" fair e-cash, i.e., minimize number of added requirements, security assumptions and overhead while extending the e-cash systems into fair ones. We utilize the recent result [TY98,NR97] showing equivalence of the semantic security (namely, security in the sense of indistinguishability) of ElGamal encryption and the decision Diffie-Hellman assumption.

The model: Fair off-line electronic cash (FOLC), independently introduced by [FTY96] and [CMS96], extends anonymous off-line electronic cash and involves a bank ($\mathcal{B}$), a collection of users (a single user is called $\mathcal{U}$), a collection of receivers/shops (a single receiver is denoted by $\mathcal{R}$), and a collection of Trustees (judges/escrow agents) which act like one party[1] (and

---

* CertCo, NY, NY. e-mail: `frankely@certco.com`
** GTE Laboratories, Inc., Waltham, MA. e-mail: `ytsiounis@gte.com`
*** CertCo, NY, NY. e-mail: `moti@certco.com, moti@cs.columbia.edu`

[1] It is outside the scope of this paper to show how the power of the Trustees can be equally distributed. $\mathcal{T}$ should be envisioned as being a single trusted entity.

K. Ohta and D. Pei (Eds.): ASIACRYPT'98, LNCS 1514, pp. 257–270, 1998.
© Springer-Verlag Berlin Heidelberg 1998

are denoted as $\mathcal{T}$). FOLC includes five basic protocols, three of which are the same as in off-line electronic cash: a *withdrawal protocol* with which $\mathcal{U}$ withdraws electronic coins from $\mathcal{B}$ while his account is debited, a *payment protocol* with which $\mathcal{U}$ pays the coin to $\mathcal{R}$, and a *deposit protocol* with which $\mathcal{R}$ deposits the coin to $\mathcal{B}$ and has his account credited.

The two additional protocols are: *owner tracing* in which $\mathcal{B}$ gives to $\mathcal{T}$ the view of a deposit protocol and $\mathcal{T}$ returns a string that contains the identifying information of the coin's owner (which $\mathcal{B}$ can use to identify the owner via its account databases); and *coin tracing* in which $\mathcal{T}$, given the view of a withdrawal protocol from $\mathcal{B}$, returns some information that originated from this withdrawal. $\mathcal{B}$ can use the returned value to find the coin(s) by accessing its views of the deposit protocols. Hence, owner tracing allows tracing of suspicious payments, while coin tracing allows the authorities to find the destination of suspicious withdrawals. We do not consider the strong bank robbery attacks [JY96].

Previous work: [FTY96] introduced the notion of "indirect discourse proofs" and used it to implement FOLC; however, payments had to be interactive, while security required novel assumptions. Here we implement non-interactive indirect discourse proofs, while our complete solution is more secure and as efficient as owner tracing alone on that system. [FTY96] also proved that anonymity in FOLC cannot be unconditional. [CMS96] introduced efficient owner and coin tracing protocols; coin tracing in particular was much faster than [FTY96]. However, security was not analyzed, while owner tracing was performed against the database of withdrawn coins, i.e., $\mathcal{T}$ returns to $\mathcal{B}$ a value appearing in a withdrawal transcript instead of the user's identity; this reduces the computational requirements at withdrawal and payment (i.e., "enforcement" of owner tracing capability), but requires more time for owner tracing. Here we perform owner tracing against the account database (i.e., we escrow the "users' identities") while retaining the efficiency of [CMS96]. [DFTY97] simplified the protocols of [FTY96] using faster coin tracing techniques, on par with [CMS96]; security however still required novel assumptions while payments were again interactive. [dST98] recently presented efficient protocols (for account-based owner tracing) with non-interactive payments, but their anonymity depends on more complex assumptions (these are not specified in a strict sense, but our evaluation shows that the main assumption is a variant of the decision Diffie-Hellman assumption, similar to the "matching Diffie-Hellman" introduced in [FTY96]). Our efficiency is on par with this system but we can concretely prove anonymity under the decision Diffie-Hellman assumption.

Security assumptions: Security of the basic off-line e-cash scheme is based on the blind signature protocol that we use as an underlying block; in the case we demonstrate here, this is the same as in [Bra93b] but other protocols can be used. All such protocols are based on the random oracle model and although the unforgeability of the resulting signatures is provable [PS96a] their restrictive properties are still unproven. We prove the anonymity of our system based on the decision Diffie-Hellman assumption.

Structure of the paper: In section 2 we present the ElGamal encryption scheme and the decision Diffie-Hellman assumption, as well as some known impossibility results for FOLC. In section 3 we present the building blocks for our protocols, namely a blind signature scheme with some restrictive properties, proofs of equality of logarithms and non-interactive indirect discourse proofs. In section 4 we show how FOLC can be added in a modular way in existing systems, while in section 5 we show how to achieve FOLC efficiently and securely if we have more freedom in the system design phase. We discuss the security in section 6 and we conclude with open problems in section 7.

2   Preliminaries

In [FTY96] it was shown what are the cryptographic assumptions needed for FOLC as summarized in the following Theorems.

Theorem 1 *(1) Unconditional unlinkability is impossible in FOLC even if only owner tracing or coin tracing is supported. (2) Further, any implementation of FOLC based on black box reduction from an arbitrary one-way permutation will separate P and NP (thus, it seems implausible, since it will yield a breakthrough in complexity theoretic proof techniques).*

Theorem 2 *Given off-line e-cash and public-key encryption, there exists a FOLC system in which anonymity is semantically secure (in the sense of secure encryption [GM84]).*

A semantically secure encryption which has homomorphic properties is the ElGamal encryption scheme [ElG85]:

Definition 1. (ElGamal public-key encryption scheme) *The* ElGamal public-key encryption *scheme is defined by a triplet* (G, E, D) *of probabilistic polynomial-time algorithms, with the following properties:*
  - *The* system setup algorithm, S, *on input* 1^n, *where* n *is the security parameter, outputs the system parameters* (p, q, g), *where* (p, q, g) *is an instance of the DLP collection, i.e.,* p *is a uniformly chosen prime of length* $|p| = n + \delta$ *for a specified constant* δ, *and* g *is a uniformly chosen generator of the subgroup* G_q *of prime order* q *of* Z_p^*, *where* $q = (p-1)/\gamma$ *is prime and* γ *is a specified integer.*
  - *The* key generating algorithm, G, *on input* (p, q, g), *outputs a public key,* $e = (p, q, g, y)$, *and a private key,* $d = (p, q, g, x)$, *where*
    - x *is a uniformly chosen element of* Z_q, *and*
    - $y \equiv g^x \bmod p$.
  - *The* encryption algorithm, E, *on input* (p, q, g, y) *and a message* $m \in G_q$, *uniformly selects an element* k *in* Z_q *and outputs*

$$E((p, q, g, y), m) = (g^k \pmod p, my^k \pmod p) .$$

  - *The* decryption algorithm, D, *on input* (p, q, g, x) *and a ciphertext* (y_1, y_2), *outputs*

$$D((p, g, x), (y_1, y_2)) = y_2(y_1^x)^{-1} \pmod p .$$

For simplicity we write $E(m) = (g^k, my^k)$ for public key y.

Definition 2. (Decision Diffie-Hellman problem) *For security parameter* n, p *a prime with* $|p - 1| = \delta + n$ *for a specified constant* δ, *for* $g \in Z_p^*$ *a generator of prime order* $q = (p-1)/\gamma$ *for a specified integer* γ *and for* $a, b \in_R Z_q$ *random, given* $[g^a, g^b, y]$ *output 0 if* $y \equiv g^{ab} \pmod p$ *and 1 otherwise, with probability better than* $1/2 + 1/n^c$ *for any constant* c *for large enough* n.

The decision Diffie-Hellman assumption states that it is infeasible to solve the decision Diffie-Hellman problem. In [TY98] a proof of the following is presented:

Theorem 3 *The ElGamal encryption scheme is semantically secure, if and only if there does not exist a p.p.t. TM that solves the decision Diffie-Hellman problem.*

We remark here that theorem 3 is true even for a modified **"inverted" ElGamal encryption,** i.e., when $E(m) = (y^k, mg^k)$ with y the public key.

3   Building Blocks

All off-line electronic cash schemes to date utilize a blinding protocol that allows the bank to verify that users embed their identity in the coin. In turn, all fair off-line e-cash schemes, employ a protocol for proving relations between committed values. We devote one subsection to each concept. In addition we show an implementation of "indirect discourse proofs" [FTY96,DFTY97] based on proofs of equality of logarithms.

3.1   The Blinding Protocol

There are several blind signature protocols in the literature which allow the signer to verify that some values are correctly embedded by the requester. The first was proposed by [CFN90] but here we will use protocols that avoid the costly (in terms of both speed and storage) "cut-and-choose" technique, such as the withdrawal protocols in [CP93a,BCC+92,CP93b], the "restrictive blinding" in [Bra93b], the protocol "P" in [CMS96], or the "blind signature" protocol in [dST98]. Here we will demonstrate one particular such protocol, Brands' "restrictive blind signature," but it should be noted that the ideas presented are applicable to any of the other sub-protocols used as building blocks.

We now describe the blinding protocol in [Bra93b], between a signer S and a verifier V.

Setup:

Let p and q be primes such that $|p - 1| = \delta + k$ for a specified constant δ, and $p = \gamma q + 1$, for a specified integer γ. Define a unique subgroup G_q of prime order q of the multiplicative group Z_p^* and generators g, g_1, g_2 of G_q. Let $\mathcal{H}, \mathcal{H}_0, \mathcal{H}_1, \ldots$ be hash functions from a family of collision intractable hash functions.

Let $X_S \in_R Z_q$ be the secret key of the signer. The signer publishes its public keys $h = g^{X_S}$, $h_1 = g_1^{X_S}, h_2 = g_2^{X_S}$.

Let $u_1 \in G_q$ be the verifier's private key and $I = g_1^{u_1}$ his public identification information (knowledge of private keys should be verified as pointed out in [CFMT96], using e.g., a Schnorr proof of knowledge [Sch91]).

The protocol creates a blind signature of I. V will end up with a Schnorr-type [Sch91] signature on $(Ig_2)^s$, where s is a random number (chosen by V and kept secret). The exact form of the signature is $sig(A, B) = (z, a, b, r)$ satisfying:

$$g^r = h^{\mathcal{H}(A,B,z,a,b)}a \quad \text{and} \quad A^r = z^{\mathcal{H}(A,B,z,a,b)}b \tag{1}$$

The **blinding protocol** (over an authenticated channel between V and S) appears in figure 1.

This protocol produces a signed number A of the form $I^s g_2{}^s$, i.e., A is an unconditionally-hiding commitment of the verifier's identity I. There are no complete security proofs for such protocols, but they are used in every efficient e-cash scheme and have received continuous scrutiny in recent years. There do however exist security arguments under the random oracle model [PS96a] for the existential unforgeability of such signature schemes—but not for their "restrictive" properties (i.e., we cannot yet prove that A is a correct commitment on I).

3.2   Proving Equality of Logarithms

A basic tool for both owner and coin tracing is an efficient blind proof of equality of logarithms. Such proofs are used for FOLC either in isolation, or as a block in constructing non-interactive indirect discourse proofs, which can then provide some of the functionality needed for FOLC.

$\mathcal{S}$ blindly signs A, such that A embeds the identity I of $\mathcal{V}$

$\mathcal{V}$ $\hspace{10cm}$ $\mathcal{S}$

$$w \in_R Z_q$$

$\xleftarrow{a',b'}$ $\qquad a' = g^w, b' = (Ig_2)^w$

$s \in_R Z_q$

$A = (Ig_2)^s$

$z' = h_1^{u_1} h_2 [= (Ig_2)^{X_S}]$

$z = z'^s$

$x_1, x_2, u, v \in_R Z_q$

$B = g_1^{x_1} g_2^{x_2}$

$a = (a')^u g^v$

$b = (b')^{su} A^v$

$c = \mathcal{H}(A, B, z, a, b)$

$c' = c/u$ $\qquad \xrightarrow{c'}$

$r = r'u + v \bmod q$ $\qquad \xleftarrow{r'} \qquad r' = c'X_S + w$

Fig. 1. *Blind signature protocol, embedding the verifier's identity. At the end of the protocol* $\mathcal{V}$ *verifies:* $g^r \stackrel{?}{=} h^c a, A^r \stackrel{?}{=} z^c b.$

Setup: A probabilistic polynomial-time *(p.p.t.)* prover $\mathcal{P}$ and a p.p.t. verifier $\mathcal{V}$.
Common **input** is $A, B, a, b, G_1, G_2, G_3$, with a, b, G_1, G_2, G_3 generators of G_q, a subgroup of prime order q of the multiplicative group Z_p^* for some large prime p. The prover is assumed to not know the relative discrete logarithms of a, b, G_1, G_2, G_3.
Secret input to $\mathcal{P}$ is x, v, w, such that $A \equiv a^x G_1^v \pmod{p}, B \equiv b^x G_2^w \pmod{p}$ (for simplicity we henceforth use the notation $A = a^x G_1^v$).
Notation: $\mathbf{EqLog}[(A, a), G_1, (B, b), G_2]$ denotes that $A = a^x G_1^v$ and $B = b^x G_2^w$ for some $x \in G_Q$, and G_1, G_2 generators of G_Q. The reader may wish to think of that as $\log_a A = \log_b B$ for intuition (computations are always $\bmod P$).
The **proof** appears in Figure 2.

EqLog$[(A, a), G_1, (B, b), G_2]$
Input: A, B
$\mathcal{P}$ proves that $A = a^x G_1^v, B = b^x G_2^w$, i.e., $\log_a A = \log_b B$:

$\mathcal{P}$ $\hspace{11cm}$ $\mathcal{V}$

$y, s_1, s_2, s_3 \in_R Z_q$

$A' = a^y G_1^{s_1}, B' = b^y G_2^{s_2}$

$\xrightarrow{A', B'}$ $\qquad\qquad c \in_R Z_q$ or

$\xleftarrow{c} \quad c = \mathcal{H}(A, A', a, G_1, B, B', b, G_2, \text{Date/Time}, \text{Info})$

$r = c \cdot x + y$

$r_1 = c \cdot v + s_1, r_2 = c \cdot w + s_2$

$\xrightarrow{r, r_1, r_2}$ $\qquad\qquad$ Verify:

$$a^r \cdot G_1^{r_1} \stackrel{?}{=} A^c \cdot A' \quad \text{and}$$

$$b^r \cdot G_2^{r_2} \stackrel{?}{=} B^c \cdot B'$$

Fig. 2. *Proof of equality of logarithms.*

The proof is essentially a set of parallel Schnorr knowledge proofs and can be used to prove equality of more than two logarithms (see "extensions" below). As is the case in [Sch91], this minimal-knowledge proof can be made non-interactive and transferable under the random oracle model, with the challenge c being computed as a hash function of $\{A, A', a, G_1, B, B', b, G_2, \text{Date/Time}, \text{Info}\}$ and the hash function behaving like a random oracle.

We now discuss the correctness and zero-knowledge of the proof.

Correctness: It suffices to show that if a prover can answer to two challenges then s/he knows two representations as required (i.e., $A = a^x G_1{}^v$ and $B = b^x G_2{}^w$); then, if the prover cannot break the discrete log problem, s/he cannot know any other representations of A, B w.r.t. $(a, G_1), (b, G_2)$ respectively [Bra93b], since the relative logarithms of a w.r.t. G_1 and b w.r.t. G_2 are secret. Therefore there are only two possibilities: either the prover can answer to exactly one challenge (which depends on the construction of (A, B), i.e., it is "pre-selected" via the choice of (A, B)) or s/he knows the correct representations. But since the challenges are produced at random, the prover has only negligible probability of answering the "pre-selected" challenge without knowing the correct representations.

Now it is easy to see that given two answers to different challenges, $r = c{\cdot}x + y, r' = c'{\cdot}x + y$ and $[r_1 = c \cdot v + s_1, r_2 = c \cdot w + s_2], [r_1' = c' \cdot v + s_1, r_2' = c' \cdot w + s_2]$ one can solve the system of equations (where $r, r', r_1, r_2, r_1', r_2'$ and c, c' are known values) to compute x, y, v, w, s_1 and s_2; thus if the prover can answer to two challenges, it knows (can compute) the correct representations.

Zero-knowledge: The proofs can be simulated w.r.t. an honest verifier. In the interactive setting this is done by the verifier selecting a random challenge c and random "responses" r, r_1, r_2, and computing $A' = A^{-c} a^r G_1{}^{r_1}, B' = B^{-c} b^r G_2{}^{r_2}$. Here we assume that the verifier is honest, i.e., that c is indeed randomly chosen (and can be learned in a simulation).

In the non-interactive setting the simulations are performed under the random oracle model, as in [PS96b]. Briefly, here the challenge is constructed using a hash function: $c = \mathcal{H}(A, A', a, G_1, B, B', b, G_2, \text{Date/Time}, \text{Info})$ where the hash function H is modeled as (i.e., assumed to act like) a "random oracle," or "perfect hash function". The simulator proceeds as previously; the random oracle assumption is used in the construction of c. I.e., we want to guarantee that after choosing c, r, r_1, r_2 and computing A', B', the equation $c = \mathcal{H}(A, A', a, G_1, B, B', b, G_2, \text{Date/Time}, \text{Info})$ still holds. For this we let the simulator "change" the output of the random oracle H, such that on input this particular vector it outputs c. Then the resulting "modified" random oracle cannot be distinguished from the original, since c was originally chosen as a random value. As the random value c is here substituted by the output of the random oracle, the "honest verifier" assumption is guaranteed; i.e., in the non-interactive version, and under the random oracle assumption, the equality of logarithm proofs are zero-knowledge. Full proof to appear in extended version.

Extensions: The same proof can be used for more than two values; thus we can define $\text{EqLog}[(A, a), G_1, (B, b), G_2, (C, c), G_3]$ to prove equality between the respective logarithms of A, B and C. The protocol and security proofs are similar; we omit description for conciseness. (Although it is simple to observe that two consecutive proofs of equality of logarithms for (A, B) and (B, C) respectively achieve the same result—but with slightly higher computation.) This extended version is used in section 5.

3.3   Indirect Discourse Proofs

We now show how proofs of equality of logarithms can be used to create indirect discourse proofs. These will be used for the protocols of section 4 but *not* for section 5; if interested only in simplicity and not backwards compatibility we encourage the reader to move directly to section 5.

In this particular example of indirect discourse proofs, tailored to our purposes, we will construct a proof which shows a specific construction for three numbers A, B, C. This is a more general construction than we actually need for section 4.

The proof appears in figure 3. The interactive form is shown, but the proof can be made non-interactive by computing the challenge using a random oracle $\mathcal{H}$: $c = \mathcal{H}(A, B, C, A',$ $B', a, b, G_1, G_2, G_3, \text{Date/Time, Info})$, where "Info" is some transaction-related information (such as the identity of $\mathcal{V}$ or the transaction purpose/description/amount).

Notation: we use $\mathbf{IndPrf}[(A, a), G_1, (B, C|G_3), G_2]$ to denote that $A = a^x G_1{}^v$, $B = C^x G_2{}^z G_3{}^t = b^{ex} G_2{}^w$.

$$\mathbf{IndPrf}[(A, a), G_1, (B, b, C|G_3), G_2]$$
$$\text{Input: } A, \quad B = b^s G_2{}^w, \quad C = b^e G_3{}^u$$
$$\mathcal{P} \text{ will prove to } \mathcal{V} \text{ that } A = a^x G_1{}^v, B = C^x G_2{}^z G_3{}^t = b^{ex} G_2{}^w:$$

$\mathcal{P}$ $\hfill$ $\mathcal{V}$

$y, s_1, s_2, s_3 \in_R Z_q$
$A' = a^y G_1{}^{s_1}, B' = C^y G_2{}^{s_2} G_3{}^{s_3}$

$\qquad\qquad\qquad\qquad \xrightarrow{\quad A', B' \quad}$

$\qquad\qquad\qquad\qquad \xleftarrow{\quad c \quad} \qquad\qquad c \in_R Z_q$

$r = c \cdot x + y$
$r_1 = c \cdot v + s_1, r_2 = c \cdot w + s_2, r_3 = s_3 - r \cdot u \xrightarrow{\quad r, r_1, r_2, r_3 \quad}$ $\qquad$ Verify:

$$a^r \cdot G_1{}^{r_1} \overset{?}{=} A^c \cdot A' \quad \text{and}$$
$$C^r \cdot G_2{}^{r_2} \cdot G_3{}^{r_3} \overset{?}{=} B^c \cdot B'$$

Fig. 3. *Indirect discourse proof.*

We omit the proof of security due to lack of space; its construction is similar to the correctness and zero-knowledge proof of the protocol for proving equality of logarithms in section 3.2 above.

4   Retaining Existing Infrastructure

Changing systems that have already been implemented sometimes requires a disproportionate amount of effort, compared to the changes required. Thus it is important to devise techniques that enhance functionality without affecting existing systems. In this section we show how modular additions to off-line electronic cash systems can be used to construct FOLC in a seamless manner. We elect to show our additions on the Brands' protocol, but similar solutions are possible in other blinding protocols. As mentioned earlier, our focus is primarily security (i.e., basing anonymity on the decision Diffie-Hellman assumption) and efficiency.

4.1   Coin Tracing

Coin tracing can be performed efficiently using the techniques of [CMS96,DFTY97], modified to allow for provable security. To add it in a modular way we need a preliminary stage, in which the Trustee entity $\mathcal{T}$ is created, and an addition to the withdrawal protocol. The following steps are performed: during the withdrawal protocol an additional value $I' = I g_3{}^{s^{-1}} g_4{}^t$ is created (where g_4 is an additional generator of G_q) and its relationship to an ElGamal encryption $E_1 = (I g_2 g_4{}^t)^s f_1{}^m, E_2 = g_1{}^m$ is proven using indirect discourse proofs; here $f_1 = g_1{}^{X_{\mathcal{T}}}$ is a public key published by the Trustee. The coin then embeds I' instead of I and becomes $A = I^{s'} g_2{}^{s'} g_3{}^{s' \cdot s^{-1}} g_4{}^{t \cdot s^{-1}}$, where s' is the user's blinding factor.

At payment the verifier checks that the coin is of the form $A = g_1{}^x g_2{}^y g_4{}^z g_3$, thereby indirectly forcing the user to set $s' = s$.

Coin tracing is then performed by the trustee decrypting (E_1, E_2) to obtain the paid coin $\bar{A} = A/g_3 = (Ig_2g_4{}^t)^s$.

This method retains the anonymity of the user (based on the decision Diffie-Hellman assumption) with minimal computational overhead, while it requires no changes to the existing blind signature protocol. However we do not describe it in detail as (1) it can be derived in a straightforward manner from [DFTY97] and section 3.3 above, while (2) in section 5 we show a more efficient method achieving both owner and coin tracing.

4.2   Owner Tracing

An off-line coin by its nature has its owner's identity embedded in it. Thus for owner tracing all we need is an encryption of the user's identity using a public key encryption system, in such a way that the encryption is linked to the coin. Hence, Trustees can open the ciphertext to obtain the identity. An indirect discourse proof during payment assures the receiver that the encrypted identity is the same as the one embedded in the coin. The additions to the basic protocol are limited to a preliminary stage, in which the Trustee entity $\mathcal{T}$ is created, and to a modular addition to the payment protocol. Here we show the payment protocol that corresponds to the blinding protocol of section 3.1.

$\mathcal{T}$'s public information: Public key $f_2 = g_2{}^{X_{\mathcal{T}}}$ associated with private key $X_{\mathcal{T}} \in_R G_q$.

The new payment protocol:

$$\mathcal{U} \hspace{8cm} \mathcal{R}$$

$m \in_R Z_q$
$D_1 = Ig_2{}^{X_{\mathcal{T}} m}, D_2 = g_2{}^m$
$V_1 = \mathrm{EqLog}[(D_1, f_2), g_1, (D_2, g_2), \mathrm{nil}]$
$V_2 = \mathrm{IndPrf}[(\bar{A}, \{g_2, g_4\}), g_1, (\bar{A}, g_1, D_1|f_2), g_2]$
In $\mathbf{V_2}$, $\mathcal{U}$ uses $\mathbf{B = g_1{}^{x_1}g_2{}^{x_2}}$ from
withdrawal, instead of random $\mathbf{A'}$

$$\xrightarrow{D_1, D_2, V_1, V_2} \qquad D_2 \overset{?}{\neq} 1$$
$$\text{Verify } V_1, V_2$$

This protocol proves to $\mathcal{R}$ that (D_1, D_2) is an ElGamal [ElG85] encryption of I, based on f_2, where I is the same identity as the one embedded in the coin A. In particular, first V_1 proves that $D_1 = g_1{}^x g_2{}^{X_{\mathcal{T}} m}, D_2 = g_2{}^m$ for some x, m. Then V_2 proves that $x \cdot s \equiv u \cdot s$ (mod Q) where $\bar{A} = g_1{}^{us} g_2{}^s g_4{}^{ts}$ is the user's coin; therefore, $x \equiv u$ (mod Q) and thus $D_1 = Ig_2{}^{X_{\mathcal{T}} m}$ as required.

Efficiency: The protocol poses minimal additional communication and computation requirements (on the order of 7 exponentiations for $\mathcal{U}$ and 9 for $\mathcal{R}$), while keeping $\mathcal{T}$ off-line in all cases.

5   Simplified FOLC

Although the protocols of the previous sections are efficient and secure, it turns out that if we can alter some design aspects of the basic e-cash system it is possible to perform coin and owner tracing in one step, thus effectively reducing in half the computational requirements, while remaining within the same security assumptions.

The idea is to combine the identity of the user with a "coin identifier" (as in [CMS96]) to an *unconditional* commitment. Then, this commitment is signed using the blinding protocol. The commitment is constructed such that the resulting coin is itself part of an ElGamal encryption of the user's identity (this idea has its root in [dST98]). Thus, one execution of the blinding protocol (which is the bulk of the computation at withdrawal) in effect performs two tasks at once: tracing the coin and encrypting the user's identity. The blinding protocol used is a modification of the one appearing in section 3.1 that operates on 3 instead of 2 generators, but whose security is unchanged [Bra93a]. The fact that the commitment is unconditional allows us to prove anonymity under the decision Diffie-Hellman assumption.

For coin tracing an ElGamal encryption of the "coin identifier" is constructed at withdrawal, and its correct construction (with respect to the commitment) is verified using proofs of equality of logarithms. For owner tracing one additional value is constructed (at payment) to form an ElGamal encryption in conjuction with the coin; the correctness of this value requires proofs of equality of logarithms instead of indirect discourse proofs. We proceed with the details.

Bank's setup protocol: (performed once by $\mathcal{B}$)

Primes p and q are chosen such that $|p-1| = \delta + k$ for a specified constant δ, and $p = \gamma q + 1$, for a specified integer γ. Then a unique subgroup G_q of prime order q of the multiplicative group Z_p^* and generators g, g_1, g_2, g_3, g_4 of G_q are defined. Secret key $X_\mathcal{B} \in_R Z_q$ is created.[2] Hash functions $\mathcal{H}, \mathcal{H}_0, \mathcal{H}_1, \ldots$, from a family of collision intractable hash functions are also defined. $\mathcal{B}$ publishes $p, q, g, g_1, g_2, g_3, g_4, (\mathcal{H}, \mathcal{H}_0, \mathcal{H}_1, \ldots)$ and its public keys $h = g^{X_\mathcal{B}}$, $h_1 = g_1^{X_\mathcal{B}}, h_2 = g_2^{X_\mathcal{B}}, h_3 = g_3^{X_\mathcal{B}}$.

Trustee's setup protocol: (performed once by $\mathcal{T}$)

Public keys $f_2 = g_2^{X_\mathcal{T}}, f_3 = g_3^{X_\mathcal{T}}$ associated with private key $X_\mathcal{T} \in_R Z_q$ are published.

User's setup (account opening) protocol: (performed for each user $\mathcal{U}$)

The bank $\mathcal{B}$ associates user $\mathcal{U}$ with $I = g_1^{u_1}$ where $u_1 \in G_q$ is generated by $\mathcal{U}$ and $g_1^{u_1} g_2 \neq 1$. $\mathcal{U}$ also proves (using the Schnorr identification scheme [Sch91]) to $\mathcal{B}$ that he knows how to represent I w.r.t. g_1.

Withdrawal: (over an authenticated channel between $\mathcal{B}$ and $\mathcal{U}$)

An intermediate value $I' = g_1^{u_1 s^{-1}} g_3^{s^{-1}} g_4^t$ is created. The user constructs an ElGamal encryption $E_1 = g_2^s f_3^m, E_2 = g_3^m$ of g_2^s and proceeds to prove its correct construction w.r.t. I'. The constructions of I', E_1, E_2 are proven using proofs of equality of logarithms. The blinding protocol of section 3.1 then proceeds with I' replacing I.

Note that during the payment protocol the user is expected to present a coin of a specific structure; this forces him to use the committed value s as the blinding factor. Thus the coin contains g_2^s and can be traced by decrypting (E_1, E_2).

The withdrawal protocol results in a signature of the form appearing in equation (1) (see section 3.1):

$\mathcal{U}$ $\qquad\qquad\qquad\qquad\qquad\qquad\qquad\qquad\qquad\qquad\qquad\qquad$ $\mathcal{B}$

$m, s, t \in_R Z_q$
$I' = g_1^{u_1 s^{-1}} g_3^{s^{-1}} g_4^t$
$E_1 = g_2^s f_3^m, E_2 = g_3^m$
$V_1 = \mathrm{EqLog}[(E_1, f_3), g_2, (E_2, g_3), \mathrm{nil}]$
$V_2 = \mathrm{EqLog}[(g_3, I'), (g_1, g_4),$
$\quad (E_1, g_2), f_3, (I, I'), (g_3, g_4)]$

$\qquad\qquad\qquad\qquad \xrightarrow{I', E_1, E_2, V_1, V_2} \qquad\qquad\qquad\qquad \overset{?}{E_2 \neq 1}$
$\qquad\qquad\qquad\qquad\qquad\qquad\qquad\qquad\qquad\qquad$ Verify V_1, V_2
$\qquad\qquad\qquad\qquad\qquad\qquad\qquad\qquad\qquad\qquad$ $w \in_R Z_q$
$\qquad\qquad\qquad\qquad \xleftarrow{a', b', b''} \quad a' = g^w, b' = (I'g_2)^w, b'' = g_4^w$

---

[2] We assume, for simplicity, that only one denomination is used. A different key for each denomination is necessary.

$$A = (I' g_2 g_4{}^{t^{-1}})^s = g_1{}^{u_1} g_2{}^s g_3$$
$$z = h_1{}^{u_1} h_2{}^s h_3 \; [= A^{X_B}]$$
$$x_1, x_2, u, v \in_R Z_q$$
$$B = g_1^{x_1} g_2^{x_2}$$
$$a = (a')^u g^v$$
$$b = (b' b''^{t^{-1}})^{su} A^v \; [= A^{wu+v}]$$
$$c = \mathcal{H}(A, B, z, a, b)$$
$$c' = c/u \qquad\qquad \xrightarrow{\;c'\;}$$
$$\qquad\qquad\qquad \xleftarrow{\;r'\;} r' = c' X_B + w$$
$$r = r'u + v \bmod q$$

At the end of the protocol $\mathcal{U}$ verifies: $g^r \overset{?}{=} h^c a,\; A^r \overset{?}{=} z^c b$.

Payment: (performed between $\mathcal{U}$ and $\mathcal{R}$ over an anonymous channel)
At payment time $\mathcal{U}$ supplies information to the receiver $\mathcal{R}$ (which is later forwarded to the bank) so that if a coin is double-spent the user $\mathcal{U}$ is identified.

The user provides the signature on the coin $A = g_1^x g_2^y g_3$ and uses $A_1 = A/g_3$ for the verifications of the payment protocol. I.e., the user is forced to use s as the blinding factor, in order to "neutralize" the exponent s^{-1} of g_3.

The user also provides the value $A_2 = f_2{}^s$ and proves that this, together with the coin, forms a (modified) ElGamal encryption of g_1^x which, from the withdrawal protocol, can only be $g_1{}^{u_1} = I$, i.e., the user's identity. To prove the construction all that is needed is the proof of equality of logarithms $V_3 = \mathrm{EqLog}[(A_1, g_2), g_1, (A_2, f_2), \mathrm{nil}]$.

The payment protocol ($\mathcal{U}$ and $\mathcal{R}$ agree on date/time, to be used as input to the non-interactive challenge):

$\mathcal{U}$ $\qquad\qquad\qquad\qquad\qquad\qquad\qquad\qquad\qquad\qquad\qquad$ $\mathcal{R}$

$$A_1 = g_1{}^{u_1} g_2{}^s \; [= A/g_3]$$
$$A_2 = f_2{}^s$$
$$V_3 = \mathrm{EqLog}[(A_1, g_2), g_1, (A_2, f_2), \mathrm{nil}]$$
$\mathcal{U}$ uses $\mathbf{B}$ instead of $\mathbf{A'}$
$\quad$ in the construction of $\mathbf{V_3}$

$$\xrightarrow{\;A_1, A_2, A, B, (z, a, b, r)\;} \qquad A_1 \overset{?}{\neq} 1,\, A_1 g_3 = A$$
$$sig(A, B) \overset{?}{=} (z, a, b, r)$$
$$\text{Verify } V_3$$

Deposit: (performed between $\mathcal{R}$ and $\mathcal{B}$ over an authenticated channel)
$\quad$ $\mathcal{R}$ sends a transcript of the payment protocol to $\mathcal{B}$ who verifies the (non-interactive) proofs.

Owner tracing: (performed between $\mathcal{B}$ and $\mathcal{T}$ over an authenticated channel)
$\quad$ The bank simply sends the deposited coin to the trustee $\mathcal{T}$. $\mathcal{T}$ uses the private key to decrypt the ElGamal encryption (A_1, A_2) and sends the decrypted value (i.e., $I = g_1{}^{u_1}$) to $\mathcal{B}$. The bank indexes this against its account database to find the coin's owner.

Coin tracing: (performed between $\mathcal{B}$ and $\mathcal{T}$ over an authenticated channel)
$\quad$ The bank sends a withdrawal transcript to $\mathcal{T}$. The trustee decrypts the ElGamal encryption (E_1, E_2) to obtain the value $g_2{}^s$; the bank then searches its deposit databases for the coin $A = I g_2{}^s g_3$, where I is the user's identity.

Efficiency: The protocols require around 8 and 11 exponentiations for the user and bank at withdrawal[3] and 4 and 2 for the user and receiver at payment.

6 Security

The security of FOLC can be described in three parts: (1) security for the payees and bank (i.e., unreusability, unforgeability, and unexpandability of coins; see [FY93] for a precise model), (2) security of the extensions (i.e., the ability of the trustees to trace), and (3) security (anonymity) for the legitimate users. Our protocols guarantee the following:

- (1) above is unchanged from the underlying basic off-line e-cash protocol. This can be seen since the blinding protocol is either unmodified (section 4) or (in section 5) the modifications do not impair its security [Bra93a]. See appendix A for a sketch of the proof.
- (2) above is based on the correctness property of the proof of equality of logarithms, i.e., it is guaranteed based on the existence of hash functions that behave like random oracles. The proof here is straightforward (verify that the user is constrained in the construction of the ElGamal encryptions, based on the proofs of equality of logarithms) but relatively lengthy. See appendix A for more details.
- Finally, (3) above is based on the semantic security of the (inverted) ElGamal encryption, i.e., on the decision Diffie-Hellman assumption. Intuitively, note that the disclosed values do not reveal any information; a sketch of an actual proof which shows that if anonymity is broken then the decision D-H problem does not hold, is given in appendix B.

7 Discussion and Open Problems

We have constructed a simple solution for fair off-line electronic cash, utilizing recent security proofs for homomorphic encryption schemes [TY98]. We believe that the biggest open problem is to prove security under even more strict assumptions while keeping the efficiency of our constructions. A first step to this direction may be a recently proposed encryption scheme with homomorphic properties, whose semantic security is equivalent to factoring [OU98]. Similarly, we would like to see blinding protocols whose restrictive properties can be proven secure.

References

BCC+92. S. Brands, D. Chaum, R. Cramer, N. Ferguson, and T. Pedersen. Transaction systems with observers, August 13 1992. Unpublished manuscript.

Bra93a. S. Brands. An efficient off-line electronic cash system based on the representation problem. Technical Report CS–R9323, CWI (Centre for Mathematics and Computer Science), Amsterdam, 1993. anonymous ftp: ftp.cwi.nl:/pub/CWIreports/AA/CS-R9323.ps.zip.

Bra93b. S. Brands. Untraceable off-line cash in wallets with observers. In *Advances in Cryptology — Crypto '93, Proceedings (Lecture Notes in Computer Science 773)*, pages 302–318. Springer-Verlag, 1993. Available at http://www.cwi.nl/ftp/brands/crypto93.ps.Z.

CFMT96. A. Chan, Y. Frankel, P. MacKenzie, and Y. Tsiounis. Mis-representation of identities in e-cash schemes and how to prevent it. In *Advances in Cryptology — Proceedings of Asiacrypt '96 (Lecture Notes in Computer Science 1163)*, pages 276–285, Kyongju, South Korea, November 3–7 1996. Springer-Verlag. Available at http://www.ccs.neu.edu/home/yiannis/pubs.html.

---

[3] Here we count the additional burden over basic e-cash that is required for the "fairness" extensions.

CFN90.   D. Chaum, A. Fiat, and M. Naor. Untraceable electronic cash. In *Advances in Cryptology —Crypto '88 (Lecture Notes in Computer Science)*, pages 319–327. Springer-Verlag, 1990.

CMS96.   J. Camenisch, U. Maurer, and M. Stadler. Digital payment systems with passive anonymity-revoking trustees. In *Esorics '96*, (Lecture Notes in Computer Science 1146), pages 33–43. Springer-Verlag, Italy, 1996. Available at http://www.inf.ethz.ch/personal/camenisc/publications.html.

CP93a.   D. Chaum and T.P. Pedersen. Wallet databases with observers. In E. Brickell, editor, *Advances in Cryptology — Crypto '92, Proceedings (Lecture Notes in Computer Science)*, pages 90–106. Springer-Verlag, New York, 1993. Santa Barbara, California.

CP93b.   R. Cramer and T. Pedersen. Improved privacy in wallets with observers. In *Advances in Cryptology: Eurocrypt '93, Proceedings (Lecture Notes in Computer Science 765)*, pages 329–343. Springer-Verlag, 1993.

DFTY97.   G. Davida, Y. Frankel, Y. Tsiounis, and M. Yung. Anonymity control in e-cash. In *Proceedings of the 1st Financial Cryptography conference (Lecture Notes in Computer Science 1318)*, Anguilla, BWI, February 24-28 1997. Springer-Verlag. To appear. Available at http://www.ccs.neu.edu/home/yiannis/pubs.html.

dST98.   A. de Solages and J. Traore. An efficient fair off-line electronic cash system with extensions to checks and wallets with observers. In *Proceedings of the 2nd Financial Cryptography conference*, Anguilla, BWI, February 1998. Springer-Verlag. To appear.

ElG85.   T. ElGamal. A public key cryptosystem and a signature scheme based on discrete logarithms. *IEEE Trans. Inform. Theory*, 31:469–472, 1985.

FTY96.   Y. Frankel, Y. Tsiounis, and M. Yung. Indirect discourse proofs: achieving fair off-line e-cash. In *Advances in Cryptology, Proc. of Asiacrypt '96 (Lecture Notes in Computer Science 1163)*, pages 286–300, Kyongju, South Korea, November 3–7 1996. Springer-Verlag. International patent pending. Available at http://www.ccs.neu.edu/home/yiannis/pubs.html.

FY93.   M. Franklin and M. Yung. Secure and efficient off-line digital money. In *Proceedings of the twentieth International Colloquium on Automata, Languages and Programming (ICALP 1993), (Lecture Notes in Computer Science 700)*, pages 265–276. Springer-Verlag, 1993. Lund, Sweden, July 1993.

GM84.   S. Goldwasser and S. Micali. Probabilistic encryption. *Journal of Computer and System Sciences*, 28(2):270–299, April 1984.

JY96.   M. Jakobson and M. Yung. Revokable and versatile e-money. In *3rd ACM Symp. on Computer and Communication Security*, March 1996.

NR97.   M. Naor and O. Reingold. On the construction of pseudo-random permutations: Luby-Rackoff revisited. In *38th Annual Symp. on Foundations of Computer Science (FOCS)*, 1997.

OU98.   T. Okamoto and S. Uchiyama. An efficient public-key cryptosystem. In *Eurocrypt 98*, Espoo, Finland, May 31–June 4 1998. Springer-Verlag. To appear. Preliminary announcement in Workshop on Public Key Cryptography, Feb. 5-6 1998, Yokohama, Japan.

PS96a.   D. Pointcheval and J. Stern. Provably secure blind signature schemes. In *Advances in Cryptology, Proc. of Asiacrypt '96 (Lecture Notes in Computer Science)*, Kyongju, South Korea, November 3–7 1996. Springer-Verlag. To appear. Available at http://www.ens.fr/dmi/equipes_dmi/grecc/pointche/pub.html.

PS96b.   D. Pointcheval and J. Stern. Security proofs for signature schemes. In U. Maurer, editor, *Advances in Cryptology, Proc. of Eurocrypt '96*, pages 387–398, Zaragoza, Spain, May 11–16, 1996. Springer-Verlag. Available at http://www.ens.fr/dmi/equipes_dmi/grecc/pointche/pub.html.

Sch91.   C. P. Schnorr. Efficient signature generation by smart cards. *Journal of Cryptology*, 4(3):161–174, 1991.

TY98.   Y. Tsiounis and M. Yung. On the security of El Gamal-based encryption. In *International workshop on Public Key Cryptography (PKC '98)*, Yokohama, Japan, February 5-6 1998. Springer-Verlag. To appear. Available at http://yiannis.home.ml.org.

A   Security for the Bank and Receivers (Shops)

We show a sketch of the proof for (1) and (2) of section 6; for shortness we limit the discussion to the protocol of section 5.

At payment, V_3 proves that $A_1 = g_2{}^x g_1{}^y$ and $A_2 = f_2{}^x$ for some x, y; i.e., that (A_1, A_2) forms an ElGamal encryption of $g_1{}^y$ based on the Trustee's public key f_2. Also notice that V_3 is always carried out with the same randomness $B = g_1{}^{x_1} g_2{}^{x_2}$, therefore if it is executed twice it will reveal x (which, as we will see, is the user's private key).

Then, at withdrawal, V_1 proves that $E_1 = g_2{}^s f_3{}^m, E_2 = g_3{}^m$ for some s, m, i.e., that (E_1, E_2) forms an ElGamal encryption of $g_2{}^s$. Also, V_2 proves that $g_3 = (I')^v g_1{}^w g_4{}^t, E_1 = g_2{}^v f_3{}^u, I = (I')^v g_3{}^r g_4{}^z$ for some v, w, t, u, r, z. But from V_1 we have that $E_1 = g_2{}^s f_3{}^m$, thus $v = s, u = m$ and therefore $g_3 = (I')^s g_1{}^w g_4{}^t, E_1 = g_2{}^s f_3{}^m, I = (I')^s g_3{}^r g_4{}^z$. By rearranging the equations involving I' we get $I' = g_3{}^{s^{-1}} g_1{}^{w'} g_4{}^{t'}$ and $I' = I^{s^{-1}} g_3{}^{r'} g_4{}^{z'}$, where $w' = -ws^{-1}, t' = -ts^{-1}$, etc. Also at user setup it has been proven that $I = g_1{}^{u_1}$, hence we have that $I' = (g_1{}^{u_1})^{s^{-1}} g_3{}^{r'} g_4{}^{z'} = g_1{}^{u_1 s^{-1}} g_3{}^{r'} g_4{}^{z'}$, and (from the first equation on I'), $I' = g_1{}^{u_1 s^{-1}} g_3{}^{s^{-1}} g_4{}^{t'}$, where t' is unknown to the bank, and s is the same as in E_1.

Now, if we assume that the withdrawal protocol is a restrictive blind signature protocol (an assumption initially made and argued for in [Bra93a]), i.e., under the terminology of [FY93] it satisfies unforgeability and unexpandability, then the signed number A must be of the form $A = (I' g_2)^u g_4{}^v$, for some u, v, i.e., $A = g_1{}^{u_1 s^{-1} u} g_3{}^{s^{-1} u} g_2{}^u g_4{}^{t' u} g_4{}^v$. From the payment above we have seen that $A = A_1 g_3 = g_2{}^x g_1{}^y g_3$. Therefore, it must be that $s^{-1} u \equiv 1$ (mod q) and $t' u + v \equiv 0$ (mod q); in particular, $u \equiv s$ (mod q). Putting these values in A we get $A = g_1{}^{u_1} g_2{}^s g_3$, and therefore $A_1 = g_1{}^{u_1} g_2{}^s, A_2 = f_2{}^s$, as required for tracing.

Thus we have shown that if unforgeability and unexpandability are satisfied for the starting scheme (in this case [Bra93a]) then traceability and bank/shop security also hold for FOLC.

B   Anonymity

For anonymity (i.e., untraceability as defined in [FY93]) we want to prove that given a pair of withdrawal protocols and the corresponding paid coins, a collaboration of bank and shops cannot decide which coin came from which withdrawal. Again we limit the discussion to the protocol of section 5. The data that is available for this linking is the following[4] (we omit the values I_0', I_1' since they are unconditionally blinded by the random t_0, t_1):

At withdrawal: $\left[V_1^0, V_2^0, E_1^0 = g_2{}^{s_0} f_3{}^{m_0}, E_2^0 = g_3{}^{m_0}, c'^0 \right]$ and

$\left[V_1^1, V_2^1, E_1^1 = g_2{}^{s_1} f_3{}^{m_1}, E_2^1 = g_3{}^{m_1}, c'^1 \right]$.

At payment: $\left[A_1^i = g_1{}^{u_i} g_2{}^{s_i}, A_2^i = f_2{}^{s_i}, V_3^i, z^i, a^i, b^i, r^i, B^i \right]$ and

$\left[A_1^{\bar{i}} = g_1{}^{u_{\bar{i}}} g_2{}^{s_{\bar{i}}}, A_2^{\bar{i}} = f_2{}^{s_{\bar{i}}}, V_3^{\bar{i}}, z^{\bar{i}}, a^{\bar{i}}, b^{\bar{i}}, r^{\bar{i}}, B^{\bar{i}} \right]$, $i, \bar{i} \in \{0, 1\}, i \neq \bar{i}$.

The linking problem is to determine whether i is 0 or 1.

Suppose now we have a machine $\mathcal{M}$ which given the above information can find i. Then we can use this machine to break the ElGamal encryption in the sense of indistinguishability, i.e., break the decision D-H assumption [TY98], as follows (sketch):

Let $\mu_i = g_2{}^{s_i}, \mu_{\bar{i}} = g_2{}^{s_{\bar{i}}}$ be two messages, and let $(E_1^0, E_2^0), (E_1^1, E_2^1)$ be the encryptions of μ_0, μ_1 respectively. Then we feed $\mathcal{M}$ with these encryptions, plus $(A_1^i, A_2^i), (A_1^{\bar{i}}, A_2^{\bar{i}})$, which we can construct for a random $u_i, u_{\bar{i}}$, since we know $s_i, s_{\bar{i}}$. We then simulate V_j^l, for $j = \{1, 2\}, l = \{0, 1\}$ and $V_3^i, V_3^{\bar{i}}$; the simulations for V_3 require random values to be chosen for $B^i, B^{\bar{i}}$. Then the signatures of the coins are simulated, i.e., random values $R_i, c^i, R_{\bar{i}}, c^{\bar{i}}$ are chosen and $a^i = g^{R^i}, r^i = c^i X_\mathcal{B} + R^i, z^i = (A^i)^{X_\mathcal{B}}, b^i = (A^i)^{R^i}, a^{\bar{i}} = g^{R^{\bar{i}}}, r^{\bar{i}} = c^{\bar{i}} X_\mathcal{B} + R^{\bar{i}}, z^{\bar{i}} =$

---

[4] Here X^i or X_i denotes value X at protocol i.

$(A^{\bar{i}})^{X_B}, b^{\bar{i}} = (A^{\bar{i}})^{R^{\bar{i}}}$ are calculated. Finally c'^0, c'^1 are chosen at random (it is easy to verify that for any choice of c, c', R, setting $u = c/c', v = R - wu$ satisfies both $c' = c/u$ and the values of a, b, as calculated using R; thus the simulation is perfect). These values are then inserted into $\mathcal{H}(A^i, B^i, z^i, a^i, b^i), \mathcal{H}(A^{\bar{i}}, B^{\bar{i}}, z^{\bar{i}}, a^{\bar{i}}, b^{\bar{i}})$ and the values of the hash function at these points are changed so that the results are $c^i, c^{\bar{i}}$ respectively.

The whole output of the simulator (consisting of the above values) is then fed to $\mathcal{M}$, which returns the value of i, and thus breaks the semantic security of ElGamal encryption.

Finally, the above problem of distinguishing between two ciphertexts can be embedded in a context of polynomially many withdrawals using standard methods.

Off-line Fair Payment Protocols using Convertible Signatures

Colin Boyd and Ernest Foo*

Information Security Research Centre
School of Data Communications
Queensland University of Technology
Brisbane, Australia
{boyd,ernest}@fit.qut.edu.au

Abstract. An exchange or payment protocol is considered *fair* if neither of the two parties exchanging items or payment at any time during the protocol has a significant advantage over the other entity. Fairness is an important property for electronic commerce. This paper identifies a design framework based on existing fair protocols which use offline trusted third parties, but with convertible signatures as the underlying mechanism. We show that in principle any convertible signature scheme can be used to design a fair payment protocol. A specific protocol is detailed based on RSA undeniable signatures which is more efficient than other similar fair payment schemes. Furthermore, in this protocol the final signature obtained is always an ordinary RSA signature.

1 Introduction

As more and more electronic transactions are being conducted on insecure networks, it is becoming obvious that electronic transactions are governed by different forces from the ones which affect normal physical exchanges of currency and goods. The possibility that transactions can occur remotely is one of the greatest advantages of electronic transactions as well as one of its biggest challenges to protocol designers.

In a typical physical exchange two entities, for example a customer and a shopkeeper, are present at the same location. During the exchange the customer hands the shopkeeper some notes and coins. In return the shopkeeper hands the desired goods to the customer. Unfortunately, in electronic commerce the security of this scenario is suspect because of the remoteness of the shopkeeper and the customer. It is possible that, once the customer's coins have passed through cyberspace and have been received by the shopkeeper, the shopkeeper refuses to deliver the goods; or if the shopkeeper hands the goods to the customer first the customer may log off instead of paying the shopkeeper. These problems arise with electronic transactions because the customer and shopkeeper are separated by cyberspace. In a physical situation, if the customer attempts to take the goods without paying the shopkeeper has the option to detain him.

---

* Sponsored by Commonwealth Bank and the Australian Research Council

K. Ohta and D. Pei (Eds.): ASIACRYPT'98, LNCS 1514, pp. 271-285, 1998.
© Springer-Verlag Berlin Heidelberg 1998

This problem is an obvious one to electronic transaction protocol designers. In the course of development of electronic commerce protocols, many schemes have been developed to solve the problem of electronic exchange. These protocols are referred to in the literature as *fair exchange* protocols. The main objective of all fair exchange protocols is to ensure that at no point during the execution of the protocol can either of the entities participating in the exchange gain any (significant) advantage over the other if the protocol is suddenly halted.

1.1   Previous Work

Until recently there have been two main approaches for achieving fair exchange. The first approach is to ensure that the exchange occurs simultaneously. One way of providing simultaneous exchange is to have the participants exchange information bit by bit in an interleaving manner [15].

The second approach is to ensure that the exchange will be completed even though one of the entities participating in the exchange refuses to continue. Fair exchange protocols which employ this approach often use a trusted third party to store the details of the transaction [8, 18]. These details are released if one of the entities refuse to complete the protocol.

The use of the trusted third party greatly reduces the efficiency of the protocol. For a once off transaction such as, say, exchange of an important contract, high efficiency need not be a priority. But for regular electronic transactions, such as remote purchase of electronic goods, efficiency is a critical issue. So most of the recent fair exchange protocols attempt to reduce the need for the trusted third party in the online execution of the transaction while ensuring that a trusted third party is always available to resolve disputes. Protocols which do not require a trusted third party during the online execution are referred to as being *offline*.

The basic method for fair exchange using an offline third party has been established in a few recent papers. This method seems first to have been presented by Mao [12] and was followed further by Asokan, Shoup and Waidner [1] and Bao, Deng and Mao [2]. The general idea in all these papers is for one party (sometimes both parties) to send a signature to the other in such a way that:

- the recipient is convinced that the signature is correct but cannot transfer the proof of correctness to other parties.
- the recipient is convinced that *if necessary* the offline third party will be able to make the signature available to any verifier.

The recipient of such a signature should then be willing to proceed with the transaction with the knowledge that in case of dispute the third party can make the signature universally verifiable. But normally the third party is not involved, thereby allowing great efficiency savings over protocols with an online trusted third party.

The way that the above properties have been achieved in previous work is that the signature is encrypted with the public key of the third party. A *verifiable encryption* protocol is then executed between the sender and recipient of the signed message in order to achieve the second property above. Although these are all ingenious protocols they do suffer from some potential drawbacks. One is that the verifiable encryption protocols currently available are computationally expensive, perhaps too much so for practical use of these schemes in everyday transactions. Another drawback is that these protocols also require a large amount of storage. In order to reduce complexity of both computation and communications, non-interactive verifiable encryption has been proposed. However, this raises the question of whether a non-interactive proof that a signature is encrypted is really any different from a signature itself, since it alone is sufficient to prove to any third party that the signer has committed to the message. We believe that there is little difference in functionality and that convertible signatures with non-interactive proofs of correctness should be avoided in our fair payment protocols.

1.2   Our Approach

In this paper new fair exchange protocols using an offline trusted third party are proposed. The principal new idea is to make use of a well known cryptographic primitive known as a *convertible signature*. All the previously published offline fair exchange schemes use the same basic idea of allowing one party, say the merchant, to be able to verify that *if necessary* he can employ the third party to convert a restricted commitment, verifiable by the merchant, into a full signature providing non-repudiation. In other words, a signature verifiable only by the merchant is converted into a universal signature. Convertible undeniable signatures provide exactly this property.

Undeniable signatures were introduced by Chaum and van Antwerpen [5]. These are digital signatures which can only be verified with the assistance of the signer. The signer is able to confirm or deny the ownership of the signature. No entity other than the signer is able to verify ownership of the signature. The signer is unable to prove that a valid signature is invalid or similarly that an invalid signature is valid. Convertible undeniable signatures developed by Boyar, Chaum and Damgård [3] build on the properties of undeniable signatures. Like undeniable signatures, convertible undeniable signatures can only be verified with the assistance of the signer but in addition the signer is able to selectively convert a single undeniable signature into a normal digital signature or collectively convert all the signer's signatures into normal digital signatures which can be verified by anyone.

An extension of the idea of convertible signatures are *designated converter* signatures, defined by Chaum [4] in which conversion may be achieved by a designated third party separate from the original signer. (Actually Chaum called them *designated confirmer* signatures, but we have changed the name to emphasize the conversion property which we are interested in. In fact in all known examples either confirmation or conversion may be achieved according to whether an interactive or non-interactive protocol is used.) These appear even more suited to application in fair exchange than ordinary convertible signatures.

Surprisingly, the use of convertible signatures does not appear to have been proposed before in the context of fair exchange. Despite this each of the offline fair exchange protocols proposed in previous papers [1, 2, 12] can be seen as a new designated converter signature algorithm! This is because verifiable encryption of a signature with a designated third party's public key clearly allows that third party to convert the signature into a universally verifiable one simply by decryption. In this paper we will use existing convertible signature schemes and adapt them to work for fair exchange protocols.

We explore the use of convertible undeniable signatures in fair exchange protocols with an offline third party. We mainly concentrate on the convertible property of these signatures as the undeniable function is not necessary for fair exchange. We are able to propose a number of new protocols which are at least as efficient as any other known protocols of this type. We regard the following as the three main contributions of the current paper.

- A general framework for fair payment in which any convertible signature scheme may be used.
- A new fair payment protocol which is more efficient than similar fair exchange schemes.
- A new designated converter signature for which converted signatures are ordinary RSA signatures.

Asokan, Shoup and Waidner [1] and Mao [12] exchange signatures fairly between two parties. In this paper we focus on more specific goals in that we wish to conduct a payment transaction between a customer and a merchant. Bao, Deng and Mao [2] present two fair exchange protocols which may be used for payment. Their first protocol is inefficient since it relies on use of verifiable encryption protocols which require a high number of rounds for security. Their second protocol uses a more efficient verifiable encryption protocol, but unfortunately this protocol is faulty and allows anyone to verify the customer's signature.

In section 2, we present a general design model for fair payment. Section 3 discusses use of existing convertible signature schemes within the model. A new designated converter signature is presented in detail inside the framework in section 4. An attack on the second Bao, Deng and Mao protocol is presented in the appendix.

2   A Framework for Offline Fair Payment Protocol Design

2.1   Definitions and Notation

The following symbols will be used to represent common parameters for the entire paper. Other parameters which are only used by specific protocols will be defined in the protocol description.

C The customer entity.

M The merchant entity.

B The bank, acquirer or notary entity.

TTP The trusted third party. It is possible that the bank could play the role of the trusted third party also but for the purpose of this paper we assume trusted third party and the bank are separate entities.

m Purchase Information. This is information regarding the goods' *product ID*, the *price* to be paid for the goods as well as the *merchant account number*. It is assumed that this information will uniquely identify the transaction and the merchant entity.

$Cert_X$ The certificate which verifies the public key of entity X with the appropriate certification authority. It also contains the customer's banking details which can only be decrypted by the bank entity and the customer's public key.

Goods The goods which are described in m. These are assumed to be software goods which can be transmitted securely encrypted across open networks.

The following notation is used to denote cryptographic operations. X and Y always represent communicating parties and may be any of the four entities defined above.

$E_{XY}(Message)$ *Message*, encrypted with the key XY using symmetric key cryptography. It is assumed that the key is known only by X and Y and that only these entities may know the contents of *Message*.

$E_X(Message)$ *Message*, encrypted with a public key belonging to X using public key cryptography. It is assumed that the public key belonging to X is known to all entities but only the entity X knows the corresponding private key to decrypt the contents of *Message*.

$Sig_X(Message)$ *Message*, digitally signed by X using public key cryptography. This implies that X's public key is used to ensure that the message was transmitted by X. A message signed in this fashion can be verified by any entity.

$S_X(Message)$ *Message*, digitally signed by X using a convertible undeniable signature.

$H(Message)$ A cryptographic function which results in a digest and checksum of *Message*, using an algorithm such as the Secure Hash Algorithm (SHA) one-way hash function.

2.2   The Design Framework

The following design framework is the model which has been used to develop the offline fair payment protocols described in this paper. This model can be used with any convertible signature scheme to construct new offline fair payment protocols as long as there is a way to ensure that only the third party is able to convert signatures.

The basic protocol ensures fairness by having TTP force the completion of a transaction if a dispute occurs. If no dispute occurs only C and M need to participate in the transaction.

Registration A registration protocol between the customer and third party is required for our efficient protocol in section 4. It will be correctly argued that the need for registration is an overhead which somewhat reduces the efficiency of the new protocol. However, we would like to point out that in practice trusted third parties will not be offering their services free of charge, and registration is probably a necessary phase. It need only be carried out once to initialize the relationship between C and TTP. The purpose of the registration process is to ensure that C has been identified and approved by TTP. In section 4 it is specifically used to ensure that both the trusted third party and C share keys which are to be used in the case of a dispute.

Payment The payment phase of the protocol must be conducted for each transaction. It is during this phase that M and the customer exchange goods.

It is assumed that in this phase C has already gone through a bidding process with M and that the two entities have already settled on the items to be purchased and the price to be paid. This process may be as simple as C selecting fixed priced goods from M's web site. Thus C should already have all the information included in m defined above.

$$P1. \; C \; \to M : S(m)$$
$$P2. \; C \; \leftrightarrow M : M \text{ verifies interactively that } S(m) \text{ is valid}$$
$$P3. \; M \to C \; : E_C(Goods)$$
$$P4. \; C \; \to M : Sig_C(m)$$

In step $P1$, C generates a partial signature of the transaction information m. The partial signature must be in such a form that only M can verify its correctness. In all our protocols M and C have to interact to verify this partial signature and this verification is done in step $P2$. Another property of the partial signature is that the trusted third party must be able to convert it into a normal signature which anyone could verify. This property is only used in case of a dispute.

Once M is satisfied that C's partial signature is valid he sends a signed copy of the requested goods to C along with the transaction information. This is done in step $P3$ of the protocol.

In step $P4$, C, on receipt of the goods, sends a normal signature to M. M can now show everyone, including the bank, that C has agreed to the transaction details in m. In practice M will follow this step with a deposit process, but we omit this from further discussion.

Disputes If M decides not to send C the goods requested in the purchase request, C does not send M her full signature approving the transaction. If C decides to cheat M by refusing to send her full signature in step $P4$, M can begin the dispute process in which the trusted third party forces the transaction to occur.

$$D1.\ M\quad \to TTP : Sig_M(S(m), E_{TTP}(Goods))$$
$$TTP \text{ converts } S(m) \text{ to } Sig_C(m)$$
$$D2.\ TTP \to M\quad : Sig_C(m)$$
$$D3.\ TTP \to C\quad : E_C(Goods)$$

In step $D1$, M sends to TTP the partial signature $S(m)$ and an encrypted copy of the goods $E_{TTP}(Goods)$. The trusted third party can now convert the partial signature, which can only be verified by M, into a normal signature which anyone can verify.

In step $D2$, TTP sends the normal signature to M. TTP also sends the goods to C in step $D3$, in case M is trying to falsely obtain C's converter string.

We assume here that since the goods in question are information ('soft') goods neither party will gain if the goods are in fact sent twice to C in a dispute resolution. In particular for the system to work it is essential that neither party should gain from falsely engaging in a dispute.

One problem that we have not addressed here is what should happen if the soft goods become old before they can be used by C, such as might happen with travel tickets or betting slips. This is an important issue in practical applications although somewhat out of scope of our concern here which is only to ensure that M and customer fairly exchange payment for goods. In practice use of validity windows and expiry times could solve this problem; for example, TTP would use the time of dispute in conjunction with the expiry time of the soft goods to resolve the issue. Note that previous fair exchange solutions have also left this issue unresolved. Another approach to this problem was taken by Asokan, Shoup and Waidner [1] in which users are allowed to send abort messages to TTP, which keeps a record of all aborted transactions.

Security and Efficiency The security of any protocol designed using this framework relies on the following properties.

Property 1. Only C can create the partially signed message $S(m)$.

If this does not hold a fraudulent customer can impersonate C in step $P1$ of the payment protocol by generating the partial signature and illegitimately purchase goods. Transactions would be forced despite the denial of C.

Property 2. Only M and TTP can confirm that the partial signature generated by C is valid or can convert the partial signature into a universally verifiable signature.

In most cases only M needs to verify that C has produced the partial signature. If other entities were able to verify C's partial signature at any time the fairness of the payment would not be present and M would have the advantage.

Property 3. If M accepts the validity of the transaction, then TTP can convert partial signature $S(m)$ into a normal signature $Sig_C(m)$.

This property of the protocol ensures that the transaction will be completed fairly and that C does not gain an advantage over M. If this property was not provided C could refuse to send her signature in step $P4$ and receive the goods without payment.

3   Solutions using Existing Signatures

The framework of section 2 is applicable for use with a number of existing convertible signature algorithms. Due to space limitations we give only a brief outline here to allow room for more detailed discussion of the new protocol in the next section. We highlight two distinct options for using the framework. The first is to use convertible signature schemes together with verifiable encryption while the second is to use designated converter signatures.

3.1   Convertible Signatures with Verifiable Encryption

In the first practical convertible undeniable signature scheme of Boyar, Chaum and Damgård [3], an undeniable signature consists of a triple (T, r, s) of elements in the integers modulo a large prime p^1. The element required to convert such a signature into a universally verifiable signature is the discrete log t of T. A partial signature can thus be formed by adding a copy of t encrypted with the TTP's public key to the undeniable signature. If the merchant is convinced (i) that (T, r, s) is correct and (ii) that the ciphertext really is t encrypted with TTP's public key, then he can be sure that TTP can convert the undeniable signature into a universally verifiable one.

The biggest problem with such a solution is that known protocols for verifiable encryption of discrete logs are not very efficient. For example, the protocol of Stadler [17] requires around 40 rounds in its interactive version. Alternative, more general, protocols due to Asokan, Shoup and Waidner [1] have the same requirement. More recent convertible undeniable protocols, such as those of Damgård and Pedersen [6] could also be used in a similar fashion. The problem

---

[1] It should be noted that although this scheme was successfully attacked by Michels, Petersen and Horster [13], the attack only affects the situation where signatures are converted all at once and not converted individually as in our application.

with all these is to find an efficient verifiable encryption scheme which can be matched to the conversion information. This problem is the reason why previous fair exchange protocols have not been efficient.

Some schemes, such as those of Michels and Stadler [14] do not seem appropriate to use in this way since conversion of individual signatures works by converting an interactive proof to a non-interactive one. This means that verifiable encryption of a non-interactive proof would be required to use this method.

3.2   Designated Converter Signatures

Designated converter signatures can be used in a very direct way in the framework. Confirmation by the customer during payment is essentially identical to signature confirmation. TTP takes the role of the designated converter and so can complete the dispute procedure when presented with the signature.

The first designated converter signature protocol proposed by Chaum [4] is based on RSA signatures, but these signatures are never used as plain RSA signatures in the protocol. Instead the correctness of signatures is linked to knowledge of a certain discrete log. The definition also relies on the existence of a function which destroys the multiplicative property of RSA signatures while at the same time being easy to invert.

Converted signatures in Chaum's scheme are not ordinary RSA signatures but non-interactive proofs of knowledge of a discrete log. In fact it is impossible for the signature owner in Chaum's scheme to convert signatures in the same way as the designated converter. We believe it is important in our application that signatures converted either by the owner (merchant) or the designated converter (TTP) are indistinguishable. To achieve this in Chaum's scheme, a signer who converts must recalculate a brand new designated converter signature, using a designated converter public key for which it knows the corresponding private key, and provide a non-interactive proof of correctness.

Further designated converter signatures were provided by Okamoto [16]. His constructions rely on different assumptions from those of Chaum but share the same properties that converted signatures are non-interactive proofs and also that conversion by owner and designated converter are different.

In conclusion we may say that use of existing designated converter signatures may be used within our framework. These solutions are efficient in that they require only two rounds (4 moves) to achieve high security. Their major drawback is that converted signatures are not in the form of ordinary RSA or ElGamal-type signatures which are likely to be required in electronic commerce schemes.

4   Offline Fair Payment using RSA Based Designated Converter Signatures

The cryptographic tools used in this new protocol are entirely based on RSA public key encryption and signatures. C splits her secret key in such a way that TTP is able to complete a partial signature of the customer. TTP can force the transaction to completion by ensuring that a complete signature can be generated.

The scheme is an adaptation of the recent RSA-based undeniable signature scheme of Gennaro, Krawczyk and Rabin (GKR) [10]. Although their scheme does allow for designated confirmer signatures this still leaves the same drawbacks identified in the previous section if used directly for fair exchange, in particular converted signatures would not be ordinary RSA signatures.

4.1   Registration

This is an efficient protocol requiring only one signature by each party. The registration stage of the protocol need only be conducted once (or at periodic intervals) and can be used to support any number of payments whether they are disputed or not. No state information need be stored by the third party once registration is complete.

C has an RSA key pair consisting of secret exponent d, public exponent e and modulus n. In order to use the results of GKR we assume that n is a *strong prime* so that $n = pq$ where $p = 2p' + 1$ and $q = 2q' + 1$ for primes p, p', q, q'. C's public key is certified by some certification authority which, in general, has no connection with TTP, but which can be used by TTP or any merchant to verify the correctness of the key. We denote this certificate $Cert_C$. The certificate must assert that the modulus is correctly formed. A method for achieving this is given in the GKR paper [10].

$$R1.\ C \rightarrow TTP : Cert_C$$

When TTP receives this certificate he generates a random number d_1 which is less than n. We require that $(d_1, \phi(n)) = 1$ but since $\phi(n) = 4p'q'$ this can be practically ensured by demanding that d_1 is odd. This is to be part of the secret key which is shared between C and TTP. TTP must be able to reconstruct d_1 from the identity of C. A practical way to achieve this without demanding TTP to store data for each customer is to make $d_1 = 2H(K, C) + 1$ where K is a secret known only to TTP and H is a suitable hash function.

TTP then sends this key encrypted to C. This can be achieved using the public key in the certificate $Cert_C$.

$$R2a.\ TTP \rightarrow C : E_C(d_1)$$

C now calculates the second part of the secret key d_2 such that $d_1 d_2 e = 1 \bmod \phi(n)$. C must also create a reference message ω and calculate a reference signature $S(\omega) = \omega^{d_2}$. It is shown by GKR that we may safely choose $\omega = 2$.

The reference message and signature will be used by M to verify that TTP knows d_1 and can force a transaction to completion. The reference message and signature are sent to TTP.

$$R2b.\ C \rightarrow TTP : \omega, S(\omega)$$

On receipt of the reference message and signature the trusted third party checks that the reference signature is valid by verifying that the following equation holds:

$$S(\omega)^{d_1 e} \bmod n = \omega$$

If the equation holds then C must have generated the reference signature correctly. TTP then creates a ticket which consists of C's public keys and the reference message and signature. TTP now signs this ticket and sends it to C.

$$R2c.\ TTP \rightarrow C : Sig_{TTP}(Cert_C, \omega, S(\omega))$$

C can now use this ticket to purchase goods from merchants. TTP's signature is a guarantee to the merchant who receives the ticket that the transaction can be completed by TTP if C refuses, or is unable, to complete the transaction. This is achieved by proving that a partial signature signed with d_2 is signed with the same exponent as was used to sign $S(\omega)$. This is the basis of the GKR scheme.

4.2 Payment

C has to generate a partial signature of the purchase information $S(m) = \bar{m}^{d_2}$. (Here and below, $\bar{m}$ denotes m after preprocessing by any desired hashing and padding processes which we will not detail here.) C indicates that she wishes to conduct a payment by sending the purchase information, a partially signed version of the purchase information and the ticket received from TTP to M.

$$P1.\ C \rightarrow M : m, S(m), Sig_{TTP}(Cert_C, \omega, S(\omega))$$

M and C now complete a confirmation protocol which convinces M that TTP can complete the transaction. This is exactly the signature confirmation protocol of the GKR scheme. An efficient 4-move zero knowledge protocol shown below is given in their paper [10].

Customer	Merchant
	Choose $i, j \in_R [1..n]$
	Set $Q = S(m)^{2^i} S(\omega)^j \bmod n$
P2a. $\xleftarrow{\quad Q \quad}$	
Set $A = Q^{d_1 e}$	
P2b. $\xrightarrow{\ \texttt{commit}(A)\ }$	
P2c. $\xleftarrow{\quad i,j \quad}$	
P2d. $\xrightarrow{\quad A \quad}$	
	Verify
	$A = \bar{m}^{2^i} \omega^j \bmod n$

The function `commit` is a commitment function to ensure the zero knowledge property. It may be implemented as a hash or as RSA encryption with an unknown secret exponent if it is designed to avoid further security assumptions.

If M is satisfied the exchange can take place in step $P3$ and $P4$ of the protocol.

$$P3.\ M \rightarrow C\ :\ E_C(Goods)$$
$$P4.\ C\ \rightarrow M : Sig_C(m)$$

4.3   Disputes

If C does not complete the protocol by aborting after receiving the goods, M contacts TTP to resolve the dispute. M sends to TTP the ticket and signature received from C and the goods.

$$D1.\ M \rightarrow TTP : Cert_C, m, S(m)$$
$$E_{TTP}(Goods)$$

TTP first recovers $d_1 = 2h(K,C) + 1$ then calculates $S(m)^{d_1}$. TTP checks whether $S(m)^{d_1} = Sig_C(m)$ since $Sig_C(m) = m^{d_1 d_2}$. TTP may also check that the description of the goods in m corresponds with $Goods$ sent to TTP. If so, TTP accepts the claim of M and proceeds to send $Sig_C(m)$ to M and the goods to C.

$$D2.\ TTP \rightarrow M : Sig_C(m)$$
$$D3.\ TTP \rightarrow C\ : E_C(Goods)$$

4.4   Security and Efficiency

Let us again examine the three security properties for this protocol. It is intuitively reasonable that property 1 holds if RSA signatures are secure. In fact it has been shown that breaking a *multisignature* with two private keys d_1 and d_2 is as hard as breaking RSA [9]. The basic idea is that if the multisignature can be broken given known signatures and partial signatures then RSA may be broken by simulating partial signatures with random d_1 values and complete signatures with the public e value. This proof easily can be adapted to include the trusted party for whom d_2 is also known.

Property 2 can also be proven from the security of RSA multisignatures. Similar to the above case, an algorithm that can convert a partial signature into a complete one can be used to forge ordinary RSA signatures.

Finally, to prove property 3 we can use the properties of the GKR signature. It is proven [10, Theorem 1] that the prover (customer) in the payment protocol cannot convince the verifier (merchant) to accept an incorrect signature except with negligible probability. Thus the merchant will only accept if $S(m) = \bar{m}^{d_2}$.

It must be pointed out that the proofs in GKR only give confidence that signatures are true RSA signatures up to multiple by an element of order 2. To be precise, it is proven that $S(m) = \alpha \bar{m}^{d_2}$ where α is an element of order at most 2. Thus a customer could give this slight variant instead of the true RSA signature. However, in this case, on conversion the third party will obtain $\alpha \bar{m}^{d_1 d_2}$ and can hence obtain α. But there are only two non-trivial elements of order 2 (since it is certified that n is the product of only two primes) and knowledge of one of these, say β, is sufficient to find a factor $(\beta - 1, n)$ of n. Hence, although C could attempt to cheat in this way, the result is that the third party can forge any signature of C.

To summarize, we can prove the following.

Lemma 1. *Properties 1, 2 and 3 all hold for the scheme. At the end of the transaction, C obtains the goods if and only if M gains a true RSA signature from the customer of the order.*

The use of RSA signatures in this protocol allows it to be more efficient than protocols using verifiable encryption. Asokan, Shoup and Waidner [1] present a general fair exchange protocol which can also be used with a range of signature and encryption schemes. This includes a scheme which also uses all RSA signatures and an encrypted signature verification step. But Asokan, Shoup and Waidner's protocol is less efficient in terms of messages sent by a factor of 10 when compared to the ones using designated converter signatures.

5   Acknowledgements

Thanks to Wenbo Mao for suggesting that we study the area of fair exchange protocols. Thanks also to the anonymous referees who found critical typographical errors in our manuscript.

References

1. N. Asokan, Victor Shoup, and Michael Waidner. Optimistic Fair Exchange of Digital Signatures. In *Advances in Cryptology - Proceedings of EUROCRYPT '98*, pages 591–606, Espoo Finland, May 1998. Springer-Verlag.
2. Feng Bao, Robert H. Deng, and Wenbo Mao. Efficient and Practical Fair Exchange Protocols with Off-line TTP. In *Proceedings of the 1998 IEEE Symposium on Security and Privacy*, 1998.
3. Joan Boyar, David Chaum, and Ivan Dåmgard. Convertible Undeniable Signatures. In *Advances in Cryptology - Proceedings of CRYPTO '90*, pages 189–205. Springer-Verlag, 1991.
4. David Chaum. Designated Confirmer Signatures. In *Advances in Cryptology - Proceedings of EUROCRYPT '94*, pages 86–91, Perugia Italy, May 1994. Springer-Verlag.
5. David Chaum and Hans van Antwerpen. Undeniable Signatures. In *Advances in Cryptology - Proceedings of CRYPTO '89*, pages 212–216, 1989.
6. Ivan Damgård and Torben Pedersen. New Convertible Undeniable Signature Schemes. In *Advances in Cryptology - Proceedings of EUROCRYPT '96*, pages 372–386, Berlin Heidelberg, 1996. Springer-Verlag.

7. T. ElGamal. A Public Key Cryptosystem and a Signature Scheme Based on Discrete Logarithms. In *IEEE Transactions on Information Theory*, volume IT-31(4), pages 637–647, 1985.
8. Matthew K. Franklin and Michael K. Reiter. Fair Exchange with a Semi-Trusted Third Party. In *Proceedings of the 4th ACM Conference on COmputer and Communications Security*, April 1997.
9. Ravi Ganesan and Yacov Yacobi. A Secure Joint Signature and Key Exchange System. Technical report, Bellcore Technical Memorandum, 1994.
10. Rosario Gennaro, Hugo Krawczyk, and Tal Rabin. RSA-Based Undeniable Signatures. In *Advances in Cryptology - Proceedings of CRYPTO '97*, pages 132–149. Springer-Verlag, 1997.
11. L. C. Guillou and J. J. Quisquater. A Paradoxical Identity-Based Signature Scheme Resulting from Zero Knowledge. In *Advances in Cryptology - CRYPTO '88*, pages 216–231. Springer-Verlag, 1988.
12. Wenbo Mao. Publicly Verifiable Partial Key Escrow. In *ACISP'97*, pages 240–248. Springer-Verlag, 1997.
13. Markus Michels, Holger Petersen, and Patrick Horster. Breaking and Repairing a Convertible Undeniable Signature Scheme. In *Proceedings of the 3rd ACM Conference on Computers and Communications Security*, pages 148–152, New Delhi, 1996. ACM Press.
14. Markus Michels and Markus Stadler. Efficient Convertible Undeniable Signature Schemes. In *SAC '97*, 1997.
15. T. Okamoto and K. Ohta. How to Simultaneously Exchange Secrets by General Assumption. In *Proceedings of the 2nd ACM Conference on Computer and Communications Security*, pages 184–192, 1994.
16. Tatsuaki Okamoto. Designated Confirmer Signatures and Public Key Encryption are Equivalent. In *Advances in Cryptology - Proceedings of CRYPTO '94*, pages 61–74, Santa Barbara California, August 1994. Springer-Verlag.
17. Markus Stadler. Publicly Verifiable Secret Sharing. In *Advances in Cryptology - Proceedings of EUROCRYPT '96*, pages 190–199, Berlin Heidelberg, 1996. Springer-Verlag.
18. Jianying Zhou and Dieter Gollman. A Fair Non-repudiation Protocol. In *Proceedings of the 1996 IEEE Symposium on Security and Privacy*, pages 55–61, Oakland, CA, 1996. IEEE Computer Press.

A   Breaking the Bao, Deng and Mao Fair Exchange Protocol

The second protocol of Bao, Deng and Mao [2] uses verifiable ElGamal encryption [7] of a Guillou-Quisquater (GQ) signature [11] to provide fair exchange. The system wide public parameters are n, g, q, v where $n = PQ$ is the modulus used for GQ signatures and $P = 2p'q + 1$ and $Q = 2pq + 1$ where P, Q, p, p', q are all primes, g is an element of order q and v is the public exponent used for GQ signatures.

A GQ signature of a message M is a pair (d, D) for which $d = h(M, D^v J^d \bmod n)$ where h is a published one way hash function. In the protocol only D is encrypted using the public key PK_{TTP} of TTP. ElGamal encryption is used to form the ciphertext pair $(W, V_{TTP}) = (g^w \bmod n, D(PK_{TTP})^w \bmod n)$ for a randomly chosen w. In order to bind D to the ciphertext, the value $V = D^v \bmod n$ is also calculated and used as part of the 'challenge' c generated using a hash function $\mathcal{H}$.

$$c = \mathcal{H}(g, W, (PK_{TTP})^v, V_{TTP}^v/V, a, A)$$

where $a = g^u \bmod n$ and $A = PK_{TTP}^{vu} \bmod n$ for a random value u. Finally the 'response' $r = u - cw \bmod q$ is calculated. The following parameters are then sent from the prover to the verifier.

$$M, (W, V_{TTP}), r, c, V, d$$

The verifier can use these parameters to ensure that the third party is able to decrypt the ElGamal ciphertext (W, V_{TTP}) to obtain the correct D value so that (d, D) is the GQ signature of M.

The attack consists of showing that the verifier is able to calculate $PK_{TTP}^w \bmod n$ and hence decrypt the ElGamal ciphertext to obtain D without the help of TTP. In other words the verifier (or any observer) can convert that signature without the help of TTP. The main observation is that since PK_{TTP} is in the orbit of g, to remove exponents of PK_{TTP} it is necessary only to invert them modulo q (which is known) and not modulo n (which is not known). Thus the verifier first calculates $A = (PK_{TTP}^v)/(V_{TTP}^v/V)^c \bmod n = PK_{TTP}^{uv} \bmod n$ (this is part of the intended verification process). Then the verifier calculates $A^{v^{-1} \bmod q} \bmod n = PK_{TTP}^u \bmod n$ and also $PK_{TTP}^r \bmod n$. This allows calculation of $PK_{TTP}^{cw} \bmod n$ since the following holds.

$$PK_{TTP}^r = PK_{TTP}^u / PK_{TTP}^{cw} \bmod n$$

Finally the verifier obtains $(PK_{TTP}^{cw})^{c^{-1} \bmod q} \bmod n = PK_{TTP}^w \bmod n$ as required.

Efficient Fair Exchange
with Verifiable Confirmation of Signatures

Liqun Chen

Hewlett-Packard Laboratories,
Filton Road, Stoke Gifford, Bristol BS34 8QZ, UK
liqun@hplb.hpl.hp.com

Abstract. We propose a new efficient protocol, which allows a pair of potentially mistrusting parties to exchange digital signatures over the Internet in a fair way, such that after the protocol is running, either each party obtains the other's signature, or neither of them does. The protocol relies on an off-line Trusted Third Party (TTP), which does not take part in the exchange unless any of the parties behaves improperly or other faults occur. Efficiency of the protocol is achieved by using a cryptographic primitive, called *confirmable signatures* (or *designated confirmer signatures* in its original proposal [9]). We recommend using a new efficient confirmable signature scheme in the proposed fair exchange protocol. This scheme combines the family of discrete logarithm (DL) based signature algorithms and a zero-knowledge (ZK) proof on the equality of two DLs. The protocol has a practical level of performance: only a moderate number of communication rounds and ordinary signatures are required. The security of the protocol can be established from that of the underlying signature algorithms and that of the ZK proof used.

1 Introduction

Since electronic commerce is playing a more and more important role in today's world, a related security issue - how to exchange electronic data, particularly digital signatures, between two parties over the Internet in a fair and efficient manner - is becoming of more and more importance. Imagine the following scenario that may happen in, for instance, signing electronic contracts and purchase of electronic goods. Two parties Alice and Bob need to exchange their digital signatures on agreed messages; but neither wants to send her/his signature before obtaining the other's because they do not trust each other. The basic requirement for Alice and Bob on the fairness of exchanging signatures is that either each of them gets the other's signature, or neither of them does.

1.1 The Related Previous Work

How to sort out the fair exchange problem has attracted much research attention. The original idea for the realisation of fair exchange is that two parties "simultaneously" disclose messages by many steps. Two mathematical models for realising simultaneous disclosure of messages have been proposed as follows.

K. Ohta and D. Pei (Eds.): ASIACRYPT'98, LNCS 1514, pp. 286–299, 1998.

The first is a computational model (e.g., [10,12,15,19,24,30]). In this approach, Alice and Bob exchange digital signatures (or agreed secret messages) piece by piece (e.g. bit by bit), where the correctness of each bit is verifiable. If both of them follow the approach correctly, they will receive the signatures at the end of a successful protocol run. If either of them aborts in the middle of the protocol running, this early stopper will at most obtain one more bit than the other party. This extra bit does not result in a significant advantage in finding the remaining secret bits unexchanged. Obviously, a virtue of this approach is that Alice and Bob can sort out the fair exchange problem without any intervention of a third party. The cost of this virtue is in two respects. (1) This approach is based on the assumption that Alice and Bob have equal computing power. However, this assumption may not be realistic and desirable for them. (2) This approach has a poor performance: many rounds (usually hundreds) of interactions between them are required.

The second type of model is a probabilistic model (e.g., [5,26]). For exchanging signatures on an agreed message, Alice and Bob sign and exchange many signatures on different events. Each event has a small probability binding with the agreed message. In order to increase the probabilities of their commitment to the message, they have to exchange a great number of signatures. This approach removes the requirement on equal computing powers of Alice and Bob. But it needs intervention of a third party in a weak form. In [26], an active third party defines the events by broadcasting a random number each day. In [5], a passive third party is invoked, only when a dispute between Alice and Bob occurs, to arbitrate the dispute according to a simple computation on events. Similarly to the first model, the major drawback of this approach is a poor performance.

In order to reduce the communicational and computational cost of simultaneous disclosure of messages, recent fair exchange research has proposed a variety of interventions of a Trusted Third Party (TTP), which can be on-line or off-line.

In an on-line TTP based approach (e.g. [11,13,17,31]), the TTP, who acts as a mediator between Alice and Bob, checks the validity of every transaction and then forwards correct data to both parties. The major disadvantage in this approach is that the TTP is always involved in the exchange even if both Alice and Bob are honest and no fault occurs, so that it results in another big cost of maintaining availability of the on-line TTP.

A number of off-line TTP based approaches have been proposed to reduce the requirement of TTP availability. In these approaches, the TTP does not take part in normal exchanges, it gets involved only where dishonest parties do not perform properly or other faults occur.

In [1,32], the TTP provide either of the following two services to guarantee the fairness. (i) The TTP is able to undo a transfer of an item, and/or produce a replacement for it. (ii) When a misbehaving party gets the other party's data and refuses to give his/her own one, the TTP will issue affidavits attesting to what happened. Obviously, neither of these TTP services meets the needs of many applications.

Bao, Deng and Mao in [4], which is based on the solution of [20], and Asokan, Shoup and Waidner in [2] separately proposed a novel off-line TTP based approach that uses verifiable public-key encryption to ensure fairness of signature exchanges. In [4], Alice first encrypts her ordinary signature under the TTP's public key and demonstrates the correctness of the encryption to Bob via an interactive ZK proof. Next Bob sends his ordinary signature to Alice, and Alice returns her ordinary one back. If Bob does not receive Alice's signature correctly, he will send Alice's encrypted signature and his own ordinary signature to the TTP. The TTP will do the corresponding decryption and check the validity of both signatures. If all the checks pass, the TTP will transfer these two signatures between Alice and Bob.

The approach of [2] is based on a primitive, called *a homomorphic inverse of a signature* (e.g., a DL for DSS [16] and Schnorr [28] signatures, and an RSA inverse for RSA [27] signatures). Alice and Bob first reduce a "promise" of a signature to the "promise" of a particular homomorphic inverse. Then, they encrypt their promised inverses under the TTP's public key and demonstrate the correctness of the encryption in a non-transferable way to each other. Once demonstrated of encryption, they disclose their promised inverses. If anyone of them (say Bob) does not receive a correct inverse of the other (Alice), he will send the encrypted homomorphic inverse of Alice and a promised inverse of his own to the TTP. The TTP will decrypt and check the validity of both signatures. After all the checks pass, the TTP will send Alice's inverse to Bob and then record Bob's one for Alice's possible requirement.

Although the idea of using verifiable encryption in an off-line TTP based fair exchange is clever, it is difficult to implement this idea in an efficient and generic manner because so far there has not been a generic and efficient construction of publicly verifiable encryption. A well-known solution of publicly verifiable encryption, [29], is based on inefficient "cut and choose" method. Bao recently in [3] proposed a more efficient scheme using Okamoto-Uchiyame trapdoor one-way function [25], which is not a generic construction. How to design an efficient and generic construction of publicly verifiable cryptographic systems is still an interesting and hard open problem.

In order to improve efficiency, [4] recommended the use of a modified Guillou-Quisquater signature algorithm [18] with the ElGamal encryption algorithm [14]. This protocol was recently attacked by Boyd and Foo [6] as the verifier is able to obtain the signer's signature without the help of TTP. For a more closed look at the properties of fair exchange, there is another problem in this protocol that the encrypted signature can not be simulated. Again to improve efficiency, [2] proposed a solution called off-line coupons where each party needs to retrieve the TTP's coupons before starting a fair exchange protocol. Clearly, it will increase the cost for maintaining availability and security of the off-line TTP service.

We finally state, in the author's view, that the previous work has not produced an efficient and widely acceptable approach for fair exchange of digital signatures over the Internet.

1.2   The New Contribution

In this paper, we propose a new approach for fair exchange of digital signatures which uses verifiable confirmation of signatures in place of verifiable encryption of signatures in [2,4]. Both verifiable encryption and verifiable confirmation of signatures can be used to provide off-line TTP based fair exchange. However, the existing constructions of verifiable confirmation are much more efficient and generic than that of verifiable encryption.

The contribution of the paper is organised as two parts. In the first part (the next section) we introduce a new off-line TTP modelled fair exchange protocol which is based on a cryptographic primitive, called *confirmable signatures* (or *designated confirmer signatures* in the original proposal [9]), to guarantee the fairness. In this protocol, the TTP acts as a designated confirmer. There is no restriction for the protocol as to which confirmable signature scheme will be used. In the second part (Section 3), we present a new realisation of confirmable signatures which is constructed by using the family of DL problem based digital signature algorithms. It is one of suitable confirmable signature schemes for the proposed fair exchange protocol.

2   Protocol for Fair Exchange

In this section, we present a fair exchange protocol, which allows a pair of parties to exchange digital signatures with an off-line TTP's intervention in a fair manner.

The protocol involves three players: two exchange parties, Alice (A) and Bob (B), plus one off-line TTP, Colin (C), who acts as a designated confirmer. Each of these players has a secret and public key pair denoted by S_X and P_X respectively (where $X \in \{A, B, C\}$), which is used for digital signature and verification. Suppose that there exists a secure binding between each player's identity and the corresponding public key. Such a binding may be in the form of a public key certificate that was issued by a certification authority. Suppose further that the communication channels between these three players are protected to guarantee integrity and confidentiality (if required).

2.1   Model, Notation and Explanation

We denote $Sig_X(m)$ ($X \in \{A, B, C\}$) as an ordinary signature on a message m signed using S_X, which can be universally verified using P_X. We denote $CSig_Y(m)$ ($Y \in \{A, B\}$) as a confirmable signature on m signed using S_Y. We denote $Sta\_of\_CSig_Y(m)$ as a validity statement of $CSig_Y(m)$, for instance, in the recommended confirmable signature scheme, as described in Section 3, $Sta\_of\_CSig_Y(m)$ is the equality of two DLs. It can be proved by using either S_Y or S_C.

A confirmable signature bound with its statement is universally verifiable and is as valid as an ordinary signature. Thus,

$$\{CSig_Y(m), Sta\_of\_CSig_Y(m)\} \equiv Sig_Y(m).$$

Without the statement, the binding between Y and $CSig_Y(m)$ cannot be claimed.

In order to prove $Sta\_of\_CSig_Y(m)$ from one party (as signer named Y) to the other (as verifier) in a non-transferable way, we make use of an interactive ZK proof between the two parties, named $Conf_Y$, which, on common inputs of m, P_Y, P_C, a string $Claim$ and on secret input of S_Y, outputs "true" or "false". That is,

$$Conf_Y(Sta\_of\_CSig_Y(m)|m, P_Y, P_C, Claim) = \text{true } or \text{ false .}$$

If output is "true", it is proved that $Claim$ is $CSig_Y(m)$; if output is "false", it is proved that $Claim$ is not $CSig_Y(m)$.

In a confirmable signature scheme, the confirmer can make either a non-transferable confirmation or a transferable confirmation of $Sta\_of\_CSig_Y(m)$. For the purpose of the proposed fair exchange protocol, we only need the transferable one. In the protocol of the next subsection, an ordinary signature on $Sta\_of\_CSig_Y(m)$ signed using S_C will be used for the transferable confirmation of $CSig_Y(m)$. A confirmable signature suitable for the proposed fair exchange protocol has the following three properties.

– *Invisibility.* $CSig_Y(m)$ can be simulated by using a polynomial-time algorithm.
– *Unforgeability.* No polynomial-time algorithm can forge such a signature that can be confirmed to have a validity statement.
– *Undeniability.* Signer of $CSig_Y(m)$ cannot deny having issued this confirmable signature if $CSig_Y(m)$ is bound to $Sta\_of\_CSig_Y(m)$.

2.2   The Protocol

Suppose that Alice and Bob have agreed on a message (such as a contract) M. The protocol for fair exchange of signatures on M between Alice and Bob proceeds as follows. Without loss of generality, we assume that Alice is the protocol initiator.

Protocol FE

1. Alice computes her confirmable signature on M, $CSig_A(M)$, and sends it to Bob.
2. Alice and Bob run an interactive ZK protocol $Conf_A$, e.g. as described in Section 3.2, proving $Sta\_of\_CSig_A(M)$. If

$$Conf_A(Sta\_of\_CSig_A(M)|M, P_A, P_C, CSig_A(M)) = \text{false},$$

the proof is rejected and the protocol stops. If

$$Conf_A(Sta\_of\_CSig_A(M)|M, P_A, P_C, CSig_A(M)) = \text{true},$$

Bob computes and sends Alice his ordinary signature $Sig_B(M)$.

3. After receiving $Sig_B(M)$, Alice verifies whether it is a valid signature. If not, Alice halts; if it is valid, Alice accepts the signature, and then computes and sends Bob her ordinary signature $Sig_A(M)$.
4. Upon the receipt of $Sig_A(M)$, Bob verifies whether it is a valid one. If it is, Bob accepts the signature, and the protocol completes.
5. If Bob receives an invalid signature or nothing during a designed time period, Bob sends both $Sig_B(M)$ and $CSig_A(M)$ to Colin. Colin first checks whether $Sig_B(M)$ is Bob's valid signature on M, and secondly checks, by using his secret key S_C, whether $CSig_A(M)$ is Alice's valid confirmable signature on M. If either of these two checks does not pass, Colin does not provide a confirmation service. If both of the checks pass, Colin computes and sends Bob his signature on $Sta\_of\_CSig_A(M)$, and in the meantime, he forwards $Sig_B(M)$ to Alice.

2.3   Analysis of Protocol FE

We now consider the behavior of Alice and Bob. If both of them follow the protocol properly, it is easy to see that Alice and Bob will obtain each other's signatures without any involvement of Colin.

If Bob performs improperly, Bob may send Alice either an incorrect $Sig_B(M)$ or nothing in Item 2. In both of the cases, Alice does not send $Sig_A(M)$ to Bob in Item 3, and Bob has to ask Colin for confirmation of $CSig_A(M)$ if he wants Alice's signature. Based on Item 5, Colin makes such a confirmation for Bob only if Bob gives a valid $Sig_B(M)$, which will be forwarded to Alice.

If Alice does not follow the protocol properly, either of the following two situations may happen. (i) Alice sends Bob a non-confirmable signature in Item 1. In this case, she cannot demonstrate

$$Conf_A(Sta\_of\_CSig_A(M)|M, P_A, P_C, CSig_A(M)) = \text{true}$$

in Item 2 to Bob. (ii) She sends an invalid $Sig_A(M)$ or nothing to Bob in Item 3. In this case, Bob can obtain the confirmation of $CSig_A(M)$ from Colin.

As mentioned earlier, the fairness of exchanging signatures between two parties means that either each party gets the other's signature, or neither party does. In terms of the definition of fairness, we can conclude that neither Alice nor Bob can gain any benefit by performing improperly, so that Protocol FE can achieve fair exchange between Alice and Bob.

However, in Protocol FE, after accepting $CSig_A(M)$, Bob has the advantage of choosing stop or continuation. If it makes Alice feel unfairly treated, the protocol can be slightly changed. Following Alice having proved her confirmable signature to Bob, Bob proves his confirmable signature to Alice. Then Alice releases her ordinary signature and Bob releases his ordinary one. Both Alice and Bob can ask Colin for a confirmation service. As in Protocol FE, Colin always makes confirmation of a signature for one party and forwards an ordinary signature to another party. Before Colin provides the confirmation, Alice is able to ask Colin for invoking *abort* (i.e. by an *abort* sub-protocol as in [2]). Here Colin needs to maintain an extra record about "abort" and "confirmed".

A normal procedure of the protocol, where there is non-intervention of Colin, includes only five communication rounds: three rounds for non-transferable confirmation of $CSig_A(M)$ (Item 1 and 2 by using the recommended scheme of Section 3); and two rounds for exchange of $Sig_B(M)$ and $Sig_A(M)$ (Item 2 and 3).

Note that both parties' identifiers must be indicated in $CSig_A(M)$, which could be a part of the message M. Otherwise, Colin can know only that Alice is one of the exchange parties, and he cannot know who is another. In this case, an intruder (who may be Bob's colluder), given $CSig_A(M)$, can obtain the confirmation of $CSig_A(M)$ from Colin by providing his own signature on M. After the protocol is running, Alice will get an unexpected intruder's signature in place of Bob's one, which is not what she wants.

Protocol FE can be modified to meet the following different requirements of message styles.

Assume that Alice and Bob want to keep M confidential to Colin. They can use a one-way hash function, $h()$, and replace M with $h(M)$ in Protocol FE.

Assume that Alice and Bob want to sign two messages M_A and M_B, where both Alice's signature on M_A and Bob's signature on M_B can be universally verified. In this case Colin should be able to check if he is making a confirmation service for a real agreement between Alice and Bob. For this purpose, each file signed by one party must include an indicator of the file signed by the other. For example, as used in [4], Alice signs $M_A||h(M_B)$ and Bob signs $M_B||h(M_A)$, where $||$ denotes concatenation. Otherwise (e.g., Alice and Bob directly sign M_A and M_B respectively for such M_A and M_B that have no explicit relationship explanation), Bob may send Colin $CSig_A(M_A)$ with $Sig_B(M'_B)$ for the confirmation service. Finally Bob get a real confirmed signature of Alice, who will get only a signature on a meaningless message M'_B. Furthermore, if it is required that both M_A and M_B are confidential to Colin, Alice and Bob can have extra secret and public key pairs for encryption and decryption. In this case, M_A will be replaced by encrypted M_A under Bob's encryption public key and M_B will be replaced by encrypted M_B under Alice's encryption public key as well.

If it is required with certain applications, the protocol can be modified by including multiple confirmers instead of a single one.

3   A Confirmable Signature Scheme

The concept and the first realisation of confirmable signatures (or called designated confirmer signatures in [9]) was proposed by Chaum, [9], where he presented a realisation on the RSA signature algorithm. Following Chaum's idea, Okamoto proposed a more generic confirmable signature scheme [23]. However, that scheme was later attacked by Michels and Stadler [22] as the confirmer can forge signatures.

Michels and Stadler also proposed their own confirmable signature scheme based on a primitive called *the confirmer commitment scheme*. The scheme places a message in the position of a committal (i.e., commit to a message), and the confirmer is able to prove whether or not a given commitment contains a certain message. Using this scheme, two classes of ordinary digital signatures can be transformed into related confirmable signatures. The first class consists of the signatures that are based on proofs of some particular style of knowledge. Both the Schnorr signature and the Fiat-Shamir signature can be used in this way. The second class consists of the signatures that have the property of existential forgeability. For this kind of signature, an attacker can compute a universally verifiable message-signature pair without further constraint on the message. The RSA signature and the ElGamal signature are two good examples of this class.

This section presents a new confirmable signature scheme. In this scheme, a *confirmable signature* contains a *validity statement*, which is the equality of two DLs, and which can efficiently be proved either via running a ZK protocol, or via verifying an ordinary digital signature signed by the confirmer. Any DL based signature algorithm and any ZK protocol for proving the equality or the inequality of two DLs can be used in this scheme. The security of the scheme can be established from that of the underlying signature schemes and that of the ZK protocol used. In terms of efficiency the scheme is similar to the most efficient one of [22], which is based on the Schnorr signature scheme.

3.1 System Setup

Let p be a prime, and q be another prime which divides $p - 1$. Let $G =< g >$ be a subgroup of $\mathbb{Z}_p^*$ of order q, in which computing DLs is infeasible. Let $h()$ denote a one-way hash function, and $a \in_R N$ denote to choose element a from the set N at random according to the uniform distribution.

A confirmable signature scheme involves three players: a Signer (say Alice), a Verifier (say Bob) and a designated Confirmer (say Colin). In the proposed fair exchange protocol described in Section 2.2, both the exchange parties, Alice and Bob, can be such a signer and verifier.

Alice, as a signer, has a secret and public key pair, denoted by (S_A, P_A); and Colin has another secret and public key pair, denoted by (S_C, P_C). These two key pairs can be generated as follows. Alice chooses $x \in_R \mathbb{Z}_q^*$ as S_A, and computes $P_A = (g, y)$ where $y = g^x \bmod p$. Colin chooses $w \in_R \mathbb{Z}_q^*$ as S_C, and computes $P_C = (g, z)$ where $z = g^w \bmod p$.

A confirmable signature scheme consists of the following two procedures: *signature issuance* and *signature confirmation*.

3.2 Signature Issuance

A signature issuance procedure runs between Alice and Bob. It consists of (i) Alice generating $CSig_A(m)$; and (ii) Alice demonstrating to Bob that $CSig_A(m)$ is a confirmable signature on a message m.

To generate $CSig_A(m)$, Alice chooses $u \in_R \mathbb{Z}_q^*$, computes $\tilde{y} = y^u \bmod p$ and $\hat{y} = z^{xu} \bmod p$. Next she generates a signature on a message m signed using u and ux as private keys. The basic idea of this signature is to make a transferable

294   L. Chen

proof that: (i)someone knows how to express $\tilde{y}$ as a power of y and how to express $\hat{y}$ as a power of z; and (ii)this person has signed m using the DLs of both $\tilde{y}$ to the base y and $\hat{y}$ to the base z as private keys. Any existing secure signature algorithm, based on the DL problem, can be used to make this signature. The following is an example using the Schnorr signature [28],

$$k_1, k_2 \in_R \mathbb{Z}_q^*, \; r_1 = y^{k_1} \bmod p, \; r_2 = z^{k_2} \bmod p,$$
$$c = h(m, r_1, r_2), \; s_1 = k_1 - uc \bmod q, \; s_2 = k_2 - uxc \bmod q,$$
$$CSig_A(m) = (c, s_1, s_2).$$

The signature verification is to check if

$$c = h(m, y^{s_1}\tilde{y}^c, z^{s_2}\hat{y}^c)$$

holds. This signature is universally verifiable. However, because anyone can construct (c, s_1, s_2) by randomly choosing $\tilde{y}$ as a power of y and $\hat{y}$ as a power of z, without further proof, no one can see who is the issuer of the signature.

Proposition 1. *The above $CSig_A(m)$ is a confirmable signature with a validity statement $Sta\_of\_CSig_A(m)$, $\log_{\tilde{y}}\hat{y} = \log_g z \pmod q$.*

Proof. On the assumption that a random oracle model holds, the proposition is proved if the following three assertions can be proved: (i) given that $\log_{\tilde{y}}\hat{y} = \log_g z$, it can be proved that the issuer of $CSig_A(m)$ must be Alice; (ii) without the verification of $\log_{\tilde{y}}\hat{y} = \log_g z$, it cannot be claimed that the issuer of $CSig_A(m)$ is Alice; (iii) $\log_{\tilde{y}}\hat{y} = \log_g z$ can independently be verified by Alice and Colin.

By verifying the correctness of the digital signature, it can be proved that the issuer of (c, s_1, s_2) must know both $\log_y \tilde{y}$, denoted by u, and $\log_z \hat{y}$, denoted by v. The value $\log_g \hat{y}$, denoted by t, must be the product of three values: $\log_g y = x$, $\log_y \tilde{y} = u$, and $\log_{\tilde{y}}\hat{y}$. If $\log_{\tilde{y}}\hat{y}$ is $\log_g z = w$, then $t = xuw \bmod q$ and $v = xu \bmod q$. The person who knows v and u must know x. Since x is known only to Alice, the issuer of $CSig_A(m)$ must be Alice. The first assertion holds.

Without verifying $\log_{\tilde{y}}\hat{y} = \log_g z$, no one can claim that $CSig_A(m)$ was signed by Alice, since anyone knowing y and z is able to generate the signature (see the proof of Proposition 3 of Section 3.4). The second assertion holds.

Colin is able to prove $\log_{\tilde{y}}\hat{y} = \log_g z$, because $\log_g z$ is S_C. Alice can prove the knowledge of u and x, and hence she can demonstrate this statement (see the next subsection). The third assertion holds.

According to the definition of a confirmable signature and the above three assertions, it has been proved that $Sta\_of\_CSig_A(m)$ is $\log_{\tilde{y}}\hat{y} = \log_g z$ so that $CSig_A(m)$ is a confirmable signature. The proposition holds.   □

The following interactive protocol, denoted by $Conf_A$, is used for Alice to demonstrate $Sta\_of\_CSig_A(m)$ to Bob.

Protocol $Conf_A$
Suppose that before the protocol starts, both Alice and Bob have $\tilde{y}$, $\hat{y}$ and $CSig_A(m)$.

1. Alice computes $\ddot{y} = z^x \bmod p$ and sends it to Bob.
2. Alice and Bob run an interactive ZK protocol proving

$$\log_g y = \log_z \ddot{y} \ (\bmod q).$$

3. Alice and Bob run an interactive ZK protocol proving

$$\log_y \tilde{y} = \log_{\ddot{y}} \hat{y} \ (\bmod q).$$

4. If both ZK proofs are accepted, Bob is convinced that $CSig_A(m)$ is a confirmable signature. Otherwise, the proof is rejected.

Several efficient ZK protocols for proving equality in DLs, e.g. [7,8], can be used for the proof.

Proposition 2. *Upon acceptance of $Conf_A$, Alice proves $\log_g z = \log_{\tilde{y}} \hat{y}$ (mod q) to Bob.*

Proof. Suppose $\tilde{y} = y^u \bmod p = g^{xu} \bmod p$ where $u \in \mathbb{Z}_q^*$. From the first ZK proof, Bob is convinced of $\ddot{y} = g^{xw} \bmod p$. From the second ZK proof, Bob is convinced of $\hat{y} = \ddot{y}^u = g^{xwu}(\bmod p)$. So the proposition follows, i.e. $\hat{y} = \tilde{y}^w \bmod p$. $\qquad \square$

3.3   Signature Confirmation

In order to let Bob know whether or not a given statement is $Sta\_of\_CSig_A(m)$. Colin needs to demonstrate to him either

$$\log_g z = \log_{\tilde{y}} \hat{y} \ (\bmod q), \quad \text{or} \ \ \log_g z \neq \log_{\tilde{y}} \hat{y} \ (\bmod q).$$

A number of efficient protocols for a ZK proof on the equality or inequality of two DLs, e.g. [21], can be used for the proof. Colin can either run an interactive ZK protocol with Bob to make a non-transferable confirmation, or sign $Sta\_of\_CSig_A(m)$ for Bob to make a transferable confirmation. For the purpose of our fair exchange protocol, we need a transferable confirmation. A number of existing efficient interactive protocols for ZK proof of the equality or inequality of two DLs can be turned into non-interactive protocols, which can be used. The following is one example based on the Schnorr signature [28]. Colin signs $(g, z, \tilde{y}, \hat{y})$ using $S_C = w$ by two ordinary signatures.

The first signature makes a transferable proof in that there exist two values r_1 and r_2 satisfying $r_1 = g^k \bmod p$ and $r_2 = \tilde{y}^k \bmod p$ where $k \in \mathbb{Z}_q^*$. The signature is (c, s') generated as follows.

$$k' \in_R \mathbb{Z}_q^*, \ r_1' = g^{k'} \bmod p, \ r_2' = \tilde{y}^{k'} \bmod p,$$
$$c = h(r_1', r_2'), \ s' = k' - kc \bmod q.$$

The signature verification is to check if

$$c = h(g^{s'} r_1^c, \tilde{y}^{s'} r_2^c)$$

holds. If it does not hold, Bob can claim that Colin did not send a proper signature to him.

Based on acceptance of the first signature, the second signature provides a transferable proof on either $\log_g z = \log_{\tilde{y}} \hat{y}$ or $\log_g z \neq \log_{\tilde{y}} \hat{y}$. The resulting signature is (r_1, r_2, s), where

$$s = k + wh(r_1, r_2) \bmod q.$$

The signature verification is to check if

$$g^s = r_1 z^{h(r_1, r_2)} (\bmod p), \quad \tilde{y}^s = r_2 \hat{y}^{h(r_1, r_2)} (\bmod p)$$

holds. If the first equality does not hold, Bob can claim that Colin did not send a proper signature to him. Otherwise, Bob accepts the conviction of the signature. In this case, if the second equality holds, Bob accepts $\log_g z = \log_{\tilde{y}} \hat{y}$, and then further accepts that the related signature, $CSig_A(m)$, is a confirmable one. If the second equality does not hold, Bob accepts $\log_g z \neq \log_{\tilde{y}} \hat{y}$, and further accepts that the related signature is not a confirmable one.

Note that before generating the above two signatures, Colin may check if $\hat{y} = \tilde{y}^w \bmod p$ holds firstly. If it does hold he can simply make a transferable proof on $\log_g z = \log_{\tilde{y}} \hat{y}$ by using the second signature only. With this signature, anybody is able to verify the correctness of $Sta\_of\_CSig_A(m)$. Hence $CSig_A(m)$ is universally verifiable.

3.4   Security of the Scheme

The confirmable signature scheme, specified above, allows the players of the scheme free to choose any DL based signature algorithms and to choose any efficient protocols for ZK proof on the equality or the inequality of two DLs. As long as the security property of those algorithms and protocols have been proved, i.e., (i) the verification of a digital signature is complete and sound; (ii) the error probability of an acceptance for a ZK protocol is negligible; (iii) they guarantee not to reveal useful information about x and w, the following three security properties hold under this scheme.

Proposition 3. *A confirmable signature, $CSig_A(m)$, can be simulated.*

Proof. A simulator, who knows g, y, z, q, p and m, is always able to generate a triple (c', s'_1, s'_2) in the following way. He/she simply chooses $u' \in_R \mathbb{Z}_q^*$ and $v' \in_R \mathbb{Z}_q^*$, computes $\tilde{y}' = y^{u'} \bmod p$ and $\hat{y}' = z^{v'} \bmod p$, and then signs m using u' and v' as private keys, by the same approach described in Section 3.2, to obtain (c', s'_1, s'_2). For two fixed public keys y and z, and any message m, let $\mathcal{A}$ be any polynomial-time algorithm which, on input of a signature pair (m, σ), outputs whether or not (m, σ) is valid with respect to y and z. The value

$$Pr\{\mathcal{A}(m, (c', s'_1, s'_2)) = valid\} - Pr\{\mathcal{A}(m, (c, s_1, s_2)) = valid\}$$

is negligible.

Note that there is no binding between z^x and (c, s_1, s_2), hence z^x does not reveal any useful information for distinguishing a real $CSig_A(m)$ and a simulated one. Furthermore, the set $(g, g^x, z^x, \tilde{y}, \hat{y})$ is indistinguishable from the set $(g, g^x, z^x, \tilde{y}', \hat{y}')$, otherwise the Decision Diffie-Hellman assumption is not valid in the random oracle model. So the proposition holds. □

Proposition 4. *A confirmable signature, $CSig_A(m)$, is unforgeable, i.e., under the assumption on that it is computationally infeasible to compute DL in G, there is no polynomial-time algorithm which, on input of y, z, w, and any value $m' \in \{0,1\}^*$, outputs $CSig_A(m')$, with respect to $\tilde{y}'$ and $\hat{y}'$ satisfying $\log_g z = \log_{\tilde{y}'} \hat{y}' (\bmod q)$.*

Proof. It has been proved in Proposition 1 that, if $\log_g z = \log_{\tilde{y}} \hat{y}'$, the value $\log_z \hat{y}'$ must be equal to $\log_g y * \log_y \tilde{y}'$. If there is a polynomial-time algorithm $\mathcal{A}$ which, on input of y, z, w and m', outputs $CSig_A(m')$ with respect to $\tilde{y}'$ and $\hat{y}'$ satisfying $\log_g z = \log_{\tilde{y}'} \hat{y}'$, $\mathcal{A}$ must be able to obtain $\log_g y$. This contradicts the assumption. Hence the proposition holds. □

This proposition proves that no one, including the confirmer Colin, is able to forge such a confirmable signature, $CSig_A(m)$.

Proposition 5. *A confirmable signature, $CSig_A(m)$, is undeniable.*

Proof. It is impossible for Alice to find any $\tilde{y}$, $\ddot{y}$ and $\hat{y} \in \mathbb{Z}_p^*$ satisfying $\log_g y = \log_z \ddot{y}$, $\log_y \tilde{y} = \log_{\ddot{y}} \hat{y}$ and $\log_g z \neq \log_{\tilde{y}} \hat{y}$. As has been proved in Proposition 1, given that $\log_g z = \log_{\tilde{y}} \hat{y}$, only the person knowing $\log_g y$ is able to make $CSig_A(m)$, so that Alice cannot deny having issued this confirmable signature. Therefore the proposition holds. □

4 Conclusions

Previous work on fair exchange of digital signatures did not produce an efficient approach that would be widely acceptable in electronic commerce. This paper has proposed a new efficient protocol for fair exchange of digital signatures between two potentially mistrusting parties. In the protocol, a TTP, acting as a designated confirmer, is needed only when one of the exchange parties does not follow the protocol properly or other fault occurs. This protocol has a practical level of performance: only a moderate number of communication rounds (e.g. 5 rounds for a normal procedure) and ordinary signatures (e.g. two Schnorr signatures for a confirmable signature and one Schnorr signature for a normal confirmation service) are required. It will be suitable for many electronic commerce applications over the Internet, such as contract signing and electronic purchase. The fairness property of the protocol is based on verifiable confirmation of digital signatures. The paper has presented an efficient and generic confirmable signature scheme recommended being used in the proposed fair exchange protocol.

Acknowledgements

I would like to thank Wenbo Mao, Markus Stadler, Markus Michels, Graeme Proudler and Siani Pearson for invaluable discussions and/or comments. I am also grateful to anonymous referees for helpful comments.

References

1. Asokan, A., Schunter, M., Waidner, M.: Optimistic protocols for fair exchange. In *Proceedings of 4th ACM Conference on Computer and Communications Security*, Zurich, Switzerland, (1997) 6 - 17
2. Asokan, A., Shoup, V., Waidner, M.: Optimistic fair exchange of digital signatures. In *Advances in Cryptology - EUROCRYPT '98, LNCS 1403*, Springer-Verlag, (1998) 591–606
3. Bao, F.: An efficient verifiable encryption scheme for encryption of discrete logarithms. To appear in CARDIS '98
4. Bao, F., Deng, R., Mao, W.: Efficient and practical fair exchange protocols with off-line TTP. In *Proceedings of 1998 IEEE Symposium on Security and Privacy*, Oakland, California, IEEE Computer Press, (1998) 77-85
5. Ben-Or, M., Goldreich, O., Micali, S., Rivest, R.: A fair protocol for signing contracts. IEEE Transactions on Information Theory. 36(1) (1990) 40-46
6. Boyd, C., Foo, E.: Off-line fair payment protocols using convertible signatures. ASIACRYPT '98 (these proceedings)
7. Boyar, J., Chaum, D., Damgård, I., Pedersen, T.: Convertible undeniable signatures. In *Advances in Cryptology - CRYPTO '90, LNCS 537*, Springer-Verlag, (1991) 189–205
8. Chaum, D.: Zero-knowledge undeniable signatures. In *Advances in Cryptology - EUROCRYPT '90, LNCS 473*, Springer-Verlag, (1991) 458–464
9. Chaum, D.: Designated confirmer signatures. In *Advances in Cryptology - EUROCRYPT '94, LNCS 950*, Springer-Verlag, (1994) 86-91
10. Cleve, R.: Controlled gradual disclosure schemes for random bits and their applications. In *Advances in Cryptology - CRYPTO '89, LNCS 435*, pages. Springer-Verlag, (1990) 572-588
11. Cox, B., Tygar, J., Sirbu, M.: NetBill security and transaction protocol. In *Proceedings of First USENIX Workshop on Electronic Commerce*, (1995) 77-88
12. Damgård, I.: Practical and provably secure release of a secret and exchange of signatures. In *Advances in Cryptology - EUROCRYPT '93, LNCS 765*, Springer-Verlag, (1994) 201-207
13. Deng, R., Gong, L., Lazar, A., Wang, W.: Practical protocol for certified electronic mail. Journal of Network and Systems Management. 4(3) (1996) 279-297
14. ElGamal, T.: A public-key cryptosystem and a signature scheme based on discrete logarithms. IEEE Transactions on Information Theory. 31(4) (1985) 469-472
15. Even, S., Goldreich, O., Lempel, A.: A randomized protocol for signing contracts. CACM. 28(6) (1985) 637-647
16. U.S. Department of Commerce/National Institute of Standards and Technology, *Digital Signature Standard*. Federal Information Processing Standard Publication (FIPS PUB) 186, May 1994.
17. Franklin, M., Reiter, M.: Fair exchange with a semi-trusted third party. In *Proceedings of 4th ACM Conference on Computer and Communications Security*, Zurich, Switzerland, (1997) 1-5

18. Guillou, L., Quisquater, J.: A paradoxical identity-based signature scheme resulting from zero-knowledge. In *Advances in Cryptology -CRYPTO '88, LNCS 403*, Springer-Verlag, (1990) 216-231
19. Luby, M., Micali, S., Rackoff, C.: How to simultaneously exchange a secret bit by flipping symmetricall-based coin. In *Proceedings of the 24th IEEE Symposium on the Foundations of Computer Science (FOCS)*, (1983) 11-22
20. Mao, W.: Verifiable escrowed Signature. In *Proceedings of Second Australasian Conference on Information Security and Privacy, LNCS 1270*, Springer-Verlag, (1997) 240-248
21. Michels, M., Stadler, M.: Efficient convertible undeniable signature schemes. In the Proceedings of the 4th Annual Workshop on Selected Areas in Cryptography (SAC '97), (1997)
22. Michels, M., Stadler, M.: Generic constructions for secure and efficient confirmer signatures. In *Advances in Cryptology - EUROCRYPT '98, LNCS 1403*, Springer-Verlag, Berlin, (1998) 406–421
23. Okamoto, T.: Designated confirmer signatures and public-key encryption are equivalent. In *Advances in Cryptology - CRYPTO '94, LNCS 839*, Springer-Verlag, (1994) 61-74
24. Okamoto, T., Ohta, K.: How to simultaneously exchange secrets by general assumption. In *Proceedings of 2nd ACM Conference on Computer and Communications Security*, (1994) 184-192
25. Okamoto, T., Uchiyama, S.: A new public-key cryptosystem as secure as factoring. In *Advances in Cryptology - EUROCRYPT '98, LNCS 1403*, Springer-Verlag, Berlin, (1998) 308–318
26. Rabin, M., Transaction protection by beacons. Aiken Computation Lab. Harverd University Cambridge, MA, Tech. Rep. (1981) 29-81
27. Rivest, R.L., Shamir, A., Adleman, L.: A method for obtaining digital signatures and public key cryptosystems. Communications of the ACM. **21** (1978) 294–299
28. Schnorr, C.: Efficient identification and signatures for smart-cards. In *Advances in Cryptology - EUROCRYPT '89, LNCS 435*, Springer-Verlag, (1990) 239–252
29. Stadler, M.: Publicly verifiable secret sharing. In *Advances in Cryptology - EUROCRYPT '96, LNCS 1070*, Springer-Verlag, (1996) 190-199
30. Tedric, T.: Fair exchange of secrets. In *Advances in Cryptology - CRYPTO '84, LNCS 196*, Springer-Verlag, (1985) 434-438
31. Zhou, J., Gollmann, D.: A fair non-repudiation protocol. In *Proceedings of the 1996 IEEE Symposium on Security and Privacy*, Oakland, California, IEEE Computer Press, (1996) 55-61
32. Zhou, J., Gollmann, D.: An efficient non-repudiation protocol. In *Proceedings of 10th IEEE Computer Security Foundations Workshop*, Rockport, Massachusetts, (1997) 126-132

Adaptively Secure Oblivious Transfer

Donald Beaver *

Transarc Corp.

Abstract. Oblivious Transfer (OT) is a ubiquitous cryptographic tool that is of fundamental importance in secure protocol design. Despite extensive research into the design and verification of secure and efficient solutions, existing OT protocols enjoy "provable" security only against static attacks, in which an adversary must choose in advance whom it will corrupt.

This model severely limits the applicability of OT, since it provides no verifiable security against attackers who choose their victims adaptively (anytime during or after the protocol) or may even corrupt both players (which is not a moot point in a larger network protocol). This issue arises even if the communication model provides absolutely secure channels.

Recent attention has been given to accomplishing adaptive security for encryption, multiparty protocols (for $n > 3$ participants, with faulty minority), and zero-knowledge proofs.

Our work fills the remaining gap by demonstrating the first (provably) adaptively secure protocol for OT, and consequently for fully general two-party interactive computations. Based on the intractability of discrete logarithms, or more generally on a minimally restricted type of one-way trapdoor permutation, our protocols provably withstand attacks that may compromise Alice or Bob, or both, at any time.

1 Introduction

In the *Millionaires' Problem* [Yao82a], Alice and Bob wish to determine who has more money, without revealing how much each one respectively has. This problem is a special case of the more general *two-party function computation* problem, in which Alice and Bob wish to compute some arbitrary discrete function $f(x, y)$, where Alice holds x and Bob holds y, without revealing anything more about x and y than what $f(x, y)$ reveals.

Kilian [K88] provided an elegant general solution based on the fundamental primitive known as *Oblivious Transfer* (OT). Introduced by Rabin [R81], OT is a process by which Alice transmits a bit b to Bob over a "noisy" channel: Bob learns b with probability $1/2$, but Alice does not discover whether Bob succeeded or failed in learning b. This simple asymmetry in knowledge provides the basis not only for two-party function computation but for a variety of other

---

* Transarc Corp., 707 Grant St., Pittsburgh, PA, 15219, USA; 412-338-4365; beaver@transarc.com, http://www.transarc.com/~beaver

K. Ohta and D. Pei (Eds.): ASIACRYPT'98, LNCS 1514, pp. 300-314, 1998.
© Springer-Verlag Berlin Heidelberg 1998

cryptographic tasks, including bit commitment and zero-knowledge proofs [K88, BCC88, GMW87, GMR89].

Because of its importance, many implementations for OT exist [R81, EGL85, BCR86a, BCR86b, BM89, KMO89, HL90, dB91, B92], based on a variety of unproven intractability assumptions and providing varying degrees of efficiency and security. Some provide unconditional security for Alice; some provide unconditional security for Bob.

For most, a proof of security against static 1-adversaries has been offered or is straightforward to construct. In other words, most approaches support a case-by-case analysis: an always-honest Alice is protected against Bob (adversary corrupted Bob in advance), or an always-honest Bob is protected against Alice (adversary corrupted Alice in advance).

Such verification is technically insufficient, in and of itself, to demonstrate security against *adaptive* attacks. This does not immediately provide a means to break existing protocols, but it does mean that they remain at best intuitively secure. Worse, a partial verification (*i.e.* for static attacks only) is misleading when it suggests robustness against adaptive attacks.

In addition, certain applications of OT protocols introduce dangerous logical deficiencies, even when only static adversaries are involved. That is, if a statically-verified OT protocol is used in a non-black-box manner within a larger protocol, then the "obvious" deduction that the larger protocol is secure against merely static attacks may be dangerously incorrect. (See §1.4.)

To utilize Kilian's foundational result in the most robust and general fashion, an OT implementation is needed that enjoys a proof of security against adaptive 2-attacks. This paper provides such an implementation for the first time, and it uses common intractability assumptions.

1.1   Network Security and Adaptive Attacks

What is Adaptive Security? Unlike static adversaries, adaptive adversaries are able to corrupt one or more players at any time during or after a protocol.

Often, security is argued through a simulator-based approach à la Goldwasser, Micali and Rackoff [GMR89] (*cf.* [MR91, B91]). A simulator S is given access to some ideal setting (*e.g.*, the rock-hard exterior of an absolutely secure channel), and it must provide a realistic virtual environment for the adversary. If the adversary cannot tell the difference between this environment and an actual execution, then the actual execution does not leak any more information (or provide more influence on results) than the ideal setting.

Encryption over public channels provides the simplest illustration of the process. A static security proof typically arranges for S to create a fake encryption[2] $E(k, 0, r)$ of 0. In accomplishing this, S clearly needs (and is granted) no access to the message protected by the ideal channel.

---

[2] It is convenient to consider just public-key encryption, although even private-key encryption such as DES suffers the same problems with adaptive attacks. Here, k is an encryption key; r is a random string.

If an adversary can later corrupt the sender, then it (as well as S) is now entitled to learn the cleartext, m. But because S cannot generally find k' and/or r' such that $E(k', m, r') = E(k, 0, r)$, an adversary can easily detect the inconsistency. Resetting the adversary is not viable, either, particularly when in the meantime it has examined thousands of other (simulated) messages being delivered within a larger-scale interaction.

Even if S uses a random or cleverly chosen message m' instead of 0, it is highly likely that it will be mistaken. The very security of the ideal channel itself makes this problem fundamentally inevitable.

Why is Adaptive Security Important? At first glance, the distinction seems an obscure technicality. In reality, however, adaptive security reflects a more natural and applicable threat model. Although analyzing a protocol according to each possible corruption pattern appears to be a convincing argument for security, the fundamental problem is that real-world attackers need not choose in advance whom they will corrupt; nor are they restricted to corrupting at most one party.

These factors are particularly evident when OT (or encryption) is used as a pluggable component in a larger-scale protocol involving many parties. Any particular OT execution might be overrun by an adversary who eventually chooses to corrupt *both* parties – whether immediately or later.

The technical issue would be moot if there were an obvious mapping from static arguments to the adaptive case. No such mapping is known. Indeed, the opposite seems to be true for certain protocols, which enjoy proofs of static security but are unlikely to enjoy proofs of adaptive security, at least using simulator-based approaches [B95a, B96].

What are the Obstacles? Even though computational encryption makes it difficult to discover the cleartext, it binds the sender and receiver to the cleartext. That is, because there is no *equivocation* of the message given the cleartext, neither sender nor receiver can find a different key or random input to map the ciphertext to a different cleartext.

This holdover from Shannon is a curse on adaptive security in the computational setting. Not only are the sender and receiver bound to the cleartext (even though hidden!), so is the *simulator* itself.

1.2 Specifics of Oblivious Transfer

For OT, the ideal setting contains a trusted third party who receives b from Alice and decides randomly whether to send $(0, 0)$ or $(1, b)$ to Bob. The simulator can inspect and control those ideal parties (Alice/Bob) if and precisely when the adversary has requested their corruption.

In particular, S must provide a view of the conversation between A and B over a public channel, even before any corruptions have been requested. When Alice (or Bob) is then corrupted, S should "back-patch" its view to show an internal history of Alice (or Bob) that is consistent with the conversation. For security against 2-adversaries, S must also be prepared to provide a fake history for Bob (resp. Alice) in the future, if the adversary Adv later requests a second corruption.

Example. For concreteness, consider Rabin's OT protocol [R81]. Alice generates $n = pq$ as a product of large Blum primes, then sends n and (for simplicity, say) $s = (-1)^b r^2 \bmod n$ to Bob, for a random $r \bmod n$. Bob chooses a secret $x \bmod n$ and sends $z = x^2 \bmod n$ to Alice. Alice chooses one of the four square roots $\{x, -x, y, -y\}$ of z and sends it to Bob. If Alice chose $\pm x$, Bob learns nothing, but if Alice chose $\pm y$, Bob can factor n and discover b.

Now, say that Adv corrupts "real" Bob. Even if the whole conversation had been encrypted, Adv now learns the traffic described above, and S must simulate it. S is entitled to learn what a trusted third party handed over to "ideal" Bob in the ideal case. With probability $1/2$, S failed to learn b, yet it must present Adv with some s.

We might try the approach that seems to suffice for the static case: just make s up using a guessed b, and Adv will never know the difference. But Adv may choose to corrupt "real" Alice a hundred years later (even for reasons completely independent of this OT execution), at which point S has to report a consistent internal history for Alice. Indeed, S is now entitled to learn b by corrupting the "ideal" Alice. But the fake value of s can be "decoded" in only one way, and with probability $1/2$, S's earlier faked value will be inconsistent with b, causing the simulation to fail.[3]

1.3 Adaptive Security: Related Work

The fundamental importance of *adaptively*-secure solutions is underlined by recent solutions for several fundamental cryptographic tasks, including:

- *Encryption* [CFGN96]
- *Multiparty computation* (for $n > 3$) [CFGN96]
- *Zero-knowledge proofs and arguments* [B95a] (*cf.* [BCC88, FS90a])
- *Bit committal* [B95a] (*cf.* [BCC88, FS90a])

Erasing. Simulation can be finessed in settings where erasing internal information is allowed [BH92, F88]. By deleting sensitive information, players remove the evidence that might otherwise indicate a simulator's mistaken guess. If a private key is no longer available, then the adversarial view, although information-theoretically improper, will reveal no contradiction.

Fake Ciphertexts with Equivocation. Using public channels while maintaining complete internal records is a significantly greater challenge. Recently, Canetti, Feige, Goldreich and Naor [CFGN96] developed a secure encryption scheme without erasing, based on honest parties' refraining from learning certain bits. This

---

[3] A simulator for the static case doesn't ever have to face this possibility; it only produces fake information for Alice when Alice is corrupt from the start, in which case it knows b already.

important idea enables the simulator to construct fake ciphertexts that can be made consistent with either 0 or 1.

Naturally, the facsimiles are imperfect (otherwise a receiver could not tell whether the message was 0 or 1), but it is computationally difficult to distinguish them from actual ciphertexts.

1.4   Previous Work Insufficient for OT

There is good reason why OT is conspicuously missing from the preceding list. Generally speaking, the earlier settings demand at most *one-sided* privacy, whereas OT requires *two-sided* privacy.

That is, in earlier settings, at most one of the parties is hiding information from the other. Therefore S holds *no* information from the ideal setting, until it gains *all* information as soon as a sensitive party (sender/receiver/prover/committer) is corrupted. Thus, S need only prepare for one "surprise" event, namely when it suddenly gains the private information and must back-patch its current simulation.

In OT, however, each party withholds information from the other. Achieving equivocation in both directions *simultaneously* is a significantly different and harder task. The simulator must be prepared to back-patch flexibly with two kinds of newly-gained data, depending on which player is first compromised. Even thereafter, the ongoing simulation must still be prepared for an eventual back-patching needed to show consistency with the still-unknown data held by the other player. This remains true even if the interaction occurs over an absolutely secure channel.

Two-Sided Equivocation. Beaver recently characterized two equivocation properties for OT [B96]: An OT implementation is **content-equivocable**[4] (C.E.) if S can generate views (whether or not B is yet corrupt) so that if A is suddenly corrupted, the views can be made consistent with A having transmitted $b = 0$ or $b = 1$. Likewise, the implementation is **result-equivocable** (R.E.) if S can patch a view consistently with "received" or "didn't receive" when Bob is suddenly corrupted.

Weaker equivocation properties are also useful to consider, particularly when the traffic itself between A and B is also encrypted. An OT protocol is **weakly content-equivocable** if S need do the appropriate patching only when Bob is already corrupt. An OT protocol is **weakly result-equivocable** if S need do the appropriate patching only when Alice is already corrupt.

For example, the Rabin protocol is result-equivocable but not weakly content-equivocable. According to need, S can use an appropriate choice from $\{x, -x, y, -y\}$ as the "actual" x that Bob chose, thereby switching whether Bob received b or not. But as described earlier, the announced value of s prevents S from adapting b itself.

---

[4] The term "equivocable" means "can be made to appear equivocal." Equivocal *ciphertexts* convey no information and are useless for communication; but equivocal *facsimiles* enable flexible back-patching.

Weak content-equivocation is virtually identical to the "chameleon" property [BCC88] for bit commitment. Unfortunately, the methods in [BCC88] do not generalize to achieve both C.E. and R.E. properties simultaneously for OT.

Notably, no known OT protocol is both weakly content- and weakly result- equivocable [B96]. This includes the protocols described in Rabin [R81], Even/Goldreich/Lempel [EGL85], Goldreich/Micali/Wigderson [GMW87], Bellare/Micali [BM89], Den Boer [dB91], and Beaver [B96].

Insufficiencies for Static *Attacks.* Even ignoring adaptive attacks altogether, there are subtle dangers in using OT protocols in larger protocols. Unless the protocol is used in a black-box manner, it can be incorrect to deduce that a larger protocol is secure against merely static attacks based on a proof that the OT subprotocol is secure against static attacks.

As an illustration, recall Rabin's protocol for OT, in the case where Alice is honest, *i.e.* where S does not have access to b. If S uses the encryption-style simulation, it sets $b = 0$ (or guesses a random b).

Now, imagine using this kind of OT protocol for commitment purposes, to tie Alice to each bit b. As long as Alice does not ever reveal the r value, it is always possible to "reveal" a b' value that is inconsistent with $s = (-1)^b r^2$. (Discovering this inconsistency is just the Quadratic Residuosity problem.)

A "black-box" use of OT would never instruct Alice to "decommit" b by revealing r. (Thus, even if b is revealed later in a larger protocol, it remains infeasible to detect whether S's facsimile has the wrong quadratic residuosity.) But a less well-bred protocol might indeed use this attractive ability to decommit b. In that case, it would be incorrect to extend a claim of security to the larger protocol, even against static attacks. This is because the quadratic residuosity of the simulator's fake s value will match an unknown b value only half the time, and S's attempts at simulation will fail. This problem is particularly acute where *encryptions* are used as committals in such a non-black-box way.

Again, the protocol may not be obviously breakable, but the deduction that it is provably secure would be incorrect.

1.5   Results

Our results are complementary to recent advances in adaptive security in the related but distinct domains of encryption, proofs and committal.

We give the first known protocol for Oblivious Transfer that admits a proof of security against attacks by adaptive 2-adversaries:

Theorem 1. *There exists an implementation of Oblivious Transfer that is secure against adaptive 2-adversaries, if the Diffie-Hellman Assumption holds.*

Our methods require a small constant number of exponentiations and are comparable to the complexity of statically-secure OT implementations.

Similar results hold for other cryptographic assumptions such as the intractability of factoring or breaking RSA. More generally, they hold for a slightly restricted type of one-way trapdoor permutation, one which allows the selection of a permutation without knowing the trapdoor [CFGN96].

Although secure channels are insufficient, we make use of methods in [B97] that employ (statically-secure) key exchange in a bizarre fashion, intentionally *revealing* the keys that are mutually generated.

Contents. §2 describes notation, formalities, and OT variants. §3 presents our solution based on the Diffie-Hellman assumption. §4 describes a proof of security against adaptive attacks. §5 discusses generalizations of the techniques.

2   Background and Notation

Notation. Let $\$(S)$ denote the uniformly random distribution over finite set S. Let p be a prime. Let $\mathbf{Z}_p^* = \{1, 2, \ldots, p-1\}$ and let $\mathbf{Z}_{p-1} = \{0, 1, 2, \ldots, p-2\}$.

Attacks: Static or Adaptive. An adversary is a probabilistic poly-time TM (PPTM) that issues two sorts of messages: "*corrupt i*," "*send m* from i to j." It receives two sorts of responses: "*view of i*," "*receive m* from j to i." Whether its send/receive message is honored depends on whether it has issued a request to corrupt i.

A **static t-adversary** is an adversary who issues up to t *corrupt* requests before the protocol starts. An **adaptive t-adversary** may issue up to t such requests at any time.

OT specification. The **specification protocol for OT** is a three-party protocol consisting of $\hat{A}$, $\hat{B}$, and incorruptible party OT. $\hat{A}$ has input b, which it is instructed to send to OT. OT flips a coin, $?b$, and sends $(?b, ?b \wedge b)$ to $\hat{B}$.[5] The communication channels between $\hat{A}$ and OT and between OT and $\hat{B}$ are absolutely private.

We also consider two variants on OT: one-out-of-two OT ($\frac{1}{2}$OT), in which Alice holds (b_0, b_1) and Bob receives (c, b_c) for a random c unknown to Alice [EGL85]; and chosen one-out-of-two OT ($\binom{2}{1}$OT), in which Alice holds (b_0, b_1) and Bob receives b_c for a c of his choice, but unknown to Alice.

Simulation-based security. The definition of simulator-based static security is the standard approach: find an appropriate simulator for the case in which Alice is bad, and another simulator for when Bob is bad. We focus on the adaptive case.

In the adaptive case, there is a single simulator, $\mathcal{S}$, who receives requests from and delivers responses to the attacker, Adv, creating an environment for Adv as though Adv were attacking a given implementation. $\mathcal{S}$ is itself an attacker acting within the specification protocol for OT, which is run with $\hat{A}$ on input b. When Adv corrupts player i, $\mathcal{S}$ issues a corruption request and is given $\hat{i}$'s

---

[5] Thus, $(0, 0)$ means "failed," while $(1, b)$ means "received b."

information.[6] S responds to Adv with a facsimile of the *"view of i"* response that Adv expects. S receives all of Adv's *"send m"* requests and provides Adv with facsimiles of *"receive m"* responses. Finally, Adv (or S on Adv's behalf) writes its output, y_{Adv}.

Let Adv, with auxiliary input x_{Adv}, attack a given OT implementation OT in which Alice holds input b. The execution induces a distribution $(A(b), B, \text{Adv}(x_{\text{Adv}}))$ on output triples, $(y_A, y_B, y_{\text{Adv}})$.

Let $S(\text{Adv}(x_{\text{Adv}}))$ attack the OT specification. The execution induces a distribution $(\hat{A}(b), \hat{B}, S(\text{Adv}(x_{\text{Adv}})))$ on output triples, $(y_{\hat{A}}, y_{\hat{B}}, y_S)$.

An extra, "security parameter" k may be included. This provides a sequence of distributions on output triples in each scenario. Let $\approx$ denote *computational indistinguishability*, a notion whose formal definition is omitted for reasons of space (*cf.* [GMR89]).

The implementation OT is **secure against adaptive t-adversaries** if, for any adaptive t-adversary Adv, there is a PPTM simulator S such that for any b, $(A(b), B, \text{Adv}(x_{\text{Adv}})) \approx (\hat{A}(b), \hat{B}, S(\text{Adv}(x_{\text{Adv}})))$. In other words, the simulator maps attacks on the implementation to equivalent attacks on the specification.

Assumptions. Let p be a "safe" prime, namely $p - 1 = 2q$, where q are prime. Let $\hat{g}$ be a generator of $\mathbf{Z}_p^*$, and define $g = \hat{g}^2 \bmod p$; g generates a subgroup denoted $\langle g \rangle$.

In the **Diffie-Hellman protocol**, Alice selects an exponent $a \leftarrow \$(\mathbf{Z}_{p-1})$ and sends $x \leftarrow g^a \bmod p$ to Bob. Alice selects $b \leftarrow \$(\mathbf{Z}_{p-1})$ and sends $y \leftarrow g^b \bmod p$ to Bob. Alice and Bob then individually calculate the shared "key" $z = g^{ab} \bmod p$. (Alice uses $z \leftarrow y^a$ and Bob uses $z \leftarrow x^b$.)

Define the **Diffie-Hellman distribution** D_p as the triple of random variables (x, y, z) obtained from an execution of the DH protocol by honest parties.

The **Decision Diffie-Hellman Assumption** (DDHA) can be described as follows:

(DDHA) Let p be a safe prime and g a subgroup generator selected as described above. Then D_p is computationally indistinguishable from $(\$(\langle g \rangle), \$(\langle g \rangle), \$(\langle g \rangle))$.

Note that without the precaution of moving to a subgroup, typical Diffie-Hellman triples can be distinguished from three random elements. The quadratic residuosity of g^{ab} can be deduced from that of g^a and g^b, hence a random element would be distinguishable from g^{ab}.

3   Solution Employing Diffie-Hellman

By Crépeau's reductions, it suffices to implement $\binom{2}{1}$OT [C87]. Alice and Bob attempt to set up a valid $\binom{2}{1}$OT execution on random bits, as in [B95b]: if successful, they can later apply this execution to the desired input bits.

---

[6] $\hat{i}$ is a player in the specification protocol and is unaware of messages being passed in a given implementation. In particular, $\hat{A}$ knows only its input b (and its message to OT), and $\hat{B}$ knows only its message from OT.

The attempt consists of four invocations of the Diffie-Hellman key-exchange protocol [DH76], some of which are "garbled" according to Beaver's approach [B97]. If an appropriate invocation remains ungarbled, then Alice and Bob have established a valid $\binom{2}{1}$OT execution, otherwise they must try again.

3.1   Honest Players

Assuming initially that neither Alice nor Bob misbehaves, a simple overview is possible. Essentially, Alice encodes bits b_0 and b_1 using a 2×2 table α_{ij} of bits, where $\alpha_{ij} = 0$ iff $b_i = j$. Bob encodes a choice c and mask m using a table β_{ij}, where $\beta_{cm} = 0$ and all other values are 1. They engage in four DH executions, some of which are garbled. Alice "garbles" whenever $\alpha_{ij} = 1$ and Bob "garbles" whenever $\beta_{ij} = 1$. Bob can detect when they both left instance cm ungarbled, in which case $\alpha_{cm} = 0$, hence $b_c = m$. Otherwise, Bob requests a retry.

The "garbling" of the Diffie-Hellman protocol occurs in one of two ways. Instead of choosing an exponent e and computing $r = g^e$, a player can choose r directly without knowing its discrete logarithm. (Thus, the player will be unable to calculate or verify the final DH key, g^{ab}.) Second, a player can garble g^{ab} by likewise choosing a uniformly random residue whose discrete logarithm is unknown. In particular, define the following random variables, which either report a deterministic output or produce a uniform, garbled distribution:

$$G(\sigma, s) = \begin{cases} \$(\mathbf{Z}_p^*) & \text{if } \sigma = 0 \\ g^s \bmod p & \text{if } \sigma = 1 \end{cases}$$

$$G(\sigma, s, r) = \begin{cases} (\$(\mathbf{Z}_p^*), \$(\mathbf{Z}_p^*)) & \text{if } \sigma = 0 \\ (g^s \bmod p, r^s \bmod p) & \text{if } \sigma = 1 \end{cases}$$

The first version is for the player who sends out the initial DH message (Alice, in the original DH protocol; but this will vary below), having made choice σ whether to garble or not. The second version is for the player who responds, having made his own choice σ about whether to garble or not.

Fig. 1 describes the details of the protocol.

Why Garble? Recall that the simulator S plays the hand of an honest player (within the proposed OT protocol) when it constructs an environment for the adversary. But S can play that hand dishonestly (for the desired purpose of deceiving an attacker, after all!), by always producing ungarbled instances. By withholding suitable exponents, S can nevertheless make any ungarbled instance look garbled, since no computationally-bounded judge can detect the difference between four DH triples (fake distribution) and four triples of which one is DH and three are wholly random (real distribution). This remains true even when the adversary obtains all information that Alice and Bob would hold; S keeps the logarithms up his sleeve.

3.2   Malicious Players

Although these techniques are strongly motivated by the application of DH to adaptively-secure encryption in [B97], note that they suffice only for the case of honest players. Malicious misbehavior is of little concern in encryption (*i.e.* it can be handled trivially), where the sender generally has little to gain by causing the receiver to accept nonsense messages. Here, however, both sender and receiver have something to gain by misbehaving.

Protecting against malicious behavior will consist of two parts: (1) using committal to enable suitable random number generation; (2) using zero-knowledge proofs of knowledge (ZKPK's) to extract effective values and ensure compliance with the rules (*cf.* [GMW86, TW87]).

The central problem with this "obvious" cryptographic solution is that the commitments and ZKPK's might defeat the simulator's ability to provide equivocal facsimiles. Thus, the tricks of [B97] are insufficient, by themselves, to achieve our desired goal.

By [B95a], however, it suffices to employ committals that are weakly content-equivocable (a.k.a. *chameleon* [BCC88], a.k.a. *trapdoor* [FS90b]). That is, the "receiver" should be able to "open" the committed bits to 0 or to 1, using knowledge held by the receiver.

Brassard, Chaum and Crépeau provide a discrete-logarithm-based implementation of chameleon blobs [BCC88]. This commitment scheme enables the simulator to extract the effective α_{ij}/β_{ij} values used by the adversary.

To complete the discrete-logarithm-based solution, we add the following straightforward complications (*cf.* [GMW87]). The random values a_{ij} and b_{ij} are constructed from precursors: $a_{ij} \leftarrow a'_{ij} + \Delta a_{ij}$; $b_{ij} \leftarrow b'_{ij} + \Delta b_{ij}$. Alice commits to a'_{ij} and Δb_{ij}, and Bob commits conversely. They then reveal the Δa_{ij}, Δb_{ij} values and proceed as before. (The guaranteed randomization of the α_{ij}'s and β_{ij}'s is similar.) Each party must then give a ZKPK that they used the proper a_{ij}, α_{ij}, or b_{ij}, β_{ij} value. Bob must give a ZKPK that $x_{cm}^{b_{cm}} == z_{cm}$.

4   Proving Security

Recall that S must simultaneously create a fake environment for Adv while "attacking" an execution of the ideal specification.

Actions in the Ideal Setting. When S engages in an extraction of knowledge from Adv that fails, S then deliberately aborts the ideal protocol. (This reflects a malicious adversary's rightful ability to stop participating.) When the extraction succeeds, S uses the value on behalf of the corrupt $\hat{A}$ or $\hat{B}$ in the ideal protocol.

4.1   Equivocation

We first sketch how the weak equivocation properties are satisfied when Alice or Bob are initially corrupted, and then discuss strong equivocation.

```
OT-Honest
0.        Public:     prime p, generator g mod p
1.1.      B:          c ← $(0,1), m ← $(0,1)          // choice and mask
                      for i = 0, 1, j = 0, 1:
                          if (i == c and j == m) then β_ij ← 1 else β_ij ← 0
                          b_ij ← $(Z_{p-1})
                          y_ij ← G(β_ij, b_ij)
1.2.      B→A:        y_00, y_01, y_10, y_11
2.1.      A:          m_0 ← $(0,1), m_1 ← $(0,1)    // masks for transferred bits
                      for i = 0, 1, j = 0, 1:
                          if (j == m_i) then α_ij ← 1 else α_ij ← 0
                          a_ij ← $(Z_{p-1})
                          (x_ij, z_ij) ← G(α_ij, a_ij, y_ij)
2.2.      A→B:        x_00, x_01, x_10, x_11, z_00, z_01, z_10, z_11
3.1.      B:          if (x_cm^{b_cm} == z_cm) then s ← 1 else s ← 0
3.2.      B→A:        s                              // success if 1
// To use successful attempts (after [B96]):
S1.1.     B:          get input choice C
                      γ = C ⊕ c
S1.2.     B→A:        γ
S2.1.     A:          get input bits M_0, M_1
                      w_0 ← M_0 ⊕ m_γ
                      w_1 ← M_1 ⊕ m_{1-γ}
S2.2.     A→B:        w_0, w_1
S3.1.     B:          M_C ← w_C ⊕ m
```

Fig. 1. Adaptively secure chosen-1/2-OT, for honest players.

Weak Result Equivocation. Assume that Alice is passively corrupted. To simulate Bob, generate $\hat{b}_{ij} \leftarrow \$(\mathbf{Z}_{p-1})$, but do not choose the β_{ij}'s yet. Set $y_{ij} \leftarrow g^{\hat{b}_{ij}}$, and hand these values to adversary Adv.

Extract Adv's choices for α_{ij} from its proof of knowledge. Select $s \leftarrow \$(0,1)$.

If the attempt is to fail ($s = 0$), then choose the β_{ij}'s conditioned on failure. In particular, let m_0, m_1 be such that $\alpha_{0m_0} = \alpha_{1m_1} = 1$.[7] Set $c \leftarrow \$(0,1)$ and take $m \leftarrow 1 - m_c$, which enforces a failure. Set $\beta_{cm} \leftarrow 1$ and $\beta_{ij} \leftarrow 0$ for $(i,j) \neq (c,m)$. Set $b_{cm} \leftarrow \hat{b}_{cm}$ (which conveniently makes $y_{cm} == g^{b_{cm}}$) and $b_{ij} \leftarrow y_{ij}$ for $(i,j) \neq (c,m)$. Thus, even though the three b_{ij} values were chosen with known discrete logarithms (*i.e.* known to the simulator), it appears as though they were chosen directly at random.

If the attempt is to succeed ($s = 1$), then we must enable result-equivocation. The nontrivial case occurs when Bob is corrupted after a successful transmission. (The analysis is similar, indeed trivial, if no bit has been transmitted.) The values w_0, w_1 are obtained from Alice. Because Bob is now corrupt, the simulator is

---

[7] Actually, m_0, m_1 may be read directly from the honest machine. Otherwise, they are calculated from the extracted α_{ij} values.

entitled to learn the choice C that Bob made, along with the transmitted bit M_C. Set $c \leftarrow C \oplus \gamma$ and $m_c \leftarrow M_C \oplus w_C$. Set $\beta_{cm} \leftarrow 1$ and $\beta_{ij} \leftarrow 0$ for $(i,j) \neq (c,m)$. Set $b_{cm} \leftarrow \hat{b}_{cm}$ (which conveniently makes $y_{cm} == g^{b_{cm}}$) and $b_{ij} \leftarrow y_{ij}$ for $(i,j) \neq (c,m)$. Again, even though the three b_{ij} values were chosen with known discrete logarithms, it appears as though they were chosen directly at random.

Weak Content Equivocation. Assume that Bob is passively corrupted. Extract c,m such that $\beta_{cm} = 1$. To simulate Alice, simply follow Alice's program, except for the calculation of (x_{ij}, z_{ij}). Instead of using $(x_{ij}, z_{ij}) \leftarrow G(\alpha_{ij}, a_{ij}, y_{ij})$, set $(x_{ij}, z_{ij}) \leftarrow (g^{\hat{a}_{ij}}, y_{ij}^{\hat{a}_{ij}})$, for randomly selected $\hat{a}_{ij} \leftarrow \$(\mathbf{Z}_{p-1})$.

In case of failure ($\alpha_{cm} = 0$), simply withhold the known discrete logarithms. That is, set $a_{0,m_0} \leftarrow \hat{a}_{0,m_0}$, $a_{0,1-m_0} \leftarrow x_{0,1-m_0}$, $a_{1,m_1} \leftarrow \hat{a}_{1,m_1}$, $a_{1,1-m_1} \leftarrow x_{1,1-m_1}$.

In case of success ($\alpha_{cm} = 1$), withhold one of the discrete logarithms by setting $a_{cm} \leftarrow \hat{a}_{cm}$, $a_{c,1-m} \leftarrow x_{c,1-m}$. (The other pair remains "indeterminate" for now, so the simulator can withhold the discrete logarithm of either member of the pair, thereby effectively reversing the unknown bit.) Obtain Bob's final choice C and the value M_C he is entitled to learn. Set $w_C \leftarrow M_C \oplus m$ but $w_{1-C} \leftarrow \$(0,1)$ (this corresponds to the masked, unchosen bit M_{1-C}). When Alice is later corrupted and bit M_{1-C} is obtained, equivocate w_{1-C} as follows. Calculate $m_{1-c} \leftarrow w_{1-C} \oplus M_{1-C}$, and set $\alpha_{1-c,m_{1-c}} \leftarrow 1$, $\alpha_{1-c,1-m_{1-c}} \leftarrow 0$, Withhold a second discrete logarithm by taking $a_{1-c,m_{1-c}} \leftarrow \hat{a}_{1-c,m_{1-c}}$, $a_{1-c,1-m_{1-c}} \leftarrow x_{1-c,1-m_{1-c}}$.

Strong Equivocation. Note that in the absence of corruptions, $\mathcal{S}$'s calculations and "public traffic" will be consistent with the steps described above for both Alice and Bob. Thus, until Adv makes its first corruption request, $\mathcal{S}$ follows the steps described above for both Alice and Bob. If Alice is corrupted first, $\mathcal{S}$ follows the weak R.E. steps to create Alice's view, then continues with the weak C.E. steps. If Bob is corrupted first, the converse programs are followed.

4.2   Reduction to Diffie-Hellman (DDHA)

The distribution that Adv obtains by interacting with the simulator differs from that obtained in a regular execution in precisely one way: for certain triples (x_{ij}, y_{ij}, z_{ij}), the fake distribution follows the correlated Diffie-Hellman distribution D_p, whereas the "real-life" distribution contains three fully independent random variables.

These triples occur only in successful attempts, and only on indices where *neither* Alice *nor* Bob has chosen to know the discrete logarithm. That is, neither $\log_g x_{ij}$ nor $\log_g y_{ij}$ is known to Alice or Bob, and in particular, Adv *never* learns them as a result of corrupting Alice or Bob.

Straightforward arguments (see [B97], for example) show that distinguishing the simulator's faked view from an actual view would enable distinguishing D_p from independently-random triples, violating the DDHA.

Note in particular that this is why failed attempts must be fully discarded.[8] If the protocol were changed to capitalize on mismatched attempts (intuitively, Alice's index choice remains secret and known only to the two of them even in case of mismatch!) the simulator proof would fail. For instance, if Bob knows $\log_g x_{ij}$, the simulation would be detectably fake, because $z_{ij} = y_{ij}^{\log_g x_{ij}}$ would hold in the simulated cases.

5   Generalizations and Applications

To use other intractability assumptions, such as RSA or factoring, a suitable key-exchange construction suffices. In particular, the dense secure public-key cryptosystems of DeSantis and Persiano are appropriate [DP92].

General Assumptions. A more general construction (*cf.* [DP92, CFGN96]) employs one-way trapdoor permutation families with the property that permutations can also be generated (indistinguishably) without simultaneously generating a trapdoor. Two modifications are needed.

First, in the honest OT protocol, Alice and Bob respectively choose and report four permutations, f_{ij}, g_{ij}. For garbled channels, each generates the permutation without the trapdoor, and sends random numbers. For ungarbled channels, each chooses an accompanying trapdoor. Bob sends $y_{ij} \leftarrow f_{ij}(b_{ij})$; Alice returns $z_{ij} \leftarrow g_{ij}(f_{ij}^{-1}(y_{ij}))$. Note that $z_{ij} = b_{ij}$ precisely when Alice and Bob garble the same channel.

Second, malicious behavior is again resisted through ZKPK's; the general constructions of Feige and Shamir [FS90a, FS90b] provide the needed trapdoor/chameleon/weak-equivocation property.

Third Parties. When third parties are available – as in the case of a multiparty computation – one-way trapdoor permutations without the extra oblivious-generation property can be used. These third parties need not be individually trusted, but at least one of them must remain honest. We also require a broadcast channel.

As in the clever construction used in [CFGN96] for encryption, the ultimate permutations are composed of permutations generated by the third parties, who allow Bob and Alice to learn trapdoors selectively. Receiver Bob learns one of four (rather than of two) trapdoors by way of EGL/GMW $\binom{2}{1}$OT. Unlike [CFGN96], however, Sender Alice also learns trapdoors: one from each of two pairs. The remainder of the protocol follows the Diffie-Hellman solution proposed in this work. Malicious behavior is avoided through network-based commitment and proofs, which do not require the set of faults to be a minority.

---

[8] Note: this does not mean *erased*; the simulator is choosing what to place in the details of a *full* player history. To simulate a failed attempt, the simulator behaves *perfectly* accurately on behalf of any corrupt party/parties. Only the *successful* attempts suffer any mathematical (but still negligible) distinction from the real-life distribution.

Although this approach relies on a weaker assumption, it is far less efficient, requiring network-wide interaction for each transfer. Note that applying [CFGN96] to encrypt an information-theoretically secure OT protocol using [BGW88, CCD88] would also suffice, but it requires that faults be a strict minority.

Faulty Majority. While adaptively-secure encryption enables one to construct adaptively-secure multiparty protocols when there is a faulty minority [BH92, CFGN96], it does not directly suffice when there is a faulty majority. In separate work [B96b], we show that the tools described in this paper make possible the construction of a provably fair and secure protocol for multiparty function evaluation even in the presence of a majority of faults, using techniques of Beaver, Goldwasser and Levin [BG89, GL90].

References

[B91]   D. Beaver. "Foundations of Secure Interactive Computing." *Advances in Cryptology – Crypto '91 Proceedings,* Springer–Verlag LNCS 576, 1992, 377–391.

[B92]   D. Beaver. "How to Break a 'Secure' Oblivious Transfer Protocol." *Advances in Cryptology – Eurocrypt '92 Proceedings,* Springer–Verlag LNCS 658, 1993, 285–296.

[B95a]   D. Beaver. "Adaptive Zero Knowledge and Computational Equivocation." *Proceedings of the 28th STOC,* ACM, 1996, 629–638.

[B95b]   D. Beaver. "Precomputing Oblivious Transfer." *Advances in Cryptology – Crypto '95 Proceedings,* Springer–Verlag LNCS 963, 1995, 97–109.

[B96]   D. Beaver. "Equivocable Oblivious Transfer." *Advances in Cryptology – Eurocrypt '96 Proceedings,* Springer–Verlag LNCS 1070, 1996, 1996, 119–130.

[B96b]   D. Beaver. "Fair and Adaptively Secure Computation with Faulty Majority." Manuscript, 1996, to be submitted.

[B97]   D. Beaver. "Plug-And-Play Encryption." *Advances in Cryptology – Crypto '97 Proceedings,* Springer–Verlag LNCS 1294, 1997, 1997.

[BG89]   D. Beaver, S. Goldwasser. "Multiparty Computation with Faulty Majority." *Proceedings of the 30th FOCS,* IEEE, 1989, 468–473.

[BH92]   D. Beaver, S. Haber. "Cryptographic Protocols Provably Secure Against Dynamic Adversaries." *Advances in Cryptology – Eurocrypt '92 Proceedings,* Springer–Verlag LNCS 658, 1993, 307–323.

[BGW88]   M. Ben-Or, S. Goldwasser, A. Wigderson. "Completeness Theorems for Non-Cryptographic Fault-Tolerant Distributed Computation." *Proceedings of the 20th STOC,* ACM, 1988, 1–10.

[BM89]   M. Bellare, S. Micali. "Non-Interactive Oblivious Transfer and Applications." *Advances in Cryptology – Crypto '89 Proceedings,* Springer–Verlag LNCS 435, 1990, 547–557.

[BCR86a] G. Brassard, C. Crépeau, J. Robert. "All or Nothing Disclosure of Secrets." *Advances in Cryptology – Crypto '86 Proceedings,* Springer–Verlag LNCS 263, 1987, 234–238.

[BCR86b] G. Brassard, C. Crépeau, J. Robert. "Information Theoretic Reductions among Disclosure Problems." *Proceedings of the 27th FOCS,* IEEE, 1986, 168–173.

[BCC88]   G. Brassard, D. Chaum, C. Crépeau. "Minimum Disclosure Proofs of Knowledge." *J. Comput. Systems Sci.* **37**, 1988, 156–189.

[CFGN96] R. Canetti, U. Feige, O. Goldreich, M. Naor. "Adaptively Secure Multiparty Computation." *Proceedings of the* 28th *STOC,* ACM, 1996, 639–648.

[CCD88] D. Chaum, C. Crépeau, I. Damgrd. "Multiparty Unconditionally Secure Protocols." *Proceedings of the* 20th *STOC,* ACM, 1988, 11–19.

[C87] C. Crépeau. "Equivalence Between Two Flavours of Oblivious Transfers." *Advances in Cryptology – Crypto '87 Proceedings,* Springer–Verlag LNCS 293, 1988, 350–354.

[dB91] B. den Boer. "Oblivious Transfer Protecting Secrecy." *Advances in Cryptology – Eurocrypt '91 Proceedings,* Springer–Verlag LNCS 547, 1991, 31–45.

[DP92] A. DeSantis, G. Persiano. "Zero-Knowledge Proofs of Knowledge Without Interaction." *Proceedings of the* 33rd *FOCS,* IEEE, 1992, 427–436.

[DH76] W. Diffie, M. Hellman. "New Directions in Cryptography." *IEEE Transactions on Information Theory* **IT-22**, November 1976, 644–654.

[EGL85] S. Even, O. Goldreich, A. Lempel. "A Randomized Protocol for Signing Contracts." *Comm. of the ACM* **28**:6, 1985, 637–647. (Early version: *Proceedings of Crypto 1982,* Springer–Verlag, 1983, 205–210.)

[F88] P. Feldman. Manuscript, 1988. (Personal communication, Cynthia Dwork.)

[FS90a] U. Feige, A. Shamir. "Witness Indistinguishable and Witness Hiding Proofs." *Proceedings of the* 22nd *STOC,* ACM, 1990, 416–426.

[FS90b] U. Feige, A. Shamir. "Zero Knowledge Proofs of Knowledge in Two Rounds." *Advances in Cryptology – Crypto '89 Proceedings,* Springer–Verlag LNCS 435, 1990, 1990, 526–544.

[GMW86] O. Goldreich, S. Micali, A. Wigderson. "Proofs that Yield Nothing but Their Validity and a Methodology of Cryptographic Protocol Design." *Proceedings of the* 27th *FOCS,* IEEE, 1986, 174–187.

[GMW87] O. Goldreich, S. Micali, A. Wigderson. "How to Play Any Mental Game, or A Completeness Theorem for Protocols with Honest Majority." *Proceedings of the* 19th *STOC,* ACM, 1987, 218–229.

[GL90] S. Goldwasser, L. Levin. "Fair Computation of General Functions in Presence of Immoral Majority." *Proceedings of Crypto 1990.*

[GM84] S. Goldwasser, S. Micali. "Probabilistic Encryption." *J. Comput. Systems Sci.* **28**, 1984, 270–299.

[GMR89] S. Goldwasser, S. Micali, C. Rackoff. "The Knowledge Complexity of Interactive Proof Systems." *SIAM J. on Computing* **18**:1, 1989, 186–208.

[HL90] L. Harn, H. Lin. "Noninteractive Oblivious Transfer." *Electronics Letters* **26**:10, May 1990, 635–636.

[K88] J. Kilian. "Founding Cryptography on Oblivious Transfer." *Proceedings of the* 20th *STOC,* ACM, 1988, 20–29.

[KMO89] J. Kilian, S. Micali, R. Ostrovsky. "Minimum Resource Zero-Knowledge Proofs." *Proceedings of the* 30th *FOCS,* IEEE, 1989, 1989, 474–479.

[MR91] S. Micali, P. Rogaway. "Secure Computation." *Advances in Cryptology – Crypto '91 Proceedings,* Springer–Verlag LNCS 576, 1992, 392–404.

[R81] M.O. Rabin. "How to Exchange Secrets by Oblivious Transfer." TR-81, Harvard, 1981.

[RSA78] R. Rivest, A. Shamir, L. Adleman. "A Method for Obtaining Digital Signatures and Public Key Cryptosystems." *Communications of the ACM* **21**:2, 1978, 120–126.

[TW87] M. Tompa, H. Woll. "Random Self-Reducibility and Zero-Knowledge Proofs of Possession of Information." *Proceedings of the* 28th *FOCS,* IEEE, 1987, 472–482.

[Yao82a] A. Yao. "Protocols for Secure Computations." *Proceedings of the* 23rd *FOCS,* IEEE, 1982, 160–164.

[Yao82b] A. Yao. "Theory and Applications of Trapdoor Functions." *Proceedings of the* 23rd *FOCS,* IEEE, 1982, 80–91.

[Yao86] A. Yao. "How to Generate and Exchange Secrets." *Proceedings of the* 27th *FOCS,* IEEE, 1986, 162–167.

ML-Sequences over Rings $Z/(2^e)$ * :
I. Constructions of Nondegenerative ML-Sequences
II. Injectivness of Compression Mappings of New Classes

WenFeng Qi[1], JunHui Yang[2], JingJun Zhou[1]

[1] Zhengzhou Information Engineering Institute, HeNan, China

[2] Institute of Software, Academia Sinica,
State Key Lab. of Information Security, Beijing, China
yangdai@mimi.cnc.ac.cn

Abstract

Pseudorandom binary sequences derived from the ML-sequences over the integer residue ring $Z/(2^e)$ are proposed and studied in [1-10]. This paper is divided into two parts. The first part is on the nondegenerative ML-sequences. In this part the so-called quasi-period of a ML-sequence is introduced, and it is noted that a ML-sequence may degenerate in the sense that it has the quasi-period shorter than its period, and the problem of constructing the nondegenerative ML-sequences is solved by giving a criterion for nondegenerative primitive polynomials. In the second part, based on the constructions [1, 6, 7] of some classes of injective mappings which compress ML-sequences over rings to binary sequences, some new classes of the injective compression mappings are proposed and proved.
Keywords: nondegenerate ML-sequence, quasi-period, injective compression mapping

1 Introduction

The maximal length sequences of elements in the integral residue ring $Z/(2^e)$ (ML-sequences over $Z/(2^e)$), whose definition will be recalled in the next section, and the binary sequences derived from ML-sequences are proposed and studied in [1-9]. The research shows that the binary sequences derived from ML-sequences may provide a good source of pseudorandom sequences and have a potential perspective in cryptographic applications.

The integral residue ring $Z/(2^e)$ is the set of 2^e integral residue classes $\{i \pmod{2^e}) | 0 \leq i < 2^e\}$, the class $i \pmod{2^e}$ will be written simply as i or any integer of the form $i + k2^e$ with k being an integer. Any element b belonging to $Z/(2^e)$ has a binary decomposition as $b = \sum_{i=0}^{e-1} b_i 2^i, b_i \in \{0,1\}$, where b_i is called the ith level bit of b, and b_{e-1} the highest level (or the most significant bit) bit of b. If a_t is an element in $Z/(2^e)$ with the binary decomposition $a_t = \sum_{i=0}^{e-1} a_{t,i} 2^i$, then the sequence $\alpha = \{a_t\}_{t=0}^{\infty}$ has a binary decomposition

*This work was supported by Chinese Natural Science Foundation (69773015 and 19771088).

K. Ohta and D. Pei (Eds.): ASIACRYPT'98, LNCS 1514, pp. 315-326, 1998.
© Springer-Verlag Berlin Heidelberg 1998

$\alpha = \sum_{i=0}^{e-1} \alpha_i 2^i$, where $\alpha_i = \{a_{t,i}\}_{t=0}^{\infty}$ is a binary sequence called the ith level component of α.

The highest level component sequence of a ML-sequence over $Z/(2^e)$ is the most naturally derived binary sequences. More binary sequences can be derived from a ML-sequence over $Z/(2^e)$ by mixing the bits at its highest level with the bits at the lower levels. This can provide a convenient way of generating pseudorandom binary sequences on computers when e is chosen as the processor word length. It is shown that the derived binary sequences have guaranteed large periods [5] and guaranteed large lower bound of linear complexities [4]. It is also shown that the distributions of the elements 0 and 1 of the derived binary sequences are close to be balanced [8, 9, 10]. In addition to these, it is proved [1, 6, 7] that the mapping which compresses the ML-sequences over $Z/(2^e)$ to its highest level component sequences is injective, and that a large class of mappings which compress the ML-sequences over $Z/(2^e)$ to the binary sequences by mixing the highest level component sequences with the lower level ones are also injective. The injectiveness of these compression mappings is desirable when the ML-sequences are used as a source of pseudorandom sequences, since in this case, different initial states of a ML-sequence do lead to different pseudorandom sequences.

In this paper we keep studying the ML-sequences and the compression mappings, the contents are divided into two parts. In the first part, the work is started by noticing the phenomenon that a ML-sequence may degenerate in the sense that its quasi-period (which will be defined in section 2) is shorter than its period, and that the deganerative ML-sequences are undesirable in applications. So we study the problem how to construct nondegenerative ML-sequences. As results, it is shown (Theorem 3) that an ML-sequence degenerates if and only if the corresponding primitive polynomial (*i.e.*, its minimal polynomial) degenerates in the same sense that its quasi-period (which will be defined in section 2) is shorter than its period, thus the problem constructing nondegenerate ML-sequences is reduced to the problem constructing nondegenerate primitive polynomials, and the latter is solved (Theorem 4) by giving a criterion for nondegenerative primitive polynomials. In the second part, based on the constructions [1, 6, 7] of some classes of injective compression mappings, some new classes of injective compression mappings are proposed and proved.

2   Constructions of Nondegenerative ML-Sequences

Before coming to the main topic, we recall some basic concepts and basic facts which we need. Let $\alpha = \{a_i\}_{i=0}^{\infty}$ be a sequence of elements in $Z/(2^e)$, obeying the linear recursion of the form $a_{i+n} = -\sum_{i=0}^{n-1} c_j a_{i+j} \pmod{2^e}, \forall i \geq 0$, with $(a_0, a_1, \cdots, a_{n-1})$ specifying the initial condition, and with c_j constants in $Z/(2^e)$. As usual, the monic polynomial $f(x) = x^n + \sum_{j=0}^{n-1} c_j x^j$ is called a characteristic polynomial of α, the characteristic polynomial with the least degree is called the minimal polynomial of α. The polynomial $f(x)$ has the binary decomposition $f(x) = \sum_{i=0}^{e-1} f_i(x)2^i$, where $f_i(x) = \sum_{i=0}^{n-1} c_{j,i}x^j$ and $c_j = \sum_{i=0}^{e-1} c_{j,i}2^i$ is the binary decomposition of c_j.

In this paper we always assume $c_0 \equiv 1 \pmod{2}$.

Definition: The *period* of $\alpha = \{a_i\}_{i=0}^{\infty}$, denoted by $per(\alpha)$, is defined to be the least positive integer t satisfying $a_{t+i} = a_i, \forall i \geq 0$.

Definition: The *period* of $f(x)$ over $Z/(2^e)$, denoted by $per(f(x))_{2^e}$, is defined to be the least positive integer t satisfying $x^t \equiv 1 \pmod{2^e, f(x)}$.

Both of $per(f(x))_{2^e}$ and $per(\alpha)$ are upper bounded by $2^{e-1}(2^n - 1)$ [5], and this upper bound is attainable.

Definition: α is called a ML-sequence of degree n if its period attains this upper bound $2^{e-1}(2^n - 1)$; and the polynomial $f(x)$ is called *primitive* over $Z/(2^e)$ if $per(f(x)_{2^e}$ attains this upper bound $2^{e-1}(2^n - 1)$.

If $f_0(x)$ is primitive over $Z/(2^e)$, then there exists a polynomial $r(x) \in Z/(2^e)[x]$ such that

$$x^{2^n-1} - 1 \equiv f_0(x)r(x) \pmod{2} \tag{1}$$

it is clear that $r(x) \pmod{2}$ is uniquely determined; and there exists $h(x)$ over $Z/(2^e)[x]$ such that

$$
\begin{aligned}
x^{2^n-1} &\equiv 1 + f_0(x)r(x) + 2h(x) \\
&\equiv 1 + (f_0(x) + \sum_{i=1}^{e-1} f_i(x)2^i)r(x) + 2(h(x) - r(x)\sum_{i=1}^{e-1} f_i(x)2^{i-1}) \\
&\equiv 1 + 2(h(x) - r(x)\sum_{i=1}^{e-1} f_i(x)2^{i-1}) \\
&\equiv 1 + 2h_f(x) \pmod{2^e, f(x)}
\end{aligned}
$$

where $h_f(x) = h(x) - r(x)\sum_{i=1}^{e-1} f_i(x)2^{i-1}$, hence

$$h_f(x) \equiv h(x) - r(x)f_1(x) \pmod{2, f_0(x)} \tag{2}$$

and

$$x^{2^n-1} \equiv 1 + 2h_f(x) \pmod{2^2, f(x)} \tag{3}$$

Taking $f_1(x) = 0$ in (3), we get

$$x^{2^n-1} \equiv 1 + 2h(x) \pmod{2^2, f_0(x)} \tag{4}$$

It is also clear that both $h(x) \pmod{2, f_0(x)}$ and $h_f(x) \pmod{2, f_0(x)}$ are uniquely determined.

We know the following theorem.

Theorem 1 *[2, 5]*

1. *Let $per(f(x))_2 = T$, then $per(f(x))_{2^e} = 2^k T$, where k is an integer with $0 \leq k < e$.*

2. α *is a ML-sequence of degree n if and only if* $f(x)$ *is primitive over* $Z/(2^e)$ *and* $\alpha_0 \neq 0$; *and in this case,* $f(x)$ *is the minimal polynomial of* α.

3. *The following conditions are equivalent:*

   (a) $f(x)$ *is primitive over* $Z/(2^e)$, *i.e.,* $per(f(x))_{2^e} = 2^{e-1}(2^n - 1)$.

   (b) $f_0(x)$ *is primitive over* $Z/(2)$, *and* $h_f(x) \neq 0$ (mod $2, f_0(x)$) *when* $e = 2$ *and* $h_f(x)(h_f(x) + 1) \neq 0$ (mod $2, f_0(x)$) *when* $e \geq 3$.

   (c) $f_0(x)$ *is primitive over* $Z/(2)$, *and* $f_1(x) \neq r(x)^{-1}h(x)$ (mod $2, f_0(x)$) *when* $e = 2$ *and*

$$f_1(x) \neq \begin{cases} r(x)^{-1}h(x) & (\text{mod } 2, f_0(x)) \\ r(x)^{-1}(h(x) + 1) & (\text{mod } 2, f_0(x)) \end{cases}$$

   when $e \geq 3$.

Lemma 1 *[2] Denote the formal derivative of* $f_0(x)$ *by* $f_0'(x)$, *we have*

1. $r(x)^{-1} \equiv xf_0'(x)$ (mod $2, f_0(x)$).

2. *Denote* $f_0(x) = \sum_{i \in S} x^i$ *where* S *is a subset of* $\{i | 0 \leq i \leq n\}$, *and denote* $\rho(x) = (\sum_{i,j \in S, i < j} x^{i+j})^{2^{n-1}}$ (mod $2, f_0(x)$), *then* $r(x)^{-1}h(x) \equiv \rho(x)$ (mod $2, f_0(x)$).

Remark 1 Based on Lemma 1, The equivalent conditions for primitive polynomials given in Theorem 1 can be easily checked.

Definition: The *quasi-period* of $\alpha = \{a_i\}_{i=0}^{\infty}$, denoted by $Qper(\alpha)$, is defined to be the least positive integer t satisfying $a_{t+i} = ca_i, \forall i \geq 0$, with $c \in Z/(2^e)$.

Definition: The *quasi-period* of $f(x)$ over $Z/(2^e)$, denoted by $Qper(f(x))_{2^e}$, is defined to be the least positive integer t satisfying $x^t \equiv c$ (mod $2^e, f(x)$) with $c \in Z/(2^e)$.

Definition: We say a ML-sequence α is *nondegenerative* if $Qper(\alpha) = per(\alpha)$; and say a primitive polynomial $f(x)$ is *nondegenerative* if $Qper(f(x))_{Z/(2^e)} = per(f(x))_{Z/(2^e)}$.

The following theorem is on the relation between the quasi-periods and the periods of the polynomials over $Z/(2^e)$.

Theorem 2 *Let* $per(f(x))_2 = T$, *and* $per(f(x))_{2^e} = 2^k T$, *then* $Qper(f(x))_{2^e} = 2^m T$ *for some non-negative integer* m *with* $m \leq k$.

Proof Let $Qper(f(x))_{2^e} = t$, first we claim $T|t$, hence $t = bT$ for some integer b. In fact, we have $x^t \equiv c$ (mod $2^e, f(x)$) for some $c \in Z/(2^e)$; since $(2^e, f(x)) \subseteq (2, f_0(x))$, so $x^t \equiv c$ (mod $2, f_0(x)$). We claim $c \equiv 1$ (mod 2), hence $T|t$; otherwise, we have $c \equiv 0$ (mod 2), then $1 \equiv x^{(2^k T)t} \equiv x^{t(2^k T)} \equiv 0$ (mod $2, f_0(x)$), a contradiction. Now consider the following set (where Z is the integer ring):

$$\mathcal{T} = \{t | x^t \equiv c \quad (\text{mod } 2^e, f(x)), t \in Z, c \in Z/(2^e)\} \tag{5}$$

It is clear that $\mathcal{T}$ is an ideal of Z containing $2^k T$, and $bT = Qper(f(x))_{2^e}$ is the positive generator of $\mathcal{T}$, so bT must be a factor of $2^k T$, thus $b = 2^m$ for an integer m with $m \leq k$. $\qquad\square$

It is easy to prove the following theorem.

Theorem 3 *If α is an ML-sequence of degree n, then $Qper(\alpha) = Qper(f(x))_{2^e}$, as a consequence, α is nondegenerative degenerate if and only if $f(x)$ is nondegenerative.*

Based on Theorem 1 and 2, the problem constructing nondegenerative ML-sequences is reduced to the problem constructing nondegenerative primitive polynomials. The latter can be solved by the following Theorem, which gives a criterion for nondegenerative primitive polynomials.

Theorem 4 *Let $f(x)$ be primitive over $Z/(2^e)$, and let $h(x)$ (mod $2, f_0(x)$) be the polynomial defined as (4). We have*

1. *When $e = 2$, then the following conditions are equivalent:*

    (a) *$f(x)$ is nondegenerative.*

    (b) *$h_f(x) \neq 1$ (mod $2, f_0(x)$).*

    (c) *$f_1(x) \neq r(x)^{-1}(1 + h(x))$ (mod $2, f_0(x)$).*

2. *When $e \geq 3$ and n is odd, then $f(x)$ is always nondegenerative.*

3. *When $e \geq 3$ and n is even, then the following conditions are equivalent:*

    (a) *$f(x)$ is nondegenerative.*

    (b) *$h_f(x)(1 + h_f(x)) \neq 1$ (mod $2, f_0(x)$).*

    (c)

    $$f_1(x) \neq \begin{cases} r(x)^{-1}(x^{(2^n-1)/3} + h(x)) & \text{(mod } 2, f_0(x)) \\ r(x)^{-1}(1 + x^{(2^n-1)/3} + h(x)) & \text{(mod } 2, f_0(x)) \end{cases}$$

Proof *Write $T = 2^n - 1$. Taking squares on the two sides of the equation (3), we get*

$$x^{2T} \equiv 1 + 2^2 h_f(x)(h_f(x) + 1) \quad \text{(mod } 2^3, f(x))$$

continueing this way we get

$$x^{2^{i-2}T} \equiv 1 + 2^{i-1} h_f(x)(h_f(x) + 1) \quad \text{(mod } 2^i, f(x)), \forall i \leq e$$

In particular, we get

$$x^{2^{e-2}T} \equiv 1 + 2^{e-1} h_f(x)(h_f(x) + 1) \quad \text{(mod } 2^e, f(x)) \qquad (6)$$

For $e = 2$, we have

$$Qper(f(x))_{2^e} < per(f(x))_{2^e}$$
$$\longleftrightarrow \quad Qper(f(x))_{2^2} = T \ (by \ Theorem \ 2)$$
$$\longleftrightarrow \quad c \equiv x^T \equiv 1 + 2h_f(x) \pmod{2^2, f(x)} \ (by \ (3))$$
$$\longleftrightarrow \quad 2h_f(x) \equiv 2b \pmod{2^2, f(x)}, b = 0 \text{ or } 1 \pmod 2$$
$$\longleftrightarrow \quad h_f(x) \equiv 1 \pmod{2, f_0(x)} \ (by \ the \ assumption \ and \ Theorem \ 1)$$
$$\longleftrightarrow \quad f_1(x) \equiv r(x)^{-1}(1 + h(x)) \pmod{2, f_0(x)} \ (by \ (2))$$

For $e \geq 3$, we get

$$Qper(f(x))_{2^e} < per(f(x))_{2^e}$$
$$\longleftrightarrow \quad Qper(f(x))_{2^e} | 2^{e-2}T$$
$$\longleftrightarrow \quad c \equiv x^{2^{e-2}T} \equiv 1 + 2^{e-1}h_f(x)(h_f(x) + 1) \pmod{2^e, f(x)} (by(6))$$
$$\longleftrightarrow \quad 2^{e-1}h_f(x)(h_f(x) + 1) \equiv 2^{e-1}b \pmod{2^e, f(x)}, b = 0 \text{ or } 1$$
$$\longleftrightarrow \quad h_f(x)(h_f(x) + 1) \equiv 1 \pmod{2, f_0(x)}$$
(by the assumption and Theorem 1).

If we identify $(Z/(2))[x]/(f_0(x))$ to the finite field $GF(2^n)$, then it is clear that the fact "$h_f(x)(h_f(x) + 1) \equiv 1 \pmod{2, f_0(x)}$" holds true if and only if $h_f(x)$ is a root of the irreducible polynomial $x^2 + x + 1$ over $Z/(2) = GF(2)$, i.e., one of the two elements of order 3. It is known that there exists such $h_f(x)$ if and only if n is even. Hence the item 2. is true. Now for the item 3., we know that the two roots of $x^2 + x + 1$ are $x^{T/3} \pmod{2, f_0(x)}$ and $1 + x^{T/3} \pmod{2, f_0(x)}$ (the two elements of order 3), so "$h_f(x)(h_f(x) + 1) \equiv 1 \pmod{2, f_0(x)}$" holds true if and only if $h_f(x) \equiv x^{T/3} \pmod{2, f_0(x)}$ or $1 + x^{T/3} \pmod{2, f_0(x)}$, which is further equivalent to the conditions shown in (3c)(by (2)). □

Remark 2 Based on Lemma 1, The equivalent conditions for nonprimitive primitive polynomials given in Theorem 4 can be easily checked.

In studying the injective compression mappings, the so-called strongly primitive polynomial is introduced [1], it is defined to be the primitive polynomial with $h_f(x) \neq 1 \pmod{2, f_0(x)}$ when $e = 2$, and to be the primitive polynomial with $h_f(x)(h_f(x) + 1) \neq 1 \pmod{2, f_0(x)}$ when $e \geq 3$. Now from Theorem 3 we get imediately

Corollary 1 $f(x)$ *is strongly primitive if and only if* $f(x)$ *is nondegenerative primitive, i.e.,* $Qper(f(x))_{2^e} = per(f(x))_{2^e}$.

3   Compressing Mappings on ML-Sequences

Let $f(x)$ be a primitive polynomial of degree n over $Z/(2^e)$, We denote $G(f(x))_{2^e}$ the set of all sequences over $Z/(2^e)$ generated by $f(x)$, $S(f(x))_{2^e} = \{\alpha \in G(f(x)) \mid \alpha_0 \neq 0\}$ the set of all ML-sequences over $Z/(2^e)$ generated by $f(x)$ and $GF(2)^\infty$ the set of all sequences over $GF(2)$. For $\alpha \in G(f(x))_{2^e}$, we denote α_i the ith level component of α. Set $T = 2^n - 1$, by (3), we have

$$x^{2^{k-1}T} - 1 = 2^k h_k(x) \pmod{f(x), 2^e}$$

where $k = 1, 2, \ldots, e-1$, $\deg h_k(x) < n$ and $h_k(x) \neq 0 \pmod 2$. In fact $h_1(x) = h_f(x) \pmod 2$, $h_2(x) = \ldots = h_{e-1}(x) = h_f(x)(h_f(x) + 1) \pmod{2, f(x)}$.

Let $\alpha = \{a_i\}_{i=0}^{\infty}$ and $\beta = \{b_i\}_{i=0}^{\infty}$ be two sequences over $Z/(2^e)$, define $\alpha + \beta = \{a_i + b_i\}_{i=0}^{\infty}$, $\alpha\beta = \{a_i b_i\}_{i=0}^{\infty}$ and $x\alpha = \{a_i\}_{i=0}^{\infty} = \{a_{i+1}\}_{i=0}^{\infty}$. For $g(x) = \sum_{j=0}^{n} c_j x^j$ over $Z/(2^e)$, then $g(x)\alpha = g(x)\{a_i\}_{i=0}^{\infty} = \{\sum_{j=0}^{n} c_j a_{j+i}\}_{i=0}^{\infty}$.

[1, 6, 7] propose the following injectiveness theorem.

Theorem 5 *[1, 6, 7] Let $f(x)$ be a primitive polynomial over $Z/(2^e)$, $\alpha, \beta \in G(f(x))_{2^e}$, then $\alpha = \beta$ if and only if $\alpha_{e-1} = \beta_{e-1}$. If $f(x)$ is strongly primitive over $Z/(2^e)$, $\varphi(x_0, x_1, \ldots, x_{e-1}) = x_{e-1} + cx_{e-2} + \eta(x_0, x_1, \ldots, x_{e-3})$ is a Boolean function of e variables, where $\eta(x_0, x_1, \ldots, x_{e-3})$ is a Boolean function of $e - 2$ variables, $c = 0$ or 1, then for $\alpha, \beta \in G(f(x))_{2^e}$, $\alpha = \beta$ if and only if $\varphi(\alpha_0, \alpha_1, \ldots, \alpha_{e-1}) = \varphi(\beta_0, \beta_1, \ldots, \beta_{e-1})$ over $GF(2)$.*

By theorem 5, the compression mapping x_{e-1} or $x_{e-1} + cx_{e-2} + \eta(x_0, \ldots, x_{e-3})$ on $G(f(x))_{2^e}$ is injective, that is, the binary sequence α_{e-1} or $\alpha_{e-1} + c\alpha_{e-2} + \eta(\alpha_0, \alpha_1, \ldots, \alpha_{e-3})$ can uniquely determine its original sequence α, in other words, α_{e-1} or $\alpha_{e-1} + c\alpha_{e-2} + \eta(\alpha_0, \alpha_1, \ldots, \alpha_{e-3})$ contains all information of α.

We study the injectiveness of general compression mappings in this section. Let $\varphi(x_0, \ldots, x_{e-1})$ be a Boolean function with e variables, if the mapping

$$\varphi : \begin{cases} G(f(x))_{2^e} \to GF(2)^{\infty} \\ \alpha = \alpha_0 + \alpha_1 2 + \ldots + \alpha_{e-1} 2^{e-1} \mapsto \varphi(\alpha_0, \ldots, \alpha_{e-1}) \end{cases}$$

is injective, then $\varphi(x_0, \ldots, x_{e-1})$ contains x_{e-1} clearly, i.e., $\varphi(x_0, \ldots, x_{e-2}, 0) \neq \varphi(x_0, \ldots, x_{e-2}, 1)$.

Definition: Let $B = \{x_0^{i_0} x_1^{i_1} \ldots x_{e-1}^{i_{e-1}} - i_k = 0 \text{ or } 1, k = 0, 1, \ldots, e-1\}$ be the set of all single terms of Boolean functions of e variables, define the order in B as follows:

$$x_0^{i_0} x_1^{i_1} \ldots x_{e-1}^{i_{e-1}} > x_0^{j_0} x_1^{j_1} \ldots x_{e-1}^{j_{e-1}}$$

provided that

$$i_0 + i_1 \cdot 2 + \ldots + i_{e-1} \cdot 2^{e-1} > j_0 + j_1 \cdot 2 + \ldots + j_{e-1} \cdot 2^{e-1}$$

Lemma 2 *[10] Let $f(x)$ be a strongly primitive polynomial of degree n over $Z/(2^e)$, $e \geq 3$, $\varphi(x_0, x_1, \ldots, x_{e-1})$ is a Boolean function of e variables and $\varphi(x_0, x_1, \ldots, x_{e-1}) \neq 0$ and 1. Let $x_{k_0} x_{k_1} \ldots x_{k_{t-1}}$ be the term of the maximal order in $\varphi(x_0, x_1, \ldots, x_{e-1})$ and the product $x_0 x_1$ of x_0 and x_1 is not a divisor of $x_{k_0} x_{k_1} \ldots x_{k_{t-1}}$, where $1 \leq t \leq e-1$, $0 \leq k_0 < k_1 < \ldots < k_{t-1} \leq e-1$. Then for $\alpha, \beta \in S(f(x))_{2^e}$, $\varphi(\alpha_0, \ldots, \alpha_{e-1}) = \varphi(\beta_0, \ldots, \beta_{e-1})$ implies $\alpha_0 = \beta_0$.*

Lemma 3 *[10] Let $f(x)$ be a primitive polynomial of degree n over $Z/(2^e)$, $e \geq 3$, $\alpha, \beta \in G(f(x))_{2^e}$ and $\alpha_0 = \beta_0$, then, for $3 \leq k \leq e-1$, over $GF(2)$*

$$(x^{2^{k-2}T} - 1)(\alpha_k + \beta_k) = (\alpha_{k-1} + \beta_{k-1})h_2(x)\alpha_0 + h_2(x)(\alpha_1 + \beta_1)$$

and

$$(x^T - 1)(\alpha_2 + \beta_2) = (\alpha_1 + \beta_1)h_1(x)\alpha_0 + h_1(x)(\alpha_1 + \beta_1)$$

Lemma 4 *[10] Let $f(x)$ be a primitive polynomial of degree n over $Z/(2^e)$, $e \geq 3$, $\alpha, \beta \in G(f(x))_{2^e}$ and $\alpha_0 = \beta_0 \neq 0$. If $(\alpha_1 + \beta_1)h_1(x)\alpha_0 h_2(x)\alpha_0 = h_1(x)(\alpha_1 + \beta_1)h_2(x)\alpha_0$ over $GF(2)$, then $\alpha_1 = \beta_1$*

Theorem 6 *Let $f(x)$ be a strongly primitive polynomial of degree n over $Z/(2^e)$, $e \geq 3$, $\varphi(x_0, \ldots, x_{e-1}) = x_{e-1} + \eta(x_0, \ldots, x_{e-2})$ is a Boolean function of e variables, for $\alpha, \beta \in S(f(x))_{2^e}$, if*

$$(\varphi(\alpha_0, \ldots, \alpha_{e-1}) + \varphi(\beta_0, \ldots, \beta_{e-1}))h_2(x)\alpha_0 = 0 \qquad (7)$$

then $\alpha = \beta$.

Proof *First we show $\alpha_0 = \beta_0$. Set $T = 2^n - 1$. $x^{2^{e-2}T} - 1$ acts on (7), then $(h_2(x)\alpha_0 + h_2(x)\beta_0)h_2(x)\alpha_0 = 0$ since $(x^{2^{e-2}T} - 1)\alpha_{e-1} = h_2(x)\alpha_0$, $(x^{2^{e-2}T} - 1)\beta_{e-1} = h_2(x)\beta_0$ and the periods of $\eta(\alpha_0, \ldots, \alpha_{e-2})$ and $\eta(\beta_0, \ldots, \beta_{e-2})$ divide $2^{e-2}T$. So $h_2(x)(\alpha_0 + \beta_0)h_2(x)\alpha_0 = 0$ which implies $\alpha_0 + \beta_0 = 0$ since $\alpha_0 + \beta_0$ is 0 or an ML-sequence. Thus $\alpha_0 = \beta_0$.*

If $e = 3$, then $\varphi(\alpha_0, \alpha_1, \alpha_2) + \varphi(\beta_0, \beta_1, \beta_2) = \alpha_2 + \beta_2 + \eta(\alpha_0, \alpha_1) + \eta(\beta_0, \beta_1)$. The period of $\alpha_1 + \beta_1$ divides T since $\alpha_0 = \beta_0$. So the period of $\eta(\alpha_0, \alpha_1) + \eta(\beta_0, \beta_1)$ divides T. Thus the period of $(\eta(\alpha_0, \alpha_1) + \eta(\beta_0, \beta_1))h_2(x)\alpha_0$ divides T. $x^T - 1$ acts on

$$(\alpha_2 + \beta_2 + \eta(\alpha_0, \alpha_1) + \eta(\beta_0, \beta_1))h_2(x)\alpha_0 = 0 \qquad (8)$$

then $0 = (x^T - 1)((\alpha_2 + \beta_2)h_2(x)\alpha_0) = (x^T - 1)(\alpha_2 + \beta_2)h_2(x)\alpha_0$. And by lemma 3, we have

$$(\alpha_1 + \beta_1)h_1(x)\alpha_0 h_2(x)\alpha_0 = h_1(x)(\alpha_1 + \beta_1)h_2(x)\alpha_0$$

Thus $\alpha_1 = \beta_1$ by lemma 4. So $(\alpha_2 + \beta_2)h_2(x)\alpha_0 = 0$ by (8). $\alpha_2 + \beta_2$ is 0 or an ML-sequence since $\alpha_1 = \beta_1$ and $\alpha_0 = \beta_0$. Therefore $\alpha_2 = \beta_2$ because the product of two ML-sequences over $GF(2)$ is not 0.

If $e > 3$, set

$$\begin{aligned} \eta_{e-2}(x_0, \ldots, x_{e-2}) &= \eta(x_0, \ldots, x_{e-2}) \\ &= x_{e-2}\eta_{e-3}(x_0, \ldots, x_{e-3}) + \mu_{e-3}(x_0, \ldots, x_{e-3}) \end{aligned}$$

and in general, we set

$$\eta_k(x_0, \ldots, x_k) = x_k \eta_{k-1}(x_0, \ldots, x_{k-1}) + \mu_{k-1}(x_0, \ldots, x_{k-1})$$

$k = e - 2, e - 3, \ldots, 2$. $x^{2^{e-3}T} - 1$ acts on (7), we have

$$\begin{aligned} (x^{2^{e-3}T} - 1)(\alpha_{e-1} + \beta_{e-1} + \alpha_{e-2}\eta_{e-3}(\alpha_0, \ldots, \alpha_{e-3}) \\ + \beta_{e-2}\eta_{e-3}(\beta_0, \ldots, \beta_{e-3}))h_2(x)\alpha_0 = 0 \end{aligned}$$

that is

$$(x^{2^{e-3}T} - 1)(\alpha_{e-1} + \beta_{e-1} + \eta_{e-3}(\alpha_0, \ldots, \alpha_{e-3}) + \eta_{e-3}(\beta_0, \ldots, \beta_{e-3}))h_2(x)\alpha_0 = 0$$

By lemma 3,

$$((\alpha_{e-2} + \beta_{e-2})h_2(x)\alpha_0 + h_2(x)(\alpha_1 + \beta_1)$$
$$+ \quad \eta_{e-3}(\alpha_0, \ldots, \alpha_{e-3}) + \eta_{e-3}(\beta_0, \ldots, \beta_{e-3}))h_2(x)\alpha_0 = 0$$

that is

$$((\alpha_{e-2} + \beta_{e-2} + \eta_{e-3}(\alpha_0, \ldots, \alpha_{e-3}) + \eta_{e-3}(\beta_0, \ldots, \beta_{e-3}))h_2(x)\alpha_0$$
$$= \quad h_2(x)(\alpha_1 + \beta_1)h_2(x)\alpha_0 \tag{9}$$

If $e > 4$, $x^{2^{e-4}T} - 1$ acts on (9) continuously, and so on, then we get

$$((\alpha_k + \beta_k + \eta_{k-1}(\alpha_0, \ldots, \alpha_{k-1}) + \eta_{k-1}(\beta_0, \ldots, \beta_{k-1}))h_2(x)\alpha_0$$
$$= \quad h_2(x)(\alpha_1 + \beta_1)h_2(x)\alpha_0 \tag{10}$$

where $k = e - 2, e - 3, \ldots, 2$. Finally, $x^T - 1$ acts on

$$((\alpha_2 + \beta_2 + \eta_1(\alpha_0, \alpha_1) + \eta_1(\beta_0, \beta_1))h_2(x)\alpha_0 = h_2(x)(\alpha_1 + \beta_1)h_2(x)\alpha_0$$

and we get $(\alpha_1 + \beta_1)h_1(x)\alpha_0 h_2(x)\alpha_0 = h_1(x)(\alpha_1 + \beta_1)h_2(x)\alpha_0$. So $\alpha_1 = \beta_1$ by lemma 4 and $\alpha_k = \beta_k$ by (10), $k = 2, 3, \ldots .e - 2$. Lastly, $\alpha_{e-1} = \beta_{e-1}$ by (7). Therefore $\alpha = \beta$. $\square$

Corollary 2 *Let $f(x)$ be a strongly primitive polynomial of degree n over $Z/(2^e)$, $e \geq 3$, $\varphi(x_0, \ldots, x_{e-1}) = x_{e-1} + \eta(x_0, \ldots, x_{e-2})$ is a Boolean function of e variables, then for $\alpha, \beta \in S(f(x))_{2^e}, \alpha = \beta$ if and only if $\varphi(\alpha_0, \ldots, \alpha_{e-1}) = \varphi(\beta_0, \ldots, \beta_{e-1})$*

Theorem 7 *Let $f(x)$ be a strongly primitive polynomial of degree n over $Z/(2^e)$, $e \geq 3$, $\varphi(x_0, x_1, \ldots, x_{e-1})$ is a Boolean function of e variables containing x_{e-1}, and $x_{k_0}x_{k_1} \ldots x_{k_{t-1}}$ is the term of the maximal order in $\varphi(x_0, x_1, \ldots, x_{e-1})$. If $x_{k_0}x_{k_1} \ldots x_{k_{t-1}}$ is not divided by x_0 and x_1, i.e. $k_0 \geq 2$, then the compression mapping*

$$\varphi : \left\{ \begin{array}{c} S(f(x))_{2^e} \rightarrow GF(2)^\infty \\ \alpha = \alpha_0 + \alpha_1 2 + \ldots + \alpha_{e-1}2^{e-1} \mapsto \varphi(\alpha_0, \ldots, \alpha_{e-1}) \end{array} \right.$$

is injective, i.e., for $\alpha, \beta \in S(f(x))_{2^e}$, then $\alpha = \beta$ if and only if $\varphi(\alpha_0, \ldots, \alpha_{e-1}) = \varphi(\beta_0, \ldots, \beta_{e-1})$.
Proof *If $t = 1$, the result follows immediately from corollary 2. Assume $t > 1$ in the following.*

Let $\alpha, \beta \in S(f(x))_{2^e}$ and $\varphi(\alpha_0, \ldots, \alpha_{e-1}) = \varphi(\beta_0, \ldots, \beta_{e-1})$, then $\alpha_0 = \beta_0$ by lemma 2.

$\varphi(x_0, x_1, \ldots, x_{e-1})$ contains x_{e-1}, that is, $k_{t-1} = e - 1$, so let

$$\varphi(x_0, \ldots, x_{e-1}) = x_{e-1}\eta(x_0, \ldots, x_{e-2}) + \lambda(x_0, \ldots, x_{e-2}) \tag{11}$$

where $\eta(x_0, \ldots, x_{e-2}) \neq 0$. *The term of maximal order in* $\eta(x_0, \ldots, x_{e-2})$ *is* $x_{k_0} x_{k_1} \ldots x_{k_{t-2}}$. *Thus we set* $\eta_{k_{t-2}}(x_0, \ldots, x_{k_{t-2}}) = \eta(x_0, \ldots, x_{e-2})$ *and*

$$\eta_{k_{t-2}}(x_0, \ldots, x_{k_{t-2}}) = x_{k_{t-2}} \eta_{k_{t-3}}(x_0, \ldots, x_{k_{t-3}}) + \mu_{k_{t-2}-1}(x_0, \ldots, x_{k_{t-2}-1})$$

In general, we set

$$\eta_{k_s}(x_0, \ldots, x_{k_s}) = x_{k_s} \eta_{k_{s-1}}(x_0, \ldots, x_{k_{s-1}}) + \mu_{k_s-1}(x_0, \ldots, x_{k_s-1}) \tag{12}$$

where $s = t-2, t-1, \ldots, 2, 1$, *and*

$$\eta_{k_0}(x_0, \ldots, x_{k_0}) = x_{k_0} + \mu_{k_0-1}(x_0, \ldots, x_{k_0-1}) \tag{13}$$

Set $g_i(x) = \prod_k (x^{2^{k-1}T} - 1)$, *where* k *takes over* $k_i, k_{i+1}, \ldots, k_{t-1}$ *and* $i = 1, 2, \ldots, t-1$. $g_1(x)$ *acts on* $\varphi(\alpha_0, \ldots, \alpha_{e-1}) = \varphi(\beta_0, \ldots, \beta_{e-1})$, *then, by (11), (12) and (13), we get*

$$(\alpha_{k_0} + \beta_{k_0} + \mu_{k_0-1}(\alpha_0, \ldots, \alpha_{k_0-1}) + \mu_{k_0-1}(\beta_0, \ldots, \beta_{k_0-1}))h_2(x)\alpha_0 = 0$$

So $\alpha = \beta \pmod{2^{k_0+1}}$ *by theorem 6.*
   (i) If $t = 2$, *then*

$$\alpha_{e-1}\eta_{k_0}(\alpha_0, \ldots, \alpha_{k_0}) + \beta_{e-1}\eta_{k_0}(\beta_0, \ldots, \beta_{k_0})$$
$$+ \quad \lambda(\alpha_0, \ldots, \alpha_{e-2}) + \lambda(\beta_0, \ldots, \beta_{e-2}) = 0$$

that is

$$(\alpha_{e-1} + \beta_{e-1})\eta_{k_0}(\alpha_0, \ldots, \alpha_{k_0}) + \lambda(\alpha_0, \ldots, \alpha_{e-2}) + \lambda(\beta_0, \ldots, \beta_{e-2}) = 0 \tag{14}$$

By lemma 3

$$\begin{aligned}(x^{2^{e-3}T} - 1)(\alpha_{e-1} + \beta_{e-1}) &= (\alpha_{e-2} + \beta_{e-2})h_2(x)\alpha_0 + h_2(x)(\alpha_1 + \beta_1)\\ &= (\alpha_{e-2} + \beta_{e-2})h_2(x)\alpha_0\end{aligned}$$

$x^{2^{e-3}T} - 1$ *acts on (14) if* $e - 3 > k_0$, *then by the period of* $\eta_{k_0}(\alpha_0, \ldots, \alpha_{k_0})$ *dividing* $2^{e-3}T$,

$$(\alpha_{e-2} + \beta_{e-2})h_2(x)\alpha_0\eta_{k_0}(\alpha_0, \ldots, \alpha_{k_0})$$
$$+ \quad (\lambda_{e-3}(\alpha_0, \ldots, \alpha_{e-3}) + \lambda_{e-3}(\beta_0, \ldots, \beta_{e-3}))h_2(x) = 0$$

that is

$$\begin{aligned}((\alpha_{e-2} + \beta_{e-2})\eta_{k_0}(\alpha_0, \ldots, \alpha_{k_0})\\ + \quad \lambda_{e-3}(\alpha_0, \ldots, \alpha_{e-3}) + \lambda_{e-3}(\beta_0, \ldots, \beta_{e-3}))h_2(x) = 0\end{aligned} \tag{15}$$

where $\lambda_{e-3}(x_0, \ldots, x_{e-3})$ *is determined by*

$$\begin{aligned}\lambda_{e-2}(x_0, \ldots, x_{e-2}) &= \lambda(x_0, \ldots, x_{e-2})\\ &= x_{e-2}\lambda_{e-3}(x_0, \ldots, x_{e-3}) + \sigma_{e-3}(x_0, \ldots, x_{e-2})\end{aligned}$$

$x^{2^{e-4}} - 1$ *acts on (15) continuously if* $e - 4 \geq k_0$. *In general we have*

$$((\alpha_k + \beta_k)\eta_{k_0}(\alpha_0, \ldots, \alpha_{k_0}) + \lambda_{k-1}(\alpha_0, \ldots, \alpha_{k-1}) + \lambda_{k-1}(\beta_0, \ldots, \beta_{k-1}))h_2(x) = \mathbf{0} \tag{16}$$

where $k = e - 2, \ldots, k_0 + 2, k_0 + 1$. $\lambda_{k_0}(\alpha_0, \ldots, \alpha_{k_0}) = \lambda_{k_0}(\beta_0, \ldots, \beta_{k_0})$ *since* $\alpha = \beta \pmod{2^{k_0+1}}$.

By the case $k = k_0 + 1$ *in (16), we have*

$$(\alpha_{k_0+1} + \beta_{k_0+1})\lambda_{k_0}(\alpha_0, \ldots, \alpha_{k_0})h_2(x)\alpha_0 = \mathbf{0} \tag{17}$$

Since $(\alpha_{k_0+1} + \beta_{k_0+1})$ *is* $\mathbf{0}$ *or an ML-sequence over* $GF(2)$ *and* $k_0 \geq 2$, *if* $x^{2^{k-1}T} - 1$ *acts on (17), where* $k = k_0$, *then*

$$[(x^{2^{k-1}T} - 1)\eta_{k_0}(\alpha_0, \ldots, \alpha_{k_0})](\alpha_{k_0+1} + \beta_{k_0+1})h_2(x)\alpha_0 = \mathbf{0} \tag{18}$$

By $\eta_{k_0}(\alpha_0, \ldots, \alpha_{k_0}) = x_{k_0} + \mu_{k_0-1}(\alpha_0, \ldots, \alpha_{k_0-1})$, *(18) implies*

$$(\alpha_{k_0+1} + \beta_{k_0+1})h_2(x)\alpha_0 = \mathbf{0}$$

So $\alpha_{k_0+1} = \beta_{k_0+1}$. *And by (16), we obtain* $\alpha_k = \beta_k$, $k = k_0 + 1, \ldots, e - 2$. *Finally,* $\alpha_{e-1} = \beta_{e-1}$ *by (14).*

  (ii) If $t = 3$, $g_2(x)$ *acts on* $\varphi(\alpha_0, \ldots, \alpha_{e-1}) = \varphi(\beta_0, \ldots, \beta_{e-1})$, *then*

$$(\alpha_{k_1}\eta_{k_0}(\alpha_0, \ldots, \alpha_{k_0}) + \beta_{k_1}\eta_{k_0}(\beta_0, \ldots, \beta_{k_0}))h_2(x)\alpha_0 = \mathbf{0}$$

that is

$$(\alpha_{k_1} + \beta_{k_1})\eta_{k_0}(\alpha_0, \ldots, \alpha_{k_0})h_2(x)\alpha_0 = \mathbf{0} \tag{19}$$

As in case (i), $r_k(x) = \prod_{i=k}^{k_1-1}(x^{2^{i-1}T} - 1)$ *acts on (19), then we obtain*

$$(\alpha_k + \beta_k)\eta_{k_0}(\alpha_0, \ldots, \alpha_{k_0})h_2(x)\alpha_0 = \mathbf{0} \tag{20}$$

$k = k_1 - 1, \ldots, k_0 + 2, k_0 + 1$. *So* $(\alpha_{k_0+1} + \beta_{k_0+1})\eta_{k_0}(\alpha_0, \ldots, \alpha_{k_0})h_2(x)\alpha_0 = \mathbf{0}$. *By the process of proof in (i), we have* $\alpha_{k_0+1} = \beta_{k_0+1}$. *Thus* $\alpha_j = \beta_j, j = k_0 + 2, \ldots, k_1$, *by (19) and (20).*

  Finally, as $r_k(x)$ *acts on (19),* $s_k(x) = \prod_{i=k}^{e-2}(x^{2^{i-1}T} - 1)$ *acts on,*

$$(\alpha_{e-1} + \beta_{e-1})\eta_{k_1}(\alpha_0, \ldots, \alpha_{k_1}) + \lambda(\alpha_0, \ldots, \alpha_{e-2}) + \lambda(\beta_0, \ldots, \beta_{e-2}) = \mathbf{0}$$

Similarly, we get $\alpha_j = \beta_j, j = k_1 + 1, \ldots, e - 1$. *Therefore* $\alpha = \beta$.   □

References

[1] M.Q.Huang, Analysis and Cryptologic Evaluation of Primitive Sequences over an Integer Residue Ring, Doctoral Dissertation of Graduate School of USTC, Academia Sinica. 1988.

[2] Z.D.Dai, M.Q.Huang, A Criterion for Primitiveness of Polynomials over $Z/(2^d)$, Chinese Science Bulletin, Vol.36,No.11,June 1991.pp.892-895.

[3] Z.D.Dai and M.Q.Huang, Linear Complexity and the Minimal Polynomials of Linear Recurring Sequences Over $Z/(m)$, System Science and Mathematical Science, Vol.4,No.1,Feb.1991. pp.51-54.

[4] Z.D.Dai, Beth T., Gollman D, Lower Bounds for the Linear Complexity of Sequences over Residue Rings, Advances in Cryptology-EUROCRYPT'90, Spring-Verlag LNCS 473 (1991), Editor: I.B. Damgard. pp.189-195.

[5] Z.D.Dai, Binary Sequences Derived from ML-Sequences over Rings I:Periods and Minimal Polynomials, J. Cryptology, Vol 5, No4, 1992, pp.193-207.

[6] M.Q.Huang, Z.D.Dai, Projective Maps of Linear Recurring Sequences with Maximal p-adic Periods, Fibonacci Quart 30(1992), No.2, pp.139-143.

[7] K.C.Zeng, Z.D.Dai and M.Q.Huang, Injectiveness of Mappings from Ring Sequences to Their Sequences of Significant Bits, Symposium on Problems of Cryptology, State Key Laboratory of Information Security, Beijing, China, 1995,pp.132-141.

[8] W.F.Qi, J.J.Zhou, Distribution of 0 and 1 in Highst Level of Primitive Sequences over $Z/(2^e)$, Science in China, Series A, 40(6),1997,606-611.

[9] W.F.Qi, J.J.Zhou, Distribution of 0 and 1 in Highst Level of Primitive Sequences over $Z/(2^e)$ (II), Chinese Science Bulletin, 43(8),1998, 633-635.

[10] W.F.Qi, Compressing Maps of Primitive Sequences over $Z/(2^e)$ and Analysis of Their Derivative Sequences, Doctoral Dissertation of ZhengZhou Information Engineering Institute, 1997.

Analysis Methods for (Alleged) RC4

Lars R. Knudsen[1], Willi Meier[2], Bart Preneel[3*], Vincent Rijmen[3], and Sven Verdoolaege[3]

[1] Department of Informatics, University of Bergen, N-5020 Bergen
[2] HTL Brugg-Windisch, CH-5210 Windisch
[3] SISTA/COSIC Lab, Dept. ESAT, K.U.Leuven, K. Mercierlaan 94, B-3001 Leuven

Abstract. The security of the alleged RC4 stream cipher and some variants is investigated. Cryptanalytic algorithms are developed for a known plaintext attack where only a small segment of plaintext is assumed to be known. The analysis methods reveal intrinsic properties of alleged RC4 which are independent of the key scheduling and the key size. The complexity of one of the attacks is estimated to be less than the time of searching through the square root of all possible initial states. However, this still poses no threat to alleged RC4 in practical applications.

Keywords. Cryptanalysis. Stream Cipher. RC4.

1   Introduction

Many key stream generators proposed in the literature consist of a number of possibly clocked linear feedback shift registers (LFSRs) that are combined by a function with or without memory. LFSR-based generators are often hardware oriented and for a variety of them it is known how to achieve desired cryptographic properties [3]. For software implementation, a few key stream generators have been designed which are not based on shift registers. One of these generators, known as (alleged) RC4, has been publicized and described in [1]. RC4 is widely used in commercial products and standards (one example is the Secure Sockets Layer standard SSL 3.0).

RC4 takes an interesting design approach which is quite different from that of LFSR-based stream ciphers. This implies that many of the analysis methods known for such ciphers cannot be applied. The internal state of RC4 consists of a table of 2^n n-bit words and two n-bit pointers, where n is a parameter (for the nominal version, $n = 8$). The table varies slowly in time under the control of itself. As discussed by Golić in [2], for such a generator a few general statistical properties of the key stream sequence can be measured by standard statistical tests, but these criteria are hard to establish theoretically. A noticeable exception are the results in [2], which show a (slight) statistical deviation of the output stream of RC4. These results are mainly of theoretical interest, as a large amount

---

* F.W.O. postdoctoral researcher, sponsored by the Fund for Scientific Research, Flanders (Belgium).

K. Ohta and D. Pei (Eds.): ASIACRYPT'98, LNCS 1514, pp. 327–341, 1998.

of output stream is necessary before this deviation can be detected. It remains an open problem whether these results can be used to cryptanalyze RC4.

The aim of this paper is to derive some cryptanalytic algorithms that find the correct initial state of the RC4 stream cipher using only a small segment of output stream, and to give precise estimates for the complexity of the attacks where possible. The cryptanalytic algorithms in this paper exploit the combinatorial nature of RC4 and allow to find the initial table, i.e., the state at time $t = 0$. Knowledge of this table enables to compute the complete output sequence without knowing the secret key.

If the first portion of about 2^n output words are known, our basic algorithm allows to find the initial table in a reduced search with complexity much lower than exhaustive search over all possible initial states. A careful analysis, which is confirmed by numerous experiments for different values of the word length n, shows that the complexity of the best attack is lower than the square root of all possible initial states. Our algorithms become infeasible for $n > 5$ and thus pose no threat to RC4 with $n = 8$ as used in practice. However, our attacks give new insight into the design principles of RC4 and the estimates of the complexity should give some realistic parameters for the security of RC4. Our results are intrinsic to the design principles of RC4 and are independent of the key scheduling and the size of the key.

This paper is organized as follows. In Sect. 2 we give a description of RC4. In Sect. 3 we discuss an attack on a simplified version of RC4. Section 4 describes attacks on the full RC4, and Sect. 5 presents a possible optimization. We conclude in Sect. 6.

2   Description of RC4

We follow the description of RC4 as given in [1,2]. RC4 is a family of algorithms indexed by a positive integer n (in practice $n = 8$). The internal state of RC4 at time t consists of a permutation table $S_t = (S_t[l])_{l=0}^{2^n-1}$ of 2^n n-bit words and of two pointer n-bit words i_t and j_t. Thus the internal memory size is $M = \log(2^n!) + 2n$, where log denotes logarithm to the base 2. The pointers i_0 and j_0 are initialized to zero. Let Z_t denote the output n-bit word of RC4 at time t. Then the next-state and output functions of RC4 for every $t \geq 1$ are defined by

$$i_t = i_{t-1} + 1 \tag{1}$$
$$j_t = j_{t-1} + S_{t-1}[i_t] \tag{2}$$
$$S_t[i_t] = S_{t-1}[j_t], \quad S_t[j_t] = S_{t-1}[i_t] \tag{3}$$
$$Z_t = S_t[S_t[i_t] + S_t[j_t]] \tag{4}$$

where all additions are modulo 2^n. In one update, all the words in the table except the swapped ones remain the same (and swapping is only effective if $i_t \neq j_t$). The output n-bit word sequence is $Z = (Z_t)_{t=1}^{\infty}$. Every word Z_t is XORed with a piece of plaintext of length n bits to produce ciphertext, or

XORed with ciphertext to produce plaintext. The initial table S_0 is derived from the secret key. The details of this derivation are not important for our attacks.

3   Attacking Simplified RC4

The swap operation in (3) makes the recovery of the table S very difficult. In this section we develop an attack on simplified versions of RC4, where the swap operation occurs less often.

3.1   No Swap Operation

RC4 without the swap operation (3) is useless as a key stream generator. The following theorem illustrates this.

Theorem 1. *If the swap operation in the state update is omitted, the key stream of RC4 becomes cyclic with a period of 2^{n+1}.*

Proof: Equation (4) gives: $Z_{t+2^n} = S[S[i_{t+2^n}] + S[j_{t+2^n}]]$. Because of the modular addition $i_{t+2^n} = i_t$. Since S is constant now, (2) can be applied repeatedly on j_{t+2^n}. We get: $Z_{t+2^n} = S[S[i_t] + S[j_t + \sum_{u=0}^{2^n-1} S[u]]]$. Because S is a permutation, we can evaluate the summation, and $Z_{t+2^n} = S[S[i_t] + S[j_t + 2^{n-1}]]$. In a completely analogous way, we can derive $Z_{t+2^{n+1}} = S[S[i_t] + S[j_t]] = Z_t$. ∎

The algorithm to recover S works as follows. Initially, we guess a small subset of the entries of S. We derive the other entries from the observed key stream and (4). If we get a contradiction at some point, we know that we guessed one of the initial values wrongly.

There are four possibly unknown variables in (4): $j_t, S[i_t], S[j_t]$ and $S^{-1}[Z_t]$. If all four variables are known and a contradiction arises, we guessed one of the initial values wrongly. If three variables are known, we can determine the fourth.

– If $S^{-1}[Z_t], j_t$ and $S[i_t]$ are known, we can determine $S[j_t]$ as follows:

$$S[j_t] = S^{-1}[Z_t] - S[i_t].\qquad(5)$$

($S^{-1}[Z_t]$ is known if the value Z_t is already filled in somewhere in S.)
– If $S[i_t], S[j_t]$ and thus also j_t are known, then

$$S[S[i_t] + S[j_t]] = Z_t.\qquad(6)$$

– If $S[i_t], S[j_t]$ and $S^{-1}[Z_t]$ are known, then

$$j_t = S^{-1}[S^{-1}[Z_t] - S[i_t]].\qquad(7)$$

– If $S^{-1}[Z_t], j_t$ and $S[j_t]$ are known, then

$$S[i_t] = S^{-1}[Z_t] - S[j_t].\qquad(8)$$

The initial value of j is known. If we guess the values of v entries at the beginning of S, we know the value of the j-pointer for the first v steps. In these steps we use (5) and (6) to determine new values of S. If we have not determined $S[v + 1]$ after v steps, we "lose" knowledge of the j-pointer. We discard the following Z_t-values until we can use (7) to recover the value of j. Once j is recovered we can use (5) and (6) again, but we can also work backwards and use (8) to determine more entries of S. If v is too small, we will lose the value of j too fast and we will not be able to recover the table in this way.

3.2   Reduced Swap Frequency

In this version of RC4 we swap two entries after every s iterations. We start by applying the same algorithm as above, until the first swap occurs. If we do not know the value of j at this moment, we do not know with what value $S_t[i_t]$ gets swapped. At this point we can only remove $S_t[i_t]$ from our (incomplete) table. If the unknown j actually points at a table entry that we have already filled in, this entry will change in the RC4 table, but not in our partial solution. In this way, errors are introduced in our S_t table. After a while we will observe contradictions; however, it is not possible to determine which element is responsible for the contradiction. A naive solution is to remove the three entries involved when we encounter a contradiction. However, in this way we will destroy more good values than we are able to produce, and we will end up with an empty table. For a good solution strategy it is important that the number of removed correct values is minimal. We have developed a number of heuristics to solve this problem; the details are omitted because of space restrictions. The resulting algorithm converges very fast.

If we increase the swap frequency $1/s$ towards 1, the algorithm needs a larger number of correctly guessed table entries before it can deduce the remainder of the table. Figure 1 shows the experimentally determined success probability as a function of the number of correctly guessed entries at the start, for swapping frequencies increasing from $1/128$ to $1/2$ (actual RC4 has swapping frequency 1). For a success ratio of 50% we need 40 correctly guessed entries at the start if the swapping frequency equals $1/128$. If the swapping frequency increases to $1/2$, we need about 240 correct entries. For a success ratio of 5%, we need 30, respectively 210 values. The complexity of this attack is proportional to the average number of trials required to guess the initial values correctly; e.g., there are approximately 2^{315} possible ways to assign 40 8-bit values of the permutation table.

4   Attacking the Full RC4

This section presents cryptanalytic attacks on RC4 which allow to find the initial table $S = S_0$, without guessing values initially. Instead, values are only guessed when they are needed. First the attacks are described and their efficiency is analyzed. Then some special cases are discussed and experimental results are presented.

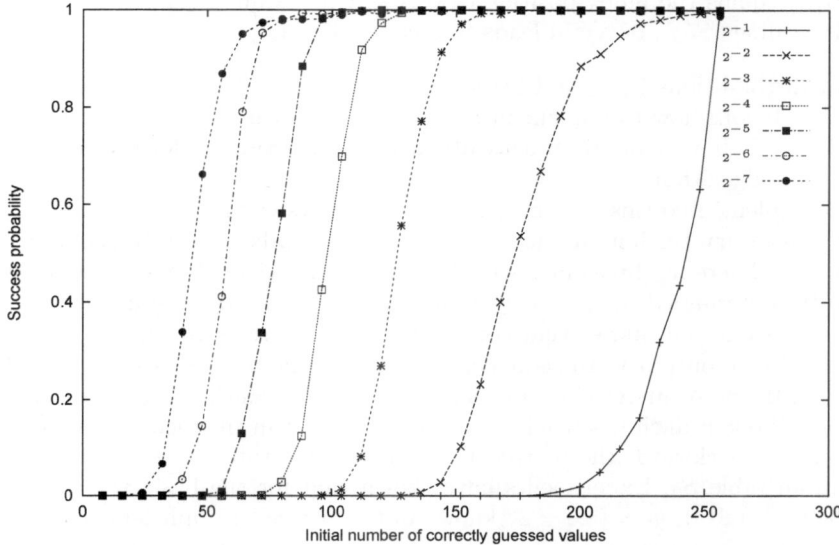

Fig. 1. Success ratio for various simplified versions of RC4 for which the swap frequency is reduced to $1/s$.

4.1 Description

The idea of the algorithm may informally be described as follows. For times $t = 1, 2, \ldots, m$, if $S_{t-1}[i_t]$ or $S_{t-1}[j_t]$ have not already been assigned values in a previous time, choose a value v for $S_{t-1}[i_t]$, $0 \leq v < 2^n$, compute j_t and then choose $S_{t-1}[j_t]$. This is in order to be able to follow up the next update of the RC4 algorithm, i.e., in order that steps (1) to (4) are defined. We proceed so that at each time t an output word $\bar{Z}_t$ is produced with the property that $\bar{Z}_t$ has the correct value $\bar{Z}_t = Z_t$. This imposes several restrictions on the possible choices for $S_{t-1}[i_t]$, $S_{t-1}[j_t]$:

i) As S is a permutation table, every new value $S_{t-1}[i_t]$ or $S_{t-1}[j_t]$ to be assigned has to be different from a value already chosen as a word in the table.

The next two conditions represent two alternatives and are specific consequences of the design of RC4.

ii) If the known output word Z_t differs from all words which have previously been fixed in the S table, the sum $i_s = S_t[i_t] + S_t[j_t]$ occurring in step 4 has to differ from all index positions which have already values assigned. If this is satisfied, set $S_t[i_s] = Z_t$. Otherwise we have a contradiction in our search.

iii) If Z_t is equal to a word previously assigned in the S table then $i_s = S_t[i_t] + S_t[j_t]$ equals the index position of this assigned value. This either uniquely determines $S_t[j_t]$ or again leads to a contradiction.

Although conditions i), ii) and iii) follow directly from the description of RC4, it is not obvious how to implement an efficient algorithm that exploits these restrictions and how to obtain practically meaningful estimates for the complexity of such an algorithm.

We implemented this attack by means of a recursive function $guess(t)$. In the most elementary version, at each parameter t one update following steps 1 to 4 is effected. Thereby, three entries in the S table are affected or suitably chosen, one entry determined by i_t, one by j_t and one by Z_t, so that the update at time t can be carried out and so that conditions i) to iii) are satisfied.

For a given output word sequence of length m the programs start by calling $guess(1)$. In the recursive calls for increasing t most branches end up by contradictions. If one branch has reached depth $t = size + 1$ in the recursive algorithm, we compute backwards the (correct) actual state to state $t = 0$, in order to get the initial table S_0. Experiments have shown that for the basic version of the attack as sketched, $m = size = 2^n$ known output words are sufficient to uniquely determine the correct state. Note that for RC4 with n-bit words, there are a total of $2^n!$ different initial states. Thus, the required number of output words m can be estimated as the smallest integer such that $2^{nm} > 2^n!$. Clearly, 2^n upper bounds m for any value of n. (For $n = 8$, $m \simeq 211$.)

We investigated several variants of the attack. In order to accelerate the attack in simulations, we pre-assigned the first few words in the S table at the beginning of the program execution. This has motivated a modification of the function $guess(t)$ which is based on the following observation: if $S_{t-1}[i_t]$ has a value assigned one can compute j_t according to step 2. Thus one can swap $S_{t-1}[i_t]$ and $S_{t-1}[j_t]$ even if $S_{t-1}[j_t]$ was not assigned a value before swapping. After swapping, $S_t[j_t]$ is assigned but $S_t[i_t]$ is not.

As a consequence, suppose $S_{t-1}[i_t]$ has a value assigned but $S_{t-1}[j_t]$ has not. Assume now that the value Z_t is different from all previously assigned values in the S table. Then instead of guessing the value of $S_{t-1}[j_t]$ one can check whether $S_{t-1}[i_{t+1}]$ has already been assigned a value and whether the value of Z_{t+1} equals a value previously assigned in the S table. Under this condition it may pay off not to check all possible values for $S_{t-1}[j_t]$ because a check can be done at time $t + 1$ without guessing any additional values. This variant has in experiments shown to be particularly attractive for parameter values $n = 7$ and 8. Moreover note that for this variant the known output segment has to be slightly longer than for the basic attack.

There are even further refinements of the variant which we will not describe here. In another direction, computer experiments have lead to the following observation: suppose two initial tables S_0 and $\bar{S}_0$ are given with the property that $S_0[i] = \bar{S}_0[i]$ for $i = 1, 2, \ldots, k$. Then for k sufficiently large, suitable segments of the corresponding output sequences Z and $\bar{Z}$ of the RC4 algorithm are correlated. This correlation is illustrated in Fig. 2. We have built this statistical property into our attack in order to make a preliminary test at a suitable time t whether a choice of values $S_0[i]$, $i = 1, 2, \ldots, t - 1$, is correct. It turned out that this in fact can lead to an acceleration of the attack but at the cost of a decreased success probability, as often a correct choice is excluded erroneously.

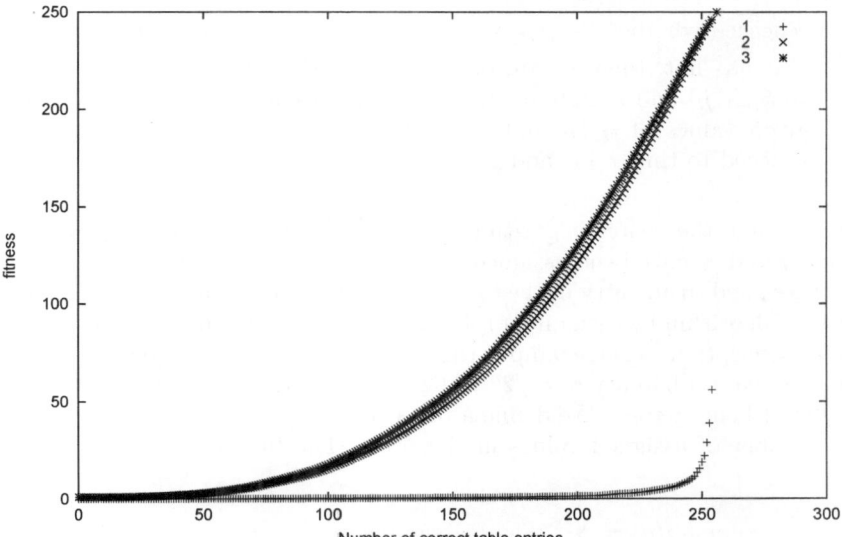

Fig. 2. Correlation between key streams as a function of the number of equal table entries. Three measures for the correlation are shown: (1) the number of equal outputs until the first difference occurs, (2) the number of equal outputs in the first 250 values and (3) the number of equal outputs in the first 250 values, added with a weighting function that emphasizes the first outputs of the row. It is clear that the last two functions are better measures.

4.2   Efficiency of the Attack

The complexity of the attacks is measured in terms of the total number of assignments made for all entries in the initial table. It is necessary at this point to explain some further details of our search algorithm. The algorithm uses recursive function calls with the time variable t as parameter. Assume we are at some given time t, and let a_t denote the number of entries in the initial table, which were assigned a value at time t.

1. It is checked whether $S_{t-1}[i_t]$ has been assigned a value:
   a) if it has, proceed to step 2.

b) if it has not, then assign, one after one, the $2^n - a_t$ remaining values to $S_{t-1}[i_t]$, increment a_t and go to 2.

2. It is checked whether Z_t has a value which has been used in an assignment:

a) if it has, we can calculate the expected value of $S_t[j_t]$ from (4) of the RC4 description. If this does not lead to a contradiction, proceed to time $t + 1$ and go to step 1.

b) if it has not, go to 3.

3. It is checked whether $S_{t-1}[j_t]$ has already been assigned a value:

a) if it has not, then assign, one after one, the $2^n - a_t$ remaining values to $S_{t-1}[j_t]$ and update a_t. Subsequently, it can be checked whether the given values of i_t, j_t and Z_t lead to a contradiction. If they do not, proceed to time $t + 1$ and go to step 1.

It follows that the search algorithm can be split into 8 cases, depending on whether i_t and j_t have been assigned a value or not and whether Z_t has a value already assigned to an entry in the table. It is possible to simulate the behavior of the search algorithm by assigning probabilities to the different cases in the above informal description. As an example, the case "$S_{t-1}[i_t]$ has been assigned a value" has an average probability of $a_t/2^n$ of being true and an average probability of $1 - a_t/2^n$ of being wrong. We define a function $complex(\cdot)$, which takes as input a, the number of assigned values in the table. The function has the following form:

$$complex(a) = \sum_{i=0}^{3} p_i \cdot \text{no-assignments}_i \cdot complex(a + i). \qquad (9)$$

Our approximation reduces the 8 above cases to 4 cases, each one with a recursive call of the function $complex$. The four recursive calls are explained as follows: p_i denotes the probability of the particular case, no-assignments$_i$ denotes the total number of assignments we do for $S_{t-1}[i_t]$ and $S_{t-1}[j_t]$.

By definition, $complex(255) = 1$ and $complex(a) = 0$ for all $a \geq 256$. Given the values for $complex(a+3)$, $complex(a+2)$, $complex(a+1)$ and expressions for p_i and no-assignments$_i$, (9) can be solved for $complex(a)$. In this way $complex(0)$ can be determined.

Solving the Recurrence: Instead of determining p_i and no-assignments$_i$ directly, we will rewrite (9). We define three new functions $c_1(\cdot), c_2(\cdot)$ and $c_3(\cdot)$, representing the complexity of each individual step in our algorithm. We start with the equation for $c_1(a)$. The first test of step 1 will succeed on average $a/2^n$ times. If it succeeds, we go to step 2 without assigning a value. If it does not succeed (probability $1 - a/2^n$), we will do for every possible value of $S_{t-1}[i_t]$ one assignment and call step 2. Thus we have:

$$c_1(a) = \frac{a}{2^n} c_2(a) + (1 - \frac{a}{2^n})(2^n - a)c_2(a + 1). \qquad (10)$$

In a similar way, we can derive the expressions for $c_2(a)$ and $c_3(a)$:

$$c_2(a) = \frac{a}{2^n}\left((1-\frac{a}{2^n})^2(1+c_1(a+1)) + \frac{1}{2^n}c_1(a)\right) + (1-\frac{a}{2^n})c_3(a) \quad (11)$$

$$c_3(a) = (1-\frac{a}{2^n})\left(f(a) + \frac{2a+1}{2^n}c_1(a+1) + (2^n-a)e(a)c_1(a+2)\right), \quad (12)$$

where $e(a) = (1-(a+1)/2^n)(1-1/(2^n-a))$ and $f(a) = (2^n-a)(1+e(a))+a/2^n$. Again we start with the known values $c_i(2^n)$ and work downwards. The maximal number of assignments in our algorithm is given by $complex(0) = c_1(0)$. The results of the calculation are presented in Table 2, where they are compared with some experimental results.

4.3   Special Streams

There are streams of output words for which our attack has an increased performance. Consider the above description of our algorithm. In step 2 of the algorithm we check whether Z_t has a value which has previously been used in an assignment. If this is the case we can calculate an expected value for the entry $S_t[j_t]$. This either leads to a contradiction or it gives an assignment of an additional entry in the (unknown) table. If this is not the case we try and assign values to $S_t[j_t]$ and proceed from there. Assume now that Z_t equals Z_{t+1}. Then in our algorithm at time $t+1$ the condition in step 2 is satisfied, since the value of Z_t was used in an assignment in a previous step without reaching a contradiction, since we assume we are at time $t+1$. Thus, the performance of the algorithm can be improved if many of the given words are equal. We have incorporated this in the above approximations, but we leave out the exact details. Table 1 lists the results of our tests for versions of RC4 with $n = 4, 5$. It follows that the performance of our algorithm for RC4 with $n = 5$ increases with more than a factor of two if the first two words of the given stream are equal, and that the improvement is a factor of about 2^{k-1} if the first k words are equal. Clearly, a similar phenomenon can be expected if the number of different values in the first k words of the stream is greater than 1, but small.

Table 1. Approximations of the complexities of the attack on RC4, when the first k words in the target stream are equal.

n	$k=1$	$k=2$	$k=3$	$k=4$	$k=5$	$\sqrt{2^n!}$
4	2^{21}	$2^{20.5}$	$2^{19.9}$	$2^{19.4}$	$2^{18.9}$	2^{22}
5	2^{53}	$2^{51.6}$	$2^{50.5}$	$2^{49.4}$	$2^{48.4}$	2^{58}

4.4   Experimental Results

The first interesting value for n is $n = 4$, where the number of entries in S_0 is 16 and the number of possible initial tables is $16! = 2.09 \cdot 10^{13} \approx 2^{44}$. It turns out that the basic algorithm for our attack always finds the correct initial table in a few seconds, which represents a considerable improvement over exhaustive search. It is interesting to compare our result for $n = 4$ with a result in [2]: the method developed in [2] needs about 2^{6n-8} output words of the RC4 stream cipher to detect a statistical deviation. This is about 2^{16} output words for RC4 with $n = 4$, whereas we need 16 or 17 output words and about 2^{20} computations to find the correct initial table.

As measure of complexity we take the total number of calls of the function $guess(t)$ that are necessary to find the initial table. For $n = 4$ the average number of function calls turns out to be about 2^{20}. For $n = 5$ the complexity of the attack is too high for the computing power we have available. Therefore, in simulations for $n \geq 5$ we accelerate the programs by giving the correct values of the first few entries of the S table. Experiments show that the amount of computing time can differ some orders of magnitude depending on the initial table to be found.

In Table 2 we give the results of our experiments for parameter values $n = 4, \ldots, 8$. Hereby k denotes the number of preassigned entries $S_0[i]$, $1 \leq i \leq k$. Complexity means the average number of calls of the function $guess(t)$ in the program with given parameter k in 1000 test cases. We should mention however, that the figures for the complexity are only rough estimates as the distribution for these numbers has a large variance. When the k preassigned entries have wrong values, the search terminates rather quickly with a contradiction in most cases. For $k > 0$ the total complexity is computed as the number N of all possible choices of the first k entries multiplied by the average complexity. Note that N is computed as $2^n!/(2^n - k)!$. It can be seen that our test results for the cases $n = 4$ and 5 correspond well to the estimated complexity given in Sect. 4.2. Furthermore, for $n = 5$, $k = 3$ one can apply a program variant using the statistical property as described in Sect. 4.1. It turns out that the complexity in this case is about 2^{30}, thus the total complexity is about 2^{45}. However the algorithm often terminates unsuccessfully. The average success rate may be below 50%. For comparison, in the last column of Table 2 the magnitude of square root of $2^n!$ is shown. It follows that the estimated total complexity is slightly below the square root of $2^n!$.

We already mentioned that our search algorithm works better if the first words of the output stream are equal. We close this section by listing the results for RC4 with $n = 4$ in Table 3 and leave it as an open question how large the improvement is for RC4 with $n > 4$ in these cases.

5   A Possible Improvement

In this section we explain a technique that can be used to improve the efficiency of the RC4 attack of Sect. 4.

5.1   Description

The basic principle of the technique is the following. The initial state of the permutation table S depends on the cipher key and is unknown. We assume that

Table 2. Complexities of attacks on n-bit RC4. One column gives estimates based on the analytical calculations of Sect. 4.2. Other values are based on extrapolations of experimental results on simplified versions (preassigning k values). It follows that the (total) complexities are close to $\sqrt{2^n!}$.

	calculated		experimental			
n	k	complexity	k	complexity	total complexity	$\sqrt{2^n!}$
3	0	2^8	0	2^8	2^8	2^8
4	0	2^{21}	0	2^{20}	2^{20}	2^{22}
5	0	2^{53}	7	2^{21}	2^{55}	2^{58}
6	0	2^{132}	20	2^{23}	2^{138}	2^{148}
7	0	2^{324}	45	2^{26}	2^{302}	2^{358}
8	0	2^{779}	100	2^{30}	2^{797}	2^{842}

Table 3. Complexities of the attack on RC4 with $n = 4$, when the first k words in the target stream are equal, averaged over 1000 tests.

n	$k = 1$	$k = 2$	$k = 3$	$k = 4$	$\sqrt{2^n!}$
4	$2^{20.5}$	$2^{19.5}$	$2^{18.4}$	$2^{17.6}$	2^{22}

all $2^n!$ possibilities are equally likely, or that the a priori probability distribution of S_0 is uniform. We observe the generated values Z_t and try to calculate an a posteriori probability distribution for S_0. The method can easily be extended to deal with a non-uniform a priori probability distribution.

We represent our information about the value of j and the state of S by means of probability distributions. We define the functions f_t as $f_t(a) = \Pr(j_t = a)$ and the array of functions g_t as $g_t[x](a) = \Pr(S_t[x] = a)$. Since we know that $j_0 = 0$, the function f_0 is 1 at the origin, and zero elsewhere. Also, because S is a permutation at all times, we know that for all values of t and for $a \in [0, 255]$: $\sum_{x=0}^{2^n-1} g_t[x](a) = 1$.

During the attack we observe the generated key stream $Z_t, t = 0, 1, \ldots$, and we try to extract information about the value of j and the state of S after iteration t, by using (4) and Bayes' rule. The extracted information is manifest in the functions f_t and $g_t[x]$: the closer these functions are to a delta-function, the less uncertainty we have about the values of j_t and $S_t[x]$.

In order to calculate the updated probability distributions, we have to take into account two effects: observation of Z_t, which gives us more information, or "narrows" the probability distributions, and the change of state for j and two elements of S, which tends to "flatten" the probability distributions. The derivation of the rules for updating the probability distributions is given in Appendix A. We assume that the different entries of S_t are independent from each other, except that there cannot be two equal values because S_t is a permutation. This assumption is only an approximation.

5.2   Implementation

The algorithm reads one word of the key stream and calculates the values for f_1 and $g_1[x]$. The complexity is determined by the determination of g_1: for each of the 2^n x-entries there are 2^n probabilities to calculate and every probability is the sum of $(2^n)^3$ terms (cf. (24)). This gives a total complexity of 2^{5n} steps for each value Z_t that is analyzed. In theory, we need less than 2^n values in order to determine the initial table uniquely.

Since the complexity of this algorithm is too high to test it on the full version of RC4, we tested it with a table that is partially filled in correctly, adapting the probability distributions accordingly. A partially filled table can result in a unique determination of $j_1, j_2, \ldots$ As long as j_t is known, there is no "flattening effect" and the Bayes method works as predicted. Experimental results suggest that it is difficult to get convergence when the uncertainty on j_t grows. A possible explanation for the convergence problems is that the dependence of the different entries of S_t on one another is too high to be neglected. If 160 entries or more of S_0 are given, the algorithm always succeeds in completing the table, the complexity being less than 2^{30}. If 150 entries are given, the success ratio is 70%, and it is expected to drop very quickly from here.

Figure 3 shows some experimental results for a simplified algorithm. The input of the algorithm consists of the values for k entries of S_0. The algorithm performs the attack, until knowledge of j_t is lost. The algorithm restarts and processes the key stream again with the updated information on S_0 until no new information is obtained anymore. Since j_t is known, the complexity of the algorithm is reduced; it is now about $k(2^n - k)^3$. The figure shows how many table entries can be successfully recovered as a function of k. One can deduce that the algorithm is most successful when $k \approx 120$. Since the algorithm does not output a complete table, we can use its output table as input for the attack of Sect. 4. Experiments suggest that for values of k between 100 and 200, the prior application of the simplified Bayes algorithm before starting the attack of Sect. 4 increases the efficiency. However, the problem of determining the first k values remains. Since the latter attack also works without predetermined entries of S_0, it could be used to generate a guess for these first k values. Estimating the complexity of attacks based on combining the Bayes technique with the attack of Sect. 4 is a rather involved task. We leave it as an open problem to which extent this combination will improve the attacks on RC4.

6   Conclusions

We have demonstrated several cryptanalytic algorithms on the alleged RC4 stream cipher. The algorithms try to deduce the initial state in a known plaintext attack. First we demonstrated the importance of the swapping operation in RC4. Our results show that a less frequent use of the swapping operation enables stronger cryptanalytic attacks.

The second algorithm has the best overall performance. It finds the correct initial state using only a small segment of known plaintext. The complexity of

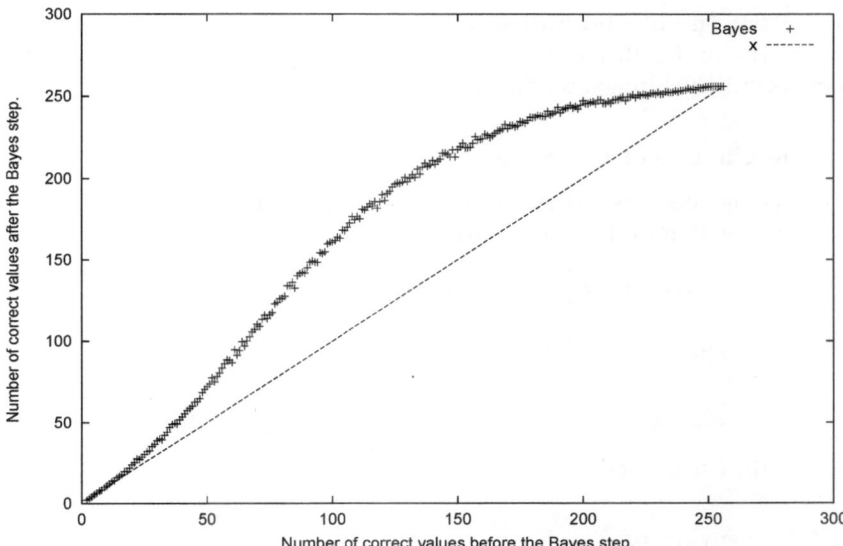

Fig. 3. Average number of entries successfully recovered by the Bayes method as function of the number of known entries on beforehand.

the attack was estimated by analytical calculations and verified by extensive testing. The complexity was approximated to be less than the time of searching through the square root of all possible initial states. We have also identified certain streams of words of RC4 for which the search algorithm has an increased performance. The third algorithm is based on probability theory. It involves no guessing, but it only works if a certain number of table entries is already known. Although our attacks are by far not practical for the specified word size of RC4, they give new intrinsic insight into the algorithm. It is our hope that our results will stimulate further research on RC4.

References

1. B. Schneier, *Applied Cryptography*, Wiley, New York, 1996.
2. J. Dj. Golić, "Linear Statistical Weakness of Alleged RC4 Keystream Generator," *Advances in Cryptology - EUROCRYPT'97, Lecture Notes in Computer Science, Vol. 1233,* Walter Fumy (Ed.), Springer-Verlag, pp. 226-238.
3. R. A. Rueppel, *Analysis and Design of Stream Ciphers*, Springer-Verlag, Berlin, 1986.

A   Calculating the a Posteriori Probability Distributions

There are two effects: observation of Z_t, which gives us more information, or "narrows" the probability distributions, and the change of state for j and two elements of S, which tends to "flatten" the probability distributions.

A.1   The Change of the State

The "flattening effect" is described by the following equations, denoting the new probability distribution functions with $f', g'[x]$:

$$f'_t(a) = \sum_b f_{t-1}(a - b)g_{t-1}[i_t](b) \tag{13}$$

$$g'_t[i_t](y) = \sum_b f'_t(b)g_{t-1}[b](y) \tag{14}$$

$$g'_t[x](y) = (1 - f'_t(x))g_{t-1}[x](y) + f'_t(x)g_{t-1}[i_t](y) . \tag{15}$$

Equation (13) corresponds to a convolution.

A.2   Observation of Z_t

The information of the known Z_t value can be used to calculate the functions f_t and $g_t[x]$. Bayes' rule gives the following equations:

$$\Pr(j_t = a \mid Z_t = d) = \frac{\Pr(j_t = a)\Pr(Z_t = d \mid j_t = a)}{\Pr(Z_t = d)} \tag{16}$$

$$\Pr(S_t[x] = y \mid Z_t = d) = \frac{\Pr(S_t[x] = y)\Pr(Z_t = d \mid S_t[x] = y)}{\Pr(Z_t = d)} . \tag{17}$$

In terms of f_t and $g_t[x]$ this becomes

$$f_t(a) = \frac{f'_t(a)\Pr(Z_t = d \mid j_t = a)}{\Pr(Z_t = d)} \tag{18}$$

$$g_t[x](y) = \frac{g'_t[x](y)\Pr(Z_t = d \mid S_t[x] = y)}{\Pr(Z_t = d)} . \tag{19}$$

The remaining probabilities can be expressed as functions of f'_t and $g'_t[x]$.

Equation (4) gives for the probability distribution of Z_t:

$$\Pr(Z_t = d) = \sum_a \sum_b \sum_c \Pr(j_t = a, S_t[a] = b, S_t[i_t] = c, S_t[b + c] = d) . \tag{20}$$

We do not need to calculate the probability $\Pr(Z_t = d)$ explicitly, because it can be determined from the renormalization requirements:

$$\sum_a \Pr(j_t = a \mid Z_t = d) = 1$$

$$\sum_y \Pr(S_t[x] = y \mid Z_t = d) = 1 .$$

The value $\Pr(Z_t = d \mid j_t = a)$ can be calculated as

$$\Pr(Z_t = d \mid j_t = a) = \sum_b \sum_c \Pr(S_t[a] = b, S_t[i_t] = c, S_t[b+c] = d) \quad (21)$$

$$= \sum_b \sum_c \Pr(S_t[a] = b) \Pr(S_t[i_t] = c \mid S_t[a] = b)$$

$$\Pr(S_t[b+c] = d \mid S_t[a] = b, S_t[i_t] = c) . \quad (22)$$

In order to rewrite this in terms of f_t' and $g_t'[x]$, we assume that for two different values x_1, x_2, the values of $S_t[x_1]$ and $S_t[x_2]$ are independent.

- $\Pr(S_t[a] = b) = g_t'[a](b)$.
- $\Pr(S_t[i_t] = c \mid S_t[a] = b)$: if both $i_t = a$ and $c = b$, the probability is one; if only one of the equalities holds, the probability is zero; else it is $\Pr(S_t[i_t] = c)/(1 - \Pr(S_t[i_t] = b)) = g_t'[i_t](c)/(1 - g_t'[i_t](b))$.
- $\Pr(S_t[b+c] = d \mid S_t[a] = b, S_t[i_t] = c)$: In the generic case, the probability is $\Pr(S_t[b+c] = d)/(1 - \Pr(S_t[b+c] = b) - \Pr(S_t[b+c] = c)) = g_t'[b+c](d)/(1 - g_t'[b+c](b) - g_t'[b+c](c))$. Special cases occur when $a = i_t$, $b = c$, $a = b+c$, $d = b$, $i_t = b+c$, and/or $c = d$.

Similarly, the value of $\Pr(Z_t = d \mid S_t[x] = y)$ can be calculated as

$$\Pr(Z_t = d \mid S_t[x] = y)$$

$$= \sum_a \sum_b \sum_c \Pr(j_t = a, S_t[a] = b, S_t[i_t] = c, S_t[b+c] = d \mid S_t[x] = y) \quad (23)$$

$$= \sum_a \sum_b \sum_c \Pr(j_t = a \mid S_t[x] = y) \Pr(S_t[a] = b \mid S_t[x] = y, j_t = a)$$

$$\Pr(S_t[i_t] = c \mid S_t[x] = y, j_t = a, S_t[a] = b)$$

$$\Pr(S_t[b+c] = d \mid S_t[x] = y, j_t = a, S_t[a] = b, S_t[i_t] = c) . \quad (24)$$

These equations can also be reworked in terms of f_t' and $g_t'[x]$.

Reduced Complexity Correlation Attacks on Two Clock-Controlled Generators

Thomas Johansson[*]

Dept. of Information Technology
Lund University, P.O. Box 118, 221 00 Lund, Sweden

Abstract. The *Shrinking Generator* and the *Alternating Step Generator* are two of the most well known clock-controlled stream ciphers. We consider correlation attacks on these two generators, based on an identified relation to the decoding problem for the deletion channel and the insertion channel, respectively. Several ways of reducing the decoding complexity are proposed and investigated, resulting in "divide-and-conquer" attacks on the two generators having considerably lower complexity than previously known attacks.

1 Introduction

A binary additive stream cipher is a synchronous stream cipher in which the keystream, the plaintext and the ciphertext are sequences of binary digits. The output of the keystream generator, $z_1, z_2, \ldots$ is added bitwise to the plaintext sequence $m_1, m_2, \ldots$, producing the ciphertext $c_1, c_2, \ldots$. Each secret key k as input to the keystream generator corresponds to an output sequence. Since the secret key k is shared between the transmitter and the receiver, the receiver can decrypt by adding the output of the keystream generator to the ciphertext, obtaining the message sequence.

The goal in stream cipher design is to efficiently produce random-looking sequences that in some sense are "indistinguishable" from truly random sequences. From a cryptanalysis point of view, a good stream cipher should be resistant against a *known-plaintext attack*. In a known-plaintext attack the cryptanalyst is given a plaintext and the corresponding ciphertext, and the task is to determine a key k. For a synchronous stream cipher, this is equivalent to the problem of finding the key k that produced a given keystream $z_1, z_2, \ldots, z_N$.

In stream cipher design, one usually use linear feedback shift registers, LFSRs, as building blocks in different ways, and the secret key is often used as the initial state of the LFSRs. A general methodology for producing random-like sequences from LFSRs that recently has been popular is *using the output of one or more LFSRs to control the clock of other LFSRs*. The purpose is to destroy the linearity of the LFSR sequences and hence provide the resulting sequence with a large linear complexity.

---

[*] Supported by the Foundation for Strategic Research - PCC under Grant 97-130.

K. Ohta and D. Pei (Eds.): ASIACRYPT'98, LNCS 1514, pp. 342–356, 1998.

The most important general attacks on LFSR-based stream ciphers are *correlation attacks*. Basically, if one can in some way detect a correlation between the known output sequence and the output of one individual LFSR, this can be used in a "divide-and-conquer" attack on the individual LFSR [13,11,5,6].

Two of the most well known clock-controlled stream ciphers are the Shrinking generator and the Alternating step generator. In this paper we consider correlation attacks on these two generators. Some basic attacks have been considered when the generators were introduced [1] and [8], and further studies in [7] and [4]. For an overview, see [12].

Our considerations are based on an identified relation to the decoding problem on the deletion channel and the insertion channel, respectively. Several ways of reducing the decoding complexity are proposed and investigated, resulting in "divide-and-conquer" attacks on the two generators mentioned above having considerably lower complexity than previously known attacks. For example, for the Shrinking generator with shift register length 61 as suggested in [10], but with known feedback polynomial, the complexity of breaking this generator is reduced from around 2^{80} [1] to $2^{40} - 2^{50}$ depending on the length of the received sequence.

In Section 2 we describe the Shrinking generator and the Alternating step generator, respectively. We also show the relation to the decoding problem for the deletion/insertion channel. In Section 3 we consider a procedure for MAP decoding on the deletion channel. In Section 4 we propose a suboptimal MAP decoding procedure with reduced complexity and then demonstrate how certain "weak" subsequences that appear in the output sequence can be used to further reduce the complexity of a "divide-and-conquer" attack on the Shrinking generator. In Section 5 and 6 the same ideas are used on the Alternating step generator and the insertion channel, essentially showing the same type of complexity reduction.

2   Preliminaries

The Shrinking Generator, or SG for short, uses two sources of pseudorandom bits to create a third source of pseudorandom bits, having better cryptographic quality than the original sources. The output sequence is a subsequence of the first source, which is selected according to the values of the second source. The two original sources are in the proposal [1] chosen to be two maximal length linear feedback shift registers (LFSR).

The output sequence is more precisely defined as follows. Let $\mathbf{a} = a_1, a_2, \ldots$ denote the output of the first LFSR, denoted LFSR_A, and let $\mathbf{s} = s_1, s_2, \ldots$ denote the output of the second LFSR, denoted LFSR_S. The two LFSRs have length L_A and L_S respectively. The output sequence of the generator, denoted $\mathbf{z} = z_1, z_2, \ldots$, is the sequence obtained from $\mathbf{a} = a_1, a_2, \ldots$ by removing all a_i's for which $s_i = 0$. This is depicted in Figure 1.

The Alternating Step Generator, or ASG for short, is closely related to the stop-and-go generator and was proposed by Günther [8] in 1987. See [8] for a

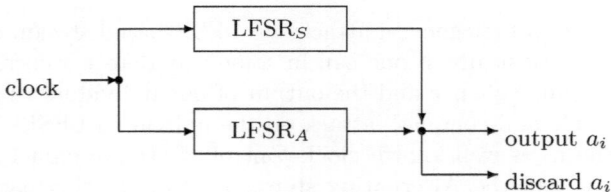

Fig. 1. The Shrinking Generator

further description of the ASG. Let us describe a modified version of the ASG, which we call ASG'.

Description of ASG': Again, we have three LFSRs, where LFSR$_S$ controls the clock of the two other LFSRs. Let LFSR$_S$ generate the sequence $\mathbf{s} = s_1, s_2, \ldots$. If $s_i = 1$ then the output symbol z_i is the output symbol from LFSR$_A$, and LFSR$_A$ is clocked. Otherwise, if $s_i = 0$ then the output symbol z_i is the output symbol from LFSR$_B$, and LFSR$_B$ is clocked. The ASG' is shown in Figure 2. It is not hard to show that ASG and ASG' are equivalent and hence we only

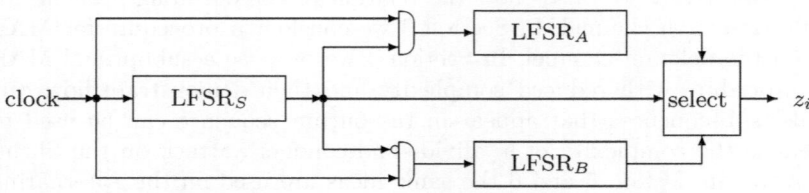

Fig. 2. The modified Alternating Step Generator, ASG'.

consider the ASG' in the sequel.

In the case of the SG, it was observed by Golic and O'Connor [4] that the sequence $\mathbf{a}$ can be recovered from the output sequence $\mathbf{z}$ if we can solve the corresponding *decoding problem on the deletion channel*. The deletion/insertion channel is a communication channel where the input symbols are deleted with a probability p and between any two undeleted input symbols i random symbols are inserted with distribution $P(i \text{ insertions}) = q^i(1 - q)$, $i \geq 0$. If there are no insertions we call the channel the deletion channel, and if there are no deletions we call it the insertion channel.

For the SG we regard the sequence $\mathbf{s}$ from LFSR$_S$ as random and try to decode the output $\mathbf{z}$ to the correct sequence $\mathbf{a}$. It can be easily verified that if we assume that the sequence $\mathbf{a} = a_1, a_2, \ldots$ is the input to the deletion channel and the sequence $\mathbf{z} = z_1, z_2, \ldots$ is the output, the requirements for the deletion channel is fulfilled and the parameter p is $p = 1/2$. Since there are only 2^{L_A} possible input sequences an output sequence is uniquely decodable if it is long enough and if the channel has a positive channel capacity [3]. With a fixed set of possible initial states we decode by simply checking each possible sequence with a MAP decoding algorithm, to be described in Section 5.

Having modified the ASG to ASG' we can then see that if we assume that the sequence $\mathbf{a} = a_1, a_2, \ldots$ is the input to the insertion channel and the sequence $\mathbf{z} = z_1, z_2, \ldots$ is the output, the requirements for the insertion channel is fulfilled and the parameter q is $q = 1/2$.

3   MAP Decoding on the Deletion Channel

By definition, a MAP decoding algorithm finds an input sequence $\mathbf{a}$ that for given $\mathbf{z}$ maximizes $P(\mathbf{a} \text{ transmitted}|\mathbf{z} \text{ received})$, whereas a ML decoding algorithm finds a sequence $\mathbf{a}$ maximizing $P(\mathbf{z} \text{ received}|\mathbf{a} \text{ transmitted})$. The derivation to be given is related to [9,4].

Assume that $a_1, \ldots, a_{L_A}$ is the given initial state of LFSR$_A$ at time zero. Each initial state gives rise to a corresponding infinite sequence $\mathbf{a} = a_1, a_2, \ldots$. Denote by $\mathcal{A}$ the set of possible sequences. Assume also that the output sequence $\mathbf{z}$ is an infinite sequence $\mathbf{z} = z_1, z_2, \ldots$ obtained by transmitting some sequence $\mathbf{a}$ over the deletion channel, i.e. the sequence $\mathbf{a} = a_1, a_2 \ldots$ gives the output $\mathbf{z} = z_1, z_2 \ldots$. Let $\mathbf{A} = A_1, A_2, \ldots$ and $\mathbf{Z} = Z_1, Z_2, \ldots$ be the corresponding random variables. Continuing, we consider input sequences of fixed length t. Thus let $\mathbf{a}^t$ denote the sequence $\mathbf{a}^t = a_1, a_2, \ldots, a_t$, and let $\mathbf{A}^t = A_1, A_2, \ldots, A_t$ be the corresponding random variable. For a fixed length t the MAP decoding procedure calculates

$$P(\mathbf{A}^t = \mathbf{a}^t | \mathbf{Z} = \mathbf{z}), \tag{1}$$

for all sequences in $\mathcal{A}$ and selects a sequence $\mathbf{a} \in \mathcal{A}$ maximizing (1).

The length of the output sequence after t input symbols can be any value in $[0, t]$. Hence, introduce the random variables $\phi_t, t \geq 0$ as the number of output symbols after t input symbols. We can then write the above equation as

$$P(\mathbf{A}^t = \mathbf{a}^t | \mathbf{Z} = \mathbf{z}) = \sum_{i=0}^{t} P(\mathbf{A}^t = \mathbf{a}^t, \phi_t = i | \mathbf{Z} = \mathbf{z}). \tag{2}$$

The calculation of $P(\mathbf{A}^t = \mathbf{a}^t, \phi_t = i | \mathbf{Z} = \mathbf{z})$ can then be done iteratively by observing that

$$P(\mathbf{A}^t = \mathbf{a}^t, \phi_t = i | \mathbf{Z} = \mathbf{z}) = \tag{3}$$
$$P(\mathbf{A}^{t-1} = \mathbf{a}^{t-1}, \phi_{t-1} = i | \mathbf{Z} = \mathbf{z}) P(A_t = a_t, \phi_t = i | \phi_{t-1} = i, \mathbf{Z} = \mathbf{z})$$
$$+ P(\mathbf{A}^{t-1} = \mathbf{a}^{t-1}, \phi_{t-1} = i - 1 | \mathbf{Z} = \mathbf{z}) P(A_t = a_t, \phi_t = i | \phi_{t-1} = i - 1, \mathbf{Z} = \mathbf{z}).$$

We further observe that

$$P(A_t = a_t, \phi_t = i | \phi_{t-1} = i, \mathbf{Z} = \mathbf{z}) = \frac{1}{4}, \tag{4}$$

since a deletion occurs with probability $1/2$ and then $A_t = a_t$ also with probability $1/2$. Furthermore

$$P(A_t = a_t, \phi_t = i | \phi_{t-1} = i - 1, \mathbf{Z} = \mathbf{z}) = \begin{cases} \frac{1}{2} \text{ if } a_t = z_i \\ 0 \text{ otherwise} \end{cases}, \quad (5)$$

because in this case there should be no deletion, which occur with probability $1/2$. Then $A_t = z_i$ and thus $A_t = a_t$ has probability 1 if $a_t = z_i$ and 0 otherwise.

With given sequences $\mathbf{a}, \mathbf{z}$, each $\mathbf{A}^t = \mathbf{a}^t, \phi_t = i, 0 \le t\ T, 0 \le i \le T$ can be considered as a node, denoted (t, i). Then the iterative calculation gives rise to a trellis, where $P(\mathbf{A}^t = \mathbf{a}^t, \phi_t = i | \mathbf{Z} = \mathbf{z})$ is the *metric* associated with each node. For simplicity, denote $P(\mathbf{A}^t = \mathbf{a}^t, \phi_t = i | \mathbf{Z} = \mathbf{z})$ simply by $\mu(t, i)$. The metric of new nodes will be updated according to whether $a_t = z_i$ or not. The metric update is obtained by combining (3), (4) and (5) as

$$\mu(t, i) = \mu(t - 1, i)\frac{1}{4} + \mu(t - 1, i - 1)\frac{1}{2}\delta(a_t, z_i), \quad (6)$$

where

$$\delta(x, y) = \begin{cases} 1 \text{ if } x = y \\ 0 \text{ otherwise} \end{cases}.$$

As previously shown, we have

$$P(\mathbf{A}^t = \mathbf{a}^t | \mathbf{Z} = \mathbf{z}) = \sum_{i=0}^{t} \mu(t, i).$$

Let $N(t, i)$ be the number of different paths from node $(0, 0)$ to node (t, i). Then $\mu(t, i) = N(t, i)/2^{2t-i}$. This implies that we only have to consider the number of paths to each node (t, i) and that we can choose $N(t, i)$ as the metric to calculate. The advantage is that $N(t, i)$ is always an integer. The metric update using $N(t, i)$ is

$$N(t, i) = N(t - 1, i) + N(t - 1, i - 1)\delta(a_t, z_i), \quad (7)$$

with initial value $N(0, 0) = 1$. We illustrate the procedure of creating the trellis and calculating the $N(t, i)$ metric by a small example given in Figure 3.

As stated for the probabilistic attack described in [4] the length of the sequence on which the decoding is performed need to be at least $3L_A$ for unique decoding, and we here choose to use the length $4L_A$. A straightforward implementation of the MAP decoding procedure is quadratic in the length. Hence the obtained complexity will be roughly $(4L_A)^2$ simple operations (about $(4L_A)^2/4$ nodes in the trellis each requiring one calculation of $\mu(t, i)$).

4   Reduced Complexity Decoding – Deletion Channel

We reduce the decoding complexity using two different approaches. Firstly, we propose and examine a suboptimal decoding algorithm, i.e., an algorithm with

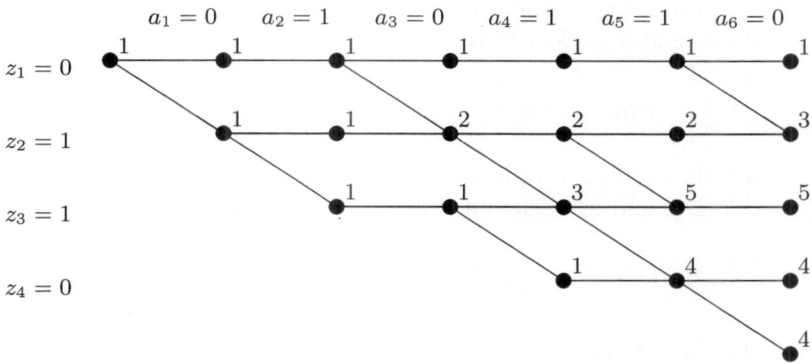

Fig. 3. A trellis with metric $N(t, i)$ for $\mathbf{a} = 0, 1, 0, 1, 1, 0, \ldots$ and $\mathbf{z} = 0, 1, 1, 0, \ldots$.

reduced complexity that has an almost optimal behavior. We use a stopping rule for the decision together with a list decoding approach (we keep only a fixed number of nodes at each time instant). Properties of this suboptimal decoding procedure is considered in the appendix. Let $C_{MAP'}$ be the expected complexity of testing one sequence with the above suboptimal algorithm. The algorithm implies a divide-and-conquer attack on LFSR_A by exhaustively testing all initial states. The complexity of such an attack is then approximately $2^{L_A} \cdot C_{MAP'}$.

Our second objective is to demonstrate that certain subsequences of the output sequence are weak in the sense that when they occur, they can be used to find the initial state of LFSR_A with lower complexity than exhaustively testing as mentioned above.

Assume that the output sequence $Z = z_1, z_2, \ldots$ contains a subsequence $z_T, z_{T+1}, \ldots, z_{T+M}$ such that either

$$(z_T, z_{T+1}, \ldots, z_{T+M}) = (0, 0, \ldots, 0, 1, 0, \ldots, 0) \tag{8}$$

or

$$(z_T, z_{T+1}, \ldots, z_{T+M}) = (1, 1, \ldots, 1, 0, 1, \ldots, 1). \tag{9}$$

The subsequence $z_T, z_{T+1}, \ldots, z_{T+M}$ is of length $M + 1$. W.l.o.g we can assume that (8) holds. Define the time t to be zero *exactly* where the occurrence of the single 1 is in the subsequence. In our notation, this means that $a_0 = 1$ and $s_0 = 1$. Let us now calculate $P(a_1 = 0)$ as follows,

$$P(a_1 = 0) = P(a_1 = 0|s_1 = 0)P(s_1 = 0) + P(a_1 = 0|s_1 = 1)P(s_1 = 1) \tag{10}$$

$$= \frac{1}{2} \cdot \frac{1}{2} + 1 \cdot \frac{1}{2} \tag{11}$$

$$= \frac{3}{4}, \tag{12}$$

since if $s_1 = 1$ then $a_1 = z_1 = 0$, and if $s_1 = 0$ then a_1 take any value in $\{0, 1\}$ with approximately equal probability.

The same arguments as above can be applied to $P(a_2 = 0)$ etc, as well as to $P(a_{-1} = 0)$ etc, and it is clear that

$$P(a_i = 0) = \frac{3}{4}, \quad -M_1 \leq i \leq M_2, \quad i \neq 0.$$

Furthermore, the deletion rate is $1/2$. Hence, assuming M_1 deletions appearing in $a_{-2M_1}, \ldots, a_{-1}$, and M_2 deletions in $a_1, \ldots, a_{2M_2}$, we would end up with

$$P(a_i = 0) = \begin{cases} \frac{3}{4}, & 2M_1 \leq i \leq 2M_2, i \neq 0 \\ 0, & i = 0. \end{cases} \tag{13}$$

If the number of deletions is not exactly M_1 and M_2 respectively, they are at least close to these values and the distribution is close to the above.

With such a strong correlation identified, we can use it to reduce the complexity of the exhaustive search. We simply define the initial state to include the positions $a_{-2M_1}, \ldots, a_{2M_2}$ and search according to the above distribution. This idea can then be extended in different ways. We here examine three different approaches.

A. **Direct exhaustive search:** Using the proposed decoding procedure in the appendix we exhaustively search all 2^{L_A} initial states. The complexity of finding the correct initial state is on average $C_{MAP'} \cdot 2^{L_A-1}$, and the length of $\mathbf{z}$ can be very small.

B. **Search using one weak subsequence:** We identify one weak subsequence of the form (8) or (9) of length $M+1$. Assume $2M \leq L_A-1$. Define the initial state to include the $2M + 1$ index positions for which (13) hold, possibly together with some additional index positions. Search through all initial states having at most $M/2$ 1's in the corresponding $2M$ index positions and $a_0 = 1$, using the proposed decoding procedure. If the correct initial state is not found, an error is declared. The complexity of finding the correct initial state is on average approximately

$$C_{MAP'} \cdot 2^{L_A-2M-1} \binom{2M}{M/2},$$

and the required expected length of z for the weak subsequence to occur is approximately $2^M/M$.

C. **Search using several weak subsequences:** We identify W weak subsequences of the form (8) or (9) all of length $M+1$, where $M \leq L_A - 1$. Then define the initial state to include the $2M + 1$ index positions for which (13) hold, possibly together with some additional index positions. Search through all initial states having at most w ones in the corresponding $2M$ index positions and $a_0 = 1$, using the proposed decoding procedure. If the correct initial state is not found, take a new weak subsequence and do the same again. If the correct initial state is not found after all weak subsequences have been used, an error is declared.

The complexity is approximately $C_{MAP'} \cdot W2^{L_A-2M-1} \binom{2M}{w}$, and the expected observed length of $\mathbf{z}$ for W weak subsequences to occur is approximately $W2^M/M$. For the probability of finding the correct sequence to be large, W must be chosen such that

$$1/W \approx \sum_{i=0}^{w} (3/4)^{2M-w} (1/4)^w (1/2)^{L_A-2M-1}.$$

In order to show different possibilities and choices of parameters we consider an example where LFSR_A of the SG has $L_A = 61$ with known feedback polynomial. Our attack then applies to any LFSR_S having arbitrary degree L_S and possibly unknown feedback polynomial. In a comparison we choose $L_S \approx L_A = 61$. (In [10] it was suggested to choose length $61 - 64$ for both LFSRs and using secret feedback polynomials). A very rough estimate of the complexity in simple instructions for recovering the initial state of LFSR_A for different lengths of $\mathbf{z}$ and different methods are given in Table 1.

	Length of $\mathbf{z}$		
	2^{20}	2^{30}	2^{40}
Exhaustive search on LFSR_S [12]	2^{80}	2^{80}	2^{80}
Exhaustive search on LFSR_A [4]	2^{77}	2^{77}	2^{77}
A.	2^{71}	2^{71}	2^{71}
B.	2^{58}	2^{56}	2^{56}
C. with $2M = L_A - 1$		2^{50}	2^{40}

Table 1. Rough estimate of complexity for different attacks on the SG with $L_A = 61$.

4.1   Comments on the Values of Table 1:

As described in [12], the divide-and-conquer attack on LFSR_S requires approximately $2^{L_S} L_A^3$ operations which for $L_S \approx L_A = 61$ is around 2^{80} independent of output length. Furthermore, using the probabilistic attack described in [4] in an exhaustive search requires approximately $2^{L_A} \cdot (4L_A)^2$ operations, since the length of the sequence on which the decoding is performed need to be at least $3L_A$ for unique decoding (here chosen to be $4L_A$) and the decoding complexity is quadratic in the length.

For method A., the complexity is $2^{L_A} \cdot C_{MAP'}$, where the parameters of the suboptimal decoding algorithm is chosen such that $C_{MAP'} = 2^{10}$, giving an error probability of 0.34 as shown in the appendix. For method B., and output length 2^{20}, M is chosen to be $M = 25$. We then search through all sequences with at most 13 ones in $2M = 50$ index positions, one position fixed to 1, and the remaining 10 positions arbitrarily. This gives complexity

$$\sum_{i=0}^{13} \binom{50}{i} \cdot 2^{10} \cdot C_{MAP'} \approx 2^{58}.$$

For output length 2^{30} or 2^{40}, we have $M = 30$ and searching through all sequences with at most 15 ones in $2M = 60$ index positions, one position fixed to 1, gives complexity

$$\sum_{i=0}^{15} \binom{60}{i} \cdot C_{MAP'} \approx 2^{56}.$$

Finally, for method C., we only consider the case when $M = 30$, which rules out the length 2^{20}. For length 2^{30} we expect to find about $2 \cdot 2^{30}/(2^{31}/31) = 31$ weak subsequences of the form (8) or (9). For each of these subsequences, we search through all sequences with at most 10 ones in $2M = 60$ index positions (one position fixed to 1). The probability of the event that the correct sequence has 10 or less ones in the $2M = 60$ index positions is approximately

$$\sum_{i=0}^{10} (3/4)^{60-i}(1/4)^i \binom{60}{i} \approx 0.08.$$

Hence the probability that at least one such event occurring among the 31 trials is large. The complexity of this procedure is roughly

$$\frac{1}{0.08} \cdot \sum_{i=0}^{10} \binom{60}{i} \cdot C_{MAP'} \approx 2^{50}.$$

Finally, for output length 2^{40} we expect about 2^{15} weak subsequences. The probability that the correct sequence has 3 or less ones in the $2M = 60$ index positions is

$$\sum_{i=0}^{3} (3/4)^{60-i}(1/4)^i \binom{60}{i} \approx 0.000047.$$

Searching through all sequences with at most 3 ones in the $2M = 60$ index positions gives complexity

$$\frac{1}{0.000047} \cdot \sum_{i=0}^{3} \binom{60}{i} \cdot C_{MAP'} \approx 2^{40}.$$

Note that in method A.–C. we only succeed with a certain probability when the selected $\mathbf{a}$ is correct, since the suboptimal MAP decoding fails with probability 0.34 etc.. If we want a very high probability of success, we can perform the whole process several times, each time on a new part of the output sequence. This slightly increases the complexity and the required length of the output sequence, compared to the above given numerical values.

4.2   Recovering the Initial State of LFSR$_S$

After having recovered the initial state of LFSR$_A$, we need to recover initial state of LFSR$_S$. This problem has not been addressed before. Due to the MAP decoding algorithm of Section 3, our candidate for initial state of LFSR$_A$ is correct with arbitrarily large probability (just run the algorithm long enough). We now proceed as follows. Again, run the MAP decoding algorithm and create the trellis. We have

$$P(s_t = 1|\mathbf{A} = \mathbf{a}, \mathbf{Z} = \mathbf{z}) = \sum_i P(\phi_t = i|\mathbf{A} = \mathbf{a}, \mathbf{Z} = \mathbf{z})P(s_t = 1|\phi_t = i, \mathbf{A} = \mathbf{a}, \mathbf{Z} = \mathbf{z})$$

$$= \sum_i P(\phi_t = i|\mathbf{A} = \mathbf{a}, \mathbf{Z} = \mathbf{z})P(s_t = 1|\phi_t = i, A_t = a_t, Z_i = z_i)$$

and

$$P(s_t = 1|\phi_t = i, A_t = a_t, Z_i = z_i) = \begin{cases} 0, & \text{if } a_t \neq z_i, \\ 2/3, & \text{if } a_t = z_i. \end{cases}$$

Furthermore,

$$P(\phi_t = i|\mathbf{A} = \mathbf{a}, \mathbf{Z} = \mathbf{z}) = \frac{\mu(t, i)}{\sum_j \mu(t, j)},$$

and hence we get

$$P(s_t = 1|\mathbf{A} = \mathbf{a}, \mathbf{Z} = \mathbf{z}) = \sum_i \frac{\mu(t, i)}{\sum_j \mu(t, j)} \cdot \frac{2}{3}\delta(a_t, z_i).$$

This procedure creates an a posteriori probability for each symbol s_t. Restoring the $\mathbf{s}$ sequence is now exactly the problem of decoding a received word to its nearest codeword on a noisy channel. One advantage is that the received word is very long and hence different ways of doing a fast decoding can be applied. One possibility is to use an iterative decoding process as suggested in [11] for fast correlation attacks. Another simpler method is to search for positions where the a posteriori probability $P(s_t = 1|\mathbf{A} = \mathbf{a}, \mathbf{Z} = \mathbf{z})$ is very small. This means that these positions are very likely to have $s_t = 0$. After finding L_S such positions one can perform a search over sequences having a low weight on these positions. The complexity of recovering the initial state of LFSR$_S$ using this approach is very low, and more details will be given in the full paper.

5   MAP Decoding on the Insertion Channel

In order to consider the ASG, we now consider MAP decoding on the insertion channel. The procedure is almost identical to the decoding procedure for the deletion channel. From Bayes rule,

$$P(\mathbf{A} = \mathbf{a}|\mathbf{Z}^t = \mathbf{z}^t) = P(\mathbf{Z}^t = \mathbf{z}^t|\mathbf{A} = \mathbf{a}) \cdot \frac{P(\mathbf{A} = \mathbf{a})}{P(\mathbf{Z} = \mathbf{z})}.$$

Since $P(\mathbf{A} = \mathbf{a})$ and $P(\mathbf{Z} = \mathbf{z})$ are both uniformly distributed it is clear that MAP and ML decoding is equivalent, i.e.,

$$\max_{\mathbf{a}} P(\mathbf{A} = \mathbf{a}|\mathbf{Z}^t = \mathbf{z}^t) = \max_{\mathbf{a}} P(\mathbf{Z}^t = \mathbf{z}^t|\mathbf{A} = \mathbf{a}).$$

It will now be apparent that the easiest way to describe a decoding process is in the form of ML decoding. Define the random variables ϕ_t, $t \geq 0$ to be the number of symbols from $\mathbf{a}$ that has appeared in $\mathbf{z}$ after observing t symbols from $\mathbf{z}$ (i.e. after observing $\mathbf{z}^t$). Clearly,

$$P(\mathbf{Z}^t = \mathbf{z}^t|\mathbf{A} = \mathbf{a}) = \sum_{i=0}^{t} P(\mathbf{Z}^t = \mathbf{z}^t, \phi_t = i|\mathbf{A} = \mathbf{a}),$$

and

$$\begin{aligned} P(\mathbf{Z}^t = \mathbf{z}^t, \phi_t = i|\mathbf{A} = \mathbf{a}) = \\ P(\mathbf{Z}^{t-1} = \mathbf{z}^{t-1}, \phi_{t-1} = i|\mathbf{A} = \mathbf{a})P(Z_t = z_t, \phi_t = i|\mathbf{z}^{t-1}, \phi_{t-1} = i, \mathbf{A} = \mathbf{a}) \\ + P(\mathbf{Z}^{t-1} = \mathbf{z}^{t-1}, \phi_{t-1} = i - 1|\mathbf{A} = \mathbf{a})P(Z_t = z_t, \phi_t = i|\mathbf{z}^{t-1}, \phi_{t-1} = i - 1, \mathbf{A} = \mathbf{a}). \end{aligned}$$

Furthermore,

$$P(Z_t = z_t, \phi_t = i|\phi_{t-1} = i, \mathbf{A} = \mathbf{a}) = \frac{1}{4} \tag{14}$$

since an insertion occurs with probability $1/2$ and then $Z_t = z_t$ also with probability $1/2$. Finally

$$P(Z_t = z_t, \phi_t = i|\phi_{t-1} = i - 1, \mathbf{A} = \mathbf{a}) = \begin{cases} \frac{1}{2} & \text{if } z_t = a_{\phi_{t-1}} \\ 0 & \text{otherwise} \end{cases}. \tag{15}$$

We can now see that the ML decoding procedure in this case is *exactly* the MAP decoding procedure for the deletion channel if the sequences $\mathbf{a}$ and $\mathbf{z}$ are switched. Hence all the results from Section 3 are valid also for the insertion channel if $\mathbf{a}$ and $\mathbf{z}$ are switched. With this conclusion we leave the details out.

6   Reduced Complexity Decoding – Insertion Channel

The ML decoding algorithm demonstrated in the previous section implies a divide-and-conquer attack on the ASG' by exhaustively testing all initial states of LFSR$_A$. The complexity of such an attack is then approximately $2^{L_A} \cdot C_{MAP'}$. We now demonstrate that again certain subsequences of the output sequence of the ASG' are weak in the sense that when they occur, they can be used to find the initial state of LFSR$_A$ with lower complexity than exhaustively testing as mentioned above.

The basic observation is the following. Assume that the output sequence $\mathbf{z}$ contains a subsequence $z_T, z_{T+1}, \ldots, z_{T+M}$ such that either

$$(z_T, z_{T+1}, \ldots, z_{T+M-1}) = (0, 0, \ldots, 0) \tag{16}$$

or

$$(z_T, z_{T+1}, \ldots, z_{T+M-1}) = (1, 1, \ldots, 1). \tag{17}$$

Redefine the time t to be zero at time T and w.l.o.g assume (16). This means that now $(z_0, z_1, \ldots, z_{M-1}) = (0, 0, \ldots, 0)$. Then assuming that at least $M/2$ of the symbols in $\mathbf{z}^M$ (which has probability $> 1/2$) came from LFSR$_A$, we have $a_0 = 0, a_1 = 0, \ldots, a_{M/2} = 0$. Hence one can perform an exhaustive search over all possible initial states of LFSR$_A$ with the first $M/2$ index positions set to zero. This will reduce the complexity with a factor $2^{M/2}$ compared with straightforward exhaustive search.

Having described the basic idea, we can now improve the performance in several ways. Instead of subsequences of the form (16) or (17), we consider any sequences of length $\geq M$ containing at most w ones (or at most w zeros). Each of the w ones comes from LFSR$_A$ with probability $1/2$ and hence with probability 2^{-w} none of the ones comes from LFSR$_A$. If this occur, the first $(M - w)/2$ symbols of $\mathbf{a}$ are all zero with probability $> 1/2$. Hence a possible procedure is as follows.

1. Search for a length M subsequence of $\mathbf{z}$ containing at most w ones (or zeros).
2. Let t be zero at the beginning of the subsequence and assume that $a_0 = 0, \ldots, a_{(M-p)/2} = 0$. Then perform an exhaustive search over the remaining index positions $a_{(M-w)/2}, \ldots, a_{L_A-1}$.
3. Go to 1.

The conclusion is that by the basic observation the search is reduced by roughly a factor $\sqrt{L}$ where L is the length of the observed sequence, and by the above improvement the reduction factor can be made a bit larger.

Finally, the concept of weak subsequences are always present for the two considered generators. It is always possible that a "very weak" subsequence appear, implying a successful attack with very low complexity, even though the probability of such a sequence is very low. For example, an subsequence of $2L_A$ consecutive zeros or ones from the ASG' implies a successful attack with complexity almost zero.

References

1. D. Coppersmith, H. Krawczyk, and Y. Mansour, "The shrinking generator, *Lecture Notes in Computer Science* 773 (CRYPTO'93), pp. 22–39, 1994.
2. T. Cover, A. Thomas, *Elements of Information Theory*, Wiley and Sons, 1991.
3. A.S. Dolgapolov, "Capacity bounds for a channel with synchronization errors", *Problemy Peredachi Informatsii*, 26, pp. 27–37, 1990.
4. J. Golic', and L. O'Connor, "Embedding and probabilistic correlation attacks on clock-controlled shift registers", *Lecture Notes in Computer Science* 950 (EUROCRYPT'94), pp. 230–243, 1995.
5. J. Golic', M. Mihaljevic', "A generalized correlation attack on a class of stream ciphers based on the Levenstein distance", *Journal of Cryptology*, 3 (1991), pp. 201–212.
6. J. Golic', "Towards fast correlation attacks on irregularly clocked shift registers", *Lecture Notes in Computer Science* 921 (EUROCRYPT'95), pp. 248–262, 1995.

7. J. Golic', "Intrinsic statistical weakness of keystream generators", *Lecture Notes in Computer Science* 917 (ASIACRYPT'94), pp. 91–103, 1995.
8. C.G. Günther, "Alternating step generators controlled by de Bruijn sequences", *Lecture Notes in Computer Science* 304 (EUROCRYPT'87), pp. 5–14, 1988.
9. P. Hall, G. Dowling, "Approximate string matching", *Computing Surveys*, 12, pp. 381–402, 1980.
10. H. Krawczyk, "The shrinking generator: Some practical considerations, *Lecture Notes in Computer Science* 809 (FSE), pp. 45–46, 1994.
11. W. Meier, and O. Staffelbach, "Fast correlation attacks on certain stream ciphers", *Journal of Cryptology*, 1, pp. 159–176, 1989.
12. A. Menezes, P. van Oorschot, S. Vanstone, *Handbook of Applied Cryptography*, CRC Press, 1997.
13. T. Siegenthaler, "Correlation-immunity of nonlinear combining functions for cryptographic applications", *IEEE Trans. on Info. Theory*, 30 (1984), pp. 776–780.

Appendix: A Suboptimal MAP Decoding Algorithm

Introduce the random variables $X_t = P(\mathbf{A}^t = \mathbf{a}^t | \mathbf{Z} = \mathbf{z})$, i.e., $X_t = \sum_{i=0}^{t} \mu(t, i)$. Using the recursion (3) we have

$$X_t = \sum_{i=0}^{t} \left(\frac{1}{4} \mu(t-1, i) + \frac{1}{2} \mu(t-1, i-1) \delta(a_t, z_i) \right),$$

which simplifies to

$$X_t = \frac{1}{4} X_{t-1} + \frac{1}{2} X_{t-1} \frac{\sum_{i:a_t=z_i} \mu(t-1, i-1)}{X_{t-1}}.$$

Introduce the random variables $S_t = 2 \frac{\sum_{i:a_t=z_i} \mu(t-1,i-1)}{X_{t-1}}$. Then

$$X_t = \frac{1}{4} X_{t-1} + \frac{1}{4} X_{t-1} S_t = \frac{1}{2} X_{t-1} \frac{1 + S_t}{2}$$

and after taking logarithms one gets

$$\log X_t = -1 + \log X_{t-1} + \log \frac{1 + S_t}{2} = -t + \sum_{i=1}^{t} \log \frac{1 + S_t}{2}$$

Clearly, for $\mathbf{a}$ being a random sequence $P(a_t = z_i) = 1/2$ for all t, i and hence $E(S_t) = 1$ implying $E(\frac{1+S_t}{2}) = 1$. Now, the Jensen's inequality [2] states that $E(\log \frac{1+S_t}{2}) \leq \log E(\frac{1+S_t}{2})$ with equality only if S_t has a deterministic distribution. But S_t has *not* a deterministic distribution and hence $E(\log \frac{1+S_t}{2}) < \log 1 = 0$. Hence

$$E(\log X_t) = -t + \sum_{i=1}^{t} E(Y_i), \tag{18}$$

where each $E(Y_i) < 0$.

Next, consider **a** being the correct sequence. Then if P_t is the number of output symbols after t input symbols we have

$$P(a_t = z_i) = \begin{cases} 1/2, \text{ if } i \neq P_t \\ 3/4, \text{ if } i = P_t \end{cases}$$

and hence $E(S_t) = 1 + \frac{1}{2}E(\mu(t-1, P_t))$. Without being able to formally prove the fact, simulations show that $E(\log \frac{1+S_t}{2}) > 0$ for this case. Thus we have the same expression as in (18), but now with $E(Y_i) > 0$.

These facts have been investigated by simulations. The value of $\log X_t - t$ expressed in the form $\log X_t - t = C \cdot t$ have been investigated for different t, covering both cases (random sequence, correct sequence). The result is tabulated in Table 2.

$\log X_t - t$		
t = Length of $\mathbf{a}^t$	CORRECT **a**	RANDOM **a**
10	$0.090775 \cdot t$	$-0.096476 \cdot t$
20	$0.072374 \cdot t$	$-0.097060 \cdot t$
30	$0.064135 \cdot t$	$-0.083986 \cdot t$
40	$0.059176 \cdot t$	$-0.069533 \cdot t$
60	$0.053739 \cdot t$	$-0.057280 \cdot t$
80	$0.050644 \cdot t$	$-0.051867 \cdot t$
100	$0.048625 \cdot t$	$-0.049880 \cdot t$
200	$0.044149 \cdot t$	$-0.051356 \cdot t$
500	$0.041362 \cdot t$	$-0.042727 \cdot t$
1000	$0.040404 \cdot t$	$-0.036148 \cdot t$
5000		$-0.033180 \cdot t$

Table 2. Tabulation of $\log X_t - t$ for **a** being a correct/random sequence.

Clearly, $\{X_t, t \geq 1\}$ is a stochastic process, for which a stopping rule can be introduced. For implementation purposes, we simplify this to apply only on certain index positions, e.g., $D \cdot n$ for $n = 1, 2, \ldots$ and some integer D. Such a stopping rule will introduce a small probability of error in our hypothesis testing problem, i.e., $P(\text{"not correct"}|\mathbf{a} \text{ "correct"}) = \epsilon > 0$. On the other hand, this will significantly reduce the computational complexity since in an exhaustive search the algorithm will terminate very quickly for most random sequences **a**. One also has to select a decision region for stopping/not stopping. Looking at Table 2 a suitable choice might be to stop if $\log X_t - t < 0$.

Secondly, a closer look at $\mu(t, i)$ for given t and a correct sequence **a** shows that the probability mass of $\mu(t, i)$ is concentrated to a few nodes (t, i) on each level. Therefore, one can consider a suboptimal decoding algorithm that only stores the L most probable nodes on each level. Furthermore, if I_{max} is the largest i such that $N(t, i) \neq 0$, then the nodes $(t, i), i = I_{max-L+1}, \ldots, I_{max}$ is a good approximation of the L most probable nodes, which we use.

These considerations give the following proposed algorithm.

1. Initialize $N(0,0) = 1$, $I_{max} = 1$.
2. If $a_t = z_{I_{max}}$ then $I_{max} = I_{max} + 1$. Update

$$N(t,i) = N(t-1,i) + N(t-1,i-1)\delta(a_t, z_i),$$

   for $i = I_{max} - L + 1, \ldots, I_{max}$.
3. If $t = 0 \pmod D$ do the following. Calculate $X_t = \sum_{i=I_{max}-L+1}^{I_{max}} N(t,i)/2^{2t-i}$.
   If $\log X_t - t < 0$ output "wrong sequence" and stop. If $t \geq T_{max}$ output "correct sequence" and stop.
4. Increase t by 1 and go to 2.

The above algorithm is given to be easily understood. When implementing it, several steps above should be done differently.

The performance of the algorithm relies on the relation between two important parameters, the probability of declaring a wrong sequence when having the correct one and the average complexity of the decoding algorithm for a random sequence (until it stops and outputs "wrong"). To measure the average complexity we consider the average depth of the trellis before stopping, i.e., if T_{stop} is the value of $t = D \cdot n$ when the algorithm stops, i.e., when $\log X_{D \cdot n} - D \cdot n < 0$ for the first $n = 1, 2, \ldots$. This is suitable since for a fixed number L of remaining states in each level of the trellis, the decoding complexity is (essentially) a linear function of T_{stop} and hence the expected decoding complexity a linear function of $E(T_{stop})$. Some simulated values of the above parameters are given in Table 3. The final conclusion of this section is a choice of parameters for complexity cal-

D	$P(\text{"wrong" output}|\mathbf{a}\text{ correct})$	$E(T_{stop})$
10	0.34	25.4
20	0.24	34.8
30	0.21	50
50	0.16	70
100	0.10	117
200	0.01	209

Table 3. Performance of the proposed algorithm in terms of error probability and decoding complexity for different D when $L = 10$.

culations. Selecting $D = 10$ and $L = 10$ will give an error probability of 0.34 and expected trellis depth 25.4. In this case the expected number of nodes in the trellis is less than 200 (there are fewer than L nodes on each level in the beginning of the trellis). Each node requires a few instructions to be updated, resulting in a very rough estimate of $C_{MAP'} = 2^{10}$ simple operations as an average of the complexity of testing one sequence $\mathbf{a}$.

A New and Efficient All-Or-Nothing Disclosure of Secrets Protocol

Julien P. Stern

[1] UCL Crypto Group,
Batiment Maxwell, Place du levant, 3
B-1348 Louvain-la-Neuve, Belgique
stern@dice.ucl.ac.be
[2] Laboratoire de Recherche en Informatique,
Université de Paris-Sud,
Batiment 490, F-91405 Orsay Cedex, France
stern@lri.fr

Abstract. Two-party protocols have been considered for a long time. Currently, there is a renewed effort to revisit specific protocols to gain efficiency. As an example, one may quote the breakthrough of [BF97], bringing a new solution to the problem of secretly generating RSA keys, which itself goes back to the pioneering work by Yao [Yao86]. The All-Or-Nothing Disclosure of Secrets protocol (ANDOS) was introduced in 1986 by Brassard, Crépeau and Robert [BCR87]. It involves two parties, a vendor and a buyer, and allows the vendor, who holds several secrets, to disclose one of them to the buyer, with the guarantee that no information about the other secrets will be gained. Furthermore, the buyer can freely choose his secret and has the guarantee that the vendor will not be able to find out which secret he picked. In this paper, we present a new protocol which achieves the same functionality, but which is much more efficient and can easily be implemented. Our protocol is especially efficient when a large number of secrets is involved and it can be used in various applications. The proof of security involves a novel use of computational zero-knowledge techniques combined with semantic security.

1 Introduction

The All-Or-Nothing Disclosure of Secrets protocol was introduced in 1986 by Brassard, Crépeau and Robert [BCR87]. It involves two parties, a vendor and a buyer, and allows the vendor, who holds several secrets, to disclose one of them to the buyer, with the guarantee that no information about the other secrets will be gained. Furthermore, the buyer can freely choose his secret and has the guarantee that the vendor will not be able to find out which secret he picked.

As in [BCR87], we make the following assumption: *we assume that the vendor is honest when he claims to be willing to disclose one secret, that is, he is not, for example, going to send junk or to swap several of his secrets.*

We will not discuss the issue of verification: it much depends on the trading environment and can easily be achieved by additional protocols, possibly involving third parties.

K. Ohta and D. Pei (Eds.): ASIACRYPT'98, LNCS 1514, pp. 357–371, 1998.

Before presenting our protocol, it is interesting to note that the security we obtain slightly differs from what was obtained in [BCR87]. While their protocol was computationally secure for the vendor and unconditionally secure for the buyer, our protocol provides unconditional security to the vendor and computational security to the buyer.

Our paper is organized as follows: we first present related work. Then we describe the properties required by the encryption systems we are going to use, and give a few examples of such systems. We next describe the algorithm itself, and we finally discuss its complexity and its practical cost.

2   Related Work

ANDOS is also known under the name *One-out-of-t* Strings Oblivious Transfer, denoted $\binom{t}{1} - \mathcal{O}T_2^k$ when t secrets of k bits are involved. Historically, the first case considered was for $t = 2$ [Wie83]. Then came natural restrictions ($t = 2$ and $k = 1$) [EGL83], and natural extensions [BCR87] (ANDOS). A large part of the work done on Oblivious Transfer aimed at finding efficient reductions of $\binom{t}{1}-\mathcal{O}T_2^k$ to $\binom{2}{1} - \mathcal{O}T_2^1$ [BCS96]. In our context, we chose to keep the name ANDOS, as we are building our protocol without using reductions among Oblivious Transfers.

Salomaa and Santean [SS90] have designed a very efficient ANDOS algorithm when several buyers are involved. The drawback is that they need a majority of honest buyers to achieve security.

Another efficient ANDOS protocol is proposed in [NR94], but relies on *ad hoc* assumptions.

The problem of blind decoding was recently introduced by Sakurai and Yamane [SY97] and its goal appears close to ANDOS. In their scheme, the buyer is supposed to have an encrypted secret and has it decoded by the vendor in such a way that the vendor does not get any information either on the plaintext or on the vendor's private key. However, the buyer might be able to combine several secrets in a single decoding, or might try to organize an oracle attack to recover the secret key (as in [Oht97]). Furthermore, to apply the scheme in an ANDOS setting, one has to assume that the buyer can anonymously recover the ciphertext for some specific secret, which, on the web for instance, seems to need in itself an ANDOS protocol if the encrypted secrets are not widely distributed.

Finally, the schemes which are probably the most closely related to the ANDOS problem are the *Private Information Retrieval* (PIR) schemes [CGKS95], and more precisely the computational PIR schemes [CG97]. In PIR protocols, the vendor is a database, which can be modeled as holding bits of information, and the buyer is a user of the database who is willing to query the database privately. Still, there are two major differences between ANDOS and PIR protocols: PIR schemes have only considered bit-per-bit retrieval so far and do not try to enforce any security for the database (a user might recover several bits in a single query).

3   The Encryption System

We now describe the generic system that will be used throughout our protocol. It is a probabilistic encryption system with a few additional properties. The system that we use can be described as follows:

- A security parameter n from which are derived several finite domains, $(R(n), X(n), Y(n))$, which we identify with initial subsets of the integers. Thus we use $R(n)$ for $\{x : 0 < x < r(n)\}$, $X(n)$ for $\{x : 0 \leq x < x(n)\}$, and similar notation for $Y(n)$.
- A public probabilistic encryption function $f : R(n) \times X(n) \to Y(n)$, and a private decryption algorithm $g : Y(n) \to X(n)$, such that :

$$\forall(r, x) \in R(n) \times X(n) \quad g(f(r, x)) = x$$

Note that the existence of a decryption algorithm implies that the function is injective with respect to its second parameter, that is, for $(r_1, x_1), (r_2, x_2) \in R(n) \times X(n)$, if $f(r_1, x_1) = f(r_2, x_2)$ then $x_1 = x_2$.

We now describe the further requirements needed for our protocols.

1. We require that the encryption function is homomorphic, that is:

$$\forall(r_1, x_1), (r_2, x_2) \in R(n) \times X(n),$$

$$f(r_1, x_1)f(r_2, x_2) = f(r_3, x_1 + x_2 \bmod x(n))$$

   where r_3 can be computed in polynomial time from r_1, r_2, x_1 and x_2. (A similar definition was given in [BD90] when $x(n) = 2$.)
2. We ask that the encryption function has *semantic security*. Informally, this means that, for a polynomially bounded adversary, the analysis of a set of ciphertexts does not give more information about the cleartexts than what would be available without knowledge of the ciphertexts. We refer the reader to [GM84] for a formal definition.
3. We assume the existence of a reliable way to prove that the public parameters of the system were correctly constructed. This might be done with the help of a certification authority or by a zero-knowledge proof. For example, to prove the validity of a composite modulus, (e.g. the modulus is the product of *exactly* two primes), one could use the protocol described in [vdGP88].
4. The last and exotic looking property is that the number 2 is invertible in $X(n)$. The reason of this choice will appear later.
5. From the previous properties, we can deduce two more, which we will use. The first one is the existence of a "hiding" function $hide : R(n) \times Y(n) \to Y(n)$, depending only on the public parameters of the system and such that:

$$\forall(r, x) \in R(n) \times X(n), \ \forall s \in R(n) \quad hide(s, (f(r, x)) = f(sr' \bmod r(n), x)$$

   where r' can be computed in polynomial time from r, x. As a matter of fact, *hide* can be defined by $hide(s, x) = f(s, 0)x$

6. The second property which is a consequence of the previous ones, is the existence of a way to prove that two ciphertexts represent the encryption of the same integer without revealing this integer. Let $(r_1, x_1), (r_2, x_2) \in R(n) \times X(n)$ and consider $y_1 = f(r_1, x_1)$ and $y_2 = f(r_2, x_2)$. Then, there exists r_3 such that $f(r_1, x_1)/f(r_2, x_2) = f(r_3, x_1 - x_2 \bmod x(n))$. In order to prove that $x_1 = x_2$, one can simply reveal r_3. Verification is performed by computing both y_1/y_2 and $f(r_3, 0)$ and checking their equality.

4 Sample Encryption Systems

We present several encryption systems which satisfy the requirements described in the previous section.

4.1 The Goldwasser-Micali Cryptosystem

This encryption system was introduced in [GM84]. We only give a brief sketch of the system here and refer the reader to [GM84] for details. Note that this system satisfy all properties but property 4, and thus cannot be used. We only present it as it was the first example of a probabilistic encryption scheme.

- It can only encrypt single bits. ($x(n) = 2$).
- Let N be the product of two large primes, and y be an non quadratic residue modulo N.
  The encryption function f is $f(r, x) = r^2 y^x \bmod N$.
  Decryption is done by calculating (with the factorization of N) whether or not the ciphertext is a quadratic residue.
- The semantic security of this system is proved in [GM84] under the *Quadratic Residuosity Assumption*.

4.2 The Benaloh Cryptosystem

This encryption system was derived from the previous one and introduced in [Ben87]. We only give a brief sketch of the system here and refer the reader to [Ben87] for details.

- It can encrypt several bits. ($x(n)$ usually varies from 2^{10} to 2^{40} depending on the required speed).
- Let Φ denote the Euler Totient function. Let N be the product of two large primes, choose a prime n and an integer y so that n divides $\Phi(N)$ but n^2 does not divide $\Phi(N)$ and y is a non n^{th} residue modulo N.
  The encryption function f is $f(r, x) = r^n y^x \bmod N$.
  Decryption is done by calculating (with the knowledge of $\Phi(n)$) the residuosity class of the ciphertext modulo n.
- The semantic security is implicit in [Ben87] under the *Prime Residuosity Assumption*.

4.3   The Naccache-Stern Cryptosystem

This system was recently introduced in [NS98]. We only give a brief sketch of the system here and refer the reader to [NS98] for details.

- It can encrypt several bits ($x(n)$ is usually around 2^{160}).
- Let Φ denote the Euler Totient function. Let N be the product of two large primes, choose $n_1, \ldots, n_p$ to be small primes so that for all $i \in \{1, \ldots, p\}$, n_i divides $\Phi(N)$ but n_i^2 does not divide $\Phi(N)$. Also choose y to be, for all i, a non n_i^{th} residue modulo N. Set $n = \prod_{i=1}^{p} n_i$.
  The encryption function f is $f(r, x) = r^n y^x \bmod N$.
  Decryption is done by calculating (with the knowledge of $\Phi(n)$) the residuosity class of the ciphertext modulo each of the n_i and by recovering the cleartext by means of the Chinese remainder theorem.
- The semantic security is proved in [NS98] under the *Prime Residuosity Assumption*.

4.4   The Okamoto-Uchiyama Cryptosystem

We only give a brief sketch of the system here and refer the reader to [OU98] for details.

- It can encrypt several bits ($x(n)$ is usually around 2^{160}).
- Let p and q be two large primes with p and $q - 1$ relatively prime. Let $N = p^2 q$. Let $y \in (\mathbf{Z}/n\mathbf{Z})$ such that the order of $y^p \bmod p^2$ is p.
  The encryption function f is $f(r, x) = r^N y^x \bmod N$.
  Decryption is performed by raising the encrypted message to the power $p - 1$ and using the fact that it is easy to compute discrete logarithm in the subgroup $\{x \in (\mathbf{Z}/p^2\mathbf{Z})^* | x \equiv 1 \bmod p\}$.
- The semantic security is proved in [OU98] under the *p-subgroup Assumption*.

5   The new ANDOS Protocol

5.1   Overview

An ANDOS protocol involves two participants. The first one, who holds several secrets, will be called the vendor. The second one, who is willing to buy one of these secrets, will be called the buyer.

Our basic idea is to have the buyer send an encrypted index of the secret he is willing to buy, and to let the vendor perform all computation on his side. The computation of the vendor takes as entries the buyer's index and his own family of secrets. Provided the buyer's index is valid, the result of this computation will be the corresponding secret, encrypted in such a way that only the buyer can properly decrypt it. The core of the protocol is to efficiently prove the validity of the index. Apart from the use of probabilistic homomorphic encryption, this proof method is our main technical contribution. Similar proofs have already been investigated in [PS96], but turn out to be much less efficient than the proposed one.

The protocol is a one-round protocol, plus an additional interactive proof of validity.

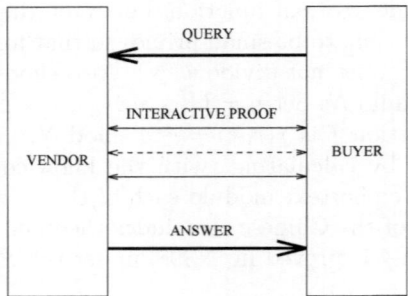

Fig. 1. The ANDOS protocol: the buyer sends his query, proves its validity, and gets the secret he selected

5.2 Preliminary Zero-Knowledge Proof

We present here a protocol which achieves the following: given

- a probabilistic encryption system $\mathcal{E}$ verifying the properties stated in 3,
- an integer t,
- a security parameter k (not necessarily related to the security parameter of $\mathcal{E}$),

we obtain the following:

- the buyer is able to convince the vendor that a sequence of t values represents the encryption of $t-1$ zeros and a single 1, say $x_1, \ldots, x_t$, encrypted under $\mathcal{E}$,
- the protocol does not reveal any information on the index of the non-zero element,
- any cheating buyer who attempts to perform the protocol with a sequence which is not of the proper form will fail with probability $1 - (4/5)^k$,

The protocol goes as follows: The buyer first creates an encryption system $\mathcal{E}$ verifying the properties stated in 3, sends its public parameters to the vendor and proves their validity. He then picks t random numbers $h_1, \ldots, h_t$ in $R(n)$, and sends to the vendor the sequence σ of t values $v_1 = f(h_1, x_1), \ldots, v_t = f(h_t, x_t)$, Then, they repeat k times the following steps:

1. The buyer sends a zero and a one in encrypted form.
2. The vendor picks a random number between 1 and 5, and:

   Case 1 if the number is 1, asks the buyer to reveal the cleartexts corresponding to the encrypted pair.

   Case 2 else, he splits the set $\{1, \ldots, t\}$ in two distinct random subsets A
   and B, computes $a = \prod_{i \in A} v_i, \bmod y(n)$ $b = \prod_{i \in B} v_i \bmod y(n)$, sends
   the buyer the sets A and B and asks him to prove (using property 5)
   that the pair (a, b) represents the same numbers as the encrypted pair
   he has sent in step 1.

5.3   Correctness

If the buyer is playing the protocol fairly (with a sequence σ of the correct form),
he will be able to answer all the vendor's questions.

Assume that the buyer is dishonest and is not playing the protocol fairly,
but uses a sequence which does not have the requested form. We will show that,
whatever strategy he uses, the cheating buyer cannot answer one round correctly
with probability greater than 4/5.

Let us first deal with the case where the sum (mod $x(n)$) of all the integers
in the buyer's sequence is not 1. Recall that property 2 implies that multiplying
several encrypted numbers gives the encryption of their sum (mod $x(n)$).

When **case** 2 occurs, whatever the vendor picks for subsets A and B, the
cleartexts corresponding to a and b cannot be 0 and 1. Hence, the buyer cannot
answer **case** 1 and **case** 2 at the same time.

Now, assume the sum of the numbers in the buyer's sequence is 1, but that
the sequence is not valid. Then at least two integers in the sequence are non-zero.

Lemma 1. *Assume that 2 is invertible in $X(n)$. Let $\alpha_1, \ldots, \alpha_t$ be in $X(n)$ with
α_i and α_j non zero. Let A be a subset of $\{1, \ldots, t\}$ such that $i \notin A, j \notin A$. Define
$A_0 = A$, $A_1 = A \cup \{i\}$, $A_2 = A \cup \{j\}$, $A_3 = A \cup \{i, j\}$. Then, none of the four
pairs*

$$p_l = \{\sum_{q \in A_l} \alpha_q, \sum_{q \notin A_l} \alpha_q\}$$

can be equal.

Proof. Let $p_0 = \{u, v\}$. Then $p_1 = \{u + \alpha_i, v - \alpha_i\}$, $p_2 = \{u + \alpha_j, v - \alpha_j\}$,
$p_3 = \{u + \alpha_i + \alpha_j, v - \alpha_i - \alpha_j\}$. Assume all the pairs coincide, then,

- From p_0 and p_1, we deduce that $\alpha_i = v - u$ (or that $\alpha_i = 0$).
- From p_0 and p_2, we deduce that $\alpha_j = v - u$ (or that $\alpha_j = 0$).
- So, we can rewrite $p_3 = \{u + 2\alpha_i, v - 2\alpha_i\}$. Hence, from p_0 and p_3, we deduce
  that $2\alpha_i = v - u$ (which leads to $\alpha_i = 0$) or that $2\alpha_i = 0$ (which also leads
  to $\alpha_i = 0$ as 2 is invertible).

Hence, all cases lead to a contradiction.

From the lemma, it follows that a buyer who can answer **case** 1 is only able to satisfy at most $3/4$ of the queries in **case** 2. Hence, at the end of the protocol, the vendor should be convinced, with probability $1 - (4/5)^k$, that the encrypted sequence he received is made of one 1 and $t - 1$ zeros.

Remark 1. We can note that the previous lemma does not work if we use the Goldwasser-Micali encryption scheme (where $x(n) = 2$). And, as a matter of fact, when using this scheme, any sequence containing a odd number of 1 will pass the protocol.

The proof that the protocol does not leak any information on the position of the non-zero element can be found in the appendix.

5.4   The Protocol

Let t be the number of secrets of the vendor, and let $s_1, \ldots, s_t$ be the secrets themselves.

Initialization The buyer creates an encryption system $\mathcal{E}$, which verifies the properties stated in 3, sends the public parameters of this system and proves their validity or provides a certificate.

Secret Selection The buyer sends a sequence of t numbers, encrypted under $\mathcal{E}$, and gives a zero-knowledge proof that there is actually $t - 1$ zeros and a one among them. Let $f(r_1, x_1), \ldots, f(r_t, x_t)$ be the t encrypted values.

Vendor computation The vendor picks a random h and computes:

$$S = hide(h, \prod_{i=1}^{t} f(r_i, x_i)^{s_i}) = f(hr' \bmod r(n), \sum_{i=1}^{t} x_i s_i \bmod x(n))$$

where r' can be computed in polynomial time from the r_i and the x_i.

Secret recovery Upon receipt of S, the buyer can retrieve $\sum_{i=1}^{t} x_i s_i \bmod x(n)$ which is equal to one of the s_i, depending on his initial choice.

5.5   Correctness

The security for the buyer is a consequence of the security of the previous proof. Now, let us analyze what additional information the buyer could try to get.

The questions of the vendor during the interactive proof of knowledge are coming from a random source which is unrelated from his secrets. Hence, the buyer might only be able to gain extra information (than the secret he retrieved) by analyzing the final reply string.

When decrypting this reply string, the buyer gets the value of one secret, which cannot be of any help to figure out what other secrets are. To see this, consider the second parameter of the encryption function, namely: $Z = hr' \bmod r(n)$. Let us fix the r_i and the s_i. r' is thus fixed. When h ranges over $R(n)$, Z ranges over $R(n)$ too. Hence, the distribution of Z on all the possible values of

h is uniform. This means that if we only fix the r_i and the very s_a retrieved by the buyer, the distribution of Z on all the possible values of h and the other s_i is also uniform. Consequently, the buyer is unable to get any information from the analysis of S.

5.6   Recovery of Large Secrets

A problem occurs in case the secrets are larger than $x(n)$. As a matter of fact, our protocol only allows the recovery of a secret modulo $x(n)$. Nevertheless, this difficulty can easily be avoided. Simply split each secret into blocks of size lower than $x(n)$, and apply the vendor computation, with the *same* query string, on the different sequences of blocks. The fact that the same query string is used provides the security, and allows a very small overhead: the query cost remains the same, and the reply cost is simply multiplied by the size of the larger secret divided by $x(n)$.

5.7   The Recursive Protocol

The complexity of the protocol is $O(t)$, while in fact, we are only wishing to send an index, which could be achieved in $O(\log t)$ without encryption (nor privacy). By using the same trick as Kushilevitz and Ostrovsky [KO97], we can reduce the query cost to $y(n)2^{O(\sqrt{\log t})}$ while the reply cost is only increased to $y(n)2^{O(\sqrt{\log t})}$. It is interesting to note that, by using the Naccache-Stern cryptosystem instead of the quadratic residuosity cryptosystem, we slightly improve their complexity result.

We now proceed as follows:

Let t be the number of secrets of the vendor, and let $s_1, \ldots, s_t$ be the secrets themselves. Fix an integer m and split the t secrets into t/m buckets of m elements. The distribution of the secrets in each bucket is known by both participant (say the m first secrets in the first bucket, and so on), and the order of the secrets in each bucket is also fixed by the protocol.

We now apply almost the same protocol as before, with a sequence of m integers:

- The buyer sends his query and proves its validity.
- The vendor performs the previous computation, for each bucket, *with the same query string* but keeps all the results.

By applying the vendor computation independently to each bucket, we have virtually extracted a set of t/m secrets out of t secrets. So, we can apply the protocol again to this new set of secrets until the size of the set is less than m. The sole difference is that the secrets in the new set are encrypted and will necessarily be of size greater than $x(n)$. This is not a problem as we know how to recover large secrets. Ultimately, when the number of secrets in the set is less than m, we apply the basic protocol.

Of course, the size of the secrets will grow at each step. After, t/m steps, their size will be $(y(n)/x(n))^{t/m}$ times bigger than the original ones, so the value of m should be chosen to obtain the best tradeoff between the size of the query strings, and the reply string.

Let us now analyze the complexity of this algorithm and discuss the values for m.

5.8   Complexity

Let L be the number of steps of the protocol. At each step we apply the protocol with $m = m_i$ (hence $t \leq \prod_{i=1}^{L} m_i$). Let us choose all the m_i equal, that is $m_i = t^{1/L}$.

- The size of each of the query strings is: $y(n)m_i$ bits, so the total communication cost of the queries is: $y(n) \sum_{i=1}^{L} m_i = y(n)t^{1/L}L$.
- If k is fixed, the communication cost of the zero-knowledge proof is of the form $C + Dm_i$, so, the cost of the zero-knowledge proofs is $(C + Dt^{1/L})L$, where C and D are some constants (which depend on k).
- The communication cost of the final reply string, (if we assume that the size of the original secrets is less than $x(n)$), is $y(n)(y(n)/x(n))^L$.

The global communication cost of the protocol, for t secrets, is

$$CC = (t^{1/L}(y(n) + D) + C)L + y(n)(y(n)/x(n))^L$$

When we use the Naccache-Stern or the Okamoto-Uchiyama cryptosystem, the ratio $y(n)/x(n)$ remains constant when n grows. Let $E = y(n)/x(n)$.

If we solve for the value of L which makes both terms equal, we get:

$$L = O(\sqrt{\log t})$$

which gives a complexity of:

$$CC = y(n)2^{O(\sqrt{\log t})}$$

This result is to be compared with the complexity obtained in [KO97], which is $2^{O(\sqrt{\log t \log y(n)})}$.

6   Applications

The possible applications of our ANDOS protocol are numerous, and we only briefly comment on them. It allows, for instance, the implementation of multi-players mental games as claimed in the original ANDOS paper [BCR87].

It can also be used to implement a pay-per-access database with private queries. This case is a very straightforward application. The implementation issues, which are discussed in the next section, show that this would lead to a really practical protocol.

It can also serve as a building block for more complicated protocols, such as electronic voting, where the basic idea is to use an ANDOS protocol to distribute "eligibility tokens", which are used later to prove one's right to vote [NSS91,Ive91].

This protocol can also be used as an important building block in asymmetric traitor tracing [CFN94,Pfi96] or asymmetric fingerprinting schemes [PS96,PW97]. In traitor tracing, the buyer can use our protocol in order to get a part of his key, say the half, while the other half would be chosen and kept by the vendor along with the query string. Tracing would be performed by comparing a set of recovered keys with the known halves, trial can be achieved by exhibiting the recovered key and the query string. An innocent buyer can prove himself innocent by revealing his cleartexts to show they do not match the recovered key. Details about these families of protocols, resistance against collusions, and good choices for sets of keys can be found in [Pfi96,CFN94,BS95].

For fingerprinting purposes, we can apply the very same process, but instead of sending back the selected secret, which would be chosen by the buyer among a set of acceptable fingerprints, the vendor would insert the (encrypted) secret inside the data to be fingerprinted, using the homomorphic properties of the encryption function (Prop. 2) and send this data to the buyer. The reader can find additional precision in [BM97] where the authors show the existence of a protocol for collusion-secure asymmetric fingerprinting with the help of what they define as a "committed" ANDOS protocol. This means that the buyer has to commit to the secret he is willing to buy at the beginning of the protocol, which is the case in our scheme.

7   Implementation Issues

Our protocol is very efficient for real-life applications, since it does not hide a very large constant beyond its asymptotic behavior. We give here a few examples of costs when the Naccache-Stern cryptosystem is used.

A reasonable size for the modulus N, in order to prevent factorization, is 640 bits. As suggested in [NS98], we will choose n around 2^{160}.

Note that in order to perform an implementation of the protocols, several small tricks can be used to improve the communication cost by a constant factor. For instance, at the beginning of each round of the zero-knowledge proof, the buyer can send one encrypted bit, say $f(h_1, x_1)$, instead of two, and then, in **case** 2, can show the mapping between the pair $\{a, b\}$, and the pair $\{f(h_1, x_1)/f(1, 1), f(1, 1)/f(h_1, x_1)\}$. We assume that these tricks are used when computing the real costs.

The table below summarizes the communication costs, in kilobits for different values of the number of secrets and of the security parameter of the zero-knowledge proof.

	$t = 1000$	$t = 10000$	$t = 100000$	$t = 1000000$
$k = 20$	94	128	176	224
$k = 30$	119	166	214	275
$k = 40$	145	205	252	326

With a 33600 modem, the protocol takes between 3 and 10 seconds to complete. This is a reasonable time to retrieve a key of up to 160 bits. If this key is used to decrypt a piece of data that has previously been retrieved anonymously (say on a newsgroup), the key retrieval time is likely to be small compared to the time needed to retrieve the encrypted data.

If one is willing to directly retrieve large data, (e.g. images), the overhead due to our protocol is roughly a multiplicative factor of 16, which is important but reasonable. Of course, for too large data, the vendor computation becomes very important and might not be negligible any more compared to the transmission time.

8   Conclusion

The primary contribution of this paper is a new and efficient zero-knowledge protocol which allows to prove that a committed string contains one 1 and otherwise 0's. We would like to stress that this protocol is an important building block for many schemes. ANDOS in a straightforward manner, and from there asymmetric fingerprinting, asymmetric traitor tracing or electronic voting. As pointed out in the last section, it is efficient enough to allow, for the first time, a viable and provably secure implementation of an ANDOS protocol.

Acknowledgments

I am grateful to Jean-Jacques Quisquater for fruitful advices and many helpful hints, as well as to my fellow students at the UCL Crypto group for valuable discussions. I also wish to thank Markus Jakobsson and Miklos Santha for proofreading the manuscript.

References

BCR87.   G. Brassard, C. Crépeau, and Jean-Marc Robert. All-or-nothing disclosure of secrets. In A.M. Odlyzko, editor, *Proc. CRYPTO 86*, pages 234–238. Springer-Verlag, 1987. Lecture Notes in Computer Science No. 263.

BCS96.   G. Brassard, C. Crépeau, and M. Sántha. Oblivious transfers and intersecting codes. In *IEEE Transactions on Information Theory*, pages 1769–1780, 1996.

BD90.   M. V. D. Burmester and Y. Desmedt. All languages in NP have divertible zero-knowledge proofs and arguments under cryptographic assumptions. In *Advances in Cryptology — Eurocrypt '90*, pages 1–10, 1990.

Ben87.   J. D. C. Benaloh. Verifiable Secret-Ballot Elections. PhD thesis, Yale's University, 1987.

BF97.   D. Boneh and M. Franklin. Efficient generation of shared RSA keys. In B. S. Kaliski Jr, editor, *Proc. CRYPTO '97*, number 1294 in Lecture Notes in Computer Science, pages 425–439, Springer-Verlag, 1997.

BM97.   I. Biehl and B. Meyer. Protocols for collusion secure asymmetric fingerprinting. In *STACS '97*, pages 399–412, 1997.

BS95.   D. Boneh and J. Shaw. Collusion-secure fingerprinting for digital data. pages 452–465. Springer, 1995. Lecture Notes in Computer Science No. 963.

CFN94.   B. Chor, A. Fiat, and M. Naor. Tracing traitors. In Y. G. Desmedt, editor, *Proc. CRYPTO '95*, pages 257–270. Springer, 1994. Lecture Notes in Computer Science No. 839.

CG97.   B. Chor and N. Gilboa. Computationally private information retrieval (extended abstract). In *Proceedings of the Twenty-Ninth Annual ACM Symposium on Theory of Computing*, pages 304–313, El Paso, Texas, 4–6 May 1997.

CGKS95. B. Chor, O. Goldreich, E. Kushilevitz, and M. Sudan. Private information retrieval. In *36th Annual Symposium on Foundations of Computer Science*, pages 41–50, Milwaukee, Wisconsin, 23–25 October 1995. IEEE.

EGL83.   S. Even, O. Goldreich, and A. Lempel. A randomized protocol for signing contracts. In R. L. Rivest, A. Sherman, and D. Chaum, editors, *Proc. CRYPTO 82*, pages 205–210, New York, 1983. Plenum Press.

FFS88.   U. Feige, A. Fiat, and A. Shamir. Zero knowledge proofs of identity. *Journal of Cryptology*, 1(2):77–94, 1988.

GM84.   S. Goldwasser and S. Micali. Probabilistic encryption. *JCSS*, 28(2):270–299, April 1984.

Ive91.   K. R. Iversen. A cryptographic scheme for computerized general elections. In J. Feigenbaum, editor, *Advances in Cryptology—CRYPTO '91*, volume 576 of *Lecture Notes in Computer Science*, pages 405–419. Springer-Verlag, 1992, 11–15 August 1991.

KO97.   E. Kushilevitz and R. Ostrovsky. Replication is not needed: Single database, computationally-private information retrieval (extended abstract). In *38th Annual Symposium on Foundations of Computer Science*, pages 364–373, Miami Beach, Florida, 20–22 October 1997. IEEE.

NR94.   V. Niemi and A. Renvall. Cryptographic protocols and voting. In *Result and Trends in Theoretical Computer Science*, number 812 in Lecture Notes in Computer Science, pages 307–316, 1994.

NS98.   D. Naccache and J. Stern. A new candidate trapdoor function. To appear in *5th ACM Symposium on Computer and Communications Security*, 1998.

NSS91.   H. Nurmi, A. Salomaa and L. Santean. Secret ballot elections in computer networks. In *Computers and Security*, volume 10, pages 553–560, 1991.

Oht97.   K. Ohta. Remarks on blind decryption. In *Information Security Workshop*, pages 59–64, 1997.

OU98.   T. Okamoto and S. Uchiyama. An efficient public-key cryptosystem. In *Advances in Cryptology—EUROCRYPT 98*, pages 308–318, 1998.

Pfi96.   B. Pfitzmann. Trials of traced traitors. In R. Anderson, editor, *Information Hiding*, volume 1174 of *Lecture Notes in Computer Science*, pages 49–64, Springer-Verlag, 1996.

PS96.   B. Pfitzmann and M. Schunter. Asymmetric fingerprinting (extended abstract). In Ueli Maurer, editor, *Advances in Cryptology—EUROCRYPT 96*, volume 1070 of *Lecture Notes in Computer Science*, pages 84–95. Springer-Verlag, 12–16 May 1996.

PW97.   B. Pfitzmann and M. Waidner. Asymmetric fingerprinting for larger collusions. In *4th ACM Conference on Computer and Communications Security*, 1997.

SS90.   A. Salomaa and L. Santean. Secret selling of secrets with several buyers. In *42th EATCS Bulletin*, pages 178–186, 1990.

SY97.   K. Sakurai and Y. Yamane. Blind decoding, blind undeniable signatures, and their applications to privacy protection. In R. Anderson, editor, *Information Hiding*, pages 257–264. Springer-Verlag, 1997. Lecture Notes in Computer Science No. 1174.

vdGP88.   J. van de Graaf and R. Peralta. A simple and secure way to show the validity of your public key. In C. Pomerance, editor, *Proc. CRYPTO '87*, pages 128–134. Springer-Verlag, 1988. Lecture Notes in Computer Science No. 293.

Wie83.   S. Wiesner. Conjugate coding. In *Sigact News*, volume 18, pages 78–88, 1983. Original manuscript written circa 1970.

Yao86.   A. C. Yao. How to generate and exchange secrets. In *Proc. 27th IEEE Symp. on Foundations of Comp. Science*, pages 162–167, Toronto, 1986. IEEE.

A   Proof of Claims of Section 5.2

We now show that the protocol does not leak any information on the position of the non-zero element by constructing a simulator. We use a zero-knowledge type argument. (For more information on zero-knowledge proofs and simulators, see [FFS88]). However, it is important to stress that we do not prove in zero-knowledge that the commitment σ is correct. This would entail a simulation of the protocol with input σ. Rather, we show how to simulate (up to computational indistiguishability) the *whole* protocol, including the commitment creation step. In other words, we show that the *whole* protocol is independent (up to computational indistiguishability) of the choice of the unique index of the buyer.

We will do this in several steps. Consider the following simulator, that we call $S(q, m)$: this simulator is given two inputs, m an integer in $Y(n)$, which is an encryption of 1, and q an index in $\{1, \ldots, t\}$. It works as follows:

- First, he creates a sequence of t integers, all of which represent encryptions of 0, except for the one in position q which is simply the application of the function *hide* on m. Let $v_1 = f(r_1, x_1), \ldots, v_t = f(r_t, x_t)$ be these integers (with $v_q = hide(r_q, m)$).

- Then the simulator anticipates the question of the vendor: he picks a random number between 1 and 5. He also chooses two random numbers h_1 and h_2 in $R(n)$.
- If he picks 1, he sends the pair $\{f(h_1, 0), f(h_2, 1)\}$ else he sends the pair $\{f(h_1, 0), hide(h_2, m)\}$.
- He waits for the vendor question. If his guess is not correct, he resets and starts again, otherwise:
- In **Case** 1, he reveals the cleartext corresponding to the encrypted pair.
- Else, he receives two subsets A and B which are a partition of $\{1, \ldots, t\}$. Suppose that q is in A. Then, the simulator sends the pair $\{\frac{\prod_{i \in A} r_i}{h_2}, \frac{\prod_{i \in B} r_i}{h_1}\}$; else he swaps h_1 and h_2.

We will now prove that, for any pairs $(q, q') \in \{1, \ldots, t\}$, the outputs of the simulators $S(q, m)$ and $S(q', m)$ are indistiguishable by a polynomially bounded adversary.

Fix $q \in \{1, \ldots, t\}$. The simulator $S(q, m)$ simulates the protocol, (but this does not prove anything as he uses as input the index of the non-zero element in the initial sequence, together with a ciphertext of 1).

Now consider the simulator $S(q, m')$ when m' is an encryption of 0. The existence of a polynomial (probabilistic) time algorithm which distinguishes between the outputs of both simulators would directly yield an algorithm which distinguishes between the encryption of a 0 and the encryption of a 1. This would go against the assumed semantic security of the system (property 3).

But, when m is a ciphertext of 0 the index q does not play any role any more, as each of the t integers of the initial sequence represents an encryption of 0. Let q' be in $\{1, \ldots, t\}$, $q' \neq q$. The output of the simulator $S(q', m')$ is thus indistinguishable from $S(q, m')$. And finally, with the same argument based on the semantic security, the output of $S(q', m')$ is indistinguishable from $S(q', m)$. This shows that our proof does not leak any information on the index of the non-zero element.

Remark 2. The simulators we have considered work in *expected* polynomial time, while the assumption made on the semantic security only requires resistance against polynomial time algorithms. Actually, by limiting the number of resets to say kn (where k and n are the two security parameters in use), we complete the simulation of the k rounds with probability exponentially close to 1. This is enough for computational indistinguishability.

The Béguin-Quisquater Server-Aided RSA
Protocol from Crypto '95 is not Secure

Phong Nguyen and Jacques Stern

École Normale Supérieure
Laboratoire d'Informatique
45, rue d'Ulm
F – 75230 Paris Cedex 05
{Phong.Nguyen,Jacques.Stern}@ens.fr
http://www.dmi.ens.fr/~{pnguyen,stern}/

Abstract. A well-known cryptographic scenario is the following: a smart card wishes to compute an RSA signature with the help of an untrusted powerful server. Several protocols have been proposed to solve this problem, and many have been broken. There exist two kinds of attacks against such protocols: passive attacks (where the server follows the instructions) and active attacks (where the server may return false values). An open question in this field is the existence of efficient protocols (without expensive precomputations) provably secure against both passive and active attacks. At Crypto '95, Béguin and Quisquater tried to answer this question by proposing an efficient protocol which was resistant against all known passive and active attacks. In this paper, we present a very effective lattice-based passive attack against this protocol. An implementation is able to recover the secret factorization of an RSA-512 or RSA-768 key in less than 5 minutes once the card has produced about 50 signatures. The core of our attack is the basic notion of an orthogonal lattice which we introduced at Crypto '97 as a cryptographic tool.

1   Introduction

Small units like chip cards or smart cards have the possibility of computing, storing and protecting data. Today, some of these cards include fast and secure coprocessors allowing to quickly perform the expensive operations needed by public key cryptosystems. But most of the cards are cheap cards with too limited computing power for such tasks. To overcome this problem, extensive research has been conducted under the generic name "server-aided secret computations" (SASC). In the SASC protocol, the client (the smart card) wants to perform a secret computation (*e.g.*, RSA signature generation) by borrowing the computing power of an untrusted powerful server without revealing its secret information. One distinguishes two kinds of attacks against such protocols: attacks where the server respects the instructions are called *passive attacks*, while attacks where the server may return false computations are called *active attacks*.

The first SASC protocol was proposed by Matsumoto, Kato and Imai [9] in the case of RSA signatures [14]. Pfitzmann and Waidner [13] presented several

K. Ohta and D. Pei (Eds.): ASIACRYPT'98, LNCS 1514, pp. 372–379, 1998.

passive attacks against all the protocols of [9], and Anderson [1] described an efficient active attack against one of the protocols of [9]. Several new protocols such as [8,5,4,2,7] have been proposed since. Among these, the protocol of Béguin and Quisquater [2] was quite attractive: it was relatively efficient (since it was based on the fast exponentiation algorithm due to Brickell, Gordon, McCurley and Wilson [3]), did not require expensive precomputations (contrary to most of the proposed protocols), and was secure against all known passive and active attacks, including some lattice-based passive attacks.

We present a very effective lattice-based passive attack against this protocol. Our implementation shows that a server is able to recover the secret factorization of the RSA key (512, 768 or 1024 bits) in less than 5 minutes, once the card has produced about 50 signatures, for all the choices of parameters suggested by Béguin and Quisquater. To run the attack, the server needs to store very few information. The core of our attack is the basic notion of an orthogonal lattice which we recently introduced as a cryptographic tool in [10]. As in [10,12,11], this technique enables us to use the linearity hidden in the protocol, and results in a simple heuristic attack which is devastating in pratice. An open question remains: does there exist a server-aided RSA signature protocol which is both efficient (without requiring expensive precomputations) and provably secure against passive and active attacks ?

The rest of the paper is organized as follows. In section 2, we make a short description of the Béguin-Quisquater server-aided RSA signature protocol. We refer to [2] for more details. In section 3, we recall some facts from [10] about the notion of an orthogonal lattice. Finally, we present our attack in section 4 and the experiments in section 5.

2 The Béguin-Quisquater Protocol

Let $n = pq$ be a RSA public modulus with a secret exponent s and a public exponent v. We have $sv \equiv 1 \pmod{\phi(n)}$ with $\phi(n) = (p-1)(q-1)$. Denote by $\ell(x)$ the bit-length of an integer x. Let $t = \max(\ell(p), \ell(q)) - 1$. In practice, one can assume that $\ell(p) = \ell(q) = t + 1$. Using the Extended Euclidean Algorithm, compute integers w_p and w_q less than n in absolute value such that $w_p + w_q = 1$, p divides w_p and q divides w_q. Thus, if $y_p \equiv y \pmod p$ and $y_q \equiv y \pmod q$ then $y \equiv y_p w_q + y_q w_p \pmod n$. The protocol uses two integer parameters m and h, and is as follows:

1. The card receives M to sign.
2. The card chooses random integers $a_0, \ldots, a_{m-1}$ in $\{0, \ldots, h\}$ and $x_0, \ldots, x_{m-1}$ such that $\ell(x_i) \leq t - \log_2(mh) - 2$.
3. The card computes $s_1 = \sum_{i=0}^{m-1} a_i x_i$.
4. The card sends $M, n, x_0, \ldots, x_{m-1}$ to the server.
5. The server returns $z_0, \ldots, z_{m-1}$ where $z_i = M^{x_i} \mod n$.
6. The card computes $z_p = \prod_{i=0}^{m-1} z_i^{a_i} \mod p$ and $z_q = \prod_{i=0}^{m-1} z_i^{a_i} \mod q$ using the algorithm of [3] for fast exponentiation with precomputation.

7. The card computes $s_2 = s - s_1$ and represents s_2 under the form:

$$\sigma_p = s_2 \quad \mathrm{mod} \ (p-1) + \varrho_p(p-1)$$
$$\sigma_q = s_2 \quad \mathrm{mod} \ (q-1) + \varrho_q(q-1)$$

where ϱ_p is a random number in $\{0, \ldots, q-2\}$ and ϱ_q is a random number in $\{0, \ldots, p-2\}$.

8. The card sends σ_p and σ_q to the server.
9. The server computes and sends to the card $y_p = M^{\sigma_p} \ \mathrm{mod} \ n$ and $y_q = M^{\sigma_q}$ $\mathrm{mod} \ n$.
10. The card computes $S_p = y_p z_p \ \mathrm{mod} \ p$ and $S_q = y_q z_q \ \mathrm{mod} \ q$.
11. Next, the card computes $S = w_q S_p + w_p S_q \ \mathrm{mod} \ n$.
12. The card verifies $M \equiv S^v \ \mathrm{mod} \ n$.
13. If the verification is correct, then the card transmits S.

In their paper [2], Béguin and Quisquater analyzed several passive and active attacks, including some lattice-based passive attacks. They concluded that their protocol was secure against all known passive and active attacks, for 4 different sets of parameters (valid for both RSA-512 and RSA-768), which are summarized in the following table:

	Case 1	Case 2	Case 3	Case 4
h	10	7	17	11
m	19	22	25	29

The resulting protocol was quite efficient. It only required about 30 modular multiplications for the card. The needed RAM and the data transfers between the card and the server were small, and the precomputations were not expensive.

3   The Orthogonal Lattice

We recall a few useful facts about the notion of an orthogonal lattice, which was introduced as a cryptographic tool in [10]. Let L be a lattice in $\mathbb{Z}^n$ where n is any integer. The orthogonal lattice $L^\perp$ is defined as the set of elements in $\mathbb{Z}^n$ which are orthogonal to all the lattice points of L, with respect to the usual dot product. We define the lattice $\bar{L} = (L^\perp)^\perp$ which contains L and whose determinant divides the one of L. The results of [10] which are of interest to us are the following two theorems:

Theorem 1. *If L is a lattice in $\mathbb{Z}^n$, then $\dim(L) + \dim(L^\perp) = n$ and:*

$$\det(L^\perp) = \det(\bar{L}).$$

Thus, $\det(L^\perp)$ divides $\det(L)$. This implies that if L is a low-dimensional lattice in $\mathbb{Z}^n$, then a reduced basis of $L^\perp$ will consist of very short vectors compared to a reduced basis of L. In practice, most of the vectors of any reduced basis of $L^\perp$ are quite short, with norm around $\det(\bar{L})^{1/(n-\dim L)}$.

Theorem 2. *There exists an algorithm which, given as input a basis $(\mathbf{b}_1, \ldots, \mathbf{b}_d)$ of a lattice L in $\mathbb{Z}^n$, outputs an LLL-reduced basis of the orthogonal lattice $L^\perp$, and whose running time is polynomial with respect to n, d and any upper bound of the bit-length of the $\|\mathbf{b}_j\|$'s.*

In practice, one obtains a simple and very effective algorithm (which consists of a single lattice reduction, described in [10]) to compute a reduced basis of the orthogonal lattice, thanks to the celebrated LLL algorithm [6]. This means that, given a low-dimensional L in $\mathbb{Z}^n$, one can easily compute many short and linearly independent vectors in $L^\perp$.

4   A Simple Attack

Throughout the attack, only steps 2, 3, 7 and 8 of the protocol will be of interest.

Assume that the card computes $r + 1$ signatures. Denote by $s_1^{[i]}, \varrho_p^{[i]}, \varrho_q^{[i]}, \sigma_p^{[i]}$ and $\sigma_q^{[i]}$ the values used by the card to compute the i-th signature. Define the following vectors in $\mathbb{Z}^r$ which consist of successive differences:

$$\Delta s_1 = \left(s_1^{[2]} - s_1^{[1]}, s_1^{[3]} - s_1^{[2]}, \ldots, s_1^{[r+1]} - s_1^{[r]}\right)$$
$$\Delta \sigma_p = \left(\sigma_p^{[2]} - \sigma_p^{[1]}, \sigma_p^{[3]} - \sigma_p^{[2]}, \ldots, \sigma_p^{[r+1]} - \sigma_p^{[r]}\right)$$
$$\Delta \sigma_q = \left(\sigma_q^{[2]} - \sigma_q^{[1]}, \sigma_q^{[3]} - \sigma_q^{[2]}, \ldots, \sigma_q^{[r+1]} - \sigma_q^{[r]}\right)$$

By definition of the $\sigma_p^{[i]}$'s and $\sigma_q^{[i]}$'s, the following equations hold:

$$\Delta \sigma_p + \Delta s_1 \equiv 0 \pmod{p-1} \tag{1}$$
$$\Delta \sigma_q + \Delta s_1 \equiv 0 \pmod{q-1} \tag{2}$$

The server knows $\Delta \sigma_p$ and $\Delta \sigma_q$ by step 8, but not Δs_1. These vectors were also considered by Béguin and Quisquater when they analyzed some lattice-based passive attacks, but this is the only similarity between these attacks and the attack we present. We will see that short vectors orthogonal to $\Delta \sigma_p$ (resp. $\Delta \sigma_q$) give information on q (resp. p). If we find enough such independent vectors, then q (resp. p) is revealed. Fortunately, the previous section shows that it is not hard to do so, provided that r is sufficiently large.

We start with two simple remarks:

Lemma 3. *Let $\mathbf{u} \in \mathbb{Z}^r$. If $\mathbf{u} \perp \Delta \sigma_p$ then $\mathbf{u} \perp \Delta s_1$ or $\|\mathbf{u}\| \geq (p-1)/\|\Delta s_1\|$.*

Proof. By (1), we have $\mathbf{u}.\Delta s_1 \equiv 0 \pmod{p-1}$ and the result follows by Cauchy-Schwarz. □

Lemma 4. *Let $\mathbf{u} \in \mathbb{Z}^r$. If $\mathbf{u} \perp \Delta s_1$ then $(q-1)$ divides $\mathbf{u}.\Delta \sigma_q$.*

Proof. Straightforward from (2). □

This shows that if $\mathbf{u} \perp \Delta\sigma_p$ then $(q-1)$ divides $\mathbf{u}.\Delta\sigma_q$, or $\|\mathbf{u}\| \geq (p-1)/\|\Delta s_1\|$. We notice that the latter case implies that $\mathbf{u}$ is relatively long, because the entries of Δs_1 are smaller than $p-1$, as the following lemma shows:

Lemma 5. *Each entry of Δs_1 is in absolute value less than 2^{t-2}.*

Proof. In Step 2, each $s_1^{[i]}$ is a sum of m integers of form ax where $0 \leq a \leq h$ and $\ell(x) \leq \lfloor t - \log_2(mh) - 2 \rfloor$. Therefore:

$$0 \leq s_1^{[i]} \leq mh2^{\lfloor t - \log_2(mh) - 2 \rfloor} \leq 2^{t-2}.$$

The result follows.   □

Actually, the previous upper bound is quite pessimistic. In practice, experiments show that when the choices of Step 2 are indeed random, the entries of Δs_1 are in absolute value less than 2^{t-5}, and on the average around 2^{t-6}. This has to be compared with $\ell(p) = \ell(q) = t+1$. This phenomenon is explained by the following technical lemma:

Lemma 6. *If the random choices of Step 2 are independent and uniformly distributed, then the entries of Δs_1 have zero mean and a variance equal to*

$$\frac{(2h+1)(2^k-1)(2^{k+1}-1)}{18}mh + \frac{2^{2k}h^2}{8}(m^2 - m),$$

where k is the integer $\lfloor t - \log_2(mh) - 2 \rfloor$.

Proof. A simple calculation shows that:

$$E(a_i) = \frac{h}{2} \qquad\qquad E(a_i^2) = \frac{h(2h+1)}{6}$$

$$E(x_i) = \frac{2^k - 1}{2} \qquad\qquad E(x_i^2) = \frac{(2^k-1)(2^{k+1}-1)}{6}$$

Therefore $E(s_1) = \frac{(2^k-1)}{4}mh$ and by independence,

$$E(s_1^2) = E\left(\left(\sum_{i=0}^{m-1} a_i x_i\right)^2\right) = mE(a_0^2)E(x_0^2) + (m^2 - m)E(a_0)^2E(x_0)^2.$$

Hence, each entry of Δs_1 has zero mean and a variance equal to $2E(s_1^2)$.   □

Let σ be the standard deviation of the entries of Δs_1. The following table gives the value of $(t+1) - \log_2 \sigma$ (which indicates the size difference between $q-1$ and the entries of Δs_1) for the 4 different choices of parameters. This value is almost independent of t: there is no difference between RSA-512, RSA-768 and RSA-1024.

	Case 1	Case 2	Case 3	Case 4
h	10	7	17	11
m	19	22	25	29
$(t+1) - \log_2 \sigma$	5.4	5.7	5.2	5.7

Thus, an orthogonal vector to $\Delta\sigma_p$ (resp. $\Delta\sigma_q$) is either relatively long, or such that $q-1$ (resp. $p-1$) divides its dot product with $\Delta\sigma_q$ (resp. $\Delta\sigma_p$). Note that, since vectors $\Delta\sigma_p$ and $\Delta\sigma_q$ are generated using the random values $\rho_p^{[i]}$'s and $\rho_q^{[i]}$'s, there is no intrinsic reason why a vector orthogonal to one of them should also be orthogonal to the other. Thus, if $\mathbf{u}$ is orthogonal to $\Delta\sigma_p$, the dot product $\mathbf{u}.\Delta\sigma_q$ is a non zero multiple of $q-1$. This implies that if we find several short vectors orthogonal to $\Delta\sigma_p$ (resp. $\Delta\sigma_q$), then $q-1$ (resp. $p-1$) will be revealed by simple gcds.

The previous section shows that one can expect to find (in polynomial time) many independent vectors orthogonal to $\Delta\sigma_p$ with norm around

$$\|\Delta\sigma_p\|^{1/(r-1)} \approx (2^{2t}\sqrt{r})^{1/(r-1)}.$$

When r is sufficiently large, the vectors are short enough to reveal $q-1$, and therefore the factorization. Finally, our attack is the following:

1. Compute a reduced basis of $(\Delta\sigma_p)^\perp$.
2. Consider the shortest vectors in this basis (a few are enough) and compute their dot product with $\Delta\sigma_q$.
3. Compute the gcd of all these dot products and check whether it is $q-1$.

In practice, only Step 1 takes a little time. Note that the server only needs to store the $\sigma_p^{[i]}$'s and the $\sigma_q^{[i]}$'s (not even the signatures) to run the attack.

5   Experiments

We implemented the attack using the NTL package [15] which includes efficient lattice-reduction algorithms. We used the LLL floating point version with extended exponent to compute orthogonal lattices, since the entries of $\Delta\sigma_p$ were too large (about the size of n) for the usual floating point version. In practice, the attack reveals the secret factorization as soon as r (the number of signatures) is large enough, and the total computation time is less than 5 minutes on a UltraSparc-I clocked at 167 MHz, when r is less than 70. It actually takes more time to generate the signatures along with the different parameters than to recover the factorization.

The following table shows the practical number of RSA signatures which are necessary to make the attack successful, for different key sizes and choices of parameters.

Minimal number of signatures				
	Case 1	Case 2	Case 3	Case 4
h	10	7	17	11
m	19	22	25	29
RSA-512	53	50	56	53
RSA-768	54	52	56	54
RSA-1024	62	60	63	62

When r reaches these values, at least the 10 shortest vectors of the reduced basis are also orthogonal to Δs_1. Generally, 5 of them are enough to reveal $q - 1$.

When r is larger, most of the vectors of the reduced basis are very short and have similar norms, and their dot product with $\Delta \sigma_q$ is a non-zero multiple of $q - 1$. As previously, we only need a few of them to discover the factorization.

6   Conclusion

We presented a simple passive attack against the Béguin-Quisquater server-aided RSA protocol. It is based on the basic notion of an orthogonal lattice. This notion was introduced as a useful tool in a paper published last year, which cryptanalyzed a knapsack-like cryptosystem proposed by Qu and Vanstone. We applied this technique in a different manner, but the success of our attack relies on the main property of orthogonal lattices as well: given a low-dimensional lattice, one can easily find many short and linearly independent vectors in the corresponding orthogonal lattice.

The attack has been implemented, and is devastating in practice, for all the choices of parameters suggested by Béguin and Quisquater. Once the card has produced about 50 signatures, the server can quickly recover the secret factorization of the RSA key, without storing much information. This shows that the Béguin-Quisquater server-aided RSA protocol is not secure, and stresses the importance of provable security as opposed to security against all known attacks. The existence of a server-aided RSA signature protocol which is both efficient (without requiring expensive precomputations) and provably secure against passive and active attacks remains open.

References

1. R. J. Anderson. Attack on server assisted authentication protocols. *Electronic Letters*, 28(15):1473, 1992.
2. P. Béguin and J.-J. Quisquater. Fast server-aided RSA signatures secure against active attacks. In *Proc. of Crypto '95*, volume 963 of *LNCS*, pages 70–83. Springer, 1995.
3. E. Brickell, D. M. Gordon, K. S. McCurley, and D. Wilson. Fast exponentiation with precomputation. In *Proc. of Eurocrypt '92*, volume 658 of *LNCS*, pages 200–207. Springer, 1993.

4. J. Burns and C. J. Mitchell. Parameter selection for server-aided RSA computation schemes. *IEEE Transactions on Computers*, 43, 1994.
5. S. Kawamura and A. Shimbo. Fast server-aided secret computation protocols for modular exponentiation. *IEEE Journal on Selected Areas Communications*, 11, 1993.
6. A. K. Lenstra, H. W. Lenstra, and L. Lovász. Factoring polynomials with rational coefficients. *Math. Ann.*, 261:515–534, 1982.
7. C. H. Lim and P. J. Lee. Security and performance of server-aided RSA computation protocols. In *Proc. of Crypto '95*, volume 963 of *LNCS*, pages 70–83. Springer, 1995.
8. T. Matsumoto, H. Imai, C.-S. Laih, and S.-M. Yen. On verifiable implicit asking protocols for RSA computation. In *Proc. of Auscrypt '92*, volume 718 of *LNCS*, pages 296–307. Springer, 1993.
9. T. Matsumoto, K. Kato, and H. Imai. Speedings up secret computation with insecure auxiliary devices. In *Proc. of Crypto '88*, volume 403 of *LNCS*, pages 497–506. Springer, 1989.
10. P. Nguyen and J. Stern. Merkle-Hellman revisited: a cryptanalysis of the Qu-Vanstone cryptosystem based on group factorizations. In *Proc. of Crypto '97*, volume 1294 of *LNCS*, pages 198–212. Springer-Verlag, 1997.
11. P. Nguyen and J. Stern. Cryptanalysis of a fast public key cryptosystem presented at SAC' 97. In *Proc. of SAC '98*, LNCS. Springer-Verlag, 1998.
12. P. Nguyen and J. Stern. Cryptanalysis of the Ajtai-Dwork cryptosystem. In *Proc. of Crypto '98*, volume 1462 of *LNCS*. Springer-Verlag, 1998.
13. B. Pfitzmann and M. Waidner. Attacks on protocols for server-aided RSA computation. In *Proc. of Eurocrypt '92*, volume 658 of *LNCS*, pages 153–162. Springer, 1993.
14. R. Rivest, A. Shamir, and L. Adleman. A method for obtaining digital signatures and public-key cryptosystems. *Communications of the ACM*, 21:120–126, 1978.
15. V. Shoup. NTL computer package version 2.0. Can be obtained at http://www.cs.wisc.edu/~shoup/ntl.

Equitable Key Escrow with Limited Time Span
(or, How to Enforce Time Expiration Cryptographically)

Extended Abstract

Mike Burmester[1], Yvo Desmedt[2,1]*, and Jennifer Seberry[3]

[1] Information Security Group, Royal Holloway – University of London
Egham, Surrey TW20 OEX, U.K.
m.burmester@rhbnc.ac.uk,
http://hp.ma.rhbnc.ac.uk/~uhah205/
[2] Center for Cryptography, Computer and Network Security, and
Department of EE & CS, University of Wisconsin – Milwaukee, U.S.A.
desmedt@cs.uwm.edu,
http://www.uwm.edu/~desmedt
[3] Center for Computer Security Research, University of Wollongong, Australia,
j.seberry@uow.edu.au,
http://www.cs.uow.edu.au/people/jennie

Abstract. With equitable key escrow the control of society over the individual and the control of the individual over society are shared fairly. In particular, the control is limited to specified time periods. We consider two applications: time controlled key escrow and time controlled auctions with closed bids. In the first the individual cannot be targeted outside the period authorized by the court. In the second the individual cannot withhold his closed bid beyond the bidding period. We propose two protocols, one for each application. We do *not* require the use of tamper-proof devices.

Key Words: key escrow, auctions with closed bids, time stamps.

1 Introduction

Key escrow has been proposed as a mechanism to protect society from individuals who use a communication system for criminal purposes [4, 25, 10] (an excellent survey of key escrow systems is given by D.E. Denning and D.K. Branstad in [11]). However key escrow can also be used to target innocent individuals. This potential targeting is a major factor which contributes to the social unacceptability of key escrow. From the point of view of an individual, key escrow may restrict his/her privacy and give controlling power to society (Big Brother [8]), which may, in certain circumstances, abuse it. In a society oriented key escrow system this power must be equally shared between the individual and society

---

* A part of this research has been supported by NSF Grant NCR-9508528.

K. Ohta and D. Pei (Eds.): ASIACRYPT'98, LNCS 1514, pp. 380–391, 1998.

(for an analysis of fair cryptosystems see [25, 23]). Furthermore it must have a limited life span. Indeed a major objection to currently proposed key escrow schemes is that there is no effective time control. Once an order to recover a key by the escrow agents has been given, there is nothing to prevent the agents from abusing their power and decrypting all wire-tapped messages, far beyond the time specified by the Court order. Various scenarios can be envisaged in which a threat against a minority is indeed serious. While the Bellare–Goldwasser[3] scheme protects a majority against Big Brother, it does not protect a minority. For example, an extremist group aiming to take control of the government can wire-tap all communication of suspect dissidents, which would then be decrypted when the group took over control.

It is essential that the control of the escrow agents be limited to specified time periods, beyond which it should not be possible for the agents to recover the "old" private keys of a targeted individual. For this purpose we have chosen in our first application of equitable key escrow, to update the keys at regular intervals, and to make it infeasible to compute old keys from the new key. The escrow agents must destroy all the shares of the old keys with each updating. We can allow for a small number of corrupted agents who keep their old shares, but these should not be sufficient to reconstruct the keys.

Our second application of equitable key escrow is contract bidding. In this case it is the individual who may try to abuse society. To prevent a tender from being opened before the specified date, it is encrypted with an escrowed key. The bidder must have some control over the encryption otherwise one can envisage situations in which the escrow agents may collude with a corrupted receiving agent. This threat can be eliminated if the bidder pre-encrypts the bid with his/her own key. However the bidder may then withhold the key. There are several scenarios in which such a threat may be of concern. For example, if altered circumstances make the bid unprofitable, or loss making. In this case, it is "society" (the receiving office) which is threatened by the individual (the bidder). The solution we propose is to force the bidder to use a weak encryption key (a nice discussion on weak encryption is given in [29]). This imposes a time limit which should make it possible for the agents to recover the bid after the tender is opened. Two keys are used: a key for the bidder and an escrowed key. The pair of these keys can be regarded as an enlarged escrow key, in which the share of the bidder is her/his key while the shares of the agents are their old shares. (In this way the bidder is included in all authorized sets.)

Our goal in this paper is to design protocols which achieve equitable key escrow. The organization of this paper is as follows. In Section 2 we present our first protocol for a time controlled key escrow system and discuss its security. In Section 3 we present a protocol for time controlled auctions with closed bids.

Notation and Background

Let p be a prime and $g \in Z_p$ an element of large order. All operations in Z_p are performed modulo p. For simplicity, and when there is no ambiguity, we drop the operator "$\mathrm{mod}\,p$". We also write $x \in_R X$ to indicate that the element x is selected uniformly at random from the set X, independently of all other selections.

The Diffie-Hellman [16] operator DH is defined by $\mathrm{DH}(g^x, g^y) = g^{xy}$. The problem of finding $\mathrm{DH}(g^x, g^y)$, given g^x, g^y, is believed to be hard, and is called the Diffie-Hellman problem. If g^x, g^y and $z \in Z_p$ are given, then the problem of deciding whether $z = \mathrm{DH}(g^x, g^y)$ is called the Diffie-Hellman *decision* problem. If this problem is hard then so is the Diffie-Hellman problem. The *squaring* Diffie-Hellman problem [24] is the problem of finding $\mathrm{DH}(g^x, g^x)$ given g^x. This problem is as hard as the Diffie-Hellman problem under some reasonable conditions [24, Theorem 2]. The problem of deciding whether $z = \mathrm{DH}(g^x, g^x)$, given z, g^x is the squaring Diffie-Hellman *decision* problem. If this problem is hard then so are the Diffie-Hellman problem, the Diffie-Hellman decision problem and the squaring Diffie-Hellman problem. We will also consider the problem of finding elements with large order in Z_p. This is related to Problem C19 in the Adleman–McCurley list of open problems in Number Theoretic Complexity [1], and is considered to be hard.

2   Time controlled key escrow

For simplicity we focus on a basic ℓ-out-of-ℓ escrow system. We will discuss generalizations to other access structures later on.

Our system uses a Discrete Logarithm setting with prime modulus p and $g \in Z_p$ an appropriate element of large order. Initially, at time $t = 0$, the private key of the receiver, Bob, is $a \in_R Z_{p-1}$ and the public key is $y_0 = g^a \bmod p$. Bob shares his private key among ℓ escrow agents EA_i, $i = 1, 2, \ldots, \ell$.

In our basic model each agent gets a share $s_i \in_R Z_{p-1}$ ($i = 1, 2, \ldots, \ell-1$), and s_ℓ is such that $s_1 \cdot s_2 \cdots s_\ell = a \bmod (p-1)$. The main feature of our system is that the private key of Bob and its shares are updated at regular intervals without the need for interaction. At time t, the private key of Bob is updated to $a^{2^t} \bmod (p-1)$, the shares are updated to $s_i^{2^t} \bmod (p-1)$, and the public key is updated to $y_t = g^{a^{2^t}} \bmod p$. The agents EA_i compute the new shares by themselves, and *must* destroy the old shares. As a consequence, the escrow agents cannot enable the decryption of a ciphertext which was encrypted with an old key at a later date, even if forced. We shall prove that the problem of decrypting encryptions with earlier keys is related to two problems: the problem of finding elements of large order in Z_p and the squaring Diffie-Hellman decision problem. Both problems are believed to be hard (*cf.* [1, 24]).

We first describe our basic protocol in more detail. For this purpose we combine the multiplicative threshold scheme of Boyd [7], the ElGamal threshold scheme of Desmedt–Frankel [14] and add time dependency using ideas from Blum-Blum-Shub [6]. For verification we adapt Pedersen scheme [27].

Setting

The parties involved: the sender Alice, the receiver Bob, a Court, the Law Enforcement Agency LEA, and the Escrow Agents EA_i, $i = 1, 2, \ldots, \ell$.

The parameters: A Discrete Logarithm setting is used. Bob chooses a prime p such that $p - 1$ has two large prime factors p_1, p_2, with $p_1 \equiv p_2 \equiv 3 \pmod 4$, so $(-1 \mid p_1) = (-1 \mid p_2) = -1$ ($p_1 p_2$ is a Blum integer [6]), and an element $g \in Z_p$ whose order is $p_1 p_2$. Bob gives p, g to all the agents EA_i, $i = 1, 2, \ldots, \ell$, and to Alice.

Bob has a long term public key which is known to all parties concerned. This key is used for authenticating (signing) Bob's encryption keys and the parameters p, g, if required.

Set-up

Set $time := 0$.

Bob chooses his private key $a \in_R Z_{p-1}^*$ and finds ℓ shares s_i of it, $i = 1, \ldots, \ell$, by choosing $s_i \in_R Z_{p-1}^*$ for $i = 1, \ldots, \ell - 1$, and taking $s_\ell = a \cdot (s_1 \cdots s_{\ell-1})^{-1}$ modulo $p - 1$. The public key of Bob is $y_0 = g^a$. Bob publishes this key. Then,

1. Bob gives privately to each agent EA_i, $i = 1, 2, \ldots, \ell$, the share s_i.
2. Bob publishes $z_1 := g^{s_1}, z_2 := g^{s_2}, \ldots, z_\ell := g^{s_\ell}$, and each agent EA_i checks that these are correct, that is that $z_i = g^{s_i}$, where s_i is its share. If any check fails then Bob has cheated and is reported to the LEA.
   Bob publishes $z_{1,2} := g^{s_1 s_2}$, $z_{1,2,3} := g^{s_1 s_2 s_3}, \ldots,\ z_{1,2,\cdots,\ell} := g^{s_1 s_2 \cdots s_\ell}\ (= y_0)$, and proves in zero-knowledge to the LEA that these are correctly constructed. That is, Bob proves that $z_{1,2,\ldots,k} = \mathrm{DH}(z_{1,2,\ldots,k-1}, z_k)$, for $k = 2, \ldots, \ell$, by using an interactive zero-knowledge proof for the Diffie-Hellman problem – an example of such a proof is given in Appendix A. If any of the proofs fails, then Bob has cheated and is reported to the LEA.

The protocol

Updating

At $time = t$

Each agent EA_i updates his share by squaring it, *i.e.*, the current share is $s_i^{2^t} \bmod (p - 1)$, and then destroys the old share ($s_i^{2^{t-1}} \bmod (p - 1)$).

Bob updates his private key to $a^{2^t} \bmod (p - 1)$ and publishes his public key $y_t := g^{a^{2^t}} \bmod p$. If necessary Bob proves to the LEA that this is correct by using an interactive zero-knowledge proof for the Diffie-Hellman problem (for example, the interactive proof given in Appendix A). That is, Bob proves that $y_t = \mathrm{DH}(y_{t-1}, y_{t-1})$.

Getting an escrowed key

1. Alice asks Bob for a new encryption key.

2. Bob sends Alice his public key which is authenticated with his long term key, $(p, g, y_t, \text{sign}_{\text{Bob}}(p, g, y_t))$.
3. If Bob's signature is valid then Alice sends Bob the encryption $\text{ElG}(m) = (g^r, m y_t{}^r)$, $r \in_R Z_{p-1}^*$, of a message $m \in Z_p^*$ with key y_t.
4. If the Court has issued an order to recover the message, then the LEA will wire-tap the communication and send g^r to agent EA_1. The agents $EA_1, EA_2, \ldots, EA_\ell$ then compute $y_t{}^r$ sequentially as follows: for $i < \ell$, each EA_i on receiving $g^{r \prod_{j=1}^{i-1} s_j^{2^t}}$ computes $g^{r \prod_{j=1}^{i} s_j^{2^t}} := (g^{r \prod_{j=1}^{i-1} s_j^{2^t}})^{s_i^{2^t}}$, which it sends to EA_{i+1}. Agent EA_ℓ then computes $(g^{r \prod_{j=1}^{\ell-1} s_j^{2^t}})^{s_\ell^{2^t}}$, which it sends to the LEA. Since this corresponds to $y_t{}^r$, the LEA can decrypt the ciphertext.

Security

Theorem 1. (Irreversible time) *If the squaring Diffie-Hellman decision problem is hard and if finding elements of large order in Z_p is hard, then decrypting old ciphertext with new shares of the escrow agents is hard.*

Proof. (Sketch) Suppose that there is a polynomial time algorithm **A** which on input $p, g, z_1, z_2, \ldots, z_\ell$, $z_{1,2}$, $z_{1,2,3}$, $\ldots$, $z_{1,2,\ldots,\ell}$, the shares $s_1^{2^t}, s_2^{2^t}, \ldots, s_\ell^{2^t}$, the old shares of $(\ell - 1)$ corrupted shareholders, Bob's long term public key, the certificates $(p, g, y_j, \text{sign}_{\text{Bob}}(p, g, y_j))$, $j = 1, 2, \ldots, t$, and an old ciphertext (w_1, w_2), with $w_1 = g^r$, $r \in Z_{p-1}^*$, $w_2 = m y_{t-u}^r$, $m \in Z_p^*$, will output the message m. Then **A** can be used to compute $g^{r a^{2^{t-u}}}$ $(= w_2/m)$. We now will use **A** to get an element in Z_p of large order. First we prepare an input for **A**.

Note that $0 < u < t$ (since public key y_0 is never used to encrypt). Assume that the dishonest escrow agents are $i_1, i_2, \ldots, i_{\ell-1}$ and let i_ℓ be the honest escrow agent. Find an appropriate long term secret key for Bob. Choose $\bar{s}_1, \bar{s}_2, \ldots, \bar{s}_\ell \in_R Z_{p-1}^*$. Compute $b_0 = \bar{s}_1 \cdots \bar{s}_\ell \bmod p - 1$, $\bar{z}_1 := g^{\bar{s}_1}$, $\bar{z}_2 := g^{\bar{s}_2}$, $\ldots$, $\bar{z}_\ell := g^{\bar{s}_\ell}$, $\bar{z}_{1,2} := g^{\bar{s}_1 \bar{s}_2}$, $\ldots$, $\bar{z}_{1,2,\ldots,\ell} := g^{\bar{s}_1 \cdots \bar{s}_\ell}$, and $\bar{y}_0 := g^{b_0}$, $\bar{y}_1 := g^{b_0^2}, \ldots$, $\bar{y}_{t-u-1} := g^{b_0^{2^{t-u-1}}}$.

Take $b \in_R Z_{p-1}^*$ and compute $\bar{s}'_{i_1} := \bar{s}_{i_1}^{2^{t-u}}$, $\bar{s}'_{i_2} := \bar{s}_{i_2}^{2^{t-u}}$, $\ldots$, $\bar{s}'_{i_{\ell-1}} := \bar{s}_{i_{\ell-1}}^{2^{t-u}} \in_R Z_{p-1}^*$. Compute $\bar{s} := \bar{s}'_{i_1} \cdot \bar{s}'_{i_2} \cdots \bar{s}'_{i_{\ell-1}}$, $\bar{s}'_{i_\ell} := b \cdot (\bar{s})^{-1}$, and the public keys $\bar{y}_{t-u} = g^b$, $\bar{y}_{t-u+1} = g^{b^2}, \ldots$, $\bar{y}_t = g^{b^{2^u}}$. Observe that even though it is highly unlikely that the public key $\bar{y}_{t-u}$ is properly constructed (that is, it is highly unlikely that $\bar{y}_{t-u} = \text{DH}(\bar{y}_{t-u-1}, \bar{y}_{t-u-1})$), it is hard for **A** to recognize this, if the squaring Diffie-Hellman decision problem is hard.

Give as input to **A**: $p, g, \bar{z}_1, \bar{z}_2, \ldots, \bar{z}_\ell, \bar{z}_{1,2}, \ldots, \bar{z}_{1,2,\ldots,\ell}$, the "shares" $\bar{s}'_1{}^{2^u}, \ldots, \bar{s}'_\ell{}^{2^u}$, the "old shares" $\bar{s}'_{i_1}, \ldots, \bar{s}'_{i_{\ell-1}}$, Bob's long term public key, the certificates $(p, g, \bar{y}_j, \text{sign}_{\text{Bob}'}(p, g, \bar{y}_j))$, $j = 1, 2, \ldots, t$, and an "old" ciphertext $(\bar{w}_1, \bar{w}_2)$ encrypted at time $t - u$, with $\bar{w}_1 = g^{\bar{r}}$, $\bar{r} \in_R Z_{p-1}^*$, and $\bar{w}_2 \in_R Z_p^*$. Algorithm **A** will output a message $\bar{m}$ such that $\bar{w}_2/\bar{m} = g^{\bar{r}d}$, where d is a 2^u–th root of b^{2^u} which is a quadratic residue in $Z_{p_1 p_2}$. However b was chosen at random in

Z_{p-1}^*, so that with probability 3/4 we get that $b \bmod p_1p_2$ is not a residue in $Z_{p_1p_2}$. (Indeed a^{2^t}, for $t > 1$, has 4 square roots in $Z_{p_1p_2}$ of which only one is a quadratic residue, because of our restrictions on the primes p_1, p_2. It follows that there is only one primitive 2^u–th root of a^{2^t} in $Z_{p_1p_2}$, $0 < u \le t$, which is a quadratic residue. in $Z_{p_1p_2}$.) Then with probability one half, $b - d$ is either a multiple of p_1 or a multiple of p_2. This means that $g^{\bar{r}d}/g^{\bar{r}b} = g^{\bar{r}(d-b)}$ has order p_1 or p_2. Consequently **A** can find an element in Z_p of large order.

(Note that, since we work modulo p, the view of the communication between the escrow agents when co-decrypting can also be included in the simulation, as discussed in the final paper. Moreover, if this communication is encrypted (to prevent an outsider to learn the ciphertext), the simulation of this part is straightforward.)   □

Theorem 2. (Privacy) *A wire-tapper may try to decipher the ciphertext. This is as hard as the Diffie-Hellman problem.*

Proof. (Sketch) We show this by using the approach in [13]. Suppose that **B** is a polynomial time algorithm which on input: $p, g, z_1, z_2, \ldots, z_\ell, z_{1,2}, z_{1,2,3}, \ldots, z_{1,2,\ldots,\ell}$, the certificates $(p, g, \bar{y}_j, \text{sign}_{\text{Bob}'}(p, g, \bar{y}_j))$, $j = 1, 2, \ldots, t$, and the ciphertext $(\bar{w}_1, \bar{w}_2)$, $\bar{w}_1 = g^r$, $\bar{w}_2 = my_t^r$, will output m. We now prove that **B** can be used to solve the Diffie-Hellman problem. Let $p, g, \bar{y}_t, \bar{w}_1$ be an instance of the the Diffie-Hellman problem. Construct $\bar{z}_1, \bar{z}_2, \ldots, \bar{z}_\ell, \bar{z}_{1,2}, \ldots, \bar{z}_{1,2,\ldots\ell}$, $\bar{y}_0, \bar{y}_1, \ldots, \bar{y}_t \in Z_p^*$, as in the previous case. Give this as input to **B** together with $(\bar{w}_1, \bar{w}_2)$, to get a "message" $\bar{m}$ such that $\bar{w}_2/\bar{m} = \text{DH}(\bar{y}_t, \bar{w}_1)$ $(= \bar{y}_t^{\bar{r}})$. The rest can all be simulated because we have used zero-knowledge proofs.   □

2.1 Generalizations

Generalizing time controlled l-out-of-l key escrow systems to l'-out-of-l systems, is straightforward when using more complex secret sharing schemes over $Z_{p-1}^*(*)$. The subset of escrow agents involved in the decryption must be known in advance. Secret sharing schemes that could be used for this purpose can be found in [15, 12, 2, 5], when using techniques such as those described in [18, 13]. Robustness can be achieved by using, for example [21, 20].

Other properties such as proactive secret sharing can also be achieved using [22, 19, 28].

3 Time controlled auctions with closed bids

We first consider a basic (additive) ℓ-out-of-ℓ escrow system, using a simple setting. Generalizations will be discussed later.

Our system uses a Discrete Logarithm setting with composite modulus $n = p_1p_2$, where p_1, p_2 are appropriate large primes. The bidder, Alice, chooses n and $g_1, g_2 \in Z_n$ such that g_1 has large order whereas g_2 has a rather small prime order q. Alice has two public keys for encryption: $y_1 = g_1^{a_1} \bmod n$, $y_2 = g_2^{a_2} \bmod n$, where $a_1 \in_R Z_{\phi(n)}$, $a_2 \in_R Z_q$. The private key a_1 is shared among ℓ escrow agents EA_i, $i = 1, 2, \ldots, \ell$. The other is not shared. For this system the public key y_2 is weak and must be used *only once*. This key must be such that it can be recovered by an exhaustive search of the key space, but the time taken for this search should not be too short.[1]

Alice "double" encrypts her contract bid m by using the keys y_1, y_2. Let $ElG^2(m)$ be the encryption. Alice sends this to the receiving agent Bob. At completion she will reveal both secret keys a_1, a_2, from which Bob will get the tendered bid m. If Alice refuses to reveal these keys, then Bob informs the escrow agents who will enable a first decryption. This will make it possible for Bob to get an encryption $ElG(m)$ of m with private key a_2. Bob then initiates a procedure to recover m, by exhaustively breaking this encryption. Bob can achieve this because the second key is relatively weak. A similar argument applies if a Court order is issued to the escrow agents to enable the decryption of $ElG^2(m)$. The security issues of this protocol will be discussed in more detail later. We first describe the protocol more formally. For this purpose we use the additive threshold scheme of Boyd and Frankel [7, 17], and/or the ElGamal threshold scheme of Desmedt–Frankel [14] and use the concept of weak encryption (see, e.g., [29]).

Setting

The parties involved: the bidder Alice, the receiving officer Bob, a Court, the Law Enforcement Agency LEA, and the Escrow Agents EA_i, $i = 1, 2, \ldots, \ell$.
The parameters: Both Alice and Bob have long term public keys which are known to each other. These keys are used for authentication (signing).
A Discrete Logarithm setting is used with a composite modulus n. Alice chooses $n = p_1 p_2$, a product of two large primes p_1, p_2, with $p_1 - 1 = 2qq_1$, $p_2 - 1 = 2qq_2$, q_1, q_2 primes, and q a rather small prime (say 140 bits).
Alice chooses $g_1 \in_R Z_n$ and $g_2 \in Z_n$ such that $\mathrm{ord}(g_2 \bmod p_1) = \mathrm{ord}(g_2 \bmod p_2) = q$. Here $\mathrm{ord}(g_2 \bmod p_1)$ is the order of g_2 in Z_{p_1} and $\mathrm{ord}(g_2 \bmod p_2)$ is the order of g_2 in Z_{p_2}. Consequently g_2 has order q in Z_n.

Set-up

Alice chooses $a_1 \in_R Z_{\phi(n)}$, $a_2 \in_R Z_q$. The public key of Alice is $(n, q, g_1, g_2, y_1, y_2)$, where $y_1 := g_1{}^{a_1} \bmod n$, $y_2 := g_2{}^{a_2} \bmod n$.
Alice finds ℓ shares of a_1, by choosing exponents $s_i \in_R Z_{\phi(n)}$ for $i = 1, 2, \ldots, \ell-1$, and taking $s_\ell = a_1 - (s_1 + s_2 + \ldots + s_{\ell-1}) \bmod \phi(n)$.

1. Alice gives privately to each agent EA_i, $i = 1, 2, \ldots, \ell$, the share s_i.
2. Alice publishes $z_1 := g_1^{s_1}, z_2 := g_1^{s_2}, \ldots, z_\ell := g_1^{s_\ell}$. Each agent EA_i checks that $z_i = g_1^{s_i}$ and reports failure to the LEA. The LEA checks that $y_1 = z_1 \cdot z_2 \cdots z_\ell$. If any of the checks of the EA_i's fails or if the LEA's check fails

---

[1] Since an exhaustive search is parallelizable, some kind of inherently sequential scheme may be used, such as the *time-lock puzzles* proposed in [29]. Our protocol can easily be adapted to allow for such schemes.

then Alice has cheated, the tender is rejected, and appropriate actions are taken.

Sending an encrypted contract bid

1. Alice sends Bob the pair of her public keys authenticated with her long term key,

$$(n, q, g_1, g_2, y_1, y_2, \text{sign}_{\text{Alice}}(g_1, g_2, n, q, y_1, y_2)),$$

and the encrypted bid $\text{ElG}^2(m) = (g_1^{r_1}, g_2^{r_2}, my_1^{r_1}y_2^{r_2})$, where $m \in Z_n^*$ is the bid and $r_1, r_2 \in_R Z_n$.
2. If the parameters are in the appropriate fields, with q a small prime, if the order of g_2 and y_2 are both q, and if Alice's public keys are authenticated properly, then Bob accepts the tender and sends Alice a receipt $\text{sign}_{\text{Bob}}(\text{Alice}, \text{ElG}^2(m))$.

Opening a tender

When the tender is due to be opened, Alice sends Bob the private keys a_1, a_2. Bob checks these for correctness. If correct, $\text{ElG}^2(m)$ is decrypted to get the bid m, which is validated.

If Alice refuses to send her keys, the LEA is informed and initiates a procedure to recover m.

The Court recovers the bid

If the Court has issued an order to recover the bid, the LEA will wire-tap the communication and send g^{r_1} to the escrow agents who will compute $y_1^{r_1}$. From this the LEA can get $\text{ElG}(m) = (g_2^{r_2}, my_2^{r_2})$. The key for this ciphertext is weak, so the LEA can recover m by brute force. However, q has to be sufficiently large to prevent a conspiracy, as explained further on.

Security

The security of this system relies on the difficulty of factoring a number $n = p_1 p_2$, p_1, p_2 primes, when a particular number $g_2 \in Z_n$ is given, with a rather small prime order q. It is important that both $g_2 \bmod p_1 \neq 1$ and $g_2 \bmod p_2 \neq 1$. Otherwise, if say $g_2 \bmod p_1 = 1$, then p_1 is a factor of $g_2 - 1$ and it becomes easy to factor n by taking the $gcd(n, g_2 - 1)$. Observe that for $g_2 = n - 1$ we have $q = 2$, but this trivial case is too small to be of any use for us.

Fair auction bidding

Alice may refuse to open her bid, on completion. Bob will inform the LEA and the Court will authorize the escrow agents to decrypt the ciphertext. The escrow agents will compute $y_1^{r_1}$ from which the LEA will get $\text{ElG}(m) = (g_2^{r_2}, my_2^{r_2})$. The key for this ciphertext is weak, so the LEA can initiate a procedure to recover m by brute force. (Note that q has to be sufficiently large, as we now explain.)

Conspiracy

The agents may be corrupted by the bidding officer Bob. They will recover $\text{ElG}(m) = (g_2{}^{r_2}, m y_2{}^{r_2})$, but if the key y_2 is not too weak they will not be able to recover the message in time. For this reason q cannot be too small.

Theorem 3. (Privacy) *A wire-tapper may try to decipher the bid m. This is as hard as breaking the Diffie-Hellman problem.*

Proof. (Sketch) For simplicity assume that the dishonest escrow agents are numbered from 1 to $\ell - 1$ (this can easily be generalized). Suppose that **A** is a polynomial time algorithm which on input: n, q, g_1, g_2, y_1, y_2, authenticated with Alice's long term key, $z_1, z_2, \ldots, z_\ell$, and $(g_1{}^{r_1}, g_2{}^{r_2}, m y_1{}^{r_1} y_2{}^{r_2})$, will output m. Let $n, g_1, \bar{y}_1, g_1{}^{\bar{r}_1}$ be an instance of the Diffie-Hellman problem similar as in [14, 13]. Take $\bar{s}_1, \ldots, \bar{s}_{\ell-1} \in_R Z_n$, and $\bar{s} = \bar{s}_1 + \ldots + \bar{s}_{\ell-1}$. Then let $\bar{z}_1 = g^{\bar{s}_1}$, $\ldots, \bar{z}_{\ell-1} = g^{\bar{s}_{\ell-1}}$ and $\bar{z}_\ell = \bar{y}_1 g_1{}^{-\bar{s}}$. Find an appropriate long term key for Alice. Finally take $\bar{r}_2 \in_R Z_q$ and compute $g_2{}^{\bar{r}_2}$ and $y_2{}^{\bar{r}_2}$.

Give as input to **A**: $n, q, g_1, g_2, \bar{y}_1, \bar{y}_2$, authenticated with Alice's public key, $\bar{z}_1, \ldots, \bar{z}_\ell$, and $(g_1{}^{\bar{r}_1}, g_2{}^{\bar{r}_2}, \bar{w})$, where $\bar{w} \in_R Z_n$. Algorithm **A** will output $\bar{m}$, such that $\bar{w}/\bar{m} = \bar{y}_1{}^{\bar{r}_1} \bar{y}_2{}^{\bar{r}_2}$, from which we get $\text{DH}(\bar{y}_1, g_1{}^{\bar{r}_1}) = \bar{y}_1{}^{\bar{r}_1}$. $\square$

Generalizations

Similar generalizations to those in Section 2.1 apply. (Although $\phi(n)$ is not public, techniques similar to those in [18, 13] will address this problem.)

Acknowledgment

The authors would like to thank an anonymous referee for pointing out the references [24, 29]. The second author thanks Moti Yung for discussions about escrowed bidding.

References

1. Adleman, L.M., McCurley K.S.: Open Problems in Number Theoretic Complexity. In: Johnson, D., Nishizeki, T., Nozaki, A., Wilf, H. (eds): Discrete Algorithms and Complexity, Proceedings of the Japan-US Joint Seminar (Perspective in Computing series, **15**. Academic Press Inc., Orlando, Florida (1986) 263–286

2. Alon, N., Galil, Z., Yung, M.: Efficient dynamic-resharing "verifiable secret sharing" against mobile adversary. In: Spirakis, P.G. (ed): Algorithms – ESA '95, Third Annual European Symposium, Proceedings (Lecture Notes in Computer Science 979). Springer-Verlag (1995) 523–537

3. Bellare, M., Goldwasser, S.: Verifiable partial key escrow. Proc. 4th ACM Conference on Computer and Communications Security (1997)

4. Beth, T.: Zur Sicherheit der Informationstechnik. Informatik-Spektrum, **13** (1990) 204–215

5. Blackburn, S.R., Burmester, M., Desmedt, Y., Wild, P.R.: Efficient multiplicative sharing schemes. In: Maurer, U. (ed): Advances in Cryptology – Eurocrypt '96, Proceedings (Lecture Notes in Computer Science 1070). Springer-Verlag (1996) 107–118
6. Blum, L., Blum, M., Shub, M.: A simple unpredictable pseudo-random number generator. SIAM J. Comput. 15(2) (1986) 364–383
7. Boyd, C.: Digital multisignatures. In: Beker, H., Piper, F. (eds): Cryptography and coding. Clarendon Press (1989) 241–246
8. Chaum, D.: Security without identification: transaction systems to make Big Brother obsolete. Commun. ACM, 28(10) (1985) 1030–1044
9. Chaum, D.: Zero-knowledge undeniable signatures. In: Damgård, I. (ed): Advances in Cryptology, Proc. of Eurocrypt '90 (Lecture Notes in Computer Science 473). Springer-Verlag (1991) 458–464
10. Clipper. A proposed federal information processing standard for an escrowed encryption standard (EES). Federal Register, July 30, 1993.
11. Denning, D.E., Branstad, D.K.: A taxonomy of key escrow encryption systems. Communications of the ACM, 39(3), (1996) 24–40
12. Desmedt, Y., Di Crescenzo, G., Burmester, M.: Multiplicative non-abelian sharing schemes and their application to threshold cryptography. In: Pieprzyk, J., Safavi-Naini, R. (eds): Advances in Cryptology – Asiacrypt '94, Proceedings (Lecture Notes in Computer Science 917). Springer-Verlag (1995) 21–32
13. De Santis, A., Desmedt, Y., Frankel, Y., Yung M.: How to Share a Function Securely. Proceedings of the twenty-sixth annual ACM Symp. Theory of Computing (STOC) (1994) 522–533
14. Desmedt, Y., Frankel, Y.: Threshold cryptosystems In: Brassard, G. (ed): Advances in Cryptology – Crypto '89, Proceedings (Lecture Notes in Computer Science #435). Springer-Verlag (1990) 307–315
15. Desmedt, Y.G., Frankel, Y.: Homomorphic zero-knowledge threshold schemes over any finite abelian group. SIAM Journal on Discrete Mathematics 7(4) (1994) 667–679
16. Diffie, W., Hellman, M.E.: New directions in cryptography. IEEE Trans. Inform. Theory, IT–22(6) (1976) 644–654
17. Frankel, Y.:. A practical protocol for large group oriented networks. In: Quisquater, J.-J., Vandewalle, J. (eds.): Advances in Cryptology – Eurocrypt '89, Proceedings (Lecture Notes in Computer Science #434) Springer-Verlag (1990) 56–61
18. Frankel, Y., Desmedt, Y.: Parallel reliable threshold multisignature. Tech. Report TR–92–04–02, Dept. of EE & CS, Univ. of Wisconsin–Milwaukee, April 1992. ftp://ftp.cs.uwm.edu/pub/tech_reports/desmedt-rsa-threshold_92.ps.
19. Frankel, Y., Gemmell, P., MacKenzie, P.D., Yung, M.: Proactive RSA. In: Kaliski, B.S. (ed): Advances in Cryptology – Crypto '97, Proceedings (Lecture Notes in Computer Science 1294). Springer-Verlag (1997) 440–454
20. Frankel, Y., Gemmell, P., Yung, M.: Witness-based cryptographic program checking and robust function sharing. Proceedings of the Twenty-Eighth Annual ACM Symp. on Theory of Computing (1996) 499–508
21. Gennaro, R., Jarecki, S., Krawczyk, H., Rabin, T.: Robust and efficient sharing of RSA functions. In: Koblitz, N. (ed): Advances in Cryptology – Crypto '96, Proceedings (Lecture Notes in Computer Science 1109). Springer-Verlag (1996) 157–172
22. Herzberg, A., Jarecki, S., Krawczyk, H., Yung, M.: Proactive secret sharing. In: Coppersmith, D. (ed): Advances in Cryptology – Crypto '95, Proceedings (Lecture Notes in Computer Science #963). Springer-Verlag (1995) 339–352

23. Kilian, J., Leighton, T.: Failsafe key escrow, revisited. In: Coppersmith, D. (ed): Advances in Cryptology – Crypto '95, Proceedings (Lecture Notes in Computer Science #963). Springer-Verlag (1995) 208–221

24. Maurer, U.M., Wolf, Y.: Diffie-Hellman Oracles. In:. Kobliz, N. (ed): Advances in Cryptology – Crypto '96, Proceedings (Lecture Notes in Computer Science 1109). Springer-Verlag (1996) 268–282

25. Micali, S.: Fair public-key cryptosystems. In: Brickell, E.F. (ed): Advances in Cryptology – Crypto '92, Proceedings (Lecture Notes in Computer Science 740). Springer-Verlag (1993) 113–138

26. Ostrovsky, R., Yung, M.: How to Withstand Mobile Virus Attacks. Proceedings of the 10-th Annual ACM Symp. on Principles of Distributed Computing (1991) 51–60

27. Pedersen, T.P.: A threshold cryptosystem without a trusted party. In: Davies, D.W. (ed): Advances in Cryptology, Proc. of Eurocrypt '91 (Lecture Notes in Computer Science #547). Springer-Verlag (1991) 522–526

28. Rabin, T.: A simplified approach to threshold and proactive RSA. To appear in the Proceedings of Crypto '98.

29. Rivest, R.L., Shamir, A., Wagner, D.A.: Time-lock puzzles and time-release Crypto. http://theory.lcs.mit.edu/~rivest/publications.html (to appear).

30. Simmons, G.J., June 22–24, 1994. Observation made at the Workshop on Key Escrow.

A   A zero-knowledge proof for the Diffie-Hellman decision problem

The zero-knowledge proof for the Diffie-Hellman decision problem in [9] is not adequate for our purpose, since it designed for the case when the group of the exponents has prime order. In our case the group of exponents has composite order. The following protocol will serve our purpose.

Input: A prime p, $g \in Z_p$ of large order, $\alpha = g^a \bmod p$, $\beta = g^b \bmod p$, $\gamma = g^{ab} \bmod p$.

Repeat independently $t = \log p$ times the following subroutine:

1. The Prover selects exponents $x, y \in_R Z_{p-1}$ and sends to the Verifier: $\kappa_x = g^x \bmod p$, $\kappa_y = g^y \bmod p$, $\kappa_{xy} = g^{xy} \bmod p$, $\kappa_{ay} = g^{ay} \bmod p$, and $\kappa_{bx} = g^{bx} \bmod p$.

2. The Verifier sends the Prover a query bit $e \in_R \{0, 1\}$.

3. If $e = 0$ the Prover sends x, y to the Verifier, and the Verifier checks that: $\kappa_x = g^x \bmod p$, $\kappa_y = g^y \bmod p$, $\kappa_{xy} = g^{xy} \bmod p$, $\kappa_{ay} = \alpha^y \bmod p$, and $\kappa_{bx} = \beta^x \bmod p$.
   If $e = 1$ the Prover sends $a' = a + x \bmod (p - 1)$, $b' = b + y \bmod (p - 1)$ to the Verifier who checks that: $g^{a'} \equiv \alpha \cdot \kappa_x \pmod p$, $g^{b'} \equiv \beta \cdot \kappa_y \pmod p$, and $g^{a'b'} \equiv \gamma \cdot \kappa_{ay} \cdot \kappa_{bx} \cdot \kappa_{xy} \pmod p$.
   If any of the checks fails, the Verifier halts and rejects the proof.

The Verifier accepts the proof of the Prover if all t rounds have been completed successfully.

Let $L = \{(p, \alpha, \beta, \gamma) \mid p$ prime, $\alpha = g^a \bmod p$, $\beta = g^b \bmod p$, $\gamma = g^{ab} \bmod p\}$. Then,

Theorem 4. *The protocol above is a perfect zero-knowledge proof of membership in L.*

Proof. (Sketch)
Completeness: Obvious.
Soundness: If the Prover can answer the queries $e = 0, 1$ then there exist a, b, x, y such that $a' = a + x \bmod (p-1)$, $b' = b + y \bmod (p-1)$, with $\kappa_{ay} = \alpha^y \bmod p$, $\kappa_{bx} = \beta^x \bmod p$, $\kappa_{xy} = g^{xy} \bmod p$, and $\gamma \equiv g^{a'b'} \cdot \kappa_{ay}^{-1} \cdot \kappa_{bx}^{-1} \cdot \kappa_{xy}^{-1} \equiv g^{ab} \pmod{p}$.
Zero-knowledge: Let α, β, γ be given. Pick $a', b' \in_R Z_{p-1}$, and let $\kappa_x = g^{a'}/\alpha \bmod p$, $\kappa_y = g^{b'}/\beta \bmod p$. Then solve $\alpha^{b'} \equiv \gamma \cdot \kappa_{ay} \pmod{p}$, $\beta^{a'} \equiv \gamma \cdot \kappa_{bx} \pmod{p}$, $g^{a'b'} \equiv \gamma \cdot \kappa_{ay} \cdot \kappa_{bx} \cdot \kappa_{xy} \pmod{p}$, for the unknowns $\kappa_{ay}, \kappa_{bx}, \kappa_{xy}$, respectively. $\square$

Audio and Optical Cryptography

Yvo Desmedt[1,2]*, Shuang Hou[2]*, and Jean-Jacques Quisquater[3]

[1] Center of Cryptography, Computer and Network Security,
CEAS, University of Wisconsin – Milwaukee, and
Dept. of Mathematics, Royal Holloway, University of London, UK
desmedt@cs.uwm.edu,
http://www.uwm.edu/~desmedt
[2] Department of EE & CS, University of Wisconsin, Milwaukee
P.O. Box 784, WI 53201 Milwaukee, U.S.A.
hou@cs.uwm.edu
[3] Dept of Electrical Eng., Microelectronic laboratory
Université Catholique de Louvain, Place du Levant, 3
1348 Louvain-la-Neuve, Belgium
Quisquater@dice.ucl.ac.be,
http://www.dice.ucl.ac.be/crypto/jjq.html

Abstract. In visual cryptography the additive property of light is used. Also the shares are random and therefore suspect to a censor. In this paper we present two new cryptographic schemes which use music and the wave properties of light. Both schemes are also secret sharing schemes in which shares are music or images and are not suspect to a human censor. Our scheme guarantees perfect privacy as well as high quality. To decrypt the message, one just plays two shares on a stereo system. There are two decryption methods which are either based on the interference property of sound or based on the stereo perception of the human hearing system. In optical cryptography, we use pictures as covers and the wave interference property of light. The privacy is perfect and the modified images are non-suspicious. The Mach-Zehnder interferometer is used as the decryption machine.

1 Introduction

Traditional hiding and steganography methods, e.g., [4,5] have the disadvantage that once their method is known, anyone can find the embedded message.

Visual cryptography [6] is secure in this prospect. Visual cryptography is a perfectly secure encryption scheme in which both the ciphertext and the key are pixels, with 1 bit depth, printed on transparencies. The decryption is done by stacking the key transparency on top of the ciphertext transparency and does not require any computer. But both ciphertext and key consist of random pixels and hence are suspect to censors.

A reason for not using computers is that in some countries high technology equipment is suspect. Also, computers may not be trustful. Indeed, Goldberg

---

* A part of this research has been supported by NSF Grant NCR-9508528.

K. Ohta and D. Pei (Eds.): ASIACRYPT'98, LNCS 1514, pp. 392–404, 1998.

and Wagner just found that at least 10 digits out of 64 bits keys in GSM system were actually zeroes [7]. Not only is it dangerous to trust software, trusting hardware is also not recommended. Today's Intel Pentium Pro microprocessor contains more than 5.5 million transistors and therefore it is easy to install a Trojan horse.

More recently cerebral cryptography [3] embeds a message in images and uses human brains to decrypt the ciphertext. It is also a perfect secret sharing schemes. It uses high quality real life images as cover images and generates two shares which maintain high quality. But it requires the cover image to have a large high frequency component, i.e., enough variation. Hence, it only allows very limited bandwidth. Also, decryption in cerebral cryptography is not so easy as the authors in [3] seem to claim. Some people have problems with 3-D perception.

In this paper we first present *audio cryptography* which uses music to embed messages. We base our scheme on the inference property of sound and phase perception of the human hearing system. Our scheme has similar features to that of cerebral cryptography. The privacy is perfect and a human censor is not able to detect that a single share is suspect. So, playing a single channel of the music, sounds as normal music. By playing two channels' sounds at the same time we can listen to the secret, i.e. the embedded message.

We then present our idea of *optical cryptography* which is based on the interference property of light waves and which uses images to hide information. This approach is completely different from the one used to obtain visual cryptography [6]. It achieves the same goal on privacy and no computer is necessary to do the decryption. As in cerebral cryptography [3], the shares are not suspicious. The privacy of our scheme is perfect and the stego-images (i.e., the modified images) are of high quality. Using a Mach-Zehnder interferometer [8] on two shares, we can see the embedded image. The scheme has the advantage of providing larger bandwidth over cerebral cryptography.

The organization of the paper is as follows. We first explain a model in Section 2. In Section 3 we discuss audio cryptography. In Section 4 we present the basic idea of optical cryptography. We conclude in Section 5.

2   Model

Before we present our schemes we introduce the model on which our cryptosystems have been built.

There are two agents (or in general n) that transport some secret message from one country to another country. Each agent carries one (or in general m) pictures/music, in which the secret message is embedded. They can not use computers.

There are human censors at each custom office who check each passenger's baggage. They cannot use a computer, either. We allow for two types of censors. Some that only censor suspicious pictures/music (then two pictures/music are sufficient). The other type of censor will randomly destroy pictures/music (then we need n agents).

There is also some counterintelligence who may intercept one suspect picture/music. They have unrestricted computer power, but we assume they will never obtain two shares.

Our goal is that at least two agents can enter the other country successfully and finally meet each other. They put their shares together and they can decrypt the message without using any computer.

Our model has the following security properties:

– Unconditional privacy, i.e., the counterintelligence has infinite computer power.
– Censors can only use human computation.

Note: modern cryptography has three levels of computation powers, i.e.,

– infinite computer power
– quantum computer power
– polynomial time (Turing machine) computer power.

We have extended this to include human computation power.

In this paper, we use "embedded message" to refer to the plaintext, "cover" to represent the original image or music which is used to encrypt the plaintext and "stego-" to refer to the modified image or music which is transported by agents.

3   Audio Cryptography

One of our approaches to hide information is based on the interference property of sound waves. The other is based on the fact that the human hearing system is capable of observing phase differences. The two methods only differ in the way to decrypt the ciphertext. In Section 3.1 we will first give a simple explanation of both concepts. In Section 3.2 we will construct our basic scheme using a harmonic sound and then we will extend it to regular music. In Section 3.3 we demonstrate our results.

3.1   Two Concepts

Interference of Sound Sound is a pressure wave traveling through air, water or any other media. Interference occurs when two sound waves encounter each other while traveling. A sound wave is a moving series of sompressions (high pressure) and rarefactions (low pressure). If the high-pressure part of one wave lines up with the low-pressure of another wave, the two waves interfere destructively and there is no more pressure fluctuation (no more sound). On the other hand, if the high-pressure part of one wave meets the high-pressure part of another wave, it results in an intensified high-pressure. Note that the matching must occur in both space and time [9]. As shown in Figure 1a, if two simple harmonic sound waves are of the same frequency and amplitude, and if they are superimposed upon one another out of phase (with a 180 difference in phase), then they will destroy each other completely. While in Figure 1b, if they are superimposed upon one another with 0 difference in phase, the resulting wave has an amplitude which is twice of the original one.

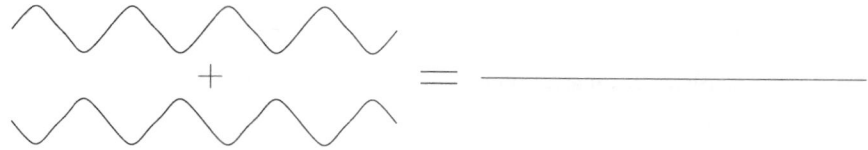

a. Destructive interference.

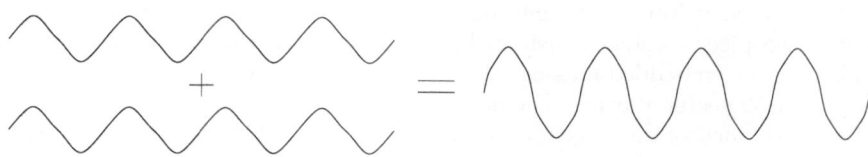

b. Constructive interference.

Fig. 1. Interference illustration.

This property has been applied to active noise control [12] where active attenuation of noise is obtained by using artificially generated acoustic waves mixed with the unwanted sound so that when the waves are in anti-phase, then destructive interference results.

We observe that the interference principle acts like a *not-exclusive-or* operation, which gives 1 (corresponding to an amplitude of 2) only when the two operands are of equal value.

Stereo Conception We can localize the direction from where the sound originate. As shown in Figure 2, the sound Source 1 has the same distance from both ears and the Source 2 is on the right side of the person in the figure. The waves from Source 1 arrive at the two ears with the same amplitudes and same phases. But the waves from Source 2 travel a little longer to get to the left ear compared to the right ear. This means that the waves striking two ears are of different amplitudes and most likely of different phase. As a result, the human hearing system can observe whether the sound comes from Source 1 or from Source 2.

The aspect of observing the phase differences is used in one of our decryption methods.

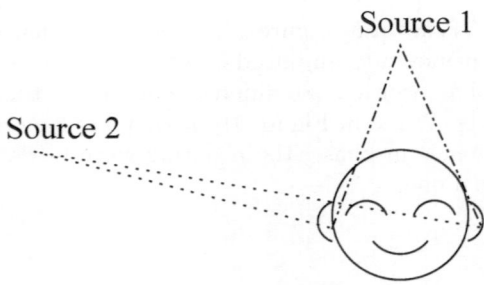

Fig. 2. Illustration of observing sound sources.

3.2   Schemes

Our goal is to use shares of the embedded message that are high quality music. We therefore start from some high quality music as the cover. We then want to produce two piece of stego-music of high quality, such that if one plays these, one obtains the embedded message. For convenience, we will refer to this scheme as a 2-out-of-2 secret sharing scheme.

The basic idea of audio cryptography is as follows. One generates the share s_1 based on random coin flips b and the second share s_2 based on $\overline{b} \oplus S$, where S is the secret bit we want to hide and $\oplus$ is the exclusive-or. It is clear from the properties of the *one-time pad* [13,11] that such schemes guarantee perfect secrecy.

In the following, we first use harmonic sound as the embedded message. We then generalize it by using music to obtain our anti-censor goal.

Harmonic Scheme Our basic scheme using harmonic sound is presented first.

The setting

S: a plaintext message which is a binary string.
L: the length of the embedded message which represents how many bits are in S.
T: a parameter which represents how many seconds of sound are used per secret bit. So, we need a total of $T \times L$ seconds of sound in order to encrypt a secret message of L bits.
B: a cover sound which is a single frequency signal lasting $T \times L$ seconds.

Procedure:

– Generate the first share s_1 as follows: Initialize s_1 to B. For every T seconds data from s_1, flip a coin b. If b is 1, multiply the corresponding T second data with -1, implying a 180 phase change. Otherwise leave them unchanged. So, one has randomly chosen to flip the T seconds data to its opposite phase or not.

– Generate the second share s_2: Initialize s_2 to B. For every T seconds data from s_2, compute $b' = \overline{b \oplus S}$. If b' is 1, multiply the corresponding T second data with -1, implying a 180 phase change. Otherwise leave them unchanged. In other words, if the secret bit is 1 then the corresponding T seconds sound from s_2 has the same phase as that from s_1. If the secret bit is 0 then the corresponding T seconds sound from s_2 has the opposite phase as that from s_1.

Two Decryption Methods There are basically two ways that can be used to decrypt the ciphertext in order to get the embedded message. They are either based on the interference property of waves or based on the stereo conception property of the human hearing system.

In the first method, we put two speakers very close and face to face. Then, we send share 1, s_1, to one speaker and send share 2, s_2, to the other speaker. We can clearly notice the effect of volume changing, in which louder represents secret bit 1 and more silent represents secret bit 0. The cancellation is not complete due to the incomplete destructive interference, the reflection from the wall, etc.

In the second method, we move one speaker to our left side and the other speaker to our right side. Then, as in Method 1 we play two shares from two speakers respectively. We can observe that the sound sources move from sides to center and from center to sides, which is due to the phase differences in two channels. If both signals from two channels are of the same phase, which encodes secret bit 1, we observe only one source which is from the center. If two signals are out of phase, which corresponds to secret bit 0, we observe two sources, one from left and one from right.

In a variant of the second method, we use a set of headphones instead of two speakers. We play one share in each ear, we obtain the same effect as in Method 2 due to the phase conception property.

Testing on Harmonic Sound We have tested our scheme on three harmonic sounds which have frequencies 300Hz, 500Hz and 1000Hz respectively. All the decryption methods worked pretty well. But, each share is suspicious. We heard some clicks at each phase changing point as shown in Figure 3. This is because the modified signal is not of a single frequency any more and the added frequencies make the click very recognizable in the pure tone environment.

Music Scheme We extend our basic scheme of using a harmonic sound to a more general one of using music. We modify the algorithm described in the harmonic method only by using a piece of music instead of a harmonic sound as the sound B uses to hide the share. Nothing else need to be changed.

The problem which exists with the harmonic method does not exist in our general scheme. We could hardly hear such clicks. When playing only one stegosound, either share 1 or share 2, we get very good quality music which sounds just as the original one. It is hard to tell any difference. When playing both, we

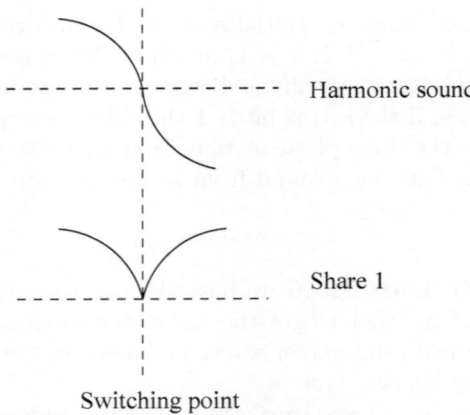

Fig. 3. Illustration of how clicks are generated in a harmonic method.

can observe the volume changing if using the decryption Method 1 and we can observe the switching of the sound sources if using the decryption Method 2 or its variant. All methods provide correct decryption.

Doing some spectrum analysis, we can see how close the two curves in Figure 4 are, one for the original music and one for the signal after being randomly phase changed. The music is rich in frequencies and therefore the added noise, which is also distributed flatly among a wide range of frequencies, has little impact on human ears.

If the volume of the music goes up and down dramatically and frequently and the cancellation is not complete by using two speakers, it may be difficult to make the right decryption using Method 1. But, in such circumstances, one can always use the methods which are based on the phase conception property, i.e., Method 2 and in particular its variant.

2-out-of-n Schemes To generalize our previous 2-out-of-2 to 2-out-of-n, we use the secret sharing scheme discussed in [2] and use $\lceil \log_2(n) \rceil$ different pieces of music as covers.

We remind the reader that the 2-out-of-n secret sharing scheme in [2] is based on $\lceil \log_2(n) \rceil$ many 2-out-of-2 sharing schemes executed independently. So if k is the secret key, one has $k = r_0^i \oplus r_1^i$, where $1 \leq i \leq \lceil \log_2(n) \rceil$. When numbering the participants from 0 to $n-1$, participant j receives share r_0^i if the ith bit of the binary representation of the integer j is 0, else r_1^i.

So, in our context, one uses $\lceil \log_2(n) \rceil$ pieces of music as covers. For practical purposes they are different. For each of the $\lceil \log_2(n) \rceil$ pieces of music one creates shares R_0^i and R_1^i as in our previous 2-out-of-2 audio cryptosystem. A participant j receives the audio channel R_0^j when the ith bit of the binary representation of j is 0, else receives R_1^i.

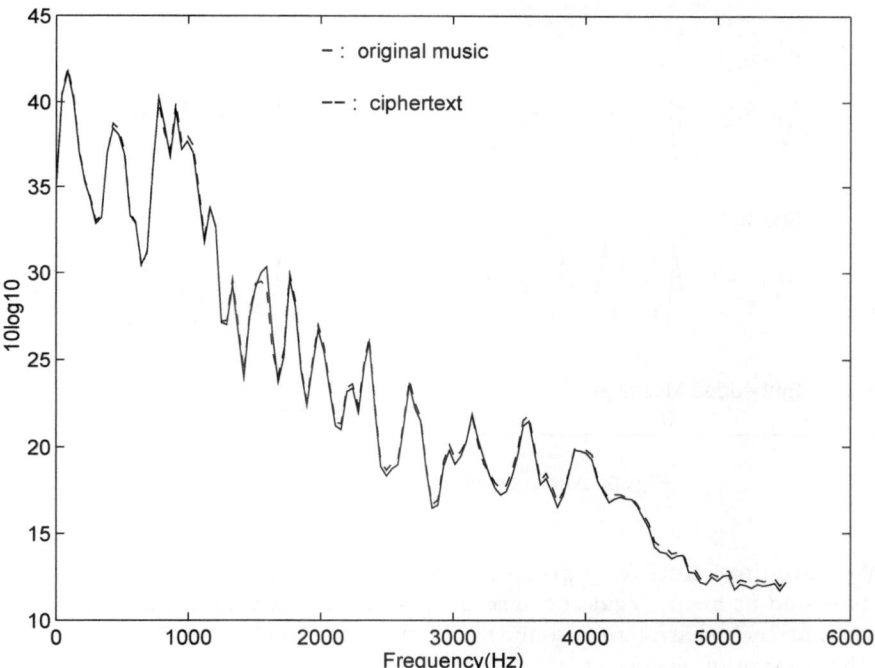

Fig. 4. Spectrum comparison of original music with ciphertext.

3.3   Demonstration

We present some sound sample showing the original music signal, two shares and corresponding secret bit in Figure 5.

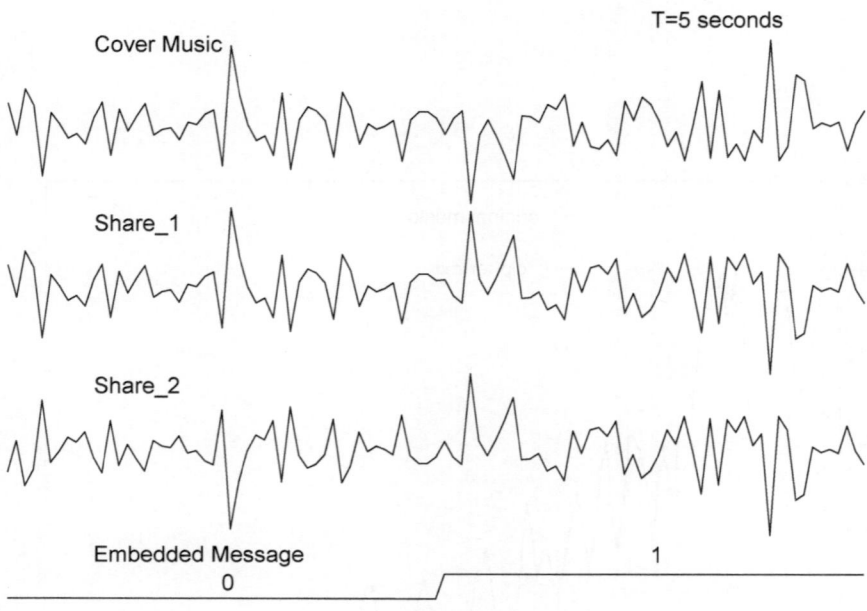

Fig. 5. Audio cryptography illustration.

We have done tests on pop music and also on classical music. These tests can be found at `http://www.cs.uwm.edu/~desmedt/audio/` Both results have shown that each share (stego-sound) is of the same quality as the cover music and the decryption is correct.

4   Optical Cryptography

Light is also a kind of wave and therefore has the interference property. If two beams of light from the same source meet out of phase, they will destroy each other and this results in total darkness. If they meet with the same phase, then they produce an intensified light.

Our idea of optical cryptography is as follows. Our plaintext is a 1 bit/pixel digital image (e.g., a blueprint). We choose a high quality n bits per pixel image which has a larger size than that of our plaintext. We pad the plaintext to make it the same size of the cover image. We generate the share 1 by randomly flipping the least mth significant bit of each pixel in the cover image. We copy share 1 to share 2 as its initial value. Then if in the plaintext a pixel has the value 1 then we flip the least mth significant bit of this corresponding pixel in share 2. So, now the mth significant bits in the generated shares are uniformly random bits. If m is small enough then we maintain the high quality. (When n is 8, m can be 4 and the alternation is unnoticeable to a human as shown in Figure 6 and Figure 7.) The two shares only differ in the least mth significant bit. Denote the least mth significant bit from share 1, share 2 and the plaintext as s_1, s_2 and s respectively. Then, they are clearly related by $s_2 = s_1 \oplus s$ which is equivalent to $s = s_1 \oplus s_2$.

Fig. 6. Share 1 for optical cryptography scheme with $n = 8$ bits/pixel and $m = 4$th least significant bit.

Now we can use a machine called Mach-Zehnder interferometer [8] to reconstruct the plaintext. As shown in Figure 8, the laser beam passes some lenses and becomes a wide parallel beam. Then, it is split into two beams, beam 1 and beam 2, which take different paths. When beam 1 passes share 1, its amplitude is changed by the corresponding pixel values in share 1. The beam 2 passes share 2 and carries similar information about share 2. When finally the two beams meet out of phase, the result is the plaintext.

Fig. 7. Share 2 for optical cryptography scheme with $n =8$ bits/pixel and $m =4$th least significant bit.

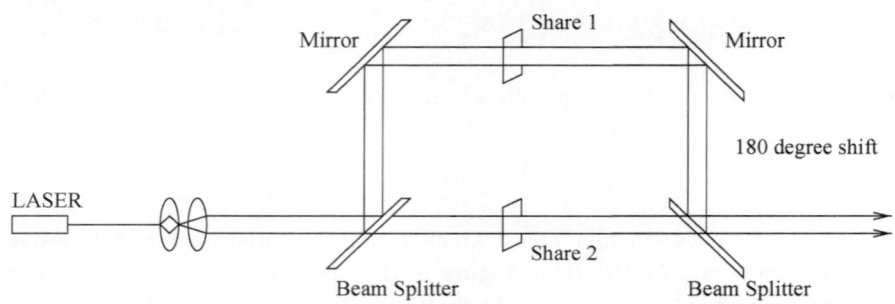

Fig. 8. Illustration of the decryption for optical cryptosystems.

Optical cryptography allows for high bandwidth encryption while still maintaining our covert property of the shares. The high bandwidth results from using the modification of each pixel.

This 2-out-of-2 perfect threshold scheme can easily be extended to a 2-out-of-n perfect threshold scheme as for audio cryptography. We use the secret sharing scheme discussed in [2] and use $\log_2(n)$ different images as cover images.

We will report about the testing results of optical cryptography in the final paper.

5   Conclusions and Open Problems

We have demonstrated that audio cryptography uses high quality music sound as shares and provides perfect privacy. Decryption is easy by playing both shares at the same time. We have discussed two decryption methods. For the decryption, we only need a stereo player and a stereo headphone (or two speakers).

We also presented optical cryptography which is different from cerebral cryptography. It has all the aspects of visual cryptography and cerebral cryptography. Only a Mach-Zehnder interferometer, a laser beam and some lenses are needed for decryption.

Both schemes can be considered as 2-out-of-2 threshold secret sharing schemes. We have shown how to generalize them to 2-out-of-n secret sharing schemes by using different cover pictures or sounds. It is not clear how to generalize them to more general t-out-of-n schemes.

Audio cryptography as well as optical cryptography do not need a digital computer to decrypt the ciphertext, however they *do* require one to encrypt the plaintext. This introduces two open questions:

- Can a cryptographic scheme be developed that does not need a digital computer or equivalent electronic hardware to encrypt plaintext and hide the share as in our schemes, and
- Can a scheme be developed that does not rely on digital computers (or electronic equipment) for encryption as well as for decryption.

References

1. Blakley, G. R.: Safeguarding cryptographic keys. In *Proc. Nat. Computer Conf. AFIPS Conf. Proc. (1979)* pp. 313–317
2. Desmedt, Y. and G. Di Crescenzo and Burmester, M. : Multiplicative non-abelian sharing schemes and their application to threshold cryptography. In *Advances in Cryptology — Asiacrypt '94*, Proceedings (Lecture Notes in Computer Science 917), pp.21–32.
3. Desmedt, Y. and Hou, S. and Quisquater, J.J.: Cerebral Cryptography. *Workshop on information hiding,* Preproceedings, April 15-17, 1998, Portland, Oregon, USA.
4. Franz, E., Jerichow, A., Möller, S., Pfitzmann, A. and Stierand, I. : Computer Based Steganography: How it works why therefore any restrictions on cryptography are nonsense, at best. *Information Hiding*, Proceedings, 1996, pp.3–21.

5. Kurak, C., McHugh, J.: A cautionary note on image downgrading. In *Proceedings of the 8th Computer Security Applications Conference (December 1992)*
6. Naor, M., Shamir, A.: Visual cryptography. In *Advances in Cryptology — Eurocrypt '94*, Proceedings (Lecture Notes in Computer Science 950) (May 9–12, 1995). A. D. Santis, Ed. Springer-Verlag pp. 1–12
7. *The New York Times*, April 14, 1998, pp.C1.
8. Nussbaum, A. and Phillips, R. A. *Contemporary Optics for Scientists and Engineers.* Prentice-Hall, 1976
9. Sears, F. W. and Zemansky, M. W.: *University Physics.* Addison-Wesley, 1964
10. Shamir, A.: How to share a secret. *Commun. ACM* **22** *(1979)* 612–613
11. Shannon, C.E.: Communication theory of secrecy systems. *Bell Systems Technical Journal*, 28 (1949), 656-715
12. Tokhi, M. O. and Leitch, R. R. : *Active Noise Control.* Oxford Science Publications 1992
13. Vernam, G.S.: Secret signaling system. *U.S. Patent # 1,310,719, 22 Jul 1919*

Strong Security Against Active Attacks in Information-Theoretic Secret-Key Agreement

Stefan Wolf

Department of Computer Science
Swiss Federal Institute of Technology (ETH Zürich)
CH-8092 Zürich, Switzerland
E-mail address: wolf@inf.ethz.ch

Abstract. The problem of unconditionally secure key agreement, in particular privacy amplification, by communication over an insecure and not even authentic channel, is investigated. The previous definitions of such protocols were weak in the sense that it was only required that after the communication not both parties falsely believe that the key agreement was successful. In such a protocol however it is possible that Eve deceives one of the legitimate partners, i.e., makes him accept the outcome of the protocol although no secret key has been generated. In this paper we introduce the notion of strong protocols which protect each of the parties simultaneously and, in contrast to previous pessimism, it is shown that such protocols exist. For the important special case of privacy amplification, a strong protocol is presented that is based on a new, interactive way of message authentication with an only partially secret key. The use of feedback in such authentication allows to reduce the size of the authenticator, hence of the additional information about the key leaked to the adversary, without increasing the success probability of an active attack. Finally, it is shown that in the scenario where the parties and the adversary have access to repeated realizations of a random experiment, previously derived criteria for the possibility of secret-key agreement against active opponents hold for the new, strong definition of robustness against active attacks rather than for the earlier definition.

Keywords. Secret-key agreement, privacy amplification, authentication, unconditional secrecy, information theory.

1 Introduction

1.1 Provably Secure Key Agreement

The security of presently used cryptosystems, for instance of all public-key cryptographic protocols, is based on unproven assumptions on the hardness of certain computational problems such as the discrete logarithm problem or the integer factoring problem. The fact that all these schemes face the risk of being broken by progress in the theory of efficient algorithms motivates the search for systems whose security can be rigorously proved. In particular, protocols for the generation of a provably secure key have attracted much attention in the past few years.

K. Ohta and D. Pei (Eds.): ASIACRYPT'98, LNCS 1514, pp. 405-419, 1998.

In [5] for instance, a general model for secret-key agreement by public communication over an authentic channel was described. Here, two parties Alice and Bob who want to generate a secret key have access to random variables X and Y, respectively, whereas the adversary Eve knows a random variable Z. The three random variables X, Y, and Z are distributed according to some distribution P_{XYZ}.

Generally, a protocol for secret-key agreement in this scenario is often described as consisting of three phases. In the first phase, called *advantage distillation*, Alice and Bob use their advantage over Eve offered by the authenticity of the public channel, to generate an advantage over Eve in terms of their knowledge about each other's information. During the second phase, *information reconciliation*, Alice and Bob agree on a mutual string S by using error-correction techniques, and in the third phase, *privacy amplification*, the partial secret S is transformed into a shorter, highly secret string S'. Bennett *et. al.* [1] have shown that the length of S' can be nearly $H_2(S|Z = z)$, the Rényi entropy of S when given Eve's complete knowledge $Z = z$ about S.

Privacy amplification, which was first introduced by Bennett *et. al.* [2], can alternatively be seen as a *special case* of secret-key agreement from common information, namely the case where Alice and Bob have identical information, i.e., where P_{XYZ} has the property that $\text{Prob}[X = Y] = 1$. Another important special class of distributions P_{XYZ} in the secret-key agreement scenario is where X, Y, and Z consist of many independent realizations of the same random experiment [5].

1.2   Strong Security Against Active Opponents

Secret-key agreement has also been studied when dropping the condition that the channel connecting Alice and Bob is authentic [4],[6]. However, it is clear that such key agreement can only be possible if Alice and Bob already have some kind of advantage over Eve initially, and if this advantage implies that Eve cannot successfully impersonate Bob towards Alice, or vice versa. The conditions on a protocol for such key agreement have been defined as follows. After the phase of insecure communication, both Alice and Bob either accept or reject the outcome and compute a string when accepting. It was demanded that if the adversary is passive only, then both parties accept and agree on a mutual highly secure string. If the adversary is active on the other hand, then with high probability at least one of the parties must reject (or the secret-key agreement must have been successful).

Unfortunately, this definition is not completely satisfactory. Since it is only required that one of the parties rejects in case of an active attack, it is not excluded that the other party is deceived by Eve, i.e., accepts although secret-key agreement was not successful. On the other hand, it is impossible to achieve that always both Alice and Bob reject in case of an active attack. Eve can always leave Alice and Bob in opposite states by blocking certain messages, as Theorem 2 shows.

However, we propose how nearly as powerful protocols, called *strong* protocols, can be defined which are not impossible to achieve. For a strong protocol it is required that, with high probability, either both Alice and Bob reject, or the secret-key agreement is successful. It is not required that both Alice and Bob accept in the latter case, but that they both compute a mutual secure key. It seems that this is the strongest possible security one can achieve against active attackers, and that such protocols are what one actually has in mind when speaking about security against active adversaries in secret-key agreement. They have the property that no party can be misled by Eve: whenever a party accepts, the key agreement has been successful. The new protocol definition and some impossibility results are given in Section 2. In the subsequent sections we will present strong protocols in the different scenarios mentioned.

For the case of privacy amplification, treated in Section 3, strong protocols are more difficult to obtain than the weaker protocols of [6], and it is shown that strong protocols necessarily are more complicated. A new way of authenticating messages must be used which is interactive rather than one-way. The crucial point is that the authenticator of a message can be much shorter, leaking less information about the partly secret string, but maintaining security even against adversaries having partial knowledge about the key.

The scenario where the parties' (and the adversary's) information consists of repeated realizations of the same random experiment is treated in Section 4. It is shown that the criteria given in [4] for the existence (in this scenario) or inexistence (in the general scenario) of protocols secure against active opponents are not correct for the protocol definition of [4], but that these (or closely related) criteria characterize the existence of *strong* protocols in this scenario. Correcting these earlier results, we show that a (weak) protocol exists if and only if Eve can either not simulate the random variable X, using Z, in such a way that someone knowing Y cannot distinguish between X and Eve's simulation, or vice versa. In [4] it was stated that a protocol exists if *both* X and Y are not simulatable by Eve this way. By modifying the protocols of [4], we show that the last condition perfectly characterizes the existence of strong protocols.

2   Secret-Key Agreement by Communication over an Insecure and Non-Authentic Channel

2.1   Definition of Weak and Strong Protocols

Definition 1. Assume that two parties Alice and Bob both know discrete random variables X and Y, respectively, and that an adversary Eve knows a random variable Z, where the joint distribution of the random variables is P_{XYZ}. In a *protocol for secret-key agreement*, Alice and Bob exchange messages $C_1, C_2, \ldots$ over an insecure channel, where the messages $C_1, C_3, \ldots$ are sent by Alice, and the messages $C_2, C_4, \ldots$ are sent by Bob. Each message C_i depends on the sender's knowledge when sending the message and possibly on some random bits R_i, i.e., $H(C_i|X, C_1 \cdots C_{i-1}, R_i) = 0$ if i is odd and $H(C_i|Y, C_1 \cdots C_{i-1}, R_i) = 0$ if i is even[1]. At the end of the protocol, both Alice and Bob either accept or reject the outcome, and decide whether to compute a string S'_A or S'_B, respectively. If a party accepts, then it always computes a string. However, a party can also decide to compute a string when rejecting the outcome of the protocol. The above decisions and the strings S'_A and S'_B are determined by X or Y, respectively, and by the messages sent and received. The protocol is called a *one-way-transmission protocol* if messages are sent only into one direction. Otherwise, a protocol is called *interactive*.

Let r be an integer, and let $\varepsilon, \delta > 0$. A $(P_{XYZ}, r, \varepsilon, \delta)$-*protocol for secret-key agreement by communication over an insecure and non-authenticated channel* (or simply $(P_{XYZ}, r, \varepsilon, \delta)$-*protocol*) is a protocol for secret-key agreement with the following properties.

1. Correctness and privacy. If Eve is a passive wire-tapper, then both Alice and Bob accept at the end of the protocol, and secret-key agreement must have been successful. The latter is the event that S'_A and S'_B are r-bit strings satisfying

$$\text{Prob}[S'_A \neq S'_B] \leq \varepsilon \qquad \text{and} \qquad H(S'_A | CZ) \geq r - \varepsilon , \tag{1}$$

where H stands for the (Shannon) entropy function, and where $C := (C_1, C_2, \ldots)$ summarizes the entire communication held over the public channel.

2. (Weak) robustness. For every possible strategy of Eve, the probability that either Alice *or* Bob rejects the outcome of the protocol or secret-key agreement has been successful, must be at least $1 - \delta$.

The protocol is called *strong* if condition *2* can be replaced by condition *2'* below. In contrast to this, a protocol satisfying *2* will also be called *weak* in the following.

2'. Strong robustness. For every possible strategy of Eve, the probability that either *both* Alice and Bob reject the outcome of the protocol or secret-key agreement has been successful, must be at least $1 - \delta$.   ∘

2.2   Impossibility Results

Of course it is most desirable to use protocols for which Alice and Bob either both accept (and secret-key agreement is successful) or both reject with high probability. However, the following theorem states that such a synchronization cannot be achieved, and makes precise what was already stated in [4].

Theorem 2. *Assume that there exists a strong $(P_{XYZ}, r, \varepsilon, \delta)$-protocol with the modified robustness property that with probability at least $1 - \delta$, either both Alice*

---

[1] Here, the C_i stand for the messages actually sent and received by the corresponding party (thus possibly modified by the active opponent).

and Bob reject, or both parties accept and secret-key agreement has been success-ful. Then either suitable strings can be computed even without communication, i.e., there exist two functions f and g, mapping $\mathcal{X}$ and $\mathcal{Y}$ to $\{0,1\}^r$, respectively, such that $S'_A := f(X)$ and $S'_B := g(Y)$ satisfy (1), or $\delta = 1$.

The proof idea is that Eve can always leave Alice and Bob in opposite acceptance states by blocking the channel completely after a certain number of rounds of the protocol. A full proof will be given in the final paper.

Clearly, secret-key agreement secure against active adversaries can only be possible if Alice and Bob have some advantage over Eve in terms of the dis-tribution P_{XYZ}. More precisely, this advantage must be such that Eve cannot generate from Z a random variable $\overline{X}$ which Bob, knowing Y, is unable to dis-tinguish from X (and vice versa). In [4], the following property of a distribution P_{XYZ} was defined.

Definition 3. [4] Let X, Y, and Z be random variables. We say that X *is simulatable by Z with respect to Y if there exists a conditional distribution $P_{\overline{X}|Z}$ such that $P_{\overline{X}Y} = P_{XY}$.*   ○

In the final paper, we will describe a simple criterion for simulatability in terms of the probabilities $P_{XYZ}(x,y,z)$. The following theorem states that a strong $(P_{XYZ}, r, \varepsilon, \delta)$-protocol can only exist if both X and Y are not simulatable by Z with respect to each other. In the scenario in which the parties obtain repeated realizations of the same random experiment, this condition is also sufficient (see Section 4). In contrast to the result of [4], a weak protocol can already exist if Eve can either not simulate X or not simulate Y. The proof of Theorem 4 is given in the full paper.

Theorem 4. *Let X, Y, and Z be random variables with distribution P_{XYZ}. If both X and Y are simulatable by Z with respect to each other, and if $r \cdot (1-\varepsilon) - \varepsilon - h(\varepsilon) > 0$, then there exists no weak $(P_{XYZ}, r, \varepsilon, \delta)$-protocol for any $\delta < 1$. If either X is simulatable by Z with respect to Y (and $r \cdot (1-2\varepsilon) - \varepsilon - h(2\varepsilon) > 0$), or Y is simulatable by Z with respect to X (and $r \cdot (1-\varepsilon) - \varepsilon - h(\varepsilon) > 0$), then there exists no strong $(P_{XYZ}, r, \varepsilon, \delta)$-protocol for any $\delta < 1$.*

3   Privacy Amplification

3.1   Protocol Definition

Privacy amplification, introduced in [2] and generalized in [1], is the technique of transforming a partially secret string into a highly secret but shorter string, and corresponds to the special case of secret-key agreement for which $X = Y =: S$ holds with probability 1. The following definition is a strengthened version of the general definition in Section 2. First, it is required that Alice and Bob end up with the same string with probability 1 if Eve is passive. Moreover, the protocol works for an entire class of distributions P_{XYZ} instead of only one distribution. More precisely, Eve's knowledge about the mutual n-bit string S is limited by assuming that $P_{S|Z=z}$ is, for all $z \in \mathcal{Z}$, contained in some subset $\mathcal{D}$ of all possible distributions over the set $\{0,1\}^n$. Typically, $\mathcal{D}$ will consist of all distributions satisfying a certain condition in terms of the Rényi- or min-entropy. The protocol definition in [6] only covered the special case $\mathcal{D} = \mathcal{D}_{\infty,t} := \{P_X \mid H_\infty(X) \geq t\}$ for some t. In this paper we will deal with $\mathcal{D}$'s of the form $\mathcal{D} = \mathcal{D}_{2,t} := \{P_X \mid H_2(X) \geq t\}$. However, it is conceivable that protocols exist for which $\mathcal{D}$ can (or must) be defined in an entirely different way.

Definition 5. Assume that Alice and Bob both know a mutual n-bit random variable S, and that the random variable Z summarizes Eve's entire knowledge about S. Let $\mathcal{D}$ be a subset of all probability distributions on the set of n-bit strings, let r be an integer, and let $\varepsilon, \delta > 0$. A *(weak or strong) $(n, \mathcal{D}, r, \varepsilon, \delta)$-protocol for privacy amplification by communication over an insecure and non-authentic channel $((n, \mathcal{D}, r, \varepsilon, \delta)$-protocol for short)* is a protocol for secret-key agreement with the following properties. Assume that $P_{S|Z=z} \in \mathcal{D}$ for all $z \in \mathcal{Z}$.

1. Correctness and privacy. If Eve is a passive wire-tapper receiving $Z = z$, then both Alice and Bob must accept at the end of the protocol, and there must exist an r-bit string S' such that $S' = S'_A = S'_B$ and $H(S'|C, Z = z) \geq r - \varepsilon$.

Finally, the same (weak or strong) *robustness* property as in Definition 1 must hold.   ∘

3.2   Entropy Measures, the Effect of Side Information, and Knowledge About Partial Strings

Let us first recall the definitions of some information-theoretic quantities used in this paper.

Definition 6. Let X be a discrete random variable with probability function P_X and range $\mathcal{X}$. The *(Shannon) entropy $H(X)$* of X is[2] $H(X) := -\mathrm{E}[\log P_X] = -\sum_{x \in \mathcal{X}} P_X(x) \log P_X(x)$. The *Rényi entropy $H_2(X)$* is defined as $H_2(X) := -\log(\mathrm{E}[P_X]) = -\log(\sum_{x \in \mathcal{X}} P_X(x)^2) =: -\log(P_C(X))$, where $P_C(X)$ is called the *collision probability* of X. The *min-entropy $H_\infty(X)$* is defined as $H_\infty(X) := -\log(\max_{x \in \mathcal{X}}(P_X(x)))$.   ∘

Because of Jensen's inequality, $H(X) \geq H_2(X)$ holds for all X, with equality if and only if X is uniformly distributed in $\mathcal{X}$ or in a subset of $\mathcal{X}$. Furthermore, $H_2(X) \geq H_\infty(X) \geq H_2(X)/2$ holds for all X.

In the remainder of this section we provide some facts necessary for the analysis of the protocols described below. We derive bounds on the amount of knowledge (e.g., of an adversary) in terms of Rényi entropy about a partial string, depending on the amount of knowledge about the entire string. This is done both for the cases where the adversary does (Corollary 9) or does not

---

[2] All the logarithms in this paper are to the base 2, except ln, which is to the base e.

(Lemma 7) obtain information about the remaining part of the string. In both cases, the result is roughly the intuitive fact that [with high probability] one cannot know [substantially] more about a part than about the whole. In the case where the adversary obtains information about the remaining part of the string, the result follows from a general upper bound on the reduction of the Rényi entropy of a random variable when side information is given (Lemma 8). A statement analogous to Lemma 7 also holds with respect to min-entropy [6].

Lemma 7. *Let $S = (S_1, S_2, \ldots, S_n)$ be a random variable consisting of n binary random variables. For any k-tuple $\underline{i} = (i_1, i_2 \ldots, i_k)$, where $1 \leq i_1 < i_2 < \cdots < i_k \leq n$, let $S_{\underline{i}}$ be the string $(S_{i_1}, S_{i_2}, \ldots, S_{i_k})$. Then $H_2(S_{\underline{i}}) \geq H_2(S) - (n - k)$.*

Proof. Consider a fixed string $s_{\underline{i}} = (s_{i_1}, \ldots, s_{i_k})$. This particular value of the random variable $S_{\underline{i}}$ corresponds to exactly 2^{n-k} values $s = (s_1, \ldots, s_n)$ of the random variable S. Let $p_1, \ldots, p_{2^{n-k}}$ be the probabilities of these strings (in decreasing order), and let $p_0 := \sum_{i=1}^{2^{n-k}} p_i$. Now, we have

$$\sum_{i=1}^{2^{n-k}} p_i^2 = p_0 \cdot \sum_{i=1}^{2^{n-k}} \left(\frac{p_i}{p_0}\right) \cdot p_i \geq p_0 \cdot \frac{p_0}{2^{n-k}} = \frac{p_0^2}{2^{n-k}} \ .$$

Because this holds for every particular string $s_{\underline{i}}$, we have for the collision probabilities of the random variables S and $S_{\underline{i}}$

$$P_C(S_{\underline{i}}) = \sum_{s_{\underline{i}} \in \{0,1\}^k} P_{S_{\underline{i}}}(s_{\underline{i}})^2 \leq 2^{n-k} \cdot \sum_{s \in \{0,1\}^n} P_S(s)^2 = 2^{n-k} \cdot P_C(S) \ .$$

Hence $H_2(S_{\underline{i}}) \geq H_2(S) - (n - k)$, and this concludes the proof.   □

Lemma 8 gives an upper bound on the reduction of the Rényi entropy $H_2(P)$ of a random variable P when side-information $[Q, R]$ (consisting of a pair of random variables) is given, where $I(P; R) = 0$. It states that this reduction exceeds $\log |\mathcal{Q}|$ substantially only with small probability in both cases. (Note that it is not trivial that no additional reduction is induced by R if $I(P; R) = 0$. For instance, $I(P; Q) = 0$ and $I(P; R) = 0$ together do *not* imply that $H_2(P|Q = q, R = r) = H_2(P)$, as the example $P = Q \oplus R$ shows.) Lemma 8 can be shown similarly to Theorem 4.17 in [3].

Lemma 8. *Let P, Q, and R be discrete random variables with $I(P; R) = 0$. Then $\mathrm{Prob}_{QR}[H_2(P|Q = q, R = r) \geq H_2(P) - \log |\mathcal{Q}| - s] \geq 1 - 2^{-(s/2-1)}$ for all $s > 2$.*

Corollary 9 is a consequence of Lemma 8. It states that a formally slightly weaker result than that of Lemma 7, concerning the knowledge (in terms of H_2) of a partial string, even holds when the rest of the string is made public.

Corollary 9. *Let S be an n-bit string, and let a partition of S be given into two strings S' and S'' of lengths l and $n - l$, respectively. Let $s > 2$ be a security parameter. Then the probability, taken over s'', that $H_2(S'|S'' = s'') \geq H_2(S) - (n - l) - s$ holds is at least $1 - 2^{-(s/2-1)}$.*

3.3   Interaction Versus One-Way Transmission

The case of *one-way-transmission* protocols for privacy amplification by public discussion over a completely insecure channel was already treated in [6]. In Appendix A of this paper, it is shown that such a protocol can never be strong, and a better analysis of the protocol in [6], called Protocol A, is given.

In Section 3.4 we present a strong, hence necessarily *interactive*, protocol for privacy amplification secure against active opponents. This protocol uses interaction for two reasons. First, feedback is necessary to prevent the sender of the first message from accepting when Eve blocks or modifies the message (Theorem 15). Second, it is advantageous to use *interactive* instead of usual one-way authentication when the adversary has some partial information about the key. Here, a message it not authenticated by the sender, but reconfirmed by the receiver by correctly answering a challenge (which is equal to the message itself). The intuitive reason is that the adversary is in a better position if she can freely choose a modified message to authenticate, instead of having to respond to a given challenge, which is necessary for attacking the interactive way of authentication described below.

Lemma 10 provides a method for interactive authentication with a partially secret key K, with the property that the adversary Eve can only answer challenges d correctly by $f_d(K)$ with substantial probability when she knows at least half of the string K (in terms of H_2). Moreover, the same is even true if Eve, given d, learns some $f_{d'}(K)$ of her choice (where $d' \neq d$). Note that this is what she can actually achieve in a substitution attack. Surprisingly, this holds although the length of d and $f_d(K)$ is only a small fraction of the length of K.

Lemma 10. *Let N and ℓ be integers such that 2ℓ divides N and $2^\ell \geq N/\ell$ holds, and let K be a random variable with range $\mathcal{K} \subseteq GF(2^N)$. Let further for any $d \in GF(2^\ell)$ the function $f_d : \{0,1\}^N \to \{0,1\}^\ell$ be defined as $f_d(x) := \sum_{i=0}^{N/\ell-1} d^i x_i$, where $(x_0, \ldots, x_{N/\ell-1}) \in (GF(2^\ell))^{N/\ell}$ is a representation of $x \in GF(2^N)$ with respect to a fixed basis of $GF(2^N)$ over $GF(2^\ell)$, the computations are carried out in the field $GF(2^\ell)$, and the elements of $GF(2^\ell)$ are represented as ℓ-bit strings with respect to a fixed basis of $GF(2^\ell)$ over $GF(2)$. Assume that there exists a (possibly probabilistic) function $d \mapsto d'$, $GF(2^\ell) \to GF(2^\ell)$, such that $d' \neq d$ holds for all d, and such that given $f_{d'}(K)$, the value $f_d(K)$ can be guessed correctly (with some strategy) with probability at least α, taken over the distribution of K, the random choice of d (according to the uniform distribution), and the coin tosses of the guessing strategy. Then $H_2(K) \leq N/2 + (2N/\ell) \cdot \log(1/\alpha)$ or equivalently, $\alpha \leq 2^{-(\ell/2N)\cdot(H_2(K)-N/2)}$.*

Proof. Note first that we can assume without loss of generality that the function $d'(d)$ and the strategy of guessing $f_d(k)$ from $f_{d'}(k)$ are deterministic, since for every possible strategy there exists a deterministic strategy that is at least as good (a randomized strategy can be seen as a combination of deterministic strategies, of which the optimal one can be chosen). Furthermore, there must exist distinct elements $d_1, \ldots, d_{N/\ell}$ of $GF(2^\ell)$ such that $f_{d_i}(k)$ is guessed correctly from $f_{d'_i}(k)$, where $d'_i := d'(d_i)$, for all $i = 1, \ldots, N/\ell$ with probability at least $\alpha^{N/\ell}$ over k. Let $\mathcal{E} (\subseteq \mathcal{K})$ be this event. We prove that[3] $|\mathcal{E}| \leq \sqrt{|\mathcal{K}|}$.

By cancelling $N/2\ell$ of the pairs (d_i, d'_i) and renumbering the remaining pairs, we can obtain $N/2\ell$ pairs (d_i, d'_i) with the property that $d_i \notin \{d'_1, \ldots, d'_{i-1}\}$ holds for all $i = 1, \ldots, N/2\ell$. (In the worst case, all the pairs (d_i, d'_i) occur twice in inverse orderings. Then, every second pair (d_i, d'_i) must be cancelled.)

The event $\mathcal{E}$ has the property that $f_{d'_1}(k) = f_{d'_1}(k^*)$ implies $f_{d_1}(k) = f_{d_1}(k^*)$ for all $k, k^* \in \mathcal{E}$. Otherwise $f_{d_1}(k)$ could not be guessed correctly from $f_{d'_1}(k)$ for all $k \in \mathcal{E}$. Hence $\mathcal{E}$ must be contained in a set $\mathcal{E}_1$ of the form $\mathcal{E}_1 = \cup \{k : f_{d_1}(k) = b(a) \text{ and } f_{d'_1}(k) = a\}$ for some function $b(a)$, where the union is taken over all $a \in GF(2^\ell)$. Analogously, $\mathcal{E}$ must also be contained in sets $\mathcal{E}_i$, $i = 2, \ldots, N/2\ell$, of the same form (with d_1 and d'_1 replaced by d_i and d'_i, respectively), hence $\mathcal{E} \subseteq \cap_{i=1}^{N/2\ell} \mathcal{E}_i$. We show that the cardinality of the set on the right hand side is $\sqrt{|\mathcal{K}|}$. First, observe that every set of at most $N/\ell (\leq 2^\ell)$ functions f_{d_i} is, for pairwise distinct $d_i \in GF(2^\ell)$, linearly independent over $GF(2^\ell)$ (the so-called Vandermonde determinant is nonzero in this case). We define $r_l := |\cap_{i=1}^l \mathcal{E}_i|$. From the linear independence of $\{f_{d_1}, f_{d'_1}\}$, we first conclude that $r_1 = 2^{N-\ell}$. Furthermore, the linear independence of $f_{d_{l+1}}$ from the set $\{f_{d_1}, \ldots, f_{d_l}, f_{d'_1}, \ldots, f_{d'_{l+1}}\}$ (because $d_{l+1} \notin \{d_1, \ldots, d_l, d'_1, \ldots, d'_l\}$ according to the choice of the pairs (d_i, d'_i)) implies that $r_{l+1} = r_l/2^\ell$ for $l = 1, \ldots, N/2\ell - 1$. Note that this also holds if $d'_{l+1} = d_i$ or $d'_{l+1} = d'_i$ for some $i < l+1$. We conclude that $|\mathcal{E}| \leq r_{N/2\ell} = 2^{N-(N/2\ell)\cdot\ell} = 2^{N/2} = \sqrt{|\mathcal{K}|}$.

On the other hand, $\mathrm{Prob}[\mathcal{E}] = \sum_{k \in \mathcal{E}} P_K(k) \geq \alpha^{N/\ell}$. In the case where P_K restricted to $\mathcal{E}$ is the uniform distribution (this case maximizes the Rényi entropy) with probability at least $\alpha^{N/\ell}/|\mathcal{E}|$, we have $\sum_{k \in \mathcal{K}} P_K(k)^2 \geq \sum_{k \in \mathcal{E}} P_K(k)^2 \geq |\mathcal{E}| \cdot (\alpha^{2N/\ell}/|\mathcal{E}|^2) \geq \alpha^{2N/\ell}/2^{N/2}$, and the claim follows when the negative logarithm is computed on both sides. $\qquad \square$

3.4   A Strong Protocol for Privacy Amplification

The new technique for authentication allows the construction of a strong protocol for privacy amplification. However, the fact that the challenge string d, which must uniquely determine the message, i.e., the specification of the hash function for privacy amplification, is short implies that one cannot use universal hash functions, whose descriptions would be too long (see for example [8] for lower bounds on the cardinality of universal classes). We use so-called *extractors* instead, which are small classes of functions allowing to extract the min-entropy H_∞ of a weak random source into a close-to-uniformly distributed string or equivalently, to transform a partially secret into a highly secret string (see Appendix B).

We are now ready to present and analyze the strong protocol for privacy amplification secure against active adversaries. Let n be a multiple of 3, let $0 < m < 1$ be such that $2mn$ is a divisor of $2n/3$, and let $d := (2n/3)/(mn)$.

---

[3] Throughout the paper, the cardinality of a set M is denoted by $|M|$.

For an n-bit string S, let S_I, S_{II}, and S_{III} be $(n/3)$-bit strings such that $S = S_I||S_{II}||S_{III}$, where $||$ stands for the concatenation of strings. Let further $f_h(S_I||S_{II})$ be defined as in Lemma 10 for $S_I||S_{II} = (S_0, \ldots, S_{d-1}) \in GF(2^{mn})^d$ (here, the S_i are interpreted as elements of $GF(2^{mn})$ with respect to a fixed representation of $GF(2^{mn})$ over $GF(2)$) and $h \in GF(2^{mn})$). Then Protocol B works as follows. The extractor function E will be specified below. By $a \in_R \mathcal{A}$, we express that a is randomly chosen in the set $\mathcal{A}$ according to the uniform distribution.

Protocol B

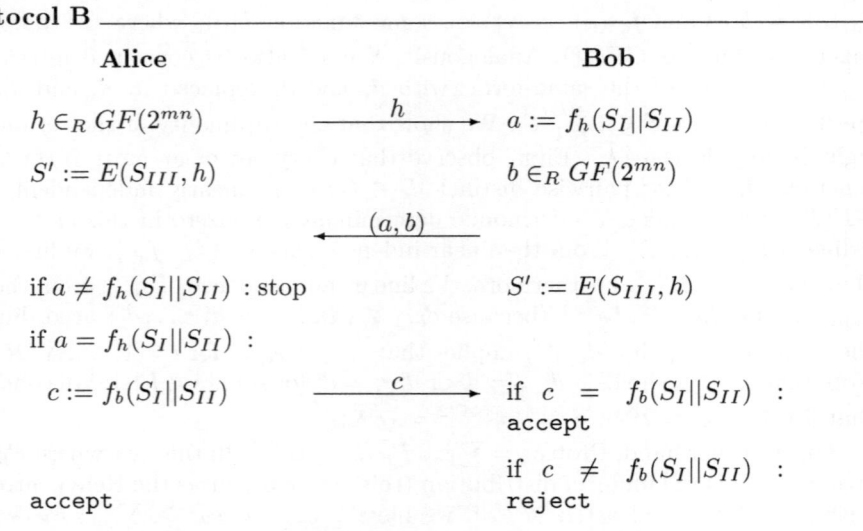

Theorem 11. *Let $t > 2/3$ be a constant. Then there exist constants m and n_0, and for every $n \geq n_0$ a function E, computable in polynomial time, such that Protocol B is a strong $(n, \mathcal{D}_{2,tn}, \Omega(n), 2^{-\Omega(n)}, 2^{-\Omega(n)})$-protocol for privacy amplification by communication over an insecure and non-authentic channel.*

Note that the assumption on Eve's knowledge about S is exactly the same for Protocol B as for Protocol A. However, the price that has to be paid for strong robustness is that the length of the extracted string is only a constant fraction of the length of the key generated by the weak Protocol A, and that a higher round complexity is required in communication.

Proof of Theorem 11. Let $0 < m < t - 2/3$ be constant, and let $z \in \mathcal{Z}$ be the particular value known to the adversary Eve. Assume first that Eve is only *passive*. We give a lower bound on the min-entropy of the string S_{III} from Eve's point of view and given the entire communication C held over the public channel. Since this communication is, given S_I, S_{II}, and $Z = z$, independent of S_{III}, we have $H_2(S_{III}|C = c, S_I = s_I, S_{II} = s_{II}, Z = z) = H_2(S_{III}|S_I = s_I, S_{II} = s_{II}, Z = z) \geq (t - 2/3)n/2$ with probability at least $1 - 2^{-((t-2/3)n/4-1)}$ according to Lemma 7. (Of course Alice and Bob could publish S_I and S_{II} at the end of the protocol, only helping a possible adversary.) Because $H_\infty(X) \geq H_2(X)/2$ for all X, we conclude that

$$H_\infty(S_{III} \mid C = c, S_I = s_I, S_{II} = s_{II}, Z = z) \geq (t - 2/3)n/4 \qquad (2)$$

holds with probability at least $1 - 2^{-((t-2/3)n/4-1)}$.

From Corollary 19 in Appendix B, we conclude that there exist n_0 and for all[4] $n \geq n_0$ numbers $w \leq mn$, $r = \Omega(n)$, and a function $E : \{0,1\}^{n/3} \times \{0,1\}^w \to \{0,1\}^r$ (computable in polynomial time) with the following property. Under the condition that T is an $(n/3)$-bit random variable with $H_\infty(T) \geq (t - 2/3)n/4$ and that V is a uniformly distributed w-bit random variable, we have for $R := E(T,V)$ that $H(R|V) \geq r \cdot (1 - 2^{-n/(6(\log(n/3))^3)}) \cdot (1 - 2^{-n/(6(\log(n/3))^3)} - 2^{-r})$. For the choice $P_T = P_{S_{III}|C=c,Z=z}$ and $P_R = P_{S'} = P_{E(S_{III},V)}$ (where V is composed by the first w bits of H in a fixed representation) we obtain, using (2) and $I(H; SZ) = 0$, $H(S'|C, Z = z) \geq r - r \cdot (2^{-n/(6(\log(n/3))^3)+1} + 2^{-r} + 2^{-((t-2/3)n/4-1)}) = r - 2^{-\Omega(n)}$.

We consider the case where Eve is an *active* adversary and give an upper bound on the probability of the event that Alice and Bob do not both reject although secret-key agreement has not been successful. It is obvious that this can only occur if Eve can either guess $f_h(S)$ from some $f_{h'}(S)$ (where $h' \neq h$) or guess $f_b(S)$ correctly, where h and b are randomly chosen. The success probability δ of such an active attack is upper bounded by

$$\delta \leq 2^{-(m/2)(t-2/3)n} + 2^{-((t-2/3-m)n/4-1)} + 2^{-(m/2)(t-2/3-m)n/2} = 2^{-\Omega(n)} . \qquad (3)$$

To see this, we first conclude from Lemma 7 that $H_2((S_I||S_{II})|Z = z) \geq (t - 1/3)n$. According to Lemma 10 (for $K = S_I||S_{II}$, $N = 2n/3$, and $l = mn$) and Lemma 8, the summands in (3) are upper bounds on the probabilities of guessing $f_h(S)$ from some $f_{h'}(S)$, of the event $\mathcal{E}$ that $H_2((S_I||S_{II})|H = h, A = a, Z = z) < n/3 + (t - 2/3 - m)n/2 \leq H_2((S_I||S_{II})|Z = z) - mn - (t - 2/3 - m)n/2$, and of finding $f_b(S)$ when given $\overline{\mathcal{E}}$, respectively. We conclude that Protocol B is a strong protocol with all the required properties. □

4   Independent Repetitions of a Random Experiment

Another important special case of secret-key agreement protocols is the scenario where the information the parties obtain consists of many independent realizations of the same random experiment (with distribution P_{XYZ}) [5]. For the

---

[4] We can assume, not changing the basic result, that n is a multiple of 3, and that $2mn$ is an integer dividing $2n/3$. Otherwise, mn can be replaced by $k := \lceil mn \rceil$ in the entire proof, and n can be substituted by the unique multiple of $3k$ in the interval $[n, n + 3k - 1]$. Alice and Bob then add the required number of zeroes to the end of S, not changing the distribution of S.

passive-adversary case, the *secret-key rate* $S(P_{XYZ})$ has been defined in [5] as the maximal rate at which a secret key can be generated. The following definition generalizes this notion to the active-adversary case with respect to weak and strong protocols.

Definition 12. The (weak) secret-key rate against active adversaries, denoted $S_w^*(P_{XYZ})$, is the least upper bound of the set of numbers $R \geq 0$ with the property that for all $\varepsilon, \delta > 0$, and for sufficiently large n, there exists a weak $(P_{XYZ}^n, \lfloor Rn \rfloor, \varepsilon, \delta)$-protocol for secret-key agreement by communication over an insecure and non-authentic channel. Here, P_{XYZ}^n stands for the distribution over $\mathcal{X}^n \times \mathcal{Y}^n \times \mathcal{Z}^n$ that corresponds to n independent realizations of the random experiment with distribution P_{XYZ}. The (strong) rate $S_s^*(P_{XYZ})$ is defined analogously, but it is required that the protocol is strong.   ○

Of course, we have $S_s^*(P_{XYZ}) \leq S_w^*(P_{XYZ}) \leq S(P_{XYZ})$ for all distributions P_{XYZ}. The following theorem expresses $S_w^*(P_{XYZ})$ and $S_s^*(P_{XYZ})$ in terms of $S(P_{XYZ})$ and P_{XYZ}, and corrects the results of [4]. Both S_w^* and S_s^* are equal to either S or 0, depending on whether X or Y (or both) are simulatable by Eve. The proof of Theorem 13 follows the lines of [4], and will be given in a final paper.

Theorem 13. *Let P_{XYZ} be a distribution of the random variables X, Y, and Z such that $S(P_{XYZ}) > 0$. Then $S_w^*(P_{XYZ}) = 0$ if and only if both X and Y are simulatable by Z with respect to each other. Otherwise, $S_w^*(P_{XYZ}) = S(P_{XYZ})$. Furthermore, $S_s^*(P_{XYZ}) = 0$ holds if and only if either X or Y is simulatable by Z (with respect to Y or X, respectively). Otherwise $S_s^*(P_{XYZ}) = S(P_{XYZ})$.*

5   Concluding Remarks

Improving earlier results, and relativizing the previous pessimism, we have shown that unconditionally secure key agreement against active opponents is possible in such a way that both parties are simultaneously protected against an adversary's active attacks. Clearly, this property is what someone would naturally request from such a protocol. In the special case of privacy amplification, interactive (instead of one-way) authentication allows to reduce the adversary's gain of information about the partially secret key by using shorter authenticators, without increasing the success probability of a message-substitution attack even by an adversary with partial knowledge about the key. Finally, we have shown that, in the situation of general random variables as well as in the scenario where the parties have access to repeated realizations of the same random experiment, previously formulated non-simulatability criteria characterize the existence of strong rather than weak protocols.

Acknowledgments

We thank Ueli Maurer and Christian Cachin for many interesting discussions. The is work was supported by the Swiss National Science Foundation (SNF).

References

1. C. H. Bennett, G. Brassard, C. Crépeau, and U. M. Maurer, Generalized privacy amplification, *IEEE Transactions on Information Theory*, Vol. 41, Nr. 6, 1995.
2. C. H. Bennett, G. Brassard, and J.-M. Robert, Privacy amplification by public discussion, *SIAM Journal on Computing*, Vol. 17, pp. 210-229, 1988.
3. C. Cachin, *Entropy measures and unconditional security in cryptography*, Ph. D. Thesis, ETH Zürich, Hartung-Gorre Verlag, Zürich, 1997.
4. U. M. Maurer, Information-theoretically secure secret-key agreement by NOT authenticated public discussion, *Advances in Cryptology - EUROCRYPT '97*, Lecture Notes in Computer Science, Vol. 1233, pp. 209-225, Springer-Verlag, 1997.
5. U. M. Maurer, Secret key agreement by public discussion from common information, *IEEE Transactions on Information Theory*, Vol. 39, No. 3, pp. 733-742, 1993.
6. U. M. Maurer and S. Wolf, Privacy amplification secure against active adversaries, *Advances in Cryptology - CRYPTO '97*, Lecture Notes in Computer Science, Vol. 1294, pp. 307-321, Springer-Verlag, 1996.
7. N. Nisan and D. Zuckerman, Randomness is linear in space, *Journal of Computer and System Sciences*, Vol. 52, No. 1, pp. 43-52, 1996.
8. D. R. Stinson, Universal hashing and authentication codes, *Advances in Cryptology - CRYPTO '91*, Lecture Notes in Computer Science, Vol. 576, pp. 74-85, Springer-Verlag, 1992.

Appendix A. One-Way Privacy Amplification

In [1], the following important theorem on privacy amplification secure against passive adversaries has been proved, which implies that there exist protocols for privacy amplification by authenticated communication which allow to extract a string S' whose length is roughly equal to the Rényi entropy of S, given Eve's knowledge.

Theorem 14. [1] *Let S be a random variable with probability distribution P_S and Rényi entropy $H_2(S)$, and let G be the random variable corresponding to the random choice (with uniform distribution) of a member of a universal class of hash functions mapping S to r-bit strings, and let $S' = G(S)$. Then $r \geq H(S'|G) \geq H_2(S'|G) \geq r - 2^{r-H_2(S)}/\ln 2$.*

We will apply Theorem 14 to the case where all the probabilities are conditioned on $Z = z$. The function G is chosen from a universal class of hash functions. Generally, a class $\mathcal{H}$ of functions mapping $\mathcal{A}$ to $\mathcal{B}$ is called *universal* if for all $x, y \in \mathcal{A}$, $x \neq y$, $\text{Prob}[h(x) = h(y)] = 1/|\mathcal{B}|$ if h is chosen randomly from $\mathcal{H}$ according to the uniform distribution. An example of such a class of functions mapping l-bit strings to r-bit strings (where $l \geq r$) is the set of functions $h_c(x) = \text{LSB}_r(c \cdot x)$ for all $c \in GF(2^l)$. This class contains 2^l different functions.

Let us now consider non-interactive privacy amplification secure against active opponents. Note first that a one-way-transmission protocol cannot be strong.

Theorem 15. *Assume that a strong $(n, \mathcal{D}_{2,t}, r, \varepsilon, \delta)$-one-way-transmission protocol exists. Then $\varepsilon \geq \min\{r, n - t\}$ or $\delta = 1$.*

The proof of this theorem will be given in the final paper. The following (weak) protocol was described already in [6]. Here, S is an n-bit string, and S_I, S_{II}, and S_{III} are the first, second, and third parts of S of length $n/3$.

Protocol A _____

Alice	**Bob**
$h \in_R GF(2^{n/3})$	
$a := h \cdot S_I + S_{II}$ $\xrightarrow{\quad (h,a) \quad}$	
accept	accept if $a = h \cdot S_I + S_{II}$
$S' := \text{LSB}_r(h \cdot S_{III})$	$S' := \text{LSB}_r(h \cdot S_{III})$

_____

The notation $h \in_R GF(2^{n/3})$ means that h is chosen randomly from $GF(2^{n/3})$ according to the uniform distribution. All the computations are carried out in the field $GF(2^{n/3})$.

Theorem 16. *Let n, s, and t be positive integers such that $n > tn > 2n/3 + s$. Then Protocol A is a weak $(n, \mathcal{D}_{2,t}, (t - 2/3)n - s, \varepsilon, \delta)$-protocol for privacy amplification by communication over an insecure and non-authentic channel for $\varepsilon = r \cdot 2^{-(s/3-1)} + 2^{-s/3}/\ln 2$ and $\delta = 3 \cdot 2^{-(t-2/3)n/4}$.*

Proof. Let $z \in \mathcal{Z}$ be the particular value known to Eve. We first assume that Eve is a passive wire-tapper. Let $(h, a) = (h, h \cdot S_I + S_{II})$ be the message sent from Alice to Bob, and let $\mathcal{E}$ be the event that $H_2(S_{III}|S_I = s_I, S_{II} = s_{II}, Z = z) \geq (t - 2/3)n - 2s/3$ Then $\mathcal{E}$ has, according to Corollary 9, probability at least $1 - 2^{-(s/3-1)}$. Let $r := (t - 2/3)n - s$, and let $S' := \text{LSB}_r(h \cdot S_{III})$. Theorem 14 now implies that $H(S'|HA, \mathcal{E}, Z = z) \geq H(S'|HAS_IS_{II}, \mathcal{E}, Z = z) = H(S'|HS_IS_{II}, \mathcal{E}, Z = z) \geq r - 2^{-s/3}/\ln 2$. We have used $I(S_{III}; HA|S_IS_{II}, Z = z) = 0$. We conclude $H(S'|HA, Z = z) \geq \text{Prob}[\mathcal{E}] \cdot (r - 2^{-s/3}/\ln 2) \geq r - r \cdot 2^{-(s/3-1)} - 2^{-s/3}/\ln 2 =: r - \varepsilon$.

Let us now consider the case where Eve is an active attacker. We give an upper bound on the probability that Eve can substitute a message (h, a) by a different message (h', a'), $h' \neq h$, without being detected. The crucial argument is that $S_I || S_{II}$ is uniquely determined by $(h, h \cdot S_I + S_{II})$ and $(h', h' \cdot S_I + S_{II})$ if $h \neq h'$. Hence the probability of a successful active attack (which can only be a substitution attack according to the definition of Protocol A, where Alice only accepts after having sent a message) is not greater than the probability of guessing S correctly when given (h, a). From Lemmas 7 and 8 we conclude that $H_2((S_I||S_{II})|H = h, A = a, Z = z) \geq (t - 2/3)n/2$ is true with probability at least $1 - 2^{-((t-2/3)n/4-1)}$. If the inequality holds, then the maximal probability of a single string $s_I||s_{II}$ is at most $2^{-H_2((S_I||S_{II})|H=h,A=a,Z=z)/2} \leq 2^{-(t-2/3)n/4}$. Hence, by the union bound, the success probability of an active attack is upper bounded by $2^{-((t-2/3)n/4-1)} + 2^{-(t-2/3)n/4} = 3 \cdot 2^{-(t-2/3)n/4} =: \delta.$ $\qquad\square$

Appendix B. Extractors

In this appendix we describe the notion of an extractor and some facts needed for Protocol B. For an introduction into the subject and the precise constructions, see [7] and the references therein. Roughly spoken, an extractor allows to efficiently distill the entire (or a substantial part of) the randomness (in terms of the min-entropy) of some source into (almost) truly random bits, using a small additional number of random bits. Theorem 18 was proven in [7], introducing one particular class of extractors. Corollary 19, which is a consequence of Theorem 18, is the statement we need in the analysis of Protocol B.

Definition 17. [7] A function $E : \{0,1\}^N \times \{0,1\}^w \to \{0,1\}^r$ is called a (δ', ε')-extractor if for any distribution P on $\{0,1\}^N$ with min-entropy $H_\infty(P) \geq \delta' N$, the distance of the distribution of $[V, E(X,V)]$ to the uniform distribution over $\{0,1\}^{w+r}$ is at most ε' when choosing X according to P and V according to the uniform distribution over $\{0,1\}^w$. The distance between two distributions P and P' on a set $\mathcal{X}$ is defined as $d(P,P') := (\sum_{x \in \mathcal{X}} |P(x) - P'(x)|)/2.$ $\qquad\circ$

Theorem 18. [7] *For any parameters $\delta' = \delta'(N)$ and $\varepsilon' = \varepsilon'(N)$ with $1/N \leq \delta' \leq 1/2$ and $2^{-\delta' N} \leq \varepsilon' \leq 1/N$, there exists a (δ', ε')-extractor $E : \{0,1\}^N \times \{0,1\}^w \to \{0,1\}^r$, where $w = O(\log(1/\varepsilon') \cdot (\log N)^2 \cdot (\log(1/\delta'))/\delta')$ and $r = \Omega(\delta'^2 N/\log(1/\delta'))$, and where E is computable in polynomial time.*

Corollary 19. *Let $\delta', m \in (0,1)$ be constants. Then there exists N_0 and for all $N \geq N_0$ a function E, computable in polynomial time, $E : \{0,1\}^N \times \{0,1\}^w \to \{0,1\}^r$, where $w \leq mN$ and $r = \Omega(N)$, such that if T is an N-bit random variable with $H_\infty(T) > \delta' N$, then $H(E(T,V)|V) \geq r \cdot (1 - 2^{-N/(2(\log N)^3)}) \cdot (1 - 2^{-N/(2(\log N)^3)} - 2^{-r})$ for uniformly distributed V.*

Proof. Let $\varepsilon'(N) := 2^{-N/(\log N)^3}$. Then there exists N_0 such that for all $N \geq N_0$ we have $\varepsilon' \geq 2^{-\delta' N}$, and a (δ', ε')-extractor E, mapping $\{0,1\}^{N+w}$ to $\{0,1\}^r$, where $w \leq mN$ (note that $w = O(N/\log N)$ for this choice of ε' and for constant δ') and $r = \Omega(N)$. By definition, this means that for a uniformly distributed random variable V and if $H_\infty(T) \geq \delta' N$, the distance of the distribution of $[V, E(T,V)]$ to the uniform distribution U_{w+r} over $\{0,1\}^{w+r}$ is at most $\varepsilon' = 2^{-N/(\log N)^3}$. Because $d([V, E(T,V)], U_{w+r}) = \mathrm{E}_V[d(E(T,V), U_r)] \leq \varepsilon'$ for uniformly distributed V, the distance of the distribution of $E(T,v)$ to the uniform distribution U_r (over $\{0,1\}^r$) is at most $\sqrt{\varepsilon'}$ with probability at least $1 - \sqrt{\varepsilon'}$ over v, i.e., $P_V[d(E(T,V), U_r) \leq 2^{-N/(2(\log N)^3)}] \geq 1 - 2^{-N/(2(\log N)^3)}$. The corollary now follows from $H(Z) \geq k(1 - d(U_k, P_Z) - 2^{-k})$, which is true for every random variable Z with $\mathcal{Z} \subseteq \{0,1\}^k$ [6]. $\qquad\square$

Some Bounds and a Construction for Secure Broadcast Encryption

Kaoru Kurosawa[1], Takuya Yoshida[1], Yvo Desmedt[2,3] *, and Mike Burmester[3]

[1] Dept. of EE, Tokyo Institute of Technology
2–12–1 O-okayama, Meguro-ku, Tokyo 152-8552, Japan
{kurosawa,takuya}@ss.titech.ac.jp
[2] Center for Cryptography, Computer and Network Security, and
Department of EE & CS, University of Wisconsin – Milwaukee
P.O. Box 784, WI 53201-0784, U.S.A.
desmedt@cs.uwm.edu
[3] Information Security Group, Royal Holloway – University of London
Egham, Surrey TW20 OEX, U.K.
m.burmester@rhbnc.ac.uk

Abstract. We first present two tight lower bounds on the size of the secret keys of each user in an unconditionally secure one-time use broadcast encryption scheme (OTBES). Then we show how to construct a computationally secure multiple-use broadcast encryption scheme (MBES) from a key predistribution scheme (KPS) by using the ElGamal cryptosystem. We prove that our MBES is secure against chosen (message, privileged subset of users) attacks if the ElGamal cryptosystem is secure and if the original KPS is simulatable. This is the first MBES whose security is proved formally.

1 Introduction

Secure broadcast encryption is one of the central problems in communication and network security. In this paper we link One-Time use Broadcast Encryption Schemes (OTBESs) [5,7,6] with Key Predistribution Schemes (KPS)[10]. Both schemes are closely related but they have a different structure. In a KPS, a Trusted Authority (TA) distributes secret information to a set of users such that, each member of a privileged subset P of users can compute a specified key k_P, but no coalition F (forbidden subset) is able to recover any information on the key k_P that it is not supposed to know. In a OTBES, the TA distributes secret information to a set of users and then broadcasts a ciphertext b_P over a network. The secret information is such that each member of a particular subset P of users can decrypt b_P, but no coalition F (forbidden subset) is able to recover any information on the plaintext m_P of b_P that it is not supposed to know.

A natural way to construct an OTBES from a KPS is to use a key k_P of the KPS to encrypt the message m_P, that is

$$b_P = k_P + m_P. \tag{1}$$

* A part of this research has been supported by NSF Grant NCR-9508528.

K. Ohta and D. Pei (Eds.): ASIACRYPT'98, LNCS 1514, pp. 420–433, 1998.

Stinson *et al.* [4,6] have shown that there is a tradeoff between $|B_P|$ and $|U_i|$ in OTBESs, where B_P is the set of ciphertexts b_P and U_i is the set of secrets of user i. That is, $|B_P|$ can be decreased by increasing $|U_i|$ and vice versa.

A $(\mathcal{P}, \mathcal{F})$-KPS is a KPS for which $\mathcal{P} \triangleq \{P \mid P$ is a privileged subset$\}$ and $\mathcal{F} \triangleq \{F \mid F$ is a forbidden subset$\}$. In particular,

- A $(t, \leq w)$-KPS is a $(\mathcal{P}, \mathcal{F})$-KPS with $\mathcal{P} = \{P \mid |P| = t\}$, $\mathcal{F} = \{F \mid |F| \leq w\}$,
- A $(\leq n, \leq w)$-KPS is a $(\mathcal{P}, \mathcal{F})$-KPS with $\mathcal{P} = 2^{\mathcal{U}}$, $\mathcal{F} = \{F \mid |F| \leq w\}$, where $\mathcal{U}$ is the set of users and $n \triangleq |\mathcal{U}|$.

We define $(\mathcal{P}, \mathcal{F})$-OTBESs, $(t, \leq w)$-OTBESs and $(\leq n, \leq w)$-OTBESs in a similar way. Below we list some of the known KPSs and OTBESs.

Key Predistribution Schemes. Blom obtained a $(2, \leq w)$-KPS in [1] by using MDS codes (also see [10]). Blundo *et al.* obtained a $(t, \leq w)$-KPS in [3] by using symmetric polynomials. Fiat and Naor presented a $(\leq n, \leq w)$-KPS in [5]. Blundo *et al.* found tight lower bounds on $|U_i|$ for $(t, \leq w)$-KPSs [3] and for $(\leq n, \leq w)$-KPSs [2].[1] Recently, Ludy and Staddon found some bounds and constructions for some classes of $(n - w, \leq w)$-OTBESs [8]. However, there is a gap between their bounds and the constructions.

One-Time Use Broadcast Encryption Schemes. Stinson *et al.* gave constructions for $(t, \leq w)$-OTBESs [4] and $(\leq n, \leq w)$-OTBESs [6] which can realize the tradeoff between $|B_P|$ and $|U_i|$. Blundo, Frota Mattos and Stinson found a lower bound on $|B_P|$ and $|U_i|$ for $(t, \leq w)$-OTBESs which reflects the tradeoff [4]. Recently, Desmedt and Viswanathan presented a $(\leq n, \leq n)$-KPS [9]. This can be considered as a complement of the Fiat and Naor $(\leq n, \leq n)$-KPS.

In this paper, we first prove that a $(\mathcal{P}, \mathcal{F})$-KPS is equivalent to a $(\mathcal{P}, \mathcal{F})$-OTBES when $|B_P| = |M|$, where M denotes the set of messages (Theorems 1, 2). Then, by using the bounds in [3,2] for KPSs we get directly a lower bound on $|U_i|$ for $(\leq n, \leq w)$-OTBESs and a lower bound for $(t, \leq w)$-OTBESs. The former is the first lower bound for $(\leq n, \leq w)$-OTBESs. The latter is more tight than the bound of Blundo, Frota Mattos and Stinson for $|B_P| = |M|$. Both bounds are tight because the natural schemes which use equation (1) meet the equalities of our bounds. We also present a general lower bound on $|U_i|$ for KPSs which includes all the previous known bounds as special cases (Theorem 3).

Next, we show how to construct a computationally secure $(\mathcal{P}, \mathcal{F})$-Multiple use Broadcast Encryption Scheme $((\mathcal{P}, \mathcal{F})$-MBES) from a $(\mathcal{P}, \mathcal{F})$-KPS by using the ElGamal cryptosystem. We prove (Theorem 4) that our $(\mathcal{P}, \mathcal{F})$-MBES is secure against *chosen (message, privileged subset of users) attacks* (Definition 1) if the ElGamal cryptosystem is secure and if the original $(\mathcal{P}, \mathcal{F})$-KPS is *simulatable* (Definition 3).

We then show that the Blundo *et al.* scheme, the Fiat-Naor scheme and the Desmedt-Viswanathan scheme are all simulatable (Theorems 5,6). By combining

---

[1] The model for broadcast encryption in [2,5] corresponds to our model for KPSs. So, for example, the bounds in [2] hold only for KPSs, and not for OTBESs.

this result with our earlier construction we get $(\mathcal{P}, \mathcal{F})$-MBESs for $(\mathcal{P}, \mathcal{F}) = (t, \leq w)$ and $(\leq n, \leq w)$ whose security is proven formally.

The proposed construction is the first MBES whose security is proven formally (Corollary 6). Furthermore, our technique can be generalized to many of the OTBESs in [6], and our argument holds for Multiple use $(\mathcal{P}, \mathcal{F})$-KPSs.

2   Mathematical Models [4,6]

Our model for key distribution and broadcast encryption consists of a Trusted Authority (TA) and a set of users $\mathcal{U} = \{1, 2, \ldots, n\}$.

2.1   Key Predistribution

In a key pre-distribution scheme, the TA generates and distributes secret information to each user. The information given to user i is denoted by u_i and must be distributed "off-band" (i.e., not using the network) in a secure manner. This secret information will enable various *privileged subsets* to compute keys.

Let $2^{\mathcal{U}}$ denote the set of all subsets of users. $\mathcal{P} \subseteq 2^{\mathcal{U}}$ will denote the collection of all privileged subsets to which the TA distributes keys. $\mathcal{F} \subseteq 2^{\mathcal{U}}$ will denote the collection of all possible coalitions (called *forbidden subsets*) against which each key is to remain secure.

Once the secret information is distributed, each user i in a privileged set P should be able to compute the key k_P associated with P. On the other hand, no forbidden set $F \in \mathcal{F}$ disjoint from P should be able to compute any information about k_P.

Let K_P denote the set of possible keys associated with P. We assume that $K_P = K$ for each $P \in \mathcal{P}$.

For $1 \leq i \leq n$, let U_i denote the set of all possible secret values that might be distributed to user i by the TA. For any subset of users $X \subseteq \mathcal{U}$, let U_X denote the cartesian product $U_{i_1} \times \cdots \times U_{i_j}$, where $X = \{i_1, \ldots, i_j\}$ and $i_1 < \cdots < i_j$. We assume that there is a probability distribution on $U_{\mathcal{U}}$, and that the TA chooses $u_{\mathcal{U}} \in U_{\mathcal{U}}$ according to this probability distribution.

We say that the scheme is a $(\mathcal{P}, \mathcal{F})$-*Key Predistribution Scheme* $((\mathcal{P}, \mathcal{F})$-KPS) if the following conditions are satisfied:

1. Each user i in any privileged set P can compute k_P:
    $\forall i \in P, \forall P \in \mathcal{P}, \forall u_i \in U_i, \exists k_P \in K_P$ s.t.,

    $$\Pr[K_P = k_P \mid U_i = u_i] = 1.$$

2. No forbidden subset F disjoint from any privileged subset P has any information on k_P:
    $\forall P \in \mathcal{P}, \forall k_P \in K_P, \forall F \in \mathcal{F}$ s.t. $P \cap F = \emptyset, \forall u_F \in U_F$ s.t. $\Pr(U_F = u_F) > 0$,

    $$\Pr[K_P = k_P \mid U_F = u_F] = \Pr[K_P = k_P]. \tag{2}$$

We denote a $(\mathcal{P}, \mathcal{F})$-KPS by $(U_1, \ldots, U_n, K)$.

2.2 One-Time Broadcast Encryption

We will use the notation from Section 2.1. We assume that the network is a *broadcast channel*, i.e., it is insecure, and that any information transmitted by the TA will be received by every user.

In a set-up stage, the TA generates and distributes secret information u_i to each user i off-band. At a later time, the TA will want to broadcast a message to a privileged subset P. The particular privileged subset P is, in general, not known ahead of time.

$\mathcal{P} \subseteq 2^{\mathcal{U}}$ will denote the collection of all privileged subsets to which the TA might want to broadcast a message. $\mathcal{F} \subseteq 2^{\mathcal{U}}$ will denote the collection of all possible coalitions (forbidden subsets) against which a broadcast is to remain secure.

Now, suppose that the TA wants to broadcast a message to a given privileged set $P \in \mathcal{P}$ at a later time. (The particular privileged set P is not known when the scheme is set up, except for the restriction that $P \in \mathcal{P}$.) Let M_P denote the set of possible messages that might be broadcast to P. We assume that $M_P = M$ for each $P \in \mathcal{P}$. Furthermore, we assume that there is a probability distribution on M, and that the TA chooses a *message* (i.e., a plaintext) $m_P \in M$ according to this probability distribution. Then the *broadcast* b_P (which is an element of a specified set B_P) is computed as a function of m_P and u_P.

Once b_P is broadcast, each user $i \in P$ should be able to decrypt b_P and obtain m_P. On the other hand, no forbidden set $F \in \mathcal{F}$ disjoint from P should be able to compute any information about m_P.

The security of the scheme is in terms of a single broadcast, so we call the scheme *one-time*. We say that the scheme is a $(\mathcal{P}, \mathcal{F})$-*One-Time Broadcast Encryption Scheme* $((\mathcal{P}, \mathcal{F})$-OTBES) if the following conditions are satisfied:

1. Without knowing the broadcast b_P, no subset of users has any information about the message m_P, even if given all the secret information $U_{\mathcal{U}}$:
   $\forall P \in \mathcal{P}$, $\forall m_P \in M_P$, $\forall u_U \in U_U$ s.t. $\Pr[U_U = u_U] > 0$,

$$\Pr[M_P = m_P \mid U_U = u_U] = \Pr[M_P = m_P]. \tag{3}$$

2. The message for a privileged user is uniquely determined by the broadcast message and the user's secret information:
   $\forall i \in P$, $\forall P \in \mathcal{P}$, $\forall u_i \in U_i$, $\forall b_P \in B_P$, $\exists m_P \in M_P$ s.t.,

$$\Pr[M_P = m_P \mid U_i = u_i, B_P = b_P] = 1. \tag{4}$$

3. After receiving the broadcast message, no forbidden subset F disjoint from P has any information on m_P:
   $\forall P \in \mathcal{P}$, $\forall F \in \mathcal{F}$ s.t. $P \cap F = \emptyset$, $\forall m_P \in M_P$, $\forall u_F \in U_F$, $\forall b_P \in B_P$,

$$\Pr[M_P = m_P \mid U_F = u_F, B_P = b_P] = \Pr[M_P = m_P]. \tag{5}$$

We denote a $(\mathcal{P}, \mathcal{F})$-OTBES by $(U_1, \ldots, U_n, M, \{B_P\})$.

2.3   Conventional Notation

We first consider key predistribution schemes. If $\mathcal{P}$ consists of all t-subsets of $\mathcal{U}$, then we will write $(t, \mathcal{F})$-KPS. Similarly, if $\mathcal{P}$ consists of all subsets of $\mathcal{U}$ of size at most t, we write $(\leq t, \mathcal{F})$-KPS. An analogous notation will be used for $\mathcal{F}$. Thus, for example, a $(\leq n, 1)$-KPS is a KPS for which there is a key associated with any subset of users (i.e., $\mathcal{P} = 2^{\mathcal{U}}$) and no key k_P can be computed by any individual user $i \notin P$. Note that in any $(\mathcal{P}, \mathcal{F})$-KPS, if $F \in \mathcal{F}$ and $F' \subseteq F$, then $F' \in \mathcal{F}$. Hence, a $(\mathcal{P}, w)$-KPS is a $(\mathcal{P}, \leq w)$-KPS.

The same notation is used for one-time use broadcast encryption schemes.

3   Known Results

For a random variable X, $H(X)$ denotes the entropy of X. Generally,

$$0 \leq H(X) \leq \log_2 |X|, \text{ where } X \triangleq \{x \mid \Pr(X = x) > 0\}.$$

In particular, $H(X) = \log_2 |X|$ iff X is uniformly distributed.

3.1   A $(t, \leq w)$-KPS (The Blundo et al. Scheme)

Blom presented a $(2, \leq w)$-KPS in [1]. This was generalized to a $(t, \leq w)$-KPS by Blundo et al. as follows [3]. Let q be a prime such that $q \geq n$ (the number of users). The TA chooses a random *symmetric* polynomial in t variables over $GF(q)$ in which the degree of any variable is at most w, that is, a polynomial

$$f(x_1, \ldots, x_t) = \sum_{i_1=0}^{w} \cdots \sum_{i_t=0}^{w} a_{i_1 \cdots i_t} x_1^{i_1} \cdots x_t^{i_t},$$

where, $a_{i_1 \cdots i_t} = a_{\pi(i_1 \cdots i_t)}$ for any permutation π on $(i_1, \ldots, i_t)$. The TA computes u_i as $u_i = f(i, x_2, \ldots, x_t)$ and gives u_i to user i secretly for $1 \leq i \leq n$. The key associated with the t-subset $P = \{i_1, \ldots, i_t\}$ is $k_P = f(i_1, \ldots, i_t)$. Each user $j \in P$ can compute k_P from u_j easily. In this scheme, $|K_P| = q = |K|$ and

$$\log |U_i| = \binom{t + w - 1}{t - 1} \log |K|.$$

This scheme is optimum because Blundo et al. have shown that the following lower bound on $|U_i|$ applies.

Proposition 1. *[3] In a $(t, \leq w)$-KPS,*

$$\log |U_i| \geq \binom{t + w - 1}{t - 1} H(K).$$

Beimel and Chor gave a combinatorial proof of Proposition 1 [7]. Blundo and Cresti obtained the following more general lower bound.

Proposition 2. *[2] In a $(\mathcal{P}, \mathcal{F})$-KPS with $\{1, 2, \cdots, n\} \setminus P \in \mathcal{F}$ for all $P \in \mathcal{P}$,*

$$\log |U_i| \geq \tau_i H(K),$$

where $\tau_i = |\{P \in \mathcal{P} \mid i \in P\}|$

Note that Proposition 1 is obtained from Proposition 2 by letting $n = t + w$.

3.2   A $(\leq n, \leq w)$-KPS (The Fiat-Naor Scheme)

Fiat and Naor presented the following $(\leq n, \leq w)$-KPS [5]. Let q be any positive integer. For every subset $F \subseteq \mathcal{U}$ of cardinality at most w, the TA chooses a random value $s_F \in Z_q$ and gives s_F to every member of $\mathcal{U} \setminus F$ as the secret information. Then the key associated with a privileged set P is defined to be

$$k_P = \sum_{F : F \in \mathcal{F}, F \cap P = \emptyset} s_F \pmod{q},$$

Here is a small example for illustration. Take $n = 3$, $q = 17$ and $w = 1$, and suppose that the TA chooses the values,

$$s_\emptyset = 11, \quad s_{\{1\}} = 8, \quad s_{\{2\}} = 3, \quad s_{\{3\}} = 8.$$

The secret information of the users is,

$$u_1 = \{s_\emptyset, s_{\{2\}}, s_{\{3\}}\}, \quad u_2 = \{s_\emptyset, s_{\{1\}}, s_{\{3\}}\}, \quad u_3 = \{s_\emptyset, s_{\{1\}}, s_{\{2\}}\}.$$

The keys determined by this information are,

$$k_{\{1,2\}} = s_\emptyset + s_{\{3\}} = 2 \bmod 17, \quad \ldots \quad , k_{\{1,2,3\}} = s_\emptyset = 11 \bmod 17.$$

In this scheme, $|K_P| = q = |K|$ and

$$\log |U_i| = \sum_{j=0}^{w} \binom{n-1}{j} \log |K|.$$

This scheme is optimum because Blundo and Cresti have shown the following Proposition and Corollary.

Proposition 3. *[2] In a $(\leq n, \mathcal{F})$-KPS,*

$$\log |U_i| \geq v_i H(K)$$

where $v_i = |\{F \in \mathcal{F} \mid i \notin F\}|$.

Corollary 1. *[2] In a $(\leq n, \leq w)$-KPS,*

$$\log |U_i| \geq \sum_{j=0}^{w} \binom{n-1}{j} H(K).$$

3.3   The $(\leq n, \leq n)$-KPS (The Desmedt-Viswanathan Scheme)

Desmedt and Viswanathan presented a $(\leq n, \leq n)$-KPS [9]. This scheme can viewed as a complement of the Fiat-Naor $(\leq n, \leq n)$-KPS. The TA initially generates $2^n - n - 1$ independent keys, i.e., one for each $P \subseteq \{1, 2, \ldots, n\}$ such that $|P| \geq 2$. Each user i receives from the TA the keys of those subsets for which $i \in P$. Hence, each user gets $2^{n-1} - 1$ keys. This scheme is optimum because of the following lower bound which follows from Corollary 1.

Corollary 2. *In a* $(\leq n, \leq n)$-*KPS,*

$$\log |U_i| \geq (2^{n-1} - 1)H(K).$$

(Desmedt and Viswanathan gave another direct proof [9].)

3.4   Lower Bounds for $(t, \leq w)$-OTBESs

Blundo, Frota Mattos and Stinson obtained the following lower bound for $(t, \leq w)$-OTBESs [4],

Proposition 4. *In any* $(t, \leq w)$-*OTBES with* $t \geq w + 1$,

$$H(B_P) + \sum_{j=1}^{w} H(U_{i_j}) \geq (2w + 1)H(M),$$

for any $P \in \mathcal{P}$.

4   New Lower Bounds on $|U_i|$

In this section we first prove that a $(\mathcal{P}, \mathcal{F})$-KPS is equivalent to a $(\mathcal{P}, \mathcal{F})$-OTBES when $|B_P| = |M|$. Then, by using the bounds in [3,2] for KPSs, we get directly a lower bound on $|U_i|$ for $(\leq n, \leq w)$-OTBESs and a lower bound for $(t, \leq w)$-OTBESs. The former is the first lower bound presented for $(\leq n, \leq w)$-OTBESs. The latter is more tight than the bound of Blundo, Mattos and Stinson for $|B_P| = |M|$. Our bounds are both tight. We also present a general lower bound on $|U_i|$ for KPSs which includes all the previous bounds as special cases.

4.1   Equivalence between KPS and OTBES

Theorem 1. *If there exists a* $(\mathcal{P}, \mathcal{F})$-*KPS* $(U_1, \ldots, U_n, K)$, *then there exists a* $(\mathcal{P}, \mathcal{F})$-*OTBES* $(U_1, \ldots, U_n, M, \{B_P\})$ *with* $|B_P| = |M| = |K|$ *for all* $P \in \mathcal{P}$.

Proof. Use a key k_P of the $(\mathcal{P}, \mathcal{F})$-KPS to encrypt a message m_P, that is

$$b_P = k_P + m_P,$$

and broadcast b_P. We then get a $(\mathcal{P}, \mathcal{F})$-OTBES.   □

Theorem 2. *If there exists a $(\mathcal{P}, \mathcal{F})$-OTBES $(U_1, \ldots, U_n, M, \{B_P\})$ such that $|B_P| = |M|$ for all $P \in \mathcal{P}$, then there exists a $(\mathcal{P}, \mathcal{F})$-KPS $(U_1, \ldots, U_n, K)$ such that $|K| = |M|$ and $H(K) = H(M)$.*

Proof. From a $(\mathcal{P}, \mathcal{F})$-OTBES construct a KPS as follows. Fix $b_P \in B_P$ arbitrarily for all $P \in \mathcal{P}$. Since $|B_P| = |M|$, there is a bijection from B_P to M for any $(u_1, \ldots, u_n)$. Then there is an $\hat{m}_P \in M$ such that each member of P decrypts the b_P as $\hat{m}_P$ for any $(u_1, \ldots, u_n)$. Now take $k_P = \hat{m}_P$ in our KPS. It is easy to see that we get a $(\mathcal{P}, \mathcal{F})$-KPS with $|K| = |M|$ and $H(K) = H(M)$. □

4.2   Lower bounds for OTBESs

From Theorem 2, Proposition 1, and Corollary 1, we obtain immediately the following lower bounds on $|U_i|$ for OTBESs.

Corollary 3. *In a $(t, \leq w)$-OTBES, if $|B_P| = |M|$ for all $P \in \mathcal{P}$, then*

$$\log |U_i| \geq \binom{t + w - 1}{t - 1} H(M).$$

Corollary 4. *In a $(\leq n, \leq w)$-OTBES, if $|B_P| = |M|$ for all $P \in \mathcal{P}$, then*

$$\log |U_i| \geq \sum_{j=0}^{w} \binom{n - 1}{j} H(M).$$

These bounds are tight because the construction in the proof of Theorem 1 meets the equalities if we use the KPSs of Section 3.1 and Section 3.2.

4.3   A General Lower Bound on $|U_i|$

We generalize Proposition 1 as follows.

Theorem 3. *In a $(\mathcal{P}, \mathcal{F})$-KPS,*

$$\log |U_i| \geq \delta_i \log |K|,$$

where
$$\delta_i = |\{P \mid i \in P \in \mathcal{P}, \{1, 2, \ldots, n\} \backslash P \in \mathcal{F}\}|.$$

The proof is given in Appendix.

Note that Proposition 3 is also obtained as a corollary from Theorem 3. Indeed, all the previous bounds for KPSs are obtained as corollaries to Theorem 3.

From Theorem 2 and Theorem 3, we get the following corollary.

Corollary 5. *In a $(\mathcal{P}, \mathcal{F})$-OTBES, if $|B_P| = |M|$ for all $P \in \mathcal{P}$, then*

$$\log |U_i| \geq \delta_i \log |M|,$$

where $\delta_i = |\{P \mid i \in P \in \mathcal{P}, \{1, 2, \ldots, n\} \backslash P \in \mathcal{F}\}|.$

5   Multiple Use Broadcast Encryption

In this section we first show how to construct a computationally secure $(\mathcal{P}, \mathcal{F})$-Multiple use Broadcast Encryption Scheme $((\mathcal{P}, \mathcal{F})$-MBES$)$ from a $(\mathcal{P}, \mathcal{F})$-KPS by using the ElGamal cryptosystem. We then prove that our $(\mathcal{P}, \mathcal{F})$-MBES is secure against chosen (message, privileged subset of users) attacks if the ElGamal cryptosystem is secure and if the original $(\mathcal{P}, \mathcal{F})$-KPS is simulatable. We also show that all the KPSs considered in Section 3 are simulatable. This construction is the first $(\mathcal{P}, \mathcal{F})$-MBES whose security is proved formally. Furthermore, our technique can be generalized to many of the OTBES presented in [6].

5.1   A Proposed Construction for $(\mathcal{P}, \mathcal{F})$-MBES

Let $(U_1, \ldots, U_n, K)$ be a $(\mathcal{P}, \mathcal{F})$-KPS. The TA distributes secret information $u_1, \ldots, u_n$ to the users in the same way as for the $(\mathcal{P}, \mathcal{F})$-KPS. Let Q be a prime power such that $|K| \mid Q - 1$. Let g be a primitive $|K|$-th root of unity over $GF(Q)$. All the participants agree on Q and g. Let

$$M \stackrel{\triangle}{=} \langle g \rangle = \{m \mid m = g^x \text{ for some } x\}$$

If the TA wishes to send a message $m_p \in M$ to a privileged set $P \in \mathcal{P}$, then the TA broadcasts

$$b_P = (g^r, m_P g^{r k_P}),$$

where k_P is the key of the $(\mathcal{P}, \mathcal{F})$-KPS for P and r is a random number. Each member of P can decrypt b_P by using k_P with the ElGamal cryptosystem.

5.2   Security

Let $\boldsymbol{u}_F$ be a $\boldsymbol{u}_F \in U_F$ with $\Pr(U_F = \boldsymbol{u}_F) > 0$. We will show that the proposed construction is secure against chosen message attacks, in which the adversary can target privileged subsets of users adaptively. Informally these attacks are defined as follows. Fix a forbidden subset F (under the control of the adversary) arbitrarily. Suppose that F has obtained a broadcast b_P of a privileged subset P, $P \cap F = \emptyset$. Then F chooses several privileged subsets P_i and messages m_{P_i} adaptively, and can obtain from the TA, by using it as an oracle, the broadcast b_{P_i}, $i = 1, 2, \ldots$.

Definition 1. *A $(\mathcal{P}, \mathcal{F})$-MBES is secure against chosen (message, privileged subset of users) attacks if there is no probabilistic polynomial time algorithm (adversary) A_0 such as follows. Give as input to A_0:*

$$Q, g, \tilde{F} \in \mathcal{F}, \boldsymbol{u}_{\tilde{F}}, \tilde{P} \in \mathcal{P}, b_{\tilde{P}} = (g^r, m_{\tilde{P}} g^{r k_{\tilde{P}}})$$

with $\tilde{F} \cap \tilde{P} = \emptyset$. A_0 then chooses $P_i \in \mathcal{P}$ and $m_i \in M$ adaptively, and sends these to the TA as a query for $i = 1, 2, \ldots, l$. The TA gives back $b_{P_i} = (g^{r_i}, m_{P_i} g^{r_i k_{P_i}})$ to A_0. Finally, A_0 outputs $m_{\tilde{P}}$ with non-negligble probability for all $(\tilde{F}, \tilde{P})$.

Definition 2. *We say that the ElGamal cryptosystem is secure if there is no probabilistic polynomial time algorithm A_1 which on input (Q, g, y, g^r, my^r) outputs m with non-negligible probability, where r is a random number and $y \in \langle g \rangle$.*

Definition 3. *We say that a $(\mathcal{P}, \mathcal{F})$-KPS is simulatable if there is a probabilistic polynomial time algorithm (the simulator) B for which the following holds. On input $(Q, g, y, P \in \mathcal{P}, \tilde{F} \in \mathcal{F})$ with $P \cap \tilde{F} = \emptyset$, B outputs $\boldsymbol{u}_{\tilde{F}}, g^{k_{P_1}}, \ldots, g^{k_{P_h}}$ with probability*

$$\Pr(K_{P_1} = k_{P_1}, \ldots, K_{P_h} = k_{P_h}, u_{\tilde{F}} = \boldsymbol{u}_{\tilde{F}} \mid K_P = k_P),$$

where $y = g^{k_P}$ and $\{P_1, \ldots, P_h\} = \{P_i \mid P_i \in \mathcal{P}, P_i \neq P, P_i \cap \tilde{F} = \emptyset\}$.

Theorem 4. *Suppose that a $(\mathcal{P}, \mathcal{F})$-KPS is simulatable. Then the $(\mathcal{P}, \mathcal{F})$-MBES obtained by using this KPS in our construction is secure against chosen (message, privileged subset of users) attacks if the ElGamal cryptosystem is secure.*

Proof. Suppose that a $(\mathcal{P}, \mathcal{F})$-KPS is simulatable and that the proposed $(\mathcal{P}, \mathcal{F})$-MBES is not secure against chosen (message, privileged subset of users) attacks. Then there is a simulator B for the $(\mathcal{P}, \mathcal{F})$-KPS, and an adversary A_0 which breaks $b_{\tilde{P}}$ for $\tilde{P} \in \mathcal{P}$ by controlling $\tilde{F} \in \mathcal{F}$ for some $\tilde{P} \cap \tilde{F} = \emptyset$.

We will describe a probabilistic polynomial time algorithm A_1 which breaks the ElGamal cryptosystem by using A_0 and B as subroutines. Let the input to A_1 be (Q, g, y, g^r, my^r). Then there is a $k_{\tilde{P}}$ such that $y = g^{k_{\tilde{P}}}$. A_1 works as follows.

1. A_1 gives $(Q, g, y, \tilde{P}, \tilde{F})$ to B. Then B outputs $\boldsymbol{u}_{\tilde{F}}, g^{k_{P_1}}, \ldots, g^{k_{P_h}}$.
2. A_1 gives $(Q, g, \tilde{F}, \boldsymbol{u}_{\tilde{F}}, \tilde{P}, g^r, my^r)$ to A_0.
3. Since A_1 has $g^{k_{P_1}}, \ldots, g^{k_{P_h}}$, A_1 can answer any query of A_0.
4. Finally, A_0 outputs m with non-negligible probability.

Then A_1 can output m with non-negligible probability. This is a contradiction. □

5.3   Simulatable $(\mathcal{P}, \mathcal{F})$-KPSs

In what follows, we assume that $\binom{t+w-1}{t-1}$ is polynomial in the length of Q for the Blundo *et al.* scheme, that $\sum_{i=0}^{w} \binom{n-1}{i}$ is polynomial in the length of Q for the Fiat-Naor scheme, and that $2^{n-1} - 1$ is polynomial in the length of Q for the Desmedt-Viswanathan scheme.

Theorem 5. *The Fiat-Naor scheme and the Desmedt-Viswanathan scheme are simulatable.*

Proof. We give a proof for the Fiat-Naor scheme. The proof for the Desmedt-Viswanathan scheme is obtained in a similar way.

We shall describe a simulator B whose input is $(Q, g, y, P, \tilde{F})$, where $P \cap \tilde{F} = \emptyset$. B chooses s_{F_i} randomly for all $F_i \in \mathcal{F}$. From the $\{s_{F_i}\}$, B can obtain $\boldsymbol{u}_{\tilde{F}}$. Note that $s_{\tilde{F}} \notin \boldsymbol{u}_{\tilde{F}}$. On the other hand,

$$k_P = \sum_{F:|F| \le w, F \cap P = \emptyset} s_F = s_{\tilde{F}} + \sum_{F:F \ne \tilde{F}, |F| \le w, F \cap P = \emptyset} s_F \pmod{q-1}$$

Therefore,

$$y = g^{k_P} = g^{s_{\tilde{F}}} \cdot g^{\sum_{F:F \ne \tilde{F}, |F| \le w, F \cap P = \emptyset} s_F},$$

$$g^{s_{\tilde{F}}} = y / g^{\sum_{F:F \ne \tilde{F}, |F| \le w, F \cap P = \emptyset} s_F}.$$

Thus B can compute $g^{s_{\tilde{F}}}$ which is consistent with k_P such that $y = g^{k_P}$. Then B can compute $g^{k_{P_i}}$ for all $P_i \in \mathcal{P}$ because B knows $\{s_F \mid F \ne \tilde{F}, F \in \mathcal{F}\}$ and $g^{s_{\tilde{F}}}$.   □

Definition 4. Let $A = \{a_{i_1 \cdots i_t} \mid 0 \le i_1 \le w, \ldots, 0 \le i_t \le w\}$. We say that A is symmetric if for any $a_{i_1 \cdots i_t} \in A : a_{i_1 \cdots i_t} = a_{\pi(i_1 \cdots i_t)}$ for all permutations π of $(i_1 \cdots i_t)$. Furthermore, let

$$f(x_1, \ldots, x_t) = \sum_{i_1=0}^{w} \cdots \sum_{i_t=0}^{w} a_{i_1 \cdots i_t} x_1^{i_1} \cdots x_t^{i_t}.$$

We say that $f(x_1, \ldots, x_t)$ is symmetric if $\{a_{i_1 \cdots i_t}\}$ is symmetric.

Lemma 1. For given $D = \{b_{j_1 \cdots j_t} \mid 1 \le j_1 \le w+1, \ldots, 1 \le j_t \le w+1\}$, let

$$a_{i_1 \cdots i_t} \triangleq \sum_{j_1=1}^{w+1} \cdots \sum_{j_t=1}^{w+1} b_{j_1 \cdots j_t} w_{j_1 i_1} \cdots w_{j_t i_t},$$

where $[w_{ij}] \triangleq C^{-1}$ and

$$C \triangleq \begin{pmatrix} 1 & 1 & \cdots & 1 \\ 1 & 2 & \cdots & w+1 \\ \vdots & \vdots & \ddots & \vdots \\ 1 & 2^w & \cdots & (w+1)^w \end{pmatrix}.$$

Then

$$b_{j_1, \ldots, j_t} = \sum_{i_1=0}^{w} \cdots \sum_{i_t=0}^{w} a_{i_1 \cdots i_t} j_1^{i_1} \cdots j_t^{i_t}.$$

Furthermore, if D is symmetric, then $\{a_{i_1 \cdots i_t}\}$ is symmetric.

Theorem 6. The Blundo et al. scheme is simulatable.

Proof. For simplicity, suppose that the input to the simulator B is

$$\tilde{F} = \{1, 2, \ldots, w\}, \quad P = \{v_1, \ldots, v_t\}, \quad y = g^{k_P}, \quad Q, \quad g.$$

B first chooses a (dummy) symmetric polynomial

$$f(x_1, \ldots, x_t) = \sum_{i_1=0}^{w} \cdots \sum_{i_t=0}^{w} a_{i_1 \cdots i_t} x_1^{i_1} \cdots x_t^{i_t},$$

randomly. Then $\boldsymbol{u}_{\tilde{F}} = (f(1, x_2, \ldots, x_t), \ldots, f(w, x_2, \ldots, x_t))$. Next we consider a (real) symmetric polynomial

$$f_c(x_1, \ldots, x_t) = \sum_{i_1=0}^{w} \cdots \sum_{i_t=0}^{w} \hat{a}_{i_1 \cdots i_t} x_1^{i_1} \cdots x_t^{i_t} \tag{6}$$

such that $f_c(i, x_2, \ldots, x_t) = f(i, x_2, \ldots, x_t)$ for $1 \le i \le w$ and $f_c(v_1, \ldots, v_t) = k_P$. We first show that there exists such a polynomial f_c. Let

$$J = \{(j_1 \cdots j_t) \mid 1 \le j_1 \le w+1, \ldots, 1 \le j_t \le w+1\} \setminus \{(w+1 \cdots w+1)\}.$$

Then B can compute $b_{j_1 \cdots j_t} = f_c(j_1, \ldots, j_t)$ for all $(j_1 \cdots j_t) \in J$ by using $\boldsymbol{u}_{\tilde{F}}$. Let $c = f_c(w+1, \ldots, w+1)$, where c is an unknown variable. From Lemma 1, B can compute $\{\hat{a}_{i_1 \cdots i_t}\}$ from $\{b_{j_1 \cdots j_t}\}$ and c. Further, it is easy to see that $\hat{a}_{i_1 \cdots i_t}$ has the form

$$\hat{a}_{i_1 \cdots i_t} = \alpha_{i_1 \cdots i_t} + \beta_{i_1 \cdots i_t} c, \tag{7}$$

for some constants $\alpha_{i_1 \cdots i_t}$ and $\beta_{i_1 \cdots i_t}$. Then from eq.(6), we have

$$k_P = f_c(v_1, \ldots, v_t) = e_0 + e_1 c$$

for some constants e_0 and e_1. This means that there exists such an f_c. Now

$$y = g^{k_P} = g^{e_0}(g^c)^{e_1}.$$

Then $g^c = (y/g^{e_0})^{1/e_1}$. Therefore B can compute $\{g^{\hat{a}_{i_1 \cdots i_t}}\}$ from equation (7). Finally B can compute $g^{k_{P_i}}$ for all $P_i \in \mathcal{P}$ by using equation (6) and $\{g^{\hat{a}_{i_1 \cdots i_t}}\}$.   □

Corollary 6. *Suppose that the ElGamal cryptosystem is secure. The MBESs obtained from the Blundo et al. scheme, the Fiat-Naor scheme and the Desmedt-Viswanathan scheme by using our construction, are all secure against chosen (message, privileged subset of users) attacks.*

5.4   Generalization of Our MBES

We can generalize the MBESs in Corollary 6 so that anyone can do broadcast encryption. In the Fiat-Naor based MBES, make each g^{s_F} public. In the Blundo et al. based MBES, make each g^{a_i} public, where a_i is the coefficient of the symmetric polynomial f. Finally in the Desmedt-Viswanathan based MBES, make each g^{k_P} public. It can be proved that these modifications maintain the security. The details will be given in the final paper.

References

1. Blom, R.: An optimal class of symmetric key generation systems. Advances in Cryptology – EUROCRYPT '84, Lecture Notes in Computer Science #209. Springer-Verlag (1985) 335–338
2. Blundo, C., Cresti, A.: Space requirements for broadcast encryption, Advances in Cryptology – EUROCRYPT '94, Lecture Notes in Computer Science #950. Springer-Verlag (1995) 287–298.
3. Blundo, C., De Santis, A., Herzberg, A., Kutten, S., Vaccaro,U., Yung, M.: Perfectly secure key distribution for dynamic conferences, Advances in Cryptology – CRYPTO '92, Lecture Notes in Computer Science #740. Springer-Verlag (1993) 471–486
4. Blundo, C., Frota Mattos, L.A., Stinson, D.R.: Trade-offs between communication and storage in unconditionally secure schemes for broadcast encryption and interactive key distribution, Advances in Cryptology – CRYPTO '96, Lecture Notes in Computer Science #1109. Springer-Verlag (1996) 387–400
5. Fiat, A., Naor, M.: Broadcast encryption, Advances in Cryptology – CRYPTO '93, Lecture Notes in Computer Science #773. Springer-Verlag (1994) 480–491
6. D.R.Stinson, On some methods for unconditionally secure key distribution and broadcast encryption, *Designs, Codes and Cryptography*, **12** (1997) 215–243
7. Beimel, A., Chor, B.: Communication in key distribution schemes, IEEE Transactions on Information Theory, **42** (1996) 19–28
8. Ludy, M., Staddon, J.: Combinatorial bounds for broadcast encryption, Advances in Cryptology – EUROCRYPT '98, Lecture Notes in Computer Science #1403. Springer-Verlag (1998) 512–526
9. Desmedt, Y., Viswanathan, V.: Unconditionally secure dynamic conference key distribution, IEEE, ISIT '98 (1998)
10. Matsumoto, T., Imai, H.: On the key predistribution systems: A practical solution to the key distribution problem. In: Pomerance, C. (ed): Advances in Cryptology – CRYPTO '87, Lecture Notes in Computer Science #293. Springer-Verlag (1988) 185–193

Proof of Theorem 3

Our proof is a generalization of the proof in [7, Theorem 3.1].

Lemma 2. *Let P and Q be distinct subsets of $\{1, 2, \ldots, n\}$.*
Let $F \stackrel{\triangle}{=} \{1, 2, \ldots, n\} \setminus Q$. If $|Q| \leq |P|$, then

$$F \cap P \neq \emptyset$$

Proof. First, suppose that $|Q| < |P|$. If $F \cap P = \emptyset$, then

$$n \geq |F \cup P| = |F| + |P| = n - |Q| + |P| > n.$$

This is a contradiction. Therefore, $F \cap P \neq \emptyset$.
   Next, suppose that $|Q| = |P|$. If $F \cap P = \emptyset$, then

$$|F \cup P| = |F| + |P| = n - |Q| + |P| = n.$$

Therefore,
$$F = \{1, 2, \ldots, n\} \setminus P.$$
This means that $P = Q = \{1, 2, \ldots, n\} \setminus P$. This is a contradiction. Hence, $F \cap P \neq \emptyset$.

$\square$

Proof of Theorem 3

For simplicity, we give a proof for $|U_1|$. Take

$$\tilde{P} \triangleq \{P \mid 1 \in P \in \mathcal{P} , \{1, 2, \ldots, n\} \setminus P \in \mathcal{F}\}.$$

Let $l = \delta_1 = |\tilde{P}|$ and let $\tilde{P} = \{P_1, P_2, \ldots, P_l\}$, where $|P_1| \geq |P_2| \geq \cdots \geq |P_l|$. Let $\boldsymbol{u} = (u_1, \ldots, u_n)$ be a vector of secret information of the users such that

$$\Pr[U_U = \boldsymbol{u}] > 0.$$

We define $\boldsymbol{u}_F$ similarly.

For all $k_1 \in K_{P_1}$, for all F such that $P_1 \cap F_1 = \emptyset$ and for all $\boldsymbol{u}_F$,

$$\Pr[K_{P_1} = k_1 \mid U_F = \boldsymbol{u}_F] = \Pr[K_{P_1} = k_1] > 0,$$

from equation (2). Therefore, for all $k_1 \in K_{P_1}$ there is a $\boldsymbol{u} = (u_1, \ldots, u_n)$ such that the key of P_1 reconstructed from $\boldsymbol{u}$ is k_1. Now let $\boldsymbol{k} = (k_1, \ldots, k_l)$ be any vector in $K_{P_1} \times \cdots \times K_{P_l}$. We claim that there is a $\boldsymbol{u}$ such that the key of P_i reconstructed from $\boldsymbol{u}$ is k_i for $1 \leq i \leq l$.

Suppose that our claim is false. Let $h(\leq l)$ be the maximum index such that the keys of $\{P_i\}$ are $(k_1, \ldots, k_{h-1}, k'_h, \ldots, k'_l)$ by some $\boldsymbol{u}$, where $k'_h \neq k_h$. Then $2 \leq h$ from our discussion. Let

$$F_h \triangleq \{1, 2, \ldots, n\} \setminus P_h.$$

Then from Lemma 2 (let $Q = P_h$ and $P = P_i$),

$$F_h \cap P_i \neq \emptyset \quad \text{for } 1 \leq i \leq h - 1. \tag{8}$$

Let $\boldsymbol{u}_{F_h}$ be a subvector of $\boldsymbol{u}$ which corresponds to F_h. Then $\boldsymbol{u}_{F_h}$ can compute $k_1, \ldots, k_{h-1}$ from equation (8). Suppose that

$$\Pr[K_{P_h} = k_h | U_{F_h} = \boldsymbol{u}_{F_h}] > 0.$$

This means that there exists a $\boldsymbol{u}$ such that the keys are $k_1, \ldots, k_{h-1}, k_h$. This contradicts the maximality of h. Therefore,

$$\Pr[K_{P_h} = k_h | U_{F_h} = \boldsymbol{u}_{F_h}] = 0.$$

However, this is against eq.(2).

Hence, for any $\boldsymbol{k} \in K_{P_1} \times \cdots \times K_{P_l}$, there exists a $\boldsymbol{u}$ such that the keys are $\boldsymbol{k}$. Remember that user 1 is included in any P_i from our definition of $\tilde{P}$. It follows that u_i must be distinct for each $\boldsymbol{k}$. Therefore,

$$|U_1| \geq |K_{P_1}| \times \cdots \times |K_{P_l}| = |K|^l.$$

Hence,

$$\log |U_1| \geq l \log |K| = \delta_1 \log |K|.$$

Author Index

Bao, F. 126,133
Beaver, D. 300
Boneh, D............................. 25
Boyd, C. 271
Burmester, M................ 380,420

Camenisch, J. 160
Canteaut, A........................ 187
Chao, J. .... .95
Chen, L. 286
Cohen, H. .... .51
Courtois, N. 35

Dai, Z. 227
Deng, R. H. 126,133
Desmedt, Y. 380,392
                                  420
Durfee, G. 25

Frankel, Y 25,257
Foo, E. 271

Goubin, L. 35

Hou, S. 392

Izu, T. 66

Johansson, T. 342

Kaliski, B. 50
Knudsen, L. R 327
Kogure, J. 66
Kurosawa, K. 420

Lam,K. Y. 227

Lee, P. J. 175
Lenstra, A. K. 1
Lim, C. H. 175,214

Mao, W. 214
Meier, W. 327
Michels, M. 160
Miyaji, A. 51

Nakamura, O. 95
Nguyen, P 372
Noro, M. 66

Ono, T. 51

Patarin J. 35
ornin, T. 148
Poupard, G. 11
Preneel, B. 327

Qi, W. 315
Quisquater, J. 392

Rijmen, V. 327

Safavi-Naini, R. 242
Sakai, Y. 80
Sakurai, K. 80
Seberry, J. ....….380
Sendrier, N. 187
Silverman, J. H. ....…........ 110
Sobataka, K. 95
Stern, J. 11,372
Stern, J. P. 357
Sun,H.-M.............................200
Suzuki, J. 110

Tsiounis, Y. 257

Tsujii, S. 95

Verdoolaege, S. 327

Wang, H. 242

Wolf, S. 405

Wu, H..........................126,133

Yang, J. 315

Ye, D. F. 227

Ye, Q. Z. 126,133

Yokoyama, K. 66

Yoshida, T. 420

Yung, M. 257

Zhou, J. 315